GLENCOE

Health

A Guide to Wellness

EIGHTH EDITION

Mary Bronson Merki, Ph.D.

Don Merki, Ph.D.

Contributing Authors
Michael J. Cleary, Ed.D.
Gale Cornelia Flynn

Glencoe
McGraw-Hill

New York, New York   Columbus, Ohio   Chicago, Illinois   Peoria, Illinois   Woodland Hills, California

About the Authors

Mary Bronson Merki, Ph.D., has taught health education in grades K–12, as well as health education methods classes at the undergraduate and graduate levels. As Health Education Specialist for the Dallas School District, Dr. Merki developed and implemented a district-wide health education program, *Skills for Living,* which was used as a model by the state education agency. Dr. Merki has assisted school districts throughout the country in developing local health education programs. Dr. Merki is also the author of Glencoe's *Teen Health* textbook series.

Don Merki, Ph.D., has taught health education for 35 years. He teaches at The University of New Mexico, featuring classes in substance abuse, mental health, adopting a healthy lifestyle, AIDS and sexually transmitted diseases, and stress and life management skills. He has taught students from broad cultural and ethnic backgrounds at every level from elementary to graduate school. Dr. Merki recently served as a consultant to the School of Family Medicine's Alcohol and Substance Abuse Prevention Program at the University of New Mexico, Albuquerque.

Michael J. Cleary, Ed.D., is Professor and School Health Education Coordinator at Slippery Rock University. Dr. Cleary taught at Evanston Township High School in Evanston, Illinois, and later became the Lead Teacher Specialist at the McMillen Center for Health Education in Fort Wayne, Indiana. Dr. Cleary has published and presented widely on curriculum development and portfolio assessment in K-12 health education. Dr. Cleary is the co-author of *Managing Your Health: Assessment for Action.* He is a Certified Health Education Specialist.

Gale Cornelia Flynn is a widely published freelance writer whose work has appeared in many well-known textbooks. Flynn has taught at both junior and senior high school levels. An educational and creative consultant, she now conducts in-service programs in a variety of schools in Delaware. She speaks to students at all levels on subjects ranging from alcoholism to creativity, and runs workshops for parents and teachers.

Glencoe/McGraw-Hill

*A Division of The **McGraw·Hill** Companies*

Send all inquiries to:
Glencoe/McGraw-Hill
21600 Oxnard Street, Suite 500
Woodland Hills, California 91367

ISBN 0-07-823864-1 (Student Edition)
ISBN 0-07-823865-X (Teacher Wraparound Edition)
ISBN 0-07-829660-9 (CNN® Video)

Printed in the United States of America.

2 3 4 5 6 7 8 9 0   071/043   07 06 05 04 03 02

Educational Consultants

Nita Auer
Health Educator
North Side High School
Fort Wayne, Indiana

Pamela Connolly
Health and Physical Education
Diocese of Pittsburgh
West Mifflin, Pennsylvania

Justin Cunningham
California Health Framework Writing
  Committee Chair
San Diego, California

Robert Wandberg, Ph.D.
Health Educator
John F. Kennedy High School
Bloomington, Minnesota

Content Reviewers

David Allen, M.D.
Infectious Disease Consultant
Dallas, Texas

Marcella Cook
Health Resource Educator
Charlotte, North Carolina

Roberta Duyff
Nutrition Education Consultant
St. Louis, Missouri

Glen C. Griffin, M.D.
Health Consultant
Mapleton, Utah

Marlene Koch, R.D., L.D.
Nutrition Education Consultant
Dublin, Ohio

Bonnie Mohnsen, Ph.D.
Health Consultant
Cerritos, California

Judy Monroe
Health Educator
St. Paul, Minnesota

Richard L. Pappenfuss, Ph.D.
Associate Professor, Health
University of Arizona
Tucson, Arizona

Howard Shapiro, M.D.
Psychiatrist
Los Angeles, California

David Sleet, Ph.D.
Injury Prevention
San Diego, California

Pamela Tollefson, R.N.
Health Education and
  HIV/STD Prevention
Olympia, Washington

Teacher Reviewers

Donna Breitenstein
Director of Health Training Center
Boone, North Carolina

Diane Bruckerhoff
Health Education Coordinator
Columbia, Missouri

Peggy Campbell
Curriculum Supervisor
Huntington, West Virginia

Alisa Debnam
Health Supervisor
Fayetteville, North Carolina

Debra Harris
Health and Physical Education Educator
West Linn, Oregon

Jo Henderson
Health Educator
Seattle, Washington

Gayle S. Jenkins
Health Education Program Specialist
Raleigh, North Carolina

Peggy V. Johns
Supervisor, Pre K–12 Health Education
Largo, Florida

Phyllis Simpson, Ph.D. CHES
Health Supervisor
Dallas, Texas

Deborah Tackmann
Health Educator
Eau Claire, Wisconsin

Betty White
Health Educator
Lexington, Kentucky

Contents

UNIT 8   Diseases and Disorders

UNIT 9

Consumer and Environmental Health

Building Health Skills

Making Responsible Decisions

CHARACTER IN ACTION

keeping Fit

connections

healthlab

Teens / Making a Difference

Drawings, Tables, Charts

CHAPTER 1

Your Health and Wellness

PRACTICING HEALTHFUL BEHAVIORS

What can you do to improve your total health? Start by completing the Personal Health Inventory Interactive Project at **health.glencoe.com** to evaluate your Health Risk Assessment.

Personal Health Inventory

> 66 *Whatever I choose to do, I'll try and make it as extraordinary as possible.* 99

—Marion Jones
Olympic Gold Medalist, track and field

Quick Write Make a can-do list of ways to make your life extraordinary each day. Include steps to improve your physical, mental, and social health. Begin each item on the list with the words *I can ...*

Self-Inventory Write the numbers 1–10 on a sheet of paper. Read each statement below and respond by writing *yes*, *no*, or *sometimes* for each item. Write a *yes* only for items that you practice regularly. Save your responses.

1	I get between seven and eight hours of sleep each night.
2	I eat at least three nutritionally balanced meals each day, beginning with breakfast.
3	I maintain a weight that is right for someone my height and frame.
4	I do at least 20 to 30 minutes of aerobic physical activity three to four times a week.
5	I wear a seat belt in cars and protective gear when bicycling or playing sports.
6	I avoid harmful substances such as tobacco, alcohol, or other drugs.
7	I ask for help when I need it and know where to turn for current and reliable health information.
8	I generally like and accept who I am.
9	I get along well with others.
10	I can express my emotions in healthy ways.

Follow-up After completing the chapter, retake this self-inventory. Pick two items that you need to work on and set a goal to improve your health behaviors.

What Is Health?

Although it may not be easy to see, you are in a constant state of change. Think about how your knowledge and skills have expanded in the past few years. What new relationships have you formed? What kind of adult will you become? Many of your answers depend on the choices and decisions you make about your health.

Defining Health

If you were to take a snapshot of your current state of health, how would it look? How are you feeling? Are you alert and well rested? Are you ready to take on whatever challenges the day holds in store for you? Is your outlook positive? Are you getting along well with family members, classmates, and teachers? What about yesterday? Did you eat well and get plenty of physical activity?

Your answers to these and other questions provide a picture of your general level of health. Does that surprise you? If it does, the reason may be that, like many people, you think of health as the absence of sickness. Health, however, is much more than that. **Health** is *the combination of your physical, mental/emotional, and social well-being.* Your personal level of health affects everything about you. It affects how you look, how you feel, even how you act. It affects your attitudes and performance in school, work, and recreation. It affects how you feel about yourself and how successful you are in your relationships. It will probably help determine some of your goals and your ability to accomplish them.

It is important to be aware that health is not an absolute state. Being healthy does not mean that you will never be sick, or that you will be guaranteed a position on the basketball team. Instead, being healthy means striving to be the best *you* can be at any given time.

The Three Elements of Your Health

Notice that people ask, "How are you?" not "Do you have any diseases?" or "Are all of your systems functioning properly?" That is because "how you are doing" involves much more than your physical condition. It also includes how you are doing mentally, emotionally, and socially. To obtain a complete picture of your health, you must take into consideration all of these elements.

Physical Health

In its broadest sense, physical health is the way the parts and systems of your body work together. It means that your body has the ability to cope with the stresses of normal daily life. It means having strength and energy to pursue physical, mental, emotional and social challenges and changes.

To gain or maintain physical health, you need to have proper nutrition, regular physical activity, and enough rest and sleep. You need to practice good hygiene to prevent disease, and get regular medical and dental checkups and treatments when you need them. Good physical health also includes paying attention to what you put into your body. It means resisting harmful substances, such as tobacco, alcohol, and other drugs.

Mental and Emotional Health

Mental and emotional health includes your feelings about yourself, how well you relate to others, and how well you meet the demands of daily life. Mental health also calls for a person to use his or her mind to develop thinking skills. People with good mental health enjoy learning, and they know that striving for information and understanding can be an exciting, lifelong process. They see mistakes as opportunities to learn, grow, and change. They accept responsibility for their actions and stand up for their beliefs and values.

A person with good emotional health is in touch with his or her feelings and expresses

▼ *You can use your talents and skills to help others succeed.*

ACTIVITY *Explain how helping other people learn new skills contributes to your mental health.*

To learn more about the health triangle, visit Glencoe's health home page at **health.glencoe.com**.

▼ *The three elements of your health—physical health, mental and emotional health, and social health—are related to each other and contribute to your total health.*

ACTIVITY *Think about your total health. Identify the activities and behaviors you do to contribute to each side of your health triangle.*

them in appropriate, healthful ways. This type of individual can usually deal with the problems and frustrations of life without being overwhelmed by them. People with good emotional health avoid dwelling on negative thoughts. Instead, they consider their situation and then use positive thoughts and actions to move them through the challenge.

Social Health

— Social health involves the way you get along with others. It includes your ability to make and keep friends and also to work and play in cooperative ways, seeking and lending support when necessary. It involves communicating well and showing respect and care for yourself and others.

Your Health Triangle

Have you ever been very tired or hungry? Did that feeling affect the way you acted toward others? Did it affect your work? If it continued for a long time, did it affect your physical well-being?

The three elements of health are interconnected, like the sides of a triangle. When one side receives too much or too little attention, the other sides change as well. The whole triangle can become lopsided and unbalanced. To be truly healthy, you need to try to keep all three sides of your health triangle—and your life—in balance.

The Health Continuum

A person with a balanced life is said to have a high degree of **wellness,** *an overall state of well-being, or total health.* It comes from a way of living each day that includes making decisions and practicing behaviors that are based on sound health knowledge and healthful attitudes. Achieving wellness is an ongoing, lifelong commitment to physical, mental/emotional, and social health.

Remember that your health is dynamic. You are constantly being bombarded with messages from advertising and television, and pressures from friends that can affect your health. The fact, however, that your health is dynamic means that it fluctuates along a *continuum.* A continuum is like a yardstick. There are many different points along it where your health can be located at any given time. From day to day and year to year, you experience different levels of total health. In any of the health areas—physical, mental/emotional, or social— there can be a sudden change. By the same token, a person may move from one side of the continuum to the other so gradually that he or she may not be fully aware of the change.

▼ *The continuum shows that your health is on a sliding scale with many degrees of health and wellness in between.*

ACTIVITY *Name three behaviors that would help a person's health move toward the right side of the Health Continuum.*

The Health Continuum

◄ **Premature Death** | **Loss of Health and Wellness** | **Improved Health and Wellness** | **High Level of Health** ►

| Chronic disorders | Lack of energy, inattention, minor aches and pains | Free from aches and pains | Moderate level of energy | Optimal level of energy, feeling of well-being |

People on this side of the continuum usually do not take responsibility for maintaining their own health.

Many people function below the wellness midpoint.

People on this side of the continuum usually exhibit a high degree of responsibility, discipline, and positive direction in life. They accept responsibility for maintaining their own health.

Sometimes you can change a situation merely by adjusting your attitude toward it. For example, instead of concentrating on what you lack, or don't have, you might instead decide to concentrate on what you *do* have.

Character Check Try these attitude boosters:

➤ Separate your *wants* from your *needs*.

➤ Notice those in the world who have less or have it tougher than you do.

➤ Learn from people who seem to thrive despite—or even because of—their setbacks.

➤ Recognize that tough times may bring out your greatest abilities and character strengths.

➤ Distinguish between what you can and can't change. Focus on the former. Let go of the latter.

Promoting Your Health

Recent discoveries in medicines and advances in technology have helped wipe out many of the diseases that killed people 100, 50, even 30 years ago. Yet, the way we live today poses new threats to our health and our lives. Millions of people get sick, become disabled, or die each year because of the decisions they make and the way they live. Their decision-making skills and personal behavior are directly related to their deaths. Many of these deaths could be prevented if people practiced a few simple health habits.

Lifestyle Factors

After years of studying many groups of people, experts have identified seven habits that make a difference in people's overall health, happiness, and *longevity*—or how long they live. People who regularly practice these important habits tend to be healthier and live longer. These habits are called lifestyle factors. **Lifestyle factors** are *personal behaviors and habits related to the way a person lives, that help determine his or her level of health.* The following are important lifestyle factors.

■ Get between seven to eight hours of sleep per night.
■ Eat nutritious foods from the various food groups each day.
■ Refrain from smoking and using tobacco products.
■ Eat breakfast daily.
■ Do 20 to 30 minutes of nonstop vigorous activity a minimum of three times a week.
■ Do not use alcohol or other drugs.
■ Maintain your recommended weight.

How many of these basic health habits do you practice regularly? What changes in habits can you make? Keep in mind that not following these guidelines can prove hazardous to your health and take years off your life.

Your Attitudes, Your Health

Practicing good health habits involves much more than just knowing what to do. Your attitudes also affect how well you take care of yourself. For example, in order to practice good health habits, you must believe that there is some benefit for you, and that by not practicing good health habits, problems will develop. You also need to become aware of your overall attitude, or outlook, on life since this can play a major role in both your quality of life and your health.

Studies have shown that optimists, people who tend to see the positive in situations, are less likely to suffer illness and die young than pessimists, those who look for and see the negative in situations. Other studies have concluded that it is not what happens to a person

Being Aware of Your Surroundings

In the past decade, Americans have witnessed many tragedies. Some were the result of natural disasters, such as Hurricane Andrew and the earthquake in Northridge, California. Other tragedies were deliberate acts of violence, including the shootings at Columbine High School and the terrorist attacks of September 11, 2001.

Although these events were terribly tragic, there are lessons to be learned. For one, we must not take our health and safety for granted, but rather make them a top priority in our daily lives. You can accomplish this task by studying and applying the health skills discussed in this book. Start by being more aware of your surroundings. Let an adult know about anyone who talks about committing acts of violence. Being aware of warning signs and taking action can help prevent a dangerous situation from occurring.

Look for other *Update: Our Changing World* features located throughout this book. In them, you will find important information about health-related concerns that have arisen in today's society.

1. What are some other ways in which being aware of your surroundings can help keep you healthy and safe?

2. Why is it so important to learn from recent tragedies? Is it possible for anything positive to result from a tragedy? Explain your answer.

but the person's attitudes and responding behaviors that determine how well that person will cope and how happy he or she will be.

Wellness and Prevention

A key to your health and wellness is **prevention**, or *practicing healthy habits to keep a person well and free from disease and other ailments*. Wearing seat belts, applying sunscreen, avoiding unsafe areas, and using protective gear when playing sports are just a few preventive measures you can take. What others do you regularly practice?

The Importance of Health Education

Because health is so critical to the quality of your life, learning how to become and stay healthy should be a priority. That is why health education is so important. **Health education** is *the providing of accurate health information in such a way as to influence people to change attitudes so that they take positive action about their health*. Its goal is to help people live long, zestful, and productive lives.

Health education is not just about learning health facts. Its goal is to give students—and that includes you—the tools needed to achieve and maintain total well-being. It is about gaining health literacy.

Being Health Literate

The fact that you are reading the words on this page means you are *literate*—able to read. Are you "health literate," however? **Health literacy** describes *an individual's capacity to obtain, interpret, and understand basic health information and services and use such information and services in ways that promote his or her health and wellness.*

To be health literate, a person must be:

■ **A critical thinker and problem-solver.** Such an individual is able to evaluate information from reliable sources before making a decision. She or he also knows how to make responsible decisions.

■ **A responsible, productive citizen.** A health-literate person acts in a way that promotes the health of the community, nation, and the world at large. He or she chooses safe, healthful, and legal behaviors that keep with family guidelines and show respect of others and himself or herself.

■ **A self-directed learner.** A self-directed learner is able to gather and use accurate, current health information throughout life. This includes the wealth of information available through newspapers, magazines, and modern technology, including computers, fax, and television.

■ **An effective communicator.** Effective communication is the ability to express one's knowledge, beliefs, and ideas in a variety of forms.

In the lessons and chapters to follow, you will find tools that can help you become a more health-literate person.

LESSON 1 *Review*

Reviewing Facts and Vocabulary

1. In a paragraph, relate the terms *health, wellness*, and *lifestyle factors*.
2. What are the three elements of health?
3. List five lifestyle factors that promote good health.
4. Identify four properties of a health-literate person.

Thinking Critically

5. *Synthesizing.* Review your responses to the Health Barometer Self-Inventory on page 23. Based on your answers, draw your own health triangle. Is it balanced or lopsided? If it is lopsided, what can you do to make the sides more even?

6. *Analyzing.* In your Health Journal list five actions you took in the past week that promote good health.

Applying Health Skills

7. *In Your School.* Make two lists—one of places at school and in the community where health is promoted—and one of places where it is *not* promoted. Compare these lists with those of classmates in a general discussion. Discuss in what ways you and your classmates have taken a step toward increased health literacy.

Influences on Your Health

Imagine that the story of your health were made into a video. The video would portray your health from the day you were born until today. It would show how you felt and functioned at each stage. The uniqueness of your video would be partly a result of the decisions you have made in your life that affected your overall well-being.

HEALTH TERMS

heredity
environment
peers
culture

HEALTH CONCEPTS

- Your health is affected by a number of factors over which you have no control.
- Your heredity, environment, and culture influence your health.
- Your behaviors and the choices and decisions you make can affect your health.

hotlink

heredity For more information on heredity and its impact on health, see Chapter 20, page 461.

Heredity

To some degree, your general level of health was determined before you were born. You are a product of **heredity**. **Heredity** is *all the traits and properties that are passed along biologically from both parents to child.* The most obvious traits are physical ones such as the color of your hair and eyes, the shape of your nose and ears, and your body type and size. You also inherit basic intellectual abilities. Tendencies toward specific diseases can also be inherited.

Environment

Your health is also influenced by your environment. **Environment** is *the sum total of your surroundings—your family, where you grew up, where you live now, and all of your experiences.* Environment includes all the places you go in a given day and the physical conditions in which you live. It also includes the people in your life—your *social environment*. Yet another aspect of your environment is your culture.

Physical Environment

Your physical environment can affect all areas of your health. How would you describe your environment? Are there parks, jogging paths, and recreational facilities? Is the environment clean and are the streets safe? A person living in this environment may be more likely to enjoy good physical and mental health. In contrast, a person living in an area with a high crime rate, for example, may experience stress and feel threatened for his or her personal safety.

Other aspects of your physical environment that can influence your health include air quality. Pollutants, such as smog and smoke from other people's cigarettes, can increase your chances of developing lung disorders, whereas growing up in a community with clean air lessens your risks of such diseases. Indoor aspects of your environment, such as a frayed electrical cord plugged into a wall socket, can also affect your personal safety.

Access to medical care is another aspect of one's physical environment that influences health. Because of the rising costs of medical care and health insurance in recent years, many people are unable to afford health services. Childhood immunizations are often overlooked, and this has led to a re-emergence of diseases that were once thought to be wiped out.

▼ *Your physical environment influences your total health and contributes to your sense of well-being.*

ACTIVITY *Describe characteristics of your physical environment. What parts contribute to a healthful environment? Are there aspects that pose risks to your health?*

Teens Making a Difference

Difference

...CARING...COMPASSION ...RESPECT

Joceneia, who likes to be called JoJo, is 16. She knows what it's like to move to a new country, have to learn a new language, and try to find her place within a new culture. She is now reaching out to help other young people in the same situation, putting caring and compassion into action and finding joy in the process.

JoJo begins, "I came from Cape Verde, off the coast of Africa, when I was nine. I was having a tough time with English. The teachers taught me and their caring made a big difference. I learned about YouthBuild, an after-school program in Boston that helps students with their homework and other problems. It's held at a drop-in center, and I got the help I needed there. They were kind and caring and took us on field trips and tutored me."

THE GIVE-BACK FACTOR As part of her community service last year, JoJo was a guide with second graders at the Museum of Science. She enjoyed working with children so she decided to give back to the drop-in center that had done so much for her. "I tutor the younger kids as a volunteer. They are kids like me that are in the same situation as I was. I help them after school with English. I make sure they are understanding what they are doing."

She continues, "I'm also in a program called the Summer Search Foundation that helps teens with a desire to travel and learn about other cultures. My first trip was to South Dakota. I stayed on a Native American reservation, and it was the most incredible experience I've ever had because I was with a whole different culture, and I *love* learning about different cultures. Also, the people there were really nice. While we were there, I built a wheelchair ramp for one of the centers. They also have a senior center, and we repainted the whole thing, and I worked at a health clinic filing patients' records. It was fun."

THE "CAN-DO" APPROACH JoJo's positive "can-do" approach keeps her busy and involved. "One of my dreams is to study medicine. I want to be a pediatrician. Coming from what I experienced, I enjoy helping other people a lot. When people help you, you can return that help, and I try to do just that."

JOJO'S STORY

1. Describe how JoJo's story demonstrates both the give-back factor and the can-do approach.
2. How does she also help herself in reaching out to help others?

YOUR STORY

1. What can you do to "give back" to family, friends, your school, or your community?
2. Where can you learn about service projects where you can combine the value of caring with your own interests and career goals?

Social Environment

Your social environment includes your family and other people with whom you come into daily contact. A person who is surrounded by individuals who show support, love, strength, and encouragement may have a positive self-image and, as a result, reach out and support others. A healthful, supportive social environment can even help a person to rise above adverse physical conditions, such as poverty. On the other hand, a person from an unhealthful social environment may suffer poor mental and emotional health as a result of rejection, neglect, verbal abuse, or other negative behaviors.

An important part of your social environment, especially during the teen years, is your peers. **Peers** are *people the same age who share a similar range of interests*. Your peers include your friends and classmates. Peers who are loyal and supportive friends can help you grow mentally and socially. At the same time, peers who take part in dangerous, unhealthy, or illegal behaviors like using tobacco, alcohol, or other drugs can put pressure on you to be "part of the group." Standing up to this **peer pressure** can be challenging. One way is by choosing friends who care about their health and yours.

Cultural Environment

Culture is *the collective beliefs, customs, and behaviors of a group.* This group may be an ethnic group, a community, a nation, or an entire section of the globe. The language your family speaks at home, the foods you prefer to eat, and the traditions and religion you practice are all part of your cultural environment.

hotlink

peer pressure For more information on peer pressure and strategies for dealing with it, see Chapter 13, page 304.

▼ *Your peers are an important part of your social environment.*

ACTIVITY *Identify some of the choices and decisions you have made that were influenced by your peers. How does your social environment contribute to positive health behaviors?*

A Values Vocabulary

The actions you take determine who you are. This idea was developed by Greek philosopher Aristotle who lived from 384–322 B.C. By making right choices, showing respect, and caring for yourself and for others, you increase the chances that you will live a longer, more healthful life. Begin by learning to understand and use the following terms.

Values: Your priorities; the ideas, beliefs, or things you cherish above everything else that help guide the way you live.

Character: Characteristics of thinking, feeling, and acting that demonstrate the essentials of who a person is and how he or she functions in the world.

Ethics: Principles of conduct based on objective values or highest moral principles.

Objective Values: The highest values, priorities, or principles; fundamental laws in the universe, such as *truth* and *justice*.

Core Ethical Values: These are the *highest values*, derived from among the objective values—a group of universal values such as *caring*, *responsibility*, and *respect*. These same highest values exist in many cultures and across many ages.

Good Character: Having traits or characteristics that show or imply feeling, thinking, and acting in terms of objective or core ethical values—your highest values.

1. Think of a time when you or someone close to you made a decision that went against one of the core ethical values. How might this have jeopardized that person's health?

2. If the person making the decision had acted upon the highest values instead, what might have been the result?

Understanding culture can help you understand yourself and get along with others. Culture can help you see what all people have in common. It can help you recognize the variety of ways in which people solve the same basic problems. Finally, your culture gives you a sense of identity as you take your place in a multicultural world.

Behavior

Although you have little or no control over your heredity and environment, you have a great deal of control over one factor affecting your life: your behavior. The way you choose to act within your environment and with your inherited abilities has a very important impact on who you are.

Suppose your family has a history of cardiovascular disease. Does this mean you must "follow in their footsteps"? Not at all! You can reduce your chances of developing this condition through positive choices and habits. You can reduce your intake of fried foods and other foods high in fat. You can also develop the positive habit of regularly participating in physical activity and exercise.

Similarly, if you are aware of environmental health influences, you have the ability to take positive action to protect your health. If there is a nonworking smoke detector in your home, you can replace the battery. You can wear sunscreen to protect your skin when you're in the sun. If you know about the dangers associated with cigarette smoke, you can try to avoid being near smokers.

By being aware—by becoming more health literate—you can take positive action to protect your health and the health of others. You can also take advantage of positive hereditary and environmental influences.

Your Behavior, Your Health

Can you recall your health video, discussed at the beginning of this lesson? Imagine that you could keep adding to this video, showing how the decisions you make today will affect your health tomorrow or how the decisions you make tomorrow will affect the rest of your life.

The simple fact is that the remainder of the video is, for the most part, in your hands. True, some factors influencing your health are out of your control, but most of the decisions affecting your health are yours to make. You and nobody else are the video's director. Sit down in the director's chair, and get ready to take responsibility for your health—and your life.

LESSON 2 *Review*

Reviewing Facts and Vocabulary

1. Define *heredity.* Give an example of how heredity can positively influence your health.
2. In your own words, define *physical environment, social environment,* and *cultural environment.*

Thinking Critically

3. **Synthesizing.** A *treatment* is a written description of events and images in a movie or video. Write a two-page treatment for a video of your health to date. Make sure to cover all important highlights.

4. **Analyzing.** Explain how peer pressure can be a positive or negative influence in your life. Why is it sometimes difficult to resist? Tell why it is important to resist the pressure to do something that is dangerous, unhealthy, or illegal.

Applying Health Skills

5. **In Your School.** Identify the resources in your school and community that contribute to the well-being of its citizens. Make a poster or pamphlet describing these resources.

Taking Charge of Your Health

You may be responsible for decisions such as buying your own clothes and for managing your schedule. As you move toward adulthood, you become increasingly responsible for more decisions regarding your health. This lesson will help you learn how to make choices to help you live a long and healthy life.

HEALTH TERMS

risk factors

values

abstinence

HEALTH CONCEPTS

- Accepting responsibility for your own health and for the health of others is a positive step toward wellness.
- Risk factors can be offset by behaviors, including making choices and practicing habits that promote good health.
- Abstinence, the conscious decision to avoid harmful behaviors, can increase your chances of a long, happy, and healthful life.

Taking Responsibility for Your Health

Does the prospect of taking on adult responsibilities excite you? Maybe it frightens you a little. Perhaps you are wondering how you get from the teenager you are now to the fully responsible adult you are rapidly becoming.

A first step toward bridging that gap, at least where your health is concerned, is to increase your awareness of risk factors in your life. **Risk factors** are *actions or behaviors that represent a potential health threat.* A second step is to examine your current behaviors and values and to make any necessary changes.

Risk Factors and Teens

The Centers for Disease Control and Prevention (CDC) in Atlanta annually conducts nationwide surveys of America's youth. In the

⚑ **With what responsibilities have you been entrusted so far? Which responsibilities do you look forward to?**

ACTIVITY *List three rights or privileges you have been given in previous years. Next to each, write the responsibility that goes along with that right or privilege.*

most recent survey, questionnaires on personal risk factors were gathered from over 16,000 students and young adults from 151 schools across the nation. The six categories of personal health risk factors covered in the survey are listed below.

- behaviors that contribute to unintentional and intentional injuries
- tobacco use
- alcohol and other drug use
- sexual behaviors
- unhealthy eating behaviors
- physical inactivity

Throughout this program you will learn how teens, like yourself, responded to questions addressing these risk factors. You will also learn about what you can do to reduce or eliminate the risk factors in your life.

Examining Your Habits and Other Behaviors

One finding of the CDC survey is that 33 percent of the teens interviewed smoked cigarettes. Another 36 percent admitted to having been in a physical fight during the previous year. While these numbers may sound alarming at first, they also mean that 67 and 64 percent of the teens surveyed, respectively, *did not* engage in these high-risk behaviors.

Where do you fit in? Are you doing everything you can in the interests of your own health and well-being? At the beginning of each chapter in this program, you will find a Health Barometer Self-Inventory like the one on page 3. Through these inventories, you will be able to gauge your behaviors. You will also learn what areas you need to improve.

Cumulative Risks

Cumulative risks are risks that increase gradually and may add up to a total that is greater than expected. Smoking one cigarette is not likely to result in death. Neither is getting one sunburn. If these habits are repeated over time, however, the negative effects *accumulate*, leading to serious health consequences.

Cumulative risks may also be combinations of risk factors whose impact is more serious than that of any component risk alone. Driving over the posted speed limit is a risk factor that can have deadly results. Another is not wearing seat belts when you drive or ride in a car. When these two behaviors occur at the same time, the potential for harm to yourself and to others is greatly magnified. Cumulative risks can and *do* occur in all areas of health and safety. In this program, you will learn strategies for minimizing risks of all sizes.

Taking Responsibility for the Health of Others

Have you ever skipped a stone across the calm surface of a lake or pond and noticed how it creates ripples? In a way, the "ripple effect" you noticed is a metaphor for your actions and behaviors. How you act and behave affects not only yourself, but others around you. A reckless driver risks his or her own life as well as the lives of others.

Taking responsibility for your health includes showing concern for the health of others. Be aware that this responsibility does not end with the people in your immediate environment. It extends, rather, to the community at large.

As you learned in Lesson 1, one of the measures of a health-literate person is responsible citizenship. As you grow older and more mature, you will be expected to behave as a responsible and productive citizen. This includes having a concern for the welfare of the community and a respect for public property and for the property of others. Remember, your environment is a health influence you can help to control. Your health is dependent on your environment's health. So is the health of those around you.

HEALTH Online

Visit **health.glencoe.com** and discover six types of risk behaviors. Learn steps to help you adopt healthy habits. Complete the online questionnaire to find out how you could improve your health behavior.

▼ *There are many precautions you can take each day to prevent injuries and reduce the chances of getting hurt.*
ACTIVITY *Identify cumulative risks that can be associated with driving a car. What other cumulative risks can affect your health?*

20%

Traffic collisions are the leading cause of teen deaths.

SPEED LIMIT 55

Building Character

Building character is an important part of your overall health. You can build good character the same way you would a strong, sturdy building—with planning, practice, and commitment. How can you get started? By taking a look at your values and how you put them into practice.

Whenever you are faced with a decision, it is important that you consider and act on your highest beliefs and principles, or core ethical values. These universal principles and ideals, such as *caring*, *responsibility*, and *respect* are time-tested concepts that still work, not just old-fashioned ideas stored in books on dusty bookshelves. In fact, these values and principles are "living ideas" that can shape your attitudes, guide your behavior, and help you become the best person you can be.

Character education is the deliberate attempt to help people build good character. Just what does that mean for you? It means learning to recognize what these highest values are and finding ways to measure your behavior against them. It means recognizing that what you do and say affects not only your well-being but also the well-being of your family, your friends, and the people in your community.

You can "build good character" by working with only the finest "materials"—the highest values. By identifying, discussing, and coming to understand what the core ethical values are, you can work to put them into practice in all areas of your life. You can, in fact, construct a life that, like a well-built skyscraper, is solid and upright. You will not sway or topple when other lesser values pull at you. You will stand tall.

▲ *Values help shape your behavior.*

ACTIVITY *What values might prompt the teen in this photo to donate his time to clean up his environment?*

Protective Factors

You do not have to do this character building alone. Just as you can make a difference in the health of your community, so the people around you—parents, teachers, and others—can help you become a successful adult. The Search Institute, a nonprofit group in Minneapolis, Minnesota, has found that when certain *protective factors* are present in a teen's life, the amount of risk-taking behaviors decreases and the chances for growing up as a healthy, caring, and responsible adult increase. Some of these factors, including having support from the people in your life, are part of your social environment. Other protective factors include positive role models and values.

- **Positive Role Models.** Role models are peers, or others that a young person looks up to. Positive role models inspire you to work harder, to look toward the future, and to choose healthful behaviors. By *being* a positive role model, you can inspire others around you.

- **Positive Values.** Your **values** are *beliefs and standards of conduct that you find important.* Positive values put into practice lead to character traits such as honesty, integrity, courage, loyalty, and hard work. The earliest source of values for most people is the family. Your values also reflect to some extent those of society, which is governed by a code of what is right and wrong.

Your values impact your health and the decisions you make. A person who values perseverance, or "stick-to-it-iveness," is more likely to maintain a new exercise program. A person with the courage of his or her own convictions will less likely give in to pressure from peers to participate in high-risk behavior. Instead, he or she will choose abstinence. **Abstinence** is *voluntarily choosing not to do something*.

Abstinence and Your Health

Responsible teens, who value their health, abstain from sexual activity before marriage and from other high-risk behaviors, such as using tobacco, alcohol, and other drugs. As you will learn through this program, abstinence from high risk behaviors is one of the most important health behaviors you can make as a teen.

Although you may not relate your present actions to how they will affect you in the future, it is important to remember that the behaviors you practice now are setting the stage for the health of the adult you will become.

LESSON 3 *Review*

Reviewing Facts and Vocabulary

1. Explain how protective factors can offset risks.
2. Explain the differences and similarities between attitudes and values with respect to their role in health.

Thinking Critically

3. *Analyzing.* Why might a teen who is informed about health not practice good health habits? Would the teen be considered health literate?
4. *Comparing and Contrasting.* Divide a sheet of paper into two columns. In one column list all the responsibilities you have gained in the past year. In the other column identify the responsibilities that are directly related to your health.

Applying Health Skills

5. *In Your School.* Visit a branch of the public library that maintains back files of newspapers on film. Alternatively, if the classroom computer is hooked by modem to an on-line service that maintains an electronic version of one or more daily newspapers, log on and use the Search command to locate articles having to do with health. Select and read several articles. Conclude by writing a report on the health knowledge you have gained through your research.

Health Skills Activities

Activity 1 — Promoting Health Literacy

So, you've decided to take charge of your health. What health resources are available in your community to help you meet your goal? You are about to find out.

Directions

1. Look through local newspapers for articles, calendars of upcoming health events, and ads for activities that promote health or wellness.
2. List two or three activities or events. Identify the area(s) of health each promotes—physical, social, and/or mental and emotional.
3. Determine the target population for the activity or event (e.g., teens, expectant mothers, senior citizens).
4. Attach a copy of the information about the event to your paper.

Time

30 minutes

Materials

local newspapers, health newsletters, paper

Self-Assessment

✓ Selected two or three community health events and explained how each event selected promotes wellness.
✓ Identified target population for each activity or event.

Activity 2 — Awareness, Then Action

Being aware of factors that influence your health is a first step toward becoming the healthiest "you" possible. Find out what influences your health.

Directions

1. Take the Self-Inventory on page 3.
2. Carefully review each of your responses in terms of hereditary and environmental influences that shaped them.
3. With a group, brainstorm ways of decreasing negative influences and maximizing positive ones. You may want to reread Emanuel's story (page 13) for possible ideas.
4. Compile your findings into a group editorial to be submitted to the school newspaper.

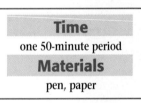

Time

one 50-minute period

Materials

pen, paper

Self-Assessment

✓ Demonstrated awareness of how health influences can positively and negatively impact wellness.
✓ Described how knowledge of influences can be used to strengthen health behaviors.

Doctors Learn Diversity

How well do you communicate with your doctor? Do you speak easily and honestly about your health? This communication link is an important part of your health. But communication is never a one-way street. Doctors need to communicate effectively with all of their patients. That can be challenging when dealing with very diverse communities. An unusual program at the Yale School of Medicine helps train doctors to talk to people from different backgrounds. The program also helps medical students learn ways to accommodate a patient's cultural or ethnic background.

Play the Video

Think About It

- ▶ What is the primary goal of the cultural diversity seminars held at Yale? What strategies do teachers use to achieve these goals?

- ▶ Give three examples of ways that a patient's cultural background can affect communication with a doctor.

- ▶ Although most students support the program, some feel that doctors naturally learn the skills taught in this seminar. Do you agree or disagree with this opinion? Why?

Using Health Terms

On a separate sheet of paper, write the term that best matches each definition below.

LESSON 1

1. The providing of accurate health information in such a way as to influence people to change attitudes so that they take positive action about their health.
2. An overall state of well-being, or total health.
3. An individual's capacity to obtain, interpret, and understand basic health information and services and use such information and services in ways that promote his or her health and wellness.
4. The combination of your physical, mental/emotional, and social well-being.
5. Practicing healthy habits to keep a person well and free from disease and other ailments.
6. Personal behaviors and habits related to the way a person lives that help determine his or her level of health.

LESSON 2

7. People the same age who share a similar range of interests.
8. All the traits and properties that are passed along biologically from parent to child.
9. The collective beliefs, customs, and behaviors of a group.
10. The sum total of your surroundings—your family, where you grew up, where you live now, and all of your experiences.

LESSON 3

11. The conscious decision to avoid harmful behaviors, including sexual activity during the teen years and the use of tobacco, alcohol, and other drugs.
12. Actions or behaviors that represent a potential health threat.
13. Beliefs and standards of conduct that you find important.

Recalling the Facts

Using complete sentences, answer the following questions.

LESSON 1

1. What are two measures of physical health?
2. Name two characteristics of a person who is mentally healthy.
3. Why is a balanced triangle a good symbol of someone's total health?
4. What is the Health Continuum?
5. Why is health education important?

LESSON 2

6. Name two ways you are affected by your physical environment.

7. How can one's behavior have a negative influence on one's health?
8. What can you do to resist pressure from peers?

LESSON 3

9. What are two steps that permit a person to take greater responsibility for his or her health?
10. Describe how cumulative risks affect a person's health.
11. Give an example of how a person can assume responsibility for the health of his or her community.
12. Explain why choosing abstinence is the best health decision a teen can make.

Thinking Critically

LESSON 1

1. **Synthesizing.** Amy is an honors student, is head of the debate team, and plays first violin in the school orchestra. She also has lots of friends and feels the need to be perfect at everything. In addition, Amy lives almost entirely on fast-food burgers and is 25 pounds overweight. Draw her health triangle.

2. **Analyzing.** Consider the seven lifestyle factors. Decide whether each one applies to you always, sometimes, or never.

LESSON 2

3. **Comparing and Contrasting.** Divide a sheet of paper into two columns. In one column, list negative hereditary and environmental influences on your health. In the other, list positive influences.

LESSON 3

4. **Analyzing.** "I am the master of my fate; I am the captain of my soul." In what way could this quote be applied to decisions about engaging in high-risk behavior?

Making the Connection

1. **Social Studies.** In the 1300s, bubonic plague was a serious risk factor to health in Europe. Research this health problem, and compare it to one of the following current health problems: HIV/AIDS, oil spills, and nuclear power by-products. Explain in what ways each period of history has its own health problems.

2. **Language Arts.** Write a script for a video titled "A Day in the Life." The video should depict a day in the life of a typical American teen in your community. It should probe the various external risk factors facing this teen, as well as ways in which he or she can respond through behaviors, decisions, and choices.

BEYOND THE CLASSROOM

PARENTAL INVOLVEMENT Ask a parent, guardian, or other adult to tell you about health risks that faced him or her as a teen. Find out how he or she dealt with these risks. What role did values play in the person's success at overcoming these risks? What other factors contributed to overcoming or dealing with the risks?

COMMUNITY INVOLVEMENT Work with classmates to create a survey on health habits and risks. Each class member can then conduct the survey with at least five volunteers in your community or neighborhood. Ask respondents to describe what good health means to them.

SCHOOL-TO-CAREER

Exploring Careers. Health specialists, who work for universities and government agencies such as the Centers for Disease Control and Prevention, specialize in getting at the root of diseases and other issues that threaten the health of the general population. Preparation includes a master's degree in public health.

If you would like to learn more about a future in this exciting health field, contact the American Medical Association, 515 North State St., Chicago, IL 60610, or the American Public Health Association, 800 I St. N.W., Washington, DC 20001-3710.

CHAPTER 2

Making Healthful Choices

GOAL SETTING

Check out Career Corner to discover whether your goals for the future might include a career in sports medicine, health care services, or medical research. Browse through a variety of health careers at **health.glencoe.com**.

Personal Health Inventory

Self-Inventory Write the numbers 1–10 on a sheet of paper. Read each statement below and respond by writing *yes*, *no*, or *sometimes* for each item. Write a *yes* only for items that you practice regularly. Save your responses.

1	I am able to communicate my thoughts and feelings to others.
2	I am aware of sources of stress in my life and have developed ways of reducing those stresses.
3	I think carefully about media messages before making decisions based on those messages.
4	I can list at least three adults I feel comfortable turning to for help with my problems.
5	I make important life decisions carefully.
6	When faced with a difficult choice, I list my options before going ahead and deciding.
7	Before making a decision, I try to anticipate the short- and long-term consequences.
8	I have thought about the life goals I hope to achieve.
9	I am aware of the short-term goals I will need to reach on the road to achieving my life goals.
10	I have established a time table for reaching my life goals.

Follow-up After completing the chapter, retake this self-inventory. Pick two items that you need to work on and set a goal to improve your health behaviors.

> **" You have to concentrate on the good things. Life presents as many opportunities for happiness as it does for tragedy. "**
>
> —RUDY GIULIANI
> MAYOR OF NEW YORK CITY, 2001

Quick Write Write down one important personal goal to improve your health and list the steps you will take to achieve it.

Building Health Skills

HEALTH TERMS

health skills

communication

refusal skills

self-esteem

stress

HEALTH CONCEPTS

- Developing good communication and building self-esteem are health skills central to achieving total health and wellness.

- Learning to evaluate messages from the various media can help you make informed, healthful choices.

- Learning to obtain and evaluate information is an important skill in our fast-paced information age.

Taking responsibility for your health begins with a commitment to take charge of your actions and behaviors in a way that reduces risks and promotes wellness. Once you have agreed to make this commitment, how do you begin making informed decisions? The answer to this question is "by learning and practicing *health skills.*"

What Are Health Skills?

Also known as life skills, **health skills** are *specific tools and strategies that lead to better and more informed health choices.* Health skills are for use not just now, during your teen years, but throughout your entire life. As with other skills you may have mastered, developing health skills takes time and practice. The immediate and long-term benefits to your physical, social, and mental/emotional health, however, make the effort worthwhile.

Social Health Skills

One of the traits of being a health literate person is being an effective communicator. Communicating effectively means being able to express your knowledge, beliefs, and ideas in many different ways and forms. It also includes the ability to say no to behaviors that threaten your health and well-being. Learning and applying these two skills—communicating and saying no—are essential to good social health.

Communication Skills

You may not think of communicating as a skill. You may be saying to yourself, "I already *know* how to communicate"—but do you? If, in a heated moment, you and a friend shout at each other so loudly that neither of you hears the other, are you communicating? Obviously, there is more to communication than just words. In its deeper sense, **communication** is *a process through which you send messages to and receive messages from others*. Effective communication involves not only making yourself heard but also being a good listener.

The skill of communicating, which is explored more fully in Chapter 11, includes the following:

- **Clearly say what you mean.**
- **Pay attention to *how* you say something.**
- **Be a good listener.**
- **Be aware of your facial expressions and gestures.**

Refusal Skills

Spending time with people who share the same likes and interests, especially during the teen years, is important to your social development. It is equally important to know when another person's needs and desires conflict with your own. Picture a situation where you are asked to do something that compromises your values or that you know or believe is wrong. This may be a high-risk behavior, such as not wearing seat belts, smoking cigarettes, or using alcohol or other drugs.

In such circumstances, a knowledge of refusal skills is vital. **Refusal skills** are *techniques that can help you refuse when you are urged to take part in unsafe or unhealthful behaviors*. This strategy includes the following:

1. **Say no.** Do this calmly at first. Use an expression such as "Sorry, I don't want to" or "I'd rather not."
2. **Explain why you are refusing.** State your feelings. Tell the other person that the suggested activity or behavior goes against your values or beliefs.

▼ *Good communication requires good listening skills.*
ACTIVITY *Name three features of a good listener.*

COMMUNICATION STYLES

When you communicate, is it through words only? What other methods might you use to express yourself? How do others interpret what you say? In this activity, you will find out.

3. **Suggest alternatives to the proposed activity.** Give a list of safe, healthful activities. Speak calmly.

4. **Back up your words using body language.** Make it clear that you don't intend to back down from your position. Look directly into the other person's eyes.

5. **Leave if necessary.** If the other person continues to put pressure on you, or simply won't take no for an answer, just walk away. Carry money in case you have to call for a ride or take a taxi.

Mental and Emotional Health Skills

Another trait of a health-literate person is being a responsible, productive citizen. This means, in part, respecting yourself and others. Doing this is sometimes easier said than done, especially during the teen years. Two health skills, building **self-esteem** and managing **stress**, can help restore perspective and give you the emotional boost you need during these years.

Building Self-Esteem

Think of five words that describe your personality and characteristics. How many of these words paint a positive picture? How many are based on how others see you? How many are based on how you see yourself? Your answers provide a window on your level of self-esteem. **Self-esteem** is *the confidence and worth that you feel about*

hotlink

self-esteem For more information on self-esteem and its role in good mental health, see Chapter 8, page 188.

stress For more information on stress and strategies for managing stress, see Chapter 9, page 214.

What you will do

1. Write down a question of five to ten words. Make it the sort heard in everyday conversation. Examples might include "Would you please hand me that pencil?" or "Why don't you have a seat?"

2. Practice reading the sentence aloud. Each time you read it, emphasize or stress a different word. For example: "Why don't you have a *seat?*" and "Why don't *you* have a seat?" Make a recording of yourself saying the sentence five different ways.

3. Find several volunteers to take part in your experiment. Ask each to number a sheet of paper from 1 to 5. Play back a recording of your reading of the sentence the first way, then stop the tape player.

4. Instruct the respondents to write a feeling or attitude they hear in the voice of the speaker. Proceed in a similar fashion for each of the remaining versions of the sentence.

In conclusion

1. How many different emotions did respondents detect in the readings of the sentence? Did the respondents agree in their reactions?

2. Which readings were perceived as sounding negative? Which were seen as positive?

3. What other nonverbal clues can you think of that influence the act of communicating?

---

yourself. Self-esteem affects everything you do, think, feel, and are. A strategy for building or improving self-esteem includes:

- **Examining the messages you send yourself.** Are you one of your own worst critics? If so, stop sending yourself negative messages. If you need to improve in a given area, don't put yourself down. Instead, find a positive way to state your goals.

- **Focusing on the things you do well.** Think about past successes you've had. This will gradually help you build more opportunities for success and expand the range of things you are good at doing.

Stress Management Skills

Your ride to school is late, making *you* late. In class, you realize your history project is due in two days. Situations like these are sources of **stress,** *the body's and mind's reactions to everyday demands.* Stress is an unavoidable part of life. However, when stress threatens to become overwhelming, there *are* solutions. These include:

- **Rechanneling your energy.** Redirect all the pent-up negative energy you are feeling into something positive. Work out your frustrations through physical activity.

- **Relaxing.** Take it easy after a hard day. Try listening to soothing music or taking a warm bath.

- **Laughing.** When things get tough, the tough get laughing. Tune in to your favorite TV sitcom, open a favorite joke book, or get together with friends with whom you have a good time.

Accessing Reliable Health Information On-Line

You are in the midst of a digital revolution that is making health information available to anyone with a modem and a connection to the Internet. Just about any health topic, from sunburn to stroke, is a mouse click away.

Is all the information on the World Wide Web equally reliable? According to Dr. George Lundberg, editor of the *Journal of the American Medical Association*, the answer is a resounding *no*. Some information, he warns, is posted on the Internet by unreputable sources that at best have no medical value and at worst can be dangerous to your health.

Mindful of this problem, the U. S. government has added its own home page to the Net. Titled "Healthfinder," the page provides links to hundreds of health-related sites that have been screened for accuracy. The Healthfinder site also enables users to reach state health departments, support organizations, and non-profit health groups.

Total Health Skills

Another trait of a health-literate person is being a self-directed learner—having the ability to gather and use reliable health information. Mastering this skill, and seeking help when you have a problem, can benefit your total health and well-being. Developing an awareness of illness symptoms and staying up-to-date on medical research are habits that can actually help prolong your life.

Accessing Reliable Information

You live in an information age. With the wealth of messages you receive—some are conflicting—how can you tell what to believe and what to disregard? The following strategies can help:

■ **Consider the source.** Pay attention to the reputation of a given media source. Is the source widely considered a "popularizer" of fad information or a legitimate provider of documented facts?

■ **Consider the "angle."** Are advertisements for products that are "guaranteed to make you look and feel better" as reliable as newspaper reports on health advances? Of course not. When evaluating a media source, ask yourself, "Are the publishers of this information trying to sell me something? Do they have my best interests in mind?" When advisable, proceed with caution.

Getting Help

Meeting life's demands means facing problems when they arise. When the problems are big, this means being able to reach out and ask for help. When you need help with a problem:

- **Think of people in your life who can offer assistance.** You might turn to a parent, a teacher, a counselor, or a religious leader. Keep a list of such names handy for times when you may need it.

- **Learn about resources in your community.** Many communities offer resources and outreach services for people in need. Many of these can be located in the Yellow Pages of your local phone directory. A health professional in your school may be able to recommend others.

- **Learn about print and electronic resources.** Sometimes, help is only a mouse click away. Yet, caution is needed, especially when using the Internet in search of help. A good starting point for reliable information is Glencoe's Health Web site, which may be found at: **health.glencoe.com**.

keeping Fit

Stay Safe in Cyberspace

Beware! There are many ways that information about you can be stored, shared, or sold on the Internet:

- ➤ Avoid giving out personal information such as your name, gender, age, interests, phone number, street address, e-mail address, family credit card numbers, or social security number to anyone.

- ➤ Don't include personal information in a personal home page.

- ➤ Stay away from discussion logs, which may keep records of your conversations or opinions for years afterward.

LESSON 1 *Review*

Reviewing Facts and Vocabulary

1. Write a paragraph that includes the terms *communication* and *stress*. The first time each of these terms is mentioned, define it in your own words.
2. Divide a sheet of paper into two columns. Label one column *Mental and Emotional Health* and one *Social Health*. Write in the appropriate column the name of a health skill covered in the lesson. Then identify Total Health skills.

Thinking Critically

3. *Analyzing.* Think about your hobbies, pastimes, and other activities you enjoy doing. Describe specific ways in which the activities you named might be used as emotional outlets when you experience stress.
4. *Synthesizing.* Aldo, a freshman, has just become a member of his school's track team. Today in the locker room just before practice, two of the older members of the team offered Aldo a pill that they said would improve his time in the 100-meter dash. Aldo has heard bad things about such pills and does not want to take chances with his health. Explain in detail the steps Aldo can take to refuse the offer.

Applying Health Skills

5. *In Your Home and School.* In your private Health Journal, make a list of adults at home and at school that you could approach if you had a problem. Next to each name, write special qualities that make the person a good source of help (e.g., is a good listener, has 25 years of experience helping teens with troubles).

Making Decisions and Setting Goals

Does it seem that people expect a lot of you? The truth is, each time you make a major decision, you are exercising enormous power—power over how healthy, happy, and productive you may be for the rest of your life.

Making responsible decisions and setting meaningful goals are important skills to learn.

HEALTH TERMS

goals

action plan

HEALTH CONCEPTS

- Decision making is a multi-step process that can be used to make responsible health choices.
- Practicing your decision-making skills can prepare you to handle real-life situations.
- Setting and achieving goals is important to the quality of your life.
- A key to effective goal setting is learning to develop and implement an action plan.

Making Responsible Decisions

Imagine finding gift-wrapped boxes at your doorstep along with a note that states, "Whichever box you choose will determine how your life proceeds." Which box would you open? Would you just grab the one nearest to you and hastily tear off the ribbon? Would you instead take your time and carefully inspect each box, looking for subtle clues as to its contents?

Making decisions about major life issues must be done carefully and deliberately. Just as you would slow down and look for approaching cars when arriving at a busy intersection, so you will need to approach life decisions with caution. You will need to "look in all directions" for possible risks, then act decisively and without hesitation once the risks have been identified and weighed.

The Decision-Making Model

One of the traits of a health-literate person is being a critical thinker and problem solver—having the ability to evaluate information from reliable sources and then make a responsible decision. The decision-making model can help you act in a way consistent with this trait. The model is designed to help you make decisions that will protect your rights, health, and self-respect, while respecting the rights, health, and self-respect of others.

There are six basic steps in making an important decision. These are as follows.

▼ *Evaluating a decision you have made will help you make good decisions in the future.*

Step 1 STATE THE SITUATION
Examine the situation and ask yourself: What decision needs to be made? Identify others who may be affected by your decision.

Step 2 LIST THE POSSIBLE OPTIONS
Ask yourself: What are the possible choices that I could make? Remember, to include "not act at all," if appropriate. Share your options with responsible family members, teachers, or friends. Ask for their advice.

Step 3 WEIGH THE POSSIBLE OUTCOMES
Ask yourself if there are both positive and negative results of each choice. Weigh the outcome, or consequence, of each option. Ask yourself: Is this decision healthful, safe, and legal? Does it show respect for myself and others?

Step 4 CONSIDER YOUR VALUES
Evaluate whether your course of action is in keeping with the highest values for yourself, your family, and community. Ask yourself: Am I comfortable with the possible outcome? What will my family and other responsible adults think about this decision? What will I feel about this decision in the weeks and months ahead?

Step 5 MAKE A DECISION AND TAKE ACTION
Use everything you know at this point to make a responsible decision. You can feel good that you have carefully prepared and thought about the situation and your options.

Step 6 EVALUATE YOUR DECISION
After you have made the decision and taken action, reflect on what happened. You might ask yourself: What was the outcome? Was it what I expected? How did my decision affect my health? What effect did my decision have on others? What did I learn? Would I take the same action again?

Developing a Moral Compass

Imagine you had a moral compass to guide you in the right direction each time you had to make an important decision. Imagine at the marking for north, the compass said *Right Way,* at the marking for south, *The Wrong Way,* and at east and west, *Possibly the Right Way.* Making ethical decisions would then be easy—you would choose *north* every time.

Character Check To develop a well-defined sense of right and wrong when making decisions:

➤ First, distinguish between ethical and unethical options. Throw out the unethical ones.

➤ Then, choose from among the highest ethical options, those that reflect core ethical values.

Practicing Decision-Making Skills

Practicing the steps in the decision making process will increase your familiarity with the process, along with the likelihood that you will use it the next time a major problem arises. An even more important benefit is that mastering this skill gives you an added measure of control over your total health.

Of course, decision making is not always easy or clear-cut, but remembering to choose only from among ethical options or choices when making a decision will point you in the right direction.

Setting Goals

Do you view your life as a series of events that simply happen to you? Do you see it as a work of art that you are constantly shaping and creating? Think about your plans for the future. What do you want to do with your life? What do you hope to become someday? Do your plans include further education and a family? What type of job do you hope to have? What do you hope to have accomplished by the age of 20? What kind of life do you want to be able to look back on when you are 70?

How you view your life can have major effects on your health and well-being. Having and setting goals is one way to help shape your life in positive directions. A **goal** is *something you aim for that takes*

Making Responsible Decisions

Missing or Making Tryouts

Lately, Amanda has spent much of her free time rehearsing for tryouts for the school play, which are to be held after school on Wednesday. Amanda's mind has been so focused on the tryouts that she has forgotten until now that every Wednesday afternoon she has a standing family commitment to take care of her younger brother. Amanda values hard work, which explains the long hours she has put into rehearsal. However, she also values the trust her parents have placed in her by asking her to take on the responsibility of babysitting. What should she do?

What Would You Do?

Apply the six steps of the decision-making process to Amanda's problem.

1. **State the situation.**
2. **List the options.**
3. **Weigh the possible outcomes.**
4. **Consider your values.**
5. **Make a decision and act.**
6. **Evaluate the decision.**

 Setting realistic goals and achieving your goals leads to increased self esteem.

ACTIVITY **What goals have you accomplished that contributed to your self-esteem?**

keeping Fit

Recipe for Success

When setting goals, here are some additional pointers that can maximize your chances of success:

➤ **Make your goals *your* goals, not someone else's.** Although other people in your life have hopes and dreams for you, be sure you agree that they match your hopes and dreams.

➤ **Be flexible.** If you do not accomplish your goal the first time, try again. Maybe you weren't realistic enough about how much time it would take. Make a new action plan, and start over.

➤ **Be the best *you* can be.** Although your goals should be realistic, do not be afraid to dream. If your goals are beyond what you can do now, you can sometimes achieve goals you might otherwise not have thought possible.

planning and work. People who identify and work at achieving goals feel more satisfaction with themselves and their lives.

Kinds of Goals

Every goal involves planning, and planning involves time. Some goals can be achieved fairly easily and in a short period of time. Such *short-term goals* include getting your homework done by nine o'clock. Other goals, such as becoming a teacher or a professional dancer, pose a greater challenge. Such *long-term goals* take a longer period—sometimes months or even years—to achieve.

Many long-term goals can be achieved by breaking them down into short-term goals. In order to meet the long-term goal of playing on the school ice hockey team, for example, you must first satisfy the beginning goal of becoming a strong skater. What kinds of short-term goals do you think might be necessary to pursue a career in politics? What short-term goals might help a person work toward the long-term goal of becoming a professional athlete?

Goals and an Action Plan

While goals can differ in the amount of time and degree of effort necessary to reach them, all can be achieved by creating an action plan. Like the decision-making process, an **action plan** is *a multi-step strategy for identifying and achieving goals.*

Goals for Life

What are your personal goals right now—today? If your answer is that you do not have any, ask yourself why.

If you do not have positive goals, you need to ask yourself: *Why? How can I remove the roadblocks that stand in the way of my having positive goals?*

Remember, goal setting, like decision making and the other health skills you learned about in this chapter, can move you toward the

Building Health Skills

Setting Goals: Making an Action Plan

AN ACTION PLAN consists of six action-based steps that can help you accomplish your goals. These are:

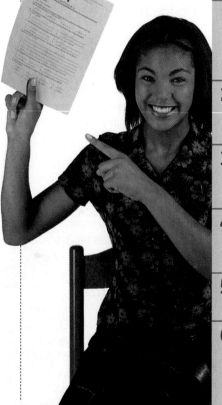

1. **Select a goal to work on.** In selecting a goal, you need to be specific and realistic. Also, state your goal as something positive. Do not settle for just "not failing." Focus your energies instead on succeeding. This will help motivate you to work toward achieving your goal.

2. **List what you will do to reach the goal.** Look for ways to break your goal down into smaller, more manageable tasks. If your goal is to become a long-distance runner, begin by training yourself to run shorter distances.

3. **Identify sources of help and support.** Sources of support and encouragement are important to achieving any goal. Such sources might include friends, family members, teachers, or neighbors.

4. **Set a reasonable time frame for reaching your goal.** When first setting out toward any goal, you should establish a reasonable time limit for reaching that goal and put it in writing.

5. **Establish checkpoints to evaluate your progress.** As with establishing a time frame, such checkpoints should be reasonable and realistic.

6. **Reward yourself after reaching your goal.** Once you arrive, congratulate yourself and enjoy the personal satisfaction. One way is to buy yourself something you have wanted. Knowing that a reward waits at the end of the journey will help you work that much harder.

ultimate goal of total health and wellness. Who would deliberately pass up the chance for improved physical, mental and emotional, and social health; for higher self-esteem; for a better quality of life? Go for it! Start today. Aim for total health!

Other Guidelines for Setting Goals

When setting a goal, keep these additional guidelines in mind:

- Make certain your goal will not harm your health or anyone else's.
- Be sure that your goal shows respect both for you and for everyone else affected by it.
- Set a goal because it will help you grow, not because you want to outdo someone or win someone else's attention.
- If you fail to reach your goal, use what you learn from the failure to set a new goal.

LESSON 2 *Review*

Reviewing Facts and Vocabulary

1. Why are questions about consequences so important when using the decision-making process?
2. Explain the difference between long-term and short-term goals, giving examples of each.

Thinking Critically

3. **Synthesizing.** Write an *interior monologue* (the thoughts of one person written from the "I" point of view) in which a teen uses the decision-making model to decide whether to attend a party where alcohol will be served.
4. **Synthesizing.** Julius, who is 16, has ambitions to become a physician some day. Create an action plan Julius might follow in reaching this life goal.

Applying Health Skills

5. ***In Your School.*** Goal setting is not limited to individuals. Groups, too, can have goals, such as raising funds for a charity, for another worthy cause, or cleaning up a vacant lot. Think about a goal your class or some other group in your school could work toward achieving. Devise an action plan for this goal. Share your "blueprint" with the school's student council.

Health Skills Activities

Activity 1 — Responsible Decision Making

Responsible decisions are choices that protect your rights, health, and self-respect. They also respect the health and rights of others. How do you apply decision-making skills?

Directions

1. With a group, review the six steps of the decision-making process on page 35, and practice applying it to Amanda's story on page 36.
2. Next, apply the decision-making model to one of the problems handed out by your teacher.
3. Elect a chairperson to present your solution to the class.
4. Review each groups solution, assigning each a rating of 1 to 5, where 5 is most responsible and 1 is least responsible.Be sure to include reasons.

Time
50 minutes
Materials
pen, paper

Self-Assessment

✓ Demonstrated how to apply the decision-making model to solve problems in a way that promotes health.
✓ Discussed how solutions promote or fail to promote health and respect for oneself and others.

Activity 2 — Rating the Media

The TV networks rate programs according to their content (G for General Audience, MA for Mature Audiences Only, etc.). Do these ratings accurately convey the messages these shows are sending? You be the judge.

Directions

1. Prepare a media rating sheet with space for the show's title, type of program (sitcom, action drama), and a brief summary of the overall message (e.g., "glorifies risk-taking," "encourages compromise").
2. At the bottom of the page make two boxes for ratings.
3. View the program your teacher airs in class. Complete your rating sheet. Share your ratings and observations with the class. How do your ratings compare with the network's? How does this show's message compare with that of other shows of the same type? Of other types?

Time
50 minutes
Materials
pen, paper

Self-Assessment

✓ Viewed and rated a TV program using rating sheet.
✓ Analyzed rating and overall message.
✓ Compared personal and class ratings with those of network.

HEALTH NEWS
VIDEO

The Winning Equation

For those who dream of winning a medal in the Olympics, long hours in the gym are only part of the winning equation. Good nutrition is as important to an athlete's performance as strength or skill. A balanced diet of carbohydrates, protein, and fat has a direct effect on an athlete's energy level and can boost his or her resistance to sickness.

To help the Olympic athletes achieve their goals, experts are on hand to provide guidance in training and nutritional planning. In the end, the athletes know that setting a goal for good nutrition is a key step in getting to the winner's circle.

Play the Video

Think About It

◉ What are some of the steps these Olympic athletes take to achieve their goal of winning a medal?

◉ What is nutrition's role in helping Olympic athletes to achieve their goals?

◉ Note the serving size of the food in the cafeteria, pointed out by the cafeteria manager. Why do you think it is important for the athletes to get help from experienced resources?

Using Health Terms

On a separate sheet of paper, write the term that best matches each definition below.

LESSON 1

1. The confidence and worth that you feel about yourself.
2. A process through which you send messages to and receive messages from others.
3. Techniques that can help you refuse when you are urged to take part in unsafe or unhealthful behaviors.
4. Specific tools and strategies that lead to better and more informed health choices.
5. The body's and mind's reactions to everyday demands.

LESSON 2

6. A multi-step strategy for identifying and achieving goals.
7. Something you aim for that takes planning and work.

Recalling the Facts

Using complete sentences, answer the following questions.

LESSON 1

1. In what way are health skills similar to other practical skills you may have learned?
2. What are three steps toward positive communication?
3. Why are refusal skills important during the teen years?
4. Why are having high self-esteem and knowing how to manage stress important?
5. What are three ways of reducing the amount of stress in your life?
6. Name four different media sources.
7. Why is it important to "consider the source" when attempting to determine whether the information received through a particular medium is reliable?
8. Identify three kinds of people you might turn to for help.

LESSON 2

9. Why are decision-making skills so vital, especially during the teen years?
10. What are the six steps in the decision-making process?
11. What are some of the questions you need to ask yourself at Step 2 in the decision-making process? What are some questions you need to ask yourself at Step 3?
12. What are the benefits of practicing decision making?
13. In what way can long-term and short-term goals be interrelated?
14. What are the steps in an action plan?
15. Why is it not a good idea to let someone else set your goals for you?
16. What are some reasons people fail to set personal goals for themselves?
17. What are three ways you can improve your goal-setting skills.

Thinking Critically

LESSON 1

1. ***Analyzing.*** Review the four traits of a health-literate person in Chapter 1 (page 10). Explain how each of these traits emphasizes the importance of one of the following skills: communication, refusal skills, building self-esteem, managing stress, accessing reliable information, obtaining help.

2. ***Synthesizing.*** Beth is constantly being ridiculed and put down by her older sister. Which of the skills covered in the lesson could best help Beth? Explain how she could use this skill to improve her overall health and well-being as well as her relationships with her sister.

LESSON 2

3. ***Synthesizing.*** Explain how the following statement applies to the skill of goal setting: A person's reach should exceed his or her grasp.

Making the Connection

1. ***Math.*** Learn more about flow charts and what the different geometric shapes in them represent. Then create two flow charts, one for a decision you recently made, another for a goal you have achieved. Your flow charts should mirror the decision-making process and action plan steps covered in the chapter.

2. ***Language Arts.*** Working with classmates, gather articles on health breakthroughs from an assortment of print media, including a supermarket tabloid, a magazine ad for a health product or beauty aid, and a newspaper or magazine article. Discuss which source provides the most reliable health information and why.

BEYOND THE CLASSROOM

PARENTAL INVOLVEMENT Ask a parent or other adult at home about a decision he or she has made and what process, if any, was used to make the decision. Share the decision-making model from the chapter, and ask the person whether having access to such a model would have made the decision easier.

COMMUNITY INVOLVEMENT In certain professions—law and teaching, for instance—effective communication is especially critical. Interview an individual from one of these professions and learn about the guidelines he or she uses to ensure good communication.

SCHOOL-TO-CAREER

Technology. Modern technology has reshaped our concept of the mass media. The most recent innovations in this area are on-line communication services and the Internet. This technology enables many industries to process large amounts of information from one place to another more quickly than ever dreamed possible. Learn how health-related industries are using this technology to process health claims and provide information to consumers.

CHAPTER 3

Physical Fitness and Your Health

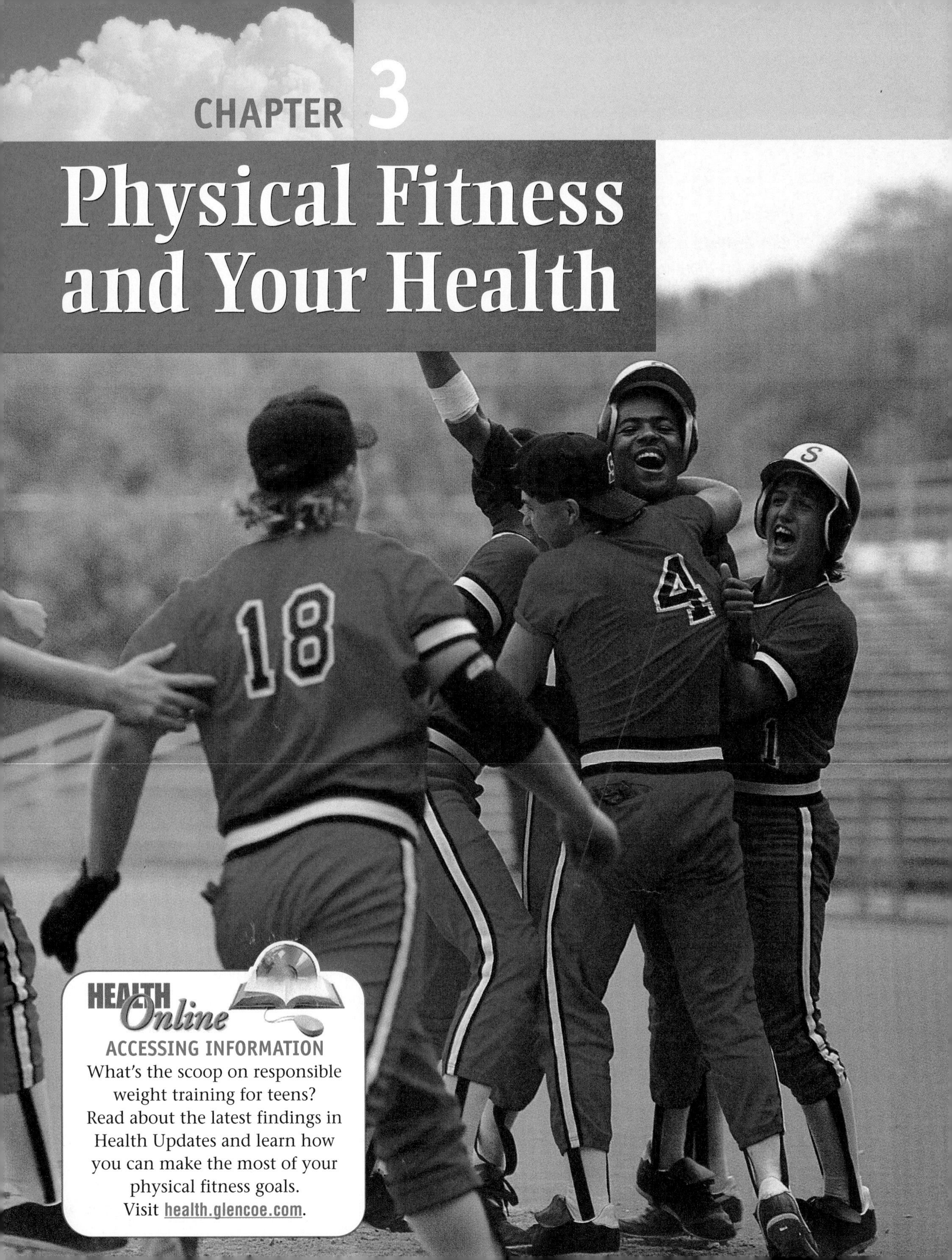

HEALTH Online

ACCESSING INFORMATION

What's the scoop on responsible weight training for teens? Read about the latest findings in Health Updates and learn how you can make the most of your physical fitness goals. Visit health.glencoe.com.

> ## **Exercise is absolutely essential to good health. It's a major key to an energetic, long life.**
>
> —DR. KENNETH H. COOPER
> FOUNDER, COOPER INSTITUTE FOR AEROBIC RESEARCH

Quick Write If exercise is a "major key" to a long and healthful life, list some of the doors this key might help to unlock for you in the near future.

Personal Health Inventory

Self-Inventory Write the numbers 1–10 on a sheet of paper. Read each statement below and respond by writing *yes*, *no*, or *sometimes* for each item. Write a *yes* only for items that you practice regularly. Save your responses.

1	I do at least 20 minutes of nonstop vigorous activity that improves the condition of the heart and lungs a minimum of three times a week.
2	I use the stairs instead of escalators or elevators whenever possible.
3	I regularly participate in lifetime sports, such as cycling, swimming or in-line skating.
4	I am more active than I am sedentary.
5	I enjoy a variety of physical activities.
6	I usually warm up before starting an exercise session and cool down after an exercise session.
7	I plan regular times for exercise.
8	I take in about the same number of calories as I burn.
9	I eat nutritious meals and snacks and avoid consuming high-fat foods and snacks.
10	I get at least 8 hours of sleep each night.

Follow-up After completing the chapter, retake this self-inventory. Pick two items that you need to work on and set a goal to improve your health behaviors.

Physical Fitness and You

Jerry is a star soccer player. He moves up and down the field with speed and grace. Yet, he isn't very good at doing push-ups. Patty competes on the balance beam but gets completely out of breath after running half a block. Would it surprise you to learn that the physical fitness program of each of these teens is lacking?

HEALTH TERMS

physical fitness
body composition
flexibility
muscular strength
muscular endurance
cardiorespiratory endurance

HEALTH CONCEPTS

- Your level of physical fitness affects your total health.
- A number of tests can be used to measure your health-related fitness levels.
- Reaching a healthy level in all areas of health-related fitness is vital to total health.

What Is Physical Fitness?

Are you able to get through your day easily without tiring? Does your body respond quickly in an emergency? Are you mentally alert in class? Do you feel good about your body? Can you climb five flights of stairs without getting tired?

All of these questions have to do with your level of **physical fitness**, *the ability to carry out daily tasks easily and have enough reserve energy to respond to unexpected demands.* Maintaining a high level of fitness is a lifelong challenge.

Benefits of Physical Fitness

Your level of physical fitness affects all aspects of your health and life. Your level of physical fitness affects your physical, mental, and social health. It affects how you sleep, eat, and learn. If you are fit, you look good, you have energy, and you generally feel good about yourself. Physical fitness has many benefits, including the following:

PHYSICAL HEALTH

- Reduces your chances of acquiring diseases, such as cardiovascular disease, and crippling conditions, such as obesity, that are linked to inactivity.
- Allows you to be more active and capable at any age.
- Gives you higher energy levels for longer periods.
- Improves your posture.

MENTAL/EMOTIONAL HEALTH

- Makes you intellectually more productive.
- Provides relief from stress.
- Helps control depression.
- Gives you a sense of pride and accomplishment for taking care of yourself.
- Contributes to positive self-esteem because you will look and feel better about yourself.

SOCIAL HEALTH

- Reduces stress that can interfere with good relationships.
- Builds self-confidence, making you more able to deal effectively in social situations such as meeting new people.
- Gives you the opportunity to interact and cooperate with others.

How physically fit is this gymnast?

ACTIVITY *With a partner, discuss the question "Are all athletes physically fit?"*

Basic Components of Physical Fitness

Not every person's level of physical fitness is the same. A teen who lifts weights probably has good muscular strength but may lack the cardiorespiratory endurance of a classmate who is a long-distance runner. Having total fitness means achieving a healthy level in each of the five areas of *health-related fitness*. These areas, which affect your overall health and well-being, include:

- **Body composition.** This is *the ratio of body fat to lean body tissue, including muscle, bone, water, and connective tissue such as ligaments, cartilage, and tendons.*
- **Flexibility.** This is *the ability to move a body part through a full range of motion.*
- **Muscular strength.** This is *the amount of force a muscle can exert.*

10 Reasons to Work Out

Regular exercise brings benefits to many areas of your life. The following are just some of these benefits:

➤ improved cardiovascular health

➤ better weight control

➤ improved flexibility, muscular strength, and muscular endurance

➤ improved appearance, such as rosy cheeks and well-toned muscles

➤ improved self-esteem

➤ increased productivity

➤ a chance to socialize when you participate in group sports

➤ increased mental alertness

➤ increased ability to handle stress

➤ less fatigue and improved sleep

■ **Muscular endurance.** This is *the ability of the muscles to do difficult physical tasks over a period of time without causing fatigue.*

■ **Cardiorespiratory endurance.** This is *the ability of the heart, lungs, and blood vessels to send fuel and oxygen to the body's tissues during long periods of vigorous activity.*

Each of these components can be measured through various tests and activities. Once you know your strengths and weaknesses, you can take steps to improve your health-related fitness.

Measuring Body Composition

Appearance is probably one of the biggest reasons people exercise and watch what they eat. Since there is a strong relationship between the thickness of lean body tissue and the amount of fat inside your body, a reliable test for body composition is the pinch test. The skin and underlying layer of fat are pinched together on the upper arm and calf. These are measured with an instrument called *calipers*. The measurements are taken three times, then compared with those on a chart for an estimated percentage of body fat. Males with 25 or more percent body fat and females with 30 or more percent body fat are at risk of developing cardiovascular problems. Carrying too much weight also puts added stress on the skeletal system. If you have too much body fat, you can lose some of this fat through moderate physical activity and by reducing the number of calories you take in from food.

Making Responsible
Decisions

To Work or to Run?

Rhonda has recently taken a part-time job at a local restaurant. She enjoys the people she works with and the new skills she is learning. She is especially happy about all the things she can do with the money she is earning. The only bad part about the job is that she

had to quit running track in order to work the necessary hours. She noticed that since she started working she has been gaining weight and feeling sluggish, probably due in part to her love for the restaurant's famous double fudge sundaes.

What should Rhonda do?

Provide an answer by putting yourself in her place. Then answer the questions below.

What Would You Do?

Apply the six steps of the decision-making process to Rhonda's problem.

1. **State the situation.**
2. **List the options.**
3. **Weigh the possible outcomes.**
4. **Consider your values.**
5. **Make a decision and act.**
6. **Evaluate the decision.**

Measuring Flexibility

Can you touch your bent knees to your chest? Can you place your palms on the floor while standing or, while sitting, twist at the waist until your shoulders are perpendicular to your feet? If so, you have good flexibility. Flexibility is important because it helps reduce muscle strains and lower back problems.

Although flexibility is specific to each moving joint, the following test gives an idea of your general level of flexibility. Before taking the test, do some light stretching to warm up your muscles.

BODY FLEXIBILITY

1. Position a yardstick on the top of a 12-inch-high box so that it protrudes 9 inches over the edge with the lower numbers facing toward you.
2. Sit on the floor. Fully extend one leg so that the sole of the foot is flat against the side of the box under the yardstick. Bend your other leg with the knee turned out and the foot 2 to 3 inches to the side of the extended leg.
3. Placing the palm of one hand over the back of the other hand, stretch your arms forward over the yardstick. Lean and reach as far as you can.
4. Repeat Step 3 four times. On the fourth try, hold the position for the count of 3, and notice where your fingertips come on the yardstick. Record your score to the nearest inch.
5. To rate your flexibility, find your score on the chart.

Measuring Muscular Strength

Can you lift a heavy stack of books? Activities of this type require muscular strength. Muscular strength is vital to activities that involve lifting, pushing, or jumping. When you have good muscular strength, you are able to perform daily tasks more efficiently. This helps you conserve energy and enables you to get more things done in a typical day.

Because the body has many different muscle groups, there are different measures of muscular strength. Two broad measures are push-ups, which measure upper body strength, and curl-ups, which measure abdominal strength.

▼ *The backsaver sit and stretch measures flexibility of the lower back and hamstrings.*

ACTIVITY *Ask a friend or family member to perform this test, then do it yourself. Is the other person's flexibility measurement similar to yours?*

SCORING (NUMBER OF INCHES)		
MALE	FEMALE	RATING
8 or more	10 or more	Healthy Range
7 or less	9 or less	Unhealthy Range

UPPER BODY STRENGTH

1. Lie facedown on a mat or carpet with your hands palm-down beneath your shoulders. Your fingers should be spread. Keep your legs straight and slightly apart, toes tucked under.
2. Raise your body until your arms are straight. Lower your body by bending your elbows until your upper arms and forearms are at right angles. Do one push-up every 3 seconds.
3. To rate your upper body strength, find your score on the chart.

▶ *What part of the body is used when doing push-ups?*

ACTIVITY *List daily activities that require upper body strength and endurance.*

SCORING (NUMBER OF PUSH-UPS)			
AGE	MALE	FEMALE	RATING
13	12 or more	7 or more	Healthy Range
14	14	7 or more	Healthy Range
15	16 or more	7 or more	Healthy Range
16+	18 or more	7 or more	Healthy Range
13	11 or fewer	6 or fewer	Unhealthy Range
14	13 or fewer	6 or fewer	Unhealthy Range
15	15 or fewer	6 or fewer	Unhealthy Range
16+	17 or fewer	6 or fewer	Unhealthy Range

ABDOMINAL STRENGTH

1. Start by lying on your back with your knees at about a 45-degree angle. Your feet should be slightly apart and your arms at your sides.
2. With your heels flat on the floor, curl your shoulders slowly off the ground. As you rise, move the fingers of each hand sideways until your hands are about 8 inches away from your body.
3. Slowly return to the original position. Do one curl-up every 3 seconds.

▲ *Curl-ups measure abdominal strength.*

ACTIVITY *Explain why abdominal strength is beneficial.*

4. To rate your abdominal strength, find your score on the chart.

SCORING (NUMBER OF CURL-UPS)			
AGE	**MALE**	**FEMALE**	**RATING**
13	21 or more	18 or more	Healthy Range
14+	24 or more	18 or more	Healthy Range
13	20 or fewer	17 or fewer	Unhealthy Range
14+	23 or fewer	17 or fewer	Unhealthy Range

Measuring Muscular Endurance

If you are in the healthy range for doing curl-ups, you probably have not only muscular strength but muscular endurance. People with good muscular endurance generally have better posture and fewer back problems. They are also better able to resist fatigue.

One activity that focuses primarily on muscular endurance is the leg lift.

MUSCULAR ENDURANCE

1. Lie on your stomach on a padded table with both feet planted on the floor. Your body should be positioned so that your thighs are just off the edge of the table.

2. Lift one leg straight out behind you. Hold the leg in the air for the count of one.

3. Slowly lower your leg to the floor. Do one leg lift every 3 seconds.

4. To rate your muscular endurance, find your score on the chart.

◄ *Leg lifts are an indicator of muscular endurance.*

ACTIVITY *Explain why it is important to have good muscular endurance.*

SCORING (NUMBER OF LEG LIFTS)	RATING
8 to 25 or more	Healthy Range
7 or fewer	Unhealthy Range

Measuring Cardiorespiratory Endurance

Can you run a mile without stopping? Can you walk all day at the mall without getting tired? If so, you have good cardiorespiratory fitness.

One way to measure cardiorespiratory endurance is to find your pulse recovery rate. This is the rate at which your heart beats following activity. The 3-minute step test determines pulse recovery rate:

STEP TEST

1. Use a sturdy bench about 12 inches high. Step up with your right foot, then your left. Step down with your right foot first. Stepping should be continuous. Fully extend each leg as you step.
2. Step at the rate of 24 steps per minute for 3 minutes.
3. Find your pulse on your wrist. To do this, find a pulse point on your wrist using the first two fingers of the other hand. *Do not use the thumb.* Count the number of pulses you feel for 1 minute.
4. To rate your cardiorespiratory endurance, find your pulse recovery rate on the chart.

▲ *The number of heartbeats increases during the step test.*
ACTIVITY *Why is endurance important?*

SCORING (NUMBER OF HEARTBEATS)	RATING
85–95	Excellent
96–105	Good
106–125	Fair
125 or more	Needs Improvement

LESSON 1

Review

Reviewing Facts and Vocabulary

1. What are the benefits of physical fitness?
2. How is lower back flexibility measured?
3. What aspect of health-related fitness do push-ups measure? What do curl-ups measure?
4. What is pulse recovery rate? What test can be used to measure it?

Thinking Critically

5. *Analyzing.* Marcella is 15. Her health-related fitness scores are as follows: flexibility, 14; upper body strength, 5; abdominal strength, 10; muscular endurance, 9; and cardiorespiratory endurance, 106. Describe Marcella's level of overall health-related fitness.

Tell in what areas she needs to improve. What reasons can you give Marcella for wanting to improve?
6. *Evaluating.* Discuss the accuracy of this statement: "Peter is overweight because he eats too much."

Applying Health Skills

7. *In Your Home.* If you are beginning or continuing a personal exercise program, encourage your parents or adult members of your family to join you. Keep an ongoing record of resting heart rate at various times throughout the year. Make a graph of the readings of each family member and analyze improvements as you become more fit.

Exercise and Fitness

Ever since the early 1970s, the United States has been in the middle of a fitness boom. At almost any time of day, you can see people of all ages exercising.

How about you? Are you physically active? Are you reaping the benefits of total fitness and health that exercise offers?

HEALTH TERMS

sedentary lifestyle
metabolism
basal metabolism
calories
aerobic exercise
anaerobic exercise
isometric exercise
isotonic exercise
isokinetic exercise

HEALTH CONCEPTS

- A variety of exercises contribute to overall fitness.
- Exercise is essential to the total health of the individual.
- Exercise is a significant contributor to weight management.

Benefits of Exercise

Exercise provides health benefits that last a lifetime. It helps strengthen not only the physical but the mental and social sides of your "health triangle."

Benefits to Physical Health

Exercise improves the physical part of your health by building a strong body. It can help reduce the feeling of chronic fatigue and stiffness, and can improve motor responses. Exercise strengthens the body's muscles, skeleton, and other moving parts and helps slow the onset of osteoporosis, a condition in which bones become brittle and weak. Another important benefit of exercise is that it enhances the body's protection against disease by building up resistance through

hotlink

nervous system For more information on the nervous system, see Chapter 16, page 364.

circulatory system For more information on the circulatory system, see Chapter 17, page 388.

respiratory system For more information on the respiratory system, see Chapter 17, page 400.

Check out some fun physical fitness activities and learn how your body responds to exercise at **health.glencoe.com.**

hotlink

overweight For more information on overweight and other weight problems, see Chapter 6, page 133.

improving fitness. A strong, toned body is capable of recuperating—or restoring itself—more quickly following an illness.

In addition, exercise contributes to the functioning of the **nervous system**, **circulatory system**, and **respiratory system**.

- **Nervous System.** Exercise can improve your reaction time by helping you respond more quickly to stimuli. This is especially helpful when driving or cycling.
- **Circulatory System.** Regular exercise strengthens the heart. This permits the heart to pump blood more efficiently, so that more work can be done with less effort.
- **Respiratory System.** With regular exercise, your respiratory system begins to work more slowly and efficiently so that you take fewer but deeper breaths. Your lung capacity increases, meaning you do not lose your breath as quickly running to catch a bus.

Exercise and Weight Control

One out of every three American adults and one in five teens is overweight or obese. This situation can be traced to overeating and a **sedentary lifestyle**, *a way of life that requires little movement or exercise.*

YOUR METABOLISM

The problem of **overweight** is related to two concepts:

- **Metabolism** is *the process by which your body gets energy from food.*
- **Basal metabolism** is *the minimum amount of energy required to maintain the life processes in a body.*

You get energy from food, and the energy value of food is measured in *units of heat* called **calories.** Your body requires a minimum number of calories each day in order to maintain itself. Additional calories must be used, or they will be stored in the body as fat.

Your metabolic rate increases during exercise. During exercise, the body burns up more calories than it does when at rest. The number of calories burned up depends on the nature of the activity. The benefit of physical activity remains for a short while even after you stop exercising. Your metabolic rate takes some time to return to normal, so during that time you are still burning more calories than before you began exercising.

Approaches to Everyday Activities

SEDENTARY	NON-SEDENTARY
Taking the car to the store	Walking to the store
Using a golf cart	Walking with your golf clubs
Taking the elevator	Walking the stairs
Playing video games	Playing tennis

YOUR WEIGHT

You are probably familiar with dieting, weight reduction, obesity, and exercise. More information on these topics can be found in Chapter 6. For now, the following statements provide an overview:

- If you take in fewer calories than you burn, you lose weight.
- If you take in more calories than you burn, you gain weight.

If you take in more calories than you can use, the excess calories are stored in the body as fat. One pound (0.5 kg) of fat is equal to about 3,500 calories. A person must control calories to control weight.

Exercise can help a person from becoming obese or overweight by changing the equation. Obesity and overweight have both been linked to heart disease and can be a problem among people of all age groups. Vigorous exercise can help reduce body fat and contribute to weight reduction.

Benefits to Mental and Emotional Health

Exercise can contribute to mental health by helping to reduce emotional stress. A few stretching exercises, for example, can help you relax tense muscles and sleep better. Exercise refreshes people with desk jobs and leads to more productive work time. It may also increase creativity by releasing body chemicals that stimulate the brain's creative centers.

Exercise can be a healthy outlet for tension, anger, or frustration. Being physically fit gives you a sense of pride and accomplishment in taking care of yourself. Getting fit and staying fit contributes to positive self-esteem because you will look better and feel better about yourself.

Benefits to Social Health

Exercise can improve your social health. Are you a member of a recreational or school team? Do you swim laps at a community pool? Do you like hiking or exploring trails in your community? If your answer to

Burning Calories

These activities, performed by a 110-pound woman for 10 minutes, can burn the following numbers of calories:

ACTIVITY	CALORIES BURNED
sitting quietly	11
playing piano	20
dancing	26
walking	41
playing tennis	55
climbing hills	61
swimming	78
running	97

▼ *Getting exercise provides opportunities to meet other people.*

ACTIVITY *List the friends you have met through physical activities.*

Managing Stress: Exercise—A Release Valve

RECHANNELING YOUR ENERGY into exercise is a good way to manage stress. While studying for a test, for example, take a break for some physical activity. Any kind of movement will help, even washing the car or cleaning your room.

Here are some other relaxation exercises for stress management. These exercises are specifically designed to reduce muscle tension:

- **Elastic Jaw.** Take a few deep, relaxing breaths. Open your mouth and shift your jaw to the right as far as possible. Hold for a count of three. Repeat to the left. Do this exercise ten times.

- **Sleeper.** Lie on your side with your arms over your head. Stiffen your body, then relax your muscles, and let your body fall where it wants to go, as though you are asleep. Repeat on the other side.

- **Tense-Relax.** Lie on your back in a comfortable position. Make a fist and tense your hand and forearm. Then relax. Repeat with the other hand. You can also tense and relax your upper arm, forehead, shoulders, abdomen, thighs, buttocks, and toes.

▲ *To contract your shoulders and upper back, hunch your shoulders to your ears.*

ACTIVITY *Compare your body tension before and after trying this exercise.*

any of these questions is *yes*, it is likely that you have met—and possibly formed friendships with—others who share your interests. Because exercise makes you look and feel better and enhances self-esteem, it increases your preparedness to meet new people.

Many find that exercising with a friend or in a group makes the workout more enjoyable. Following a fitness regime with someone else with a similar fitness profile also can help motivate a person to continue with an exercise program.

Improving Your Health-Related Fitness

Sensible exercise is good for you. The more muscles and joints you work, the greater the total health gain. To strengthen the heart and lung capacity, you might consider jogging. To increase muscular strength and endurance, you might lift weights. Chapter 4 provides details of recreational activities, such as hiking, dancing, and skiing, that also help keep the body fit.

Whatever you choose, it is important to add variety to your exercise routine. Doing a variety of exercises develops your overall level of fitness. It also places less strain on certain parts of the body and keeps you from "burning out" through repeating the same activity over and over.

Improving Cardiorespiratory Endurance

Although there are many different exercises you can do, all generally fall into one of two categories, *aerobic* or *anaerobic*. **Aerobic exercise** is *vigorous activity in which oxygen is continuously taken in for a period of at least 20 minutes.* During this time, the heart rate increases, sending more oxygen to the muscles to be used as energy to do more work.

Aerobic exercise increases cardiorespiratory endurance. It raises the lungs' capacity to hold air and strengthens the heart, making it a more efficient pump. Jogging, swimming, dancing, cycling, and brisk walking are examples of aerobic exercise.

Caution: Forcing yourself to go on if you become exhausted while doing aerobic exercise can be dangerous. People with diseases of the heart or lungs should check with their doctors before trying this test.

Running track is a good form of aerobic exercise.

ACTIVITY *Describe the aerobic activities you enjoy.*

connections   Math

Finding Your Target Heart Range

Your *target heart range* is the range in which your heart rate should be during exercise for maximum cardiorespiratory endurance. To find your target range:

1. Find your *resting heart rate* by sitting quietly for five minutes and then taking your pulse.

2. Subtract your age from 220 to find your maximum heart rate.

3. Subtract your resting heart rate (the result of Step 1) from the number you arrived at Step 2, your maximum heart rate.

4. Multiply the number you arrived at in Step 3 twice—first by 85 percent and again by 60 percent.

5. Add your resting heart rate to the result from Step 4 when you multiplied by 85 percent; then add your resting heart rate to the number you got when you multiplied by 60 percent.

6. The resulting totals represent your target heart range. Compare your target heart range with other classmates.

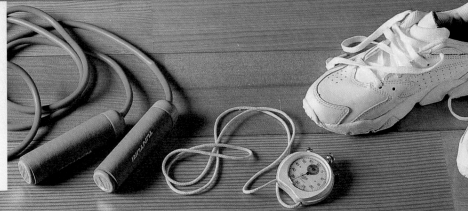

EVALUATING AN AEROBIC EXERCISE

Y̶ou know that aerobic exercise should raise your heart and breathing rate. How much vigorous exercise is enough for you? How effective is the aerobic activity you are currently doing? You are about to find out.

keeping Fit

An Aerobic Exercise Checklist

Are you considering trying a new sport or making a new physical activity part of your lifestyle? If you are and you want to make sure the activity is aerobic, look for these characteristics:

➤ The activity must be brisk. It should be able to raise the heart rate and breathing rate to within your target zone.

➤ The activity must be continuous. It should be done for 20 to 30 minutes without stopping.

Try *low-impact aerobics*—bicycling, swimming, jumping on a trampoline, and the like—which require less forceful movements.

Improving Muscular Strength, Endurance, and Flexibility

Anaerobic exercise involves *intense bursts of activity in which the muscles work so hard that they produce energy without using oxygen.* Running the 100-meter dash is an example of an anaerobic activity. Calisthenics and weight training are other anaerobic exercises. Resistance training, another type of anaerobic exercise, builds muscles by requiring muscles to resist a force. The more work the muscles do, the stronger they become. Resistance can be provided by using weights or machines, or your own body weight. Resistance training is a good way to tone muscles, improving muscular strength and endurance.

There are three types of resistance training exercises:

■ **Isometric exercise** is *activity that uses muscle tension to improve muscular strength with little or no movement of the body part.* Isometric exercises involve muscles pushing against muscles. Putting the palms of your hands together in front of you and pushing is an example of an isometric exercise.

■ **Isotonic exercise** is *activity that combines muscle contraction with repeated movement.* Push-ups and pull-ups are isotonic exercises. So is lifting weights.

■ **Isokinetic exercise** is *activity that involves resistance through an entire range of motion.* Isokinetic exercises increase the flexibility of the joints, at the same time improving muscular strength and endurance. Pushing or pulling against a hydraulic lever of certain exercise equipment is a type of isokinetic exercise.

What you will need

- Stopwatch or other timing device
- Any equipment as might be needed, such as a jump rope and running shoes
- Your target heart range

What you will do

1. Begin by taking your pulse before you exercise. Find your pulse, at either your wrist or neck. Count the number of beats for 15 seconds and multiply by four.
2. Perform some form of aerobic exercise for 20 minutes. Set a timer so you are sure to continue for 20 minutes. Make sure to exercise briskly and without stopping throughout.
3. Take your pulse again as soon as you stop the exercise. Again, count the number of beats for 15 seconds and multiply by four.
4. Compare your "before" and "after" pulse rates.

In conclusion

1. How many more beats per minute did your heart work after exercise than before exercise?
2. Were you in your target heart range?
3. What can you do when exercising to more closely match your target heart range?
4. Were you surprised by your pulse after exercising? If so, explain why.
5. If your aerobic fitness level is not where it should be, what can you do to improve it?

LESSON 2

Review

Reviewing Facts and Vocabulary

1. Describe a sedentary lifestyle.
2. What is *basal metabolism* and how does it relate to calories?
3. Which type of resistance training requires muscles to move against resistance through an entire range of motion?

Thinking Critically

4. **Synthesizing.** Suggest ways that people who need regular exercise and are opposed to it can be encouraged to participate.
5. **Evaluating.** Discuss the accuracy of the statement "Aerobic exercise is better for you than anaerobic exercise."

Applying Health Skills

6. **In Your Home.** Interview family members, teachers, or other adults and ask: How important has exercise been in your life? Why? Do you still exercise? If so, what kinds of exercise do you engage in now? What kinds of obstacles to exercising do you encounter? How do you deal with the obstacles? What would you do differently in the area of physical fitness if you had life to live over?

Planning a Fitness Program

What are your fitness goals? How fit are you? What special skills do you possess? You'll want to take all of these into account when designing your personal fitness program. If you seldom engage in physical activity, plan a program that is not overly vigorous at first and check with a qualified health professional before beginning.

HEALTH TERMS

cross-training

overload

progression

specificity

warm-up

cool-down

resting heart rate

HEALTH CONCEPTS

- To be effective, the exercise program you choose should address your specific needs and purposes.
- Realistic goals are essential to the success of an exercise program.
- Warming up and cooling down are vital parts of any exercise regime.

Setting Fitness Goals

Do you "keep meaning to get involved" in physical activity but somehow put it off? Setting fitness goals can help by providing you with a plan for action.

Planning a Fitness Program

If you've started exercise programs before only to stop after a few days or weeks, take some time to assess why you dropped out and what changes you need to make to avoid those pitfalls again. Perhaps you stopped going to an aerobics class because it was difficult to get there on time. To get back on pace, you might as an alternative choose an aerobics exercise such as walking or jogging that you can do on your own time. Another possibility would be to buy or rent an aerobics tape and do the activities in the comfort of your own home.

Getting Started

Plan your exercise a week ahead of time, and mark the activities and times on a calendar. Set short-term goals at first. If 45 minutes seems too long, start by scheduling only 20 minutes for a warm-up, workout, and cool-down. You can increase duration later when that level of exercise becomes comfortable.

You may want to reward yourself at the end of the week. For example, buy yourself something you have wanted, such as tickets to a concert. After you begin to see benefits from your workouts, you'll eventually become motivated by the results alone.

THE ACTIVITY TRIANGLE

REST OR INACTIVITY
watching TV, playing computer games, sitting for more than 30 minutes at a time

LEISURE ACTIVITIES
golf, bowling, softball, yardwork

FLEXIBILITY AND STRENGTH
stretching, pushups, weight lifting

AEROBIC EXERCISE
brisk walking, cross country skiing, bicycling, swimming

RECREATIONAL
soccer, basketball, martial arts, hiking, tennis, dancing

LIFESTYLE PHYSICAL ACTIVITY
walk the dog, take longer routes, take the stairs instead of the elevator

REST OR INACTIVITY

LEISURE ACTIVITIES

FLEXIBILITY AND STRENGTH

AEROBIC EXERCISE

RECREATIONAL

LIFESTYLE PHYSICAL ACTIVITY

Adapted with permission by Park Nicollet HealthSource® Institute for Research and Education.

➤ Each mile you walk or run adds 21 minutes to your life and saves 24 cents in medical costs.

➤ Thirty-three percent of children who watch television more than five hours a day are overweight, compared with only 12 percent of children who watch less than two hours of TV a day.

hotlink

asthma For more on asthma and ways of treating this disease, see Chapter 17, page 404.

hotlink

personal safety For more information on the issues related to personal safety when out alone, see Chapter 34, page 760.

Selecting the Right Activity

A number of factors affect the kind of fitness program you follow. These include:

- **Where you live.** Consider the local terrain. Is the land in your part of the country flat or hilly? To which kinds of activities does the region best lend itself? Temperature—especially extremes in heat or cold—should also be a consideration in selecting an activity.

- **Your range of interests.** Pick activities you like. Remember, exercise should be enjoyable.

- **Your level of health.** A person with **asthma**, a disease of the lungs that can be aggravated by physical activity, will need to take his or her physical condition into account in designing a fitness program. Other health problems also carry risks that will need to be considered.

- **Time and place.** Are you a morning person? If not, do not plan to jog each day at 6 A.M. Instead, pick a time of day when you will be most likely to stick to your goals. Build your program into your daily routine.

- **Personal safety.** Make sure that your plan takes your **personal safety** into account. If you plan to run long distances, avoid high-crime areas or running after dark.

- **Comprehensive planning.** Pick activities that address all five areas of health-related fitness.

Cross-Training

Regardless of which activity you choose, you will probably find yourself engaging in a variety of physical activities. Boxers, for example, use various exercises to get themselves into top physical shape. You have probably seen boxers jumping rope or lifting weights.

Most sports require **cross-training**. This is *combining various exercise routines to help work different body systems.* Jumping rope, swimming, jogging, and cycling are good cross-training activities for athletes.

Basics of an Exercise Program

Every exercise program, whether it is cycling or an aerobics class, should follow the same basic guidelines and include the same basic parts or stages. Consider the following principles for an effective workout:

- **Overload.** This is *working the body harder than it is normally worked.* This might be done by increasing repetitions of a specific exercise or by doing more *sets*—groups of repetitions—of the exercise. Overload builds muscular strength and contributes to overall fitness.

- **Progression.** Related to overload, progression is *a gradual increase in overload necessary for achieving higher levels of fitness*. As it becomes gradually easier to do an exercise or activity, you increase the number of repetitions or sets. Thus, you take on ever greater challenges.
- **Specificity.** This principle states that *particular exercises and activities improve particular areas of health-related fitness*. Resistance training, as you have seen, contributes to muscular strength and endurance but does little to improve cardiorespiratory fitness. A specific aerobic activity, such as swimming or running, is needed to meet this fitness goal.

In order to derive maximum benefit from an exercise program, you need to include three basic stages. These are the *warm-up*, the *workout*, and the *cool-down*. Each stage needs to be included in every session, even when you are pressed for time.

The warm-up is an important part of any exercise program.

ACTIVITY *Explain how stretching helps to prepare the muscles for exercise.*

The Warm-up

Before physical activity, your muscles are stiff. The **warm-up** is *engaging in activity that prepares the muscles for the work that is to come*. The first step is to raise your body temperature with a brisk walk. The second step is to stretch large muscles slowly and smoothly. This increases elasticity and thus prevents injury. The third step is to perform the activity slowly for about five minutes. If you are bicycling, for example, you will ride at an easy pace for five minutes, then increase the pace. Warming up allows your pulse rate to increase gradually. A sudden increase in the pulse rate puts unnecessary strain on the heart and the blood vessels.

The Workout

This part of an exercise program is where you perform the activity at its highest peak. To be effective, the activity needs to follow the *F.I.T.* formula. The letters in this name stand for:

- **Frequency**—how often you do the activity each week.
- **Intensity**—how hard you work at the activity during a session.
- **Time**—how much time you devote to a given session.

Together, these factors determine whether a workout helps you achieve the principle of overload and, ultimately, your workout goal.

FREQUENCY

Workouts should be scheduled three to four times a week, with only one or two days between sessions. Frequency depends on the type of activity you are doing and on your health-related fitness goal.

In general, exercising more than three times a week for six months should help get you physically fit. You will then need to keep up your program at least three times a week to maintain your fitness level.

INTENSITY

To improve physical fitness, you need to work your muscles and cardiorespiratory system at a level of intensity that permits you to achieve overload. To accomplish this goal, you must start slowly and build endurance. Doing too much too soon is harmful because it can cause sleeplessness or chronically sore muscles.

In weight training, start with a lighter weight and build to the heavier ones. In aerobics programs, work toward your target heart range. If you're out of shape, give yourself six months to reach it. Target heart range is 60 to 85 percent of your maximum heart rate and the rate in which your heart should beat for optimal exercise benefits.

DURATION

Time spent doing aerobic exercises should be built up gradually. The goal in aerobics is to spend 20 to 30 minutes working at your target heart range. In weight training, do the exercises slowly, taking at least two seconds each time you lower a weight. Rest for one or two minutes between sets, and do a variety of exercises to strengthen your muscles in the full range of motion. An exercise set consists of six to fifteen repetitions.

▼ *A fitness program should always include activities that you enjoy.*

ACTIVITY *List factors you would need to consider in planning your personal fitness program.*

The Cool-Down

The **cool-down** is *engaging in activity to gradually decrease activity.* Just as your body needs to be readied for increased activity, it needs to be returned gradually to a less active state. The reason is that vigorous or prolonged activity causes increased blood flow to the muscles. If you stop suddenly, the blood *pools*—or collects—in those muscles, resulting in less blood flow to the brain. This can lead to dizziness or fainting.

The best way to cool down is simply to slow down as you continue the activity. Slowed activity should be done for about five minutes, followed by five minutes of stretching. You have cooled down adequately when your heart rate is within 20 to 30 beats of your regular heart rate.

Monitoring Your Progress

Occasionally, you will want to stop and evaluate your fitness program. Ask yourself these questions: "Do I feel better? Am I walking or bicycling or jogging farther in a shorter amount of time?" If lifting weights, you might ask: "Can I lift more weights for a longer period of time?" Keep in mind, too, that most people will have minor sore or stiff muscles over the first several days of a "new" exercise program. It is important, therefore, to be realistic about your progress. Patience is critical.

Many people keep exercise journals. Begin the journal the day you begin your exercise program. List your goals and keep track of the frequency, intensity, and duration of your workouts. At the end of 12 weeks and every six weeks after that, compare the figures. You'll have a record of your fitness progress!

Your Resting Heart Rate

Another way to monitor your progress is to take your **resting heart rate.** This is *the number of times your heart beats in one minute when you are not active.* A person of average fitness has a resting heart rate of between 72 and 84 beats a minute. After only four weeks of an exercise program, that rate can decrease by five to ten beats a minute. A resting heart rate below 72 beats a minute indicates a good fitness level. A teen at the top of his or her form may have a resting rate as low as 40 beats a minute.

LESSON 3 *Review*

Reviewing Facts and Vocabulary

1. Why do some athletes engage in cross-training?
2. What are the three parts of an exercise program?
3. What do the warm-up and cool-down have in common?
4. How does being physically fit affect your resting heart rate?
5. What can you do to help yourself get started on an exercise program?

Thinking Critically

6. ***Evaluating.*** Tell how the following weight training session could be improved to include the basics of a good exercise program: stretching—five minutes, lifting heavier weights—25 repetitions, resting—five minutes, lifting lighter weights—50 repetitions.
7. ***Analyzing.*** Explain how your resting heart rate is an indicator of your fitness.

Applying Health Skills

8. ***In Your Home and School.*** Plan your exercise a week ahead of time, and mark the times on a calendar. Keep a record in your Health Journal of the physical activities you actually do at home or school, noting the frequency, intensity, and duration of each workout.

Health Skills Activities

Activity 1 — Aerobic Workout Video

Experts agree that you are more likely to stick with an aerobic workout if it's one you enjoy. Imagine that you were asked to plan an aerobic workout suited to your fitness level and interests. What kinds of activities would you include?

Directions

1. Working with one or two partners, choose music that you like and that would be appropriate for a workout video.
2. Devise a 20- to 30-minute aerobic workout made up of aerobic exercises or activities that you enjoy. Some possibilities are dance steps, running in place, jumping rope, and kick boxing.
3. As one partner performs the routine, another is to explain safety considerations of each exercise and how it promotes physical fitness. The third partner can manage the videotaping responsibilities.
4. Share your workout video with the class.

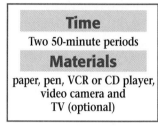

Time
Two 50-minute periods

Materials
paper, pen, VCR or CD player, video camera and TV (optional)

Self-Assessment

✓ Exercises and activities selected were aerobic, varied, and filled a 20- to 30-minute workout.
✓ Exercises and activities were demonstrated with personal safety in mind.

Activity 2 — Personal Trainer

Exercise provides physical health benefits. It can also help you perform everyday activities more easily. For this activity, act as a personal trainer to customize an exercise program for a "client."

Directions

1. In small groups or working independently, choose a client from the list your teacher provides.
2. Identify which components of fitness your client needs most to work on.
3. Develop an exercise plan for your client describing specific ways in which he or she can improve in the areas of fitness you have isolated.
4. Share and compare with the class your fitness plan for the client you chose.

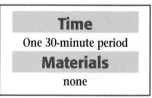

Time
One 30-minute period

Materials
none

Self-Assessment

✓ Correctly identified components of fitness client needed most to work on.
✓ Created an exercise plan that would help client achieve his or her fitness goals.

Supplement Warning

Many products sold as nutritional supplements aren't as safe as you might think. Just because a product is sold in a health store doesn't mean it's healthy.

A supplement called ephedra is a good example. Manufacturers often make many big claims for this herbal supplement. Ephedra, however, can do a lot more than boost your energy. It can give you a heart attack, stroke, or cause complications that can lead to death. The FDA has proposed new warning labels that tell customers exactly how dangerous this unnecessary supplement can be.

The way to develop your physical health is to stick to a healthy fitness program. Skip the supplements in favor of healthy activity.

Play the Video

HISTORICAL STATEMENT: For over 2000 years, the Chinese have relied upon ma-huang or ephedra in their traditions of using herbs. The plant is a straggly shrub, seemingly leafless to the untrained eye. Extensive research, which has brought about its well-deserved reputation, has been conducted on Chinese ephedra.

CAUTION: This product should NOT be used by individuals with heart disease, high blood pressure, thyroid disease, diabetes, or those who have difficulty in urination. It should NOT be taken concurrently with antidepressant or antihypertensive drugs containing monoamine oxidase (MAO) inhibitors. NOT recommended for children under 12 years of age.

DIRECTIONS: As a dietary supplement, take one to two capsules daily with meals or a glass of water. Store in a cool, dry place.

INGREDIENT: One capsule supplies 375 mg. Chinese ephedra (ma-huang).

Think About It

❯ Why has the FDA requested warning labels for supplements that contain ephedra? What will the labels say?

❯ Suppose a friend tells you "Anything herbal is safe. After all, it comes from nature." How would you respond?

❯ What are some safe alternatives to these dangerous supplements?

Using Health Terms

On a separate sheet of paper, write the term that best matches each definition below.

LESSON 1

1. The ability to carry out daily tasks easily and have enough reserve energy to respond to unexpected demands.
2. The ability to move a body part through a full range of motion.
3. The ability of the muscles to do difficult physical tasks over a period of time without causing fatigue.

LESSON 2

4. Activity that combines muscle contraction with repeated movement.
5. Vigorous activity in which oxygen is continuously taken in for a period of at least 20 minutes.

6. Activity that uses muscle tension to improve muscular strength with little or no movement of the body part.
7. The minimum amount of energy required to maintain the life processes in a body.

LESSON 3

8. Engaging in activity to gradually decrease activity.
9. Engaging in activity that prepares the muscles for the work that is to come.
10. Working the body harder than it is normally worked.
11. Combining various exercise routines to help work different body systems.
12. Number of times your heart beats in one minute when you are not active.

Recalling the Facts

Using complete sentences, answer the following questions.

LESSON 1

1. How does your level of physical fitness affect your total health?
2. What are the two categories used for measuring physical fitness?
3. How is body composition measured?
4. What two activities can be used to measure strength and endurance?
5. What two organs of the body does cardiorespiratory endurance measure?

LESSON 2

6. How are exercise and physical fitness related?
7. How does exercise help the nervous system?
8. How do metabolism and calories relate to a person's weight?

9. Describe ways in which exercise might improve your self-esteem.
10. How does anaerobic exercise differ from aerobic exercise?

LESSON 3

11. Explain the principles of overload, progression, and specificity, and tell how they are important in designing a physical fitness program.
12. What is the significance of the F.I.T. formula? What are the parts of this formula?
13. How is warming up beneficial to a person's heart rate?
14. How long will it likely take for a person who is out of shape to become physically fit when following a good fitness program?

Review

Thinking Critically

LESSON 1

1. ***Analyzing.*** How might body composition affect a person's total fitness?
2. ***Analyzing.*** Compare the fitness levels of a 75-year-old non-smoking female who bicycles three times a week to a 16-year-old male whose only physical activity is walking three blocks to school.

LESSON 2

3. ***Synthesizing.*** Participating in an aerobics class will contribute to cardiorespiratory endurance. Some people cannot afford this, or do not want to exercise in front of a group. What would accomplish the same goal and be more private, as well as less expensive?

LESSON 3

4. ***Evaluating.*** Percy plays football in the fall, hockey in winter, and baseball in the spring and summer. Analyze his program of physical fitness. Tell what is missing and what he could do to make up for these omissions.

Making the Connection

1. ***Social Studies.*** Soccer, long a popular sport in countries the world over, has developed a big following in the United States in recent years. Write a two-page report about this sport. On the first page, describe soccer, using outside resources if you are familiar with it. On the second, identify the exercise benefits that come from playing the sport.

2. ***Science.*** Find articles in your local newspaper or magazines that have to do with the costs of poor fitness. Look, in particular, for information on the rise in cardiovascular diseases and overweight and its relationship to sedentary living. Share your findings with the class in a brief oral report.

BEYOND THE CLASSROOM

PARENTAL INVOLVEMENT Observe members of your household for several days, taking note of physical activities done by each member that provide—or fail to provide—some fitness benefit. Afterward, conduct a roundtable discussion with interested family members, sharing suggestions for improvement where needed. Work together to set up a regular plan of family fitness and exercise.

COMMUNITY INVOLVEMENT Call or visit a health spa, physical fitness center, or your local YMCA or YWCA. Find out what kinds of fitness exercises they recommend for teenagers. Discover what types of equipment and facilities are available. Also, find out what other services they provide. Report to your class on your findings.

SCHOOL-TO-CAREER

Exploring Careers. Interview a personal trainer or other expert on careers in the area of health-related fitness. Ask questions to determine what kind of preparation and experience is required for such careers. Also, find out about the various settings in which such professionals work.

Physical Activity for Life

Personal Health Inventory

Self-Inventory Write the numbers 1–10 on a sheet of paper. Read each statement below and respond by writing *yes*, *no*, or *sometimes* for each item. Write a *yes* only for items that you practice regularly. Save your responses.

1	I am more active than I am sedentary.
2	I incorporate activities into my life that provide exercise.
3	I use the stairs instead of escalators or elevators whenever possible.
4	I enjoy a variety of physical activities and sports.
5	I regularly participate in sports, such as cycling, swimming, or in-line skating.
6	I take into consideration my unique skills and physical abilities when choosing a sport.
7	I know and follow safety rules for the physical activities I participate in.
8	I follow a nutritious diet, avoid harmful substances such as tobacco and alcohol, and get adequate rest.
9	I avoid "winning at all costs" in sports.
10	I take proper precautions to minimize the risk of injury.

Follow-up After completing the chapter, retake this self-inventory. Pick two items that you need to work on and set a goal to improve your health behaviors.

> ❝ *Those who think they have not time for exercise will sooner or later have to find time for illness.* ❞
>
> —EDWARD STANLEY
> 15TH EARL OF DERBY, (1826–1893)

Quick Write List all of the physical activity and exercise you have done in the past three days. Now think about which of these activities you might practice into adulthood or even over a lifetime.

Physical Activity and Skills-Related Fitness

W hat kinds of physical activities do you enjoy? Do you like to play basketball? Maybe you prefer riding mountain bikes, skiing, or playing volleyball. Whatever your preference, physical activity can provide enjoyable ways of keeping fit.

HEALTH TERMS

physical activity

lifestyle activities

agility

balance

coordination

speed

reaction time

power

HEALTH CONCEPTS

- Physical activity can take place in many forms.
- Recreational activities and sports can help you maintain a high level of physical fitness.
- Skills-related fitness includes those aspects of fitness that help you perform well in sports and other physical activities.
- A number of tests can be used to measure skiils-related fitness levels.

Choices for Physical Activity

P hysical activity includes *any form of movement—whether purposeful, as in exercise and sports or recreation, or incidental, as when carrying out domestic chores.*

All forms of physical activity provide varying amounts of exercise and benefits to one's overall health and fitness. Since many forms of physical activity involve working or playing with others, it can also be a healthful way to socialize. Generally, physical activities can be grouped into two main classes. These are *lifestyle activities* and *sports activities*.

Lifestyle Activities

You probably already do some physical activity as part of your daily routine, such as biking or playing basketball. Maybe you perform a regular task at home, such as raking leaves or walking your dog. These are examples of **lifestyle activities**, *forms of physical activity that are a normal part of your daily routine or recreation and that promote good health throughout a lifetime.*

Lifestyle activities provide many physical and social benefits. Activities associated with camping, such as carrying a backpack, hiking, and setting up tents, for example, all work the body's muscles. Dancing is an excellent aerobics activity, and so is cross-country skiing.

Sports Activities

Sports activities differ from lifestyle activities in that they usually involve competition and are guided by a set of rules. When you think of sports, you may think of team sports such as football, basketball, and hockey, but other possibilities exist.

- **Individual sports.** These are skills-oriented activities that you can do by yourself, such as swimming, bicycling, or playing golf. Many individual sports also are called lifetime sports, because they are more likely than team sports to become part of a person's routine over a lifetime.
- **Partner sports.** These are activities carried out with a partner, such as playing tennis or racquetball.
- **Nature sports.** These are activities in which there is some interaction with one of the elements of nature, such as surfing, rock climbing, and sailing.

Choosing Physical Activities

When selecting new sports or physical activities, it is best not to limit yourself to a single type. Alternating physical activities works different muscles and body systems, thus contributing to different aspects of total fitness. It also helps reduce your chances of injury.

Another reason for varying the activities you do is variety itself. Doing the same routine day in and day out can cause boredom and ultimately may lead you to stop altogether. Even slightly changing your routine can give you more enthusiasm. You might try swimming one day of the week, in-line skating the next, and power walking on still another.

Skills-Related Fitness

Regular physical activity develops skills-related fitness. Like health-related fitness, skills-related fitness contributes to your total physical health. There are six basic measures of skills-related fitness.

▼ *Many people take aerobics classes to stay fit.*

ACTIVITY *What physical activities are part of your routine? Are they individual, partner, or nature sports?*

- **Agility.** This is *the ability to control the body's movements and to change the body's position quickly.*
- **Balance.** This is *the ability to remain upright either while standing still or moving.*
- **Coordination.** This is *the ability to use two or more body parts together well, or to use the senses along with the body parts.*
- **Speed.** This is *the ability to move a distance or complete a body movement in a short period of time.*
- **Reaction time.** This is *the rate of movement once a person realizes the need to move.*
- **Power.** This is *the ability to use force with great speed.*

It is important to recognize that different sports require different parts of skills-related fitness. For example, a figure skater needs good agility, but not the power of a linebacker. Most sports require varying degrees of several skills. Some people have more natural ability in skills-related fitness than others. Although you have less control over your levels of physical skill, you can work to improve them. Knowing which skills you do well can help you decide which sports or physical activities are best for you. No matter how you score on the skills-related parts of fitness, you can still enjoy some type of physical activity.

Measuring Your Agility

Have you ever noticed how tennis players slide quickly and gracefully from side to side to reach the ball? These players have a high degree of agility. One test that measures agility is the side shuttle. Preparation for the test includes placing five lines of masking tape on the floor, about three feet apart, as in the picture.

The side shuttle measures agility.

ACTIVITY *List several sports in which players use a side shuttle.*

SIDE SHUTTLE

1. Start with your feet outside the first line.
2. Slide over all the lines without crossing your feet, until your outside foot passes over the last line.
3. Then slide back, until your other foot passes over the first line. Only one foot should cross the outside lines.
4. Repeat, sliding across and back as many times as you can in ten seconds. Keep track of your slides.
5. Freeze in place when your partner yells "stop." Count one point for each line you crossed.
6. To rate your agility, find your score on the chart.

SCORING (LINES CROSSED)		
MALE	FEMALE	RATING
31 or more	28 or more	Excellent
26–30	24–27	Good
19–25	15–23	Fair
less than 19	less than 15	Needs Improvement

Measuring Your Balance

If you've ever watched a gymnast on the balance beam, you can see how crucial the skill of balance must be to this sport. The body balance test is one good way to measure balance. You'll need a yardlong piece of wood that's about 1-inch square. The stick balance consists of two parts. To rate yourself, add the scores for both parts together.

BODY BALANCE—PART 1

1. Place the stick on the floor. Stand so that the balls of both feet are on the stick and both heels are on the floor.
2. Raise both heels off the floor while keeping your balance on the stick for 15 seconds. Have a partner time you. Keeping your arms straight out and focusing on an immovable point in front of you will help you keep your balance. Place your heels back on the floor.
3. Repeat Step 2.
4. Score two points if you could balance for 15 seconds on your first try. Score one point if you could balance for 15 seconds on your second try. If you were successful on both tries, your score is three.

BODY BALANCE—PART 2

1. Stand on the stick with your foot running lengthwise on it. Use the foot you would balance on when you kick a ball.
2. Bring your other foot off the floor and balance for 10 seconds. Then rise on your toes and balance for another 10 seconds.
3. Score one point if you balanced for 10 seconds before rising on your toes. Score one point if you balanced for 10 seconds on your toes. Score a bonus point if you were able to maintain your balance for both. The highest score is three.
4. To rate your balance, add your scores from Parts 1 and 2 and find your total score on the chart.

▼ *The stick balance measures balance.*

ACTIVITY *List several sports figures that you think possess good balance skills.*

SCORING	RATING
6	Excellent
5	Good
3 or 4	Fair
less than 3	Needs Improvement

Measuring Your Coordination

A baton twirler in a parade throws the baton high into the air and continues walking. As the baton falls toward him, he reaches out, grabs it, and continues twirling. The twirler has good coordination. Coordination usually involves either the eyes and hands, the eyes and feet, or the hands and feet. People with good eye-hand or eye-foot coordination are good at hitting and kicking games such as baseball, soccer, and golf. A test that measures coordination is the stick toss and catch. This test requires three thin sticks or dowels, each one to two feet long. Give yourself three practice tries before doing this activity for a score.

➤ *Wand juggling measures the skill of coordination.*

ACTIVITY *Explain why good coordination skills are needed in soccer.*

STICK TOSS AND CATCH

1. Hold two sticks out in front of you, one in each hand. Have a helper place the third stick across the two you are holding.
2. Toss the top stick into the air, causing it to make a one-half turn. Then catch it with the sticks in your hands.
3. Repeat, tossing the stick five times to the right and five times to the left, for a total of 10 tries.
4. Score one point for each time you caught the stick. To rate your coordination, find your total score on the chart.

SCORING	RATING
9–10	Excellent
7–8	Good
5 or 6	Fair
less than 4	Needs Improvement

Measuring Your Speed

A runner moves rapidly toward the finish line. She is demonstrating speed. The short sprint is a test that measures speed. You will need a space of at least 30 yards with a clearly marked starting line and a way to measure distances in yards from that line. To prepare, you may want to mark the starting line and distance lines of 10 to 25 yards with masking tape. Your partner will need a stopwatch and a whistle.

SHORT SPRINT

1. Start off a few steps behind the starting line.
2. When your partner blows the whistle, signaling "go," begin running as quickly as you can. As your feet cross the starting line, your partner will begin timing you.
3. Your partner will blow the whistle again exactly three seconds later, then mark the spot where you were. At the sound of the second whistle, slow down gradually to a stop.
4. Your score is the distance you covered in the three seconds after crossing the starting line. To rate your speed, find your score on the chart.

SCORING (YARDS RUN)		
MALE	**FEMALE**	**RATING**
24 or more	22 or more	Excellent
21–23	19–21	Good
16–20	15–18	Fair
less than 16	less than 15	Needs Improvement

Measuring Your Reaction Time

Perhaps you've seen runners on blocks, ready to take off as soon as they hear the starting signal. The best runners can take off quickly, and even gain a second or two over their nearest competitor. This is because they have quick reaction time.

The yardstick drop is one good way to measure reaction time. You will need a yardstick for this activity. Try the activity three times and choose your best score.

YARDSTICK DROP

1. Have a partner hold the top of a yardstick between the thumb and index finger.
2. Place your hand around the yardstick at 24 inches, but without touching it. Allow your arm to rest on the edge of a table. Your partner can adjust the yardstick to help you do this.
3. Be alert and focus on the stick. Your partner will drop the yardstick without warning. Catch the yardstick as soon as you can.
4. Your score is the inch marked on the yardstick where you catch it. To rate your reaction time, find your score on the chart.

The yardstick drop measures reaction time.

ACTIVITY *Discuss which part of a track or swim race most requires excellent reaction time.*

SCORING (INCHES)	RATING
more than 21	Excellent
19–21	Good
14–18	Fair
less than 14	Needs Improvement

Measuring Your Power

The muscular swimmer moves quickly through the water, pulling with strong arms while kicking rapidly. He has power, the ability to use force with great speed. The standing long jump is one barometer of a person's power. To prepare, make a starting line on the floor with masking tape. Do the standing long jump twice, and record your better score.

STANDING LONG JUMP

1. Begin by standing behind the line. Use your arms to swing yourself forward, and jump as far as you can. Do not hop or run before you jump, and keep both feet together.
2. A partner can use a tape measure to find the distance from the starting line to the spot where you landed. Measure to the spot closest to the starting line where any body part touched the floor.
3. To rate your power, find your score on the chart.

SCORING (INCHES JUMPED)		
MALE	**FEMALE**	**RATING**
87 or more	74 or more	Excellent
80–86	66–73	Good
70–79	58–65	Fair
less than 70	less than 58	Needs Improvement

LESSON 1

Review

Reviewing Facts and Vocabulary

1. How do lifestyle activities differ from sports activities?
2. Name the six areas of skills-related fitness.
3. Name three tests that can be used to measure the above areas of skills-related fitness.

Thinking Critically

4. ***Analyzing.*** How does the skill of agility differ from the health-related fitness of flexibility?
5. ***Comparing and Contrasting.*** In a chart, show the similarities and differences between the skills-related fitness used to play baseball and hockey.

Applying Health Skills

6. ***In Your Home and School.*** Make a two-column chart. In the first column, list the physical activities that you engaged in during the past week. Analyze each activity for the different parts of skills-related fitness. In the second column, list which skills are addressed in each activity.

Physical Activity and Total Health

Physically active teens are healthy teens. You can try to make physical activity a goal no matter where you are and what you are doing. When you get together with your friends, do something active such as riding bicycles, playing tennis, or taking a walk. These activities add to your total health, and being fit feels great!

HEALTH TERMS

training program

hydration

anabolic steroids

HEALTH CONCEPTS

- Most of the risks of physical activity can be reduced or eliminated through some common sense decisions and practices.
- Preparing your body and learning the rules are important precautions to take before playing sports.

Getting Started

Just as a well-designed exercise program begins with a warm-up, it is wise not to begin a new sport or physical activity without careful preparation. Although professional athletes often have individual trainers, you can consult your physical education teacher, coaches, or family physician to help you set training goals.

Sports and Nutrition

What you eat and drink is an important part of a **training program.** This is *a program of formalized physical preparation for participation in a sport.* Food provides the energy necessary for top performance. You will learn more about nutrition and its role in sports in Chapters 5 and 6. Getting adequate hydration when engaged in vigorous activity also is important. **Hydration** is *the addition of body fluids,* which you get through drinking liquids, especially water. During physical activity, the body loses water primarily by sweating and intense breathing. This process, called dehydration, can be a real threat. One of the first signs of dehydration is fatigue. Your body cannot effectively work when it is dehydrated. Thirst is not a good indicator of fluid loss. Exercise can blunt the thirst mechanism. Also, thirst is the body's way of telling you that the body is already depleted. To prepare for activity, an athlete should drink several cups of fluids two hours before, and then 15 minutes before, a heavy workout.

Avoiding Harmful Substances

Avoiding harmful substances such as tobacco, alcohol, anabolic steroids, and other drugs is another part of making healthful decisions and maintaining an athletic training program. **Anabolic steroids** are *chemicals similar to the male hormone testosterone.* They are sometimes taken illegally by athletes to increase muscle mass and

h⬤t link

anabolic steroids For more information on the harmful effects of anabolic steroids, see Chapter 26, page 586.

▼ *Hydration is important during vigorous physical activity.*

performance. The negative consequences of taking anabolic steroids are enormous. These include:

- increased risk of cancer and heart disease.
- sterility, or the inability to have children.
- skin problems, such as acne and hair loss.
- unusual weight gain or loss.
- sexual underdevelopment and dysfunction.
- violent, suicidal, or depressive tendencies.

Anabolic steroids mean trouble for athletes in other ways. Illegal distribution of steroids is a felony, and possession of steroids without a prescription is illegal. Athletes who test positive for steroids risk their careers. Purchasing "street steroids" adds risks, because these drugs can be mixed with other dangerous substances. The best choice regarding steroids, as with other illegal drugs, is abstinence.

Adequate Rest

Another important component of training is sleep. The rest that goes along with healthful sleeping helps the body re-energize. Too little sleep disrupts the **nervous system** causing such problems as slowed reaction time, lack of concentration, and depression. On average, teens need between eight and ten hours of sleep each night.

If you have trouble falling asleep at night, it is important to look for a cause. You may also try rearranging your schedule to allow time to unwind before bed. Since physical activity energizes the body, it is best not to exercise for several hours before bedtime. Instead, try

h⊙t link

nervous system For more information on the nervous system, its care and function, see Chapter 16, page 372.

Making Responsible Decisions

Asking a Frank Question

Jerry and his friend Dave are on their school's competitive swim team. The two boys have always shared a commitment to good health and fitness. Recently, Jerry has noticed that Dave seems to be getting more muscular and seems

to have become more aggressive. Jerry suspects that Dave may be using steroids. He doesn't know for sure. He wants to confront his friend, but if he is wrong, he could ruin a great friendship. What should Jerry do?

What Would You Do?

Apply the six steps of the decision-making process to Jerry's problem.

1. **State the situation.**
2. **List the options.**
3. **Weigh the possible outcomes.**
4. **Consider your values.**
5. **Make a decision and act.**
6. **Evaluate the decision.**

Drug Testing

According to the National Institute on Drug Abuse, on any given day in the United States, 25 percent of workers between the ages of 18 and 40 would test positive for drugs. Some experts estimate that drug use costs employers over $60 billion a year in decreased productivity, absenteeism, and accidents. Therefore, in the interest of health, safety, and economics, many companies are now testing employees for drug use. The practice is stirring a heated debate.

Presently, drug testing is used in hospital emergency rooms for suspected drug overdoses and when arrests for driving violations suggest drug use. Some schools are now suggesting random drug testing for students.

1. Who, if anyone, do you think should be tested for drugs? Why? In what kinds of situations?

2. What do you think about schools testing students for drugs? Why? Do you think this testing should be random or "across the board"?

▲ *A pep talk before a competition can motivate athletes to do their best.*

ACTIVITY *Name other steps you can take to be prepared to do your best physically and mentally.*

reading or taking a hot bath. Avoid watching stress-producing videos or TV before going to bed. Also, avoid eating before bed or consuming drinks that contain caffeine. The relaxation techniques you learned about in Chapter 3 may also help.

Sports and the Mind

There is more to sports than just playing the game. As you learned in Lesson 1, your levels of skills-related fitness have some impact on your ability to play certain sports. Your thoughts affect your performance as well.

Effort and Ability

We are all born with different physical abilities. Heredity endows some people, for example, with greater speed, others with the endurance to run long distances without tiring.

In choosing a new sport or activity, be realistic about aspects of your natural ability. Does this mean that you should not try out for the sport of your dreams or "give it your all" on the playing field? Of course not. The sports world is full of stories of professional athletes who were once told they didn't have the skills to excel in their sport.

Mind-Body Connection

Having a positive mind-set is important in sports, especially in team sports. When you think you can do a particular activity, such as jumping a hurdle in track, you are more likely to be successful than if you doubt your ability to perform. That's why coaches often give "pep talks" to their teams before an important game.

Sports and Competition

Emotions at sporting events often run high. Each team has a strong desire to win. Competition can be a positive force. Wanting to excel to "bring their team to victory" helps motivate many teenagers to develop fitness and perform at their best. It also builds character and generates team spirit and pride, leading team members to become close friends.

An excessive need to win or be first, however, can be harmful to yourself and to others. Remember that sports are games, not life. There cannot be a winner without there also being a loser. Demonstrating good sportsmanship at sports events helps you avoid conflict. It also shows that you have a healthy attitude toward the game.

LESSON 2 *Review*

Reviewing Facts and Vocabulary

1. What role does training play in sports?
2. How can your thoughts affect your physical performance?

Thinking Critically

3. **Analyzing.** Gilbert, who is trying out for the track team, has heard of a pill that "makes you fly like the wind." Give at least three reasons Gilbert should avoid using this pill.
4. **Synthesizing.** Search sports magazines or the sports section of a daily newspaper for stories that show good sportsmanship. In your private Health Journal, note qualities and traits of the athletes you admire and would like to adopt for yourself.

Applying Health Skills

5. **In Your Home.** Interview at least three relatives to find out about the kinds of sports or physical activities each enjoys. Ask what benefits he or she gains from taking part in this activity. Also, ask about the person's training program and how he or she keeps a positive attitude toward the sport or physical activity. Then answer the same questions for yourself with regard to a sport or physical activity in which you participate.

Avoiding Injuries

With any activity that involves movement, there is always a risk of accident or injury. The risk of injury during exercise increases when a person is not in good physical condition or has not sufficiently warmed up and cooled down. Attempting physical activities beyond your level of ability also increases the risk of injury.

HEALTH TERMS

muscle cramp

strain

sprain

overexertion

heat cramps

heat exhaustion

frostbite

hypothermia

HEALTH CONCEPTS

- Physical activities and sports carry an inherent risk of injury.
- Taking proper precautions can minimize the risk of injury.
- Paying attention to the weather is among the most important safeguards you can take against injury from outdoor physical activities.
- Wearing the proper attire and using the proper equipment help protect against injuries.

hotlink

muscular and skeletal systems For more information on injuries of the muscular and skeletal systems, see Chapter 15, pages 344 and 352.

Minor Exercise-Related Injuries

Have you ever had sore muscles after exercising or experienced the pain of a twisted ankle? The most common injuries that occur from exercise are to the **muscular** and **skeletal systems**. These injuries, which usually result from too much stress being placed on a joint or muscle, include the following:

- **Muscle cramp.** This is *a spasm or sudden tightening of a muscle,* usually the result of irritation within the muscle from being tired, overworked, or from dehydration—a lack of water. If you get a muscle cramp, drinking cool water may help to alleviate the problem. Muscle cramps are a danger to swimmers because they could prevent a person from being able to swim, causing drowning.

- **Strain.** This is *a condition in which muscles have been overworked.* Strains can occur from participating in strenuous activity you are not used to. To avoid strains, warm up properly and don't go "all out" the first day of exercise.

- **Sprain.** This is *an injury to tissues surrounding a joint.* Ligaments, strong bands or cords of tissue that connect the bones to one another at a moveable joint, may be stretched and torn. A sprain may be accompanied by severe pain, swelling, and difficulty in moving. Warming up properly and using proper equipment can help you avoid sprains. A sprain may take more time to heal than a broken bone, and severe sprains are major injuries that require medical treatment.

Treatment for Minor Injuries

The injuries described above are often minor and, therefore, easily treated. Muscle cramps can be relieved through light massage and by applying heat after 72 hours. Minor strains and sprains can be treated by using the *R.I.C.E.* procedure, a method whose name comes from the first letter of each of its parts:

- **Rest.** Avoid using the affected muscle or joint. This may mean staying in bed for a day or two.

- **Ice.** Ice helps reduce pain and swelling. Place ice cubes in a plastic bag and hold it on the affected area for 20 minutes, remove the ice for 20 minutes, and then apply again for another 20 minutes.

- **Compression.** Light pressure through the use of an elastic bandage can help reduce swelling. The bandage should not be so tight that it cuts off blood flow to the area.

- **Elevation.** Raising the affected limb above heart level helps reduce pain and swelling.

Major Exercise-Related Injuries

When injuries are severe, medical treatment is required. You will learn about first aid procedures for medical emergencies in Chapter 35.

- **Fractures** are any type of break in a bone. Fractures usually require immobilization to heal properly. Fractures in which the two parts of the bone have been separated must be moved back into place. In some cases, the parts may

▼ *Injuries to the skeletal system can occur during many activities.*

ACTIVITY *Name three common exercise-related injuries.*

need to be held in place with clamps and screws so that the break can heal.

- **Dislocations** result when a bone slips from its normal position at a joint. A doctor must put the bone back into place and immobilize the joint so that the tissue can heal.

- **Tendinitis** is a condition in which the tendons, bands of fiber that connect muscles to bones, are stretched or torn from overuse. This type of injury requires rest, medications, and physical therapy to heal.

- **Blows to the head,** another sports-related injury, can cause swelling of the brain, resulting in unconsciousness and even death. If you experience a headache or dizziness after a blow to the head, report it to your coach or see a physician as soon as possible. You may have suffered a concussion, a temporary disturbance of the brain's ability to function. If you receive two concussions from playing a particular sport, it is recommended that you change sports, as concussions can lead to serious neurological problems. You will learn more about brain injuries in Chapter 16.

Helmets, knee pads, and gloves are proper equipment when skateboarding.

ACTIVITY *Explain why protective equipment is necessary.*

h t link

heat cramps For more information on heat cramps and how to treat them, see Chapter 35, page 789.

Weather-Related Risks

Certain health problems can occur in hot or cold weather. You can avoid weather-related health risks while exercising if you pay attention to how your body is reacting. Do not exercise when temperatures are extremely high or extremely low, and pay attention to the wind-chill factor and smog index.

Hot Weather Health Risks

Many of the risks of hot weather are related to either **overexertion**—*overworking the body*—or dehydration, a lack of fluids. You should not exercise in hot weather without rehydrating. Drink plenty of water, even if you don't feel thirsty. Smog is usually worse in hot weather. Don't exercise outdoors during smog alerts, or damage to the lungs can result.

Heat cramps are *muscle spasms that are the result of loss of large amounts of salt and water through perspiration.* To avoid **heat cramps**, make sure you are drinking plenty of water while doing physical activity in hot weather.

Heat exhaustion is *an overheating of the body resulting in cold, clammy skin and symptoms of shock.* It is caused by overexertion in a hot, humid atmosphere. Other symptoms of heat exhaustion include dizziness, headache, shortness of breath, and nausea. If you experience any of these symptoms, move to a cool place and lie down with your feet raised.

Continuing to exercise in hot weather with the symptoms of heat exhaustion and dehydration can lead to a life-threatening condition called **heatstroke**. The body loses its ability to rid itself of excessive heat through perspiration. Body temperature rises, and a person might have difficulty breathing and collapse suddenly. Spectators at sporting events also sometimes experience heatstroke. If heatstroke occurs, call for help immediately, move the person to a cool place, and sponge him or her with cold water until help arrives.

Cold Weather Health Risks

Exercising in cold weather, especially cross-country or alpine skiing, has its own health risks. **Frostbite** is *a condition that results when body tissue becomes frozen.* Dressing warmly in cold weather, covering all exposed skin—especially the head, face, feet, and fingers, where frostbite most often occurs—keeps the body warm and prevents **frostbite**. It also protects the skin from windburn, skin irritated by freezing wind. Dressing in layers is beneficial, because air becomes trapped between the layers, adding to warmth. If you notice a lack of feeling in your toes, fingers, nose, or ears while exercising in cold weather, go indoors to warm up. Don't risk frostbite, which requires medical care.

Hypothermia is *a condition in which body temperature becomes dangerously low.* Although hypothermia is usually associated with cold weather, it can also result from long exposure in windy or rainy weather where the body becomes cold and loses its ability to warm itself. When hypothermia occurs, body temperature becomes dangerously low. The brain cannot function at a low temperature, and body systems shut down. Hypothermia is a serious condition that can lead to death. A person with hypothermia may act disoriented and lose motor control. Seek medical help as soon as possible.

Thinking About Safety

Because of the risk of injury, safety is a major concern in sports programs. Become safety conscious by:

- **Being aware of the people around you.** This includes other players in a sport and spectators, if any.
- **Playing at your skill level.** Know your physical limits and don't exceed them.
- **Obeying rules and restrictions.**
- **Accepting responsibility for your own safety.**

hot link

heatstroke For more information on heatstroke and how to treat this condition, see Chapter 35, page 789.

hot link

frostbite For more information on frostbite and emergency measures for this weather-related health emergency, see Chapter 35, page 788.

You can promote safety by keeping personal safety in mind and using the right equipment or protective gear.

Personal Safety

Risks to personal safety can be minimized by choosing the right time and place to exercise. This is especially true when you will be working out alone. If you are planning to run or jog, choose a well-used park during daylight hours, when plenty of runners and other people are out. Wearing a whistle, which you can blow to attract attention if in danger, is always a good practice.

Using Proper Equipment

Exercise equipment and clothing is big business, but you do not have to spend a lot of money to exercise. If you are starting a new sport, rent or borrow the equipment to see how you like it before buying your own. To avoid injury, make sure that the equipment fits

Building Health Skills

Safety vs. Personal Conflicts

WHEN CHAD SKATEBOARDS, he never wears knee or elbow pads. "They make it hard to move," Chad tells himself. Many teens, like Chad, are inwardly torn over issues such as sports safety. They recognize the risks associated with not wearing a helmet when bicycling, for example, but believe that helmets are only for people who aren't skilled in the activity. The truth is that Chad doesn't really believe that an accident can happen to him.

How about you? Do you secretly avoid using safety equipment because you don't want to appear to your peers as someone who can't do the activity? Do you believe "it won't happen to you"? Here's how to find out how safe you are:

1. **Make a list of activities you do regularly.** Include both sports activities and lifestyle activities. Use a page in your Health Journal for your list.

2. **List protective gear and equipment that should be worn while doing each activity.** Use information provided in this lesson, along with knowledge you already have.

3. **Circle in red each piece of gear or equipment that you do not use.** Be honest with yourself. Do not include items that you own but never use.

4. **Examine your reasons.** Think about the real reasons you fail to take proper precautions against these risks.

5. **Decide how you are going to handle the situation.** If, like Chad in the story above, you are afraid what your peers might think, try talking to them. Maybe they aren't aware of the risks themselves!

properly and is in good condition. Learn all you can about the proper use of the equipment.

Footwear is an important consideration for many sports. Shoes should have a cushioned heel, good arch support, and ample toe room. Laced shoes are best for proper control of your foot in the shoe. Avoid buying shoes that must be broken in before wearing them.

Choose clothing that is comfortable and doesn't restrict movement. When it's warm outside, dress lightly. When it's cool outside, wear loose-fitting layers of clothes. You can easily remove or add layers to ensure a safe, comfortable body temperature. Always wear socks, to cushion and pull perspiration away from your feet.

Protective Equipment

Many sports require protective equipment such as helmets, mouth guards, and padding. Athletic cups protect the genitals of males during contact sports such as hockey and football. Helmets should also be worn each time you bicycle or skateboard to prevent serious head injuries. Knee and elbow pads are important equipment for bikers, skateboarders, and skaters. Wearing colorful clothing, placing reflective tape on the bicycle, or using a light at night makes bicyclists more visible to drivers and pedestrians.

keeping Fit

Avoiding Swimmer's Ear

Swimmer's ear occurs when bacteria grow in the outer ear. The condition is called swimmer's ear because it happens often to swimmers who get water in their ears. Here's how you can avoid swimmer's ear:

➤ Drain water from your ears after every swim. Do this by gently tapping your head with a flat palm.

➤ Use swimmer's eardrops, or place two or three drops each of rubbing alcohol and vinegar into your ears after every swim.

➤ Avoid putting cotton swabs in your ears after you swim. The cotton removes protective ear wax, and can scratch the skin in the ear canal.

LESSON 3 *Review*

Reviewing Facts and Vocabulary

1. How is a strain different from a sprain?
2. How do heat cramps differ from muscle cramps?
3. What should you watch for when purchasing used athletic equipment?

Thinking Critically

4. **Comparing and Contrasting.** Tell what injury is most likely to result from each of the following situations: (a) Although Josh hasn't played hockey since last season, he pushes himself to perform physically to make a good impression. (b) Jenny is an avid alpine skier. She accepts an invitation to go skiing, even though it is 10 degrees below zero.

5. **Evaluating.** After jogging five miles in 96-degree heat, Flora felt she could not go on. She was perspiring a lot. She became pale, dizzy, nauseated, and had trouble breathing. Tell what injury Flora has suffered and what she could have done to prevent it.

Applying Health Skills

6. **In Your Home.** Talk to your parents or other adult family members about procedures that might be followed in your home in the event of a physical activity-related injury. Then post emergency information, such as your family physician's phone number, the type of medical insurance your family has, and the names and numbers of responsible adults who might be contacted in an emergency.

Health Skills Activities

Activity 1 — A Personal Fitness Plan

Becoming and staying fit is essential to good health. It is up to each individual to take charge of his or her own fitness. Start by creating a fitness action plan.

Directions

1. Write your name and today's date at the top of a sheet of paper.
2. Divide the page in half lengthwise to form two columns. In the left column, list the elements of a comprehensive plan to improve and maintain your fitness.
3. In the right column, make a physical fitness action plan (see page 38). Give careful thought to your goals, making sure your objectives are measurable.
4. Carry out your fitness plan, checking your action plan from time to time.
5. On a date specified by your teacher, bring your plan to class for review.

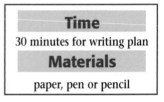

Time
30 minutes for writing plan
Materials
paper, pen or pencil

Self-Assessment

✓ Identified the elements of a comprehensive fitness plan.
✓ Listed at least two realistic goals and an action plan that you can work toward to achieve health-related fitness.

Activity 2 — What's Wrong with This Picture?

To avoid injury related to physical activity, you need to know the causes of such injuries. In this activity, you will raise the consciousness of people in your own school or community.

Directions

1. Create a sign that shows correct and incorrect ways of performing a physical action, such as lifting or stretching. Use international symbols where possible. (For example, to show the proper way to lift heavy objects, you might draw a silhouette of a person bending at the knees with a red slash through it.)
2. Sketch out ideas on scrap paper before transferring them to poster board. Make your sign as colorful and eye-catching as possible.
3. Display your sign in the school hallway or, with permission, in a public place.

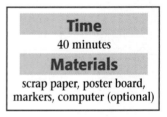

Time
40 minutes
Materials
scrap paper, poster board, markers, computer (optional)

Self-Assessment

✓ Created visually appealing signs that communicate proper safety and injury prevention techniques.
✓ Showed at least two clearly correct or incorrect actions.

HEALTH NEWS
ARTICLE

Playing It Safer

Sports-related injuries send an average of 2.6 million young people to the hospital each year, according to a new study done by the Centers for Disease Control and Prevention in Atlanta, Georgia. Dr. Michael Busch, of Children's Healthcare of Atlanta, says that the most common injuries are relatively minor.

"A lot of them are simple musculoskeletal injuries," Busch said. "Your traditional sprains and fractures."

Experts estimate two-thirds of all sports injuries are preventable.

In the past, medical training emphasized the treatment of sports injuries. Today doctors are highlighting injury prevention.

"The real key is education," says Busch. "We know a lot more about the importance of equipment, diet, and rules related to safety."

The use of protective equipment is vital. Kneepads, elbow pads, and shin guards help to prevent bruises and abrasions. Although wrist guards can't thwart every wrist fracture, they do prevent hand abrasions and sprains. Bike helmets are essential for roller-blading, skateboarding, scooters, snowboarding and cycling.

"You should never see a child on a bike without a helmet," Busch said.

Read This ▼

How Risky Is Your Favorite Sport?

Which sports put players at the greatest risk? Researchers examined three years of data about young people and sports injuries. This chart shows the sports that were the source of the most emergency room visits.

Sport	Average Number of ER Visits Per Year
Basketball	447,000
Cycling	421,000
Football	271,000
Baseball	245,000
Skating/Skateboarding	150,000
Gymnastics/Cheerleading	146,000
Snow Sports	111,000
Soccer	95,000
Source: CDC	

Think About It

1. Give two examples of preventable sports injuries. Explain how someone might avoid each injury.
2. How can you advocate for safe sports at your school?

Using Health Terms

On a separate sheet of paper, write the term that best matches each definition below.

LESSON 1

1. The ability to use two or more body parts together well, or to use the senses along with the body parts.
2. The rate of movement once a person realizes the need to move.
3. Physical activity that is a normal part of your day-to-day routine or recreation.
4. The ability to control movements and to change the body's position quickly.
5. Any form of movement, whether purposeful, as in exercise and sports, or incidental, as when doing domestic chores.
6. The ability to use force with great speed.
7. The ability to remain upright either while standing still or moving.
8. The ability to move a distance or complete a body movement in a short period of time.

LESSON 2

9. A program of formalized physical preparation for participation in a sport.
10. Chemicals similar to the male hormone testosterone.
11. The addition of body fluids.

LESSON 3

12. A condition that results when body tissue becomes frozen.
13. Overheating of the body resulting in cold, clammy skin and symptoms of shock.
14. Spasm or sudden tightening of a muscle.
15. Muscle spasms that are the result of loss of large amounts of salt and water through perspiration.
16. An injury to tissues surrounding a joint.
17. Condition in which muscles have been overworked.
18. Condition in which body temperature becomes dangerously low.

Recalling the Facts

Using complete sentences, answer the following questions.

LESSON 1

1. Identify three activities that could be either lifestyle or sport activities. Give examples to support your claims.
2. What skills-related fitness does the side shuttle measure?
3. What skills-related fitness does a discus-thrower in the Olympic Games possess?
4. Which part of a swim race most requires excellent reaction time?

LESSON 2

5. How are nutrition and adequate rest beneficial to an athlete?

6. Why are anabolic steroids not part of a good training program for a weight lifter, even though they do increase muscle bulk?

LESSON 3

7. What causes and prevents muscle cramps?
8. Why must players of contact sports take concussions seriously?
9. Why should you avoid exercising outdoors in heavy smog?
10. What medical condition results when body tissue becomes frozen?

Thinking Critically

LESSON 1

1. ***Comparing and Contrasting.*** List several lifestyle activities that are chores and several that are forms of recreation. Tell which of the measures of physical fitness are supported by each activity.

2. ***Evaluating.*** Conrad's skill-related fitness scores are as follows: agility, 20; balance, 4; coordination, 2; power, 88; reaction time, 20; and speed, 25. In which skills does he excel? Name three sports that Conrad might have success in.

LESSON 2

3. ***Evaluating.*** List several questions you could ask about a team's training program to determine if all the aspects of a good training program have been included.

LESSON 3

4. ***Analyzing.*** Mr. Vasquez had been working for three hours in the sun. Suddenly, he fell to the ground. He was not perspiring, and he felt very hot. His pulse was racing and breathing was difficult. Tell what problem he was suffering.

Making the Connection

1. ***Science.*** Develop a physical activity program that someone in good health could perform outdoors in each season in your locality. Note any risks of weather-related health problems that might exist when carrying out these activities, as well as precautions that could be taken against each possible risk.

2. ***Language Arts.*** Jim Abbott has pitched at the professional level for several baseball teams despite missing one hand. Tony Dempsey is a professional football place kicker who lacks toes on his kicking foot. Research one such individual to learn about the special properties that enabled him or her to excel as an athlete.

BEYOND THE CLASSROOM

PARENTAL INVOLVEMENT Some family members may have medical conditions that preclude certain kinds of exercise. If possible, identify someone in your family or a family friend that has, or has had, such a problem. Work with this person to develop a modified exercise program that covers as many of the 11 basic measures of fitness as possible.

COMMUNITY INVOLVEMENT Observe 20 people doing physical activity in your neighborhood. Record your answers to these questions in a chart: How old are they? What are they doing? Are they alone, or with a partner or group? At what time do they participate in physical activities? What conclusions can you draw from the information you gathered?

SCHOOL-TO-CAREER
Interpersonal. Invite a physical therapist to speak to your class for more information on becoming a physical therapist. Find out in what ways physical therapists help people with sports-related injuries, what training you would need, where you might work, and the range of pay. Write a summary of your findings and add the information to a class booklet on careers.

CHAPTER 5

Nutrition and Your Health

HEALTH *Online*

ACCESSING INFORMATION

How will you know what's going into the food you eat and what you're getting out of it? Read "Biotechnology: Miracle or Monster," to understand the pros and cons of biotech foods. Go to <u>health.glencoe.com</u> and click on Health Updates for the latest.

> **Reverse the typical American meal pattern and instead eat like a king for breakfast, a prince for lunch and a pauper for dinner.**
>
> —JANE BRODY
> NUTRITIONIST

Quick Write List some of the main ingredients that make up a healthful eating plan for breakfast, for lunch, and for dinner.

Self-Inventory Write the numbers 1–10 on a sheet of paper. Read each statement below and respond by writing *yes*, *no*, or *sometimes* for each item. Write a *yes* only for items that you practice regularly. Save your responses.

1	I eat a variety of foods that provide nutrients my body needs.
2	I include plenty of fruits, vegetables, and grain products such as pasta, rice, and bread in my eating plan.
3	I cut away visible fat or choose lower-fat meats and remove the skin from chicken.
4	I make an effort to trade off my intake of fried foods and other foods I think might be high in fat with lower-fat foods.
5	I taste food before salting it.
6	I choose nutritious snacks.
7	I eat the recommended servings from the five food groups from the Food Guide Pyramid.
8	I follow a nutritious eating plan at breakfast every day.
9	I know how to read nutrition labels and use that information when shopping.
10	I am able to spot false or misleading claims and promises in food ads.

Follow-up After completing the chapter, retake this self-inventory. Pick two items that you need to work on and set a goal to improve your health behaviors.

Food in Your Life

Picture yourself biting into a crisp, juicy apple or a slice of pizza oozing with cheese and zesty tomato sauce. Which picture appeals to you most? What foods do you enjoy eating?

Not all foods supply the same nutrients in the same amounts. Making informed, healthful food choices is important to your health and to your energy level.

HEALTH TERMS

nutrients

hunger

appetite

nutrition

HEALTH CONCEPTS

- The body has a physical need for food, which is signaled by hunger.
- Many people's eating habits are governed by appetite, rather than by hunger.
- Factors that influence your food choices include culture, family and friends, advertising, lifestyle, and mood.
- Learning the basics of nutrition can help you become a more healthful eater both now and later in life.
- Proper nutrition is a tool in disease prevention.

Why Do You Eat?

The foods you eat are your body's chief source of **nutrients** (NOO-tree-uhnts), the *substances in food that your body needs to function properly to grow, to repair itself, and to supply you with energy.* The nutrients in food affect all sides of your health triangle. They affect how you look, feel, act, grow, and even your abilities—how well you function each day.

Have you ever wondered why you eat and why you make certain food choices? The reasons may be more complex than you realize. Your eating habits stem from both a physical *need* for food and a psychological *desire* for food. Learning to recognize the difference between the two helps you to make more healthful food choices.

Your Body's Physical Need for Food

The most basic reason for eating is physical. Food, along with air and water, is one of life's basic needs. Your body tells you through hunger when it needs food. **Hunger** is *a natural drive that protects you from starvation.*

When your stomach is empty, its walls contract, stimulating nerve endings. The nerve endings signal your brain that your body's food supply needs replenishing. Once you have responded to this message, the walls of the stomach are stretched and the nerve endings are no longer stimulated. By eating, you have satisfied your physical need for food. You feel "full."

Your Mind's Desire for Food

Have you ever "made room" for dessert at the end of a big meal? Maybe you have eaten in response to the aroma of fresh-baked cookies, or maybe, like Pete in the story that opened this chapter, you ate to be sociable. In such cases, you have eaten not in response to hunger but to **appetite.** Appetite is *a desire, rather than a need, to eat.*

Appetite is a learned, rather than an inborn, response. It is shaped by factors in your environment and by your emotions.

Your Environment

There are a number of environmental factors that influence your food choices. These include your cultural heritage, your family and social relationships, media messages, and your lifestyle.

CULTURE

What foods do you associate with picnics, county fairs, the movies, baseball games, and holidays such as Thanksgiving, and birthday parties? Your food choices reflect the culture you live in, as well as your ethnic background and perhaps your religious beliefs. Teenagers have a culture of their own, too. What eating practices seem to be part of teen culture?

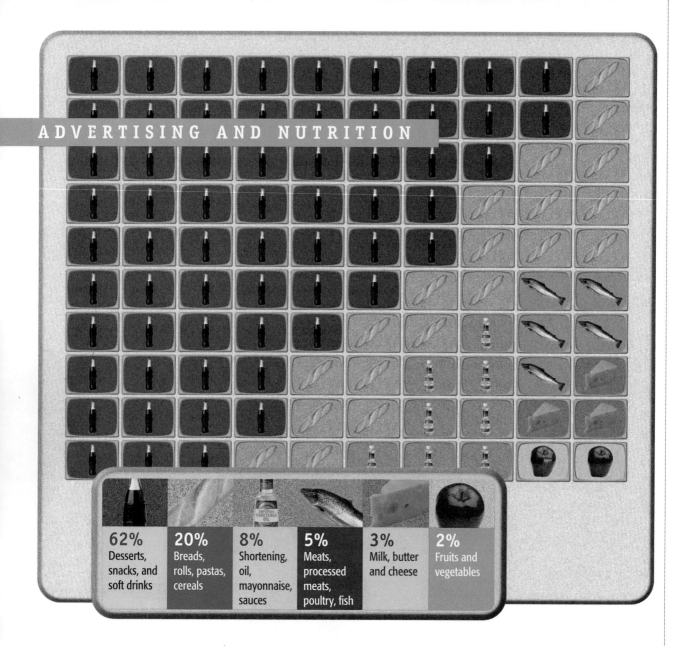

62%	20%	8%	5%	3%	2%
Desserts, snacks, and soft drinks	Breads, rolls, pastas, cereals	Shortening, oil, mayonnaise, sauces	Meats, processed meats, poultry, fish	Milk, butter and cheese	Fruits and vegetables

Does it appear to you that advertising promotes wellness through good nutrition?

ACTIVITY **Determine which categories of food products receive the most attention and which receive the least from advertisers.**

FAMILY AND FRIENDS

What you ate as a child, what you learned to like and dislike, and when you ate meals were all influenced by your family. These influences affect your food decisions and preferences now, and they will continue to influence you throughout your life.

As you have grown older, friends have influenced your food choices. Perhaps you tried new foods at their homes or tasted different foods at parties. Because eating can be a social experience, food is the focus of many gatherings.

ADVERTISING

Food ads are everywhere—on television, in magazines, and on billboards. Food advertisements are created to make you aware of certain foods and, perhaps, to sell you on their benefits. Most importantly, they can shape food decisions. Think about food ads you see and hear on television. Which foods have you bought or tried as a result of such ads?

Many people believe everything they read in newspapers and see and hear on television and radio. While many ads are responsible, others may be misleading. For example, an ad may state that a food is low in fat without stating that it is also high in calories. Advertisers spend millions of dollars on powerful persuasion techniques. Ads may try to persuade you that status, sex appeal, weight loss, or a terrific appearance will be yours if you buy the product. To make informed food choices, you need to know about food and health. You need to listen and judge advertising messages carefully. That way, you—not advertisers—control what foods you buy and eat.

TIME AND MONEY

Taste and nutrition are the two top factors that influence food shopping decisions. Cost, convenience, and food safety come next. With today's busy lifestyles, people rely more on foods they can cook and eat quickly, such as microwavable meals and other convenience foods. To stay healthy, choose some foods that will provide you with essential nutrients and that can be prepared and eaten within the time you have available. Skipping meals cheats your body of the nutrients food provides. Cost can also affect food choices. How has cost affected food decisions you have made?

Your Emotions

Emotions are another factor that affects eating habits. Have you ever headed to the refrigerator just because you had nothing else to do? Do you tend to eat more—or less—when you feel stressed, frustrated, or depressed? Eating to relieve tension or boredom can result in overeating. At the same time, if you lose your appetite when you are upset or bored, you may miss out on getting important nutrients that your body needs.

Your Eating Habits

Choosing foods that taste good *and* provide nutrients without too much fat, cholesterol, and sodium, is one of the most healthful ways to reduce major risk factors for chronic diseases, including **obesity**, high blood pressure, and high blood cholesterol. Why, then, is eating linked to six out of ten leading causes of death in the United States, including heart disease, stroke, and cancer? One answer is that many people are unable to distinguish between appetite and hunger. They eat past the point of feeling full because their appetite continues to be stimulated after their hunger has been satisfied. Unfortunately, many of the foods that stimulate the appetite are also high in fat and calories.

keeping Fit

Managing Your Eating Habits

Here are some tips for managing your eating habits.

➤ **Avoid being influenced by others in making your food choices.** Make choices with *your health* in mind—not just your appetite.

➤ **Pay attention to quantity.** Start off with reasonably sized servings, and, if possible, use a smaller plate. Listen to your body's "hunger clock" rather than to your appetite. When you feel full, set down your fork or spoon and stop eating. Remember, it takes 20 minutes for your stomach to completely signal your body that it is satisfied.

➤ **Make something other than food the focus of everyday social occasions.** If you are getting together with friends, consider a setting other than a restaurant. This might be a park, a community swimming pool, a skating rink, or the home of one of the group members.

hotlink

obesity For more information on obesity and the health risks associated with it, see Chapter 6, page 134.

Nutrition Throughout Your Life

At every stage in life, good nutrition is essential for health. **Nutrition** is *the process by which the body takes in and uses food.* Even before you were born, then as an infant and a child, and now as a teen, nutrients in food provided and continue to provide you with substances you need to grow and develop. At each age you have required the same nutrients. As you have grown and developed, however, you have needed them in increasing amounts.

Getting the nutrients your body needs also enables you to have energy, feel and look your best, and stay mentally alert. Another important benefit of good nutrition is that it can help prevent chronic diseases such as heart disease, certain cancers, diabetes, and stroke.

Next to the first years of life, adolescence is the fastest period of growth a person experiences. For growth and active living, the body uses more energy from food and has higher nutrient needs than ever before. In spite of this, many teens skip meals and make poor food choices. Think about what you have eaten today. Would you describe your food choices as healthful?

LESSON 1 *Review*

Reviewing Facts and Vocabulary

1. Explain the difference between hunger and appetite.
2. What factors influence decisions that affect food choices?
3. Why is good nutrition so important during adolescence?

Thinking Critically

4. ***Analyzing.*** Give three examples of how your culture and family have influenced your eating habits.
5. ***Comparing and Contrasting.*** Compare your food habits with those of a friend. What might account for the differences and similarities?
6. ***Synthesizing.*** In what ways beyond those mentioned in the lesson can emotions affect your food choices?

Applying Health Skills

7. ***In Your Home.*** Analyze factors that influence your eating patterns. Make a chart showing the food purchased in one grocery shopping trip. Indicate whether foods were selected for reasons of cost, convenience, culture, or any other factor described in the lesson. Analyze the chart, and determine which factors represented the greatest influence on your family's food choices. Share your findings with your family, discussing the impact these choices make on the nutritional value of your meals.

Nutrients: Carbohydrates, Proteins, and Fats

I n order to survive, the human body needs the nutrients found in food. These nutrients, which perform a number of life-sustaining functions in the body, are divided into six main categories: carbohydrates, proteins, fats, vitamins, minerals, and water. Each has a unique function in the normal growth and functioning of your body.

HEALTH TERMS

carbohydrates

glucose

glycogen

proteins

amino acids

lipid

linoleic acid

cholesterol

HEALTH CONCEPTS

- The nutrients found in food are essential to life.
- Carbohydrates are the body's chief fuel.
- A healthful eating plan includes appropriate amounts of protein to build and repair body tissue.
- Limiting fat and dietary cholesterol is a guideline for health.

Carbohydrates

Do you enjoy eating potatoes, pasta, and bread? These foods are rich in carbohydrates. Made up of carbon, oxygen, and hydrogen, **carbohydrates** are *the starches and sugars found in foods*. Carbohydrates are the body's preferred source of energy, providing four calories per gram.

Depending on their chemical makeup, carbohydrates are classified into one of two types—simple or complex. Health experts recommend that 55 to 65 percent of your daily calories come from carbohydrates, mainly complex carbohydrates.

Simple Carbohydrates

Simple carbohydrates, or sugars, are present naturally in fruits, some vegetables, and milk. These sugars are called fructose in fruit, lactose in milk, maltose in grain, and sucrose in table sugar. Sugars are also added to many manufactured food products, such as candy, cookies, soft drinks, and other concentrated sweets. In recent decades, food manufacturers have also begun adding corn syrup and other forms of sugar to soups, salad dressings, breads, and other foods you may not characterize as being sweet.

Complex Carbohydrates

Complex carbohydrates, or starches, are found in great supply in rice and other grains, seeds, nuts, legumes (dried peas and beans), and tubers (potatoes, cassava, yams, taro). Starches are called complex carbohydrates because they are chemically more complex than simple carbohydrates. They are made of many sugars linked together.

During digestion, starches break down into sugars.

The Role of Carbohydrates

Before your body can use carbohydrates, it must first convert them to **glucose**, *a simple sugar and the body's chief fuel.* Glucose that is not used right away is stored in the liver and muscles as *a starch-like substance* called **glycogen** (GLY-kuh-juhn). Later, when more glucose is

Which of these foods do you eat regularly? What other foods do you enjoy eating?

ACTIVITY *List the foods in the picture that are high in complex carbohydrates.*

needed, the glycogen is converted back to glucose. When people consume more carbohydrates than their body needs for energy or can store as glycogen, this excess is stored as adipose tissue, or body fat.

Fiber

Found in the tough, stringy part of vegetables, fruits, and grains, fiber is a special form of complex carbohydrate. Although it cannot be digested and used as energy, fiber serves other vital functions. It helps move waste through your **digestive system** and helps prevent constipation, appendicitis, and other intestinal problems. Eating enough fiber throughout your life may reduce your risk of some cancers and heart disease. It is also instrumental in controlling diabetes. Some types of fiber seem to help lower blood cholesterol and control blood sugar, though this connection is only partially understood.

For people watching their weight, fiber offers other benefits. Fiber-rich foods are bulky, so they offer a feeling of fullness. They tend to be lower in fat and calories, and they may take longer to chew, thereby slowing the pace of your meal.

You can increase your fiber intake by eating an abundance of vegetables and fruits, especially those with edible skins and seeds. Other good sources include whole-grain products, such as bran cereals, whole-wheat breads and pasta, whole rye bread, brown rice, oatmeal, corn tortillas, and popcorn. It is recommended that you eat 25 grams of fiber a day.

h⬤t l⬤nk

digestive system For more information on the digestive system and its functions, see Chapter 18, page 412.

Proteins

A vital part of every body cell, **proteins** are *nutrients that help build and maintain body tissues.* Muscle, bone, connective tissue, teeth, skin, blood, and vital organs all contain protein. Like carbohydrates, proteins provide four calories per gram. Like both carbohydrates and fats, excess protein calories are converted to fat for storage.

Just as letters of the alphabet are arranged to make different words, proteins are made of chains of building blocks called amino acids. These **amino** (a-MEE-noh) **acids,** *substances that make up body proteins,* can be arranged in numerous ways. Your body can make all but nine of the 20 different amino acids. These nine are called *essential amino acids,* because they must come from foods you eat.

Complete and Incomplete Proteins

Protein-rich foods are categorized into *complete protein* or *incomplete protein* sources depending on the amino acids these foods contain.

- **Complete proteins** are foods that contain all the essential amino acids that the body needs and in the proper amounts. These sources include animal products, such as fish, meat, poultry, eggs, milk, cheese, yogurt, and many soybean products.

⬤id You Know?

➤ Americans eat their own weight in sugar every year.

➤ The term *protein* comes from a Greek word meaning "of prime importance." The name is fitting because without protein, life could not exist.

■ **Incomplete proteins** are foods that lack some of the essential amino acids. Such sources are foods derived from the seeds of plants: legumes, nuts, whole grains, and the seeds themselves. Eating various incomplete protein sources—legumes with grains, for example—yields the equivalent of a complete protein. They need not be eaten at the same meal as long as the day's meals supply both of them. The illustration below shows some examples of complete proteins from incomplete sources.

The Role of Proteins

During each of the normal periods of marked growth—infancy, childhood, adolescence, and pregnancy—amino acids build new body tissues. Throughout life, new proteins form constantly to replace damaged or worn-out body cells.

Proteins in enzymes, hormones, and antibodies also help regulate many body processes. Enzymes are substances that control the rate of thousands of biochemical reactions in your body cells. Hormones regulate reactions. Antibodies help identify and destroy bacteria and viruses that cause disease in the body.

▼ *By combining incomplete protein sources over the course of a day, you can be sure your body is getting complete sources of protein.*

ACTIVITY *Look at the puzzle pieces and identify as many of the seeds pictured as you can. They represent foods you can combine to get complete proteins.*

PROTEIN COMBINATIONS

Incomplete Proteins ➤

1 slice of bread
+ 2 oz. of peanut butter

2 oz. of tofu
+ 1 cup of rice

1 tortilla
+ 1 cup of beans

Complete Proteins ➤

Fats

You have no doubt seen the following words printed on food packages: *"Now with less fat." "Reduced fat." "Low fat." "No fat."* With all the media attention that fat has received in recent years, you might wonder why it is considered a nutrient at all. Although consuming too much fat is unhealthful, as these labels may indicate, the fact is your body needs some fat. Fats represent the most concentrated form of energy available. Gram for gram, fats deliver more than twice the energy of either carbohydrates or proteins.

Chemically, fats are a type of **lipid** (LIP-uhd), *a fatty substance that does not dissolve in water.* Like carbohydrates, fats are composed of carbon, hydrogen, and oxygen atoms. Fats are made of fatty acids. Fats are generally classified as either saturated or unsaturated, depending on their chemical composition. Fats are a combination of both types.

Saturated Fats

A fatty acid is said to be saturated when the fatty acid holds all the hydrogen atoms it can. Animal fats and tropical oils, such as palm oil, palm kernel oil, and coconut oil, have a high proportion of saturated fats. Fats in beef, pork, egg yolks, and dairy foods are higher in saturated fatty acids than fats in chicken and fish. Foods high in saturated fats are usually solid or semi-solid at room temperature. High intake of saturated fats is associated with an increased risk of heart disease.

Unsaturated Fats

A fatty acid is described as unsaturated when it is missing one or more pairs of hydrogen atoms. Most vegetable fats, including olive, canola, soybean, corn, and cottonseed oils, contain a higher proportion of unsaturated fatty acids. Such fats become liquids, or oils, at room temperature. Unsaturated fats have been associated with a reduced risk of heart disease. Be careful, however, when selecting products made with vegetable oils since processing can change a fat's characteristics. Hydrogenation—the adding of missing hydrogen atoms—makes them more saturated and firmer in texture. Margarine, for example, is vegetable oil but in hydrogenated form.

The Role of Fats

Besides providing nine calories per gram of energy, fats are integral to other important health functions as well. They carry vitamins A, D, E, and K into your blood and serve as sources of **linoleic** (lih-noh-LAY-ik) **acid.** This is *an essential fatty acid not made in the body but which is essential for growth and healthy skin.* Fats in food add flavor, and they help satisfy hunger since they take longer to digest than

Olive oil   Canola oil   Vegetable oil

▲ *More and more, Americans are switching to less saturated forms of fat in their diets.*

ACTIVITY *Can you think of other trends that show Americans are becoming more health-conscious?*

HEALTH Online

Using a research tool at **health.glencoe.com**, become familiar with good sources of each nutrient. Record what you have eaten in the last three meals and check which nutrients the foods contain. Are you lacking important nutrients?

carbohydrates and proteins. Body fat plays a different role than dietary fat does. Body fat surrounds and cushions your vital organs, protecting them from injury, and it insulates your body against excessive heat and cold.

Your body needs only a moderate amount of dietary fat each day. The average teenage girl, who needs about 2,200 calories daily, should have no more than 66 grams of fat daily. Teenage boys, who use an average of 2,800 calories daily, should have no more than 84 grams of fat daily. Too much fat is linked to obesity, heart attacks, and other health problems. The *Dietary Guidelines for Americans* and other reports from advisory groups recommend that most Americans cut their fat intake to no more than 30 percent of calories. These groups further suggest replacing some saturated fats with unsaturated fats.

Cholesterol

Cholesterol is *a fatlike substance produced in the liver of all animals and, therefore, found only in foods of animal origin*—meats, poultry, fish, eggs, and dairy products. Your body needs some cholesterol, like fat, but it can make what it needs. Cholesterol is instrumental, for example, in the production of the sex hormones, of vitamin D (in the presence of sunlight), and of the protective sheath around nerve fibers. At the same time, like fat, elevated blood cholesterol levels in the blood constitute a major risk factor for heart and other circulatory diseases. Consumption of dietary fat, especially saturated fat, tends to raise blood cholesterol levels. Limiting these fats may reduce the risk.

LESSON 2 *Review*

Reviewing Facts and Vocabulary

1. What three nutrients provide energy?
2. What is protein? What does it do?
3. Name three functions of fats.

Thinking Critically

4. *Synthesizing.* What other products besides those mentioned in the lesson do you think might contain hidden sugar?
5. *Evaluating.* How would you distinguish a healthful meal from an unhealthful one?

Applying Health Skills

6. *In Your Home and School.* Think back to the meals you ate over the last two or three days. Divide a sheet of paper into three columns labeled *Carbohydrate-rich Foods, Protein-rich Foods,* and *High-fat Foods.* Identify which foods you ate that belong to each of these categories. Which changes in your eating patterns, if any, do you need to make?

Nutrients: Vitamins, Minerals, and Water

Some of the body's most essential nutrients are every bit as important as carbohydrates, fats, and proteins. These important nutrients are vitamins, minerals, and water. In this lesson you will learn about the unique function of each one and the best food sources of these nutrients.

HEALTH TERMS

vitamins

minerals

HEALTH CONCEPTS

- Healthful eating includes consuming ample amounts of vitamins and minerals.
- Water is the body's most essential nutrient.

Vitamins

Vitamins are *compounds that help regulate many vital body processes, including the digestion, absorption, and metabolism of other nutrients.* Vitamins are known as *micronutrients* because they are needed in small amounts. Although vitamins do not supply calories, some of them speed up reactions that produce energy in body cells.

Of the 13 vitamins that play a key role in good nutrition, only one—Vitamin D—is manufactured by the body. The rest must be derived from food. Vitamins are classified into two groups: *water-soluble* and *fat-soluble*.

Water-Soluble Vitamins

Water-soluble vitamins include Vitamin C and the eight vitamins in the Vitamin B complex. As their name suggests, water-soluble

Water-Soluble Vitamins

VITAMIN	ROLE IN BODY	FOOD SOURCE
C (ascorbic acid)	Protects against infection; helps with formation of connective tissue; helps wounds heal; maintains elasticity and strength of blood vessels; promotes healthy teeth and gums.	Citrus fruits, cantaloupe, tomatoes, cabbage, broccoli, potatoes, peppers
B_1 (thiamine)	Changes glucose into energy or fat; helps prevent nervous irritability; necessary for good appetite.	Whole-grain or enriched cereals, liver, yeast, nuts, legumes, wheat germ
B_2 (riboflavin)	Is essential for producing energy from carbohydrates, fats, and proteins; helps keep skin in healthy condition.	Milk, cheese, spinach, eggs, beef liver
Niacin	Important to maintenance of all body tissues; helps in energy production; needed by body to utilize carbohydrates, to synthesize human fat, and for tissue respiration.	Milk, eggs, poultry, beef, legumes, peanut butter, whole grains, and enriched and fortified grain products
B_6	Essential to amino acid and carbohydrate metabolism. Helps turn the amino acid tryptophan into serotonin (a messenger to the brain) and niacin.	Wheat bran and germ, liver, meat, whole grains, fish, vegetables
Folic acid	Necessary for the production of RNA and DNA and normal red blood cells; reduces risk of birth defects.	Nuts and other legumes, green vegetables, orange juice, folic acid-enriched breads and rolls, liver
B_{12}	Necessary for production of red blood cells and normal growth.	Found in animal products, such as meat, fish, poultry, eggs, milk, other dairy foods, some fortified foods
Pantothenic acid	Functions in the breakdown and synthesis of carbohydrates, fats, and proteins; necessary for synthesis of some of the adrenal hormones.	Milk, cheese, poultry, wheat germ, whole-grain cereals and breads, legumes, green vegetables

keeping Fit

Cooking Good!

Foods containing water-soluble vitamins need to be cooked carefully so that the vitamins are not destroyed by heat or lost through steam or in cooking water. Follow these tips:

➤ Cook fruits and vegetables quickly, or steam them.

➤ Cover food during cooking.

vitamins dissolve in water and thus pass easily into the bloodstream in the process of digestion. Excess amounts are excreted in urine. Since these vitamins are not stored in the body, you need to replenish your supply of them regularly through the foods you eat. Foods that contain these vitamins need to be cooked carefully so that only a minimum amount of vitamins are lost. Adding variety to the foods you eat will also ensure that you obtain these nutrients.

Fat-Soluble Vitamins

Fat-soluble vitamins—vitamins that are absorbed and transported by fat—include Vitamins A, D, E, and K. Your body obtains Vitamin A in two ways: directly from plant-eating organisms and by manufacturing it from carotenoids in plants such as *beta-carotene*, a substance found in carrots, broccoli, spinach, and other vegetables.

Fat-Soluble Vitamins

VITAMIN	ROLE IN BODY	FOOD SOURCE
A	Maintenance of epithelial tissue; strengthens tooth enamel and promotes use of calcium and phosphorus in bone formation; growth of body cells; keeps eyes moist; helps eyes adjust to darkness; possible aid in cancer protection.	Milk and other dairy products, green vegetables, carrots, deep-orange fruits, liver
D	Promotes absorption and use of calcium and phosphorus; essential for normal bone and tooth development.	Fortified milk; eggs; fortified breakfast cereal; sardines; salmon; beef; margarine; produced in the skin upon exposure to ultraviolet rays in sunlight
E	May relate to transporting oxygen through blood and longevity; may be a protection against red blood cell destruction.	Widely distributed in foods; vegetable oils, legumes, nuts, seeds, and wheat germ
K	Essential for blood clotting; assists in regulating blood calcium level.	Spinach, broccoli, eggs, liver, cabbage, tomatoes; produced by intestinal bacteria

Unlike water-soluble vitamins, which are eliminated through the urine, fat-soluble vitamins are stored in the body's fatty tissue, the liver, and the kidneys. Excess buildup of these vitamins can have a toxic or other damaging effect on the body. People who take nutrient supplements with very large doses of fat-soluble vitamins are especially vulnerable to these effects.

Minerals

Minerals are *inorganic substances that the body cannot manufacture but that act as catalysts, regulating many vital body processes.* Like vitamins, minerals are micronutrients. Despite the small amounts your body needs, each mineral has its own unique function in health.

Your body requires larger amounts of some minerals than others. So-called *trace* minerals—the ones your body needs in tiny, or trace amounts—include iron, iodine, copper, and others. During the teen years, when growth is rapid, iron is especially important. It is essential for the hemoglobin in your blood, which carries oxygen throughout the body. Without ample iron, you may feel tired and have little endurance.

Another important mineral to the body is calcium. Giving structure to your bones, calcium helps develop and maintain bone strength. It also aids muscle contraction, blood clotting, and the proper functioning of the nervous system. Milk and most other dairy products, some leafy green vegetables, and canned salmon are good sources of calcium. When you fail to get enough calcium through foods such as these, your body draws upon deposits of the mineral in the bones and sends these to the muscles, blood, and nerves. This

The best source of vitamins and minerals is in the foods you eat.

ACTIVITY *Identify which nutrients are in these foods.*

Minerals

MINERAL	PRIMARY FUNCTION	FOOD SOURCE
Calcium	Building material of bones and teeth (about 99 percent of body calcium is in your skeleton); regulation of body functions: heart muscle contraction, blood clotting.	Dairy products, leafy vegetables, canned fish with soft, edible bones, tofu processed with calcium sulfate
Phosphorus	Combines with calcium to give rigidity to bones and teeth; essential in cell metabolism; helps to maintain proper acid-base balance of blood (calcium and phosphorus are the most abundant minerals in the body).	Milk and most other dairy foods, peas, beans, liver, meat, fish, poultry, eggs, broccoli, whole grains
Magnesium	Enzyme activator related to carbohydrate metabolism; aids in bone growth and muscle contraction.	Whole grains, milk, dark green leafy vegetables, legumes, nuts
Sodium	Regulates the fluid and acid-base balance in the body; aids in transmission of nerve impulses.	Table salt, prepared sauces, soy sauce, milk, processed foods, foods in a brine such as pickles
Potassium	Part of the system that controls the acid-base and liquid balances; thought to be an important enzyme activator in the use of amino acids.	Legumes, potatoes, bananas, oranges, meat, milk
Sulfur	Component of the hormone insulin and some amino acids; builds hair, nails, skin.	Nuts, dried fruits, barley, oatmeal, eggs, beans, cheese
Chloride	Associated with sodium and its functions; a part of the gastric juice, hydrochloric acid; also functions in the starch-splitting system of saliva.	Table salt, milk, meat, fish, poultry, egg whites
Iron	Part of the red blood cells' oxygen and carbon dioxide transport system; important for use of energy in cells and for resistance to infection.	Meat, shellfish, poultry, legumes, peanuts, dried fruits, egg yolks, liver, fortified breakfast cereal, enriched rice
Iodine	Essential component of the thyroid hormone, thyroxin, which controls the rate of cell oxidation; helps maintain proper water balance.	Iodized salt, saltwater fish
Zinc	Function still under study; a component of many enzyme systems and an essential component of the pancreatic hormone insulin; essential for growth; promotes cell reproduction and repair.	Shellfish, meat, milk, eggs
Selenium	Works with Vitamin E to prevent cell damage.	Grain products, milk, eggs, meat, kidney, liver, seafood
Copper	An essential ingredient in several enzymes; needed for development of red blood cells.	Beans, Brazil nuts, whole-meal flour, lentils, seafood, kidney, liver
Fluoride	Essential to normal tooth and bone development and maintenance.	Fluoridated water, fish with edible bones
Manganese	Enzyme activator for carbohydrate, protein, and fat metabolism; also important in growth of cartilage and bone tissue.	Whole-grain products, nuts, green leafy vegetables, kidney, liver, beans, Brazil nuts, lentils

can result in weakening of the skeleton and can increase your body's susceptibility to bone **fractures**. A lack of calcium in the teen years can lead to poor bone density and later in life to osteoporosis, a condition in which bones become brittle and weak.

Three other important minerals—sodium, chloride, and potassium—belong to a group of minerals known as *electrolytes*. They are called this because they become electrically charged when in solution, as they are in the body fluids. Sodium and potassium help maintain the balance of fluid within body cells. You probably get enough sodium in the form of salt—sodium chloride. Bananas and orange juice are excellent sources of potassium.

h⦾t link

fractures For more information on fractures and other problems of the skeletal system, see Chapter 15, page 344.

Water

If you were asked to guess which nutrient makes up the greatest percentage of your body, what would you say? If your answer was "water," you would be right.

Water is a regulator and is vital to every body function. It carries nutrients to and transports waste from your cells, mainly through the plasma in your blood. Water lubricates your joints and mucous membranes. It enables you to swallow and digest foods, absorb nutrients, and eliminate wastes. Through perspiration, water helps your body cool down and prevents the buildup of internal heat.

Your body uses about 10 cups (2.4 liters) of water a day. If you perspire from fever, hot weather, or strenuous exercise, you use more. Some water can be replaced by drinking fluids such as juice, milk, or water itself—about six to eight cups (1.4 to 1.9 liters) daily. Food is also a source of water. On average, fruits, vegetables, and milk products contain about 75 percent water.

LESSON 3 *Review*

Reviewing Facts and Vocabulary

1. Write a short paragraph that defines the terms *vitamin* and *mineral* and explains the chief importance to the body of these micronutrients.
2. Compare and contrast water-soluble and fat-soluble vitamins.

Thinking Critically

3. *Analyzing.* Since few foods naturally contain Vitamin D, manufacturers fortify milk with this vitamin. Why do you think milk was the food chosen for this purpose?

4. *Evaluating.* Consider the validity of the statement *Water should not be considered a nutrient because it does not provide calories or energy.*

Applying Health Skills

5. *In Your School.* Some critics claim that lunches offered on school campuses could be more healthful. Take a position on this issue with respect to your school's own options for lunch. Back up your views with information from the lesson.

Guidelines for a Healthful Eating Style

Having information about nutrition is an important and necessary step toward healthful eating. Yet, it is only a start. Think about the thousands of food products lining supermarket shelves. Which of these items will you choose to get the nutrients and food energy your body needs? How do you make healthy food choices?

HEALTH TERMS

Recommended Dietary Allowances (RDA)

HEALTH CONCEPTS

- The *Dietary Guidelines for Americans* help you make healthful food choices.

- Varying the foods you eat based on availability, affordability, and personal taste adds to the enjoyment of eating.

- Balancing the types of foods and nutrients consumed over the course of several days is part of a sound eating plan.

- Moderation—the controlling of portion size as well as the fat, saturated fat, cholesterol, sugars, and sodium in your food choices—can also make you a more healthful eater.

Dietary Guidelines for Americans

To help you meet this challenge to healthful eating, the U.S. Department of Agriculture (USDA), with the support of the Department of Health and Human Services, has published a booklet titled *Nutrition and Your Health: Dietary Guidelines for Americans*. This booklet spells out the **Recommended Dietary Allowances (RDA)—** *the amounts of nutrients that will prevent deficiencies and excesses in most healthy people*—for Americans two years old and older. These recommendations may be seen as nutritional standards against which you can evaluate—and, where needed, modify—your eating habits.

Following the *Dietary Guidelines* will help decrease your risk of getting eating-related chronic diseases now and in the future. It will also help ensure variety, balance, and moderation among the foods you choose.

Eat a Variety of Foods

No single food provides all of the nutrients your body needs in the right amounts. To eat healthfully, you need to eat a variety of foods. Varying your food choices based on what is available, affordable, and personally enjoyable to you also helps make eating a more pleasurable experience.

THE FOOD GUIDE PYRAMID

The Food Guide Pyramid on page 114 is a graphic tool for expressing the *Dietary Guidelines*. The Food Guide Pyramid categorizes foods into five food groups, indicating a range of servings for each that a person is advised to eat daily. Notice that these recommendations are not meant to apply just to one food or to a single meal but to all the foods you eat over the course of several days—your eating pattern.

The Pyramid's food groups are presented in different sizes. In general, the greater the number of servings recommended from a food group, the larger the group in the Pyramid.

Notice that the ranges of servings are broad. This is because specific nutritional needs vary depending on age, gender, physical condition, body size, and activity level. Teenage boys and active men usually need the most servings, whereas young children generally require less. Except for additional iron and calcium needed by females (ages 12–50), eating the recommended number of servings should supply all the nutrients most healthy people need.

Balance the Foods You Eat with Physical Activity

Balancing the foods you eat with physical activity can help you stay at or reach a weight that is right for you. Follow these guidelines:

- **Balance the amount of energy in food with the amount of energy your body uses.** Many teens lead a too-sedentary life, spending far too much time in front of the television or the computer. Counter some of this inactivity by getting enough physical activity.

- **Be aware that controlling body fat is more important to health than controlling body weight.** The location of body fat can be a risk factor. In particular, excess fat in the abdomen poses a greater health risk than excess fat in the hips and thighs.

- **Keep in mind that all calories add up in the same way, no matter what their source.** Calories count. Excess calories, whether from carbohydrates, fats, or proteins, are converted into fat for storage.

▼ *Good nutrition habits are important throughout life.*
ACTIVITY *Name and list some good nutrition habits that you can follow.*

Food Guide Pyramid
A GUIDE TO DAILY FOOD CHOICES

FATS, OILS, AND SWEETS
Nutrients: Fats, Carbohydrates

MILK, YOGURT, AND CHEESE
Nutrients: Protein, calcium, Vitamins A, D, B₂, and phosphorus

MEAT, POULTRY, FISH, BEANS, EGGS, AND NUTS
Nutrients: Protein, iron, B vitamins, and phosphorus

VEGETABLES
Nutrients: Vitamins A, C, and K, calcium, iron, magnesium, fiber, and carbohydrates

FRUITS
Nutrients: Vitamins A, C, magnesium, and potassium, fiber, and carbohydrates

BREAD, CEREAL, RICE, AND PASTA
Nutrients: Complex carbohydrates, fiber, iron, B vitamins

FATS, OILS, AND SWEETS
Servings: Use sparingly.
Found in: candy, soft drinks, butter, margarine, salty snack foods such as chips, mayonnaise, salad dressing, jams and jellies

MILK, YOGURT, AND CHEESE
Servings: 2–3

SINGLE SERVING EQUIVALENTS:
- 1 cup of milk or yogurt
- 1½ ounces of natural cheese
- 2 ounces of processed cheese

MEAT, POULTRY, FISH, BEANS, EGGS, AND NUTS
Servings: 2–3

SINGLE SERVING EQUIVALENTS:
- 2–3 ounces of cooked lean meat, poultry, or fish
- 1 egg
- ½ cup of cooked dry beans
- 2 tablespoons of peanut butter

The Food Guide Pyramid shows the types of foods you need and in which amounts.

ACTIVITY *Determine single serving equivalents within particular sections of the pyramid.*

VEGETABLES
Servings: 3–5

SINGLE SERVING EQUIVALENTS:
- 1 cup of raw leafy vegetables
- ½ cup of other vegetables, cooked or raw
- ¾ cup of vegetable juice

FRUITS
Servings: 2–4

SINGLE SERVING EQUIVALENTS:
- 1 medium apple, banana, or orange
- ½ grapefruit or melon wedge
- ¾ cup of 100-percent fruit juice
- ½ cup of berries
- ½ cup of canned fruit, water or natural juice pack
- ½ cup of dried fruit

BREAD, CEREAL, RICE, AND PASTA
Servings: 6–11

SINGLE SERVING EQUIVALENTS:
- 1 slice of bread
- ½ hamburger bun or English muffin
- 1 small roll or biscuit
- 3 to 4 small crackers
- 1 ounce of ready-to-eat breakfast cereal
- ½ cup of cooked cereal
- ½ cup of cooked rice
- ½ cup of cooked pasta

Choose Plenty of Grain Products, Vegetables, and Fruits

Why do vegetables, fruits, and grain products get special attention? It is because they are excellent sources of complex carbohydrates and fiber. They are usually low in fats and calories, and they provide essential vitamins and minerals.

A high intake of fiber and complex carbohydrates has been shown to decrease the risk for heart disease, obesity, and some cancers. The National Cancer Institute recommends 20 to 35 grams of fiber a day, in contrast to the 10 to 15 grams currently consumed daily by most Americans.

Choose an Eating Style Low in Fat, Saturated Fat, and Cholesterol

The top section of the Food Guide Pyramid contains foods you are advised to use sparingly—fats, oils, and sweets. At present, fat makes

HEALTH Online

Visit **health.glencoe.com** to learn about the five food groups and the Food Guide Pyramid.

up about 34 percent of the calories in the average American diet. This is well in excess of the no more than 30 percent of calories from fat called for in the *Dietary Guidelines*. Eating styles high in fat are linked to obesity and some cancers. A diet high in saturated fat and cholesterol also contributes to increased cholesterol levels, a risk factor for heart disease.

To control the amount of fat you eat:

- Cut off the fat you see on meat.
- Eat lean meat and poultry.
- Remove the skin from chicken and turkey.
- Eat more fish, including oilier fishes such as salmon or halibut. Omega-3 fatty acids, a polyunsaturated fat in fish, have been linked with a decreased risk of heart disease.
- Occasionally, perhaps one or two times a week, have a meal based on dried beans or other legumes instead of meat.
- Choose lower-fat milk, cheese, and yogurt.
- Eat less salad dressing and mayonnaise. Spread only a little margarine or butter on bread or potatoes.
- Substitute vegetables, fruits, and whole-grain snacks for foods with a high fat content.
- Cut down on fried foods, including french fries. Eat roasted, baked, broiled, or grilled meat, poultry, or fish instead. Choose vegetables that are steamed, boiled, or baked.

For most people, including teens, many of the above tips help control cholesterol as well as fat. For individuals with a tendency toward

Making Responsible Decisions

Valuing and Helping Friends

Denise is watching her intake of fat, added sugars, and salt. Yet, every time she goes out with her closest friends, Rae and Yvonne, the three end up at the same fast-food restaurant. Rae and Yvonne always order shakes and fries, and Denise feels pressured to order the same as her friends. Denise wants to suggest a different plan, but she has known Rae and Yvonne since the second grade and doesn't want to seem like a troublemaker. At the same time, she doesn't want to compromise her health and nutrition goals. What can Denise do?

What Would You Do?

Apply the six steps of the decision-making process to Denise's problem.

1. **State the situation.**
2. **List the options.**
3. **Weigh the possible outcomes.**
4. **Consider your values.**
5. **Make a decision and act.**
6. **Evaluate the decision.**

high blood cholesterol levels, additional precautions may need to be taken. These include increasing one's awareness of and limiting foods high in dietary cholesterol such as egg yolks, organ meats like liver, and even some low-fat foods, such as shellfish.

Choose an Eating Style Moderate in Sugars

Americans eat sugar in many forms, and most like its taste. Healthy people can eat a moderate amount of sugar. As with fats, the guideline is to watch the size and frequency of foods with added sugars, such as sweet desserts, candy, and soft drinks, and to balance these with foods that provide the amounts of nutrients your body needs.

Some tips for using sugar in moderation are:

- Become aware of your intake of foods with added sugars but few nutrients. If you drink a lot of soda, reach instead for a natural fruit juice or even plain water. Substitute fruit for doughnuts, candy, or other sweets made with added sugar.
- Learn to identify added sugars by their names on product packages, such as corn syrup, honey, and sucrose.
- Choose canned fruits packed in water or juice rather than in heavy syrup.
- Eat sweets as part of a meal, rather than as between-meal snacks. Other foods in the meal may help neutralize damaging acids from carbohydrates that build up on the teeth. When sweets are eaten, be sure to brush your teeth afterward, using a fluoride toothpaste, and floss daily.

Choose an Eating Style Moderate in Salt and Sodium

Sodium is one of the body's essential minerals. It helps transport nutrients into your cells and helps wastes move out. It also helps maintain normal blood pressure and nerve function. Yet, most Americans consume far more than the amount advised: 2,400 mg or less sodium a day.

Where does all the sodium come from? About 10 percent is naturally present in foods. The remainder comes from table salt—sodium chloride—and processed foods. In fact, about 75 percent of the sodium we eat is derived from processed foods. The remainder comes from the salt shaker. Too much sodium may put some people at risk of high blood pressure, although body weight, genetics, and amount of physical activity are some other factors that affect this condition.

Follow these tips to ensure a moderate intake of sodium and salt:

- Become "sodium-literate." The Nutrition Facts panel on food labels identifies the sodium content. Learn to look for and read this information when you buy processed foods.

Sweet desserts and sugary snacks provide little nutritional value. Instead, substitute with melon, grapes, and other fresh fruits.

ACTIVITY *What nutrients are found in these fruits?*

- Season foods with herbs and spices rather than salt, and encourage the family member who prepares meals at home to use less salt in cooking.
- Taste foods before you salt them. If you must add salt, shake once, then taste again.
- Go easy on the salty snacks you eat—such as chips and pretzels.

Healthful Eating Patterns

Whether you eat three meals a day, or four, five, or six "mini-meals," *variety, moderation,* and *balance* are the foundation of a healthful eating plan. Meals and snacks with adequate servings from all five food groups in the Food Guide Pyramid provide the nutrients and energy you need.

Building Health Skills

Setting Goals: Improving Your Snacking Habits

BECAUSE THE BODY continues to grow throughout adolescence, your nutritional and caloric needs right now are at a high point. One way of meeting the increased needs is through smart snacking. As with other aspects of health, you can become a smarter snacker. In order to do this, you have to make up your mind that a change is in order, then follow a logical plan of action.

1. **Make a list of your current favorite snacks.** Divide a page of your private Health Journal into three columns. Write the names of your favorite snacks in the first column. Include any food consumed between meals, including beverages such as soda or milk. Be as thorough as possible.

2. **Determine where each listed item belongs on the Food Guide Pyramid.** Fruits and vegetables are self-evident. Yogurt and cheese belong in the Milk, Yogurt, and Cheese group. Crackers, pretzels, and popcorn belong in the Bread, Cereal, Rice and Pasta group. Soft drinks and candy belong with the Fats, Oils, and Sweets group. Write this information in the second column next to the corresponding items in Column 1.

3. **Identify the nutrients the snack provides.** Again, refer to the Food Guide Pyramid on page 114. Look in particular for foods that provide calcium, iron, protein, and vitamins A and C. All of these are nutrients that are especially important to consume in adequate amounts. Note your findings in Column 3.

4. **Review your list.** Which snacks belong with the Fats, Oils, and Sweets group? To what food groups are your combined snacks contributing most? What foods might you change to moderate fat, sugar, or sodium intake or to add more food variety?

Some Sensible Snacks

FOOD	FAT (in grams)	% CALORIES FROM FAT
Air-popped popcorn, 1 cup	0	0
Applesauce, ½ cup	0	0
Bagel, 1	0.8	11
Bread sticks, 1	1	15
Frozen fruit bar, 4 ounces	0	0
Fruit roll-ups, 1	0.5	9
Gelatin with sliced banana, ½ cup	0	0
Graham crackers, 2	1	15
Popcorn cake, 2	0	0
Pretzel sticks, 1 ounce	1	10
Skim milk, 1 cup	0	0
Yogurt, plain, low-fat, 4 ounces	1.8	23

When planning menus, remember that there are no good or bad foods. Any food that supplies calories and nutrients can be part of a nutritious eating style. Nutrition guidelines apply to all your food choices for a day or more, not for just a single meal or food.

Breakfast

Breakfast may be your most important meal. After 10 to 14 hours without fuel, your body needs to be recharged. According to breakfast studies, eating a nutritious morning meal is linked with better mental and physical performance in late morning. Those who ate breakfast also reacted faster and experienced less muscle fatigue than those who skipped breakfast.

As with other meals, a key to successful breakfast planning is variety. This helps break some of the monotony of the same traditional breakfast foods; a varied meal provides a variety of nutrients. You might choose peanut butter on toast, pizza, or even a stuffed tomato for a healthful and eye-opening beginning. To get enough vitamin C during the day, add a citrus juice or fruit or tomato juice for breakfast. Breakfast is also a good time to get one calcium-rich serving of milk, cheese, or yogurt and a perfect opportunity to add needed fiber by eating a high-fiber cereal.

A *What other foods that you enjoy eating would make healthful snacks?*

ACTIVITY *Which of the foods listed contain the least fat? Which contain the lowest percentage of calories from fat? Which do you think are sources of the following nutrients: Carbohydrates? Calcium? Protein?*

Lunch and Dinner

Typically, Americans eat a sandwich or something similar for lunch and then a large dinner. Other cultural groups follow a reverse pattern, eating their large meal at midday. Either way, the focus of lunch and dinner should provide a variety of foods from several food groups in the Food Guide Pyramid. The protein at lunch or dinner might come from eggs, a lean meat, poultry, fish, some form of legumes, or a dairy food. Again, including pasta, rice, or bread at both these meals will help ensure that you satisfy the 6 to 11 servings of grain from the Food Guide Pyramid that many active teenagers need. A turkey and cheese sandwich piled high with lettuce and tomato provides one serving each from the protein, dairy, and vegetable sections of the pyramid and two from the grain group. A slice of vegetarian pizza with steamed or grilled vegetables provides similar nutrient benefits.

LESSON 4 *Review*

Reviewing Facts and Vocabulary

1. Name the six sections of the Food Guide Pyramid, and identify the recommended serving ranges.
2. How are the terms *variety, balance,* and *moderation* important in any eating plan?

Thinking Critically

3. *Analyzing.* What are some of the health problems that can arise from unhealthful eating patterns? How might you benefit if you improved your eating pattern?
4. *Evaluating.* Which foods do you eat on a regular basis that may be high in sodium or salt? Which are high in fat, especially saturated fat? How could you tell?

Applying Health Skills

5. *In Your Home and School.* Keep a food diary of the foods you eat over a period of several days. Analyze your choices by making a list of the five food groups and organizing the foods you ate into the appropriate groups. (Some foods such as pizza may represent more than one food group.) What does the chart tell you about your eating habits? Discuss it with a family member and identify how you could add more balance to your eating habits.

Being a Smart Food Consumer

The Food Guide Pyramid is one way of evaluating the nutritional contribution of a food or several foods to your overall eating pattern. This task becomes more challenging when you shop for prepared and packaged foods.

To help food shoppers, all food products now carry a standardized Nutrition Facts panel.

Nutrition Label Basics

The Nutrition Facts panel on food labels indicates the nutrient and calorie content of foods. This information helps you find good sources of nutrients, compare nutrients and calories among similar products, and choose foods that meet special dietary needs. Specifically, each label contains:

■ serving size;
■ servings per container;
■ calories per serving and calories per serving from fat;
■ grams of total fat, saturated fat, total carbohydrate, fiber, sugars, protein, and milligrams of cholesterol and sodium per serving;
■ percentage of the Daily Value (DV) the product supplies of the above nutrients (except sugars and protein), plus some important minerals and vitamins in one serving.

Some nutrient labels have two lists. If a food is eaten with another food—for example, cereal with milk—nutritional information is given for the product alone and with the other food.

Foods that do not need to carry the Nutrition Facts panel include:

- food served in restaurants;
- plain coffee and tea;
- some spices and other foods that contain no nutrients;
- fresh meat, poultry, and fish;
- fresh fruits and vegetables;
- food produced by very small companies or offered in very small packages.

Ingredients List

Almost all food labels must have an ingredient list. Labels list ingredients by weight in descending order. The ingredient in greatest amount is listed first. Food labels with several similar ingredients may be confusing. For example, when three sweeteners—corn syrup, sugar, and honey—are used in the same product, each is listed separately and lower on the list than if they were listed totally as one ingredient.

▼ *The Nutrition Facts on the food label provide easy-to-read nutrition information "at the source."*

ACTIVITY *How many calories from fat are contained in this product?*

Nutrition Facts title signals that the label contains the new required information.

Serving sizes are more consistent across product lines and reflect the amounts people actually eat.

List of nutrients covers those most important to the health of today's consumers.

Daily Values are based on a daily diet of 2,000 and 2,500 calories.

Label shows calories per gram of fat, carbohydrates, and protein.

Nutrition Facts

Serving Size ½ cup (114g)
Servings Per Container 4

Amount Per Serving

Calories 90	Calories from Fat 30

	% Daily Value*
Total Fat 3g	5%
Saturated Fat 0g	0%
Cholesterol 0mg	0%
Sodium 300mg	13%
Total Carbohydrate 13g	4%
Dietary Fiber 3g	12%
Sugars 3g	
Protein 3g	

Potassium	0%	Thiamin	0%
Vitamin A	80%	Riboflavin	0%
Vitamin C	60%	Niacin	0%
Calcium	4%	Vitamin B 6	0%
Iron	4%	Folate	0%
Vitamin D	0%	Phosphorus	0%

* Percent Daily Values are based on a 2,000 calorie diet. Your daily values may be higher or lower depending on your calorie needs:

Calories		2,000	2,500
Total Fat	Less than	65g	80g
Sat Fat	Less than	20g	25g
Cholesterol	Less than	300mg	300mg
Sodium	Less than	2,400mg	2,400mg
Potassium		3,500mg	3,500mg
Total Carbohydrate		300g	375g
Dietary Fiber		25g	30g

Calories from fat help consumers meet dietary guidelines that recommend people get no more than 30 percent of their calories from fat.

% Daily Value shows how a food fits into the overall daily diet.

FOOD ADDITIVES

Additives must be listed on food labels. **Food additives** are *substances added to food intentionally to produce a desired effect*. They are used to:

- add nutrients,
- lengthen storage life and keep it safe to eat,
- give flavor or color,
- maintain texture,
- control food's acidity,
- help age foods, such as cheese.

Foods can also be enriched or fortified to improve nutrient value. An **enriched food** is *a food in which nutrients that were lost in processing have been added back*. Breads, pastas, and rice made of refined grains are enriched with B vitamins and iron. **Fortification** is *the addition of nutrients that are not naturally present*. Because vitamin D helps deposit calcium in bones, milk is fortified with vitamin D.

The U.S. Food and Drug Administration (FDA) and the USDA regulate most foods that cross state lines. This includes foods with additives. If food manufacturers want to use regulated additives in their products, they must prove to the appropriate government agency that the additives are safe in the amounts used.

Some additives, such as sugar and salt, are termed *generally recognized as safe (GRAS)*. Because they have been used safely for years, these 700 or so additives can be used without permission.

SUGAR AND FAT SUBSTITUTES

The food industry has responded to many consumer concerns about nutrition. In many cases, the industry has been very creative in substituting ingredients that lower either the caloric count or the fat content.

Fructose, natural fruit sugar, is used as a sugar substitute. Because it is sweeter than table sugar, less is needed, so it supplies fewer calories. A noncaloric sweetener, *aspartame,* is commonly added to soft drinks and frozen desserts and is considered safe for most people when used in moderation. You can also buy aspartame in powdered form.

In response to the public's recent concern about fat, the food industry has begun developing fat substitutes. They have the potential for widespread use in processed foods, fried foods, and home cooking.

Food Product Label Claims

The food labeling regulations permit labels of certain foods to claim possible benefits in combating a disease or condition. For example, labels on products that are high in calcium can claim to be a possible help in preventing osteoporosis. Labels on foods high in fiber, low in fat, or high in vitamins A and C can claim they "may help" to lessen the risk of cancer.

▲ *If you see the word "organic" on a label, it means the food product was made from foods grown without pesticides or synthetic fertilizers.*

keeping Fit

Sensitive to Additives?

Food manufacturers in the United States use almost 3,000 additives in their products, and all of them have been approved as safe by the government. However, a small percentage of people have reactions to colorings, flavorings, and preservatives in foods. Learning which ones they are sensitive to can sometimes mean the difference between feeling fit and having unpleasant reactions. Monosodium glutamate, or MSG, for example, is a food additive safe for most people but may cause discomfort to others. In the case of sulfite sensitivity, the reaction can be life threatening.

Safety Inspections: Imported Food

The safety of imported food is an ongoing concern in the United States, where 3.7 million food shipments arrive each year. The FDA inspects imported food when it enters the country, but the percentage of food inspected has dropped in recent years as the volume of imported food has risen.

In addition to the FDA food inspections, the USDA also inspects crops and livestock as they enter the United States. In the past few years, these inspections have successfully prevented mad cow disease and foot-and-mouth disease—both livestock diseases—from crossing the U.S. border.

Following the terrorist attacks in September 2001, safety concerns over imported food have been heightened. President Bush asked Congress for emergency funding for national security and recovery. His request included money that would be allocated to fund more frequent and thorough inspections of imported food.

1. Do you think that the United States should limit the amount of food imported from other countries? How might this action benefit food consumers? What problems might it cause?

2. Research the latest information on safety inspections of imported food.

Other terms that may appear on food product labels and their meanings are:

- **Healthy:** The food is low in fat and saturated fat and contains limited amounts of cholesterol and sodium—no more than 360 mg per serving. In addition, if it is a single-item food, it provides at least 10 percent of one or more of the following: Vitamin A or C, iron, calcium, protein, or fiber.

- **Light:** The calories have been reduced by at least a third, or the fat or sodium by at least half.

- **Less:** The food contains 25 percent less of a nutrient or of calories than a comparable food. Similarly, if a food label claims *more*, the food contains 10 percent more of a nutrient than the Daily Value for that food.

- **-free:** The product contains no amount, or only a slight amount, of fat, cholesterol, sodium, sugars, or calories.

- **Fresh:** The food is raw, unprocessed, contains no preservatives, and has never been frozen or heated.

- **Natural:** This term is reserved for meat and poultry only. According to the USDA, it means the food is minimally processed with no artificial or synthetic ingredients.

Open Dating

Many food products are open dated with a system that consumers can easily interpret. Look for these dates on labels:

- **Expiration Date**—last date you should use the product
- **Freshness Date**—last date a food is thought to be fresh
- **Pack Date**—the date on which the product was packaged
- **Sell Date**—Also known as the pull date, this term denotes the last date the product—for example, milk—should be sold. Note that you can store a product past its sell date.

Shelf Labeling

In recent years, stores have begun including vital information of their own to help shoppers. The best-known and perhaps most important information of this kind is **unit pricing**, *a strategy for recognizing the relative cost of a product based on the cost of a standard unit, such as an ounce or gram.* An 8-ounce can of corn that costs 88¢, for example, has a unit price of 11¢ per ounce. If a 12-ounce can of the same brand costs $1.04, it would have a unit price of 8.7¢ per ounce. Buying the larger can would give you more corn for your money. The one caution is that, before buying a larger size of a product, it is wise to determine whether you can use the extra amount.

▼ *Unit pricing labels appear below most products on supermarket shelves. Note that this helpful pricing policy is not confined to food products but applies to health and beauty aids as well.*

ACTIVITY *What other factors do you consider in making a choice besides the price?*

LESSON 5 *Review*

Reviewing Facts and Vocabulary

1. What do the terms *enriched* and *fortified* mean?
2. What are four reasons food additives are used in food?
3. What do *open dating* and *unit pricing* mean?

Thinking Critically

4. *Analyzing.* Review your own buying and shopping practices. What is at the root of your decisions?

5. *Evaluating.* Have you used the Nutrition Facts panels on foods? If not, how could this information prove helpful to you in the future?

Applying Health Skills

6. *In Your Home.* Compare two similar food products in the kitchen of your home. Use information from the products' Nutrition Facts panel, other claims made on the packaging, and any open dating codes.

Health Skills Activities

Activity 1 · Life of the Party

One key to healthful eating is to limit the fat calories in your eating plan to 30 percent or less. Is it possible to plan heathful foods for a party? You are about to rise to that challenge.

Directions

1. With a group, list foods and food combinations you associate with entertaining (for example, crackers, chips and dip).
2. Match the foods on your list with the Nutrition Facts labels provided by your teacher. Figure out what percent of the calories come from fat. (See the Nutrition Facts panel on page 122.)
3. Brainstorm creative lower-fat alternatives to any foods that are over the limit.
4. Share your findings with those of other groups. If possible, hold an in-class party featuring nutrient-dense treats.

Self-Assessment

✓ Identified the fat calories of foods and computed the percentage based on total calories.
✓ Provided lower-fat alternatives to higher-fat snack foods.

Time
50 minutes (30 minutes for activity, 20 minutes for party during a later class)

Materials
paper, pen or pencil, computer with printer (optional), Nutrition Facts panels from a variety of high- and low-fat snack-type products

Activity 2 · Fast-Food Report Card

Many restaurants—including fast-food chains—now offer separate foods and menus for people aware of the importance of good nutrition. How do various fast-food restaurants in your community stack up when it comes to nutrition?

Directions

1. As a class, make a checklist of criteria to use in evaluating a restaurant menu. Develop your criteria in terms of the Food Guide Pyramid (page 114).
2. Working as part of a smaller group, rate the menu of a particular fast-food chain. Use the nutrition pamphlets supplied by your teacher.
3. Share your findings with classmates.
4. Discuss with the class whether the results from this project will make a difference in the eating habits of class members.

Self-Assessment

✓ Included at least three items in your criteria list for evaluating menus.

Time
40 minutes

Materials
paper, pen or pencil, computer with Internet access (optional)

The Skinny on Healthy Eating

If you're heading to the soccer field, remember the shin guards . . . and four glasses of milk. You'll need both to protect your bones.

Calcium is an important nutrient in a teenager's diet, but it's not the only one. A balanced diet is essential. Health professionals often talk about what effect poor eating habits will have later, but solid nutrition is important now.

Growth occurs during adolescence. Teens who eat poorly could grow into adults with health problems. An inadequate diet could lead to poor school performance, weak bones, a lack of energy, and disease.

"Doctors talk about eating right to prevent disease later. Well, disease is starting now," said Kris Rudolph, a registered dietitian at Cincinnati's Teen Health Center Adolescent Nutrition Program.

"We're seeing an increase in diabetes, high blood pressure, and elevated cholesterol levels in teens," she said. "That's happening now. It's not waiting until they are 40."

A healthy diet includes servings from the milk, meat, vegetable, fruit, bread and fat groups. The heaviest concentration should come from the bread and cereal group. Fats should be limited. Teens should eat two to three servings of fruits each day and three to four servings of vegetables.

Read This ▼

Diets Out of Balance

What are teens eating today? The results of a recent study by the American College of Cardiology revealed many poor eating habits. Careless food choices already are having dangerous effects on these teens' health:

- 80% included more than the recommended amount of fat in their daily diets
- 49% had high cholesterol levels
- 11% had high blood pressure

Researchers also point out that fat-heavy diets greatly increase the chance that these students will develop heart disease.

Think About It

1. Explain three ways that a balanced diet can prevent disease.
2. Eating wisely one day won't make you healthy if you eat poorly the rest of the week. What strategies do you think will really help teens establish daily balanced diets?

Using Health Terms

On a separate sheet of paper, write the term that best matches each definition below.

LESSON 1

1. A desire, rather than a need, to eat.
2. Substances in food that your body needs to function properly, to grow, to repair itself, and to supply you with energy.
3. A natural drive that helps protect you from starvation.
4. The process by which the body takes in and uses food.

LESSON 2

5. Nutrients that help build and maintain body tissues.
6. A starchlike substance stored in the liver and muscles.
7. The starches and sugars found in foods.
8. A simple sugar and the body's chief fuel.
9. Substances that make up body proteins.

LESSON 3

10. Inorganic substances that the body cannot manufacture but that act as catalysts, regulating many vital body processes.

LESSON 4

11. The amounts of nutrients that will prevent deficiencies and excesses in most healthy people.

LESSON 5

12. The addition to food of nutrients that are not naturally present.
13. Substances added to food intentionally to produce a desired effect.
14. A food in which nutrients that were lost in processing have been added back.
15. A strategy for recognizing the relative cost of a product based on the cost of a standard unit, such as an ounce or gram.

Recalling the Facts

Using complete sentences, answer the following questions.

LESSON 1

1. How does your environment affect your food choices?
2. Give two examples of how eating is tied to emotions.

LESSON 2

3. Why are complex carbohydrates more beneficial than simple carbohydrates?
4. What are some benefits of foods high in fiber?
5. What is an essential amino acid?

LESSON 3

6. What is the difference between water-soluble and fat-soluble vitamins?

7. Describe whether vitamin and mineral supplements should be used as substitutes for food.

LESSON 4

8. Explain the importance of variety, moderation, and balance in your eating pattern?
9. List four ways of reducing your intake of fat. Explain which would be the most effective for you, and why.

LESSON 5

10. What is required on a Nutrition Facts panel of a food label?
11. How are ingredients listed on food labels?

Thinking Critically

LESSON 1

1. **Analyzing.** How might a limited budget influence your food choices?
2. **Synthesizing.** How do boredom, stress, and happiness affect eating habits? Give examples to support your claims.

LESSON 2

3. **Synthesizing.** Create a persuasive advertisement for a nutritious food.

LESSON 3

4. **Comparing and Contrasting.** In what ways are vitamins and minerals similar to other nutrient groups? In what ways are they different?

LESSON 4

5. **Evaluating.** What parts of the Food Guide Pyramid should provide most of the calories you currently take in?

LESSON 5

6. **Evaluating.** When Pete shops for food, he always looks for the terms *healthy* and *light*. Is Pete using enough information to make good food shopping decisions? Why or why not?

Making the Connection

1. **Language Arts.** Read a magazine or newspaper article about a nutritional issue. Summarize the article in writing.
2. **Social Studies.** Learn about the foods served by Native Americans of the Pacific Northwest in the rituals known as *potlatches*. In your research, determine how these foods are prepared. Publish a short booklet on the classroom computer that contains recipes for or descriptions of at least three of the dishes, noting which essential nutrients each provides.

BEYOND THE CLASSROOM

PARENTAL INVOLVEMENT Find recipes in cookbooks for the prepared foods you most enjoy eating. Take note of the hidden fats and sugars. Explore with family members easy-to-make alternatives that are more nutritionally balanced. Write about your discoveries and experiences with such alternative recipes.

COMMUNITY INVOLVEMENT With several classmates, create a guide to restaurants in your community that summarizes the variety on their menu. You might create a separate section for establishments that feature dishes designated "heart healthy" by the American Heart Association. In your guide, include the price range for dishes, along with such vital information as each restaurant's address, telephone number, and hours of operation. Share copies of your guide with other classes and community members.

SCHOOL-TO-CAREER
Exploring Careers. Interview the school dietitian or another registered dietitian in your community about the possibilities of a career in nutrition. Determine what preparation, including schooling and training, is necessary, the various settings in which dietitians work, and the types of interpersonal skills needed for various jobs. Share your findings with the class.

CHAPTER 6

Food and Your Health

HEALTH *Online*

ANALYZING INFLUENCES
Body image and weight management are issues teens deal with all the time. Create an electronic slide show with Presentation Software to demonstrate how you think males as well as females are influenced by society's expectations. See the Technology Projects at
health.glencoe.com.

Personal Health Inventory

Self-Inventory Write the numbers 1–10 on a sheet of paper. Read each statement below and respond by writing *yes*, *no*, or *sometimes* for each item. Write a *yes* only for items that you practice regularly. Save your responses.

1	I try to keep my weight within a healthy range.
2	I try to eat a variety of nutritious foods, even when I am attempting to lose or gain weight.
3	If I had a weight problem, I would be satisfied with losing or gaining ½ to 1 pound a week.
4	I exercise at least 20 or 30 minutes on most days of the week.
5	I would not fast or go on a quick weight-loss or weight-gain diet.
6	If I compete in athletics I follow a balanced eating plan with a variety of foods.
7	I drink plenty of water before, during, and after exercise.
8	I do not substitute nutrient supplements, such as vitamin pills, for a sensible eating style.
9	I avoid leaving perishable foods standing at room temperature for more than 2 hours.
10	I wash my hands before and after handling food.

Follow-up After completing the chapter, retake this self-inventory. Pick two items that you need to work on and set a goal to improve your health behaviors.

> 66 *The American diet is too loaded with fats and sweets and too deficient in fruits, vegetables and grains.* 99
>
> —DR. DAVID SATCHER
> U.S. SURGEON GENERAL

Quick Write List ten of your favorite foods that you enjoy eating. What food groups are most represented in your list?

Managing Your Weight

To be truly fit, you need to maintain a healthy weight—now and throughout your lifetime. Your own healthy weight probably will not be the same as the weight of a high-fashion model, a bodybuilder, or your best friend. You can use some general guidelines, however, to judge your weight and to keep it within a healthy range.

HEALTH TERMS

overweight

obesity

underweight

undernutrition

body mass index (BMI)

nutrient-dense

HEALTH CONCEPTS

- Being obese, overweight, or underweight poses risks to your total health.
- Physical activity is an important part of weight management and maintenance.
- The only way to lose weight is by burning more calories than you consume. You need to consume an adequate number of calories for someone your height and age, and include physical activity in your life.

Calorie Basics

In order to understand weight management, you need to understand calories—what they are, where they come from, and how they affect body weight. When people hear the word *calories,* they often think of fattening foods. Calories, or more correctly, kilocalories, are simply a unit to measure energy. Calories are a measure of the energy in food and the energy your body burns. Calories are not nutrients.

Calories: Their Source

Some foods have more calories than others. The specific number of calories depends on the amount of carbohydrate, fat, and protein in the food as well as the portion size. The way a food is prepared or cooked also affects the calorie count.

In the previous chapter you learned about three nutrients that supply energy, or calories. Carbohydrate, the main source, and protein each supply four calories per gram. Fat supplies more than twice as much—nine calories per gram. For this reason, even small amounts of fat in a food significantly increase its caloric content.

Calories to Burn

How many calories do you need? Several factors play a role, such as rate of growth, body size, gender, age, and metabolic rate. For example, some people have a higher metabolic rate than others, so they need more calories. Children and teens need more calories than adults do because they are still growing. Taller and bigger people need more calories than shorter and smaller people do. A person's activity level also plays a major role. Active people need more calories than sedentary people do in order to remain active.

Balancing the Energy Equation

Keeping a healthy weight is an issue of energy balance. Simply stated, calories consumed must equal calories burned. You gain or lose weight by tipping the balance. By taking in fewer calories than you expend, you lose body weight. When you take in more calories than you expend, you gain. Your body stores the extra calories as body fat.

Each pound (0.5 kg) of body fat equals about 3,500 calories. To lose 1 pound (0.5 kg) a week, which is a realistic, healthy goal, you need to consume 500 fewer calories than normal each day. Here is the calculation you can use: 500 calories per day x 7 days = 3,500 calories = 1 pound (0.5 kg) of body fat. What will happen if you also burn 250 extra calories a day through physical activity?

Weight Problems: Risky Business

Being too heavy or too thin increases the risk of developing health problems later on. In the meantime, weight problems can certainly affect the quality of life.

Body Fat versus Body Weight

Although we use the terms *overweight* and *obesity* interchangeably, these conditions are not the same. **Overweight** means *weighing more than 10 percent over the standard weight for height;* **obesity** means *excess body fat, or adipose tissue.* Usually obesity and overweight go together.

From a health standpoint, being overweight or being obese is risky. However, in

▼ *People come in all different shapes and sizes.*

ACTIVITY *Explain how to determine whether or not you are overweight or underweight.*

certain situations, being overweight might not be a risk. A football player or bodybuilder may be overweight because of excess muscle, not excess fat. Body composition, rather than weight, is often a better measure of fitness.

Obesity: A Hazard to Health

Obesity is a common health risk in the United States. Excess body fat strains the body frame and increases the workload of the heart and the lungs. Obese people have a higher risk of health problems, including hypertension, diabetes, high blood cholesterol, atherosclerosis, and some cancers. Also, obese people are often inactive, which increases their health risks even more.

Adolescent obesity is increasing. Besides the health risks later in life, excess body fat during adolescence may affect self-esteem and social health. Unfortunately, many teens who are overweight or obese as adolescents continue to be so through adulthood.

Why do people gain too much weight? There are two main reasons:

- **sedentary lifestyle**
- poor food habits

Interestingly, studies show that many obese people actually eat less than normal-weight people who exercise more.

The causes of obesity may be more complex, however. Heredity may play a role, but the exact relationship is unclear. Some scientists believe that obese people have more fat cells, which may get smaller but never go away. Other researchers are exploring the set point theory. This theory says that each person has a biological set point for weight and body fat. The body works to maintain that point by lowering the metabolic rate when caloric intake goes down. Then it is hard to lose weight and keep it off.

Underweight: A Health Risk

Being underweight can sometimes pose health risks. With so much attention placed on obesity, we sometimes forget the health risks related to being **underweight,** or *being 10 percent or more below normal weight.* Being too thin means that a person has little body fat as an energy reserve, and perhaps less of the protective nutrients the body stores. This makes it harder for an overly thin person to fight off infection and increases the risk of health problems if surgery is needed.

Underweight people may be undernourished, too. **Undernutrition** is *not consuming enough essential nutrients or calories for normal body functions.* Among other health

h⊙t l⍾nk

sedentary lifestyle For more information on factors that contribute to a sedentary lifestyle, see Chapter 3, page 54.

▼ *Regular physical exercise is a key to maintaining your proper weight.*

ACTIVITY *Describe two other benefits of a regular exercise program.*

risks, underweight people have a greater chance of developing iron-deficiency anemia.

Managing Body Weight

How many people do you know who have tried to lose weight? How many lost weight, only to regain it shortly afterward? Why? Perhaps they did not follow realistic and effective weight-control strategies.

Determining a Healthy Weight

Height and weight charts are often used to determine a person's proper weight. However, the range of weights listed on these charts can vary a great deal when accounting for different body frames. For example, two people who are the same height can have very different weights. A large-boned person will weigh more than a small-boned person of the same height.

Measuring a person's body composition is a more accurate way to determine a healthy weight.

The chart shown on page 136 provides an indicator for acceptable weight. This chart determines **body mass index (BMI).** This is the ratio of weight to height. BMI is a better measure of disease risk than body weight alone. Certain groups, however, should not use BMI as a predictor of health risk. These include athletes, such as body builders, and pregnant women, both of whom have abnormally high BMIs.

Health Risk Based on BMI

BMI CATEGORY	HEALTH RISK
Under 25	Minimal
26–27	Low
28–30	Moderate
31–34	High
35–39	Very High
40 and higher	Extremely High

connections Math

Determining Your Body Mass Index

There are several quick and easy ways to compute your BMI. One is to use the chart on the next page. A second is the following formula:

1. Multiply your weight in pounds by 703 (e.g., for a person weighing 149 pounds, this would be $149 \times 703 = 104,747$).

2. Multiply your height in inches times itself (e.g., for a person 65 inches tall, this would be $65 \times 65 = 4,225$).

3. Divide the answer in Step 1 by the answer in Step 2 (e.g., $104,747 \div 4,225 = 24.8$, or 25 when expressed as a rounded number).

Refer to the table on this page titled "Health Risk Based on BMI" to see the risk category associated with your BMI. How do you rate?

YOUR ACCEPTABLE WEIGHT

This chart provides a fairly simple way to determine whether you have too much body fat. Find your weight in the left-hand column (lb.) and your height in the right-hand column (in.). Then put a ruler between the two numbers. If the line falls within the acceptable range, in the middle of the chart, your weight is all right. If the line falls in the overweight or obese range, consult a physician.

This chart can only let you know whether you are overweight. It is not a scientific measure of healthful weight. Even if you come out in the acceptable range on the chart, talk with your physician if you think you may have a weight problem.

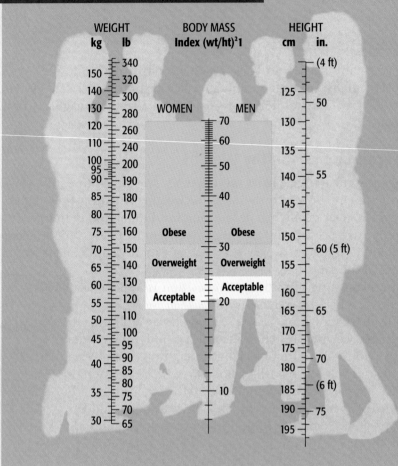

WEIGHT

BODY MASS Index (wt/ht)²1

HEIGHT

▲ *You can improve your overall health by staying within your acceptable weight range.*

ACTIVITY Find your own acceptable weight on the chart. What can you do to maintain your acceptable weight?

Starting a Weight-Control Plan

The true meaning of the word *diet* is everything a person eats and drinks, not a restrictive eating plan. The truth is teens especially need the nutrients from all the food groups for growth and should not consider restricting their food intake. A healthy eating plan and physical activity are often all you need to do to get to an appropriate weight.

These steps can get you started if you are considering a weight-control plan:

- **Target your weight.** Based on your body frame, choose a target weight that is within a healthy range and not too thin. Ask a health care professional what range is healthy for you.

- **Set smart goals.** Losing or gaining one-half to one pound (0.2 to 0.5 kg) a week is realistic, attainable, and safe.

- **Make a personal plan,** preferably one that includes both a nutritious eating plan and regular physical activity. Consider your own food preferences and lifestyle. Choose activities you will enjoy doing. It is easier to follow a plan that you create yourself.

- **Put your goal and plan in writing.**
- **Stick to your plan.** To help, keep a diary of what you eat and when, so that you become more aware of your food habits. Focus on eating a variety of foods with at least the minimum number of servings from the Food Guide Pyramid. Avoid meal skipping; try to eat three or more meals a day.
- **Think positively.** If you slip up occasionally, that is okay. Focus on your progress, and get back on track.
- **Evaluate your progress, but avoid weighing yourself every day.** Instead, weigh yourself once a week at the same time of day.
- **Recognize that plateaus are normal.** Plateaus are a period of time when your weight does not change.

Smart Weight-Loss Strategies

The best weight-loss strategies are easily summed up as follows:

- Eat fewer calories (and make them nutrient dense). **Nutrient-dense** foods are *foods high in nutrients relative to their caloric content.*
- Burn more calories through exercise.
- Better yet, do both.

This advice is the same no matter how much you need to lose—5, 15, even 50 pounds (2.3, 6.9, even 22.7 kg). These strategies can help your weight-loss plan work for you:

- As a teen, eat at least 1,400 to 1,600 calories daily. Otherwise, you may miss out on essential nutrients.
- Eat mainly low-calorie foods from the five food groups, including fruits and vegetables.
- Eat foods you like. If your favorites are high in calories, have just a tiny portion from time to time.
- Make meals last. Take small bites.
- If you are tempted to snack, choose low-calorie snacks such as carrots or celery.

Smart Weight-Gain Strategies

Some people want to gain weight to look better; others want to gain to participate in sports. Smart weight gain includes physical activity and an eating plan that is higher in calories. Without exercise, extra food calories turn mainly to body fat. Consider these tips:

- Increase caloric intake, especially with foods high in complex carbohydrates, such as bread, pasta, rice, and potatoes.
- Eat more frequently. Take second helpings.
- Eat nutritious snacks, but space them two to three hours before meals to avoid spoiling your appetite.

HEALTH Online

Learn the basics of weight management from Shape Up America, including strategies for decreasing food intake and increasing physical activity, at **health.glencoe.com**.

CHARACTER IN ACTION

Consideration and Respect

Weight management is an important part of your overall health. It is common for people to be sensitive about some aspect of his or her appearance. Yet each person, *whatever* his or her weight, build, or overall appearance, deserves basic dignity and **respect**.

You can demonstrate respect by considering the feelings of others and showing kindness toward people who may seem self-conscious about the way they look, speak, or move.

Character Check Practice respect toward those whose appearance may be different from your own. Imagine what it is like to be that person. Vow never to make fun of other people. Discourage other people from doing it, too.

Physical Activity and Weight Management

People can lose body fat just by dieting, but increased physical activity helps them reach their target weight faster, easier, and, over the long run, more effectively. Whether you need to lose, gain, or maintain weight, you need physical activity. Consider the following benefits of regular **exercise:**

h t link

exercise For more information on exercise and its importance to good physical health, see Chapter 3, page 53.

- It burns calories, which promotes loss of body fat.
- It tones and builds muscles to give a firm, lean body shape. Without exercise, the weight lost may be lean tissue as well as body fat.
- It helps promote a normal appetite response, which helps anyone trying to gain, lose, or maintain weight.
- It helps relieve the stress that often leads to overeating or undereating.
- It helps increase metabolic rate, so the body burns more calories for several hours, even while resting. It takes more calories to maintain muscle tissue than body fat. Exercise may help lower your set point.
- It increases self-esteem, which helps keep your plan on track.

To build muscles and spend calories, you really need to work your muscles on a regular basis. Adding exercise to your daily routine, such as using stairs instead of an elevator or walking instead of driving, helps. To set up a realistic, yet effective, exercise program, refer to Chapter 4.

LESSON 1 *Review*

Reviewing Facts and Vocabulary

1. Discuss the relationship between maintaining a healthy weight and energy balance.
2. Name three health risks related to obesity.
3. What role does physical activity play in weight management?

Thinking Critically

4. *Analyzing.* Compare being obese to being overweight.
5. *Synthesizing.* Suppose you want to lose 1 pound (0.5 kg) per week for the next five weeks. How would you change the amount of calories you eat and the amount of calories you burn through exercise to reach that goal?

Applying Health Skills

6. *In Your Home.* Has anyone in your family gone on a weight-loss or weight-gain diet? Interview this person about his or her eating and physical activity plan. Discuss whether the plan was successful in achieving permanent weight change.

Fad Diets and Eating Disorders

"Miracle Pill Burns Off Fat!" "Melt Fat Away While You Sleep!" You have probably seen headlines like these. They appear in ads in magazines, subways and buses, and on billboards. They promise quick and easy solutions to weight problems.

In this lesson, you will examine the risks of fad diets and other quick weight-loss strategies.

HEALTH TERMS

weight cycling

anorexia nervosa

bulimia nervosa

HEALTH CONCEPTS

- Weight control requires self-discipline and commitment. There are no shortcuts.
- Be wary of any diet or weight-loss scheme that promises to take off pounds in an abnormally short time period or without any effort.
- Eating disorders are symptoms of other problems.

Weight control products

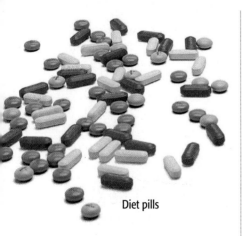
Diet pills

Fad Diets

Look up the term *diet* in the dictionary, and you will find it refers to everything you eat and drink. In this society in recent decades, however, the term *diet* has come to be associated with the idea of losing weight. Fad diets—approaches to weight control that are popular for a short time—come and go but rarely have any lasting effect. Many of these diets limit food variety and certain nutrients. They have names that tell all, such as the "grapefruit diet" or the "cabbage soup" diet. As a rule, these diets are hard to stick to for very long.

Some fad diets cost a lot of money. Others are far more costly, causing problems with one's health. As a health consumer, you need to be aware of the health risks associated with such practices and products.

Let the Dieter Beware

Beware of any diet or product that:

- involves eating only one food.
- claims that you can eat anything you want or as much as you want.
- promises quick results.
- supplies too few calories—below 1,400 calories a day—for energy and health.
- requires a weight-loss aid, such as a vitamin pill, a body wrap, a liquid shake, or an appetite suppressant, or the purchase of books, videos, or tapes.
- promises spot reducing—an unrealistic claim because weight loss occurs all over.
- does not teach a person how to make lifestyle changes to achieve permanent weight loss.

There is no safe way to take weight off quickly, no matter what claims and promises the ads make.

ACTIVITY *List the key words on the product packages that are clues to false and misleading claims.*

Weight Cycling

"Lose Pounds Fast!" At first, some diets seem to live up to claims like this. However, since the weight loss is usually from water, not body fat, the pounds lost are quickly regained. These rapid ups and downs in weight are all part of **weight cycling**. This is *the cycle of losing, regaining, losing, and regaining.* Other names are "seesaw dieting" and "yo-yo dieting."

Weight cycling may be less healthy than being slightly overweight. Why? Lean body tissue lost along with body fat is replaced by more body fat. Because body fat burns fewer calories than muscle does, the person continues to require fewer and fewer calories to maintain weight. Therefore, losing weight becomes harder and harder.

Other Risky Weight-Loss Strategies

Other weight-loss approaches not only fail to achieve permanent weight loss, but they can be dangerous and even fatal. These include:

- **Fasting.** Avoiding food, or *fasting,* is dangerous even for a short time. For health, growth, and energy, you need a fresh supply of nutrients daily. For example, without enough food energy, the body uses its own muscle tissue for energy.

- **Liquid Protein Diets.** High-protein, low-carbohydrate liquid diets can have such serious side effects that the U.S. Food and Drug Administration (FDA) requires a warning label on these products. Using them as the only source of nutrients can result in serious health problems, even death. Using them as an approach to weight loss should only be done under medical supervision.

- **Diet Pills.** Some diet pills claim to "burn," "block," or "flush" fat from the system. However, science has yet to come up with a low-risk pill that does this. Diet pills may help control the appetite, but they can have very serious side effects. Some cause drowsiness, while others may produce anxiety. Some diet pills may even be addictive.

Eating Disorders

Today's society is obsessed with being thin. The average female high-fashion model is about 5 feet 8 inches (1.7 m) tall and weighs less than 110 pounds (50 kg). Does this model represent an accurate picture of a healthy, typical female figure? In truth, no, but many people compare themselves to these models.

An obsession with thinness, along with psychological pressures and perhaps genetic factors, can lead to two eating disorders: anorexia nervosa and bulimia nervosa. Thousands of people in the United States, mainly females, suffer from these disorders.

Throughout history, each era has had its own standard for the ideal male and female form.

ACTIVITY *Describe the ideal body image represented by male and female models in advertisements today.*

Helping a Friend with an Eating Disorder

If you have a friend who has an eating disorder, you can help by following these tips:

➤ First, listen.

➤ Use your active listening skills and encourage your friend to share feelings honestly.

➤ If you think the problem is serious, help your friend find adult or professional help.

➤ *People with eating disorders should seek professional medical help.*

ACTIVITY *Explain the consequences a teen might face by not dealing with an eating disorder.*

Anorexia Nervosa

Anorexia nervosa is *a disorder in which the irrational fear of becoming obese results in severe weight loss from self-induced starvation.* *Anorexia* means "without appetite." *Nervosa* means "of nervous origin." Anorexia nervosa is a psychological disorder with emotional and physical consequences. It relates directly to an individual's self-concept and coping abilities. Outside pressures, high expectations, the need to achieve, and the need to be accepted help lead to this disorder.

Each person with anorexia is different, but the following behaviors and emotions are typical: extremely low caloric intake, an obsession with exercising, emotional problems, unnatural interest in food, unrealistic or distorted sense of body image, and denial of an eating problem. Most people with anorexia are females in their teens or twenties. This disorder is not typically associated with males, but they can be at risk as well as females.

A person with anorexia has physical symptoms related to malnutrition and starvation. These include extreme weight loss, constipation, hormonal changes, heart damage, impaired immune function, and decreased heart rate. In females, the menstrual cycle may stop because of low body fat. In severe cases, anorexia can result in death.

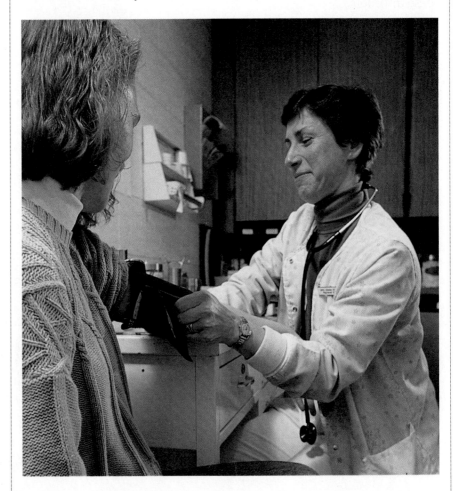

Teens Making a Difference

...RESPONSIBILITY...CARING ...CITIZENSHIP

Yennifer, 15, knows the value of food. Though she has never experienced prolonged hunger herself, she has listened to the stories of how her parents and sister suffered from hunger when they lived back in El Salvador. "When my sister was little, before I was born, my mom and dad were so poor that my sister did not have food sometimes," she begins. She has taken these stories to heart. Now a student at Lakewood High School in Florida, she is working hard to collect canned foods and make further plans to help people in need both locally and in El Salvador, the place of her birth.

FOOD FOR PEOPLE, FOOD FOR THOUGHT When a series of earthquakes hit El Salvador, Yennifer took action. "I went to my counselor at school to talk about the earthquakes in El Salvador and to see what I could do. The counselor sent me to Aspira." Aspira, a national organization, works to help Latino teens stay in school and go on to college. "Aspira helped me to find specific ways to help other people," Yennifer continues. "They gave me instruction on how I could help the earthquake victims. Along the way, they also gave me new goals. We are collecting canned foods and other things through the whole school for the earthquake victims. We have placed boxes all over for the foods, and we are having success," she says with pride. "Right now we are collecting for El Salavador," she says, "but we know there is hunger and need around us here in Florida, too, and we are planning to make more new projects to get food to the hungry right here."

LEARNING SKILLS, EARNING FRIENDS Yennifer has learned many skills along the way. "We have made posters and speeches to tell others what we are doing and what we need from them. I am drawing posters," she says. "I like to do that. No, I *love* it. We've also had to talk to the principal and teachers and other people like that and get hooked up with the community. We found churches willing to help send the boxes to El Salvador," she says in an empowered voice. "And I feel better about myself because I can reach out and do something to make a difference. You can, too."

YENNIFER'S STORY
1. What values has Yennifer put into action?
2. How did listening to other people's stories of hunger inspire Yennifer to reach out to help others?

YOUR STORY
1. What steps can you take to address hunger in your own school or community? What support might you need to help you to accomplish this goal?
2. What skills and benefits to your self-esteem can you gain in the process of helping others?

Bulimia Nervosa

Bulimia nervosa is *a disorder in which cycles of overeating are followed by some form of purging or clearing of the digestive tract.* Often the person with bulimia follows a restrictive diet, then binges—or quickly eats large quantities of food—when hungry. This behavior is followed by self-induced vomiting or purging through abuse of laxatives. After a binge a person may try to follow a severely restrictive diet in order to restore a sense of control and avoid the possibility of weight gain.

The desire to become thin, more attractive, and more physically perfect can be overwhelming until vomiting or purging becomes a daily routine. Associated with this behavior may be the misguided notion that once the perfect figure is attained, everything in life will be fine. Bulimics are often secretive, but know they have a problem.

Bingeing, purging, or fasting should never be viewed as a smart way to control weight. Bulimia can lead to serious health problems—even death. Vomiting and diarrhea can lead to dehydration, kidney damage, and irregular heartbeat. Chronic vomiting erodes tooth enamel, causes tooth decay, and damages tissue of the stomach, esophagus, and mouth. Because laxative abuse interferes with digestion and absorption, nutrient deficiencies may occur. Laxative abuse can also lead to serious damage of blood composition.

Anorexia and bulimia are not diseases; they are symptoms of other problems. Both are psychological in nature. People suffering from these disorders need medical help and qualified counseling immediately. Recovery is a long process, but early diagnosis and care improve the chance of recovery.

If you believe a friend has symptoms of anorexia or bulimia, advise your school nurse, or, in a caring way, encourage your friend to get help. Do not try to counsel your friend yourself.

LESSON 2 *Review*

Reviewing Facts and Vocabulary

1. Give three examples of an unhealthful weight-loss plan.
2. Describe what is meant by the term *weight cycling.*

Thinking Critically

3. *Analyzing.* What influences do you think might lead a person to be at risk for anorexia?
4. *Synthesizing.* If you had a friend who might have an eating disorder, what could you do to help?

Applying Health Skills

5. *In Your School.* Using library resources, write a research report on eating disorders. Consider reading about celebrities who have struggled with such problems and how they deal with them. Share your findings with the class.

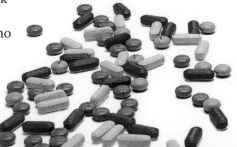

Nutrition for Individual Needs

A re you physically active? Do you engage in sports in and out of school and in other physically demanding activities? In this lesson you will explore the special nutritional requirements of athletes, vegetarians, and two other groups of people with special nutritional needs— aging persons and pregnant women.

HEALTH TERMS

electrolytes

rehydration

carbohydrate loading

vegans

nutrient supplements

megadoses

HEALTH CONCEPTS

- Nutrient-dense foods contribute to an athlete's diet by providing energy as well as nutrients.
- The vegetarian diet offers a number of benefits, although vegetarians need to ensure that they get all the necessary nutrients.
- Aging persons and pregnant women have special dietary needs.

Sports Nutrition

A re you a serious athlete? Do you engage in basketball or tennis? Do you swim for fun and relaxation? No matter what type of athlete you are, good nutrition can help you do your best. Smart food choices can help you reach your top physical performance.

The Training Diet

No one food or nutrient builds muscles or increases speed. The best training diet is balanced, moderate, and varied. Athletic training does not significantly alter the body's requirements for protein, vitamins, or minerals. The main difference is the athlete's increased need for calories, or food energy. Nutrient-dense foods are the best sources of energy and nutrients together.

Physical activity requires an increase in fluids, especially during hot weather, to prevent dehydration and heatstroke. Dehydration leads to an imbalance of **electrolytes.** These are *minerals that become electrically charged when in solution*—as they are in bodily fluids. Examples of electrolytes include sodium, potassium, and chloride. Electrolytes play an important role in regulating body fluids.

Electrolyte balance requires that the intake of water and electrolytes equal the amounts eliminated through perspiration and body wastes. For an athlete, this means drinking several cups of fluid two hours, and then 15 minutes, before a heavy workout. **Rehydration,** or *restoring lost body fluids,* is important after exercise or competition. Drink two cups of fluid for every pound of body weight lost through sweat. Water is the best source of fluid to replenish losses experienced during exercise.

"Making Weight"

In some sports, maintaining a certain body weight is important. Wrestlers, for example, compete in a specific weight class. In contact sports, a little extra body weight may offer some advantages. Wise athletes meet their weight requirements in a healthful way.

Trying to compete in a weight class that is below your healthy weight can be dangerous. Fasting, crash dieting, or trying to sweat off extra weight before weigh-in can cause dehydration and can compromise performance. Over time, these practices may result in loss of muscle

➤ *Following a varied, balanced diet is an essential part of achieving athletic performance.*

ACTIVITY *List some special concerns an athlete might have in maintaining good nutrition.*

Is Making the Right Weight Right?

Terry's boyfriend, Carlos, is the star of the school's varsity wrestling team and a top prospect for a college scholarship. Terry loves the excitement of the sport and is proud of Carlos, but she has mixed emotions. Carlos's natural weight is about 10 pounds over the 157 pounds at which he wrestles. To lose weight before wrestling season, he severely limits his food intake, exercises, and tries various other tricks. Terry knows that this is not healthy. While trying to lose weight, Carlos becomes irritable, sullen, and sometimes mean. He is counting on winning the scholarship in order to be able to attend college. His coach believes that he would not be successful wrestling in a higher weight class. Terry has spoken to Carlos about her concerns. He says he has the situation under control, but he really doesn't. What should Terry do?

What Would You Do?

Apply the six steps of the decision-making process to Terry's problem.

1. **State the situation.**
2. **List the options.**
3. **Weigh the possible outcomes.**
4. **Consider your values.**
5. **Make a decision and act.**
6. **Evaluate the decision.**

mass, too. If you must lose weight, follow the sensible plan—one-half to one pound (0.2 to 0.5 kg) a week.

Athletes who train to gain weight need to eat in a healthful way and to exercise to build muscle mass. Extra calories should come mainly from nutrient-dense foods. Slow, steady weight gain, no more than two pounds (0.9 kg) a week, is best. Using hormones such as steroids to increase muscle mass is not healthy. Hormones may stunt growth and damage the body's reproductive system.

Eating Before Competitions

Many athletes ask, "What should I eat before competing, and how far ahead of the event?" Eating three to four hours before an event allows the stomach to empty, yet keeps the athlete free from hunger pangs while competing.

Before competing, choose a meal high in carbohydrates and low in fat and protein. Fats and proteins stay in the digestive tract too long. Good sources of carbohydrates are pasta, rice, breads, vegetables, and fruits. Drinking plenty of fluids before a workout is important, too.

Carbohydrates are stored in the body in the form of glycogen. Athletes who participate in endurance sports, such as cross-country running or long-distance bicycling, may benefit by **carbohydrate**

loading, or *storing extra glycogen in the muscle,* before strenuous exercise. Several days ahead, the athlete eats a high-carbohydrate diet to store plenty of muscle glycogen. At the same time, training is tapered and often eliminated the day before the event to allow for maximum glycogen storage. Carbohydrate loading is not advised for teen athletes. Growing bodies are still developing and need an even balance of nutrients. Glycogen storage upsets this necessary balance.

Vegetarianism

More and more Americans, including teenagers, are choosing to follow a vegetarian eating pattern. Those who avoid eating meat, fish, and poultry but eat dairy foods and eggs are called lacto-ovo vegetarians. *Lacto* refers to milk, and *ovo* refers to eggs. Some people turn to vegetarianism out of concern for the environment or for the conditions under which food animals are raised and slaughtered. Others have a belief in nonviolence or a desire for a healthier lifestyle.

Vegetarian eating can have health benefits. By reducing saturated fats and cholesterol from animal products, vegetarians may reduce the risk of **lifestyle diseases** such as heart disease, high blood pressure, and some forms of cancer. Be aware, however, that vegetarians still need to watch fat intake.

At the same time, following a vegetarian food style requires greater nutritional awareness. Vegetarians must take care to consume incomplete proteins in a way that will yield complete protein during the day. It is not necessary to have the combinations at one meal as once believed, but just sometime during the day. Vegetarians must also be sure they are getting enough iron, zinc, and B vitamins. The key to a healthful vegetarian diet is to eat a wide variety of foods in adequate amounts, including fruits, vegetables, leafy greens, whole-grain products, nuts, seeds, and legumes, as well as dairy foods and eggs.

SPORTS NUTRITION MYTHS

MYTH Vitamin pills give extra energy.
FACT Because vitamins do not supply calories, extra amounts will not give extra energy.

MYTH Consuming extra protein or taking amino acid supplements build extra muscle.
FACT The only way to build muscle mass and strength is through exercise.

MYTH Eating a high-fat, high-protein meal before competition improves performance.
FACT A high-fat, high-protein meal will not digest as quickly as one high in carbohydrates and will lower performance.

MYTH Eating a candy bar before a workout provides quick energy.
FACT Energy for physical activity comes from foods you ate several days, not an hour or so, before a workout.

MYTH Drinking tea, colas, or coffee before a workout will improve performance.
FACT All three beverages contain caffeine, which can cause headaches, stomach upset, nervousness, irritability, and diarrhea.

h t l nk

lifestyle diseases For more information on lifestyle diseases, as well as their causes and dangers, see Chapter 31, page 676.

Vegans

Most vegetarians eat dairy products and eggs. The type of vegetarians known as **vegans** (VEE-gunz)—*vegetarians who eat only foods of plant origin*—do not. Because animal products are the only food sources of vitamin B_{12}, vegans must supplement their food choices with vitamin B_{12}. Since vegans do not use milk or other dairy products, they must make sure to get adequate vitamin D and calcium from other sources.

Nutrient Supplements

With ill the time ever come when people can get all the nourishment they need from pills? Probably not, but nutrient supplements *can* provide dependable sources of some vitamins and minerals. **Nutrient supplements** are *pills, powders, liquids and other nonfood forms of nutrients.* Under some health conditions or during certain stages of life, some groups of people may benefit from nutrient supplements. These groups include pregnant women and the elderly.

up date
▶ Looking at the Issues

Nutrient Supplements, Pro and Con

Annual sales of nutrient supplements have more than doubled during the last decade. This growth has spurred a debate among nutrition experts and supplement manufacturers.

ANALYZING DIFFERENT VIEWPOINTS

▶ **Viewpoint One**

Most nutrition experts are in agreement that basic nutritional needs for most people can be met by following the guidelines of the Food Guide Pyramid. Foods, they argue, also contain substances your body requires that supplements do not provide, such as fiber and phytochemicals, including beta carotene, lycopene, and others. Eating some vegetables such as broccoli and cabbage, appear to lessen the risks of some types of cancer. No nutrient supplements can make the same claim. Moreover, some supplements, such as melatonin, are potentially dangerous. At present, labeling of nutrient supplements is regulated by the FDA for the protection of the consumer. However, the FDA is not responsible for determining the effectiveness of supplements.

▶ **Viewpoint Two**

Supplement manufacturers note that antioxidant vitamins—vitamins C and E and beta carotene—may help reduce the risk of diseases and illnesses such as some cancers, heart disease, cataracts, and even the common cold. Yet, they say, to get the amount of antioxidants needed through food, a person would have to consume many more servings of fruits and vegetables than most people consume. The only way they say to ensure an adequate amount is through taking nutrient supplements.

EXPLORING YOUR VIEWS

1. Do you agree that healthful eating can give you all the vitamins and other nutrients you need, or do you feel that you should also take nutrient supplements? Explain your response.

2. A spokesperson for the American Dietetic Association has stated: "If you decide you have met your nutritional needs by taking a few tablets in the morning, you may not pay attention to how you eat the rest of the day." Do you agree or disagree?

HEALTH Online

To learn more about food and your health, including facts about nutrient supplements, visit **health.glencoe.com**.

Nutrition During Pregnancy

Healthful eating is an important aspect of prenatal care, along with avoiding tobacco, alcohol, and other drugs. Pregnant women have somewhat increased nutritional needs because they are supplying nutrients for the developing fetus as well as their own additional needs. In particular, they may need more iron, calcium, and folic acid.

Nutrition and Aging

A Tufts University study on nutrition and aging reveals that people 60 and older may need even more of certain vitamins—B_6 and vitamin D, for example—than young adults do. Older adults may not be able to process and synthesize vital nutrients as efficiently as younger people. In addition, some medications commonly prescribed for the elderly can interfere with nutrient absorption. Nutrient supplements may therefore be beneficial for older adults.

Risks Associated with Nutrient Supplements

With vitamins, as with nutrition as a whole, moderation is the key. **Megadoses,** or *very large amounts of nutrient supplements,* are potentially dangerous. Excess amounts of the fat-soluble vitamins A, D, E, and K, for example, stay in the body and become toxic. Too much vitamin A can lead to liver damage, hair loss, blurred vision, and headaches. Excess vitamin C puts a heavy strain on the kidneys.

Throughout the teen years and much of adulthood, the safest and most healthful approach to getting the micronutrients you need is through the foods you eat.

LESSON 3 *Review*

Reviewing Facts and Vocabulary

1. What types of foods should be included in the best training diet for athletes?
2. Compare the lacto-ovo vegetarian and vegan eating patterns.
3. Give three examples of situations in which nutrient supplements might be beneficial.

Thinking Critically

4. ***Evaluating.*** Describe the diet of a vegetarian, an athlete, and a pregnant female. Decide whether or not it is healthful and explain why.

5. ***Evaluating.*** Determine whether or not doubling protein intake is a good method of building muscles.

Applying Health Skills

6. ***In Your School.*** From what you know about nutrition and the Food Guide Pyramid, plan a sample one-day menu to be followed by a member of one of your school's athletic teams who is in training. Find out the athlete's average level of calorie expenditure and food preferences.

Protecting Yourself from Food Problems

Most of the foods you eat have food labels to help you make informed food choices and reduce health risks associated with certain foods. Yet, some risks are not reflected on these labels. How can you be sure the food you eat is safe? In this lesson, you will learn ways to protect yourself from food-related problems.

HEALTH TERMS

foodborne illness

contaminant

pasteurized

perishable

cross-contamination

food allergy

food intolerance

HEALTH CONCEPTS

- Foodborne illness can be caused by bacteria.
- Specific safety measures can be taken to limit the spread of foodborne pathogens and to help avoid cross-contamination.
- Food allergies stem from additives as well as from various kinds of foods.

Food Safety

Food safety has been described as one of the major health problems. Foodborne illness is on the rise. More than 6 million Americans suffer from foodborne illness each year, and the incidence may be much higher.

Foodborne Illness

Foodborne illness, or *food poisoning,* often comes from eating food that has come in contact with a **contaminant**, *a substance that spoils or infects.* In most cases, the contaminant is a bacteria, a parasite, or virus. These bacteria cannot be seen, smelled, or tasted. The best protection against foodborne illness is knowledge of the causes of contamination and ways to keep food safe.

Causes and Symptoms of Foodborne Illness

There are two main ways that food can become contaminated:

- Animals raised or caught for food may harbor disease organisms in their tissues. If meat or milk from such an animal is eaten without being thoroughly cooked or **pasteurized**—*treated by a process of heating to destroy or slow the growth of pathogens*—the organisms may cause illness.

- Food may be contaminated with bacteria spread from an infected person or animal.

Foodborne illnesses related to food spoilage are commonly caused by bacteria: *Salmonella, Staphylococcus aureus, Clostridium perfringens, Escherichia coli (E. coli),* and *Clostridium botulinum.* The last, which

Building Health Skills

Analyzing Messages About Food and Food Safety

NEWSPAPER, MAGAZINE, TELEVISION, and radio reports advise people about food and food safety on an almost daily basis. Trying to sort through all these messages can be confusing. Sometimes reports from different sources contain conflicting information. How can you tell whether the information is reliable? Which warnings should you pay attention to? The following tips can help you decide.

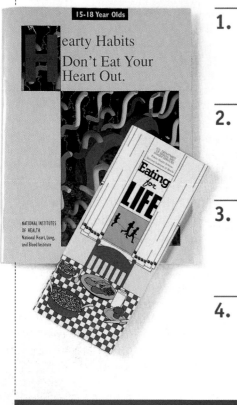

1. **Consider the source.** Where does the message come from? Information from sources such as the FDA or U.S. Department of Health are likely to be more reliable than information from a manufacturer trying to market a product. Reliable sources, such as the FDA, often have authority. They generally use scientific evidence to back up the information or warning.

2. **Consider the risk group.** Are you at risk, or is the problem limited to a specific group, such as aging people, or to a certain area of the country? For example, if you might have food that has been shipped from an area with a problem, such as contaminated strawberries from California, you need to check the source of the food.

3. **Consider the specifics.** Sometimes manufacturers recall batches of a product that may be unsafe. Most manufactured products, such as canned goods, have lot numbers. If there is a problem with a specific batch, you need to check lot numbers and discard or return any items with the lot number that is being recalled.

4. **Consider the nature of scientific research.** Messages about food and food safety can change as researchers discover new information. Early findings can be contradicted by later findings. Different researchers might even interpret the same findings in different ways! Look at their conclusions as guidelines, not established fact.

causes botulism, is found in improperly canned or preserved food. Botulism is especially dangerous, because it can be fatal.

Common symptoms of foodborne illness include nausea, vomiting, diarrhea, fever, and body aches. Since many of these symptoms are similar to those of the flu, foodborne illness is sometimes hard to diagnose. Most people recover from the symptoms in a few days. For the elderly, very young, and individuals who are malnourished or have problems with their immune system, however, foodborne illness can be serious.

Minimizing Risks of Foodborne Illness

Bacteria need three conditions for growth: nutrients, moisture, and warmth. Bacteria in food multiply rapidly between 40° and 140° F (4.4° and 60° C). At these temperatures, bacteria double in number in 30 minutes.

You can keep food safe by selecting and handling it with care. The U.S. Department of Agriculture has identified six critical control points that can limit foodborne illness:

1. **Buying.** Do not buy or eat food with damaged packaging, dents, cracks, bulging lids, or popped safety buttons. Make sure meat and poultry products are refrigerated when purchased. Keep packages of raw meat and poultry separate from other foods. Refrigerate foods that are **perishable**, or *liable to spoil,* within one hour.

2. **Home Storage.** Refrigerate or freeze meat and poultry immediately. Wash your hands before and after handling any raw meat, poultry, or seafood. Store foods according to package instructions.

3. **Pre-preparation.** Thaw meat in the refrigerator, *never* at room temperature. Bacteria can grow rapidly at certain temperatures. Avoid **cross-contamination**—*the spreading of bacteria from one food to another*—by washing your hands before and after handling food. In addition, wash work surfaces and utensils immediately after use. Do not let juices from raw meat, poultry, or seafood come in contact with cooked foods or foods that will be eaten raw.

4. **Cooking.** Always cook food thoroughly. Use a meat thermometer to determine whether food has reached a safe internal temperature. Cook food thoroughly, then refrigerate and reheat it if necessary.

▼ *Washing cutting boards and other equipment in hot, soapy water can prevent cross-contamination of foods.*

ACTIVITY *Explain why juices from raw meat, poultry, or seafood should not come in contact with other foods.*

5. **Serving.** Keep hot foods hot (above 160° F; 71.2° C) and cold foods cold (below 40° F; 4.4° C). Never leave perishable foods at room temperature for more than two hours.

6. **Handling Leftovers.** Refrigerate leftovers within two hours of cooking. Put dates on containers before refrigerating. When reheating leftovers, reheat thoroughly. Throw away suspicious foods without tasting them. Remember, if in doubt, throw it out!

Food Sensitivities

Many people experience abnormal reactions to a food substance or food additive. These reactions may stem from a sensitivity to certain foods or from a specific physiological response to a food or food additive.

Food Allergies

Do you have itchy eyes and sneeze during hay fever season? Have you ever developed a raised welt from an insect bite? These are signs of an *allergy*. An allergy is the body's reaction to an irritating substance or a toxin. Foods can also cause an allergic reaction in some people. With a true **food allergy,** *the body's immune system overreacts to substances in some foods.* These substances, called allergens, are usually proteins. The immune system responds to them as it would to **pathogens**, or foreign invaders. The body produces antibodies for defense against these substances.

h⚫t link

pathogens For more information on pathogens and their role in infectious diseases, see Chapter 28, page 620.

▶ *Foods such as bleu cheese, soy sauce, milk, eggs, nuts, and wheat can cause allergic reactions.*

ACTIVITY *How would you advise a person to find out about a reaction to a particular food item?*

The foods that cause most food allergies are nuts, eggs, wheat, and soy. Fish, shellfish, chicken, and tomatoes may also cause problems. Sulfites, or food additives that help preserve food, and certain nutrients, such as monosodium glutamate (MSG), cause allergic reactions in some people. To identify an allergy, doctors ask patients to eliminate certain foods from their diet one at a time or to keep a food diary. They may also conduct tests for antibodies.

Some people with food allergies show no symptoms. Others may experience one or more reactions. These include rash, hives, or itchiness on the skin; vomiting, diarrhea, or abdominal pain; and hay fever-like symptoms in the respiratory tract. In the most serious cases, food allergies can be deadly. If, after eating a food, you experience any of the symptoms described, be sure to consult a health care professional.

Food Intolerance

Food allergy should not be confused with food intolerance. **Food intolerance** is *a negative reaction to a food or an ingredient in food that is not related to the body's immune system or to food poisoning.* It is sometimes caused by irritants such as food additives. It may also be associated with certain foods, such as green peppers or fried foods. Food intolerance can also be caused by an inborn or acquired defect, such as the inability to digest the lactose in milk, called **lactose intolerance**.

h⦁t link

lactose intolerance For more information on lactose intolerance, see Chapter 18, p. 416.

LESSON **4** *Review*

Reviewing Facts and Vocabulary

1. Define the term *foodborne illness.*
2. What are the common symptoms of foodborne illness?
3. How does the body react in a case of food allergy?

Thinking Critically

4. *Analyzing.* Explain why some people may be more vulnerable to foodborne illness than others.
5. *Synthesizing.* Describe how a doctor might find out whether you are allergic to peanut butter.

Applying Health Skills

6. *In Your Home.* Inspect the contents of your refrigerator at home, and make a list of foods that have sell dates. Next to each item, note how often it is used in your household and whether any product is past its date of use. Discuss with family members a strategy for ensuring that all such purchases are used within the prescribed time frame after purchase.

Health Skills Activities

Activity 1 — Diet Mania

Today, you see ads for countless weight-loss diets on television and printed in publications. Diet specialists and diet centers everywhere boast plans to "take the weight off." Do these diets really work?

Directions

1. As a small group, examine the weight-loss plan your teacher provides. Note the claims made, along with features such as total calories, food choices, number of meals per day, and so on.
2. Write a report of your findings, describing any health risks and benefits of the plan.
3. Combine your report with those of classmates into a pamphlet titled "The Skinny on Weight-Loss." Offer to leave copies of your pamphlet in the school library and other high-visibility locations in the community.

Time
50 minutes plus outside research and writing time

Materials
library or Internet resources, paper, pen or pencil, computer

Self-Assessment

✓ Analyzed a weight-loss plan using information from the book.
✓ Identified risks and benefits.

Activity 2 — Nutrition for the "Teen Team"

As you have learned, athletes need to watch what they eat in order to achieve peak performance. In a sense, you are a member of a team with special nutrition needs—the "teen team." Prepare a pep talk and eating plan for your team members.

Directions

1. Using your book, review the nutrient needs of teens and teen athletes. Note similarities and differences in terms of the amounts of protein, carbohydrates, and other key nutrients. (Don't forget water—one of the most important, and neglected, nutrients.)
2. Prepare a pep talk, urging members of the teen team in your school to make healthful food choices. Explain the benefits to mental and physical performance in all areas.
3. Distribute copies of your pep talk, or arrange to deliver it over the school PA system.

Time
40 minutes

Materials
paper, pen or pencil

Self-Assessment

✓ Explained at least three performance benefits of healthful eating.
✓ Identified healthful foods consistent with the Food Guide Pyramid.
✓ Provided a clear message using effective persuasive communication strategies.

Anorexia Warning

Today, Gina has a healthy appetite and a strong self-image. But that wasn't always true. She nearly died from anorexia nervosa. Surprisingly, Gina says she didn't always feel terrible, even though she was starving herself. She often felt like she was "on top of the world."

These feelings are one reason it can be difficult to help people with anorexia. They feel good, even though they aren't getting enough nutrition. Gina says she felt like she was addicted to not eating.

Scientists are studying why anorexia can create feelings of happiness. They are also learning more about why anorexia tends to run in families. This knowledge will help people combat this critical eating disorder.

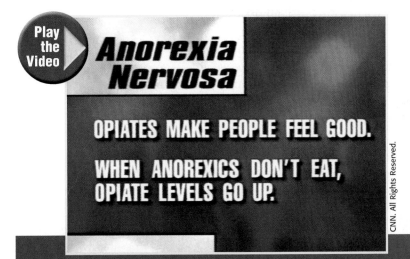

Play the Video

Anorexia Nervosa

OPIATES MAKE PEOPLE FEEL GOOD.

WHEN ANOREXICS DON'T EAT, OPIATE LEVELS GO UP.

Think About It

- How did Gina feel when she was anorexic? How did she learn to manage this disorder?
- How can anorexia affect chemicals in the body?
- According to the researcher in the video, what factors do most scientists agree lead to anorexia?
- Why is it important for people with anorexia to get treatment, even if they feel well?

Using Health Terms

On a separate sheet of paper, write the term that best matches each definition below.

LESSON 1

1. High in nutrients relative to calories provided.
2. Excess body fat, or adipose tissue.
3. Weighing more than 10 percent over the standard weight for height.
4. The ratio of weight to height.
5. Not consuming enough essential nutrients or calories for normal body functions.

LESSON 2

6. A disorder in which cycles of overeating are followed by some form of purging and clearing of the digestive tract.
7. The cycle of losing, regaining, losing, and regaining.
8. A disorder in which the irrational fear of becoming obese results in severe weight loss from self-induced starvation.

LESSON 3

9. Restoring lost body fluids.
10. Very large amounts of nutrient supplements.
11. Pills, powders, liquids and other synthetic forms of nutrients.
12. Vegetarians who eat only foods of plant origin.
13. Storing extra glycogen in the muscle for athletic activity.
14. The loss of excess body fluids.

LESSON 4

15. Condition in which the body's immune system overreacts to food substances.
16. Treated by a process of heating to destroy or slow the growth of pathogens.
17. The spreading of bacteria in food.
18. Liable to spoil.
19. Food poisoning.

Recalling the Facts

Using complete sentences, answer the following questions.

LESSON 1

1. Why is obesity considered a health risk?
2. What are two main reasons why people might be obese or overweight?
3. What health risks are associated with being underweight?
4. How does physical activity promote healthy weight?

LESSON 2

5. Why does weight cycling make permanent weight loss difficult?
6. What are four signs of anorexia nervosa?
7. What are the behavioral differences between anorexia and bulimia?

LESSON 3

8. Name some benefits of a vegetarian diet.
9. What is the best high-performance diet for sports?
10. Name one risk and one benefit associated with nutrient supplements.

LESSON 4

11. What conditions promote the growth of bacteria in food?
12. Name four steps that should be taken to avoid cross-contamination of foods.
13. What are three symptoms of a food allergy?

Review

Thinking Critically

LESSON 1

1. **Synthesizing.** Besides overeating, what personal habits could lead to obesity?
2. **Evaluating.** How can a healthy eating plan improve your life?

LESSON 2

3. **Comparing and Contrasting.** Compare the causes, behaviors, and effects of anorexia nervosa and bulimia nervosa.

LESSON 3

4. **Analyzing.** Why is it necessary for vegetarians to pay special attention to such nutrients as iron, zinc, and B vitamins?

LESSON 4

5. **Analyzing.** Why do food service establishments post signs that say, "Wash hands before returning to work"?
6. **Evaluating.** How would you decrease the risk of foodborne illness at an afternoon barbecue?

Making the Connection

1. **Science.** After it was discovered during the 1950s that diet pills containing the stimulant drug dextroamphetamine did not work and could even become habit-forming, the FDA issued a series of warnings. Learn more about appetite suppressants now being developed, their chemical composition, and the health risks involved. Share your findings in a brief oral report.

2. **Social Studies.** In developed countries, foodborne illnesses are controlled or prevented by adequate sanitation and sewage treatment, regulations that govern food production and distribution, and generally high standards of hygiene. Choose an area of the world where illnesses such as typhoid and cholera, are still prevalent. Research the causes, the public health consequences, and solutions.

BEYOND THE CLASSROOM

PARENTAL INVOLVEMENT Survey family members to determine a physical activity plan they could do together. After the family members have shared the results of their ideas, analyze the plan and offer additional suggestions of how the plan could be implemented.

COMMUNITY INVOLVEMENT Overeaters Anonymous is a group of individuals who support one another in their attempts to overcome eating problems. Contact a branch of this organization in your community. Find out what services OA provides and how "sponsors" are used to help people through recovery. Share your findings in a brief report.

SCHOOL-TO-CAREER
Exploring Careers. Write to The American Dietetic Association, 216 West Jackson Blvd., Suite 800, Chicago, IL 60606, for information on a career as a dietetic technician. Determine what schooling, in-service training, and interpersonal skills are necessary. Share your findings with the class in the form of an oral or written report.

CHAPTER 7

Personal Health

ACCESSING INFORMATION
What are the issues and health consequences to be considered when thinking about body adornments that include tattoos and piercings? Get the facts in the Health Update article at **health.glencoe.com**.

Personal Health Inventory

Self-Inventory Write the numbers 1–10 on a sheet of paper. Read each statement below and respond by writing *yes*, *no*, or *sometimes* for each item. Write a *yes* only for items that you practice regularly. Save your responses.

1	I wash my face twice daily.
2	When I am in the sun, I use appropriate sunscreen.
3	I keep my hair clean.
4	I keep my nails clean and evenly trimmed.
5	I brush my teeth more than once a day and floss regularly.
6	I have regular dental checkups.
7	When reading or studying for long periods of time, I rest my eyes periodically.
8	I have my eyes checked by a professional on a regular basis.
9	I avoid extremely loud noises— 85 decibels or more.
10	I wear some type of ear protection when I know I will be around loud noises.

Follow-up After completing the chapter, retake this self-inventory. Pick two items that you need to work on and set a goal to improve your health behaviors.

> ❝ *A man (or woman) too busy to take care of his health is like a mechanic too busy to take care of his tools.* ❞

—SPANISH PROVERB

Quick Write Write the following words in a vertical list: *hair, skin, nails, eyes,* and *ears*. Next, jot down one step you can take to improve the health, hygiene, or care of each. Estimate the amount of time that each of these caretaking steps might actually take up on an average day.

Healthy Skin, Hair, and Nails

Y ou probably know the expression "Put your best foot forward." Your physical appearance has a great effect on the people you meet. Whether you are talking to a new person at school or applying for a job, your appearance influences how people react to you. Taking care of yourself makes you feel better, too.

HEALTH TERMS

sweat glands

acne

sebaceous glands

follicles

dandruff

HEALTH CONCEPTS

- The health of your skin, hair, and nails affects the way people respond to you.
- Healthy skin, hair, and nails can be achieved through simple daily hygiene, such as bathing and washing, as well as through periodic maintenance.
- The way an individual takes care of skin, hair, and nails is often an indication of how that person feels about himself or herself.

hotlink

integumentary system For more information on the integumentary system and its chief organ, the skin, see Chapter 15, page 340.

infectious diseases For more information on the body's defense against infectious diseases, see Chapter 28, page 632.

Functions of the Skin

What do you see when you meet another person for the first time? One of the first features people notice about you is your skin. Together with your hair and nails, your skin forms the basis of one of your body's main systems, the **integumentary system**. In fact, the skin itself is the body's single largest organ!

Every living organism is protected by some kind of protective cover. In humans, that function is served by the skin. The skin also helps cushion your internal tissues and organs and is your body's first line of defense against **infectious diseases**. The skin provides protection against the ultraviolet rays of the sun. Another important function of the skin is the regulation of the body's temperature. Your skin has an enormous supply of tiny blood vessels just beneath the surface. When your internal temperature rises, circulation to these blood vessels increases. As internal heat is circulated through these surface blood vessels, it is lost through the process of radiation. You start to perspire, and as the perspiration evaporates, your skin cools. This last function is accomplished by means of the **sweat glands**, *structures within the skin that secrete perspiration through ducts to pores on the skin's surface.* When your body gets hot, sweat glands become more active and produce perspiration through pores onto your skin to cool the body down.

Healthy Skin

Every morning and every evening, you should wash your face with soap and water. If the skin on your face is very oily, wash it once more during the day. Pat your skin dry with a clean towel. If you use creams and cosmetics, select them carefully and avoid greasy preparations. Eat a well-balanced diet. Vitamin A helps promote healthy skin. Milk, egg yolks, liver, green leafy and yellow vegetables, and yellow fruits are good sources of vitamin A. Get plenty of rest and exercise. Try to keep your hands away from your face.

Skin and the Sun

Understanding the sun's effect on the skin and knowing some protective steps to take can help you better care for your skin. The sun does not have the same effect on everyone. Some people tan more easily than others. Some people with fair skin may never tan; they may just burn.

Ultraviolet (UV) rays are light rays that come from the sun. Two types of ultraviolet rays are important in considering the sun's effects on the human body. The shorter rays, which are most intense in the middle of the day, are the main cause of sunburn. The longer rays, in the morning and late afternoon, are less strong.

Do not be fooled on a hazy or cloudy day. Up to 80 percent of ultraviolet rays can penetrate haze, light clouds, or fog. Ultraviolet rays can also be reflected upward from the ground, sand, and water. Snow is an excellent reflector, sending back more than 85 percent of the rays.

The most important thing you can do for your skin is to keep it clean.

ACTIVITY *Name other ways you can keep your skin healthy.*

▼ *No matter what your skin type is, it is important to use sunscreen to prevent damage from UV rays.*
ACTIVITY *Name other ways this teen could protect herself from sun damage.*

You should not judge a sunburn by how red you look while you are still out in the sun. It takes about two to eight hours after exposure for a sunburn to show. The pain from the burn is greatest about six to 48 hours after exposure.

In addition to causing sunburn, exposure to the sun's ultraviolet rays can permanently destroy the elastic fibers that keep the skin tight. This causes the skin to age prematurely, or before its time. The layers of skin cells also thicken with repeated sun exposure, giving the skin a hard, leathery texture.

Ultraviolet radiation also damages deoxyribonucleic acid (DNA), the genetic material in skin cells. Accumulated DNA damage can result in the formation of cancerous cells. Excessive sun exposure is the primary cause of certain types of skin cancer. Therefore, you should protect your skin. Use a sunblock if you are going to be in the sun for a prolonged period of time. Sunblocks stop the sun's rays by reflecting them.

The effects of the sun on your skin may not show up for years and cannot be stopped with any cosmetic ointments. These effects are cumulative, or build up over time, and the damage is irreversible. The healthiest behavior is prevention. Avoid overexposure to the sun's ultraviolet rays.

Making Responsible Decisions

Should I Suntan?

In the past, Jessica has always taken pride in having a deep tan. However, after learning about the dangers of ultraviolet rays and their relationship to skin cancer, she is having second thoughts about her tanning habits.

On the one hand, she thinks she looks healthier and more attractive with a tan, and a lot of her friends have tans. On the other hand, she does not want to develop skin cancer later on in life. What should Jessica do?

What Would You Do?

Apply the six steps of the decision-making process to Jessica's problem.

1. **State the situation.**
2. **List the options.**
3. **Weigh the possible outcomes.**
4. **Consider your values.**
5. **Make a decision and act.**
6. **Evaluate the decision.**

Body Piercing and Tattooing

Do some of your friends wear eyebrow or nose rings? Maybe some have tattoos. People have been decorating their bodies for thousands of years. Some decorations, such as blush and other facial cosmetics, are temporary. Others, such as body piercing and tattooing, are not.

Both body piercing and tattooing pose health risks. Each involves puncturing the skin. This can permit pathogens to enter if the equipment used is not sterile or if follow-up care of the wound is inadequate. A special concern is the risk of hepatitis or **HIV** infection from dirty needles during tattooing.

Tattooing and piercing threaten not only your physical health but also your social health. A tattoo that has a current girlfriend's or boyfriend's name may not be appreciated by future dates. A nose ring or other piercing may make a poor first impression on a potential employer. Before going along with fads like these, consider the long-term consequences.

Skin Problems

Many problems of the skin are not life-threatening. They can, however, affect a person's self-image. Following healthy habits may help eliminate some of these problems. One common skin problem during adolescence is **acne.** This is *a clogging of the pores of the skin.* Some adults get acne as well. The **sebaceous** (sih-BAY-shuhs) **glands** are *structures within the skin that produce an oily secretion called sebum.* When these glands enlarge, they produce excess sebum. During adolescence, the increase in hormone production causes these glands to enlarge and produce more sebum, making the skin oily. The oil becomes trapped in a pore and plugs it, allowing bacteria to multiply and causing the area to become inflamed.

Keeping the skin clean is the most important treatment for acne. Wash the skin twice daily. Medicinal lotions and creams may also help relieve the condition. Picking at or squeezing pimples can spread the infection and cause scarring.

Your Hair

Humans have hair present on almost all the skin surfaces of their bodies. You have between 100,000 and 200,000 hairs on your head alone! The roots of hairs are made up of living cells. These grow out of **follicles**, *tiny pits in the skin.* The upgrowth of dead cells and keratin—a protein that also makes up nails and the outer skin layer—from the root forms the hair. Your hair affects your appearance greatly. Taking proper care of your hair is an important part of total health. So is wearing a style that fits your features.

Proper care includes washing your hair regularly. Brushing your hair daily keeps dirt from building up and helps distribute the natural hair oils evenly. These oils keep the hair soft and give it its shine.

hot link

HIV For more information on how HIV is spread, see Chapter 30, page 656.

keeping Fit

Perspiration

Many people think perspiration causes body odor. Perspiration itself is not the cause. Bacteria interacting with perspiration create the odor. Sweat glands are numerous under the arms, which is the reason body odor tends to be a problem in that area. A routine of regular bathing and use of an antiperspirant will help control perspiration problems. Using deodorant will help mask the body odor.

Health Online

Learn techniques for improving your personal health and hygiene at **health.glencoe.com**.

Dandruff, *a condition in which the outer layer of dead skin cells is shed from the scalp,* is one common hair and scalp problem. It becomes noticeable when white flakes of skin cling to the hair or are shed onto the collar and shoulders of clothes. Regular, thorough washing of hair—especially with anti-dandruff shampoos—can control ordinary dandruff. If itching and scaling persist, a health professional should be consulted.

Head lice are small, wingless insects that live on and suck blood from the scalp. Their bites make the scalp itchy and uncomfortable and can cause infection. Lice can usually be killed by medicinal shampoos. Head lice can be spread from one person to another. Therefore, it is wise not to use other people's combs, brushes, towels, or hats.

Your Nails

Your fingernails and toenails are dead cells that grow from the outer layer of your skin. Living cells extend from the root of the nail, below the skin, to just above the base of the nail. As living cells die and are replaced, they are pushed up, forming the rest of the nail. Good nail care includes keeping nails clean and evenly trimmed. Keep your cuticles pushed back and clip hangnails with a nail clipper. You should cut toenails straight across, leaving the nail just at or slightly above skin level. If you cut the nails too low, you increase your risk of skin infection and ingrown nails.

▼ *Clean, trimmed nails add to your overall appearance.*
ACTIVITY *List other personal hygiene habits that contribute to a healthy appearance.*

LESSON 1 *Review*

Reviewing Facts and Vocabulary

1. What is the relationship between an overactive sebaceous gland and acne?
2. What effect does the sun have on skin?

Thinking Critically

3. *Analyzing.* Your cousin who lives in another state has written to tell you she is thinking of having her lower lip pierced, insisting that it is "all the rage." What advice might you write back to her?
4. *Synthesizing.* Explain how your overall appearance makes a statement about how you feel about yourself.

Applying Health Skills

5. *In Your Home.* Think of the healthy grooming habits that are part of your morning or evening routines. Which are the most important to you? Which are your least favorite? Consider how you might make these activities more balanced so as to give equal time to each area.

Healthy Teeth and Mouth

What is the most common noninfectious disease in the United States? If you guessed tooth decay, you are right. Most Americans have or have had tooth decay. Yet, this is also one of the most preventable diseases. In this lesson, you will learn about the function and structure of the teeth and how to prevent tooth decay.

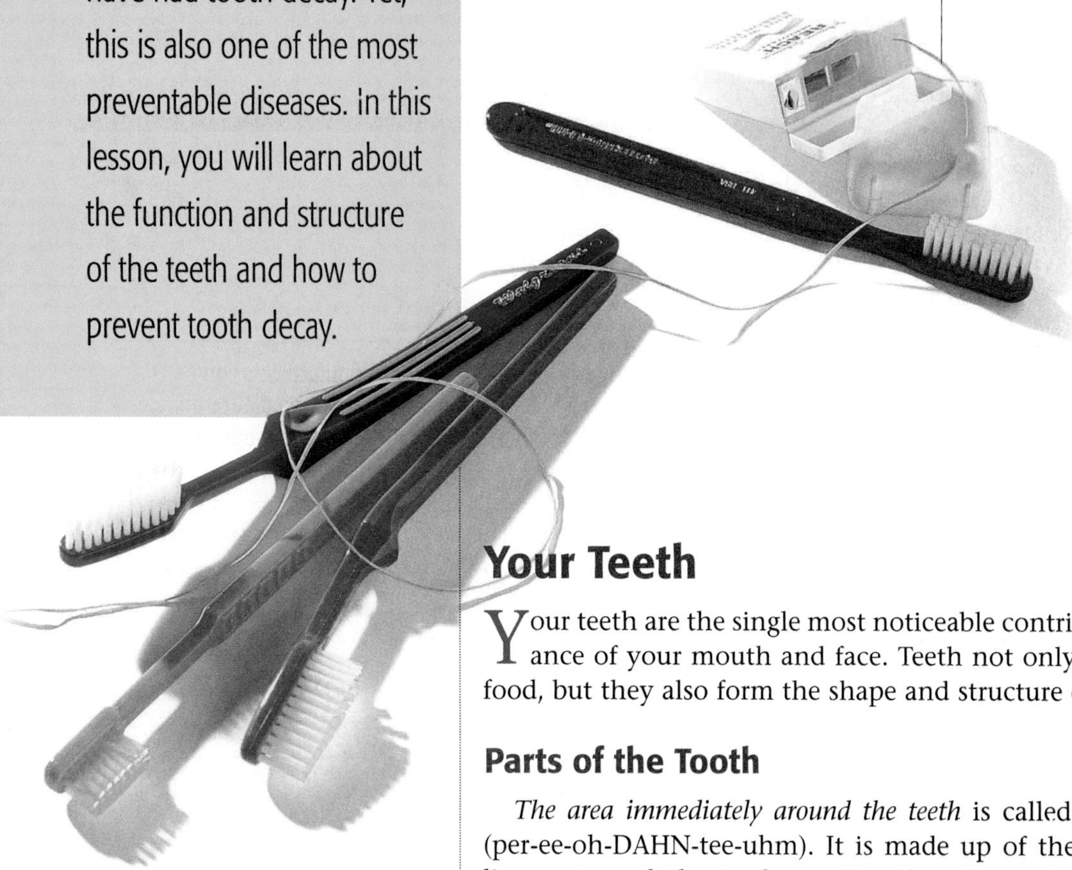

HEALTH TERMS

periodontium

pulp

plaque

periodontal disease

tartar

HEALTH CONCEPTS

- Regular oral hygiene can help you have clean, healthy teeth and breath.
- Oral hygiene is an important step in preventing periodontal disease.

Your Teeth

Your teeth are the single most noticeable contributor to the appearance of your mouth and face. Teeth not only allow you to chew food, but they also form the shape and structure of your mouth.

Parts of the Tooth

The area immediately around the teeth is called the **periodontium** (per-ee-oh-DAHN-tee-uhm). It is made up of the gums, periodontal ligament, and the jawbone. Together these structures support the teeth.

The tooth itself is divided into three major parts: the root, the neck, and the crown. The crown is the visible part of the tooth. The **pulp** is *the living tissue inside the tooth.*

CROSS-SECTION OF A TOOTH

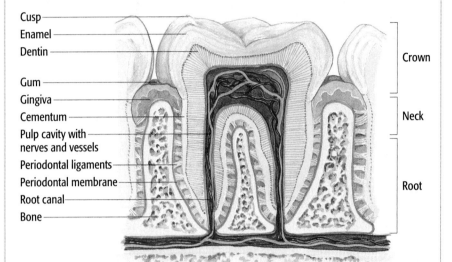

Cusp
Enamel
Dentin

Gum
Gingiva
Cementum
Pulp cavity with nerves and vessels
Periodontal ligaments
Periodontal membrane
Root canal
Bone

Crown

Neck

Root

▶ *A tooth is a living structure made up of many parts.*

ACTIVITY *Describe the structures within each of the three parts of the tooth and explain the different functions of different teeth.*

Building Health Skills

Comparing Health and Beauty Aids

"BREAKTHROUGH PRODUCT bleaches teeth whiter, faster." "Now–whiter, brighter teeth!" "Unique formula lightens teeth to a dazzling white." With all the claims being made, how do you know which product to buy? Here are a few pointers:

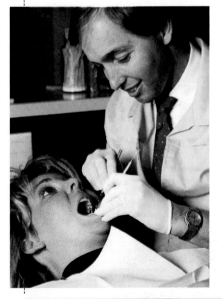

1. **If it sounds too good to be true, it probably is.** Manufacturers sometimes make claims that are false or misleading. Beware of products that promise radical changes in short periods of time. Watch for "cures" for something that science does not have a cure for.

2. **Be alert to key words.** Promoters of health and beauty aids may use key phrases such as *one-time offer, scientific breakthrough, unique formula,* or *secret ingredient.* This is a typical marketing technique used to attract and deceive consumers.

3. **Read the fine print.** Just how different are the various products? Check and compare the list of ingredients on the labels.

4. **Consult a dental professional.** Ask your dentist or dental hygienist for his or her recommendation.

Healthy Teeth and Mouth

Good, regular oral health care is necessary for healthy, clean teeth. Because a toothbrush often misses hard-to-reach spots, flossing is also important. Flossing removes **plaque**, *a sticky, colorless film that acts on sugar to form acids that destroy tooth enamel and irritate gums.* Flossing also removes food particles stuck between teeth and between teeth and gums.

Fluoride has been shown to be effective in helping to prevent tooth decay. Today, 60 percent of the nation's drinkable water supply has been treated with fluoride. Dentists may treat children's teeth by painting on a fluoride solution or by briefly holding a fitted tray filled with fluoride gel against the teeth. Fluoride mouthwashes and toothpastes can be purchased for daily use at home.

Besides regular brushing and flossing, regular visits to a dental care professional are the next most important part of oral dental health. The food choices you make are also important. Frequent consumption of sugary foods contributes to tooth decay. If you eat sweets, it is important to brush your teeth as soon as possible. Eating foods rich in phosphorus and vitamins C and D, meanwhile, can strengthen teeth and gums. Avoid smoking and the use of smokeless tobacco, which can lead to oral cancer. Smokeless tobacco causes white patches or leukoplakia, which is a forerunner to mouth cancer.

Periodontal Disease

More than 20 million Americans have lost most or all of their teeth. The culprit is **periodontal** (per-ee-oh-DAHN-tuhl) **disease**, *an inflammation of the periodontal structures.* It is almost entirely preventable.

Periodontal disease is primarily the result of the destructive action of bacteria in the mouth. Bacteria form plaque. Unless plaque is removed once every 24 to 36 hours, it can harden into **tartar**, or calculus. Either name refers to *a hard, crustlike substance.* Tartar irritates both the underlying bone and the surrounding gums.

Decay begins as the plaque eats into the enamel and then spreads to the dentin. Your tooth will become more sensitive as the decay reaches the pulp. You will get a toothache when the decay reaches the pulp and exposes the nerve. If it is not treated, the bacterial infection can spread.

A tooth becomes abscessed when decay progresses to the stage where pus collects in, and tissue becomes inflamed around, the bone sockets of a tooth. Infection from an abscessed or badly decayed tooth in the upper jaw can spread into the sinuses.

keeping Fit

Brushing Up

Removing plaque from teeth requires two minutes of proper brushing. Most people, however, brush for a maximum of 45 seconds. To make sure you brush long enough, play a radio in the background. Brush through the entire length of one song.

Here are more tips:

➤ Hold the bristle tips at a 45-degree angle against the gumline.

➤ Brush back and forth in very short strokes. Use a gentle, scrubbing motion.

➤ Brush the outer surfaces of each tooth, the inside surfaces and, finally, the chewing surfaces.

➤ To clean the inside surfaces of the front teeth, tilt the brush vertically and make up-and-down strokes.

➤ Brush your tongue to help freshen breath and remove bacteria.

Flossing reaches areas your toothbrush cannot get to, such as gaps between teeth and around the gums. See techniques on page 170.

ACTIVITY *Describe what might happen if a person does not floss in addition to brushing.*

Other Problems of the Teeth and Mouth

In addition to periodontal disease, several other tooth and mouth disorders can occur. These are often caused by poor oral health care, but they may also result from poorly aligned teeth.

Halitosis

Halitosis is the medical term for bad breath. This condition can be caused by such factors as decayed teeth, eating certain foods, smoking, and mouth infections. Mouthwashes and mints may temporarily cover up the odor. However, if halitosis is caused by tooth decay or other infections, the only way to cure it is to treat the underlying cause of the problem.

Gingivitis and Periodontitis

Gingivitis is a disorder in which the gums become red and swollen and bleed easily. The inflammation may be caused by dental plaque, misaligned teeth, or deposits of decaying food. A dentist must determine the cause of the inflammation in order to treat this condition.

If gingivitis goes untreated, a more serious form of gum disease can develop. Called *periodontitis,* this disease results in swollen, tender, or bleeding gums. Bone surrounding the teeth is gradually destroyed, causing teeth to become loose and possibly fall out. As with gingivitis, good oral health care prevents this disease.

Malocclusion

Malocclusion is a condition in which the teeth of the upper and lower jaws do not align properly. Malocclusion can lead to decay and disease. It can also affect a person's speech and ability to chew. Orthodontics is the area of dentistry that corrects malocclusion.

LESSON 2 *Review*

Reviewing Facts and Vocabulary

1. How can you protect and maintain your teeth?
2. Describe the causes of tooth decay.

Thinking Critically

3. *Synthesizing.* Develop a headline for a poster aimed at people who do not regularly brush or floss their teeth.
4. *Evaluating.* How might you be able to distinguish between a person who practices good oral health and one who does not?

Applying Health Skills

5. *In Your Home and School.* Locate three ads for dental health products and analyze the claims these ads make. Then, create your own ad on how to practice good dental health using one of the health products. Share it with your family and the class.

Healthy Eyes

Imagine video equipment that provides images so convincingly three-dimensional and lifelike that you feel as though you are in the middle of the action. Such wonders exist, although they cannot be found in any store. In fact, you already own a set. They are your eyes.

HEALTH TERMS

lacrimal gland

sclera

cornea

choroid

retina

HEALTH CONCEPTS

- The parts around the eyes provide protection for the eye.
- Measures can be taken to protect the eyes.
- Many vision problems can be corrected with professional help.

Your Eyes

More than 80 percent of the information you receive about the environment around you comes by way of your eyes. Your eyes have more than a million electrical connections and can distinguish nearly 8 million differences in color!

Situated within bony sockets in the skull, your eyes are surrounded by protective structures. These include the eyebrows, eyelids, and eyelashes, all of which keep out foreign matter. Another important structure is the **lacrimal** (LAK-rih-mul) **gland.** This is *the gland responsible for producing tears.* Tears are made mostly of water and a small amount of salt and mucus. The salt gives the tears an antiseptic effect, which helps them fight pathogens. Tears keep the eyeballs moist and help remove foreign particles from the eyes.

Tears reach the surface of the eye through tiny ducts. Some of the tears evaporate from the eye's surface. Those that do not evaporate are drained into the nasal cavity by two tear ducts located at the inner corner of each eye. These ducts open into larger ducts that run down into the nose. When the production of tears increases, the ducts are not able to carry away the extra quantity, and the tears will flow over the lower lid.

Parts of the Eye

The eye is made up of two main parts. One of these, the optic nerve, is a cable that connects the eye with the brain. The second, the eyeball wall, is itself made up of three layers.

■ The **sclera** (SKLEHR-uh) is *the tough, white outer coat of the eye.* It protects the inner structures of the eye from injury and helps maintain the eye's spherical shape. The rounded front part of the sclera forms the transparent **cornea.** This is *the main lens that performs most of the eye's focusing.*

■ The **choroid** (KOHR-oid) is *the middle layer of the eyeball wall.* Among the structures it contains is the iris, the colored part of the eye.

■ The **retina** is *the light-sensitive membrane on which images are cast by the cornea and lens.* The retina contains millions of light-sensitive receptors. These are classified, depending on their shape, as either *rods* or *cones.* The rods are highly sensitive to light but not to color. The opposite is true of the cones.

Within the shallow space formed by the cornea and lens is a watery fluid known as the *aqueous humor.* This fluid is continuously formed and drained to help maintain pressure within the eye. A second fluid, the *vitreous humor,* is a clear jelly that fills the eyeball behind the lens. The vitreous humor keeps the eyeball firm.

➤ *The eye is a complex organ.*

ACTIVITY *Name the major parts and functions of the eye.*

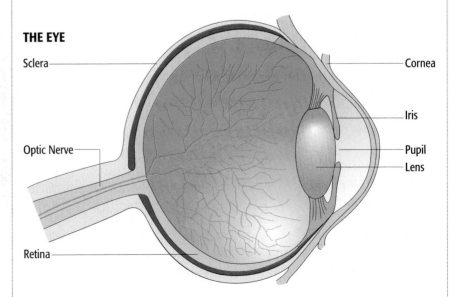

THE EYE

Sclera

Optic Nerve

Retina

Cornea

Iris

Pupil

Lens

Vision

Vision starts in the retina. As light rays pass through the cornea and aqueous humor, they are bent and directed through the pupil. The light rays then pass through the lens, which adjusts to focus the light on the retina. The lens bulges to accommodate objects that are near and flattens to accommodate objects that are distant.

The rods and cones in the retina change this "visual information" into **nerve impulses**. These impulses are passed along the optic nerve to the brain, where they are fused into a single image. Because each eye has a slightly different view of a given object, the brain must interpret depth. This "stereoscopic" vision, as it is called, is important in judging distance.

In normal vision, a sharp image is produced. If you stand 20 feet (6 m) from an eye chart and can read the top eight lines, you have 20/20 vision. If you can read at 20 feet (6 m) what a person with normal vision can read at 40 feet (12 m) you have 20/40 vision. A person who has less than 20/200 vision and who cannot see the letter at the top of the chart is considered legally blind.

hotlink

nerve impulses For more information on nerve impulses and their function, see Chapter 16, page 364.

Healthy Eyes

Sensible eye care begins with regular checkups by a trained eye care professional. If corrective lenses have been prescribed for you, wear them. Take breaks from using your eyes for long periods of time, especially when working at a computer. It is important to read and watch television in a well-lighted room. Avoid rubbing your eyes. Avoid direct sun or bright light, or wear sunglasses. Wear protective goggles or glasses when engaging in an activity or sport that could cause an eye injury.

Eye Problems

Even with regular care, problems of the eye can occur. Eye problems can be divided into two general types: vision problems and diseases of the eye.

Vision Problems

The two most common vision problems are nearsightedness and farsightedness.

Nearsightedness, or *myopia,* is a condition in which light rays are focused in front of the retina rather than on it. Objects close up are seen clearly, but distant objects are blurred. Concave corrective lenses make the rays focus farther back. Myopia can now be corrected by a surgical procedure called *radial keratotomy.* (See Update, page 174.)

Farsightedness, or *hyperopia,* occurs when the light rays are focused behind the retina. Distant objects can be seen clearly, but close objects are blurred. Convex lenses correct this condition.

▼ *Regular examinations by an eye-care professional are important in early detection of eye problems.*

ACTIVITY *Can you read the number shown in this simple test for color-blindness?*

HEALTH Online

Visit **health.glencoe.com** to learn how to care for your eyes and protect them from injury. Then take the interactive quiz on eye care facts and myths at the American Academy of Ophthalmology Web Link.

Other vision problems include the following:

- **Astigmatism.** In this condition, the curvature of the lens is uneven. As a result, the light rays focus at different points, causing the entire image to be blurred. Astigmatism can be corrected with lenses shaped to the correct curvature.

- **Strabismus.** In this condition, the muscles of both eyes do not work together. The eyes may appear crossed or one eye may appear to turn outward. A person with strabismus may have double vision since the brain cannot fuse the input from each eye into a single image.

- **Amblyopia.** If strabismus goes undetected or untreated, it may lead to *amblyopia,* or reduced vision in an eye that otherwise appears to be normal. The unused eye loses some ability to see. Treatment of amblyopia may include covering the stronger eye with a patch, wearing corrective lenses, or corrective surgery.

Most vision problems can be corrected with the use of prescription glasses or contact lenses.

up date
▶ Looking at Technology

Laser Eye Surgery

Throughout history, doctors have looked for ways to correct imperfect vision. One early advancement was RK or Radial Keratotomy—a surgical operation to improve nearsightedness by changing the curve of the cornea over the pupil. The surgeon made several deep incisions in the cornea in a radical or spoke-like pattern. Then with the advent of laser technology, in the 1980s, PRK (Photo Refractive Keratectomy) was introduced. In PRK, a computer-guided laser is used to precisely sculpt the surface of the cornea.

One of the latest advancements in laser eye treatments, developed in the 1990s, is LASIK (Laser in Situ Keratomileusis). In this procedure, a small flap in the cornea is created using a device called a micokeratome. Then, a cold (excimer) laser beam is used to either trim or to build up the surface of the cornea depending on whether the patient is nearsighted or farsighted. The entire procedure takes approximately 60 seconds and is guided by a preprogrammed computer.

There are, however, risks involved with corrective laser eye surgery. This can include sensitivity to light or scarring of the cornea, and it is not suitable for correcting some vision problems. Researchers are continuing to make advancements to reduce the risks involved in laser eye treatments.

Diseases of the Eye

Diseases of the eye range from easily treated infections to disorders and conditions that can threaten sight. Among the more common but less serious diseases are sty and pinkeye. A sty is an inflamed swelling of a sebaceous gland near the eyelash. Pinkeye, or *conjunctivitis,* is an eye infection of the sclera or related tissues, causing redness, discomfort, and discharge. Both conditions can be treated with **antibiotics**.

More serious diseases of the eye include:

- **Cataracts.** This is a clouding of the lens, which causes blurring or hazy vision and problems with night vision. The only treatment is to remove the lens surgically and restore the eye's vision with an artificially implanted lens or with special contact lenses.

- **Glaucoma.** Glaucoma is a condition in which pressure of the fluid in the eye is so high that it damages the optic nerve and may result in blindness.

- **Detached Retina.** The retina may become separated from the outer layers of the eye as a result of natural degeneration—or wearing out of the tissue—or from injury.

h⊙t link

antibiotics For more information on the class of medications called antibiotics and the kinds of infections they are used to treat, see Chapter 23, page 512.

◄ *Wear protective goggles or glasses when engaging in an activity that could cause eye injury.*

ACTIVITY *List different sports activities that require eye protection equipment.*

LESSON 3 *Review*

Reviewing Facts and Vocabulary

1. Describe the main functions of the three layers of the eyeball wall.
2. Explain the roles of the rods and cones in vision.
3. How do cataracts affect vision?

Thinking Critically

4. *Evaluating.* Do you think it is important for school-aged children to have their vision tested on a regular basis? Why or why not?
5. *Comparing and Contrasting.* Create a Venn diagram with two overlapping circles to show similarities among and differences between nearsightedness and farsightedness. Similarities should be placed in the area where the two circles overlap, differences in the nonoverlapping areas.

Applying Health Skills

6. *In Your Home and School.* Research the costs of various types of eyewear, both eyeglasses and contact lenses of different types. Identify factors that are responsible for the price differences. Share this information with your family and the class.

Healthy Ears

I f you thought ears were only for hearing, think again. If it were not for the role ears play in balance, you could not sit upright or walk. In this lesson, both these roles will be explored. You will also learn about ways of protecting these vital sense organs.

HEALTH TERMS

external auditory canal

ossicles

labyrinth

otosclerosis

tinnitus

HEALTH CONCEPTS

- Hearing is the result of sound waves moving through the structure of the ears.
- There are effective measures to care for the ears.
- Hearing loss can be prevented by avoiding exposure to excessively loud noise.

Parts of the Ear

The ear extends deep into the skull and has three main parts. These are:

- **The Outer Ear.** Known technically as the *auricle,* this is the familiar fleshy, curved part attached to each side of the head. It is made up of fatty tissue and cartilage. The auricle collects sound waves and directs them into the ear. Visible within the auricle is the **external auditory canal**, *a passageway about one inch (2.5 cm) long that leads to the eardrum.* This canal is lined with fine hairs and tiny wax-producing glands that protect the ear by trapping dust and other foreign substances. At the inner end of the auditory canal is the tympanic membrane, better known as the eardrum.

INNER EAR (LABYRINTH)　MIDDLE EAR　OUTER EAR

AUDITORY OSSICLES

Semicircular canals

Stapes

Incus

Malleus

Auricle

Cochlear nerve

Vestibule

Cochlea

Round window

Eardrum

Oval window

Mastoid process

Temporal bone

External auditory canal

Eustachian tube

The standard unit for measuring the intensity of sound is the decibel (dB).

ACTIVITY *List at least three activities during which hearing protection should be worn.*

- **The Middle Ear.** Behind the eardrum are the **ossicles** (AH-si-kuhlz), which are *three small bones linked together that connect the eardrum with the inner ear.* The malleus is the first bone. It is attached to the eardrum and is the largest of the three bones. The incus is the middle bone. It connects the malleus and the innermost bone, the stapes. The stapes is stirrup-shaped and attaches to the inner ear. It is the smallest bone in the body. The ends of the stapes are attached by ligaments to a membrane called the oval window, which leads to the inner ear.

- **The Inner Ear.** The **labyrinth** (LAB-uh-rinth), or *inner ear,* consists of a maze of winding passages divided into three parts. The cochlea, the outermost part, turns sound vibrations into nerve impulses for transmission to the brain. The central and innermost parts, the vestibule and semicircular canals, contain structures critical to the sense of balance.

Hearing

Your ears transform sound waves—vibrations in the air—into nerve impulses that your brain interprets as sounds. Sound waves entering the external auditory canal cause the eardrum to vibrate. These vibrations are carried across the middle ear by the ossicles and into the inner ear. There they are converted into nerve impulses that are then sent to the brain.

Slight differences in how sounds arrive at each ear can indicate the direction a sound is coming from. This is called *binaural hearing.* A sound is slightly louder in the ear that is closer to the sound source and reaches that ear a fraction of a second sooner than it does the other ear. Your brain notices these differences in loudness and time and uses them to determine the direction from which the sound comes.

Balance

The semicircular canals in your ears provide much of the brain's information about balance. At one end of each canal is an organ called a *crista*. The crista contains many tiny hairs bathed in a fluid. As the head moves, the fluid shifts, bending the hairs and stimulating nerve impulses. Some of these hairs are sensitive to gravity. Others respond to positions and movements—up and down, side to side, back and forth. Nerve fibers send information about changes in position to the brain. The brain then signals the muscles to make the necessary adjustments to maintain balance.

Healthy Ears

To keep your ears healthy, it is important to clean them regularly and to protect them against weather, especially the cold. Clean the outer ears with a cotton swab. Use the soft head of the swab to remove dirt and earwax, but do not push the swab into the ear. Never use pencils or other sharp items to clean your ears.

Avoiding loud noises is another measure you can take to protect the health of your ears. When you are listening to music or the TV, keep the sound at a reasonable level. When you operate noisy machinery, wear ear protectors. Exposure to loud noise over time can lead to temporary, and sometimes permanent, hearing loss. If your school offers hearing tests, have one performed on you. Early diagnosis of problems is important.

Problems of the Ear

Deafness is a complete or partial inability to hear. Total deafness is rare and is usually congenital, or present from birth. Partial deafness, ranging from mild to severe, is most commonly caused by an ear disease, injury, or the aging process.

All deafness is one of two types. These are known as *conductive* and *sensorineural*.

Conductive Deafness

In conductive deafness, sound waves are not passed from the outer to the inner ear. This can be caused by damage to the eardrum or the ossicles or by earwax blocking the auditory canal. Middle-ear infections may lead to rupture of the eardrum. Persistent buildup of fluid within the middle ear, often due to infection, is the most common cause of hearing difficulties in children.

▲ *Having regular checkups helps ensure healthy ears.*

ACTIVITY *List situations in which you would need to take steps to protect your hearing.*

A less common cause of conductive deafness is **otosclerosis** (OH-toh-skluh-ROH-suhs). This is *a hereditary disorder in which an overgrowth of bone causes the ossicles to lose their ability to move.* Otosclerosis is usually progressive. This means its severity increases with time. Surgery can be used to treat this condition.

Sensorineural Deafness

In sensorineural deafness, sounds that reach the inner ear are not sent to the brain. This is the result of damage to the cochlea, to the auditory nerve, or to part of the brain. Sensorineural deafness can be caused by many factors. These include prolonged exposure to loud noise, some medicines such as streptomycin, increased fluid pressure in the labyrinth, viral infections, and tumors.

Have you ever experienced a ringing noise in your ears? **Tinnitus** (TIN-uh-tuhs) is *a condition in which a ringing, buzzing, whistling, hissing, or other noise is heard in the ear in the absence of external sound.* Tinnitus is usually a symptom of damage to the ear. It can also be a reaction to medication, or a symptom of a physical condition, such as hypertension. About 50 million Americans have tinnitus. Overexposure to loud noise is the most common cause of tinnitus.

You can do something about hearing loss and tinnitus. Take these steps to protect your ears:

- Lower the volume of the source of the noise.
- Wear earplugs in a noisy environment.
- Limit the length of time you are exposed to loud noise. It will reduce the chance of permanent ear damage.

CHARACTER IN ACTION

Worth Hearing

One way to show care and respect is to be **considerate** of others' specific needs.

Character Check When communicating with someone who is hearing impaired, follow these guidelines.

➤ Face the person, speak clearly.

➤ Speak loudly, but do not shout.

➤ Speak slowly, but do not talk "down" to the person in terms of content.

➤ Keep lip movements and facial gestures normal.

➤ Keep your hands away from your mouth when you speak.

➤ Show the same dignity toward the hearing impaired that you do toward all people.

LESSON 4 *Review*

Reviewing Facts and Vocabulary

1. What is the function of the auditory canal?
2. Identify the parts of the labyrinth.
3. Describe the proper method for cleaning the ears.

Thinking Critically

4. *Analyzing.* Analyze the ear as a source of balance.
5. *Evaluating.* What has been the impact of this lesson on your willingness to care for your ears?

Applying Health Skills

6. *In Your School.* Think about areas in and around your school where noise is a problem. Write a letter to the school's administration proposing remedies for this problem. Find out whether your community is one of the growing number nationwide that has ordinances— or laws—to control loud noises from car stereos and other sources.

Health Skills Activities

Activity 1 — Vitamins for Health

Adjusting your diet or taking vitamin supplements can help to ensure that you are getting all the vitamins you need to maintain your personal health. Evaluate your diet to see if it lacks any of the essential vitamins that you need.

Directions

1. For one week, keep track of all the foods and beverages you intake. Include everything you eat—breakfast, lunch, dinner, and even snacks.
2. Bring in the diet information that you have been recording for the last week. Refer to page 108 in your health text.
3. Compare the foods you have been eating with the foods listed in the chart. List all the vitamins that are included in your diet for each day. Make note of any vitamins you are missing or that you receive in small amounts.
4. Next to the list of any vitamins your diet may be lacking, record what role those vitamins play in your body. Determine whether you need to add any foods or supplements to your diet.

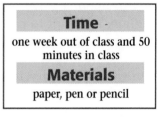

Time - one week out of class and 50 minutes in class

Materials paper, pen or pencil

Self-Assessment

✓ Recorded your diet for at least one week.
✓ Correctly compared diet to chart on page 108 and identified any vitamins that may be deficient in your diet.

Activity 2 — Promoting Personal Health Care

Teachers of elementary children are always looking for interesting ways of teaching their students about the proper care of the eyes, teeth, and hair. What creative ideas do you have about the best ways to teach personal health care to young children?

Directions

1. Create a booklet to teach young children about the care of the eyes, teeth, and/or hair. Read several children's books for ideas.
2. Make a storyboard, plotting out illustrations, and then outline the text. Complete your storyboard, making it colorful and appealing. Focus on the best way to positively influence your target age group.
3. Read your completed story to a young child—maybe a brother or sister—or to a class at a local elementary school. Ask for feedback on what was learned about improving hygiene habits.

Time two 50-minute periods

Materials children's books, storyboard, paper, pen or pencil, markers

Self-Assessment

✓ Described appropriate personal care of eyes, teeth, and/or hair illustrated with pictures.
✓ Created messages appropriate to age group of younger children.

Harmful Rays of Light

If you weren't born with a tan, the Centers for Disease Control and Prevention says you should think twice about trying to get one.

Since tanning now can lead to skin cancer later, the federal government is directing its skin cancer prevention message toward young people. The "Choose Your Cover" campaign includes upbeat, youth-oriented TV, radio, and print advertisements. The ads tell children and teenagers to use sunscreen, wear wide-brim hats and avoid the midday sun.

"Young people need to know that the risk of getting skin cancer later can be greatly reduced if they start protecting their skin from the sun now," CDC Director Jeffrey P. Koplan said.

"The effects of the sun are cumulative," said Mary Kay Sones, a spokeswoman for the CDC. "Most of a person's lifetime sun exposure occurs before 18," she said.

The CDC recommends that individuals take personal responsibility for their skin. Protective measures include wearing a hat, remaining in the shade, slathering on sunscreen with an SPV of at least 15, donning sunglasses, and covering skin with lightweight clothing.

If possible, people should avoid going outside between the peak hours of 10 a.m. and 4 p.m., when the sun's rays are most powerful.

Read This

Take the Quiz: Are You at Risk?

1. What is your skin complexion?
   - Fair
   - Dark
2. Do you have a family history of skin cancer?
   - Yes
   - No
3. Do you have freckles?
   - Yes
   - No
4. How often are you exposed to the sun?
   - Everyday
   - Only on vacation
   - Never
5. Do you use sunscreen with an SPF rating of 15 or higher?
   - Yes
   - No

Think About It

1. Do you always wear sunscreen? Why or why not?
2. Do you think you could be at risk for skin cancer?
3. Does the statement from CDC Director Jeffrey P. Koplan motivate you to be more cautious in the sun?

Using Health Terms

On a separate sheet of paper, write the term that best matches each definition below.

LESSON 1

1. Structures within the skin that secrete perspiration through ducts to pores on the surface of the skin.
2. A condition in which the outer layer of dead skin cells is shed from the scalp.
3. A clogging of the pores of the skin.
4. Structures within the skin that produce an oily secretion called sebum.
5. Tiny pits in the skin.

LESSON 2

6. The living tissue inside the tooth.
7. A hard, crustlike substance.
8. A sticky, colorless film that acts on sugar to form acids that destroy tooth enamel.
9. An inflammation of the periodontal structures.

10. The area immediately around the teeth.

LESSON 3

11. The gland responsible for producing tears.
12. The light-sensitive membrane on which images are cast by the cornea and lens.
13. The middle layer of the eyeball wall.
14. The main lens that performs most of the eye's focusing.
15. The tough, white outer coat of the eye.

LESSON 4

16. A hereditary disorder in which an overgrowth of bone causes the ossicles to lose their ability to move.
17. Three tiny, linked, movable bones.
18. A condition in which a ringing, buzzing, whistling, hissing, or other noise is heard in the ear in the absence of external sound.

Recalling the Facts

Using complete sentences, answer the following questions.

LESSON 1

1. Name three functions of your skin.
2. What can be a serious result of excessive exposure to the sun over a period of time?
3. What basic procedures can keep skin healthy?
4. How does regular brushing benefit your hair?
5. What are some basic procedures to follow for good nail care?

LESSON 2

6. What functions do teeth serve?
7. What are the parts of the periodontium, and what function do they serve together?

8. How can periodontal disease be stopped in its early stages?
9. What is malocclusion, and what are its effects?

LESSON 3

10. How does the lens of the eye change, and for what purpose does it change?
11. What part does the brain play in vision?
12. Name three things that you can do to protect your eyes.

LESSON 4

13. What is binaural hearing?
14. What is the function of the semicircular canals?
15. Name four steps you can take to protect your ears.

Thinking Critically

LESSON 1

1. ***Analyzing.*** Analyze the sense of the statement: "To avoid the sun, I'm going to a tanning salon."
2. ***Comparing.*** Describe the differences between gingivitis and periodontitis.

LESSON 2

3. ***Synthesizing.*** Conduct a survey of the number of people in your class and other grades in your school who wear braces or dental retainers. What might these numbers indicate?

4. ***Analyzing.*** What snack foods would you recommend for a person who wanted healthy teeth and who was trying to eliminate tooth decay?

LESSON 3

5. ***Synthesizing.*** What activities would require protective eyewear? When is it appropriate to wear protective eyewear?

LESSON 4

6. ***Analyzing.*** Consider the statement: "Walkmans and headsets cause more problems than they are worth."

Making the Connection

1. ***Science.*** Ask a science teacher to help you use a sound level meter to measure the noise levels in various parts of the school. Compare readings against approved safety levels. Make recommendations about improving unhealthful situations to the school administration or student council.

2. ***Music.*** The great German composer Ludwig van Beethoven lost most of his hearing before he died. Learn about Beethoven and other hearing-impaired composers. Write a brief report summarizing your findings.

BEYOND THE CLASSROOM

PARENTAL INVOLVEMENT Invite family members to take part in an experiment to determine how well brushing and flossing remove plaque from teeth. Get two disclosing tablets for each family member from your dentist or dental hygienist. Each person chews one tablet without swallowing, spits into a sink, and rinses his or her mouth with water. Dark spots on teeth and gums show where plaque has formed. Have each person brush and floss carefully, then use the second disclosing tablet. Compare and discuss the differences in the amount of plaque that is seen.

COMMUNITY INVOLVEMENT Take a sign language class or borrow a book on American Sign Language from your local library. Practice with a friend.

SCHOOL-TO-CAREER

Exploring Careers. The eye care field includes a variety of professions, including ophthalmologist, optometrist, optician, and optometric technician. For each career, determine the educational background and training, duties and responsibilities.

CHAPTER 8

Your Mental and Emotional Health

HEALTH
Online

PRACTICING HEALTHFUL BEHAVIORS

Are you mentally alert, did you get enough sleep? Teens and sleep is a subject of recent scientific research, and you may be surprised at the findings. Read about how much sleep you really need in Health Updates at **health.glencoe.com**.

> **" Positive attitudes—optimism, high self-esteem, an outgoing nature, joyousness, and the ability to cope with stress—may be the most important bases for continued good health. "**
>
> —HELEN HAYES
> INSPIRATIONAL WRITER, (1900–1993)

Quick Write Think of someone you know who has a positive attitude. Summarize in a few sentences how other people react to the person. How does being around that person make *you* feel?

Personal Health Inventory

Self-Inventory Write the numbers 1–10 on a sheet of paper. Read each statement below and respond by writing *yes*, *no*, or *sometimes* for each item. Write a *yes* only for items that you practice regularly. Save your responses.

1	I have a generally positive outlook on life.
2	Overall, I like and accept who I am.
3	I recognize my strengths and weaknesses.
4	I try to learn from my mistakes.
5	I am interested in and get along well with others.
6	I can cope with challenges and face problems rather than avoid them.
7	I take responsibility for my personal behavior.
8	I understand my needs and try to get them met in healthful ways.
9	I express my emotions in positive ways.
10	I am usually in control of my emotions more than they are in control of me.

Follow-up After completing the chapter, retake this self-inventory. Pick two items that you need to work on and set a goal to improve your health behaviors.

What Is Mental Health?

Close your eyes. Quickly think of three images that suggest positive mental health. Do you see someone smiling or chatting with friends? Do you see someone attacking a project or problem with a "can do" attitude? Do you see yourself?

HEALTH TERMS

mental health

feedback

HEALTH CONCEPTS

■ Mental health means much more than not being mentally ill.

■ There are varying levels of mental and emotional health.

■ Self-esteem is central to mental and emotional wellness.

Your Mental Health

As with physical health, mental health is much more than the absence of sickness. **Mental health** is *generally having a positive outlook, being comfortable with yourself and others, and being able to meet life's challenges and demands.* Being mentally healthy means being able to cope, adapt, and thrive on many levels. Someone who is mentally healthy can usually handle a wide variety of feelings and situations. He or she will usually make wise and safe choices that demonstrate both strong values and responsible behavior.

This is not to say that people with a high degree of mental health are never unhappy. Like Seth in the chapter-opening story, everyone's level of mental health has its ups and downs. You can have good physical health yet suffer from an occasional cold or a sore muscle. Likewise, you can have good mental health and still have a bad day or even a bad week once in a while. By the same token, just as you can work consciously at becoming more physically fit, you can also work at improving your "mental fitness."

Assessing Your Mental Fitness

As a health-literate person, your first step toward improving your mental health is to assess your general level of mental fitness. Think back to the health continuum you learned about in Chapter 1. Where on this sliding scale is your mental health at this very minute? How about during recent weeks and months? How many of the signs of mental health in the box below describe you?

How you see yourself may have a lot to do with how others see you.

ACTIVITY *Write down three adjectives that others might use to describe you and three that you would use to describe yourself.*

Signs of Good Mental Health

In general, people with good mental health:

- are realistic about their strengths and weaknesses.
- are responsible for their personal behavior.
- avoid high-risk behaviors, such as using tobacco, alcohol, or other drugs.
- are open-minded and flexible.
- are fun-loving and able to relax alone or with others.
- respect both their own and others' needs.
- respect everyone's value as a human being—including their own.
- express their emotions in ways that do not hurt themselves or others.
- invest time and energy into nourishing relationships.
- put their talents and abilities to good use.
- view change as a challenge and an opportunity.

Forgiveness

Forgiveness means letting go of the misdeeds and mistakes of others.

Character Check Can you think of someone you hold a grudge against? Remind yourself that people make mistakes. Try to understand the feelings behind the person's behavior. Wish for something good to happen to that person, despite your resentment. Take responsibility for your part in what went wrong. Be forgiving and let go of the rest.

Can you find patterns in the ways you react to different situations and people? Are there certain conditions under which you feel more alive, positive, and able to cope? The more you identify such factors, the better able you may be to control them.

Roadblocks to Mental Health

On the road to improved mental health, you may run into obstacles in your own thinking, attitudes, or behaviors. By becoming aware of these roadblocks, you can learn to bypass them. Among these roadblocks are the following:

- **All-or-nothing thinking.** Many situations have "shades of gray." Learn to recognize and accept these subtle degrees of difference.
- **Expecting the "worst" in others or yourself.** Look for the good, and you will be more likely to find it.
- **Being a perfectionist.** Trying to be perfect or thinking you can do it all often leads to failure and frustration. Remind yourself that no one is perfect. Don't be afraid to ask for help when you need it.
- **Letting your actions or words betray your values.** Stand up for what you believe in and know is right.

Building Health Skills

Promoting a Positive Self-Image

IT IS NEVER too late to begin improving your self-esteem and, in turn, your mental health. Try the following suggestions:

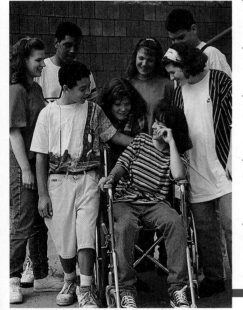

1. **List your assets or strengths.** Include your mental, emotional, and physical strengths. Read this list every day for a week.

2. **Surround yourself with positive, supportive people.** Choose friends who support you, believe in you, and respect your individual rights and needs.

3. **Find something that you love to do, and do it frequently.** If you're always too busy to do the things you enjoy, you're not fully taking care of yourself. Make time for your favorite activities and pastimes.

4. **Stop making life a contest.** Recognize that there will always be people more and less able than you in all areas of life. Be content with doing the best you can in all areas that really matter to you.

5. **Help someone else.** One way to feel good about yourself is to see the positive effects of your own words or actions on someone else's life.

Self-Esteem and Your Mental Health

Self-esteem—the confidence and worth that you feel about yourself—is directly related to your general level of wellness. How you feel mentally and physically and how you take care of yourself—your health habits—are all affected by what you think of yourself. Teens with high self-esteem are better able to take failure in their stride and move forward. They often tend to have specific long-term goals and aspirations for their future. Having high self-esteem promotes good mental health.

The Role of Positive and Negative Feedback

How is self-esteem formed? Over the years you have received **feedback**—*messages from others that indicate who they think you are or what they think you are like.* You have received positive or negative feedback from many sources—from your parents or guardians, other adults who first took care of you, as well as from your siblings, your extended family, teachers, coaches, friends, and your peers.

From the moment you were born, you began to receive, process, and store these messages, which came mostly from your family. Some messages were nonverbal. People hugged you, patted you, and smiled at you. Perhaps they frowned at or ignored you. All of these actions made deep and lasting impressions on you. These first caregivers gave you verbal messages, too, like "Oh, what a cute baby!" or "Bad boy!" With all of these verbal and nonverbal messages that you received, you began to develop your self-esteem.

By the time you reached school age, other factors started to play a role in how you viewed yourself. Now, in addition to your family, your feelings were influenced by how friends, neighbors, and teachers reacted to you. During the teen years, feedback from peers takes on a new and greater importance. Messages from the media about what you as a teenager *should* be like have also directly or indirectly begun to shape and influence your self-image.

So what does self-esteem have to do with overall mental health? A person who has received mostly positive feedback will generally have high

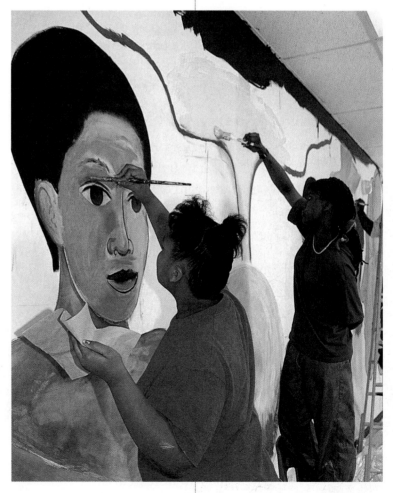

▼ *Participating in community projects and volunteering your skills and talents can contribute to positive mental health.*

ACTIVITY *Over the next month, learn a new skill or try a new and healthful recreational activity. Record your progress in your private Health Journal.*

self-esteem. Someone who has received lots of negative feedback may be more likely to have low self-esteem and fragile mental health. This person may also misinterpret the feedback she or he gets from others, and may assume messages are negative even when they are not.

Self-Talk

Feedback comes not just from others but also from yourself. Are you too hard on yourself when you do something wrong or make a mistake? Do you go overboard in focusing on your own limitations or weaknesses? *Negative self-talk*—hurtful or non-constructive messages that you send yourself—can erode your self-esteem as much and sometimes even more than negative feedback from others. Positive feedback on the other hand, can do just the opposite. If someone continually tells you you can do whatever you set out to do, you may start to believe that person—and in yourself.

Listen to the messages you send yourself, and replace any negative self-talk with **constructive criticism**. When you make a mistake, accept it as part of being human and try to learn and grow from the experience. This is one way of reducing the chances of making the same mistake in the future. Get into the habit, moreover, of giving yourself a verbal pat on the back from time to time. Tell yourself "Good job" or "Way to go" when you've done something deserving of praise. Your self-esteem and mental health will benefit.

h t link

constructive criticism For more information on constructive criticism and its benefits to social and overall health, see Chapter 11, page 209.

LESSON 1 *Review*

Reviewing Facts and Vocabulary

1. Name three signs of positive mental health.
2. Name two factors that influence a person's self-esteem.

Thinking Critically

3. *Analyzing.* Make two lists, one of positive feedback and one of negative feedback that you received in your childhood. Describe how you think each kind of feedback affected your self-image.
4. *Evaluating.* Over the next week, keep track of each time you hear a "put-down" from a peer. Take note of when and where the put-down is delivered, how it is received, and how it seems to affect the self-esteem of its recipient. See if you can find a relationship between the level of self-esteem of the people who deliver put-downs and the frequency with which they use them.

Applying Health Skills

5. *In Your Home.* Think of a caring adult in your family who has been important in your life and has given you positive feedback. Write a letter to this person, thanking him or her for caring. Indicate in the letter how this positive feedback has affected your feelings of self-worth.

Your Needs, Your Personality

Have you ever been so thirsty for a drink of water that nothing else seemed to matter? Like all people, you usually try to get your most basic needs met first. This is true not only for physical needs, but also for emotional and social needs. Getting your needs met in positive ways is essential for your total health.

HEALTH TERMS

hierarchy of needs

aesthetic

self-actualization

personality

psychologists

modeling

HEALTH CONCEPTS

- All human beings have basic needs.
- When basic needs are continuously not met, physical and mental illness may occur.
- Personality is shaped by three main factors: heredity, environment, and behavior.
- The factor over which you have the most control is your personal behavior.

A Pyramid of Needs

There are many theories that try to explain or describe human behavior and development in terms of needs. One famous theory is that of Abraham Maslow, who organized human needs into the form of a pyramid. Maslow maintained that although everyone has needs, some are more basic than others. These lower needs must be satisfied before higher-level needs can be met. Maslow's **hierarchy of needs** is *a ranked list of those needs essential to human growth and development presented in ascending order from the most basic to the most fulfilling or satisfying.*

People who do not have their needs met in healthful ways may be motivated to get them met in unhealthful or inappropriate ways. Think of the child who is constantly being scolded for misbehaving. That child has probably learned that one sure way to get attention is

Your emotional needs are an important part of your good mental health. Follow the Web Links at **health.glencoe.com** to the National Institute of Mental Health and learn how mental health professionals study mental disorders.

to act up. How do you think this child might act as an adolescent or as an adult in order to meet the need to be recognized? At any time such people can be shown more healthful ways to get their needs met. With help, they can often overcome some of the damage that may have resulted from being neglected or deprived earlier in life.

Physical Needs

At the bottom of Maslow's pyramid are physical needs. Among these are the need to satisfy hunger, thirst, sleep, and so on. People who are denied these become physically weak. A lack of essential nutrients the body needs also interferes with the normal functioning of the brain, which in turn affects a person mentally. Many people in our society take for granted that these needs are easily satisfied for everyone. They may overlook the fact that there are great numbers of people for whom food, clean water, and shelter are scarce or unavailable.

Emotional Needs

Emotional needs include the need to be loved, to belong, and to be valued and recognized. After we meet our physical needs, most of our behavior is an attempt to meet emotional needs.

- **The need to be loved.** Everyone needs to give love and to feel that he or she is valued and loved in return. Babies who are denied both physical and emotional attention may be stunted physically and mentally. They may fail to thrive. Some even die.

- **The need to belong.** Everyone has the need to belong. Human beings are social beings; that is, they need to be with and interact with people. We need to feel like we belong to and are a valued member of a group. When we are mentally healthy, we meet these needs in positive ways that benefit ourselves and those to whom we are connected. When we are not mentally healthy, we may isolate ourselves from others.

- **The need to be valued and recognized.** Another emotional need that all human beings have is feeling that they have personal value or worth. We have a need to achieve—to have ourselves and others recognize that we are competent at something and that we can make a positive contribution to the world. We must have something we can do well, and we need recognition from others.

Aesthetic Needs

At the next level of Maslow's pyramid are **aesthetic**, or *artistic*, needs. The word *aesthetic* means artistic; it applies to our response to or appreciation of

Every human being feels the need to belong.

ACTIVITY *Name three places or groups where you feel that you belong.*

MASLOW'S HIERARCHY OF NEEDS

Need for self-actualization

SELF-FULFILLING

Need to know, to explore, to understand

AESTHETIC

Need to achieve, to be recognized

EMOTIONAL

Need to belong, to love and be loved

Need to be secure and safe, out of danger

PHYSICAL

Need to satisfy hunger, thirst, sleep, etc.

that which is beautiful. We feel the need to appreciate beauty in its many forms, and we also feel the desire for order and balance in our lives. Our senses are constantly stimulated by the rhythms, forms, and colors around us, which can, in turn, affect our behavior and mental health.

Self-Fulfilling Needs

At the top of Maslow's pyramid is the need to reach one's full potential as a person. This quest for **self-actualization**—*the striving to become the best that you can be*—includes having goals that motivate and inspire you. Self-actualization is a lifelong process.

▲ *Basic needs speak the loudest.*

ACTIVITY *Describe a time when you needed food, water, or sleep, and this need overshadowed everything else.*

During the teen years, working toward self-actualization may involve volunteering to help others, making specific education and career goals, and beginning to work toward these goals. What goals have you begun to work toward?

It is important to note that not all of your needs can be met all of the time. You may have some needs met only partly and still strive to satisfy the higher ones. Even people raised in extreme conditions can create lives for themselves that reach toward self-actualization.

Understanding Your Personality

Think about words you have heard to describe other people—for example, "quiet," "pushy," or "outgoing." Words like these may describe some characteristics of a person's personality. **Personality** is, in fact, *a complex set of characteristics that makes you unique and sets you apart from everyone else.* It includes your emotional makeup, attitudes, thoughts, behaviors, and more.

Psychologists, *professionals with doctoral degrees who diagnose and treat emotional and behavioral disorders,* view personality as one window on a person's mental health. Over the years, they have isolated a

▼ *Just as one domino can knock into another, making all three fall, one positive thought, feeling, or behavior can have a positive "domino effect" on the other two.*

ACTIVITY *Think of a time when a positive feeling or thought had a positive "domino effect" on your behavior.*

number of different personality traits and investigated these in depth. Maslow's hierarchy, explained earlier in this lesson, is one model of personality.

Foundations of Personality

Your personality began taking shape before you were actually born. **Heredity**, the biological passing along of traits and characteristics from your parents, is one of the three major factors in molding personality. The other two—environment and behavior—are also important.

Personality and Heredity

Heredity is the first influence on your personality. You inherit obvious physical traits such as your hair and eye color, the shape of your nose and ears, and your body type and height. You also inherit basic intellectual abilities as well as temperament, or emotional tendencies. Studies of twins separated at birth suggest that even such characteristics as preferences for foods, colors, and scents may, in fact, have inherited components. There is also increasing evidence that heredity may play a role in behaviors such as risk-taking and in talents such as the ability to draw or sing well.

h t l nk

heredity For more information on heredity and its effect on the total person you are, see Chapter 20, page 461.

connections Social Studies

When Needs Aren't Met

Elie Wiesel, an author and concentration-camp survivor, writes that while in the horrifying camp during World War II, he had "neither the time nor the strength" to think about the meaning of the universe. "The daily bread ration was the center of our concerns," he notes. "Would it be a centimeter thicker or thinner? Would they give us margarine or jam?…I remember a Dutchman who shared his bread with a comrade sicker than he was, a comrade he did not know. 'I prefer to be hungry than to feel remorse,' he said."

1. Where on Maslow's "pyramid" do you think Wiesel was forced to spend most of his time?

2. Where on Maslow's "hierarchy of needs" would you place the Dutchman when he offered his bread to his comrade?

3. What qualities or traits in human nature do you think make it possible for people to bypass or temporarily overlook their basic needs to help another human being? Do you think you could have done what the Dutchman did? Why or why not?

When you take responsibility for your behavior, you skip the "victim mentality" and avoid blaming others for what you have done wrong. You thereby demonstrate the value of **accountability**, taking responsibility for all that you say and do.

Character Check The next time you are wrong and you know it, admit it. Avoid blaming anyone else. Quickly say you are sorry. Finally, make amends. Do something specific to right the situation.

Personality and Environment

The second factor affecting personality is your environment beggining at your birth. Your environment includes all of your surroundings, your family, your friends at school, your neighborhood, and all of the places, people, and activities you have experienced up to this point in your life. These influences can have positive or negative effects on your developing personality.

People who come from unhealthful environments may experience neglect, abuse, rejection, or other negative treatment. These experiences and actions can leave a person with emotional scars that can lead to poor mental health. People who live in healthful environments, however, feel supported, safe, loved, and valued and, therefore, often develop higher levels of mental health.

One way in which environmental "traits" are stamped on the developing personality is through modeling. **Modeling** means *copying the behaviors of those you are exposed to.* A caring adult who gives positive messages to a small child provides a positive pattern of behavior for that child to "model" or follow. That child is more likely to grow up into a trusting adult unafraid to meet life's experiences head-on.

Personality and Personal Behavior

The influence on your personality over which you have the most control is your personal behavior. How you make decisions, what decisions you make, and what actions you take can make all the difference in the world in the quality of your life and your levels of physical and mental health. In some situations, it can even mark the difference between life and death.

LESSON 2 *Review*

Reviewing Facts and Vocabulary

1. Define the word *personality*.
2. What three influences affect the development of personality?
3. Define *modeling* and give one example.

Thinking Critically

4. *Comparing and Contrasting.* Write two versions of a fictional story in which a person faces two levels of need. In one version, the person has to make a choice that meets the more basic need; in the other, she or he must make a choice that meets the higher-level need. Share your different outcomes with the class.

5. *Synthesizing.* Write a letter to an imaginary gang or cult member giving that person tips on how to get his or her needs met in more healthful ways.

Applying Health Skills

6. *In Your Home.* Go through family photo albums or interview family members to find out which relatives you act, look, sound, or behave like. Think about which of these similarities may be the result of heredity and which are the result of environment.

Understanding Your Emotions

H ow do you feel right now? Are you in a good mood? Are you down or bored? Your feelings, or emotions, influence everything you do. They affect your thinking, your relationships with others, your behavior, and even your success or failure at accomplishing a given task. Your emotions have an impact on your mental and physical health.

HEALTH TERMS

emotions

empathy

phobias

hostility

HEALTH CONCEPTS

- Your emotions influence your thoughts and actions.
- Emotions are neither good nor bad.
- During adolescence, hormones can greatly affect your emotions.

Understanding Your Emotions

E motions are *signals that tell your mind and body how to react.* They are neither good nor bad. They are simply the way your body and mind respond to input from outside your body.

Emotions can greatly affect all sides of your health triangle. Consider:

- When you are in a dangerous situation, emotions such as fear can trigger the body and mind to protect you by causing you to shout or flee the scene.
- Emotions such as joy can prompt the release of brain chemicals that not only cause warm, happy feelings but also promote mental health.

Did You Know?

➤ In the middle of the brain are two amygdalas, almond-shaped organs that receive and send all kinds of emotional messages.

➤ A woman whose amygdala had been destroyed was found to be unable to read the signs of fear and unable to feel the emotion itself.

■ Strong emotions like anger can cause physical changes within your body, including a rise in heart rate, perspiration, and a tightening of the muscles of the stomach. If no emotional outlet is found for some of this tension, it builds up inside, eventually taking a toll on your physical health.

Learning constructive ways to deal with your emotions is, therefore, extremely important. A first step toward achieving this goal is learning to identify your emotions.

Identifying Emotions

Identifying emotions can be difficult, especially in situations where you have "mixed emotions," for example, being jealous of and happy for a friend at the same time. Like two colors mixed together, it may at times be difficult to name what you are feeling.

➤ *Different activities bring about varying emotions.*

ACTIVITY *What do you do when you are feeling down? Angry? Happy?*

It is especially important to learn to identify unsettling emotions. Feeling worried may call for a different action than feeling terrified does. Feeling a bit down is different from feeling hopeless and may require different kinds of help. Identifying emotions correctly can help you to know how to express them more effectively the next time you experience them.

Love

All human beings need to give and receive love. This emotion involves strong affection, deep concern, and respect. It includes supporting the growth and individual needs of another person and respecting that person's boundaries and values as well as your own. Love can be expressed through words, actions, facial expressions, touch, and good deeds. It comes in many forms, including caring for family and friends, loyalty to siblings, and even a deep sense of being connected to your country or to all people. Being able to receive and give love is central to what it means to be mentally and emotionally well.

▲ *Everyone needs to feel loved and be able to give love.*

ACTIVITY *Name three ways you express love to family members and close friends.*

Empathy

Empathy is *the ability to imagine and understand how someone else feels*. It is being able to "walk in another's shoes." People who have empathy for others feel more connected to the world. They are better able to help others in need. They can offer insight and understanding. When you have empathy, you can reach out to others and receive their gestures of warmth and caring in return.

As with other emotions, it is important to experience this feeling with some balance. It is not healthy, for example, to be overwhelmed with concern for others' feelings at the expense of meeting all of your own needs.

Fear

Every time you hear an ambulance siren, a loud noise, or a scream, you probably feel some degree of fear. This response can be a safeguard or protection if you need to respond to a real threat.

As with other reactions, your body responds physically to the emotion, preparing itself for what it might need to do. When you experience fear, your **sympathetic nervous system** reacts by preparing your body for necessary action. Hormones cause your heart to beat faster, sending an increased supply of blood to your heart and muscles. Your breathing rate increases. Once the threatening situation has passed, your body returns to its normal state.

h🔥t link

sympathetic nervous system
For more information on the sympathetic nervous system, see Chapter 16, page 370.

A Top Ten List of Fears

Some 3,000 Americans were asked, "What do you fear most?" Here is what they answered.

1.	Speaking before a group	41%
2.	Heights	32%
3.	Insects and spiders	22%
4.	Money problems	22%
5.	Deep water	22%
6.	Sickness	19%
7.	Death	19%
8.	Flying	19%
9.	Loneliness	14%
10.	Dogs	11%

> *A fear of insects and spiders is quite common. As long as fear doesn't control your daily activities, it is a normal emotion to have.*

ACTIVITY *List your top three fears and possible ways to overcome each one.*

Some fears—the fear of falling, for example—may be inherited. Most fears, however, are learned. The fear of fire was probably instilled in you when you were small to protect you from the potential danger of playing with matches. Such fears, which are *rational,* or reasonable, are helpful as you grow. Other fears, such as a fear of heights, are not helpful. These *irrational fears,* or **phobias**, can get in the way of leading a normal life.

Anger

Everyone feels anger at one point or another. At times it may be displayed as a simple annoyance, at other times it may rise up as boiling rage. As with other emotions, how you choose to handle that anger is one of the key factors in your mental and emotional health.

When people do not handle their anger in constructive ways, they can do great damage not only to others and to other's property but also to their own bodies and minds. **Hostility**, *the intentional use of unfriendly or nasty behavior,* can be particularly damaging. In fact, experts now think that hostile behavior is the key personality trait in predicting heart disease. People who show chronic hostile behavior are four to seven times more likely to die of heart disease and cancer than those who are not prone to anger. According to Redford Williams, a researcher at Duke University, silent "seethers" are even more likely to die earlier than those who are openly hostile.

Guilt

Everyone feels guilty for their actions or thoughts some of the time. Guilt is an emotional response when you think you have done something wrong. It often results from acting against one's values or from not acting at all when direct action might have brought about a better outcome. Frequently, guilt is associated with low self-esteem. It may also act as a smokescreen, keeping you from other feelings. For example, it may seem easier to feel guilty than it is to overcome your fear of taking a particular action and perhaps failing. Though guilt can eat away at you, leaving you feeling inadequate, it can also motivate you to make positive changes. You are less likely to engage in a negative behavior if you know yourself well enough to realize that you will be left with a guilty conscience afterward.

Emotions and Adolescence

Strong emotional responses are common during your teen years. Rapid growth and other changes brought on by hormones may make you feel oversensitive on some days, insecure on others. You may overreact or suddenly feel flooded by an emotion. Such reactions are normal. Just remember, you are not alone. The other teens you know are experiencing similar kinds of emotional changes, too.

▲ *During the teen years, it is normal to experience rapid changes in emotions.*

ACTIVITY *List ways you could deal with quickly changing emotions (for example, going for a walk if you are feeling angry).*

LESSON 3

Review

Reviewing Facts and Vocabulary

1. Define the word *emotion* and give examples of three emotions.
2. Describe what happens to the body when responding to anger or fear.

Thinking Critically

3. *Analyzing.* Analyze this statement: "Emotions are neither positive nor negative, but the ways they are expressed can be either." Give examples from your own experience to support this statement.
4. *Evaluating.* Flip through your favorite magazine, identifying what emotions you think you see on the photographed faces. Find a pattern to the kinds of emotions portrayed. Which emotions seem most and least frequently featured? What effect does this have on the overall "mood" or tone created by the publication?

Applying Health Skills

5. *In Your Home.* For a week's time, practice empathy toward someone you encounter on a daily basis. Start by asking yourself, "What is it like to be that person right now? What might he or she be thinking or feeling? Why might he or she be acting in this way?" At the end of the week, record in your private Health Journal any changes in your feelings toward or understanding of that person.

Handling Emotions in Healthful Ways

As noted earlier, emotions are neither good nor bad. How you deal with your emotions, however, can strongly influence your overall level of health. Learning to recognize emotions and dealing with them in positive, healthful ways are two of the most important skills leading to good mental health.

HEALTH TERMS

defense mechanisms

resilience

HEALTH CONCEPTS

- There are positive and negative ways of dealing with emotions.
- Certain defense mechanisms are common as people face strong emotions and try to find ways to handle them.
- Your emotional health depends on your outlook on life and on protective factors.

Positive Ways of Dealing with Emotions

In growing up, you have probably learned various ways of expressing your emotions. You learn from watching others, from your environment, and from your own experiences. Suppose that as a young child you were repeatedly told that crying is a sign of weakness. Do you think that now you would be likely to express an emotion of sadness by crying? How have you learned to express joy and excitement?

Even if you learned unhealthful ways to express your emotions while growing up, it is never too late to learn new, healthful ways. There are both general strategies that can be applied to all emotions and individual strategies for coping with specific emotions, such as fear, anger, and guilt. The general strategies include the following:

- Look below the surface of your emotion. Ask yourself: What is this feeling really about? Do I have any control over what caused this feeling?
- Consider whether or not this feeling or situation will really matter so much tomorrow, next week, or next year.
- Do not take action on a strong feeling until both your head and your heart have investigated what's going on and what's at stake.
- Remind yourself that feelings are just feelings; they are not facts.
- Keep in mind that a strong feeling can be a useful signal. Listen to it. Sometimes it can even be a signal of danger.
- Use positive feelings to inspire you. Use upsetting ones to motivate you to change.
- Remember that you are not alone. All human beings have strong feelings.
- If the feeling doesn't go away, seek help from a parent, another trusted person, or a professional.

Dealing Healthfully with Emotions

Certainly the ways you express your emotions may have to do with your personality. You may be easily brought to tears or quick to fly off the handle. Many of the ways you express your feelings have been learned from observing others. Perhaps in your family, people talk about their feelings openly. Maybe they express themselves indirectly with looks or smiles or with behaviors like crying or slamming doors. Perhaps they do not talk much at all, and you learned from their example that emotions were something not to be shared. Even so, you can still learn healthful ways to express feelings. It takes practice.

There are many negative ways of dealing with feelings that do nothing to solve problems and, in fact, may create additional ones. These include exaggerating emotions for effect, acting them out instead of communicating them, pretending as if they were not there at all, or intentionally hurting another person in expressing them.

There are many positive ways to handle emotions, including playing music or creating art.

ACTIVITY *The next time you feel a strong emotion, try drawing it before you describe it with words.*

keeping Fit

What's Your Hostility I.Q.?

Do you spend too much of your life in the "anger zone"? Your answers to the following questions will help you determine your "hostility I.Q."

➤ Have you ever been so angry at someone that you've thrown things or slammed a door?

➤ Do you tend to remember irritating incidents and get mad all over again?

➤ Do you find yourself getting annoyed at little things family and friends do that get under your skin?

➤ If someone doesn't show up on time, do you find yourself thinking about the angry words you're going to say to that person?

Common Defense Mechanisms

Repression Involuntary, unconscious pushing of unpleasant feelings below the surface and out of conscious thought.

Suppression Conscious, intentional pushing of unpleasantness from one's mind.

Rationalization Making excuses to try to explain a situation or behavior rather than directly taking responsibility for it.

Regression Reverting, or turning back, to behaviors more characteristic of an earlier stage of development rather than dealing with the conflict in a more mature manner.

Denial Unconscious, involuntary lack of acknowledgment of something in one's environment that is obvious to others.

Compensation Wanting to cover up weaknesses and mistakes by making up for them through gift-giving, hard work, or other extreme efforts.

Projection Being unaware of attributing one's own feelings or faults to another person or group even when these attributes do not apply.

Idealization Seeing someone else as perfect or more ideal, or worthy, than everyone else.

Defense Mechanisms

Defense mechanisms are *strategies used to deal with strong or stressful emotions and situations.* Everyone uses them. Sometimes these strategies occur unconsciously and may be helpful over the short term in protecting you from feeling too much pain. In the long run, however, defense mechanisms can keep you from facing and dealing with what is really troubling you.

Handling Fear

In dealing with fear, it is important to identify what your fears are and to confide in someone you trust who may give you a fresh perspective or outlook. This person may help you find a constructive way of lessening your fear or suggest a resource to which you can turn.

Managing Anger

Think of ways in which you have seen anger expressed. Perhaps you have seen a child throw a temper tantrum or seen someone kick a wall or take a swing at someone else. Some people let their anger build up without saying or doing anything, until they explode and strike out at anyone who happens to be around.

How can you express your anger in a constructive way? You must first recognize your feelings and, if possible, identify the source of those feelings. Sometimes there is nothing you can do about what is causing the anger, but you can find ways to cope with the anger so that it does not build up. Diffusing your anger can help you reduce the risk that you might act on impulse and be sorry later. Here are some suggestions:

■ Rechannel your anger in positive, productive ways. Try painting, drawing, or sewing. If you need something more physical, try hammering, cleaning your room, or going on a vigorous walk or run.

■ Get away by yourself, or have a good cry. Sadness or hurt is often the emotion you're really feeling.

■ Pick up the phone. Call a close friend and talk it out.

■ Write down exactly what you are feeling and why. Express yourself freely. No one needs to see what you write.

■ Punch a pillow, or count to ten.

Learn to channel your anger in safe ways. Acting irrationally could prove dangerous to your health or someone else's health. Getting angry with someone is normal and likely if you spend much time with that person. You can clear the air by expressing the emotion. If you bury or ignore it, you will carry it around with you. Then it will begin to affect how you feel about the other person, which can be unhealthful for you and the relationship.

Ride your emotions the way you would ride a wave, knowing there will be ups and downs but that no emotion can necessarily "wipe you out."

ACTIVITY *What other simile or metaphor could you use to describe the "up and down" nature of emotions?*

Making Responsible Decisions

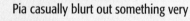

When You're Angry with a Friend

Jennifer and Pia have been friends since junior high. A mainstay of their friendship has been sharing feelings and keeping confidences. That is why today, in the locker room, Jennifer turned red with anger when she overheard Pia casually blurt out something very personal that Jennifer had shared with her. Jennifer's first reaction was to slam her locker door and storm out, expecting that Pia would follow and apologize. Pia did not, however, and now Jennifer believes that if she tells Pia how angry she feels, it might ruin their friendship. What should she do?

What Would You Do?

Apply the six steps of the decision-making process to Jennifer's problem.

1. **State the situation.**
2. **List the options.**
3. **Weigh the possible outcomes.**
4. **Consider your values.**
5. **Make a decision and act.**
6. **Evaluate the decision.**

Handling Emotions During Tragedies

It's difficult to read the newspaper or watch television without hearing bad news. Sometimes the news might be a local tragedy that occurred in your community or across the nation. In response to a tragedy, you may feel many strong emotions, including sadness, anger, fear, and guilt. All of these reactions are normal. Here are some tips for handling emotions during these times:

- **Maintain your daily routine.** Doing so will help you feel a sense of control. Plan a special activity each day so that you have something to look forward to.

- **Share your feelings.** Remember that friends and family members are probably experiencing similar emotions. If you're not ready to talk, try writing down your thoughts and feelings in a journal.

- **Turn off the news.** It's easy to become overwhelmed with nonstop media coverage of tragedies. Take a break by going for a walk, listening to a favorite CD, or watching a funny movie.

- **Channel your energy into a worthwhile cause.** Volunteer to help raise money for relief efforts, participate in a local memorial service, or create a memory book.

Dealing with Guilt

Guilt can be one of the most destructive emotions. When you feel guilty about something, it is important to get at the underlying source and address that issue. The sooner you take action, the better. Many people use their guilt as an excuse for inaction, letting the emotion paralyze them. When this happens, the guilt feeds on itself, causing the problem—and the emotion—to snowball.

One way of avoiding this vicious circle is by resisting doing something you know is wrong in the first place. Saying no to unhealthy demands or requests should never make you feel guilty. In the event you have done something wrong, admit it. If you have hurt another person in the process, try to make amends and resolve to do the right thing next time.

Qualities that Can Foster Emotional Health

You can free yourself of strong emotions for short periods of time, but sooner or later you will have to deal with them again. Two qualities can help ease your emotional load. One of these is your overall outlook on life. The other is your ability to adapt and recover from disappointment.

Your Outlook on Life

Do you think of yourself as a pessimist or an optimist? Your answer to this question—your outlook on life—can mean the difference between good and poor emotional health. While pessimists tend to view negative events as permanent and far-reaching, optimists see them as more temporary and specific.

The good news for pessimists is that strategies exist for changing their outlook. You can develop a more positive outlook by reminding yourself daily that no matter what happens to you, there is always hope. When something does go wrong, make a plan to address or solve the problem. If your behavior is causing the trouble, change it. Get support. Instead of seeing a stressful situation as a crisis, try to see it as a challenge.

Resiliency

Do you recall learning in Chapter 1 about protective factors that influence your health? One additional factor related to your outlook is **resilience.** This is *the ability to adapt effectively and recover from disappointment, difficulty, or crisis.* People with resilience are able to bounce back quickly, even in the face of great hardships and tragedies. Resilient people show an ability to survive and thrive. People who are resilient do not get overwhelmed when the going gets tough. Instead, they view what has gone wrong as a challenge to be faced head-on and then set out to find specific ways to meet that challenge.

LESSON 4 *Review*

Reviewing Facts and Vocabulary

1. Define the term *defense mechanism* and give examples of three different types.
2. Name three negative and three positive ways of handling anger.
3. Define *resilience* and name three characteristics of resilient people.

Thinking Critically

4. *Evaluating.* Discuss this saying: "The shortest way around a problem is directly through it." Relate the statement to the subject of emotional health.
5. *Synthesizing.* Talk about the following Swedish proverb. "Shared joy is double joy, and shared sorrow is half-sorrow."

Applying Health Skills

6. *In Your Home.* Keep an "anger log." For one week, record every instance of anger you feel. Rate the anger from 1 to 10. List the trigger for the anger, how it registers in your body, what you feel like doing at the time, and how you actually handle the emotion. Give yourself a healthful reward every time you handle the anger in a mature and positive way.

Health Skills Activities

Activity 1 — Pyramid of Human Needs

Psychologist Abraham Maslow presented the concept of human needs in a pyramid form. Needs at the bottom of the pyramid must be satisfied before those higher up can be met. How are your needs addressed within the community?

Directions

1. With a small group, create a schoolwide "pyramid of needs." Begin by cutting a pyramid shape from a large sheet of cardboard.
2. Take or find photos of people within your school community fulfilling needs at each level. Alternatively, you may create art that shows this. Write a caption for each image.
3. Display your pyramid in a public place.
4. Discuss where you as a class are on Maslow's Pyramid. Create a step-by-step plan describing how you will maintain this level or attain a higher level on the pyramid.

Time

50 minutes

Materials

large sheet of cardboard, markers, photos or art, manila pocket folder

Self-Assessment

✓ Identified at least three human needs being met by people in your community.
✓ Listed the names or titles of the people that met each need and explained how they fulfilled this need.
✓ Included a plan to maintain or enhance your health.

Activity 2 — Greeting Cards for Health

Have you ever sent or received a greeting card that gave you an emotional lift? Cards are a good way of communicating positive messages. Design a greeting card that sends a positive, meaningful message to someone in your life.

Directions

1. Fold a sheet of colored paper in half lengthwise. Turn the paper with the crease to the left. You are now looking at the front of the card.
2. Decorate this front panel with a picture, symbol, or a brief introductory message.
3. Open the card, and create a positive, meaningful message for the inside. The message may address a specific event in the person's life, or it can serve to provide encouragement.
4. Send the card, or save it for a time when it will do the most good.

Time

40 minutes

Materials

8-x-11-inch colored paper, felt-tip pens of different colors

Self-Assessment

✓ Created an uplifting and encouraging message through words and images.
✓ Successfully developed a message promoting mental health.

HEALTH NEWS ARTICLE

Overcoming Flying Fears

At least one of seven people has some fear of going up in an airplane. For those who refuse to get on board, that phobia can be paralyzing.

People don't have to live with flying fears. Experts suggest that therapy, workshops, self-help programs, or even a few basic tips can go a long way toward getting them off the ground. Tony Martinez, a United Airlines mechanic who serves on the board of the Fear of Flying Clinic says knowledge is the key to overcoming flying anxiety.

"We're not saying you have to like to fly, but at least you have to have the tools to fly, and of course, practice makes perfect. Over time and repeated flights, your anxiety and phobias diminish dramatically," he says. The clinic features instruction by a pilot, mechanic, and air traffic controller. They explain the basics of aerodynamics and flight safety procedures and take clients on a tour of the control tower and maintenance area. A licensed therapist also works with participants to help them determine the basis of their phobia or fear.

Each clinic ends with a short orientation flight. Every one of these flights brings people closer to overcoming their fears.

Read This ▼

Coping with Flying Fears

These expert tips help many people deal with anxiety about flying.

- Learn relaxation techniques, including deep-breathing exercises.
- Check Web sites devoted to flying fears. They may have message boards where you can swap information with other travelers.
- Learn more about aeronautics and meteorology.
- Don't be frightened by turbulence. It's a routine part of flying.
- Inform flight crewmembers that you're nervous about flying. They may be able to assist you.
- Enroll in a seminar, buy a self-help tape, or consider private therapy.

Think About It

1. How do fear of flying clinics help people control their emotional health?
2. Does this article suggest that it is possible to overcome all fears? Why or why not?

Using Health Terms

On a separate sheet of paper, write the term that best matches each definition below.

LESSON 1

1. The messages you receive from others that indicate who they think you are or what they think you are like.
2. Generally having a positive outlook, being comfortable with self and others, and being able to meet life's challenges.

LESSON 2

3. The striving to become the best that you can be.
4. Artistic.
5. A complex set of characteristics that makes you unique and sets you apart from everyone else.
6. A ranked list of those needs essential to human growth and development presented in ascending order from basic to most fulfilling or satisfying.
7. Copying the behaviors of those you are exposed to.

LESSON 3

8. The ability to imagine and understand how someone else feels.
9. Irrational fears.
10. Signals that tell your mind and body how to react.
11. The intentional use of unfriendly or nasty behavior

LESSON 4

12. The ability to adapt and recover from disappointment, difficulty, or crisis.
13. Strategies used to deal with strong or stressful emotions and situations.

Recalling the Facts

Using complete sentences, answer the following questions.

LESSON 1

1. What are five signs of good mental health?
2. What are some of the ways a person can improve his or her self-esteem?
3. List three sources of feedback that can influence a person's feelings of self-worth.
4. Give two examples of negative feedback and two examples of positive feedback.

LESSON 2

5. What is the theory underlying Maslow's hierarchy of needs?
6. What are some of the effects of not fulfilling the need for self-actualization?
7. What are the three main influences on the development of personality?

8. Over which personality influences do you have most control?

LESSON 3

9. Describe three physical reactions that occur in the body when you feel anger.
10. Name eight basic emotions.
11. What is a phobia, and what role does it play in a person's life?
12. What are three effects hormones can have on teens' emotional well-being?

LESSON 4

13. List five defense mechanisms and give an example of each.
14. Name five strategies for handling anger in healthful ways.
15. Describe three traits of optimistic, resilient people.

Thinking Critically

LESSON 1

1. *Evaluating.* List ten events that took place during your day and analyze how each affected your self-esteem.

LESSON 2

2. *Synthesizing.* Think of a question that might come from a teen whose emotional needs have not been met. Then offer suggestions on how to meet needs healthfully.

3. *Analyzing.* Recall a situation where your personal behavior did not include healthful choices, and analyze the factors that caused you to choose this behavior.

LESSON 3

4. *Evaluating.* Watch the first ten minutes of a nightly news program. List the number of stories that cause you to feel fear or anger and the number that elicit positive emotions. How does the news seem to be "weighted" emotionally?

LESSON 4

5. *Synthesizing.* Using the material in this chapter, write a pamphlet offering tips on how to manage anger in healthful ways.

Making the Connection

1. *Social Studies.* Choose a famous person from history whom you believe achieved self-actualization. The subject should have had to overcome physical, psychological, social, or other obstacles. Include details about the time in which the person lived, and investigate the kinds of resilient behaviors the person exhibited in meeting challenges. Present your findings in the form of an oral report.

2. *Language Arts.* A simile compares two seemingly dissimilar items using a comparing word such as *like* or *as*. For example, *Anger is like hot coals on the back of your neck*. Write five similes, one for each of the emotions covered in this chapter.

BEYOND THE CLASSROOM

PARENTAL INVOLVEMENT Present to your family what you have learned in this chapter about expressing anger in healthful ways. Ask members of your household to observe for several days when they become angry, what triggers the anger, how that anger is expressed or handled, and how others in the household react. Afterward, have a discussion in which each person is given a chance to present his or her findings. As a group, come up with a plan to help one another express anger in healthful ways.

COMMUNITY INVOLVEMENT To help those in your community who may not have their basic food needs met, work with classmates to organize a canned food drive.

SCHOOL-TO-CAREER

Exploring Careers. There are many kinds of careers relating to mental and emotional health, including school counselor, psychologist, and art therapist. Invite one of these professionals to your class to talk about his or her work and what kind of training is required.

CHAPTER 9

Managing Stress in Your Life

STRESS MANAGEMENT

Take a time-out to flex your mind and relieve some mental stress. Challenge yourself to some brain exercises and puzzles at **health.glencoe.com**. Look for "Think of it! A Mental Health Barometer" under Interactive Projects.

Personal Health Inventory

Self-Inventory Write the numbers 1–10 on a sheet of paper. Read each statement below and respond by writing *yes*, *no*, or *sometimes* for each item. Write a *yes* only for items that you practice regularly. Save your responses.

1	I'm aware of when I'm feeling tense.
2	I can identify many of the situations that cause me to feel tense.
3	I know how to calm myself down in healthful ways after a stressful experience.
4	I use physical activity to help reduce my stress.
5	I plan for things in advance so that I am prepared for them.
6	I take time out every day to relax and enjoy myself.
7	When I'm feeling tense or upset, I share my thoughts and feelings with family members and friends.
8	I avoid using tobacco, alcohol, and other drugs.
9	I get enough sleep and make nutritious food choices.
10	When I feel things are getting to me, I try to deal with them in healthful ways before they build up and get the best of me.

Follow-up After completing the chapter, retake this self-inventory. Pick two items that you need to work on and set a goal to improve your health behaviors.

66 *The process of living is the process of reacting to stress.* 99

—Dr. Stanley J. Sarnoff
Physician

Quick Write Jot down one recent situation or event that has caused you stress. Think about what you can do to manage this one stressor.

What Is Stress?

R ory has to give a speech to the student body at his school. As he walks onto the auditorium stage, his face suddenly feels hot, his palms begin to sweat, and his heart starts beating like a bass drum. Physical symptoms like these are evidence that Rory is experiencing stress. Has this ever happened to you?

HEALTH TERMS

stress

distress

eustress

stressor

alarm

adrenaline

resistance

fatigue

HEALTH CONCEPTS

- Stress is a normal part of everyday life.
- The response to stress is different for each individual and may change from situation to situation.
- How you manage stress can greatly affect your mental, emotional, and physical health.

Stress and Your Well-Being

S **tress** is *the body's and mind's reaction to everyday demands or threats.* Whether real or imagined, these demands produce measurable changes in both the body and the brain.

Sometimes the stress in your day is minor and goes almost unnoticed. At other times it can be so strong that you may feel as if you are walking a tightrope, trying to keep everything in balance, afraid that at any moment the pressure might get to you and bring you crashing down. The fact is, stress is a part of daily life. It can be useful or harmful, energizing or exhausting. The key is to learn to handle it in healthful ways.

Kinds of Stress

C ontrary to popular opinion, *stress* is not just a negative word. Stress can be either positive or negative, depending on how it is perceived, managed, and put to use. **Distress,** or *negative stress,* on the one hand, can result when there is too much pressure or trauma and you don't know how to cope with it. Having too much homework or running to catch a bus when you are late are both examples of distress. **Eustress,** or *positive stress,* on the other hand, can help you achieve your goals. For example, if you are concerned about your final grade, you may study harder. Research suggests that acceptable levels of stress may even help you to focus and concentrate better.

Kinds of Stressors

S tress occurs in response to a **stressor.** This is *any stimulus that produces a stress response.* Stressors can be people, objects, places, events, or situations that cause you to react. Hearing an ambulance siren, being in a new school, or going out on a first date are all potential stressors. Psychologists have identified five general categories of stressors. These are:

- **biological stressors,** such as those that come from biochemical imbalances, mental or physical illnesses, disabilities, or injuries;
- **environmental stressors,** such as poverty, pollution, crowding, noise, or natural disasters;
- **cognitive or thinking stressors,** such as the way you perceive a situation or what you expect from it;
- **personal behavior stressors,** such as those negative reactions in the body and mind caused by using tobacco, alcohol, or other drugs, or not exercising;
- **life situations,** such as having a relative or pet die, parents who separate or divorce, or trouble in relationships with peers.

◀ *Local and national emergencies cause stress that can affect different people in different ways.*

ACTIVITY *How can individuals, families, and communities help one another through stressful situations?*

keeping Fit

Overcoming Test Anxiety

Does taking tests make you tense or put you on edge? Following these guidelines will help you to address your "test stress."

➤ Plan for tests in advance, studying a little bit each night.

➤ Learn to outline material, high-lighting and numbering important points so you can spot them quickly.

➤ During the test, do some deep breathing. Get comfortable in your chair. Give yourself a quick positive message like, "You can do it!"

➤ Answer all the questions you are sure of, then go back to answer the ones that are more difficult.

➤ After getting your corrected test back, examine your mistakes and try to understand why you made them. If you don't understand them, ask for explanations.

h t link

nervous system For more information on the nervous system and its parts and functions, see Chapter 16, page 364.

endocrine system For information on the endocrine system and its parts and functions, see Chapter 16, page 377.

The Body's Stress Response

When you perceive a situation or event to be a threat, your body begins a stress response. A series of events is put into action as your body prepares itself for "danger." For example, if a car suddenly backfires, the loud sound is a stressor. How your body and mind react is your stress response. The combination of the stressor and your stress response adds up to your stress. You may jump at the sound without thinking, or your heart may suddenly start to race. If you recognize the sound for what it is and realize that there is no real danger, your response may be minimal. If, however, you mistake the sound for a gunshot, you may have a much stronger reaction.

Two major systems of the body, the **nervous system** and the **endocrine system**, are active during the body's response to stressors. The body's response is largely involuntary, or automatic. It happens in three stages and can occur whether the stress is physical or emotional, positive or negative.

Alarm

Alarm is *the first stage in the stress response, when the body and mind go on high alert.* During this stage, the hypothalamus, a small nerve center at the base of the brain, is excited by the stressor. The autonomic nervous system, the system that controls involuntary actions, is activated, as is the pituitary gland. This gland secretes a hormone that stimulates the adrenal glands, which in turn secrete a hormone called adrenaline. **Adrenaline** is *the "emergency hormone" secreted by the adrenal glands to prepare the body to respond to a stressor.* This "fight or flight" response provides energy to get you through the actual or perceived emergency. Because of adrenaline, the heart speeds up its activity, providing more blood to the brain and muscles. Breathing becomes faster and deeper, providing more oxygen to the body. Throat muscles may contract, making swallowing difficult. Your face may become flushed, you may sweat, and your arms and legs may tighten to prepare the body for action. Your mind also goes on high alert so that you can take in information and become aware of your surroundings.

Resistance

Resistance is *the second stage in the stress response, when the body tries to repair its damage from the stressful event and return to its normal state.* Usually, if the stressor is prolonged, the stage of resistance occurs. During this stage, physical resistance to the stressor reaches its peak. This is why people in extremely high-stress situations have been known to accomplish incredible feats of strength, such as lifting an automobile to save a child trapped under it. The body functions at a higher-than-normal level. If this stage continues for too long, however, both the body and mind may show ill effects.

To get a sense of how much your life may have changed in the last year and how these changes might have affected your level of stress, add up the "life-change units" for the changes you've faced during the past year.

If your score is less than 150, your life hasn't changed very much. A score between 150 and 300 means moderate change. A score of over 300 indicates you have experienced a great deal of change and may have to pay special attention to how you handle the stress that can come with it.

LIFE-CHANGE UNITS	LIFE EVENT
101	Getting married
92	Being pregnant and single
87	Having a parent die
81	Getting a visible deformity
77	Having parents divorce
77	Becoming a single father
76	Getting involved with drugs or alcohol
75	Having a parent jailed for a year or more
69	Going through a parent's separation
68	Having a brother or sister die
67	Experiencing a change in peers' acceptance
64	Having a single pregnant teenage sister
64	Discovering that you are adopted
63	Having a parent get married again
62	Experiencing a close friend's death
62	Having a visible deformity since birth
58	Being seriously ill and requiring hospitalization
56	Moving to a new school district
56	Failing a grade in school
55	Not making a team or other extracurricular activity
55	Having a parent become seriously ill
53	Breaking up with a boyfriend or girlfriend
53	Having a parent go to jail for 30 days or less
51	Beginning to date
50	Being suspended from school
50	Getting a newborn sister or brother
47	Getting in more arguments with parents
46	Having an outstanding personal achievement
46	Seeing more arguments between parents
46	Having a parent lose his or her job
45	Having a change in parents' financial status
43	Being accepted at a college of your choice
41	Having a brother or sister become seriously ill
38	Having a parent be more absent from home due to a change in occupation
37	Having a brother or sister leave home
36	Experiencing the death of a grandparent
34	Having a third adult added to the family
31	Becoming a fully committed member of a religion
27	Experiencing a decrease in parents' arguments
26	Having a mother begin to work outside the home

Fatigue

Fatigue is *the third stage of the stress response, resulting in a tired feeling that lowers one's level of activity.* When the body is continually exposed to stressors or a particular stressor is prolonged, the body and the mind become worn down. During this stage, there is little energy to resist the stressor.

There are many kinds of fatigue, and it is important to recognize and understand each.

- **Physical fatigue** may occur at the end of a long day or after exercise, when the body produces waste products in the form of lactic acid from the muscles and carbon dioxide from all the body's cells. A buildup of wastes in the muscles can produce soreness and, at higher levels, tiredness.

- **Pathological fatigue** is tiredness brought on by overworking the body's defenses in fighting disease. Anemia, the flu, being overweight, and having poor nutrition can all bring on pathological fatigue. So can using drugs such as alcohol or caffeine.

- **Psychological fatigue** can result from constant worry, overwork, depression, boredom, and isolation.

Prolonged or repeated periods of stress can lead to stress-related illnesses. Although these can be minor, they can also be life-threatening. It is not just the major stresses or traumas that lead to disease. Daily hassles can build up over time and have serious health consequences. It is important to try to control the amount of stress in your life.

LESSON 1 *Review*

Reviewing Facts and Vocabulary

1. Define the words *eustress* and *distress* and use them in a single paragraph.
2. Name and describe the three stages of the stress response.
3. What happens if a person is under stress too often or for too long?

Thinking Critically

4. **Analyzing.** Divide a piece of paper in half. At the top of one side, write a plus sign; at the top of the other, a minus sign. For one day, keep track of the eustress and distress that you feel and the stressors that caused each, recording each in the appropriate column.

5. **Evaluating.** Write down some major sources of stress. Then write the ways you typically handle the stressors. How well are you handling stress in your life?

Applying Health Skills

6. **In Your Home.** Survey your home, thinking about what things cause negative stress for you and other family members. For example, maybe the TV is on too much, there isn't enough privacy, or phone messages are not properly relayed. With other members of your household, discuss these stressors and how you might change or "defuse" them in healthful and creative ways.

Stress in Your Life

Stress is an unavoidable part of life. When it is positive, stress can make life fun, exciting, enjoyable, and challenging. When it is negative, it can severely impact your mental and physical health. Research suggests that both your brain chemistry and your personality type play a role in how you respond to stress.

HEALTH TERMS

stress tolerance

Type A personality

Type B personality

hardy personality

psychosomatic response

HEALTH CONCEPTS

- Several factors affect a person's level of stress.
- Stress can negatively impact an individual's health.
- You can learn to recognize the signs of stress in your own body and life.
- Stress can often be controlled by how you view the stressor.

Stress and the Brain

Do you thrive on challenge? Does it frighten you? Do you jump into new experiences unafraid, or does the thought of too much risk or change scare you?

Your answers to these and similar questions may be partly related to conditions in your brain that were present at birth. Scientists have determined that in some people, stress upsets a delicate balance among brain chemicals called *neurotransmitters*. This imbalance may cause sleep disturbances, panic attacks, and low enjoyment of life. The first signs of such an imbalance can include trouble falling asleep, waking up often during the night, and very vivid dreams followed by lack of energy, aches and pains, and later, depression.

Stress tolerance is *the amount of stress that you can handle before you reach a state of too much stress.* Though most people have lived through some period of overstress, it is estimated that one in ten Americans experience low stress tolerance.

Stress and Your Personality Type

Personality is another factor in how you handle stress. Some psychologists have grouped people into Type A and Type B personalities. The **Type A personality** is described as a *competitive, high-achieving personality type most likely to develop heart disease* or other significant health problem. The **Type B personality** is seen as *a "laid back," non-competitive personality type less likely to suffer from heart disease.* Research indicates, however, that the Type A personality may actually relieve stress by working, whereas the Type B is more likely to hold on to the stress, thereby becoming more open to other stress-related disorders.

➤ *People with Type A and Type B personalities react differently to the same stressor.*

ACTIVITY *List three stressors, and tell how a Type A and Type B person would respond to each.*

The fact is that different personality types and even different individuals respond to the same stressors in different ways. Some people hold up well during certain kinds of stress while others break down more quickly. Some people seem able to remain healthy even under the most severe kinds of distress. According to psychologist Suzanne Kobasa, such people have "hardy personalities." The **hardy personality** is *a personality type that seems able to stay healthy despite major or even traumatic stressors.* In general, people with hardy personalities have a higher degree of **resilience**. Kobasa also notes that such people share three other very important characteristics:

- **Change.** The hardy personality likes and welcomes change, viewing it as an opportunity for growth.
- **Commitment.** The hardy personality has a strong sense of purpose and is committed to people, activities, and principles that bring meaning to her or his life.
- **Control.** The hardy personality has a sense of power about his or her own life and feels some influence over what happens, taking action when possible. This person also recognizes that some things cannot be controlled.

Stress During Adolescence

Certain periods of life seem to have their own characteristic stressors and stress responses. Adolescence is one of these. Learning what stressors are common among teens can help you to cope. So can sharing feelings of stress with your peers. Doing so will remind you that you're not alone, and that what you are feeling is probably perfectly normal for people your age.

Stress and the Body-Mind Connection

The body-mind connection is not entirely understood by science. Nevertheless, there is a clear connection between the health of the mind and the health of the body. Too much stress can raise blood pressure, weaken the immune system, and cause other health risks. It can even lead to premature, or early, death.

Stress and High Blood Pressure

Mental and emotional stress can cause an increase in your levels of cholesterol, the fatty substance that can block arteries. When these levels are high, high blood pressure—a condition that contributes to heart disease and stroke—can result.

Stress and Headache

It is estimated that most adults and about half of all teens get headaches. For some people, these headaches are mild and brief; for others, they can be severe and get in the way of normal functioning. Many headaches are related to tension. When stressed, the muscles in the head and neck contract.

A migraine headache can also be triggered by stress, although this more severe form of headache can also be triggered by hormone changes, food additives, fluorescent lights, changes in air pressure, and more. When the arteries leading to the brain narrow, blood flow to the brain decreases. When the arteries open up again, the nerve

h⬤t link

resilience For more information on resilience and other protective factors that increase a person's likelihood for a healthy life, see Chapter 8, page 207.

CHARACTER IN ACTION

Honestly!

Your level of **honesty** with others can strongly impact your relationships, the kinds of stress you experience in those relationships, and, in turn, your level of mental and emotional health.

Telling lies or withholding important information that another person has the right to know adds stress to a relationship. Being insincere or manipulating others destroys trust that is essential in building healthy relationships. It also chips away at one's own energy and self-esteem.

Character Check Write a story called "Lying: The Domino Effect." In your story have a person tell one lie, and then demonstrate how it affects his or her life and the life of someone close. Tell how this causes mental and emotional stress to both parties.

Problem-Solving and Perfectionism

Jake excels in math and is a good hockey player. Still, his best friend, Luke, always seems to outdo him at everything. Because of his desire to do as well as Luke, Jake puts undue pressure on himself. He feels anxiety before every contest, seeing everything as a "win or lose" event. Now Jake has a chance to compete with Luke for a position on the school hockey team. Jake knows he puts too much pressure on himself and that his perfectionism is a problem, but he feels like he'd love to beat Luke just once at something this important.

What Would You Do?

Apply the six steps of the decision-making process to Jake's problem.

1. **State the situation.**
2. **List the options.**
3. **Weigh the possible outcomes.**
4. **Consider your values.**
5. **Make a decision and act.**
6. **Evaluate the decision.**

---

endings press into the artery walls, causing severe throbbing, possibly a loss of balance or coordination, and changes in mood.

Stress and Asthma

Though **asthma** may have many causes and triggers, stress can help to trigger an asthma attack. During an asthma attack, breathing becomes difficult as the bronchioles—or air-carrying tubes of the lungs—constrict. The person may cough, wheeze, or fight to get air. In some cases, if untreated, asthma can be life-threatening. If you have asthma, it is important to try to discover what triggers your attacks and to avoid those triggers. It is, therefore, important that you try to keep your stress levels low.

Stress and Immune Response

Prolonged exposure to stress can compromise your immune response. This means that your body cannot fight disease as well as it might if you had not undergone so much stress. When your immune system is not working at full capacity, you may be more prone to colds, flu, or even more severe infections or cancers. The additional stress of tobacco or alcohol use puts your immune system at a very high risk for serious problems.

Psychosomatic Response to Stress

Sometimes stress can lead to a **psychosomatic response.** This is *a physical disorder that results from stress rather than from an injury or*

h⊙t link

asthma For more information on other triggers of asthma, see Chapter 17, page 404.

Did You Know?

➤ Migraine headaches often begin with an "aura," a series of warning signs that can include seeing flickering lights, spots, or lines, ringing in the ears, strange smells, or even numbness in the limbs. These signs usually develop 10 to 30 minutes before the migraine hits, then disappear as the headache pain begins.

➤ Most migraines last 4 to 6 hours, but some have been known to last for days.

illness. Psycho- means "of the mind," and *somatic* means "of the body." These physical disorders may be minor or severe, but they are not imaginary. Some sleep disorders may be psychosomatic in origin, as are some skin disorders, stomachaches, digestive problems, and headaches.

Recognizing Signs of Stress

When stress occurs, it is important to recognize its source and then figure out how to deal with it. Train your body and mind to recognize what stressors cause distress and how your body, mind, and behaviors are affected by each. If you know that you are likely to have a large reaction to an event, consider whether or not it is worth making your body and mind "pay" in such a big way. In the next lesson, you will learn many strategies for managing stress and preventing it from getting out of hand.

Signs of Stress

- **Physical Signs:** headaches, trembling or twitching, upset stomach, migraines, sweating, rash, constipation, diarrhea, pounding heart, muscle aches and tightness, trouble sleeping, grinding teeth, dry mouth, nervous twitches or tics, dizziness, back pain, ringing in ears.

- **Emotional Signs:** frustration, nervousness, boredom, edginess, feeling powerless, being quick to anger, impatience, mood swings, worrying, loneliness, confusion, crying, low self-esteem, becoming easily upset without cause.

- **Mental Signs:** trouble reading or thinking clearly, lack of creativity, constant worry, obsessive thoughts, inability to make decisions, forgetting, losing sense of humor and perspective.

- **Behavioral Signs:** not eating, overeating, compulsive talking, verbal or physical outbursts, fidgeting, using alcohol, caffeine, or other drugs, smoking, gambling, tapping feet, drumming fingers, hurrying, forgetting one's values, withdrawing, reckless and high-risk behaviors like driving too fast.

LESSON **2** *Review*

Reviewing Facts and Vocabulary

1. Distinguish between Type A and Type B personalities, and describe how each handles stress.
2. Name three ways that stress can have negative effects on your health.

Thinking Critically

3. *Analyzing.* List the top ten stressors of your life. Rank these in order from most stressful to least stressful. Think about positive and negative effects each of these stressors has on your life.
4. *Comparing and Contrasting.* Listen to three musical numbers from each of the following categories—jazz, pop, rock, and classical. Compare and contrast your stress responses to each. Note both physical and emotional reactions.

Applying Health Skills

5. *In Your Home.* Teach your family members what you have learned about the behavioral signs of stress. For one week, have each family member keep track of those behaviors in other members that suggest they are feeling stress. In a family roundtable discussion, share these findings with one another.

Managing Stress

Identifying stressors and managing stress are among the most important steps you can take in staying healthy and preventing disease. Although it is impossible to live completely free of stress, it *is* possible to learn ways to avoid certain stressors and manage your response to others.

HEALTH TERMS

rechanneling

relaxation response

support group

time management skills

priorities

HEALTH CONCEPTS

- It is important to identify major stressors in your life.
- You can learn strategies for coping with and managing stress.
- Time management is one effective way to manage stress.

Identifying the Problem

A first step in stress management is identifying the source of the stress. At times, this source may be clear-cut—anxiety over taking a major exam, for example. At other times, the stressors may be less obvious. You may have had the experience of feeling uncomfortable in a certain place or around a certain person without knowing why. Some cases of stress are caused by a combination of stressors, making identification more difficult.

Stress Management

There are two basic ways to deal with stress that is upsetting to you. The first is to eliminate the stressor or reduce your exposure to it. The second is to change the way you perceive or react to the stressor.

Just as your natural instincts for survival tell you to jump out of the way of a vehicle that is speeding toward you, in dealing with stress, you can learn to sense the warning signs that "something is coming." You can then find ways to escape oncoming stressors. Sometimes the best strategy is simply to walk away. At other times, you may be able to "rethink," or get a new perspective on, a stressful situation, making it a learning opportunity instead of a threat.

Physical activity is one effective technique for handling stress. Other ways to manage stress include planning, rechanneling energy, relaxing, and laughing.

Planning

People who plan well tend to have less stress. When you plan, you decide in advance what you want, what you need, and what is expected of you so that you can come into situations well prepared. Planning adds to your confidence. If you are prepared for the unexpected, you are also better able to deal with changes, disappointments, frustrations, or delays when they happen, enabling you to keep your stress to a minimum.

How do you react to stressful situations? Learn how to recognize stress and manage it more effectively. At **health.glencoe.com** keep a stress diary for three days. What changes could you make to better manage stress?

Building Health Skills

Taking Control of Your Day

FOLLOW THESE SUGGESTIONS for better time management, and you'll start to feel as though you control your time instead of time controlling you.

1. **Set and prioritize goals.** Set specific goals each day. Write "A" next to any goal or task you must achieve, "B" next to any you would like to get done, and "C" for any goal or task that is not important or that can wait.

2. **Budget your time.** Set regular time slots each day for relaxation techniques, exercise, and sleep. Set deadlines for yourself. Every once in a while, go over your daily schedules for a week and make sure your "time budget" balances work and play, social time and time to yourself, time for self-improvement and time for helping others.

3. **Learn to say no.** Practice saying no to the little things, then work your way up to the bigger ones. Saying no does not mean being cruel or selfish. It means not spending your energy or time on activities that do not benefit your life or someone else's.

4. **Slow down.** Make a conscious effort to do ordinary things—talk, walk, and eat—more slowly. When you can, take a break from all schedules. Take off your watch and ignore time—at least for a little while.

You can reduce stress and find time for a wide array of activities if you plan well. Time management skills, strategies to help you use time effectively and healthfully, can help. One such skill, prioritizing, simply means deciding which tasks are more important than others.

When you prioritize your tasks, you can make time for the things that bring you the most pleasure.

ACTIVITY **Think of a way to budget your time this week so that you can do one activity you love and usually don't make time for.**

Rechanneling Energy

Rechanneling means *transferring or redirecting your energies.* You can use pent-up energy in useful ways by turning negative energy into positive actions and thoughts. When you feel stressed, why not use the energy to wash the car or straighten your room? If you are unable to put physical distance between yourself and a stressful situation, find ways to take a mental break. Let your mind wander for a few minutes, listen to soothing music, or simply daydream.

Relaxing and Laughing

Perhaps nothing restores your state of mind more than relaxation. Taking the time to rest, enjoy yourself, and simply *be* rather than *do* can work wonders for the body and the mind. You can learn specific techniques, too, that offer you deeper rest. The **relaxation response** is *a state of deep rest that can be reached if one or more relaxation techniques are practiced regularly.* Among these techniques are deep breathing, thinking pleasant thoughts, repetitive exercise, and stretching.

Laughing can instantly relieve some stress. It gets more oxygen moving through the bloodstream and works the muscles of the stomach. When you are finished laughing, your blood pressure is lower and you feel relaxed.

Seeking Support

Whatever stressors you face in life, getting support can help you to deal with them. Talking with individuals you trust is vital. Parents, teachers, coaches, siblings, close friends, clergy, neighbors, or peer helpers can prove to be helpful choices when you need support. A **support group**, *an informal or formal gathering of people who meet and share experiences, feelings, and trust,* can also be helpful.

Time Management

For many people, stress management requires time management. **Time management skills** are *specific strategies for planning and using time in effective, healthful ways.* One important time management skill is setting priorities. **Priorities** are *those goals, tasks, or activities that you judge as more important to do than others.* When you set priorities, or prioritize, you decide which things you will do in which order, ranking them from most to least important or necessary. Setting priorities can help to organize your day and reduce your stress over what must get done.

keeping Fit

Sweat Your Stress Away

The next time you're tense and don't know what to do about it, start sweating. Whack a tennis ball, run around the neighborhood, go dancing, play soccer, do anything that will keep the big muscles moving and the heart pumping. Exercise will:

➤ calm you down,

➤ wake you up,

➤ make you more alert,

➤ improve your mood,

➤ pump up your confidence,

➤ improve your appearance.

LESSON 3 *Review*

Reviewing Facts and Vocabulary

1. What are the two basic strategies for managing stress?
2. Name and describe three relaxation techniques used for reducing stress.

Thinking Critically

3. **Synthesizing.** Make a "How to Survive" booklet or video advising teens on ways to manage the stress of one of the following life events: moving to a new school, failing a grade, not making a team, winning a major award, having an ill family member, or having a parent lose a job.
4. **Analyzing.** Consider the following saying, and explain how it is tied to stress management: "Don't look back; something might be gaining on you."

Applying Health Skills

5. **In Your Home.** List those tasks you want or need to achieve for one day. Do not prioritize them. At the end of the day, check your list, noting which ones you accomplished, which ones you resisted and why, and which ones you forgot altogether. The next day, try the same exercise but prioritize your tasks first thing in the morning, using the "A-B-C" system.

Coping with Loss

Life is full of losses. Some losses are minor and temporary. Others are major and can disrupt your entire life. Any loss can put your body and mind into a state of stress.

Yet, no matter how severe or painful a loss is, you can learn to respond to it in ways that help you to cope. Doing so will help you to heal in time.

HEALTH TERMS

grief reaction

delayed grief response

closure

HEALTH CONCEPTS

- Any loss can cause a stress response.
- The loss of a loved one is one of the greatest stressors a person can face.
- People who suffer a major loss may go through a special five-stage process that enables them to deal with the loss.
- Grieving after a major loss is a normal and necessary step toward healing.

Different Kinds of Losses

Have you ever lost something that could not be replaced? Maybe a pet died or ran away. Perhaps you lost an important athletic contest, such as a championship game. These are all losses. So are breakups between girlfriends and boyfriends, rejection by a once-close friend, or the loss of a job by you or a parent. Maybe you have had to change apartments, schools, or neighborhoods, feeling the loss of whatever—or whomever—you had to leave behind.

Your reactions to each loss may vary. Any loss requires change, and that change can be stressful. Depending on its value to you, you may respond to any loss as a minor or a major stressor. Note that a loss does not have to have a dollar value to be important. Sometimes, your emotional attachment to an object, situation, pet, or person can make its loss even more painful.

The Stages of Loss

When a loss occurs, it is common and natural to experience a grief reaction. A **grief reaction** is *an individual's total response to a major loss*. This reaction can take many forms and includes many stages, from feelings of emptiness or deep sadness to feelings of intense anger.

Dr. Elisabeth Kübler-Ross, a psychiatrist who has done pioneering work on the related subjects of death and dying, has identified five emotional stages that both dying and grieving people go through. These five stages, which might be experienced by anyone suffering a major loss, include:

- **Stage 1: Denial.** Denial is a person's initial reaction to any loss. At this stage, a person who has suffered a significant loss cannot believe the loss has occurred.

- **Stage 2: Anger.** A person next moves from denial to anger, or the "Why me?" stage. During this stage, the person may be critical, demanding, or uncooperative.

- **Stage 3: Bargaining.** As the reality of the loss sets in, the anger begins to subside and is replaced by bargaining. The person may pray or promise to change if only the lost person or object can be returned, even for a while.

- **Stage 4: Depression.** This stage is often marked by silence and withdrawal. Earlier feelings of disbelief, isolation, anger, and rage are replaced with a deep sense of quiet sadness.

- **Stage 5: Acceptance.** This is the last stage in dealing with a deep loss. While the depression stage may leave a person feeling helpless, this last stage can involve a sense of power, allowing the person to face reality in constructive ways and make significant and meaningful gestures surrounding the idea of the loss.

Kübler-Ross also noted that another emotion, hope, operates through all of the five stages. This hope keeps alive the thought that the lost item, situation, or person might somehow be returned.

CHARACTER IN ACTION

Helping a Friend through Heartache

When someone you know is grieving, simple acts and words of kindness may be the best way to show your concern.

Character Check Try one or more of the following ways to demonstrate your **caring** toward someone in grief:

➤ Be available to talk or just be with the person when you're wanted.

➤ Be a good listener. Avoid asking a lot of probing questions.

➤ Be patient. The person may not be rejecting you personally but may simply need to be alone.

➤ Talk about the person who has died, sharing fond memories.

➤ Respect the other person's way of grieving even if it isn't your own.

➤ Write a note. You don't have to say anything more than, "I'm sorry that you're hurting," "I care," or "I'm here when you want to talk."

Teens Making a Difference

...INITIATIVE...COURAGE...CITIZENSHIP

Danny is 16 and lives near the coast of North Carolina. He isn't a stranger to hurricanes, but when hurricane Floyd hit, Danny jumped in and took action to help others cope with the stress and loss caused by the storm.

ENTERING TROUBLED WATERS Danny begins, "It was one of the worst storms to hit North Carolina ever. There was terrible flooding. I was fortunate enough to get away with just a few shingles off the roof, but half an hour away from here, it got pretty bad. Through the church, we saw pictures of the flooding and got a group together and started working together rebuilding." The group formed smaller disaster recovery teams of adults and teens working together to help those who'd lost the most. "We'd go down there and work on a specific house. The damage was terrible, and the way they were living was awful. They had no electricity or running water. Some of the people were poor and elderly and had spent all of their money. We were their last hope. We'd talk to them...and they were so happy for us to be with them."

HANDS-ON HELPING
Danny not only listens with compassion to the people he helps; he offers practical help and hands-on work. "We go in there and take out floors and rotted wood and replace it. I've learned a lot about carpentry and tools, and, between doing this work and being in shop at school, I've learned a lot more than I thought I ever would. "I've been going down to help out for about a year and a half," Danny says humbly. With tools, wood, caring, and hard work, he continues, after almost two years, to give up Saturdays to help the people of North River rebuild their homes and their lives.

TOOLS FOR LIVING "I've learned not just about carpentry either," Danny continues. "I've also learned to care about what other people go through. A lot of people are really stressed out by a disaster like this, but once we could show them everything would be all right, they saw there could be a better side to it all. I've learned to appreciate that I don't have it as bad as other people. I've also learned that we all need a helping hand at some time in our lives. It's been a really good experience."

DANNY'S STORY
1. What values does Danny exhibit by helping the victims of the hurricane and flood?
2. What has he learned?

YOUR STORY
1. What steps can you take to raise your awareness about the needs of others facing different kinds of losses?
2. How can you team up with other teens to offer a "helping hand" to people in a time of stress or loss?

Responding to Loss

A person who has undergone a great loss needs to talk about what has happened and express feelings. In an attempt to process what has happened, this person may need to "relive" the events through talking about or thinking about them over and over again. Through such actions, over time, and with the caring of others, the survivor can come to accept the death or other loss and continue on. Though the person left behind may never forget or stop missing the beloved one, he or she can at least reach a sense of **closure**, *a coming to an end of the most intense parts of the grieving process.*

Grief Counseling

Sometimes people are so stressed by a sudden or traumatic loss that they feel paralyzed and stop coping altogether. They may have a **delayed grief response**, *a putting off of the most intense stages of grief.* They may deny the death or loss for a while until the shock wears off. They may even try to cover up their feelings by using chemicals or by assuring everyone that they are "just fine." Such strategies, however, just delay the grieving process. Seeing a counselor who specializes in grief may prove helpful. In fact, talking with a counselor can be beneficial to anyone who has suffered a major loss.

▲ People respond to loss in different ways.

ACTIVITY *Name three different ways that people you know have responded to losing a loved one.*

Review

Reviewing Facts and Vocabulary

1. Name the five stages of grief and describe each one.
2. List some do's and don'ts when helping a friend through grief.
3. What is closure, and why is it so important?

Thinking Critically

4. *Analyzing.* Explain the benefits of communication in helping a person respond to the loss of a loved one.
5. *Comparing and Contrasting.* Investigate mourning rituals—the formal ways that people grieve—from at least two cultures. Present your findings to the class in the form of an oral report.

Applying Health Skills

6. *In Your Home.* Make a "loss line." Draw a line and divide it by years from birth till your present age. On the line, draw small perpendicular lines wherever you have suffered an important loss. Label each. Now step back and think about the number of losses in your lifetime, when they happened, and the effects of each.

Health Skills Activities

Activity 1 — Reducing Stress

Businesses across the country are developing stress management programs for employees. Exercise, relaxation techniques, and stretching are all part of these efforts. What kind of program would you devise to reduce stress in a teen's life?

Directions

1. As a class, discuss typical causes of stress among teens, such as taking a test or auditioning for a school play. Brainstorm strategies for reducing the stress.
2. Make a class video that demonstrates techniques for reducing stress in such situations.
3. Include each class member in the production. Possible tasks include writing, camera operation, research, acting, set design, and editing.
4. Air the video to another class in your school. Discuss with this class whether they think the stress-reducing video will help them in the future.

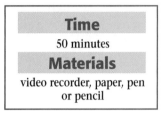

Time
50 minutes
Materials
video recorder, paper, pen or pencil

Self-Assessment

✓ Identified at least three leading causes of stress in a teen's life.
✓ Described coping strategies for each stress identified.
✓ Created a clear message on the importance of managing stress.

Activity 2 — Role-Playing to Cope with Loss

A situation can have many different outcomes—some healthful, some not—depending on the strategies used to handle it. Role-playing, or acting out various scenarios, can help you "see" these different possible outcomes more vividly.

Directions

1. In a group, brainstorm various situations in which teens might experience loss, such as breaking off a relationship or failing to make tryouts for a team.
2. Role-play several strategies for dealing with the feelings of loss—for example, allowing time to deal with the loss, accepting comfort from loved ones.
3. After each scene, discuss the effectiveness of the technique used.
4. With permission, present your scenarios to members of other health classes.

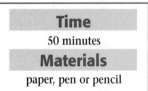

Time
50 minutes
Materials
paper, pen or pencil

Self-Assessment

✓ Identified types of loss common among teens.
✓ Devised and acted out coping strategies for various types.

Bullying and Teasing in Schools

Bullying and teasing are cited as the top school troubles of students, ages 8 to 15, in a report from the Kaiser Family Foundation. With report findings indicating that most young people aren't affected or helped by sporadic talks with their parents, experts said it was crucial for parents and their children to develop an ongoing dialogue about various important issues, starting at an early age. Of these issues, students of various ages said bullying was far more common than drinking, drugs, racism or sex at their schools.

"Some kids sometimes don't know how to tell their parents, 'I have this problem. This person is bothering me, I don't know what to do,'" said Victoria Zaras, 15, who responded to the survey. "Instead, some may take matters into their own hands."

Dominic Cappello, an expert on parent-child communications, said parents often think their children will never act out on their problems.

"Parents think, 'Oh my kids are not in high school yet. I guess I will wait to talk,'" he said. "What we say is 'Oh no–when your child starts kindergarten, you have to start conversations about how you respect people.'" Tina Hoff, who oversaw the survey, says, "These issues need to get talked about on an ongoing basis."

Read This

Pressure Poll

These survey results from the Kaiser Family Foundation show some major sources of teen stress (ages 12 to 15).

Percentage of students who say the following is a big problem in school:		Percentage of students who say students experience the following:	
Teasing & Bullying	68	Get Teased or Bullied	86
Discrimination	63	Are Treated Badly Because They're Different	67
Violence	62		
Alcohol or Drugs	68	Are Threatened With Violence	60
Pressure to Have Sex	49	Smoke Cigarettes	67

Think About It

1. Explain why Dominic Cappello sees a strong connection between respect for others and bullying at school.

2. How would you have responded to the survey about sources of teen stress? Do you think your school's results would match the survey results?

Using Health Terms

On a separate sheet of paper, write the term that best matches each definition below.

LESSON 1

1. Negative stress.
2. The third stage of the stress response, resulting in a tired feeling that lowers one's level of activity.
3. The body's and mind's reaction to everyday demands or threats.
4. Positive stress.
5. The first stage in the stress response when the body and mind go on high alert.
6. Any stimulus that produces a stress response.
7. The second stage in the stress response, when the body tries to repair its damage from the stressful event and return to its normal state.

LESSON 2

8. The amount of stress that you can handle before you reach a state of too much stress.

9. A physical disorder that results from stress rather than from an injury or illness.
10. One personality type that seems able to stay healthy despite major or even traumatic stressors.

LESSON 3

11. A formal or informal gathering of people who meet and share experiences, feelings, and trust.
12. Specific strategies for planning and using time in effective, healthful ways.
13. Transferring or redirecting your energy.

LESSON 4

14. A coming to an end of the most intense parts of the grieving process.
15. The putting off of the most intense stages of grief.
16. An individual's total response to a major loss.

Recalling the Facts

Using complete sentences, answer the following questions.

LESSON 1

1. Explain the difference between eustress and distress.
2. What occurs in your body during the alarm stage of the stress response?
3. At which of the three stages of the stress response is a person most likely to become physically ill?

LESSON 2

4. Describe the three traits of the hardy personality.

5. What are some of the physical, emotional, and behavioral signs of stress in teens?

LESSON 3

6. Name three strategies for managing stress.
7. What role does setting priorities play in stress management?

LESSON 4

8. Name and describe the five stages of loss as identified by Dr. Kübler-Ross.
9. How can friends make a difference when someone is dealing with grief?

Review

Thinking Critically

LESSON 1

1. *Analyzing.* What factors in modern-day society seem to make life so much more stressful than in the past?
2. *Evaluating.* Explain how stress can be a positive factor in someone's life.

LESSON 2

3. *Evaluating.* What are the limitations in trying to classify people and the way they handle stress by personality types?

LESSON 3

4. *Analyzing.* Choose a friend or family member. Analyze the person's time management skills. Describe suggestions you would offer to improve those skills.

LESSON 4

5. *Analyzing.* What factors affect the way you view loss in your family?
6. *Synthesizing.* What are some healthful ways that teens could help one another to deal with the loss of one of their favorite teachers or classmates?

Making the Connection

1. *Math.* Prepare a survey for the students at your school that asks what students believe to be the top ten stressors. Rank responses by age, grade, and gender. Using a computer, determine the top ten stressors for the school based on those responses. Then break down the information by gender, age, and grade. Make bar graphs to illustrate your findings.

2. *Language Arts.* In most short stories, the main character faces various stressors. How he or she responds to these stressors greatly affects the plot or the story line. Read a classic story, paying attention to the stressors that the main character faces and how he or she responds to each. Share your findings in a written report.

BEYOND THE CLASSROOM

PARENTAL INVOLVEMENT Observe members of your family for several days, taking note of how efficiently each seems to use time. Ask other family members to do the same. Afterward, discuss ways that each of you can better manage time. Make task charts and weekly schedules that include appointments, activities, and work and school hours. As a group, prioritize them together.

COMMUNITY INVOLVEMENT Identify three occupations represented in your community. Identify the key stressors in each, the necessary stress management techniques for being successful, and whether or not each suits your personality.

SCHOOL-TO-CAREER
Exploring Careers. Interview a grief counselor or other mental health worker who helps clients deal with loss, death, and dying. Ask what experience is needed for such a career. Find out the kinds of settings in which the counselor works, the kinds of interpersonal skills needed, and the most frequent types of losses and reactions to those losses the counselor encounters. Share your findings in an oral report.

CHAPTER 10

Mental and Emotional Problems

HEALTH *Online*

COMMUNICATION SKILLS

Are you good at talking and listening to people about real-life issues? The role of a Mental Health Counselor plays an important part in many people's lives. Investigate the details of this profession in the Career Corner at <u>health.glencoe.com</u>.

Personal Health Inventory

Self-Inventory Write the numbers 1–10 on a sheet of paper. Read each statement below and respond by writing *yes*, *no*, or *sometimes* for each item. Write a *yes* only for items that you practice regularly. Save your responses.

1	I'm generally comfortable with myself and enjoy being alive.
2	There are people in my life I feel close to and comfortable with, and in whom I can confide.
3	Usually, my moods don't swing from one extreme to the other.
4	Though I sometimes feel fear, I don't generally feel flooded with panic or anxiety.
5	Though I may at times feel sad, I know how to handle my depression.
6	I don't dwell on the same thought or repeat an action over and over in a ritualistic way.
7	When I'm feeling down or upset, I don't keep my feelings to myself but talk with someone.
8	I'm not opposed to talking to a professional if times get really tough.
9	I understand that mental disorders are usually treatable.
10	I wouldn't be embarrassed to seek professional help.

Follow-up After completing the chapter, retake this self-inventory. Pick two items that you need to work on and set a goal to improve your health behaviors.

❝ *Although the world is full of suffering, it is full also of the overcoming of it.* ❞

—HELEN KELLER
AMERICAN WRITER AND LECTURER, (1880–1968)

Quick Write It is important for people to realize they do not have to go through emotional problems alone. List three people you might turn to—one peer, one family member, and one adult in your school or community—during a tough time.

What Are Mental Disorders?

Everyone at times feels depressed, anxious, afraid, alone, or angry. For most people, these feelings are temporary and last only a brief time. For some people, however, the feelings can be intense or endure day after day. When such feelings begin to interfere with the demands of daily life, the person may have a mental disorder.

HEALTH TERMS

mental disorder

anxiety disorder

somatoform disorder

hypochondria

affective disorder

bipolar disorder

personality disorders

schizophrenia

HEALTH CONCEPTS

- Mental disorders are rooted in emotional, psychological, physical, or biochemical problems.
- Mental disorders can interfere with an individual's normal functioning with self, others, and even society at large.
- Mental disorders can differ from person to person and episode to episode.

HEALTH
Online

Find more about anxiety disorders such as panic and phobias at **health.glencoe.com**.

Mental Disorders

A **mental disorder** is *an illness of the mind that can affect the thoughts, feelings, and behaviors of a person, preventing him or her from leading a happy, healthful, and productive life.* People who suffer from some form of mental disorder are often identified by their inability to cope in healthful ways with life's changes, demands, problems, or traumas.

In the past, mental disorders were misunderstood and people with such disorders were feared or shunned. Science has shed new light on these problems and their causes. Mental disorders are now widely understood not only as disturbances in the emotions but also as imbalances in the chemistry of the brain.

Types of Mental Disorders

All mental disorders are classified into one of two general types: organic or functional. An *organic disorder* is one that is clearly caused by a physical illness or an injury that affects the brain. Examples of such disorders are: brain tumors, alcoholism, infections such as syphilis and meningitis, lupus, and stroke. So are some inherited chemical imbalances.

A *functional disorder* may occur as the result of psychological causes in which no clear brain damage is involved. These disorders generally include or result from such conditions as stress, emotional conflict, fear, or poor coping skills. Functional disorders may be tied to inborn causes, traumatic events in childhood, or current causes. Increasingly, research has indicated that, like organic disorders, functional disorders may be the result of chemical imbalances in the brain. Whatever their root causes, the main categories of functional disorders are *anxiety disorders, somatoform disorders, affective disorders,* and *personality disorders.*

Anxiety Disorders

Most people experience some form of anxiety from time to time, but their fears do not affect their daily lives. An **anxiety disorder** is *an illness in which real, imagined, or persistent fears prevent a person from enjoying life.* An anxiety disorder is characterized by continuous, chronic anxiety. People with anxiety disorders often arrange their lives so as to avoid the object or situation that makes them anxious or fearful. Four types of anxiety disorders are **phobias**, obsessive-compulsive disorders, panic disorders, and post-traumatic stress disorders.

PHOBIA

This is a specific fear that is so strong, a person goes to extreme measures to avoid the fear-producing object or activity. Examples of phobias include acrophobia, a fear of heights, and claustrophobia, a fear of enclosed spaces. A person with a phobia may be unable to carry out daily activities. Some mental health professionals believe that a phobia is related to some past experience that was upsetting to the individual. Although there is no longer a threat or real danger, the fear remains real.

Did You Know?

There are many phobias, including:

➤ Astraphobia, a fear of lightning.

➤ Bathophobia, a fear of depth.

➤ Dromophobia, a fear of crossing streets.

➤ Ophidiophobia, a fear of snakes.

➤ Tapephobia, a fear of being buried alive.

➤ Ailurophobia, a fear of cats.

➤ Pyrophobia, a fear of fire.

➤ Logizomechanophobia, a fear of computers and other machines.

hotlink

phobias For more on phobias, including additional examples, see Chapter 8, page 200

◄ *People have phobias about all kinds of things, from snakes to speaking in public.*
ACTIVITY *Think about any phobias you may have. What do they have in common?*

OBSESSIVE-COMPULSIVE DISORDER

A person with obsessive-compulsive disorder, or OCD, is trapped in a pattern of repeated behaviors or thoughts. *Obsessions* are persistent, recurrent, unwanted thoughts or ideas that keep people from thinking about other things. *Compulsions* are urgent, repeated, irresistable behaviors. A person with OCD might, for example, feel the urge to wash his or her hands 20 or 30 times a day. When these activities interfere with other daily functions and commitments, they are considered a problem.

PANIC DISORDER

A person with a panic disorder has a condition in which fear or anxiety prevails and gets in the way of functioning and enjoying life. The individual may feel anxious, fearful, and upset most of the time, or the feelings may arise for no apparent reason. These "panic attacks" are accompanied by severe symptoms such as trembling, a racing heartbeat, shortness of breath, dizziness, or a fear of losing control or even dying. A person can be anywhere when the attack begins, although it can usually be connected with certain "triggers"—an object, condition, or situation.

POST-TRAUMATIC STRESS DISORDER

This is a condition in which a person who has experienced or witnessed a traumatic event feels severe and long-lasting aftereffects. This disorder is common among veterans of military combat, rape survivors, and survivors of natural disasters such as floods or unnatural disasters such as plane crashes. Typical symptoms include flashbacks, nightmares, emotional numbness, dreams about the event, sleeplessness, feelings of guilt, or an extreme reaction to an image or sound that reminds the person of the event. Symptoms may appear six months or even years after the initial event.

Somatoform Disorders

A **somatoform disorder** describes *an illness in which a person complains of disease symptoms, but no physical cause can be found.* An example of this type of disorder is **hypochondria**—*a preoccupation with the body and fear of presumed diseases that are not present.* A hypochondriac constantly feels aches and pains and worries about developing cancer, heart disease, or some other serious problem. Because hypochondriacs are convinced they are suffering from some disease, they refuse to believe doctors who tell them that they are healthy.

Affective Disorders

Everyone has different moods, and these moods are always subject to change. However, some mood swings are severe, can last for long periods of time, or lead to extreme behaviors. **Affective disorder,** a mood disorder, is *an illness often with an organic cause that relates to*

▲ *Washing hands every few minutes for no particular reason may be a sign of obsessive-compulsive behavior.*

ACTIVITY *In a small group, discuss how you feel about people who exhibit some form of obsessive-compulsive disorder.*

emotions and may involve mood swings or mood extremes that interfere with everyday living.

CLINICAL DEPRESSION

This is an affective disorder in which feelings of sadness, hopelessness, or despair last for more than a few weeks and interfere with daily activities and interests. It can be a serious health problem that affects one's ability to concentrate, sleep, perform at school or work, or handle everyday decisions and challenges. It can also be the symptom of substance abuse or diseases such as alcoholism or drug addiction. Depression often runs in families and can be biologically based, but it can also be caused by life events and accumulated traumas or stressors.

BIPOLAR DISORDER

Bipolar disorder, often inherited and sometimes called manic depression, is *a psychological illness characterized by extreme mood swings between depression and extreme happiness, or mania.* During manic periods, those with bipolar disorder may feel extremely happy or energetic. They may be overly talkative, often going rapidly from one topic of conversation to another. They may make lots of plans and take part in all sorts of activities. They may even act impulsively or take unnecessary risks. Often this "high" period ends abruptly, and a period of deep depression sets in. Between episodes of extreme emotions, however, manic depressives may behave normally. Some people only experience the manic phase or the depressive phase.

Personality Disorders

Personality disorders include *a variety of psychological conditions that affect a person's ability to get along with others.* People with personality disorders may often be at odds with others and not see their part in the problem. Unlike anxiety disorders, personality disorders have no apparent distinct signs or symptoms. The individual continues to function, often effectively, in his or her environment but may respond in ways that offend or interfere with others' interactions. These patterns of behavior may be harmful to the person with the disorder or to those in his or her environment.

ANTISOCIAL PERSONALITY DISORDER

One common personality disorder is termed the *antisocial personality,* characterized by a person's constant conflict with society. The antisocial individual may display behavior that is cruel, uncaring, irresponsible, and impulsive. Although he or she can distinguish right from wrong, the antisocial personality

Empathy Builders

Empathy is the ability to feel or imagine what another is feeling. It means being sensitive to another's needs and trying to become aware of what it must be like to be the other person or to be in his or her situation.

Character Check To develop empathy for people with mental disorders:

➤ Vow never to make fun of people with mental or physical challenges.

➤ Stick up for those you see being ridiculed, ignored, or talked down to by others.

➤ Remind yourself that every human being deserves dignity.

often does not care about others' needs or society's rules and therefore is often in trouble with the law.

PASSIVE-AGGRESSIVE PERSONALITY DISORDER

People with passive-aggressive personality disorder are often uncooperative with others. They resent being told what to do, yet they rely on others' direction. Angry over issues of control, they show their anger, but only indirectly. For example, a passive-aggressive person who does not want to take part in a school activity either may forget to show up or may arrive late and leave early.

SCHIZOPHRENIA

A serious mental disorder meaning "split mind," **schizophrenia** affects about one to two percent of the population and appears most frequently among people between the ages of 15 and 35. Untreated schizophrenics may behave inappropriately, exhibit abnormal emotional responses or, in some cases, show no emotional responses at all. Some schizophrenics withdraw, often losing all sense of time and space. Others hallucinate, hear voices, talk to themselves, act in an odd manner, or neglect to care for themselves. People with paranoid schizophrenia mistrust and are often suspicious of others. They may believe that they are being followed, listened to, or targeted for harm.

Much research is being carried out to better understand schizophrenia. Causes for this condition may stem from a physical disorder or may be genetic in nature. The disorder may come and go throughout a person's life. Professional help and chemical intervention are always recommended.

LESSON 1 *Review*

Reviewing Facts and Vocabulary

1. Define the term *mental disorder* and use it in a sentence that offers hope to those who suffer from one.
2. Name three possible causes of organic disorders.
3. Define the term *functional disorder* and give three examples.

Thinking Critically

4. ***Analyzing.*** Take an in-depth look at the reasons why a stigma about mental illness continues to exist.
5. ***Synthesizing.*** Make a poster summarizing the myths and facts about mental disorders.

Applying Health Skills

6. ***In Your School.*** With your classmates, read about the insanity defense. First, find definitions of the word *insanity,* a legal term. Next, research the topic, including recent cases in which this defense was attempted or used. Hold a debate discussing the pros and cons of the use of this defense in many trials of serious crimes.

Suicide Prevention

Suicide, *the taking of one's own life,* is a major health problem in the United States. Every year, some 30,000 people commit suicide. This country's rising teen suicide rate is particularly alarming and tragic, with suicide accounting for one-third of all deaths among teens. Why are these numbers so high? How can these tragic losses be stopped?

Depression and the Teen Years

Do you ever feel like things are pulling you down and that you just can't cope? Most people do sometimes. Life can feel overwhelming. This is especially true during the teen years when new challenges, responsibilities, and pressures can pile up and seem overpowering. For some teens, this emotional overload can lead to **depression**, *feelings of helplessness, hopelessness, and sadness.* These feelings can be further complicated by troubling life events such as the divorce or separation of parents or the loss of a loved one. Alienation—feeling isolated and separated from everyone else—can occur. When such painful feelings go unchecked over long periods, some teens may feel so filled with despair that they will try drastic, self-destructive measures to escape.

➤ Of the many millions of Americans who suffer from depression in any given year, 80 percent can be effectively treated, but only 30 percent seek help.

➤ In 1997, more teens died from suicide than from cancer, heart disease, AIDS, birth defects, stroke, and chronic lung disease combined.

Suicide Risk Factors

Suicide and suicidal behavior are not normal responses to the stresses experienced by most people. In general, youth at high risk are those who are depressed, isolated, and angry. Over 50 percent of suicidal adolescents are considered depressed. Other suicide risk factors include:

- Substance abuse, violence, or emotional, physical, or sexual abuse.
- Prior suicide attempts, firearms in the house, jail time, a family history of a mental disorder, and exposure to other suicides.

In some cases, suicide is accidental—the result of alcohol or drug abuse or the misuse of firearms.

Suicide's Warning Signs

Recognizing the signs of suicide in one's self or others can mean the difference between life and death. Become alert and alarmed if someone you know exhibits any of the warning signs of suicide.

Warning Signs of Suicide

VERBAL SIGNS

- Direct statements like "I want to die," "I don't want to live anymore," or "I wish I were dead."

- Indirect statements like "I (or you) won't have to put up with this much longer," "I just want to go to sleep and never wake up," "They'll be sorry when I'm gone," "Soon this pain will be over," "I can't take it anymore," "Nothing matters," "Who cares?" "I won't be a problem for you much longer," "What's the use?"

- Poems, song lyrics, or diary entries that deal with death.

NONVERBAL AND BEHAVIORAL SIGNS

- Depression and hopelessness.
- Lack of energy and zest for life.
- Withdrawal from family, friends, and social activities.
- Drop in grades or a poor student's new concern about grades, or trouble concentrating.
- Giving away possessions or otherwise settling affairs.
- Extreme sensitivity to what others say and do.
- Increased risk-taking and other aggressive activity, such as driving recklessly, or frequent accidents.
- Personality changes such as apathy or moodiness.
- A sudden upbeat mood, which can signal that the decision to attempt suicide has been made.
- Neglect of or dramatic change in appearance.
- Rebellious behavior or running away.
- Irrational or bizarre behavior.
- Drug and alcohol use.
- Violent actions.

Tragic Impulse: Teenage Suicide

Are you Feeling...
Depressed?
Stressed?
Anxious?
Isolated?
Hopeless?
Suicidal?
Help is available...
Our non-judgmental, supportive peer counselors are available 24 hours a day to listen to you.

Preventing Suicide

The tragic fact is that the conditions leading to suicide are almost always treatable. Most suicide thoughts are temporary, but death is permanent. With help, people suffering from depression, extreme stress, or mental disorders can often find new levels of purpose and happiness.

Helping Others

The first thing to remember is that people who are suicidal often feel that no one cares. It is, therefore, critical to show your caring and concern. Remember, too, that the person needs professional help as soon as he or she can get it—immediately if possible. You may in fact be able to take action in time to save a life. What to do when you suspect someone you care about is a potential suicide includes the following:

- Take any and all talk of potential suicide seriously. Actively listen and show support, and be calm and understanding. Talk directly, openly, and freely. Allow the person to express his or her feelings in depth, and show **empathy** for his or her problems. Let the person know how much you and others care.
- Stress the temporary nature of the problems and feelings the person is going through, and emphasize that there is professional help available that can make things better.
- Make clear that you understand that the person wants to end his or her pain, but emphasize that suicide is not the answer. Add the

hot link

empathy For more information on empathy and its value as a positive emotion, see Chapter 8, page 199.

keeping Fit

Signs of Trouble

If you or someone you know is experiencing any or many of the following symptoms, seek help.

➤ feelings of sadness or anxiety that won't go away

➤ persistent feelings of hopelessness or emptiness

➤ restlessness or irritability

➤ lack of energy or interest

➤ difficulties concentrating, remembering, or thinking

➤ trouble making decisions

➤ insomnia, early waking, or oversleeping

fact that most suicide survivors later express gratitude that they did not die.

■ Ask the person whether or not he or she has a specific plan and means to follow through with it. Be sure that no weapons or drugs are available. Do not leave the potential suicidal person alone if you feel the threat is immediate. Instead, take the person to a professional for counseling.

■ Suggest that he or she talk to a parent or other trusted adult, or a trained professional. Offer to make the contacts on his or her behalf.

■ Do not agree to "keep a secret."

Multiple Suicides

Sometimes within a teen population, there are **cluster suicides.** These are *a rash of suicides occurring within a short space of time and involving several people in the same school or community.* Some cluster suicides are the result of suicide pacts—oral or written agreements between two or more people to take part in a joint suicide. When these pacts fail, as they often do, the guilt experienced by the survivor is intolerable. If you know someone engaged in such a pact, talk with a responsible adult or to the authorities immediately. Intervention must take place quickly. Counseling must start right away for all involved in such a pact.

LESSON 2 *Review*

Reviewing Facts and Vocabulary

1. Name five warning signs of suicide.
2. What two factors seem to contribute to suicides more than any other?
3. List five suggestions for dealing with a friend or relative who is threatening suicide.

Thinking Critically

4. *Comparing and Contrasting.* Distinguish those traits of individuals who experience depression but seem to work through it quickly and those who seem to become overwhelmed by their feelings.
5. *Synthesizing.* List some of the common myths about suicide. Write them up, correcting each statement with its true counterpart.

Applying Health Skills

6. *In Your Home.* Make a scrapbook of pictures from newspapers, magazines, or your own photo collection called "Faces of Hope." Inside, keep pictures of people who have overcome depression, other mental disorders, suicide attempts, or other tough times and not only gotten through them but also bounced back, thriving either in spite of or even because of them. When you or someone you know is feeling really down, flip through or share this book of hope.

Getting Help

As you have seen, there are many different types of mental disorders. Within each type, the severity of the problem varies greatly. Unlike the symptoms of a cold or rash, specific symptoms of mental disorders are much more difficult to identify. There are places to go, however, to get help for these problems.

HEALTH TERMS

psychiatrist

neurologist

clinical psychologist

psychiatric social worker

HEALTH CONCEPTS

- Treatments are now available for many types of mental disorders.
- Mental disorders require the attention of a trained health professional.
- Mental health professionals can help their patients or clients to improve their perceptions of themselves, their relationships, and the outside world.

Signs of Mental Health Problems

Recognizing early warning signs of mental disorders is one key to getting help for them. Any of the following feelings or behaviors that persist over a period of days or weeks and begin to interfere with other aspects of daily living could be a sign of a mental or emotional disorder:

- prolonged sadness for no specific reason
- hopelessness—the sense that one's life is out of control
- violent or erratic mood shifts
- inability to concentrate or to make decisions about daily life
- overwhelming fear, anxiety, or anger at the world
- severe sleep disturbances—nightmares, insomnia, fitful sleep
- compulsive behaviors such as repeated handwashing

- self-destructive behaviors such as overeating, starving oneself, drinking, or other drug use
- frequent physical ailments for which no medical cause can be found

Of course, no one symptom means a person has a mental disorder. However, any one of these symptoms may be an indication that stress in your life is building. Such stresses need to be closely examined before more serious problems arise.

Building Health Skills

Evaluating Sources of Self-Help

AMONG THE RESOURCES people sometimes turn to are self-help books and Web sites for psychological services. Although these sources may offer useful hints and guidelines, you need to be a careful consumer when it comes to seeking help. Ask the following questions before proceeding:

1. **What are the qualifications and background of the author or Web site administrator?** Do these people have training in the mental health area? In the case of Web sites, refuse to sign on with individuals who won't provide their names, addresses, phone numbers, and credentials. In the case of books, check the resources at the back to see if they include references to established medical journals such as *The New England Journal of Medicine* or the *Journal of the American Medical Association.*

2. **Is the book or site supported or backed by a nationally known and respected mental health organization?** Just because a self-help source is endorsed by a celebrity or listed on a best-seller list does not mean that its advice is psychologically sound. Look for backing from a reputable source such as the American Psychological Association or the National Institute of Mental Health.

3. **Are you being advised to try medication or some other remedy?** Before accepting such advice, check with your doctor, counselor, or therapist. Remedies bought "over the counter" in a drugstore can be harmful and even life threatening.

4. **Is there a cost involved?** Many resources are available at no cost. If you are asked on-line for a credit card number, use caution.

Remember, finally, that computers and telephones are not substitutes for real face-to-face encounters. You may be bypassing the healing benefits that face-to-face relationships and therapies offer. In addition, for those who have serious disorders or need medication, "diagnosis" or treatment through cyberspace may be inaccurate, insufficient, damaging, or even dangerous.

Myths About Seeking Help

MYTH	REALITY
Seeking help from a mental health professional means a person is weak or crazy.	Asking for needed help is a sign of strength. It shows responsibility for one's well-being.
People who set their mind to it can get better on their own.	Serious disorders, compulsions, and addictions are complex and require professional intervention.
Finding help is difficult.	Help is as close as a trusted adult, friend, family physician, clergy member, or the phone book.
Getting professional help for a mental problem is too expensive.	Some mental health care professionals have sliding pay scales. Other state and community facilities offer low-cost or no-cost help.
Sharing your deepest thoughts with a "stranger" is painful and embarrassing.	People are almost always surprised to find out that unloading their problems makes them feel better.

Kinds of Professional Help

Often it is difficult to look in the mirror and do your own mental health checkup. Sometimes others are needed to help. The principal health care providers for mental health are psychiatrists, neurologists, clinical psychologists, psychiatric social workers, and counselors of various types. These individuals may work in hospitals, clinics, or private offices.

Psychiatrist

A **psychiatrist** is *a medical doctor who specializes in diagnosing and treating mental disorders and can prescribe medications.* He or she deals with mental, emotional, and behavioral disorders of the mind.

The psychiatrist uses many therapies, or treatment techniques. Among these are:

- **psychotherapy**—an ongoing dialogue between the patient and psychiatrist designed to get to the root of the problem and find a solution.
- **psychoanalysis**—an analysis of a patient's past, particularly his or her early life, to determine the early roots of a mental problem. This is rarely used today.
- **medical psychotherapy**—the use of certain medications to treat or reduce a mental disorder or to use in conjunction with or as preparation for the above two treatments.

▲ *With time, caring, support, and proper treatment, most people with mental disorders can return to life and enjoy its simple pleasures "to the max."*

ACTIVITY *List five short-term and five long-term benefits of seeking help for a mental problem.*

Neurologist

If a psychiatrist thinks a patient may have some organic problem of the brain, the patient may be referred to a neurologist. A **neurologist** is *a physician who specializes in organic disorders of the brain and nervous system.* Those who specialize in surgery are called *neurosurgeons* or *neural surgeons.* Consultation with and testing by a neurologist may be required for patients whose mental symptoms are suspected as being caused by an organic disease.

Clinical Psychologist

The **clinical psychologist** is *a psychologist who diagnoses and treats emotional and behavioral disorders but cannot prescribe medications.* State law usually determines what kinds of training is required to earn the

up date
▶ *Our Changing World*

Mental Health Counselors

In today's challenging society, the skills of mental health counselors are called upon more than ever. School counselors, social workers, psychiatrists, and psychologists can help when you're feeling overwhelmed by situations over which you feel you have no control. Their work involves helping people deal with emotional problems, relationship issues, stress management, and conflict resolution.

In a school setting, mental health counselors are often available for guidance in crisis prevention and intervention. If a crisis or tragedy does occur, counselors help students and teachers cope with grief and loss and identify victims of psychological trauma, such as post-traumatic stress disorder. They may offer counseling and group therapy sessions to assist people in dealing with their feelings about the traumatic event. Because emotions run deep in the aftermath of a crisis or tragedy, counselors must be careful to notice and try to prevent potential alcohol and drug problems as well as suicide.

1. What health skills do you think would be essential for a career as a mental health counselor? Explain your response.

2. Interview a mental health counselor. Find out about his or her daily responsibilities. Which responsibilities are most challenging, and which are most rewarding?

title *psychologist.* The clinical psychologist can practice psychotherapy, group therapy, and individual counseling, in addition to testing for many kinds of specific mental disorders.

Counselors

There are many kinds of counselors, including school counselors. These professionals usually have a master's degree and work with young people, helping them in personal or educational matters. Pastoral counselors, who include ministers, priests, and rabbis, often help people with mental, social, and marital problems. Addictions counselors have special certification and training requirements.

Psychiatric Social Worker

A **psychiatric social worker** is *one who has concentrated on psychiatric casework, doing fieldwork in a mental hospital, mental health clinic, or family service agency that provides guidance and treatment for clients with emotional problems.* They usually have a master's degree.

Seeking Help

More and more Americans, including many teens, are seeking professional help from mental health professionals. Though mental problems are often undiagnosed and untreated, many people are working hard to change the situation. If you or someone you know has a mental problem, you no longer have to suffer in silence. Talk to a trusted adult. Get the support and the help that you need.

Did You Know?

➤ There is a new movement afoot to get more mental health services in the schools. In Baltimore, Maryland, more than 60 public schools now have full-time mental health professionals to work with students.

LESSON 3 *Review*

Reviewing Facts and Vocabulary

1. Identify five signs of mental health problems.
2. List at least five different places that a teen needing to talk with someone about mental or emotional problems or disorders might go for help.

Thinking Critically

3. *Analyzing.* What are some of the reasons a person might go to a psychiatrist instead of a psychologist or psychiatric social worker?
4. *Synthesizing.* Create a Help Wanted ad that lists the personal qualities one would need to fill a position at a mental health clinic.

Applying Health Skills

5. *In Your Home.* At a library or neighborhood bookstore, examine several books on psychology and mental health. Try to find the credentials of the authors. Now look through teen magazines that have "health" sections. Select one article about emotional or mental health and evaluate what it tells you about the author's credentials.

Health Skills Activities

Activity 1 — Mental Health Help Directory

Many people who decide to seek help may have no idea how to go about finding that help. Having information about local mental health resources can make the process of getting help easier and less stressful.

Directions

1. In a group, research mental health resources in your community, such as general community outreach programs as well as centers for child abuse, addiction, and crisis intervention. Investigate vital information such as hours, cost, and services provided.
2. Compile all findings from the class into a Mental Health Help Directory to be printed from the classroom computer.
3. If possible, make your directory available in the school library or counselor's office.

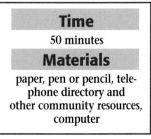

Time

50 minutes

Materials

paper, pen or pencil, telephone directory and other community resources, computer

Self-Assessment

✓ Listed at least five sources of help for mental health problems.
✓ Provided detailed information for each source identified.

Activity 2 — Building Mental Health Awareness

Despite the strides of modern research and the availability of treatment, mental problems are often a source of embarrassment to people who suffer from them. Write an editorial to explain some of the myths and misconceptions.

Directions

1. Working in a group, select one of the mental disorders covered in the chapter. Brainstorm misconceptions you know to exist or believe exist about this illness. These may be about the warning signs, behaviors, and/or symptoms.
2. Combine your misconceptions with those of other groups to create a true-false survey on mental health.
3. Administer the survey to several dozen people in the community. Tabulate the findings, and publish these as an editorial in a local newspaper.

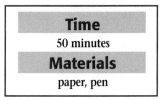

Time

50 minutes

Materials

paper, pen

Self-Assessment

✓ Described signs, behaviors, and symptoms of the mental illness you selected.
✓ Tabulated survey results.
✓ Presented findings accurately and cohesively.

HEALTH NEWS

VIDEO

Stolen Lives

Suicide is the eighth leading cause of death in the United States. It is the third leading cause of death among 15-24 year-olds. However, looking at statistics isn't enough. We need to find practical, working solutions.

Surgeon General David Satcher has announced a new suicide prevention plan. "Suicide has stolen lives and contributed to the disability and suffering of hundreds of thousands of Americans each year," he said. The plan focuses on reducing the feelings of shame surrounding suicide. It calls for better mental health screenings and more media programs that accurately depict suicide and mental illness.

Play the Video

Think About It

- What is a stigma? How does the new suicide prevention plan try to overcome the stigma of suicide?

- Why was Maggie Ming asked to speak at the press conference announcing the plan? How does her perspective help people understand the problem of suicide?

- Why does Satcher include television and movies in his suicide prevention plan? How does the media influence people's attitudes and feelings?

Using Health Terms

On a separate sheet of paper, write the term that best matches each definition below.

LESSON 1

1. A preoccupation with the body and fear of presumed diseases that are not present.
2. A serious mental disorder meaning "split mind."
3. An illness of the mind that can affect the thoughts, feelings, and behaviors of a person, preventing him or her from leading a happy, healthful, and productive life.
4. Psychological conditions that affect a person's ability to get along with others.
5. A psychological illness characterized by extreme mood swings between depression and extreme happiness, or mania.
6. An illness in which real, imagined, or persistent fears prevent a person from enjoying life.
7. An illness in which a person complains of disease symptoms, but no physical cause can be found.

8. A psychological illness often with an organic cause that relates to emotions and involves mood swings or mood extremes that interfere with everyday living.

LESSON 2

9. A rash of suicides occurring within a short space of time and involving several people in the same community.
10. Feelings of helplessness, hopelessness, and sadness.
11. The taking of one's own life.

LESSON 3

12. One who has concentrated on psychiatric casework, doing fieldwork in a mental hospital, mental health clinic, or family service agency.
13. A physician who specializes in organic disorders of the brain and nervous system.

Recalling the Facts

Using complete sentences, answer the following questions.

LESSON 1

1. What is the difference between organic and functional mental disorders?
2. Name two anxiety disorders, two affective disorders, and two personality disorders.
3. What happens to a person who suffers from bipolar disorder?

LESSON 2

4. What are some of the reasons teens experience depression?
5. Name five suicide risk factors.
6. What are the two most frequent ways that accidental suicides occur?

7. What are some of the things someone should *not* do or say to a person thinking of suicide?

LESSON 3

8. Name five signs of mental health disorders.
9. For what reasons would someone seek help from a psychiatrist instead of a clinical psychologist? From a clinical psychologist instead of a psychiatric social worker?
10. Name five places or people where a teen with a mental or emotional problem could turn to for help.

Thinking Critically

LESSON 1

1. **Evaluating.** Evaluate the following statement: "Those with mental disorders should be kept away from the rest of society because they are a potential threat to themselves and others."

LESSON 2

2. **Synthesizing.** Summarize the key strategies used in helping to prevent teen suicide in your school.

LESSON 3

3. **Analyzing.** Look carefully at this statement: *Ignorance is at the root of myths and stereotypes about mental disorders.* How would you support this statement?

4. **Evaluating.** Research individuals who have suffered from mental disorders at some time but moved on to become accomplished members of society. Compare and contrast accomplishments, moods, and relationships when they were mentally ill and when they were healthy.

Making the Connection

1. **Science.** Find out about the new fields of medical science that may have great impact on the understanding and treatment of mental disorders in the future. Choose one area from the following: *psychobiology, chronobiology, psychoneuroimmunology, psychopharmacology, neuroscience.* Read briefly about what this branch of study covers and what kinds of basic research it is adding to the understanding of mental disorders and their treatment. Present your findings to the class in an oral report.

2. **Fine Arts.** Find a painting or piece of music that seems to capture the essence of one of the following disorders: panic disorder, bipolar disorder, or clinical depression. You may create a painting or song.

BEYOND THE CLASSROOM

PARENTAL INVOLVEMENT Parents often tell their children about the physical diseases that tend to "run in the family." With your parents, review the information provided in Lesson 1, then openly discuss people in the family who have had any of these mental disorders diagnosed and treated. Discuss the effects these disorders have had on the family, how and when the person was diagnosed, and if treated, what kinds of treatment were used with what effects. Confidentially discuss with your family how it has handled these individuals?

SCHOOL-TO-CAREER

Exploring Careers. Invite a mental health worker such as a psychiatrist, psychologist, psychiatric nurse, or suicide prevention counselor to your school. Have the person discuss the kinds of disorders people present to them, the treatments or references the worker provides, and the frustrations and rewards of the profession. Also, ask the person to talk about suicide warning signs and specific ways to help potential suicide victims.

CHAPTER 11

Building Healthy Relationships

HEALTH Online

COMMUNICATION SKILLS

You live the fast-paced life of a teen, but do you take time out to nurture the relationships you have with family and friends? Computers can make written communication easier. Write a note to someone you care about using a Word Processing program or send an E-Mail Message. See Technology Projects at **health.glencoe.com** for helpful tips on these technologies.

Personal Health Inventory

Self-Inventory Write the numbers 1–10 on a sheet of paper. Read each statement below and respond by writing *yes*, *no*, or *sometimes* for each item. Write a *yes* only for items that you practice regularly. Save your responses.

1	I treat others with respect.
2	I am a good team player.
3	I am a trustworthy friend.
4	I often use compromise to resolve differences.
5	I am willing to work at my relationships.
6	I communicate well with others.
7	I am a good listener.
8	I ask questions if I'm not sure what is being said.
9	I use eye contact when communicating with others.
10	I am aware of my own body language.

Follow-up After completing the chapter, retake this self-inventory. Pick two items that you need to work on and set a goal to improve your health behaviors.

66 *You are a vital resource in and for your community. I challenge you to realize your potential, take up this cause, and reach out to other young people to make their lives better.* 99

—GENERAL COLIN POWELL
SECRETARY OF STATE, 2001

Quick Write Think of a teen who serves as a role model for helping others. Complete this sentence: *A person who helps others...*

Getting Along with Others

According to psychologist Abraham Maslow, everyone needs to be loved and to belong. Each of us also needs to feel safe, secure, valued, and recognized. By forming relationships, we are able to meet many of these basic human needs. Good relationships can affect a person's mental, social, and even physical health.

HEALTH TERMS

relationship

friendship

role

cooperation

compromise

empathy

HEALTH CONCEPTS

- Relationships affect your physical, mental, and social health.
- You play many different roles in your relationships with others.
- Cooperation and compromise are important aspects of a healthy relationship.
- Mutual trust and respect are cornerstones of a responsible relationship.
- Good relationships take time and energy.

Who Matters to You?

Think of standing in one of those photo booths where you and a friend pull a curtain, drop your coins into a slot, and get back three connected photos of the two of you. You are smiling or laughing, your faces side by side. Now imagine that you could have these three shots showing you with three different people with whom you have a significant connection—say, from your family; from your extended family, such as a grandparent or cousin; from your neighborhood; and from your school. Who would be with you in the photos?

You have many relationships in your life that affect you. A **relationship** *is a bond or connection between people.* You are part of a network of people that includes your family, extended family, neighbors, friends, as well as people from social or religious organizations, sports teams, your town or city, your nation, and the world.

If you were suddenly plunked down on a desert island and removed from all of these relationships, you might like the peace and quiet for a short time, but chances are you would soon begin to get very lonely. Having relationships with others can, in fact, not only ward off loneliness; it can also have a direct effect on a person's total health.

Choosing Relationships

As a small child, you had a limited circle of relationships. Now that you are older, you have a larger circle from which to choose your relationships. You may realize for the first time that there are people of all ages, races, religions, and backgrounds from which you can choose relationships. You can choose people who support and encourage your best qualities. You can change or back out of relationships that have a negative influence on your health, your safety, your self-esteem, or your values. No relationship can be healthy unless both parties feel valued and want the relationship.

Friendship

Whether you want to go to the movies or just chat, you turn to a friend. A **friendship** is *a significant relationship between two people based on caring, consideration, and trust.* A friend is someone whose companionship you enjoy and who can be a source of help when you have a problem. A friend also may be someone with whom you share confidences, interests, hobbies, or other friends. **Friendships** vary in importance and in how challenging and complicated they are. Maintaining friendships can be hard work, but it is often well worth the effort.

Family Relationships

Who do you turn to when you are sick or injured or need food, clothing, or a hug? You probably turn to someone in your family. **Family relationships** provide the strongest bonds with others. These are bonds that last a lifetime. Parents or guardians provide love and care for their children, as well as teach values and give guidance.

hotlink

friendships For more information on friendships and the qualities of a good friend, see Chapter 13, page 298.

family relationships For more information on family relationships and properties of a healthy family, see Chapter 12, page 276.

▼ *Relationships and roles are part of your everyday life.* ACTIVITY *Name several different kinds of relationships and roles that you experience each day.*

➤ *Each person plays many different roles in relationships.*

ACTIVITY *Name some of the relationship roles a teenager might play.*

Relationships in the Community

Your relationships extend beyond family and friends into your community. Community leaders and citizens work together for safety and to provide health services and to meet the needs of all community members. Cities and counties often sponsor classes or recreation activities at a local park. Neighbors organize block clubs. Businesses provide the community with needed products and services.

Your Many Roles

You take on many roles in your relationships with others. A **role** is *a part that you play,* especially in a relationship. You may be a sister or brother, a daughter or son; a granddaughter or grandson; a member of the orchestra; a member of the volleyball team; a Scout; a student; an employee; a member of a synagogue, church, or mosque; and even someone's boyfriend or girlfriend—all at the same time.

Sometimes the roles you play are clear-cut. You know that when you mow the neighbor's lawn or wash his or her car, you are an employee and need to act as one. Sometimes, though, roles either switch suddenly or change gradually, depending on needs and situations. For example, some days you may be the caregiver for your disabled grandfather, but at other times he is the teacher and you are the student. Perhaps your lab partner becomes the person you date. Such changes in roles can be confusing. Sometimes you may not have a clue as to what your role is in a relationship. This can make it difficult for you to know how to act.

The Healthy Relationship

A relationship consists of not only two people but also the many ways in which they relate. For a relationship to succeed, certain traits must be present.

Cooperation

A basketball team could not win a championship without teamwork. In relationships, teamwork is called **cooperation**, *working together for the good of all.* Some activities are impossible without cooperation. Susan fixes supper each night because her parents don't get home from work until six o'clock. Because of her help, the family is able to eat supper together at night. Working together through cooperation is one good way to build strong relationships.

Compromise

Jeremy wants to see a movie, but Alexis wants to play miniature golf. Have you ever found yourself in a situation like theirs? Do you remember how you solved the problem? You probably used compromise. **Compromise** is *the result of each person's giving up something in order to reach a solution that satisfies everyone.*

The "give and take" of compromise helps a relationship run smoothly. When done effectively, compromise strengthens relationships. It is a way of letting the other person know how much you value the friendship. You can learn the skills of compromise through practice. To compromise, seek a solution that is acceptable to all persons involved. Realize that you must be willing to give up something in order to reach a solution.

Making Responsible Decisions

Confronting a Friend

Carlotta and Sondra have been close friends for several years. Lately, though, Sondra has noticed a change in Carlotta. The two friends used to meet at their lockers after school. Twice in the past week, Carlotta had told Sondra she would be there, but then hadn't shown up. The last time it happened, Sondra walked home alone. The next day, she heard from another friend that Carlotta had been telling people that Sondra was "boring." What should Sondra do?

What Would You Do?

Apply the six steps of the decision-making process to Sondra's problem.

1. **State the situation.**
2. **List the options.**
3. **Weigh the possible outcomes.**
4. **Consider your values.**
5. **Make a decision and act.**
6. **Evaluate the decision.**

CHARACTER IN ACTION

Fairness in Friendship

Fairness is an important quality in a friendship. Whether you are facing a peer in a student council election or competing with a friend on the tennis court, fairness is a principle that respects the abilities, needs, and contributions of all parties. Fairness means:

➤ knowing and following the rules.

➤ participating without cheating or manipulation.

➤ taking into account the needs and rights of all parties.

➤ not showing favorites or excluding others because of your own prejudices.

Character Check Make a list of situations where you think you might have treated someone else unfairly. Now imagine how that unfair treatment may have made another person feel.

Not all disagreements can be resolved through compromise. If your friend wants you to do something that is against the law, for example, you cannot compromise. In situations like these, it is important to stand your ground. Learning when—and when *not*—to compromise is another worthwhile relationship skill.

Other Traits of a Healthy Relationship

What qualities do you look for in a friend? Most people seek the following basic traits.

■ **Respect.** Mutual respect is important in friendships. Friends may not agree on all issues, such as religious views, but they can show respect for the other person's viewpoint.

■ **Acceptance.** No one is perfect. Accepting others and being accepted leads to strong, healthy relationships.

■ **Honesty.** Relationships are built on honesty. Lying about your actions or your feelings can tear relationships apart.

■ **Trustworthiness.** Friends trust each other. If you trust someone, you know they won't do anything to hurt you.

■ **Dependability.** A dependable friend is there when you need someone. You can anticipate receiving the person's help.

■ **Loyalty.** A loyal friend speaks kindly of you even when you are not around.

■ **Empathy.** *The ability to share another person's feelings or thoughts* is called **empathy.** If a friend feels sad because of a loss, for example, you "feel for" the person, sharing his or her sadness as well.

LESSON 1 *Review*

Reviewing Facts and Vocabulary

1. Explain some of the different roles people play in relationships.
2. Describe relationships in a community.
3. Tell why compromise is an important trait in a relationship.
4. Explain how the trait of empathy adds to a relationship.

Thinking Critically

5. *Synthesizing.* Suppose your family plans to go out to a family reunion. One member wants to see the school's final basketball playoff game. Explain a plan that would resolve this problem using compromise.

6. *Evaluating.* Emiko makes all the decisions as to what she and her friend, Kate, do when they are together. What relationship trait is missing? How could the relationship be improved?

Applying Health Skills

7. *In Your Home and School.* Analyze an important relationship in your life by making a three-column chart. In the first column, list the traits of a healthy relationship from the above list. In the second column, describe the relationship in each area. In the third column, tell what you could do to improve your relationship in that area.

Communicating Effectively

To be a good athlete, you need to possess many skills. Skill development takes time and practice. In the same way, to build healthy relationships, you need to practice and master a variety of skills. Among the most important of these are skills related to the act of communication.

HEALTH TERMS

communication

"I" message

active listening

body language

constructive criticism

HEALTH CONCEPTS

- There are many ways to communicate with others.
- Effective communication means being a good listener as well as a good speaker.
- An aspect of good communication is making sure your body language and verbal communication are in sync.

Communication

Think about the messages you send to others and the messages others send to you. Think not only of messages expressed in words but also of those you deliver in the form of gestures, facial expressions, and behaviors. All of these are a part of **communication.** This is *a process through which you send messages to and receive messages from others.*

Communication is critical because it lets others know what you feel, what you want and need, and what you know. Effective communication is a two-way street. It means sending messages that are interpreted correctly, and it means correctly interpreting messages that you receive.

There are three basic skills associated with effective communication: speaking, listening, and body language. Although these skills take practice and energy, the time and effort are worth it because it helps you form healthy relationships with others.

Speaking Skills

Having good speaking skills means saying clearly what you mean. Do not assume that anyone else can read your mind or know your needs or expectations. It is your responsibility to make them clear. This is the first step to healthy communication.

The changes in your tone of voice and its pitch and loudness can also play a large role in how you communicate. Kind words delivered with a sarcastic tone, for example, may not be processed kindly. Speaking too loudly can make you sound bossy or arrogant, even if you are shy. Saying no too softly makes it seem as if you don't mean what you are saying. So it is not just *what* you say that is important to communicating but *how* you say it.

An important step in the communication process, especially when the message to be delivered has a strong emotional content, is the use of "I" messages. An **"I" message** is *a statement in which a person tells how he or she feels using the pronoun "I."* Using "I" messages can help you avoid blaming, name-calling, or antagonizing the other person in other ways.

ANTAGONISTIC MESSAGE	CONSTRUCTIVE "I" MESSAGE
You idiot! What have you done with my baseball glove?	I dislike when you borrow my things and don't return them.
Why do we always have to do what you want to do?	I'll agree to go swimming today if I get to pick the activity next time we're together.
You're always late! I don't know why I even bother being your friend.	I worry about you when I expect to meet you at 6:00 and you don't show up.

update
Our Changing World

Promoting Peace through Communication

In the aftermath of a tragedy or an act of violence, a natural human reaction is to look for someone to blame. Feelings of anger and fear sometimes cause people to try to fight back in an effort to gain control or feel that they are taking an active role. Problems can arise, however, if people react with prejudice or intolerance by condemning an entire group of people based on the actions of a few.

When we accept the differences in others, we open new lines of communication and improve relationships. Using effective communication skills can keep the doors open to promote peace and understanding among all people.

1. Describe how you could be a good role model for children, promoting peace through understanding.

2. Initiate a discussion with someone of a different religion, race, or culture from you. Encourage that person to share information about special traditions, customs, or rituals practiced in his or her culture.

Listening Skills

Listening is as important to effective communication as speaking, but it is the part of the communication process that is most often overlooked. Of the 80 percent of our waking hours that we spend communicating, we spend a high proportion of that time as hearers rather than as speakers. Hearing, however, is not the same as listening. Consider that the average listener correctly understands, properly evaluates, and retains only about 30 percent of what he or she hears in a 10-minute presentation. Within 48 hours, memory of what was said drops to an even lower percentage.

Skilled listeners use **active listening**, *really paying attention to what someone is saying and feeling.* Active listening involves careful attention to what the speaker is saying without making judgments or interrupting. Active listeners incorporate these listening techniques:

- **Reflective listening.** In reflective listening, you rephrase or summarize what the other person has said so that you are sure you understand what is intended.

- **Clarifying.** Clarifying is asking the person how he or she feels about the situation or asking questions to understand more fully what is being said.

- **Encouraging.** Encouraging is giving signals that you are really interested and involved. You can show your interest by quietly saying "Uh-huh" or "I understand" or "I see."

- **Empathizing.** Empathizing is actually feeling the other person's feelings as you listen. If a person is sad, an empathetic listener feels sad, too. If the person talking is angry, the listener feels angry, too.

▼ *A good friend is able to empathize with another friend's feelings.*

ACTIVITY *Name several other communication skills that are important to a good friendship.*

keeping Fit

Listen Up!

Here are some other tips for becoming a more effective listener:

➤ Give your full attention to the person speaking.

➤ Make direct eye contact.

➤ Do not interrupt. Wait your turn.

➤ Listen for feelings and watch for gestures. These are as much or more of a clue than words are.

Nonverbal Communication

Not all communication takes place on a verbal level. People send many messages through **body language**—*nonverbal communication through gestures, facial expressions, and behaviors.* Waving your hand to say good-bye is an example of body language. So is bringing your hands up to your mouth when you are surprised.

Most nonverbal communication is subtle and often takes place on a subconscious level. A person who is feeling embarrassed or ashamed may look at the ground when speaking rather than at his or her listener. Maybe you have found yourself leaning toward a speaker who was saying something of great interest to you.

Being aware of your body language helps you make sure you are sending the messages you intend and that those messages are understood. If your words and your face or body seem to be saying two different things, the other person may be confused or unsure of what to think or believe.

Building Health Skills

Communication: Agreeing to Disagree

IT'S NOT REALISTIC to think that you and your friends will agree on everything. When you disagree, think of it as an opportunity to learn how to handle disagreements in relationships. Follow these steps:

1. **Give the person a turn to speak.** Each of you deserves the same chance to state your opinion without hostility or rebuke from the other person. Avoid shouting the person down. Keep your ears—and mind—open.

2. **Use "I" messages.** Even if your position is not accepted by the other person, you will feel better in the end if you express your beliefs and feelings in an appropriate way.

3. **Stick to the subject.** At the height of a disagreement, it is easy to lose track of what you are arguing about. Don't bring the person's character or personality into the discussion. Avoid appeals to other people's opinions as well. They are irrelevant to the situation at hand.

4. **Keep the tone friendly.** Remember, this is a friend you are dealing with—someone whose companionship you value. If your friend holds a different view from yours on a particular topic, remember that tastes vary from individual to individual. You can still enjoy your friendship on many other levels.

Barriers to Effective Communication

A chain, it is said, is only as strong as its weakest link. The same may be said of communication. When one person in a relationship uses communication skills and another does not, the entire communication process is impeded. Other obstacles to effective communication include the following:

- **Unrealistic expectations.** If your goal is to help another person understand your feelings, you need to be prepared for the reality that he or she will not receive the message in the spirit you intended. The person may become defensive and feel attacked.

- **The need to project a tough or superior image.** During the teen years it is common to search for an **identity**—a sense of who you are and your place in the world. This search prompts some teens to develop a rough exterior or an attitude of superiority, which can make them hard to reach.

- **Prejudice. Prejudice** is an unfair opinion or judgment against a particular group of people. The term comes from the word *prejudge*, which means to judge without sufficient information or knowledge. Prejudice can keep one person from hearing what another is really saying and from freely communicating his or her own ideas.

When people put up communication barriers like these, there is little you can do. You simply need to accept the situation for what it is and move on. If you have made an effort yourself to follow the rules of good communication, you can at least walk away with the satisfaction of knowing you have done all you can in the interest of a healthy relationship.

hotlink

identity For more on the search for identity during the teen years, see Chapter 21, page 482.

prejudice For more information on prejudice and how it harms relationships, see Chapter 13, page 300.

◄ *Many statements and feelings are communicated through body language or facial expressions.*

ACTIVITY *Name the statement or emotion expressed by the gestures and facial expressions in each photo. Tell which ones the "speaker" might be doing unconsciously.*

▼ *Accept constructive criticism positively. This is one way you can learn from others and improve yourself.*

ACTIVITY *Name an example of how a critical statement can be turned into constructive criticism.*

Constructive Criticism

No one, not even your best friend or parent, is perfect. It's not realistic to think that you won't be disappointed in a relationship at least occasionally. Perhaps your brother suddenly hogs the TV remote, insisting that you watch his show, not yours. A friend that you were to meet in front of the theater is late, causing you to miss the beginning of the movie. The dry cleaners loses or damages your favorite sweater.

Giving feedback to the person can be helpful to him or her as well as to your relationship. Make sure you use **constructive criticism**, *non-hostile comments that point out problems and have the potential to help a person change.* Using constructive criticism means that you avoid attacking the other person. It means not placing blame or resorting to name-calling. You might want to start with an "I" message. Then point out what the person is doing or has done,

Communicating Across Cultural Boundaries

Terrell thought Enrique wasn't friendly because Enrique always looked at the ground when they talked. Then Terrell found out that, in Enrique's culture, looking someone in the eyes is considered rude. Becoming aware of various communication styles will help you communicate better with persons from different cultures. Read each scenario below. Describe how the same task or custom is handled in your culture.

1. Tanya greets her friends by kissing them on both cheeks.

2. Franklin stands about six inches away from friends as he talks.

3. Autumn makes immediate eye contact with her friends and maintains the eye contact throughout their conversation.

4. While in the audio store at the mall, Vernon nods his head toward a particular compact disc to show his friend the kind of music he likes.

and describe a better way to do it. You might say to your friend, "I really dislike missing the opening of the picture. Please try to arrive earlier next time." What might you say to the dry cleaners?

Acknowledgments and Compliments

Have you ever received a thank-you note or a verbal pat on the back for a job well done? Have you ever given one? Complimenting another person is a way of acknowledging his or her self worth. Unlike other forms of communication, acknowledgments and compliments are not necessarily done with an eye toward receiving a response. Yet, these small, unexpected gestures can go a long way toward improving the health of a relationship and another person's opinion of you.

Some compliments are given to acknowledge a skill or to show appreciation. An example would be telling a family member how much you enjoyed a meal he or she cooked. Other compliments are purely selfless—for example, telling another person that he or she looks nice. Still others are *self-effacing*. They are kind words offered at the expense of your own pride or personal feelings. Congratulating the team that defeats yours is an example of a self-effacing compliment.

▼ *A pat on the back and praise for a job well done leads to healthful relationships.*

ACTIVITY *Describe situations in which you can encourage someone by offering compliments.*

Review

Reviewing Facts and Vocabulary

1. Name and describe two basic communication skills.
2. In what way does sending "I" messages avoid blaming and name-calling?
3. Describe active listening.

Thinking Critically

4. *Synthesizing.* Read and respond to the following statement using reflective listening: "I don't think we should write a report. Instead, let's create a skit in which we can really show what it's like to lose a friend."
5. *Comparing and Contrasting.* Imagine that you have asked a friend to do you a favor. In your private Health Journal, create a "response grid" with four cells. Label the columns *Compliment* and *Constructive Criticism*. Label the rows *Job well done* and *Job done poorly*. Complete the grid with responses that show positive and negative communication skills.

Applying Health Skills

6. *In Your Home or School.* Think of an issue, a project, or a person you care about. How might you communicate your feelings without using words?

Health Skills Activities

Activity 1 — Building Communication Skills

One of the keys to building healthy relationships is effective communication with others. Think about the ways you communicate with the people in your life. Are there ways that you could improve your communication skills?

Directions

1. Working with several classmates, write a skit about a couple or family seeking help from a counselor. The skit should exhibit weak communication skills, such as interrupting, failing to listen, and so on.
2. Have the counselor identify communication as the problem and review communication skills, such as sending "I" messages, active listening, and accurate body language.
3. Conclude with a scene in which the clients try out some of their newly learned skills.

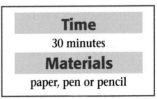

Time
30 minutes

Materials
paper, pen or pencil

Self-Assessment

✓ Correctly described at least two communication problems that can occur.
✓ Correctly described at least three communication strategies.

Activity 2 — Relationship Guidelines

Positive relationships are important to your total health. There are many do's and don'ts for having such relationships. What guidelines do you practice in your relationships?

Directions

1. Brainstorm two lists of behaviors in a friendship. One list is to be positive, the other negative.
2. Create posters, bumper stickers, and other high-visibility modes of communicating the importance of positive guidelines to follow in any relationship. Use the classroom computer or poster board and markers.
3. Distribute or display your messages to community members.

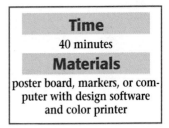

Time
40 minutes

Materials
poster board, markers, or computer with design software and color printer

Self-Assessment

✓ Described strategies for building positive relationships.
✓ Created a clear, persuasive message outlining specific communication techniques to develop healthy relationships.

HEALTH NEWS
ARTICLE

Two-Way Dialogue: A Crucial Step

When school violence blasts into the headlines, experts fully expect the news to trigger a flurry of emotion at schools nationwide. Young people across the country will be fearful, apprehensive, or confused.

The most important thing students must do, experts say, is talk about their feelings – with parents, educators, and one another. In the process, they gain perspective about school violence and community.

"Every kid in America is wondering, 'Can this happen at my school?'" said Jim Copple of the National Crime Prevention Council. "The foundation of all learning is creating a safe and secure environment. And we can learn from the good kids as to what is safe."

For the most part, experts insist, schools nationwide are very safe – in many cases safer than any other place in a community. Still, parents and teachers must not discard young people's concerns and fears, according to counselor Joanne McDaniel.

"What's more important is that parents and staff in schools listen to what the students have to say," she said. "It's important that they don't blow off those fears . . . They have to have a dialogue, to let them talk through what their fears are."

Read This
▼

Warning Signs of Violence

What are the clues that someone might be on the brink of a violent act? These warning signs suggest that intervention may be needed to prevent violence before it occurs:

- abusive behavior
- frequent loss of temper
- repeated threats to hurt others
- committing vandalism or property damage
- sudden changes in demeanor or appearance
- increase in risky behaviors, including drug and alcohol use

Think About It

1. How can violent events in other schools affect stress levels in your school?
2. What strategies do experts suggest to help students work through fears of school violence?
3. How can talking about problems help relieve stress?

Using Health Terms

On a separate sheet of paper, write the term that best matches each definition below.

LESSON 1

1. A part that you play in a relationship.
2. Working together for the good of all.
3. The result of each person's giving up something in order to reach a solution that satisfies everyone.
4. A bond or connection between people.
5. A significant relationship between two people based on caring, consideration, and trust.
6. The ability to share another person's feelings or thoughts.

LESSON 2

7. Really paying attention to what someone is saying and feeling.
8. A process through which you send messages to and receive messages from others.
9. A statement in which a person tells how he or she feels using the pronoun "I."
10. Non-hostile comments that point out problems and have the potential to help a person change.
11. Nonverbal communication through gestures, facial expressions, and behaviors.

Recalling the Facts

Using complete sentences, answer the following questions.

LESSON 1

1. Why are relationships so important to your health?
2. What role are you playing when a friend comes into a fast-food restaurant where you work?
3. Which kinds of relationships are usually the strongest and last a lifetime?
4. What quality of a healthy relationship do two students working together on a poster exhibit?
5. How does compromise help to strengthen a relationship?
6. Name several traits of a healthy relationship.

LESSON 2

7. How is backing away from someone a form of communication?
8. Why are good speaking skills an important part of effective communication?
9. What are three techniques you can use for active listening?
10. How does prejudice set up a barrier to effective communication?
11. Give an example of constructive criticism.
12. How should you deal with a disagreement in a relationship?

Thinking Critically

LESSON 1

1. *Analyzing.* Explain whether or not a compromise is the right choice in this situation: Peter is Jackie's first boyfriend. Peter wants Jackie to go to a late-night party with him, but it would mean breaking her curfew. Jackie feels that she should respect her family's house rules and come home on time.

2. *Evaluating.* Ken and William recently became friends at soccer practice. Yesterday, upon learning that Ken's dog had died, William told Ken, "Cheer up. At least it wasn't a person." Do you think this relationship will survive?

LESSON 2

3. *Evaluating.* Gustavo's girlfriend, Karen, expects him to pay for everything when they go out. Gustavo resents footing the bill each time. Write an "I" message that Gustavo could tell Karen to explain his feelings.

4. *Analyzing.* Kim's father is criticizing her report card and threatening to cut off her allowance if her grades don't improve. Kim puts her head and shoulders down and shoves her hands into the pockets of her jeans. What emotion is she probably experiencing, based on her body language?

Making the Connection

1. *Math.* Pilar gets 8 hours of sleep each night. If she spends 80 percent of her waking hours communicating and 60 percent of those hours listening, how many hours a day does Pilar spend listening?

2. *Language Arts.* Write a guest editorial for the school newspaper with one of the following titles: *Traits of a Healthy Relationship, How to Compromise,* or *Resolving Differences Through Communication Skills.*

BEYOND THE CLASSROOM

PARENTAL INVOLVEMENT Ask your parents to call a family meeting on the subject of communication among family members. Allow members to give their opinions about communication in the family. Present several communication tips, including the use of "I" messages and active listening. Discuss how your family can improve its communication skills.

COMMUNITY INVOLVEMENT Research community programs in your area to help (1) a new family in the community to make new friends; (2) a senior citizen who lives alone and is lonely;

(3) a teen who is looking for an opportunity to do volunteer work.

SCHOOL-TO-CAREER

Exploring Careers. Invite a school counselor to speak to your class about a career in family counseling. Ask this person to explain how counselors help individuals and families in crisis. Also, find out where counselors work, what training they need, and average salaries for counselors. Write a summary of your findings, and add the information to a classroom career booklet.

Healthy Family Relationships

HEALTH Online

STRESS MANAGEMENT

Strong support systems are integral to the health of the family. What approach can you take to maintain that support when families separate? Read the Health Update on "When Parents Divorce" at health.glencoe.com to understand more about dealing with this type of change in family relationships.

Personal Health Inventory

❝ *Treasure your families...* **❞**

—John Paul II
Roman Catholic Pope, (1920–)

Quick Write Write a quick thank-you note to someone in your family who has taught you that you matter and have an important role to play in this world. Think about how the person demonstrates this through actions and words.

Strengthening Family Relationships

From the time you were born, your family has had a strong influence on your life. Families not only provide food, clothing, and shelter but also give family members a sense of security and a feeling of belonging. It is through the family that a child receives his or her first opportunities for physical well-being, learning, and loving.

The Family as a System

If every student in your class were to bring in a family photo, you would probably see a wide representation of family types and sizes. Some families are made up of two parents and one or more children. Others are headed by a single parent. Still others are "blended"— headed by two adults who have remarried following a divorce or the death of a spouse, plus the children of both previous marriages.

Regardless of its makeup, every family may be viewed as a system similar to the human body. All parts of the body are interconnected to compose a whole being. No part exists in isolation. As a system, each family member's level of health—physical, mental and emotional, and social—affects the health of the total family. The reverse is also true. The health of the family system directly affects the health of its individual members. In addition, because the family is the basic social unit of society, society's health is directly related to the family's health. If we are to survive and maintain a healthy society, then everyone must work to promote healthy families.

Functions of the Family

As a social unit, the family serves several important functions. These include:

- Constituting the primary support system to which individuals turn in order to have their basic needs met.
- Meeting the emotional needs of children and providing nurturing.
- Instilling values and religious beliefs in children.
- Passing on traditions and customs from one generation to the next.

Meeting Basic Needs

Most parents work hard to earn money so they can provide basic needs such as food, clothing, and shelter for their children. Children have other basic needs as well. Have you ever watched a parent teach a toddler not to touch a hot stove? Young children need to be taught basic knowledge about how to live safely in their environment. Families also teach their children basic social skills, such as how to get along with others in society. The family is the essential mechanism by which a child develops the capability to survive and to function independently in the world. This can happen only when the child's needs are met.

Meeting Emotional Needs

Growing up and becoming a well-adjusted person is a complex process. Children need to develop a sense of belonging. They need families that help them feel secure and loved.

▼ *Instilling values and religious beliefs is an important function of the family.*
ACTIVITY *Explain how teaching cultural heritage strengthens family ties.*

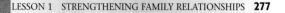

hot link

self-esteem For more information on self-esteem and ways of improving your own self-esteem, see Chapter 8, page 188.

hot link

values For more information on values and their importance, see Chapter 1, page 20.

▼ *When family members share responsibilities, all benefit.*

ACTIVITY *Identify at least two benefits for each family member in the activities pictured.*

When going through rough times, children need to know they can turn to family members for support. By providing emotional support, families promote **self-esteem** in their children. Self-esteem is the way people feel about themselves. Good self-esteem provides children with confidence to become successful and happy adults.

Instilling Values

Families teach children **values**, or beliefs and feelings about what is important. Developing a good value system helps children know right from wrong. It helps them make decisions that will affect their future, and turns them into good citizens who follow the laws and contribute in a positive way to society.

Instilling Culture and Traditions

Does your family have certain traditions, such as spending the Fourth of July at the lake or celebrating Kwanzaa at the end of the year? It is through traditions such as these that families pass their

Trends Affecting Families

In the 1950s, a typical American family included a father who worked outside the home, a mother who was a homemaker, and several children. Families have undergone many changes in the past 50 years. Mothers are now more likely to hold jobs, either as single parents or as part of a dual-income family. Child care facilities care for children while their parents are at work. Families tend to have fewer children and, in general, people are starting families later. Other trends include a rise in divorce rates and a more mobile society.

1. A rise in divorce has prompted an increase in the number of single-parent families. Do you think this factor may have contributed to an increase of women in the workforce?

2. There has been a marked increase in dual-income families. What factors could have caused this to happen?

3. Contemporary families are facing new pressures. What might these pressures be?

culture on to their children. By learning about their cultural background, children develop an ethnic identity, a feeling of belonging to a certain group of people. Having a cultural heritage enriches the lives of family members and gives them pride in who they are.

Responsibilities of Family Members

In order for a family to function as a healthy system, each member must be willing to accept his or her responsibilities to the family. Some responsibilities, such as providing basic comforts and needs, fall primarily to the parents in the household. Parents are also responsible for setting limits and maintaining rules that ensure the health and safety of family members.

Children have a number of responsibilities as well. Think about chores you may help out with at home, such as cleaning, cooking, and grocery shopping. Maybe you take care of a younger **sibling**—*a brother or sister*—while a parent is at work. Sharing these tasks not only helps the family run more efficiently, but it also equips you with life skills you will need as an adult. Knowing that you are helping out boosts your self-esteem and gives you a greater sense of responsibility.

Communication, compromise, and cooperation are essential ingredients in healthy relationships. Take the online quiz at **health.glencoe.com** to see how well you get along with family members and how you can improve your relationship skills.

Not all responsibilities, it should be noted, are practical. Some of the most important responsibilities family members have are of an emotional nature. Parents are responsible for providing love and acceptance to their children, who have the responsibility for showing love and appreciation in return.

Building Healthy Family Relationships

What are the traits of a healthy family? Good communication is one of the most important. Other traits include:

- **Affirmation.** In healthy families, members show that they love each other through words and actions. Giving **affirmation** is *providing positive input that helps others feel appreciated and supported.*

update
▶ Our Changing World

Family Support During Difficult Times

Who do you turn to during times of crisis? You probably have a few friends that you've known since childhood, while other friendships have simply come and gone. During sad, scary, or difficult times, family members and those who care for you can provide emotional support, security, and healing.

After a traumatic event, such as the terrorist attacks on America, everyone—including parents and older siblings—most likely felt shock, sadness, and fear. Talking about your feelings can help make you feel better. Don't be afraid to ask questions or show your emotions, but also remember to be a good listener when other s want to share their feelings.

Although life may never be the same after a traumatic event, returning to regular routines can help your family reestablish a sense of normalcy. Family members might prepare and eat meals together, help one another with homework or chores, or go for a daily walk or bike ride together. Keep in mind, too, that you can be a good role model for younger siblings during difficult times. You can make a real difference by helping to answer their questions, easing their fears, and letting them know that they're safe and that you care about them.

1. Why is it equally important for individuals and family members to support one another during good times as it is during difficult times?

2. Ask a parent, grandparent, or other adult family member to tell you about a tragedy or crisis that occurred during his or her adolescence. How did people support one another?

- **Trust.** Families with a high level of trust know that other members will not do anything to hurt the family. Both parents and children must earn trust, and can do so by keeping promises and being honest.
- **Commitment.** Building a strong family requires commitment. Family members are willing to work together and make sacrifices for the benefit of the whole family.
- **Time Together.** It is not possible to have strong healthy family relationships without spending time together.
- **Communication.** In families, effective communication means listening to the viewpoint of others as well as being heard.
- **Respect.** Strong families have respect for each other. They accept individual tastes, talents, and opinions.
- **Solving Problems.** Healthy families try to identify problems before they become too serious and ask for outside help if needed.
- **Love.** Healthy families give and receive love. They express love to each other, physically and verbally.

LESSON 1 *Review*

Reviewing Facts and Vocabulary

1. Name three functions of the family.
2. How can family members give affirmation to one another?

Thinking Critically

3. *Comparing and Contrasting.* Tell what need the following family members are providing: (a) A teenager stops her toddler sibling from running out into the street. (b) Parents host a bar mitzvah for their son. (c) A father and son collect goods for a local food shelf. (d) A teenager hugs his grandmother.
4. *Synthesizing.* Last year, Bart told his parents he was going over to a friend's house when he was really going to a party. Now they won't let him go out at all at night. What advice would you give Bart to help him regain his parents' trust?

Applying Health Skills

5. *In Your Home.* Practice giving affirmations by finding a situation in which you can give positive input to each member in your family. If you find it difficult to give the affirmation out loud, write the affirmation as a note that you can give to the person. Explain what affirmations are to family members and ask them to join you in giving at least one affirmation to a family member each day.

Looking at the Health of the Family

Most families experience some type of stress. When one problem leads to another, stress can become a vicious and destructive cycle. Without intervention, a family system can break down. In this lesson, you will become aware of the threats to the health of a family and learn how families can cope.

HEALTH TERMS

custody

domestic violence

spousal abuse

child abuse

emotional abuse

neglect

exploitation

HEALTH CONCEPTS

- Some families experience problems that can interfere with the normal healthy working of the family.
- Couples who cannot resolve their differences sometimes choose to separate or to end their marriages through divorce.
- Domestic violence brings fear and abuse into the family system and is the single most destructive force in American families today.
- There are techniques for coping with family problems and improving the health of the family.

Family Stress

When people live under one roof, problems are sure to arise. Maybe you have had the experience of a family member "getting under your skin." Usually, good communication and problem-solving skills can help family members successfully work out these minor problems.

Sometimes major changes occur, triggering stress in families. Sources of family stress can be sudden, such as the loss of a job, or they can occur over time, as with a chronic illness. Whatever the cause, the stress must be dealt with effectively.

Changes in Family Structure

The arrival of a new baby is a cause for great joy in a family. It can also, however, be a cause for stress among young siblings who may view the newcomer as a rival. The addition of a new baby can be stressful even on older children since the baby makes demands on the parents' time and diverts their attention from the older child's needs and wants.

Other changes to a family's structure include becoming a part of a blended family or having an older relative such as a grandparent move into the household. Either of these situations may mean that space is redefined and, hence, requires an adjustment.

Moving

Whether a family moves across town or across the country, a family faces the stress of uncertainty as they adjust to a new neighborhood. Members may miss friends or loved ones they left behind. Moving from a house into an apartment can also be a stressful adjustment, if families need to adjust to new rules.

Financial Problems

Meeting all of a family's expenses in today's society is not easy. Financial problems from overdue bills or loss of a job are a major cause of stress for families. Other financial problems are caused by impulse buying or poor planning. "Credit card abuse," the situation in which one or more family members overuse a credit card to the point of spending past the approved credit limit, can be a particularly serious source of stress for the family bill payer. Resulting arguments over this habit can further fuel the stress.

Financial problems can be a cause of family stress.

ACTIVITY *List habits you can start now, such as a regular savings account, that will help you learn to manage your money.*

Illness or Disability

When a family member becomes ill with a serious health problem, the family is faced with many stresses. When Sandy learned that her mother had cancer, for example, Sandy's worry kept her awake at night, and her grades dropped. Because Sandy's mother had to quit her job while undergoing expensive treatment, the family faced financial problems as well.

A grandparent in poor health may cause stress as family members determine how best to care for him or her. If a disability affects one member of a household, the other members of the family may need to make adjustments. The family may need to work out a schedule around work, school, and recreation activities so that everyone can share the responsibility of caring for that person.

Substance Abuse

Substance abuse within the family is almost always destructive. Parents—and others in the family who are alcoholic or who use other drugs—neglect their responsibilities, become very irritable, often lose their jobs, and may even abuse other family members.

When the health of the family is threatened by drug use, all of the members need help. By asking the right people for assistance, you can be the one who starts your family on the way back to a healthy life. The people most likely to help you are members of your extended family, a member of the clergy, a school counselor or trusted teacher, your school nurse, or a youth worker. Knowing how to get help is a way of caring for your family. These people can help you understand the problem and help you get additional assistance.

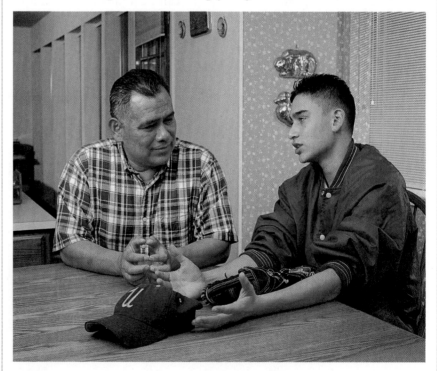

➤ *Talking with a parent is one way to cope with stress.*

ACTIVITY *Name two other ways to cope with family stress.*

Coping with Family Stress

Think of stress as water boiling in a teapot. To deal with stress, people need to find a "release valve." Depending on the nature of the problem, finding the release valve might be as easy as turning to someone within the family for help. Talking with family members about problems can help alleviate some of the stress and lead to successful problem-solving. Use these suggestions for coping with family stress:

- Talk with one or both of your parents. Find an adult who will listen to you, such as a teacher, guidance counselor, or member of the clergy. You might also talk with a brother or sister; after all, they are probably facing the same problem you are.
- Do what you can to help. If the problem is money, you could get a part-time job to pay for your own expenses. If your parents are stressed, taking on added chores or responsibilities might reduce their stress load. Regardless, helping out will make you feel better.
- Read books about people who have faced the same problem you are facing. You might also find it helpful to speak with classmates who have had similar difficulties in their families.

Separation and Divorce

Stress, as noted, is a normal part of living with other people. Most of the time, a married couple finds ways to work out their problems. When differences become too much to work out, however, a couple may go through a separation or divorce. During a separation,

CHARACTER IN ACTION

Avoiding Sibling Quibbling

One way to better sibling relationships is to exercise **self-control**. That means not overreacting. You can try to communicate in effective and caring ways that don't inflame others.

Character Check
Next time you're about to "go at it" with a brother or sister, try these tips:

➤ Talk out your differences before they escalate.

➤ When disagreeing, make an effort to stay on the subject.

➤ Use "I" messages rather than accusing with "you" messages.

➤ Learn to distinguish between the behavior and the person.

➤ Take responsibility for your part of the argument.

➤ Try saying one nice thing each day to each other.

Making Responsible Decisions

All in the Family

For the past six months Bart's dad has been ill, and the family has been under extreme stress. Bart's mother has been dividing her time between work and the hospital. Bart, who is the oldest of three brothers, has been responsible for running the house. Lately, the combined pressures of school, household chores, and looking after his younger brothers has begun to overwhelm him. Bart would like just an occasional evening or weekend afternoon to himself, but he feels it would be selfish even to ask his mother under the circumstances. What should Bart do?

What Would You Do?

Apply the six steps of the decision-making process to Bart's problem.

1. **State the situation.**
2. **List the options.**
3. **Weigh the possible outcomes.**
4. **Consider your values.**
5. **Make a decision and act.**
6. **Evaluate the decision.**

a couple lives apart from each other. Sometimes parents live apart for a while until they resolve their differences and can live together again. Other times, a separation leads to a divorce, a permanent separation. A separation or divorce is painful for all family members.

Meeting the Needs of Children

When parents divorce, it must be decided where the children will live. Usually, one parent is granted custody. **Custody** is *a legal decision about who has the right to make decisions that affect the children and who has the physical responsibility of caring for them.* Sometimes dual custody is awarded so that both parents share in the child-rearing. Adapting to a divorce requires a period of emotional adjustment for everyone. Children may experience the stages of grief—from shock and disbelief to anger, sorrow, and finally, acceptance.

Family Adjustments

Other changes occur in families after a separation or divorce. Children must learn to cope with the absence of a parent. They may have to adjust to a lower standard of living, as maintaining separate residences means less money to go around. Eventually, the children may need to adjust to a stepparent or a blended family.

Surviving a Breakup

Regardless of which parent gets custody of the children, it is important to remember that parents divorce each other, not their children. Although parents' feelings for each other have changed, their love for their children can stay the same. Sometimes, children feel they are the cause of the parents' separation. Divorce happens for many reasons, but the children are seldom the cause.

Domestic Violence

When stress explodes in a family and reactions are out of control, domestic violence can result. **Domestic violence** is *any acts of violence involving family members.* Domestic violence usually takes place at home but can occur anywhere. The violence may be directed by or at any family member and can be of a physical, sexual, or emotional nature. No one deserves to be a victim of abuse, and domestic violence is a criminal act that can be prosecuted by law.

Spousal Abuse

The amount of **spousal abuse**, *domestic abuse directed at a spouse,* in our society is disturbing. Each year women are the victims of more than 4.5 million violent abuse crimes in the United States. Spousal abuse occurs in all kinds of families regardless of income, level of education, or race. Fortunately, groups and agencies have formed to help victims of spousal abuse and their children. You may be familiar with programs in your community that are available to assist these families.

Child Abuse

No one knows exactly how much child abuse occurs in our country, since many cases go unreported. **Child abuse** is *domestic abuse directed at a child.* The abuse need not be physical or sexual. **Emotional abuse** is *a pattern of behavior that attacks a child's emotional development and sense of self-worth.* Emotional abuse can be just as damaging to a child as physical or sexual abuse. Child abuse also may include **neglect**, *a failure to provide a child's physical or emotional needs.* Physical needs include adequate food, clothing, shelter, and medical care. Emotional neglect may take the form of indifference or refusing to listen when the child has a problem.

RUNNING AWAY

Children who live in abusive homes may try to escape the abuse by running away. Living on the streets with no money or job skills, however, is a poor solution. Runaways often become victims of **exploitation**, *being used for someone else's benefit.* Runaways are prime targets for people dealing in pornography and prostitution. The best solution for children suffering abuse or neglect is to ask for help from reliable sources. Some of these resources are addressed in Lesson 3 of this chapter.

LESSON 2 *Review*

Reviewing Facts and Vocabulary

1. Name three changes that might cause stress in a family.
2. What are some options available to a teen trying to cope with family stress?
3. Why do runaways often become victims of exploitation?

Thinking Critically

4. *Analyzing.* What problems might you expect a friend to face whose sick grandfather is coming to live with the family? Tell how your friend could cope with the stress.
5. *Synthesizing.* What are the important issues for a person who is considering running away to escape an abusive situation at home?

Applying Health Skills

6. *In Your Home and School.* Think of one stress your family is currently facing and decide how you can help. Remember that one way to help is to learn to cope with stress. You might decide to read books or talk to others at school who have faced similar problems. Talk with your parents about the stress the problem is causing you. Make a list of things you can do to help.

LESSON 3

Support Systems for Families

As noted in Lesson 1, the health of a family system is dependent on the health of individual family members. When one member suffers from substance abuse or a similarly serious problem, the health of the entire family suffers. Fortunately, sources are available to which families can turn when the family system is in a state of turmoil.

HEALTH TERMS

crisis center
foster care
family counseling
mediator

HEALTH CONCEPTS

- Sources of help in the community exist for families in distress.
- A healthy family is a work in progress, requiring an ongoing effort on the part of each member.

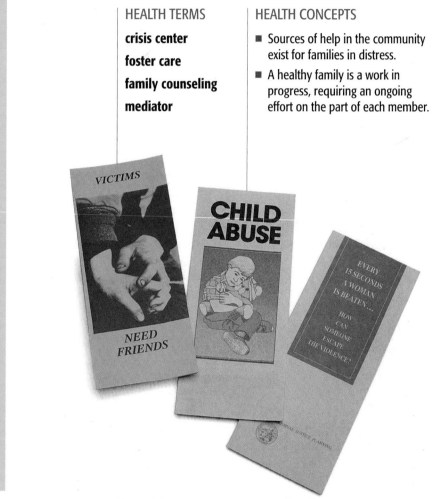

Sources of Help

Help for families in crisis is often only a phone call away. Any family member can call a **crisis center**, *a facility equipped to handle emergencies and make referrals for persons who need help.* Many communities also provide crisis hot lines, special phone numbers people can call to receive help 24 hours a day. Persons who answer the phones at crisis centers and hot lines are caring listeners. They have had training and can advise you where to get help. They are familiar with many different kinds of problems and can guide the caller to a solution. The solution often includes a referral to a community service, a support group, or a family counselor.

Community Services

Most communities have a variety of services helpful to families in distress. Both public and private agencies offer parenting and conflict resolution classes. Food, clothing, and shelter can be provided for families who are having trouble meeting their basic needs. Agencies also offer financial aid, medical care, and help in finding employment.

Parents in distress who feel they cannot safely care for their children may be able to bring them to a crisis nursery, where the children will be safe and cared for. Children in abusive situations also are sometimes removed from their families and placed in **foster care,** *under the guidance and supervision of a family headed up by parents or a parent who is not related to the child by birth.* Foster families often serve as a "port in the storm" for an abused or neglected child by providing the gentle and loving care that has been missing from the child's life. Women who are victims of spousal abuse and their children can be placed in safe houses until they are ready to start a new life free from violence.

Support Groups

Talking with others who face similar problems can be very beneficial to persons in distress. Millions of people attend **support groups**, meetings at which persons share their problems and get help from others who struggle with the same problem. Just knowing that they are not alone is helpful to many people. Hearing how others have handled the problem helps many persons cope on a day-to-day basis.

Alcoholics Anonymous (AA) is probably the best-known network of support groups in the country. Many alcoholics have found the strength to stay sober through AA. Support groups also are available for teen alcoholics as well as family members of alcoholics. Other support groups help persons who face such problems as violence and serious illness in the family.

h⊙t link

support group For more information about support groups, see Chapter 9, page 227.

Alcoholics Anonymous For more on Alcoholics Anonymous (AA) and the work this organization does to help recovering alcoholics, see Chapter 25, page 565.

➤ *Support groups help teens cope with family stress.*

ACTIVITY *Explain how support groups help people deal with problems.*

Psychological Counseling

Some families receive help from **family counseling**, *therapy to restore healthy relationships in a family.* They meet regularly with counselors to discuss the family's issues and work on finding solutions. This counseling can provide families with the skills they need for setting boundaries and solving conflicts on their own.

Occasionally, a person may benefit from **psychotherapy**. Psychotherapists may help a person realize that she or he learned abusive family patterns in childhood. These patterns can be broken by recognizing the patterns and replacing them with healthy behaviors.

Mediation

Couples going through a divorce or trying to resolve custody issues may go into mediation. A **mediator** is *a person who helps others resolve issues to the satisfaction of both parties.* The mediator sets ground rules

h t link

psychotherapy For more on psychotherapy and the problems it is used to treat, see Chapter 10, page 250.

Building Health Skills

Obtaining Help

MOST PEOPLE FIND it difficult to actually pick up the phone and place a call for help. "What will I say?" they wonder. "What if I can't think of anything to say at all?"

Imagine that you have a friend who wants to make a call to ask for help. You could assist your friend in preparing to call by helping him or her follow these steps.

1. **State the problem to yourself.** Write down on a piece of paper what the problem is and what you will say to the person who answers the phone. Then, if you become tongue-tied, you can simply read your statement from the piece of paper.

2. **List any questions you have.** Think about your reasons for calling, and write down all questions you might have for the counselor. Don't dismiss a topic because you think it might be trivial.

3. **Practice.** Rehearse the call with a close friend or family member who will act as the counselor on the phone. Practice until you feel confident.

4. **Make the call.** Go ahead and call the resource. Have a pencil and blank paper ready. If the counselor makes suggestions or offers the names of other personnel you might contact, write them down. Consider the suggestions that the counselor has for you.

5. **Be prepared.** Decide on the best course of action, in case the problem does not go away or comes up again. Being prepared and knowing how you will act can lessen the stress you feel. Also, knowing that help is just a phone call away can make the problem seem less severe.

and facilitates effective **communication** that allows each party to be heard. Mediators do not solve the problem, but help the two parties find a solution, usually through **compromise**. Mediation is less stressful than taking problems to court and can be used to solve any conflicts that family members cannot resolve on their own.

Doing Your Part

What can you do to help keep your family strong? What steps should you follow if your family is hurting? Here are some ways to show you care and to strengthen your family.

- Show appreciation for things done well. Saying "thank you" works at home, too.
- Encourage others, even your parents. Most people never get enough encouragement or know they are appreciated.
- Show concern when a family member has a problem. Offer to help or to get help.
- Stop criticizing. Be tactful and constructive. Avoid nagging.
- Show empathy by putting yourself in the other person's position. Try to see situations from his or her point of view.
- Listen to what other family members say. Listening is more than simply not talking. Avoid interrupting, daydreaming, jumping to conclusions, or just waiting for your turn to talk.

h tlink

communication For more information on communication and the steps involved in being an effective speaker and listener, see Chapter 11, page 263.

compromise For more information on the skill of compromise, see Chapter 11, page 261.

LESSON 3

Review

Reviewing Facts and Vocabulary

1. Give two reasons why a family would seek outside help for a problem.
2. What is the purpose of family counseling?
3. How does a mediator help families resolve conflicts?

Thinking Critically

4. *Evaluating.* Alicia often hears shouts and screams coming from the apartment next door. She has seen bruises on the neighbor's son. What do you think Alicia should do?
5. *Synthesizing.* Tell what kind of help each family is receiving: (a) Leon's family meets with a therapist every week to learn conflict resolution skills. (b) A person not related to the family helps the Smiths decide how to divide up their property after a divorce. (c) Dinesh meets every week with other teens whose parents have serious illnesses.

Applying Health Skills

6. *In Your Home.* Meet with family members to discuss ways in which your family could benefit from outside support systems or how your family could provide support for other families. Develop a plan and put the plan into action.

Health Skills Activities

Activity 1 — Solving Family Conflicts

Acting out problems in skits is one good way for families to practice conflict resolution. What steps do you take to solve conflicts within your family?

Directions

1. Working in a group, read the family conflict description provided by your teacher. Brainstorm a solution that would be acceptable to all family members.
2. Share and compare resolutions with the class. Vote on the best idea (which may be a composite of several or even all), and develop it into a 10-minute skit.
3. If possible, videotape the skit to share with other classes.

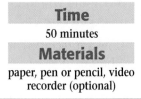

Time

50 minutes

Materials

paper, pen or pencil, video recorder (optional)

Self-Assessment

✓ Identified at least three strategies for resolving family conflicts.
✓ Demonstrated effective communication skills outlined in the chapter.

Activity 2 — Starting a Family Tradition

Does your family have traditions? These ritual celebrations can help bring about a feeling of belonging and help strengthen the family unit.

Directions

1. Explore with family members the types of activities each enjoys doing. Think about how the activity could be made appealing for all family members.
2. Based on this input, propose three new family traditions, such as an annual family biking day or a monthly movie night.
3. Get family members' reactions to your proposal. Refine ideas as needed.
4. Follow through with one or more events. Take snapshots, or write about the event. Share your experiences in class.

Time

50 minutes plus outside interview time

Materials

paper, pen or pencil, camera (optional)

Self-Assessment

✓ Created at least three ideas for new family traditions.
✓ Recorded the event and shared it with the class.

HEALTH NEWS

VIDEO

Balancing Family Stress

Healthy family relationships are an important aspect of your overall health. Stressful situations are often a natural part of living with a family. Stress creates physical changes in your body.

Researchers say that temporary stress is healthier than stress that lasts for a long time. Stressful family relationships are more harmful because they are long term. When you reduce ongoing sources of stress, you improve all aspects of your health. Recognizing this and knowing how to handle stress can help you and your family cope.

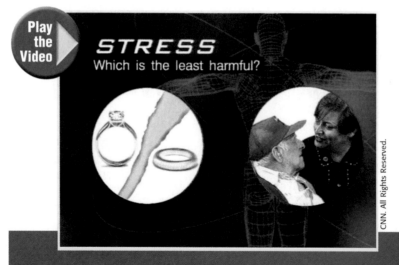

Play the Video ▶

STRESS
Which is the least harmful?

Think About It

- ◉ Explain the relationships between stress, ACTH, cortisol, and your immune system. Then tell how these physical changes can affect your mental well-being.
- ◉ Which examples are most harmful? Why are family stressors more damaging to your health?
- ◉ What criteria do researchers use to evaluate different kinds of stress?
- ◉ What advice might stress researchers give to help you build healthy family relationships?

CHAPTER 12 *Review*

Using Health Terms

On a separate sheet of paper, write the term that best matches each definition below.

LESSON 1

1. Providing positive input that helps others feel appreciated and supported.
2. Brother or sister.

LESSON 2

3. Being used for someone else's benefit.
4. Domestic abuse directed at a child.
5. A legal decision about who has the right to make decisions that affect the children and who has the physical responsibility of caring for them.
6. Any acts of violence involving family members.
7. Domestic abuse directed at a spouse.
8. A failure to provide a child's physical or emotional needs.

9. A pattern of behavior that attacks a child's emotional development and sense of self-worth.

LESSON 3

10. Therapy to restore healthy relationships in a family.
11. A facility equipped to handle emergencies and make referrals for persons who need help.
12. A person who helps others resolve issues to the satisfaction of both parties.
13. Meetings at which persons share their problems and get help from others who struggle with the same problem.
14. Under the guidance and supervision of a family headed up by parents or a parent who is not related to the child by birth.

Recalling the Facts

Using complete sentences, answer the following questions.

LESSON 1

1. What is another term for a person's brothers and sisters?
2. Why is the family called a basic unit of society?
3. Name three different kinds of basic needs of children.
4. What emotional needs do children have?
5. What are some of the traits of a healthy family?

LESSON 2

6. How might the arrival of a new baby create family stress?
7. Name three things that cause financial problems in families.

8. What is the difference between a separation and a divorce?
9. How might an illness or disability in one family member affect all family members?
10. What kinds of omissions on the part of parents can be considered neglect?

LESSON 3

11. What services do communities offer for families in distress?
12. What is a hot line?
13. In what ways might an agency protect family members in danger from abuse?
14. How might a support group help a teenager whose father is an alcoholic?

Thinking Critically

LESSON 1

1. *Analyzing.* When both his parents work late, Carlo prepares dinner for his family. Identify two benefits Carlo might derive from this action.
2. *Synthesizing.* Explain how taking responsibility and sharing family tasks can strengthen family relationships and prepare you for adulthood.

LESSON 2

3. *Synthesizing.* Your cousin Angela's parents have recently separated. While they are trying to work out their problems, Angela is coming to live with your family. What kind of support and help will Angela need?

LESSON 3

4. *Comparing and Contrasting.* How could each person best be helped? (a) Dan's parents both drink heavily, and he has no one he can talk to about it. (b) Connie is a single mother who has just lost her job and doesn't have enough food to feed her three children. (c) The Huyhns are getting a divorce and cannot agree among themselves whom their son, Pat, will live with.

Making the Connection

1. *Social Studies.* Interview a grandparent or elderly neighbor to find out how that person's family dealt with family stress or conflict when he or she was your age. Compare these methods with the ones recommended for families today.
2. *Math.* Keep track of the time you spend with your family for one week. Multiply by 52 to find out how much time you spend with your family in a year. Do the same for several other categories, such as school, sports, and friends. Then determine what percentage of time per year is spent in each category. Make a pie chart to illustrate your findings.

BEYOND THE CLASSROOM

PARENTAL INVOLVEMENT Interview a family member who has experienced a loss of job or relationship or faced financial or other hardships. Find out what he or she did to cope with the stress. Write a report on your findings to share with your class.

COMMUNITY INVOLVEMENT Investigate agencies in your community to find out about resources that are available to assist families. Make a list of community resources and what services they offer. Share the list with family members and classmates.

SCHOOL-TO-CAREER

Exploring Careers. Invite a school counselor to speak to the class and discuss the types of family problems that occur among students. Have the counselor explain how he or she works with the families to find solutions to their problems. What training and qualities are needed for someone in this position?

CHAPTER 13

Peer Relationships

HEALTH *Online*

CONFLICT RESOLUTION
What tactics do you and your peers rely on when faced with aggression or bullying in school? "Bully-proofing Programs" in the Health Updates section of **health.glencoe.com** talks about plans in place in schools across the country to deal with this social issue.

66 *...the only way to have a friend is to be one.* 99

—RALPH WALDO EMERSON
AMERICAN WRITER AND ESSAYIST, (1803–1882)

Quick Write Write five sentences, each one beginning with the words *A true friend is someone who*…. Share your definitions with your classmates of what it means to be a true friend.

Personal Health Inventory

Self-Inventory Write the numbers 1–10 on a sheet of paper. Read each statement below and respond by writing *yes*, *no*, or *sometimes* for each item. Write a *yes* only for items that you practice regularly. Save your responses.

1	I enjoy spending time with peers.
2	I have both casual and close friendships.
3	I am comfortable having friends of the opposite gender.
4	I recognize some of the limitations of belonging to cliques or clubs that exclude other teens.
5	I expect to be treated with consideration and respect by my friends or dates.
6	I spend time with groups as well as with individuals.
7	I use good communication skills and express my wishes clearly with friends or dates.
8	I try to exert positive peer pressure on my friends to behave responsibly.
9	I am able to say no to negative peer pressure.
10	I know how to assert myself when being pressured to do something I know to be wrong.

Follow-up After completing the chapter, retake this self-inventory. Pick two items that you need to work on and set a goal to improve your health behaviors.

Developing Responsible Relationships

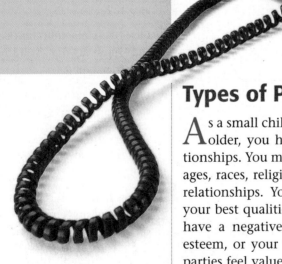

During the teen years, you begin a search for a personal identity—shaped at least in part by people the same age as you who are going through the same search. During adolescence, peers take on a new and greater importance than ever.

HEALTH TERMS

platonic friendship

clique

prejudice

stereotype

infatuation

HEALTH CONCEPTS

- Friendships take on a greater importance during the teen years, during which time teens search for an identity and sense of belonging.

- A strong need to fit in often magnifies differences that can lead to stereotyping and prejudice.

- Physical attraction to another person is a normal, healthy part of growing up.

Types of Peer Relationships

As a small child, you had a limited circle of peers. Now that you are older, you have a larger circle from which to choose your relationships. You may realize for the first time that there are people of all ages, races, religions, and backgrounds with whom you can cultivate relationships. You can choose people who support and encourage your best qualities. You can change or back out of relationships that have a negative influence on your health, your safety, your self-esteem, or your values. No relationship can be healthy unless both parties feel valued and want the relationship.

Friendships

As noted in Chapter 11, a friendship is a significant relationship between two people based on caring, respect, consideration, and trust. A friend is someone with whom you share confidences, interests, hobbies, or other friends. Having friends is a basic part of social health. It can help you define, understand, and reinforce your values.

There are many kinds of friendships. Friendships vary in importance and in how challenging and complicated they are. Maintaining friendships can be hard work, but they are usually worth the effort.

CASUAL FRIENDSHIPS

Casual friends are peers with whom you feel socially connected. You might choose to sit with casual friends at ball games or at lunchtime in the cafeteria. These friendships, however, do not fill some of the deeper needs humans have.

CLOSE FRIENDSHIPS

A close friend is more likely to share with you what he or she is really feeling and thinking and, in turn, make you feel comfortable doing the same. You may trust a close friend with your secrets or go to this person when you are hurting, confused, or in trouble. He or she might give you honest criticism and encourage you to apologize or be accountable for your mistakes. Because you may care deeply for this person, a real friend is also more likely to make you angry or hurt. Losing or having to share a close friend with someone else can be painful. It is important to remind yourself that no one owns anyone else—people must be free to choose with whom they want to be and when. Friends try to work through conflicts. This helps friendships stay healthy and grow.

PLATONIC FRIENDSHIPS

Not all close friendships are made up of same-gender pairs. Sometimes a male and a female can become real buddies in what is called a *platonic* relationship. A **platonic friendship** is *a relationship with a member of the opposite gender in which there is affection, but no sexual activity.* Such a relationship can be a wonderful way to grow to understand and feel comfortable with the opposite gender without feeling any of the pressures of dating. Such friends, in fact, can be a great source of advice in the area of dating problems. Above all else, having platonic friendships helps you begin to recognize that individuals of the opposite gender are human beings just like you, with the same kinds of fears, needs, and feelings.

HEALTH Online

Learn how good communication skills can improve relationships at **health.glencoe.com**.

▼ *Teenagers who share the same interests often become friends.*

ACTIVITY *Name several possible interests teenagers may share with their peers.*

Cliques

In their search for an identity, some teens form or become part of a **clique** (KLEEK)—*a small, narrow circle of friends, usually with similar backgrounds or tastes, that excludes people they view as outsiders.* A clique may be tightly or loosely knit and may have its own regular meeting place. This place can be something as simple as a table in the cafeteria that the clique has claimed as its private "turf." Clique members may treat non-members with scorn, ridicule, or indifference.

Although being part of a clique may give members a sense of belonging, it can also be damaging because members are often discouraged from thinking and acting as individuals. Being part of the popular crowd isn't fun if, in an effort to fit in, you cannot be yourself or if you feel pressure to do things that go against your values. Clique members may also be missing out on the benefits of meeting and interacting with a variety of people, which is important to an individual's social health.

One of the most negative aspects of cliques is that their beliefs and actions are prejudicial. **Prejudice** is *a negative feeling toward someone or something that is based not on experience but, rather, on stereotypes.* A **stereotype** is *an exaggerated and oversimplified belief about an entire group of people, such as an ethnic group, religious group, or a certain gender.* Prejudice is a type of ignorance. It denies each member of a particular group the right to be viewed as an individual. Openly rejecting a person based on superficial, or "surface," differences can damage the person's self-esteem. It can also damage your own in the long run.

V *Many teens form cliques and some may exclude others based on prejudices and stereotypes.*

ACTIVITY *List two negative impacts cliques have on teens.*

Responsible Relationships

At some time during adolescence, most teens go through a change in their feelings toward members of the opposite gender. For many, this change takes the form of a sudden stirring or awakening. Yesterday, the boy sitting across from you in math class was just another student. Today, like Max in the story that opened this chapter, you find it hard to stop staring at him. Yesterday, your younger sister's best friend was a pest or a bore. Today, you find yourself checking the mirror every time you know she is coming over to your house. These stirrings can lead to **infatuation**, *exaggerated feelings of passion for another person*. They will probably cause you to begin—or at least to begin thinking about—dating.

Dating Relationships

Dating is part of the process of learning interpersonal skills. Dating provides an opportunity for you to get to know yourself better—to recognize your strengths and weaknesses. It also gives you a chance to interact and feel comfortable with the opposite gender. By meeting and spending time with a variety of people, you learn what types of people you like and get along with best. Another benefit of dating is that it gives you a chance to practice your decision-making and communication skills.

Dating often leads to an ongoing relationship with one person. There are some advantages to this type of relationship. However, teenagers who date only one other person during their adolescence may be closing themselves off from meeting other people early in their social development. Although this type of relationship may

keeping Fit

Dangers of Positive Stereotyping

Sometimes, stereotypes come in a way that makes them hard to recognize as stereotypes. You may have heard, for example, that people of a certain ethnic background are good at math. Maybe you heard that members of some other group make the best lawyers or athletes. The list goes on.

What is wrong with observations such as these? All are *positive stereotypes,* which can be just as damaging as negative stereotypes. Like negative stereotypes, positive stereotypes make a generalization based on the identity of a group rather than an individual's identity. Remember, judging people on *any* basis other than individual strengths and weaknesses is a sign of narrow-minded, prejudicial, and faulty thinking.

connections Social Studies

Rites of Passage

Many cultures publicly recognize a person's change in status. One such change is the movement from childhood to adulthood. The Mbuti people of Africa have a special rite that recognizes passage to adulthood. In the rite, boys and girls are separated from each other for the first time. Girls are joined by friends and live in a special house called an *elima*. A festival is given by the village. Each afternoon the girls sing to the boys who sit outside the house. The boys respond with their own songs, and the ritual is a type of flirtation whereby future marriage partners may be chosen.

1. How does your family or culture recognize the transition to adult status?

2. What additional recognition, if any, would you like to see incorporated into your family or culture?

DATING AND TELEVISION

You've probably watched several different television shows in which the characters are dating. The interaction among the characters and the scenes of these shows may influence your expectations about dating. Yet, how realistically is dating portrayed on television? This investigation will help you find out.

keeping Fit

Dating Bill of Rights

1. I deserve to be treated with consideration and respect.

2. It's my right to be liked for who I am, not by the way I dress or the car I drive.

3. I have a right to have my values recognized and respected.

4. If pressured by my date, I can say no to drugs or other high-risk activities without apologizing or offering an explanation.

5. No one has the right to force or pressure me to do anything that goes against my or my family's values.

be convenient, it may not be helpful in learning to develop healthy relationships.

It is important to remember that adolescence is a time of trying different relationships and roles. Breaking up, making up, and breaking up again can be painful, but it is part of the process of becoming emotionally mature. Staying in a relationship because you do not know how to get out of it gracefully or clinging to a relationship when the other person wants to call it off are two common but painful dating situations. In both cases, honesty and open communication are essential. So is realizing that you have control over only your own actions and emotions. You cannot control the behavior or feelings of others.

These days many teens go out as groups. Going out with a group of friends of both genders is a good way to ease into dating. In a group, you have less responsibility for keeping the conversation going. Self-conscious feelings are not as likely. Because you are less nervous, you can relax and have a good time.

Choosing Not to Date

Not all teens date. Some choose not to because of other interests or time commitments, while others simply do not feel emotionally ready. It is wise to wait until you feel comfortable about dating. Do not let anyone pressure you into doing something you are not prepared to do. It is also important to talk with parents or adults in your home about their views on dating and to learn about their values.

What you will need
- Pencil and paper
- A weekly TV schedule
- A television or videotapes of several TV sitcoms in which dating occurs
- A VCR (if tapes are used)

What you will do
1. Work with several classmates in developing a questionnaire that probes the subject of TV's depiction of dating and the dating scene. Typical questions might include the following: How many characters in the show are shown dating? Is not dating presented as an acceptable alternative? What conflicts relating to dating are presented, and how is each resolved? Do dating partners show respect for each other? Are the relationships based on infatuation or on real feelings of love and caring for another person?

2. Each group member is to watch a different show in which dating occurs. While watching, the member is to fill out his or her copy of the questionnaire.

3. Conclude by rating each show on the following scale: *Excellent*–Shows realistic dating relationships and portrays healthy communication and decision-making skills. *Good*–For the most part realistic; communication and decision-making skills could be stronger. *Fair*–Dating relationship is unrealistic; few good skills are employed. *Poor*–Gives an unrealistic view of dating; employs poor communication and decision-making skills.

In conclusion
1. Which shows scored the highest rating? Which scored the lowest?

2. Did a show's rating correspond to how realistically dating was presented? Explain.

3. If you are dating or considering dating, what, if anything, did you learn about dating that might be of help?

LESSON 1

Review

Reviewing Facts and Vocabulary
1. How is a casual friendship different from a close friendship?
2. What are the positive and negative aspects of being part of a clique?
3. What is infatuation?

Thinking Critically
4. ***Comparing and Contrasting.*** Identify advantages and disadvantages of beginning to date and of not dating.
5. ***Synthesizing.*** Inez has been dating Edward for six weeks. She misses seeing her other friends but doesn't want to tell Edward for fear of hurting his feelings. What are the issues for both teens?

Applying Health Skills
6. ***In Your School.*** Analyze the cliques at your school by writing about them in your private Health Journal. First, identify several cliques. Then determine whether or not they possess the qualities of cliques discussed in your text, such as exclusion and prejudice. Describe some of the stereotyping and prejudice present at your school as well.

Peer Pressure and Refusal Skills

When Kendra learned that one of her friends was spending Saturdays serving food at a homeless shelter, Kendra began volunteering her time as well. After Don saw the progress teens in his neighborhood were making in cleaning debris from a vacant lot, he joined in the effort himself. Today the lot is a park where Don and his friends play softball.

HEALTH TERMS

peer pressure

manipulation

refusal skills

passive

aggressive

assertive

HEALTH CONCEPTS

- Peer pressure is the control and influence people your age can have over you.
- Peer pressure can have either a positive or negative influence on your actions and behaviors.
- Learning to resist negative peer pressure is an important skill.
- Refusal skills are ways of saying no to negative peer influence.

Peer Pressure

Your peers can have a great impact on what you think, feel, say, and do. They may exert direct or indirect **peer pressure**, *the control and influence people your age may have over you.* Peer pressure can occur in many kinds of relationships. The way you respond to peer pressure can have a great impact on the decisions you make and, in turn, your total health.

Kendra's and Don's stories in the opening each illustrate a positive response to peer pressure. Maybe you have felt inspired by a good example set by someone your age. Maybe you have been a positive **role model** yourself. Influencing peers to take part in a positive act or worthwhile cause is a healthful way of influencing others. It can be contagious.

Positive peer pressure is not limited to following or setting good examples of what to do. It can also provide examples of *what not to do.* A teen whose friends do not use alcohol or other drugs may be positively influenced to follow their example.

Negative Peer Influence

Sometimes, peers may pressure others to accept beliefs or take part in a behavior that has a negative consequence. A teen, for example, may try to influence a date or friend to stay out past curfew. A clique or club may have an "initiation" for would-be members that includes stealing or taking part in another crime or wrongful act.

Manipulation

One way that people exert peer pressure over others is through **manipulation.** This is *a sneaky or dishonest way to control or influence others.* A person who manipulates another does so to get what he or she wants without respect for the well-being of the person being manipulated.

h⊙t link

role model For more on the importance of positive role models and other protective factors that influence the health of the community, see Chapter 1, page 20.

◄ *A teen may feel pressured or outnumbered when others try to exert pressure to do something that goes against his or her values.*

ACTIVITY *Name some reasons you should stand up to negative peer pressure.*

Types of Manipulation

- mocking or teasing the person in mean or hurtful ways.
- bargaining, or offering to make a deal to get what one wants.
- bribing, or promising money or favors if the person will do what another asks of him or her.
- using guilt trips to get desired results.
- making threats, or using words that show a person intends to use violence or some other negative means to get his or her way.
- using blackmail, or threatening to reveal some damaging information if the person does not conform.
- using flattery or undeserved praise to influence another person.

Responding to Negative Peer Pressure

Throughout your life, people will make many requests and demands of you. Some of these will call for you to respond with a yes, others with a firm and unapologetic no. How you respond can directly affect your mental, social, or physical health—even your life. If you are in a group situation, submitting to peer pressure can sometimes make a conflict worse. For instance, if two people are about to fight, having others around to spur them on will probably increase the chances the fight will take place. You need to find ways to avoid becoming a part of the problem.

Peer pressure to take part in a potentially harmful or unsafe activity can be intense. If a friend is applying the pressure, you may have concerns about hurting the person's feelings or jeopardizing the relationship. If several people are exerting the pressure, you may worry that you will appear "uncool" or be talked about later. There are three ways in which you can respond to negative peer pressure.

- **The Passive Way.** Being **passive** means *giving up, giving in, or backing down without standing up for your own rights and needs.* People who are passive may think that they are making friends by going along with peer pressure. In fact, however, they may be viewed by their peers as pushovers and not worthy of much respect.

Building Health Skills

Resisting Peer Pressure

WHEN YOU FEEL pressure to take part in a behavior that goes against your values and ideals, such as experimenting with alcohol or driving fast, it is important to stand your ground. Your health, safety, and future hang in the balance. Ask yourself the following questions:

1. **What risks does this behavior carry?** This can help you identify the price you potentially stand to pay if you go along with the behavior. If you aren't aware of the risks, you have another valid reason for resisting.

2. **What personal or family values and goals would be compromised by engaging in this behavior?** Consider your plans, dreams, and ambitions, and how these might be altered. Don't forget to include such items as the risk of losing the respect of people who know or care for you.

3. **What is the source of the pressure?** Is the group one whose opinions and views you truly respect and trust? Is the pressure really coming from inside yourself? Keep in mind also that some teens boast about taking risks just to sound grown up. Maybe the simple fact is that "no one is doing it."

Dealing with School Bullies

Bullies have been around for decades—probably long before your grandparents were in school. What is the difference between bullies now and then? Bullying today has become a serious problem and sometimes escalates into violence. Some bullies carry weapons, and some of their victims feel the need to arm themselves in self-defense.

Experts estimate that one in ten teens is regularly bullied at some time during the school year. Bullying is often verbal, such as teasing or taunting, but it can also be physical. Bullies tend to pick on people who are different from them. Their victims might be taller or shorter than other classmates or heavier or thinner than average. They might wear glasses or braces. Sometimes bullies harass people from a different ethnic group or religious faith.

Bullies put down other people to boost their own self-esteem. By mocking or teasing others, they are trying to manipulate them and provoke a reaction. The best way to deal with bullies, then, is to simply ignore them. Eventually, they usually lose interest when they get no response to their taunts. If you are concerned about your health or safety, however, talk to a parent or other trusted adult. If you see someone else being harassed, resist peer pressure to laugh or join in. Think about how you would feel if you were the bully's target.

1. Why do you think bullying is a more serious problem now than it was years ago? What changes in society might have contributed to this problem?

2. Talk with a parent, grandparent, or other adult about bullies. Did they ever encounter bullies when they went to school? How did people deal with them?

■ **The Aggressive Way.** Being **aggressive** means being *overly forceful, pushy, hostile, or otherwise attacking in approach.* The aggressive approach to saying no might involve punching, yelling, shouting insults, or displaying other kinds of physical or verbal force. The aggressive way violates the rights of others. Though aggressive people may think they will get their way and perhaps be seen as powerful and popular, their approach usually backfires. In the long run, people either stay away from aggressors or jump in and fight back. Either reaction can hurt aggressive people emotionally and physically.

■ **The Assertive Way.** Being **assertive** means *standing up for your own rights, in firm but positive ways.* You state your position, acknowledge the rights of the other individual, then stand your ground. You do not bully or back away. You directly and honestly state your case and show that you mean what you say. Assertive people often become role models for other teens. Teens respect people who have the personal power to be true to who they really are. Assertive refusal doesn't come naturally or easily for many people. Nevertheless, it is a skill worth acquiring.

Assertive Refusal

The assertive way is often the best way to deal with negative peer influence. By learning and practicing **refusal skills,** *techniques and strategies that help you say no effectively when faced with something that you do not want to do or is against your values,* you will be prepared when a high pressure situation comes along. These skills will help you now, and later in life as well. Refusal skills involve a three-step process:

1. **State your position simply but firmly.** All you need to say is "No, I don't want to." Practice saying no in front of a mirror. Make your "no" sound like you really mean it. Then, give an honest reason why you don't want to participate. This doesn't need to be more than saying, "It goes against my values." You don't need to use phony excuses or invent reasons.

2. **Suggest alternatives to the behavior being proposed.** If a friend suggests using a parent's car without permission, recommend another form of transportation, such as, "Let's go ride our skateboards in the park instead." By offering an alternative, you give your friend a chance to continue being with you in a

Making Responsible
Decisions

Using Refusal Skills

Ever since Brandy moved to Elm City, Anne has been her closest friend. This morning when Brandy arrived at school, Anne was waiting for her on the steps, looking worried. "I just heard that we're having a pop quiz in history this afternoon," Anne said. "You've got to be a pal and let me look over your shoulder. History just isn't my subject." Brandy likes Anne. Yet, she knows that cheating is wrong. Besides, she could get into trouble herself if she goes along with Anne's idea and the teacher finds out. What should Brandy do?

What Would You Do?

Apply the six steps of the decision-making process to Brandy's problem.

1. **State the situation.**
2. **List the options.**
3. **Weigh the possible outcomes.**
4. **Consider your values.**
5. **Make a decision and act.**
6. **Evaluate the decision.**

comfortable way. Make sure your suggestion takes you away from the dangerous situation. For example, if a friend says it would be fun trying to take something from a store without paying for it, gently but firmly suggest another activity. Say, something like, "Let's go over to the video arcade."

3. **Back up your words with actions.** If your friend continues to try to persuade you to join in, make it clear that your no means no. Use strong body language and maintain eye contact. If that doesn't work, just leave. Simply say, "I'm going home." You will not be able to persuade every friend to stop pressuring you. In those cases, you may need to drop the friendship and seek another circle of friends. At the very least, you will need to speak with the person about how uncomfortable you felt and how such pressure in the future may jeopardize the relationship.

▲ *Being assertive doesn't always come easily.*

ACTIVITY *Name two things this girl can do to be assertive.*

Review

Reviewing Facts and Vocabulary

1. Give examples of both negative and positive peer pressure.
2. What is *manipulation* and how does it relate to peer pressure?
3. How does being aggressive differ from being assertive?

Thinking Critically

4. ***Analyzing.*** "If you don't do the dishes for me," Gwen tells her sister, "I'll tell Mom and Dad that you weren't really at Luisa's house last night." What type of manipulation is this?

Applying Health Skills

5. ***In Your Home and School.*** Make a two-column chart on a page in your private Health Journal. In the first column, list any incidents of negative peer influence you have experienced, explaining how you handled the situation. In the second column, identify examples of positive influence you have experienced, explaining how the experience made you feel.

Health Skills Activities

Activity 1 — Refuse to Be Used

Having a healthy dating relationship means having control over your own actions and emotions. Have you ever felt pressure in a dating situation? Refusal skills can help you resist negative peer pressure.

Directions

1. In a group, think of a slogan or line that could be the basis of a campaign for using effective refusal skills. This might be a variation on the STOP approach explained by your teacher, or it might be a slogan you create.
2. Transfer your idea to a sheet of poster board. The poster may be illustrated with original art, photos, or symbols.
3. Share and compare your group's idea with those of other groups. Make changes as needed.
4. Complete your poster using colored markers. Posters can be displayed in the hallways of your school.

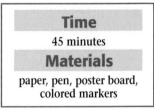

Time
45 minutes
Materials
paper, pen, poster board, colored markers

Self-Assessment

✓ Created a campaign for assertive refusal of negative peer pressure.
✓ Expressed this message in words and/or pictures.

Activity 2 — Healthful Decisions

Peer pressure can occur in many kinds of relationships. The way you respond to peer pressure can have a great impact on the decisions you make and, in turn, your total health.

Directions

1. Write a short fictional story about a teen who found him- or herself being pressured by a peer to engage in an unhealthful activity.
2. Write in the third person (*he, she, the girl, the boy*). Describe how the teen felt.
3. In your story, detail exactly what refusal techniques the teen used to resist peer pressure.
4. At the end of your story, explain how the teen benefited as a result of avoiding a high-risk situation.

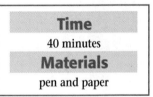

Time
40 minutes
Materials
pen and paper

Self-Assessment

✓ Identified at least one effective refusal skill.
✓ Demonstrated positive outcome of teen's decision at the end of the story.

Violence in Relationships

When you think of violence, you might think of two people who just don't like each other. However, many conflicts arise between people who think of themselves as friends or partners. Strong feelings, even strong feelings of affection and caring, can lead to violence if they are poorly managed. For example, friendly concern can turn to angry jealousy.

Domestic violence takes place in a home situation or between members of a couple. Many people are aware of the seriousness of domestic violence among adults, but the problem affects teens, too. Among high school students, approximately 1 in 10 has experienced physical violence in a dating relationship. An innovative program in San Jose, California, is helping teens recognize the warning signs and causes of domestic violence.

Play the Video

Think About It

- What is the goal of the Next Door program? Discuss your thoughts about the program's ability to affectively achieve its goals.
- How does the program get its message to teen audiences?
- Can you think of other ways to help teens identify signs and address domestic violence?

Using Health Terms

On a separate sheet of paper, write the term that best matches each definition below.

LESSON 1

1. Exaggerated and oversimplified belief about an entire group of people, such as an ethnic group, religious group, or a certain gender.
2. Exaggerated feelings of passion for another person.
3. Small, narrow circle of friends, usually with similar backgrounds or tastes, that excludes people they view as outsiders.
4. Relationship with a member of the opposite gender in which there is affection, but no sexual activity.
5. Negative feeling toward someone or something that is based not on experience but, rather, on stereotypes.

LESSON 2

6. Overly forceful, pushy, hostile, or otherwise attacking in approach.
7. Sneaky or dishonest way to control or influence others.
8. Control and influence people your age may have over you.
9. Techniques and strategies that help you say no effectively when faced with something that you do not want to do or that goes against your values.
10. Giving up, giving in, or backing down without standing up for your own rights and needs.
11. Standing up for your own rights, in firm but positive ways.

Recalling the Facts

Using complete sentences, answer the following questions.

LESSON 1

1. Why do peers take on a greater importance during the teen years?
2. How do friendships add to total health?
3. Which type of friend are you most likely to confide in when you have a problem?
4. Stereotypes can lead to what kind of behavior?
5. Name two reasons why going out as a couple may not be the best choice for a teenager.
6. Explain why teens often stay in relationships even though they want to get out of the relationship.

LESSON 2

7. Why do teens sometimes have difficulty saying no to peer pressure?
8. Give three examples of manipulation.
9. Give four examples of positive peer pressure.
10. Which of the three ways of responding to negative peer pressure is most likely to result in a fight?
11. If a teen has already said no verbally and with strong body language, and a peer continues to try and persuade him or her to do something he or she doesn't want to do, what should the teen do?

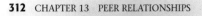

Thinking Critically

LESSON 1

1. **Comparing and Contrasting.** Jessica refers to Steven as her boyfriend, talks about him constantly, and claims to be in love with him, even though they are not actually dating. Explain to Jessica that she is experiencing an infatuation.

2. **Analyzing.** Ted thinks he would like to begin dating, but he is too shy to ask a girl out. Explain what he can do to become more comfortable around girls.

LESSON 2

3. **Comparing and Contrasting.** Darrin wants to be a friend of Sammy, but Sammy never seems to notice him. Sammy's friends spend lots of time on their computers, so Darrin begins to spend time learning how to use the Internet. Explain whether Darrin's actions are the result of direct or indirect peer pressure. Do you see this as positive or negative peer influence, and why?

Making the Connection

1. **Science.** The physical attraction to others that many people begin to experience during the teen years is largely the result of chemicals called *pheromones*. Learn more about pheromones and the complex ways they are used by social insects to communicate and send messages. Share your findings in a short report.

2. **Social Studies.** Investigate laws or efforts to create curfews in your own community. If curfews already exist, what are the terms and how effective have they been as a deterrent to teen crime? If not, what arguments were put forth by those opposed to them? Express what you have learned in a brief written report.

BEYOND THE CLASSROOM

PARENTAL INVOLVEMENT Ask a parent or adult in your home about someone with whom he or she has a long-standing relationship. Find out what the characteristics of this relationship are, and compare these with what you look for in relationships.

COMMUNITY INVOLVEMENT Interview someone in your community who lived there during the 1950s or 1960s to find out how the teen experience has changed over the years. Ask questions such as the following: What were your concerns then? Who were your role models? What kinds of problems, if any, did the neighborhood face? How has the neighborhood changed? How have teenagers changed? What resources are available now that weren't available then? Present your findings in an oral report.

SCHOOL-TO-CAREER

Interpersonal. Speak with a law enforcement official in your community who deals with hate crimes—offenses against an individual or group that are a direct or indirect result of prejudice. Ask about interpersonal skills, such as compassion, that a person would need to pursue a career in this particular area. Share your findings with the class.

CHAPTER 14

Resolving Conflicts and Preventing Violence

HEALTH Online

CONFLICT RESOLUTION

School Safety Programs are spreading across the country. Check out steps being taken to prevent violence and provide safe environments for students across the country. Read the Health Update at health.glencoe.com.

> **That message of tolerance—that message to everyone to accept and appreciate and celebrate our diversity as part of human existence—is going to be very important.**
>
> —KOFI ANNAN
> SECRETARY-GENERAL OF THE UNITED NATIONS,
> OCTOBER, 2001

Quick Write Write down three things you could do or say in a tense situation that would encourage better understanding and avoid a conflict.

Self-Inventory Write the numbers 1–10 on a sheet of paper. Read each statement below and respond by writing *yes*, *no*, or *sometimes* for each item. Write a *yes* only for items that you practice regularly. Save your responses.

1	I can recognize the signs that a conflict exists.
2	I have a good idea of how to face a conflict and when to ignore it.
3	I know several ways to keep a conflict from escalating.
4	If I see a fight building, I refuse to participate and encourage others to refuse as well.
5	When someone angers me, I know how to communicate my feelings in a way that doesn't make matters worse.
6	If I have a conflict I can't resolve on my own, I feel comfortable asking for help.
7	I know how to negotiate a conflict so that all parties feel heard and satisfied.
8	I do not use weapons to solve conflicts.
9	I do not use alcohol or drugs; I know these can cause conflicts or make them worse.
10	I do not allow others to abuse me in any way.

Follow-up After completing the chapter, retake this self-inventory. Pick two items that you need to work on and set a goal to improve your health behaviors.

The Nature of Conflict

The front-page headline of today's newspaper is about growing tensions between countries. The sports page tells of a brawl at last night's hockey game, while the "metro" section contains details of an argument between a driver and a pedestrian. Despite their differences, these stories have something in common. All are about conflict.

HEALTH TERMS

conflict

interpersonal conflicts

internal conflicts

escalate

HEALTH CONCEPTS

- Conflict is a normal part of life.
- There are common physical and emotional signs that indicate a conflict is building.
- There are times when it is wise to ignore a conflict and times when it is not.
- When conflicts are handled in a violent way, they lead to more problems.

Types of Conflict

Conflict is *any disagreement, struggle, or fight.* Conflicts are a normal part of life. Whenever your wants, needs, wishes, demands, values, or beliefs clash with someone else's, a conflict is almost certain to arise. There are two major types of conflicts—*interpersonal conflicts* and *internal conflicts.*

- **Interpersonal conflicts** are *disagreements between groups of any size, from two people to entire nations.* Conflicts of this type can start over minor issues, like the disagreement between the teens in the chapter-opening story. They can also affect the lives of entire populations, such as a dispute over whether to spend community funds to build low-income housing.

- **Internal conflicts** are *struggles within yourself.* Such conflicts, which can be common in the teen years, often involve mixed emotions. For example, a teen casting the lead role for a class play might feel "torn" between feelings of loyalty to a close friend auditioning for the part and a responsibility to select the best actor. Sometimes, internal conflicts arise over what might appear to be a good choice at the moment but what may not be best for you in the long run. In such cases, knowing how to use an effective **decision-making model** can ease you safely through the conflict with your health and self-esteem intact.

Whatever the nature of a conflict, learning to recognize conflicts when they occur, being aware of how conflicts build, and knowing how to deal with them effectively are skills that have a direct and lasting impact on your total health and well-being.

How Conflicts Build

Conflicts can begin in many ways and for many different reasons. Among these are power, property, authority, jealousy, loyalty, space, and territory. Some conflicts start innocently, such as when one person accidentally bumps another's lunch tray. Others are the result of an act or remark that provokes another person—a wet towel snapped in a locker room, for example, or a racial slur. Either way, a "fuse" is ignited.

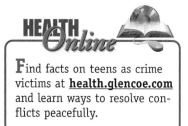

HEALTH *Online*

Find facts on teens as crime victims at **health.glencoe.com** and learn ways to resolve conflicts peacefully.

h t link

decision-making model For more information on how to make informed, healthful decisions, see Chapter 2, page 35.

connections   Social Studies

Warring Parties

Some conflicts are *chronic*, or ongoing, as when two siblings fight night after night over the TV remote control. One of the most dangerous types of chronic conflict is a *feud*, an ongoing state of hostility between people or groups that involves revenge or violent attacks. Warfare between rival gangs is one example of feuding that sometimes turns fatal. Some feuds begin over a simple misunderstanding. However, the root cause is often a need to prove something or to destroy or harm in order to feel good about oneself. For a gang member, just being in the wrong place at the wrong time is often enough to provoke a battle.

1. Using on-line or print resources, learn about the issues of feuds and gang violence in the United States. What type of injuries and fatalities have occurred from inter-gang conflicts?

2. What various steps have elected officials, law enforcement personnel, and social workers taken to help stop these senseless crimes? What recommendations can you make?

At this point, one or both parties can choose to walk away and allow the situation to drop. All too often, however, a conflict is permitted to **escalate**, or *grow into a situation that is unhealthful and even unsafe to all parties concerned.* This may result from a lack of communication, a misunderstanding, or gossip.

Learning to identify the warning signs that a conflict is brewing can help you "put out the fire" before it rages out of control. Some of the warning signs that conflict is building inside of you are physical. Others are emotional.

Warning Signs

PHYSICAL	EMOTIONAL
a knot in the stomach	feeling concerned
faster heart rate	getting defensive
a lump in the throat	wanting to cry
cold or sweating palms	wanting to lash out
a sudden surge of energy	wanting to escape
confrontational—or "fighting"—body language, such as clenching your fists or gritting your teeth	not feeling valued

Recognizing Conflict

Although conflict is an unavoidable part of life, there are healthful and unhealthful ways of responding to it. The first step is to decide whether the problem is something that really deserves your time and energy. You can identify the problem and its source by asking yourself the following questions:

- What is *really* bothering me and why?
- Is this a minor, a chronic, or a major problem?

➤ *Conflicts are often over territory, space, property, and power.*

ACTIVITY *Recall one recent conflict you witnessed that involved two teens and territory, space, or property.*

- What is triggering the conflict?
- Are there hurt feelings or other unexplored emotions lurking beneath my anger?
- Have anyone's rights been violated?
- What is my part in the problem?
- Does this conflict involve my personal values or beliefs?
- What is at stake here?

Responding to Conflict

When a conflict arises, you can either face it or ignore it. In deciding on which course of action to take, the two most important points to remember are the following: (1) Your personal health and safety should be your primary concern; (2) walking away from a volatile or dangerous situation is a healthful, mature choice—not a sign of being a coward.

Sometimes teens jump into conflicts too lightly. They think that doing so may provide a thrill or prove to those around them that they are tough, cool, or unafraid. These same teens may also believe, wrongly, that getting out of a conflict is as easy as getting in. Unfortunately, once you become embroiled in a real-life conflict, you may find that there is no turning back.

LESSON 1 *Review*

Reviewing Facts and Vocabulary

1. What is a conflict?
2. Give an original example of an interpersonal conflict and another of an internal conflict.
3. Name three physical and three emotional warning signs that a conflict may be building.

Thinking Critically

4. *Synthesizing.* Think about the ways in which a conflict can be positive. Find a newspaper or magazine article that supports this concept by summarizing the beneficial results that came directly and indirectly out of a conflict.
5. *Analyzing.* Make a chart with two columns. In the first column, list a minor, a chronic, and a major conflict in your life. In the second column, write a peaceful solution for each conflict.

6. *Comparing and Contrasting.* Compare and contrast some ways you might recognize that a conflict is brewing with different ways you can respond to the conflict.

Applying Health Skills

7. *In Your Home.* Keep a Conflict Log for a week in which you "track" and record one major or chronic conflict in your life. Pay attention to the amount of time the conflict occupies your thoughts and what emotions surround each. Write down how this conflict seems to affect your health, your eating and sleeping habits, and your emotional state. As the week goes on, brainstorm ways to face and resolve this conflict, using information provided in this chapter.

Conflict Resolution Skills

Although daily life can be full of conflicts, you don't have to think of each conflict as a battle. Instead, think of life's conflicts as opportunities to demonstrate your self-respect and integrity. During conflicts, you can practice your communication and decision-making skills.

HEALTH TERMS

conflict resolution

tolerance

negotiation

mediation

peer mediators

confidentiality

HEALTH CONCEPTS

- There are healthful and unhealthful ways to resolve conflicts.
- Good communication skills and the willingness to compromise are essential to resolving any conflict in a healthful way.
- Sometimes a conflict is so difficult that outside assistance is needed.
- People can resolve their conflicts when there is mutual respect, open-mindedness, and acceptance of other people's differences.

Conflict Resolution

When you find yourself in a conflict that is unavoidable or where you think something important is at stake, conflict resolution skills can help. **Conflict resolution** is *the process of ending a conflict by cooperating and problem solving together.* Conflict resolution involves many different interpersonal skills, several of which—communication, cooperation, and compromise—are discussed in Chapter 11. In addition to these Three C's, resolving conflict in a nonviolent way involves the following Three R's—*respect, rights,* and *responsibility.*

- **Respect.** Showing respect is an essential element in resolving conflicts in positive ways. When you show respect for others, you value each one as an individual. You also make it more likely that others will show you respect in return. People who respect others are more likely to listen with an open mind, consider the other person's views and feelings, and honor the basic values of the individual.

- **Rights.** Having respect for others also means not violating other people's basic rights. People need to remember that no one owns anyone else. No one has the right to control or harm another person or destroy another person's property. Another basic right to consider is the right to privacy. Going into other people's lockers or reading their private journals, which is a direct violation of this right, can lead to ugly, even violent, conflicts.

- **Responsibility.** With rights come responsibilities. Take responsibility for your actions. When a conflict develops, do not just blame the other person. Take a look at what your part in the conflict may be. Make responsible decisions that respect both the rights and the health of all parties. Your goal should be that any action you take is an effort to help resolve the conflict and to avoid being hurtful to you or any other human being.

Tolerance

Tolerance is important in preventing conflict and promoting peace. **Tolerance** includes *accepting others' differences and allowing them to be who they are without expressing disapproval.* People may have views and ideals that are different from your own. When people practice tolerance of different viewpoints or ideas, there are fewer conflicts.

Did You Know?

➤ Conflict resolution has become such an important skill that dozens of universities throughout the country and world now offer programs and advanced degrees in conflict analysis and resolution.

➤ The Society for Professionals in Dispute Resolutions—an organization of conflict resolution professionals—has nearly 10,000 members.

➤ People who work in conflict resolution fields include teachers, lawyers, psychologists, and individuals from a host of other professions.

◄ *Learning about others' cultural backgrounds can enrich your own life and make it more interesting.*

ACTIVITY *Make plans to learn about a culture different from your own from someone in your school or neighborhood.*

Building Health Skills

Conflict Resolution: Steps to Take When Negotiating

LIKE COMMUNICATION, decision making, and other life skills you have learned about, the skill of negotiation is one that takes practice. The steps to effective negotiation include the following:

1. **Choose a time and place conducive to working out problems.** Avoid meeting with the other person when you are feeling rushed or impatient. Choose a place that is not noisy or full of distractions.

2. **Work together at a solution.** Instead of approaching the other person as your enemy, suggest politely that you work together to brainstorm a solution.

3. **Keep an open mind.** Remember that every story has two sides. Listen carefully to what the other person has to say.

4. **Be flexible.** Be willing to bend. Meet the other person halfway.

5. **Take responsibility for your actions and role in the conflict.** There is no shame in apologizing if you see that you have unjustly hurt the other person. In fact, the ability and willingness to make amends when you are wrong is a sign that you are maturing into a responsible adult.

6. **Give the person an "out."** Your objective is to resolve your differences, not to prosecute the other person. If he or she seems embarrassed or uncomfortable about a point that is raised, suggest continuing the conversation at a later time.

Negotiation

Whereas some people think that physical fighting is the best way to settle a disagreement, a better approach involves the skill of **negotiation.** This is *a process in which compromise is used to reach agreement.* Negotiation involves talking, listening, considering the other person's point of view, compromising if necessary, and coming up with a plan of working together to solve the conflict. When two parties negotiate, each does not blame the other. Instead, they talk about what is needed to solve the problem at hand. *Before* you negotiate you should:

- Make sure that the issue is important to you.
- Check your facts. Maybe the disagreement is based on something that isn't even true.
- Remind yourself that your goal is to find a solution, not to fight or prove who is "in control."
- Rehearse what you will say, even if you have to script it out in advance.

Mediation

Sometimes during a conflict, the two parties reach a point where it may be time for **mediation.** This is *a process in which specially trained people help others to resolve their conflicts peacefully.*

Today, many schools are offering peer mediation programs. In these programs, **peer mediators,** *students trained to help other students in conflict find fair ways to settle their differences,* help other teens find solutions to the problem.

Peer mediation involves the use of problem-solving, communication, and negotiating skills. Schools with peer mediation programs report fewer fights, more cooperation, and less overall violence.

Effective Mediation

Mediation has well-defined ground rules. It is up to the mediator to set these rules and to describe them to both sides. The session should be held in a neutral location such as a classroom. Peer mediators must maintain strict **confidentiality**—*respecting the privacy of both parties and keeping details secret.* The mediator begins by asking each person, in turn, to describe the disagreement. The mediator next summarizes each side, asking for clarification of any points that are inaccurate. Each side is then invited to talk to the other with the mediator's supervision. The mediator may then ask the parties to sign an agreement to work out the problem within a certain time frame.

▲ *When teens work together for the common good, the rewards can be great.*

ACTIVITY *Identify three other life skills that play an essential role in conflict resolution. Give an example of how each could be used to resolve a conflict between two teens.*

LESSON 2 *Review*

Reviewing Facts and Vocabulary

1. Define the term *negotiation,* and describe how this skill is used to resolve conflicts nonviolently.
2. Explain the value of peer mediation in conflicts involving teens.
3. Summarize what takes place in a mediation session.

Thinking Critically

4. ***Analyzing.*** Think about some compromises that you might not be willing to make. In what kinds of situations should a compromise *not* play a part? Summarize the kinds of issues or conflicts that are not negotiable for you.

5. ***Evaluating.*** Read the following statement: *You must be the change you wish to see in the world.* Explain what these words mean to you and how they relate to the idea of responsibility.

Applying Health Skills

6. ***In Your Home.*** Keep a Relationship Conflict Journal for a week, recording conflicts that occur between you and other family members. Observe and write down what the conflicts are about, what triggers them, how they are resolved, and what factors made the conflicts better or worse. See if you can find any patterns to these conflicts and their resolutions.

Strategies for Avoiding Violence

When conflicts are permitted to escalate or go unresolved, the risk of violence increases. **Violence** is *the use of physical force to injure or abuse another person or persons.* In addition to physical harm, acts of violence can leave victims with deep emotional scars.

HEALTH TERMS

violence

homicide

assailant

random violence

aggravated assault

carjackings

HEALTH CONCEPTS

- Teens are increasingly the people who commit violent crimes as well as the victims of these crimes.
- Crimes are more random, brutal, and remorseless today than in the past.
- New measures are being taken across the nation to stop violence in schools and communities.
- Your efforts can help to make the world a safer, healthier place.

h⋅t link

prejudice For more information on prejudice and its dangers, see Chapter 13, page 300.

Violence in Society

As a society, the United States is no stranger to violence. According to the Centers for Disease Control and Prevention, over 6,000 young people ages 15–24 become victims of homicide each year. This amounts to an average of 18 youth homicide victims per day in the United States. In fact, **homicide**—*the willful killing of one human being by another*—is the second leading cause of death for persons 15 to 24 years of age. For every violent death, moreover, there are at least an estimated 100 nonfatal injuries caused by violence.

Violence happens for many different reasons. Some acts of violence are unsuccessful efforts to resolve a conflict. In many such acts, the victim knows his or her assailant. An **assailant** is *a person who commits a violent act against another.* Other acts of violence are crimes of hate, stemming from **prejudice**—negative feelings toward an individual based not on experience but on misguided generalizations about race, ethnicity, or gender. Still other violent crimes arise out of frustration or anger over poverty or lack of opportunity. Usually, these crimes occur as robberies or thefts, though sometimes people are injured or killed in the process.

An especially distressing type of violence that has emerged in recent decades is **random violence**, *violence committed for no particular reason.* Such crimes are often committed against an innocent bystander or other person who happens to be nearby at the time. One segment of the population frequently targeted for acts of random violence is the homeless.

Violence and Teens

Teens are another group that has become involved increasingly in violent acts. Nationwide, 14.8 percent of students had been in a fight on school property one or more times in 1996. Arrest rates for rape, robbery, and **aggravated assault**—*unlawful attack with an intent to hurt or kill*—are significantly higher among young people 15 to 34 years of age than among all other age groups.

Teen violence is on the rise not only on the streets but also in schools. Every day in the United States, some 16,000 crimes take place in or near schools. There are reports of fights, attacks, shootings, and gang involvement in classrooms, restrooms, hallways, locker rooms, and on school grounds. In such stressful environments, students find it difficult to learn, and teachers find it hard to teach.

◀ *Many schools have instituted new policies, such as installing metal detectors, to protect students and make them feel safe.*

ACTIVITY *In the local newspaper, find a news story that centers on an act of violence. Identify the nature of the violence. Who was the victim? Who was the assailant?*

Teens Making a Difference

...TOLERANCE...RESPONSIBILITY ...COURAGE

Nihad, age 18, is committed to the values of peace, justice, and tolerance. A senior in high school, his goal is to promote nonviolence both in his own life and in the lives of other teens around the globe. These issues are particularly close to his heart because he grew up in Bosnia, in Eastern Europe, during wartime. Nihad has seen firsthand the terrible consequences of prejudice, intolerance, and violence.

"When I was ten, the war started and people started calling me names," he begins. "I felt prejudice. Living through the war and witnessing all of the massacres and slaughtering made me hate other groups. After the war, though, when I came here, I started to realize that not all people are responsible for what happened there. I saw that people could live in harmony here, and that made me realize that I should not despise and hate people just because they belong to certain groups. Every human being deserves basic respect."

RETURNING TO HIS ROOTS Last summer Nihad went back to Bosnia with an international organization for peace to do volunteer work. "The goal of the group is to get different nationalities and cultures who are at war or in conflict to find peaceful means to get along. When we got there, we organized an English-speaking school (see photo). We taught kids English as a second language. We also helped people returning to their homeland whose houses had been destroyed. The first step for us was to help to clean up all of the ruins and debris so they could rebuild."

BUILDING PEACE, BUILDING CHARACTER "I took a class in Peace and Justice at my school here," he says, "and I gave a presentation about Bosnia and told my story. We did group discussions with Bosnian students. I belong to the International Student Forum, a school club that meets to talk about cultural differences and alleviate problems. I would like to be an ambassador...I have learned a lot about peace and conflict resolution. I believe that people should never take up arms to resolve any conflict because there is always an alternative peaceful way to resolve any kind of issue. Whether personally, culturally, or internationally, you can resolve differences without violence."

NIHAD'S STORY

1. In what ways would you consider Nihad's dedication to the values of peace, justice, and tolerance balanced in all areas of his life?
2. What other values does he demonstrate through his words and actions?

YOUR STORY

1. What steps can you take to promote conflict resolution in your own family, friendships, school, and community?
2. What safe steps can you take to help others support the values of non-violence and greater tolerance for others?

Violence Prevention and Intervention

You have probably heard or read many news stories about violence in schools and communities. Homicides, hate crimes, school shootings, and gang activities seem to make the nightly news on a regular basis. With these troubling reports, you might be worried about your own safety. In truth, though, you probably don't need to be. Statistically, schools are among the safest places in the United States. In addition, schools and communities are committing a great deal of time and resources to enhance safety and prevent violence.

Recognizing that academic failure is a risk factor for violent behavior, many schools are making changes to help students improve academic performance. For example, some schools have decreased class sizes and improved school facilities. Many schools teach conflict resolution and anger management skills, and some even offer antiviolence workshops. For increased safety, some schools not only provide metal detectors and security guards, but also offer behavioral counseling and monitoring.

Many communities also have developed strategies for preventing violence and crime. Some have neighborhood watch programs or citizen patrols, in which residents watch for and report suspicious activities. In some communities, mentoring programs provide opportunities for adult mentors to act as role models for young people. Other communities have established after-school recreation programs to teach valuable skills to at-risk students.

1. Why do you think academic failure is a risk factor for violent behavior? What might be some other risk factors?

2. Find out what violence prevention measures are being taken in your school or community.

As a reaction to this growing problem, many schools have taken preventive measures. Some have installed metal detectors to stop students from bringing guns and knives into schools. Other schools conduct physical searches or use dogs capable of sniffing out drugs and weapons.

Factors Affecting Violence

Violence, especially among teens, is a complex issue that is affected by many different factors. These include availability of weapons, territoriality, the media, and substance abuse.

AVAILABILITY OF WEAPONS

According to the CDC's 2000 *Youth Risk Behavior Survey,* nearly 7.7 percent of students have been threatened or injured with a weapon on school property. In addition to conventional weapons (such as handguns, knives, and clubs), newer "state-of-the-art" weapons—including so-called assault rifles—are finding their way into the hands of teens, particularly those with gang affiliations. Some teens also report that access to information about where to get weapons is easier than ever to come by.

TERRITORIALITY

Some teens, without a true sense of personal power or control in their lives, may turn to claiming areas not their own in an attempt to look or feel important and in control. Members of gangs may stake out their "turf" or territory, often by "tagging"—spray-painting a gang's logo or a member's initials on public property that they feel belongs to the group. Such rivalries are often deadly and may center on drug deals and drug money.

THE MEDIA

By the age of 18, the average teen has seen 22,000 hours of TV and witnessed some 200,000 acts of violence, real or staged, including 16,000 murders. In addition to TV, song lyrics, videos, movies, and video games carry images of or messages about violence.

What effect does violence in the media have on young people? Some critics feel that this media exposure provides a "recipe" for violence among young people. These critics point to a rise in the number of **carjackings**—*hijacking or stealing a car by force*—after reports of this crime were first broadcast in the early 1990s. Others insist that young viewers become desensitized, or emotionally indifferent, to acts of brutality when such images are constantly displayed.

SUBSTANCE ABUSE

A rise in recent years in abuse of alcohol and other drugs has led to a corresponding increase in violent crime. Some of these crimes, as noted earlier, are related to the sale of drugs and have even added a new term—*drive-by shooting*—to the vocabulary of violence. Other crimes related to substance abuse are committed by drug users who rob or steal to pay for their habit. Drugs and alcohol also interfere with a person's ability to reason and make healthful decisions. These substances can exaggerate what a person is feeling and greatly increase the chances that emotions such as anger and jealousy will be blown out of proportion, turning a simple argument into a violent, and potentially deadly, situation.

Across the country, Americans are reclaiming their neighborhoods, working to make them safer.

ACTIVITY *Name three steps that you and your classmates can take to make your school a safer place.*

Stopping and Preventing Violence

More and more communities across the nation are working hard to prevent violence and help their young people find healthy ways to release their energy and avoid becoming either the assailants or victims of violent crimes. There are academic after-school programs, sports and camping programs, even programs in video production and the arts to keep young people off the streets and give them useful skills and meaningful activities for life. Businesses are doing their part by funding programs and providing internships for teens who are "at risk" of violence.

What You Can Do

What can you as a responsible member of your community do to help curtail the spread of violence? The following are some practical tips:

- Avoid guns and alcohol and other drugs.
- Resist becoming a member of a gang.
- Learn and practice the skills of communication and conflict resolution, both of which can help keep your **emotions** from erupting into anger.
- Work at building your self-esteem. People who feel good about themselves seldom need to lash out at others.
- Limit your exposure to media that promote and glamorize violence and prejudice.

You can also work at seeing that younger siblings and other children in your environment follow your positive example in each of these areas. Remember, we all have a stake in curbing and preventing violence.

Did You Know?

According to the Center for Media Education:

➤ American children watch three hours of TV a day, on average.

➤ By age 21, the average viewer will have seen 1 million TV commercials.

➤ Saturday morning children's shows average about 20 to 25 violent acts per hour.

➤ Prime-time shows average five acts of violence per hour.

➤ On average, the American TV-viewing child watches 20,000 ads per year.

hot link

emotions For more information on emotions and strategies for handling them, see Chapter 8, page 197.

LESSON 3 *Review*

Reviewing Facts and Vocabulary

1. Define the terms *violence* and *assailant,* and use both in a paragraph.

2. What are some of the causes of violence, particularly among teens?

Thinking Critically

3. *Analysis.* Write down three goals you would like to achieve by age 25. After each goal, write how using violence could get in the way of achieving it.

4. *Evaluating.* In some communities, parents are required to pay for damage done by their children to community property. Do you think this is a useful policy? Why or why not?

Applying Health Skills

5. *In Your School.* Write a Public Service Announcement teaching teens some ways to prevent getting into fights. Ask if you can deliver this message over the school's public address system.

Preventing Abuse

The health of a relationship is sometimes threatened by violence between individuals in the form of abusive behaviors. It is important for you to be aware of this type of violence and to know that steps can be taken to put a stop to these behaviors.

For some people, domestic violence really hits home.

HEALTH TERMS

abuse

rape

sexual assault

HEALTH CONCEPTS

- Many cases of abuse go unreported, partly due to fear or feelings of futility on the part of the victim.
- Many teens are in abusive relationships.
- All abuse must be stopped, and there is help available to both the abused and the abuser.

Types of Abuse

Abuse is *the intentional physical, emotional, sexual, and/or verbal maltreatment or injury of one person by another.* It can take many forms, and it happens to people from all walks of life. In fact, children, teens, adults, and senior adults are all among the victims of abuse, and it crosses all economic, racial, and ethnic lines. It also happens to both sexes. Whenever or however it occurs, the emotional scars can be devastating.

Physical Abuse

Physical abuse is intentionally inflicting bodily harm or injury on a person. It may include slapping, kicking, biting, burning, shaking, beating, and other kinds of physical violence. Physical abuse is widespread. Consider these facts:

- According to the American Medical Association, between two million and four million women in the United States are assaulted by their partners every year.

- 30 percent of American women report that they have been physically abused at some time in their lives.
- About one-third of the women abused in adulthood grew up in homes where their mothers were abused, and about 20 percent were themselves abused as children.
- According to the Family Violence Prevention Fund, 34 percent of Americans have witnessed an incidence of domestic violence.

Sexual Abuse

Sexual abuse is forcing a person to engage in sexual activities or sexual advances or contact of any kind made by an adult toward a child or teen. Known as the "silent violent epidemic," sexual abuse is a widespread problem in America. Consider these facts:

- According to the American Medical Association, over 61 percent of the victims of sexual abuse are females under the age of 18.
- Males are the victims of sexual assaults approximately 5 percent of the time.
- About 75 percent of all sexual assaults or attacks are committed by people the victim knows.
- Over 700,000 women in the United States are sexually assaulted every year.
- Child sexual abuse is reported up to 80,000 times annually in this country, and unreported cases far exceed this number.

Sexual abuse can take many forms, and it does not always involve sexual intercourse. A **sexual assault** is *any intentional sexual attack against another person.* Battery—or beating—is often used in conjunction with sexual abuse.

Abuse in Dating Relationships

There is a disturbing rise in violence in dating relationships as well as an increase in the reporting of these incidents. Counselors of teens around the country report that physical, sexual, and emotional abuse are not only widespread but are also all too accepted in many teen relationships. Some teens may mistake a boyfriend's or girlfriend's dominant treatment as an expression of caring. They may confuse jealousy with demonstrations of love, when in fact true caring involves kindness, gentleness, and respect, never control or harm.

Rape and Date Rape

Rape, *or sexual intercourse by force,* is a crime of violence. It is also one of the least reported crimes. It is estimated, in fact, that half of all rapes go unreported. Anytime two people have sexual intercourse and one does not agree to the act, it is **rape**. In instances where sexual intercourse is forced upon a spouse it is considered rape.

When a person has been raped, it is critical that the victim report the rape to authorities and go to a hospital for immediate testing and

Did You Know?

➤ In the United States, there is a new victim of sexual assault every 45 seconds.

➤ According to the American Medical Association, surveys indicate that over 87 percent of the victims of sexual assault would rather tell their physicians about the attacks than anyone else.

➤ Fewer than half of all sexual assaults are reported.

➤ Rohypnol and GHB, two illegal substances also referred to as date-rape drugs, are powerful tranquilizers used in sexual crimes. Effects can include muscle relaxation, amnesia, slowing of psychomotor responses, or death.

hot link

rape For more information on rape and help for rape victims, see Chapter 34, page 762.

Make Up or Break Up?

Sara has been dating Don for almost eight months. Lately Don has begun "blowing up" unexpectedly over little things. Last weekend, when Sara arrived ten minutes late for their date, Don began screaming so loudly that people on the street stopped and stared. Sara was humiliated. Later, Don called to apologize, promising it would never happen again. Don has just invited Sara to a party this coming Saturday. Sara wants to go, but she's afraid that the whole scene might happen all over again. What should she do?

What Would You Do?

Apply the six steps of the decision-making process to Sara's problem.

1. **State the situation.**
2. **List the options.**
3. **Weigh the possible outcomes.**
4. **Consider your values.**
5. **Make a decision and act.**
6. **Evaluate the decision.**

evaluation. To prevent further illness or injury and to get physical evidence that might be used to convict the rapist, it is crucial that the rape victim act quickly.

How to Avoid Abuse

One way to lessen your chances of dating violence is to avoid using alcohol and other drugs and refuse to date people who use these substances. It is estimated that 50 percent of those who commit date violence and up to one-third of those who are its victims were using alcohol at the time of the abuse.

When it comes to preventing abuse, remember these Three R's:

- **Recognize.** Learn to recognize abusive behavior in its many forms.
- **Resist.** Should someone use or try to use offensive touching, suggestive talk, or other inappropriate behavior, resist in any way you can. Be assertive.
- **Report.** Get away and tell someone about the incident as soon as you can.

Help for Victims of Abuse

If you become the victim of abuse or rape, remind yourself that you were the victim and that *you* did nothing wrong. The first thing to remember is that physical and sexual abuse and neglect are against

▲ *Counseling can help family members find solutions to their problems.*

the law. The authorities can be brought in to prevent further abuse. Before anyone can help an abused person, however, someone must report the abuse. All states now have laws requiring doctors and other health professionals to report suspected cases of child abuse. In many states, anyone who suspects or knows of an abusive situation is required to report it.

Any teen who is being abused, has been abused, or knows someone who is being abused should talk to a caring, trusted, and knowledgeable adult. This might mean a parent or guardian, the police, a 911 operator, a teacher, coach, clergy member, counselor, physician, or someone at a rape crisis center, battered person's shelter, or hospital emergency room. Only when an abused teen can reach outside the abusive relationship will things start to improve in his or her life.

Counseling is available for both the child and the parents in abusive families. In fact, in all kinds of child abuse, as well as in those cases where teens have abused their parents, families should be brought in for evaluation and counseling.

Just as important as the rehabilitation of abusive parents is the long-range prevention of abuse in society as a whole. Parents and prospective parents need opportunities for learning about family life, child development, and parent-child relationships.

Help for the Abuser

Abuse is a problem not only for the victim but for the abuser, who needs help. Often, abusers were themselves victims of abuse. Such people are in need of intense counseling.

keeping Fit

Stopping Sexual Harassment

Sexual harassment at school is all too common an occurrence, and it doesn't even have to involve physical contact. It can take many forms, including sexual comments, jokes, stares, or looks. Knowing what constitutes sexual harassment may be a first step in stopping it. Sexual harassment includes any of the following criteria:

- making sexual comments or jokes
- writing sexual messages on notes or walls
- spreading sexual rumors
- spying on someone dressing or showering
- pulling off someone's clothes
- exposing body parts
- inappropriate touching

LESSON 4 *Review*

Reviewing Facts and Vocabulary

1. Define the words *abuse* and *sexual assault,* and use them in a single paragraph.
2. What steps should a teen being abused at home take to stop the abuse?

Thinking Critically

3. *Analyzing.* For what reasons do you think teens in abusive relationships too often stay in those relationships, suffering continued abuse?
4. *Evaluating.* Some say that the effects of abuse are worse in the long term than in the short term. Explain in what

way this statement might be true for many victims of abuse.

Applying Health Skills

5. *In Your School.* Invite a social worker, representative from the Department of Public Welfare, or a representative from Parents Anonymous to speak to the class about physical, mental, and sexual abuse, and where and how to get help. Formulate at least three meaningful questions to ask the visitor.

Health Skills Activities

Activity 1 — Resolving Conflicts

Sometimes, role-playing conflicts and their solutions can help prepare you to handle such situations when they actually occur. What strategies do you use to manage conflicts?

Directions

1. With a group, write and role-play two versions of a scene in which two teens are involved in a conflict. One version should show positive negotiating skills ("I" messages and active listening), the other a lack of skills ("you" messages and accusations).
2. After all the groups have performed their skits, discuss as a class how good communication skills can lead to a peaceful resolution of a conflict between teens.
3. Discuss whether the process of role-playing raised consciousness about types of conflict and how to avoid them.

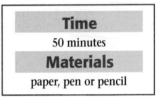

Time
50 minutes
Materials
paper, pen or pencil

Self-Assessment

✓ Demonstrated effective use of "I" messages and active listening skills.
✓ Noted at least two differences in communication that resulted from the use of "I" and "you" messages.

Activity 2 — Dating Do's and Don'ts

With cases of physical abuse, sexual abuse, and date rape on the rise, every teen needs to understand how to ensure personal safety when dating. What principles and behaviors can help make dating safe?

Directions

1. In groups, brainstorm and record guidelines that might be followed to prevent abuse or violence in a dating relationship (such as going out on group dates or recognizing abusive behavior).
2. Using the guidelines and what you learned in this chapter, create a brochure to inform incoming teens to your school (male and female) about safe dating behaviors.
3. You may want to organize your brochure into topic areas, such as "Communicating Personal Guidelines," "Handling Conflicts," and "Preventing Violence."

Time
50 minutes
Materials
newsprint, markers

Self-Assessment

✓ Listed at least three appropriate guidelines or behaviors for safe dating.
✓ Created a brochure that was persuasive and targeted to a teen audience.

Teens Taking Charge

The best way to handle school violence is to stop it before it starts. Many situations that erupt into violence can be identified and addressed, but only if people are alert and communicative.

The North Carolina Center for the Prevention of School Violence has helped to develop programs to help students resolve conflicts. Student leaders participate in discussions and seminars that help pinpoint problems before they start. Students in these programs use the power of positive peer pressure to ease tensions and head off misunderstandings. Their thoughtful and caring participation can help make one of the center's slogans a reality: "School Violence. Let's Get It Out of Our System."

Play the Video

Think About It

❯ How can student leaders help resolve conflicts that might lead to violence? Which strategies do you think are most likely to be effective?

❯ Why do you think the North Carolina program emphasizes the role of student leaders rather than adult experts?

❯ What signs indicate that a situation could turn violent?

Using Health Terms

On a separate sheet of paper, write the term that best matches each definition below.

LESSON 1

1. Struggles within yourself.
2. Grow into a situation that is unhealthful and even unsafe to all parties concerned.
3. Any disagreement, struggle, or fight.
4. Disagreements between groups of any size, from two people to entire nations.

LESSON 2

5. Respecting the privacy of both parties and keeping details secret.
6. Accepting others' differences and allowing them to be who they are without expressing disapproval.
7. A process in which compromise is used to reach agreement.
8. The process of ending a conflict by cooperating and problem solving together.

9. A process in which specially trained people help others to resolve their conflicts peacefully.
10. Students trained to help other students in conflict find fair ways to settle their differences.

LESSON 3

11. Hijacking or stealing a car by force.
12. The willful killing of one human being by another.
13. Violence committed for no particular reason.
14. A person who commits a violent act against another.
15. The use of physical force to injure or abuse another person or persons.

LESSON 4

16. Sexual intercourse by force.
17. Any intentional sexual attack.

Recalling the Facts

Using complete sentences, answer the following questions.

LESSON 1

1. What are some of the physical and emotional tip-offs that a conflict may be building?
2. In what situations is it important to avoid conflicts at all costs?
3. Name five major categories of teen conflicts—those situations over which teens are most likely to argue or fight.

LESSON 2

4. What are the Three R's of conflict resolution?
5. Name at least three ground rules for peer mediation.

LESSON 3

6. List two factors that contribute to crime in the United States.
7. If someone feels intent on fighting with you, what should you do to prevent getting into a fight?

LESSON 4

8. Name and define two different kinds of abuse.
9. What is rape, and what steps can a teen take to prevent becoming one of its victims?
10. If you know someone who is being abused, what steps should you take?

Thinking Critically

LESSON 1

1. **Synthesizing.** Graph one recent conflict in which you have been involved. Draw lines on graph paper indicating the conflict's start, buildup, climax, and resolution. Label each portion of your graph, telling what happened to your mind and body at each critical point in the conflict.

LESSON 2

2. **Synthesizing.** Make a picture book in which you teach elementary school students about the peer mediation process.

LESSON 3

3. **Evaluating.** Which techniques for reducing and managing school violence, including metal detectors and searches, do you think are most effective? Which are the least effective? Explain your responses.

LESSON 4

4. **Analyzing.** Why do you think many teens stay in relationships in which there is abuse?

Making the Connection

1. **Language Arts.** With several classmates, team-read Shakespeare's *Romeo and Juliet,* or view a videotape of the modern musical based on the play, *West Side Story.* Analyze the basic conflict in the story. What factors contributed to making the conflict turn violent? How might the conflict have been handled differently and nonviolently? Present your ideas in a written report.

2. **Social Studies.** Find out about current gun ownership laws in your town or city. What are these laws, and how were they passed? Research national debates on gun control and what federal laws have been passed regarding this issue.

BEYOND THE CLASSROOM

PARENTAL INVOLVEMENT With your parents or guardian, discuss whether or not parents should be held responsible for their children's vandalism or other crimes. Ask how they would feel if they had to pay for damage, go to prison, or do community service because of acts of vandalism committed by one of their children. Together, come up with a pledge that family members sign, promising to work to behave in ways that promote mutual respect in words and in actions, both inside and outside the home.

COMMUNITY INVOLVEMENT Help to organize a Violence Prevention Day in your neighborhood.

Begin the day with a School and Community Breakfast in which Peace Pancakes and other foods named for nonviolence are served. Have speakers from the community, the police department, and school talk about how to prevent violence in your community.

SCHOOL-TO-CAREER

Exploring Careers. Talk with a local police officer, a crime reporter for a local newspaper or TV station, or a community organizer. Ask about years of training and experience, dangers, and rewards of the career being discussed. Brainstorm ways to help prevent violence.

CHAPTER 15

Integumentary, Skeletal, and Muscular Systems

HEALTH *Online*

PRACTICING HEALTHFUL BEHAVIORS

Your skin is your body's first barrier of protection, and it's up to you to protect it for a lifetime. Stay informed about the importance of protection from the sun and environmental damage by reading the Health Update "Staying Sun Smart" at <u>health.glencoe.com</u>.

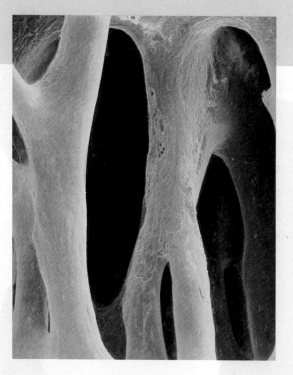

> ## Your bones...work with your muscles and the rest of your body to make you the marvelous living machine that you are.
>
> —Seymour Simon
> Contemporary Science Writer

Quick Write Write five activities you have performed today that demonstrate the importance of having healthy bones and muscles.

Personal Health Inventory

Self-Inventory Write the numbers 1–10 on a sheet of paper. Read each statement below and respond by writing *yes*, *no*, or *sometimes* for each item. Write a *yes* only for items that you practice regularly. Save your responses.

1	I wash my face twice daily.
2	I have a well-balanced eating style that includes an adequate source of vitamin A.
3	I include many sources of calcium and phosphorous in the foods I eat.
4	My physical activity includes weight-bearing exercises.
5	I take frequent breaks when working at a computer to prevent injury from repeated movements.
6	I wear proper equipment, including shoes, for the activities I participate in.
7	I exercise three to five times a week.
8	I warm up and stretch before beginning to exercise and cool down after exercising.
9	I practice good posture in order to strengthen my back muscles.
10	I participate in activities that increase my balance and coordination.

Follow-up After completing the chapter, retake this self-inventory. Pick two items that you need to work on and set a goal to improve your health behaviors.

The Integumentary System

Although it may not have occurred to you, your skin is an organ of the body, just as your heart and liver are. In fact, your skin, besides being the body's largest organ, has more functions than any other organ. Your overall appearance is affected by the condition of your skin.

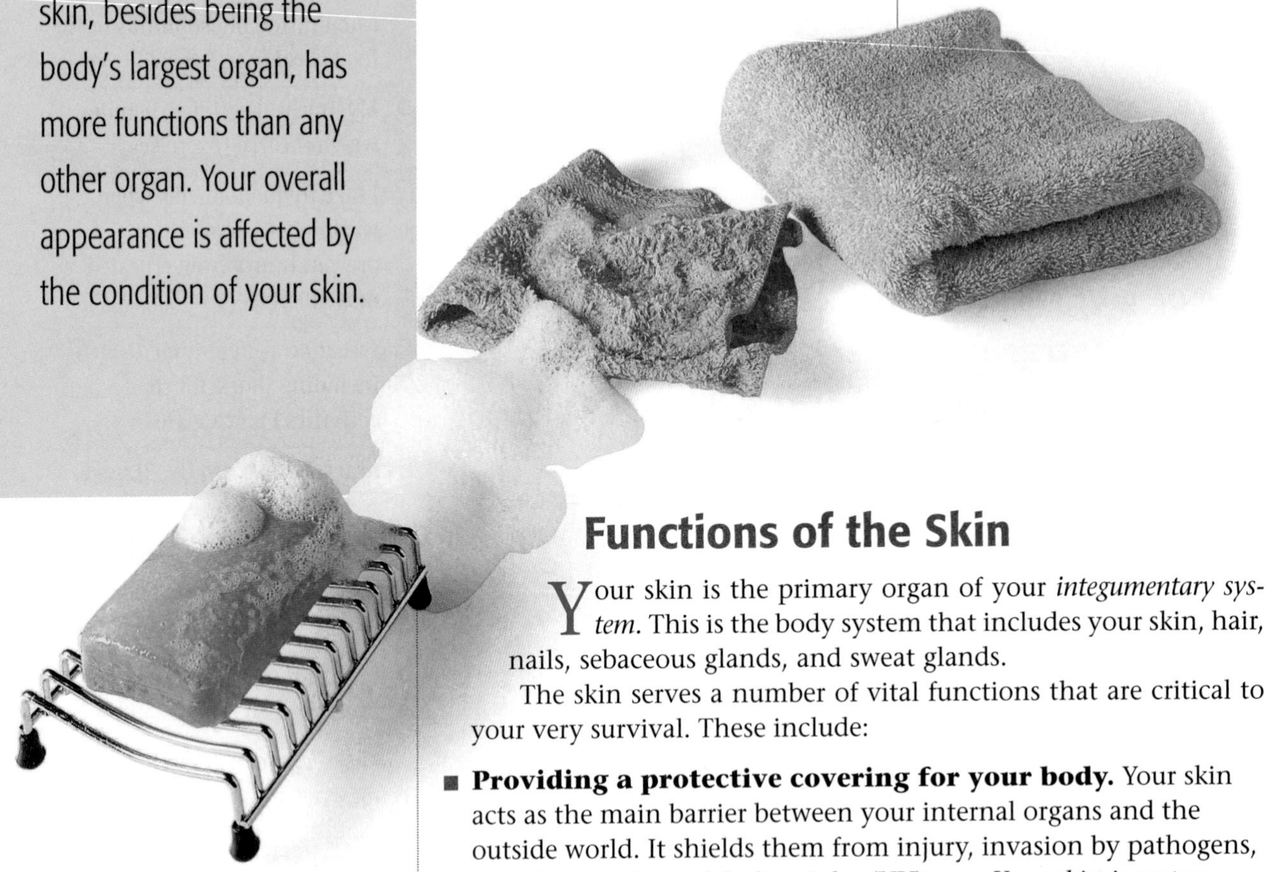

HEALTH TERMS

epidermis

dermis

melanin

athlete's foot

HEALTH CONCEPTS

- The skin serves a number of vital health functions to the body.
- Problems of the skin require varying degrees of medical treatment.
- Good skin hygiene includes regular washing and bathing.

Functions of the Skin

Your skin is the primary organ of your *integumentary system*. This is the body system that includes your skin, hair, nails, sebaceous glands, and sweat glands.

The skin serves a number of vital functions that are critical to your very survival. These include:

- **Providing a protective covering for your body.** Your skin acts as the main barrier between your internal organs and the outside world. It shields them from injury, invasion by pathogens, and the sun's harmful ultraviolet (UV) rays. Your skin is waterproof. It also has a water-holding capacity that contributes to its elasticity and helps maintain the body's balance of fluid and electrolytes.

- **Regulating body temperature.** Skin plays a role in keeping body temperature constant. When your body is hot, tiny blood vessels in the skin enlarge, permitting internal heat to escape through a process called *radiation*. The sweat glands also become active, releasing perspiration, which cools the skin as it evaporates. As your internal temperature drops, the blood vessels in the skin narrow, conserving body heat.

- **Enabling you to sense the world around you.** The skin is a major sense organ that serves as a means of communication with the outside environment. Nerve endings in your skin are responsive to touch, pain, pressure, and temperature.

Structure of the Skin

Your skin has two main layers. These are the **epidermis** (ep-uh-DUR-mihs)—*the outer, thinner layer of skin,* and the **dermis**—*the inner, thicker layer of skin.*

Epidermis

The epidermis, or outer layer, is made up of both dead and living cells. The outermost part of the epidermis is composed of dead cells that form a tough, protective coating. The epidermis contains a fatty substance called *lipids* that makes the skin waterproof.

The dead cells of the epidermis are sloughed off, or shed, when clothing rubs your skin or when you wash. As these dead cells are worn away, they are replaced by new cells. Through this shedding, your outer skin is replaced about once a month. New cells rise to the surface to replace old ones.

Some of the cells in the epidermis produce **melanin** (MEL-uh-nihn), *the pigment that gives skin, hair, and the iris of the eyes their coloring.* Skin color in humans is determined largely by the amount of melanin in the skin. The more melanin, the greater the protection from the sun and its ultraviolet rays, which have been linked to skin cancer.

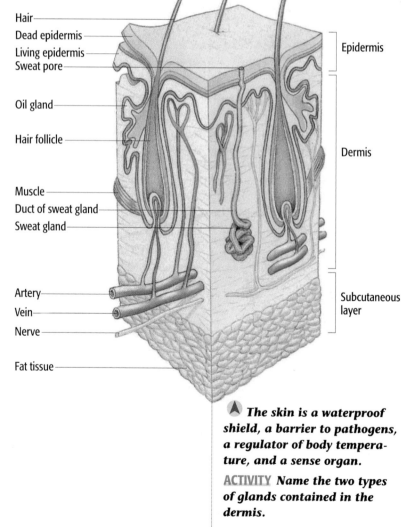

THE SKIN

Hair
Dead epidermis
Living epidermis
Sweat pore
Oil gland
Hair follicle
Muscle
Duct of sweat gland
Sweat gland
Artery
Vein
Nerve
Fat tissue

Epidermis
Dermis
Subcutaneous layer

▲ *The skin is a waterproof shield, a barrier to pathogens, a regulator of body temperature, and a sense organ.*

ACTIVITY *Name the two types of glands contained in the dermis.*

hotlink

sweat glands For more information on the function of the sweat glands, see Chapter 7, page 163.

sebaceous glands For more information on the function of the sebaceous glands, see Chapter 7, page 165.

Dermis

The dermis, the inner layer of skin, is made up of connective tissue that gives the skin its elasticity, or spongy, flexible quality. Nerve endings and hair follicles extend into the dermis. So do the **sweat glands** and **sebaceous glands**. Below the dermis is tissue called the hypodermis. The hypodermis is not part of your skin, but it attaches the skin to bone and muscle.

Skin Care

Good personal hygiene and a balanced eating style promote healthy skin. Wash your face with soap and water every morning and evening. Daily washing, bathing, or showering slows the growth of bacteria that cause body odor. Vitamin A helps promote healthy skin. Good sources of this vitamin include milk, egg yolks, liver, green leafy and yellow vegetables, and yellow fruits.

Building Health Skills

Assessing Health Information: Deodorant Claims

A DEODORANT is a substance that removes or masks bad-smelling body odors. Deodorants may contain antiseptics to destroy bacteria, perfume to mask odors, and antiperspirants—chemicals that reduce sweat production. When sweat remains on the skin, it creates a moist environment in which bacteria can thrive. The bacteria break down the chemicals in the sweat, causing body odor.

Deodorant preparations can be a useful aid against body odor, but they are no substitute for good personal hygiene. If you do decide to use a deodorant, how can you choose among all the competing claims and types? Here are a few tips:

1. **Be alert to key words.** Marketers of personal hygiene products like deodorants often use key phrases such as *superior protection, unique formula,* or *extra long-lasting.* This is a typical marketing technique aimed at getting consumers to buy on impulse rather than explore the claims that are made.

2. **Read the label.** Deodorant preparations must list their ingredients on the label. Check and compare the ingredients to determine whether there is really a difference between two products that make competing claims about effectiveness. You may be surprised.

3. **Try it out.** Which is best for you: solid stick, spray, powder? Should you buy scented or unscented? Perfumes used in deodorants can cause skin irritation in sensitive people, as can antiperspirants that contain aluminum chloride. Most deodorants are available in inexpensive sample or travel sizes. Try a few until you find the one that suits you best.

Problems of the Skin

Just as your skin has many functions, it is also a hotbed for problems, some potentially serious. One of these problems, **acne**, is common during adolescence, although it is not limited to this period. Other problems of skin include:

- **Ringworm.** Ringworm is a common fungal infection that affects various parts of the body. It gets its name from the ring-shaped, scaly, reddened, or blistery patches it forms.

- **Athlete's foot.** The same fungus that causes ringworm is also the cause of **athlete's foot,** *a fungal infection of the skin between the toes.* Athlete's foot is associated with wearing shoes and sweating. It is highly contagious. This is why it is important to wear foot coverings in locker rooms and showers.

- **Boils.** A boil is an inflamed, pus-filled area of the skin, usually an infected hair follicle. The usual cause of boils is the bacterium *Staphylococcus aureus.* Keeping skin clean helps prevent boils. Never squeeze or burst a boil; this can spread the infection. Boils can be serious and, if large, should be treated by a health care professional.

- **Warts.** Warts are contagious growths on the outer layer of the skin caused by viruses. Most warts are painless and harmless, but the virus that causes them can spread to other parts of the body and form more warts.

- **Moles.** Moles are small, usually round, slightly thickened, brown to dark brown spots on the skin. Moles are usually harmless. However, if a mole suddenly appears, grows, bleeds, or changes color, consult a physician immediately. Change in a mole may indicate a serious problem and should be checked by a doctor.

- **Psoriasis.** Psoriasis is a skin disease in which thickened patches of inflamed, red skin form, often covered by white, flaking scales. Psoriasis should be treated by a physician. The cause is not known, but this can be a lifetime skin problem if not treated.

- **Vitiligo.** Vitiligo is a disorder in which patches of skin lose their color. The affected areas of skin are extremely sensitive to sunlight and should be protected. Vitiligo is believed to be an auto-immune disorder that causes an absence of the skin cells that produce melanin. There is no cure, but in about 30 percent of cases the skin color returns naturally.

hotlink

acne For more information on acne and how to treat it, see Chapter 7, page 165.

▼ *There is a wide range of skin color and skin types among the people of the world.*

ACTIVITY *Discuss the relationship between personal hygiene, a balanced eating plan, and healthy skin.*

Shedding Light on Sunscreens

Follow these guidelines when buying and using sunscreens:

➤ Wear a sunscreen that is water-resistant and waterproof.

➤ Apply sunscreen liberally and evenly to your skin 30 minutes before you go in the sun. Reapply at least every two hours.

➤ Wear a sunscreen with an SPF of 15 or higher. *SPF* stands for *sun protection factor.* The SPF numbers indicate the sunscreen's ability to screen out the sun's harmful UV rays.

➤ *Wearing gloves while gardening can reduce your chances of developing blisters.*

ACTIVITY *Identify techniques for reducing the risk of blisters during other physical activities.*

■ **Impetigo.** A streptococcal infection in which bacteria enter a small break in the skin. This infection is highly contagious.

■ **Blisters.** Blisters are raised areas filled with a watery fluid. They usually result from the skin being rubbed (your foot rubbing against the inside of your shoe, for example) or burned. A blister should be protected to keep it from breaking and left to heal on its own. A broken blister can become infected.

■ **Callus.** A callus is an area of thickened skin that forms as a result of regular or continued friction or pressure. Musicians who play stringed instruments often develop calluses on their fingertips. Calluses can be reduced by rubbing them with a porous stone called pumice.

■ **Corn.** A corn is a callus on a toe caused by the pressure of a tight-fitting shoe. Spongy corn pads can relieve the pressure that makes corns painful. Wearing shoes that fit properly is the main way to prevent corns.

LESSON 1 *Review*

Reviewing Facts and Vocabulary

1. What are the functions of the skin?
2. Explain the unique characteristics of the epidermis.
3. What is melanin, and what is its function?

Thinking Critically

4. *Synthesizing.* Jenna has a mole on her arm that has been growing from the time she was small. Does she need to take any action? Explain.
5. *Analyzing.* What makes cleanliness so important to skin health?

Applying Health Skills

6. *In Your Home.* Have you or has anyone in your family experienced any of the skin problems discussed in this lesson? How was the problem treated? What were the results? Discuss with family members what you have learned about the problem that you did not know before. Talk about what should be done differently—if anything—in the event the problem arises again.

The Skeletal System

You may think of the skeleton as similar to the framework that supports a building. You will see that, unlike a building, the 206 bones that comprise the human skeleton work together with muscles to allow you to walk, run, jump, bend, lift, and carry.

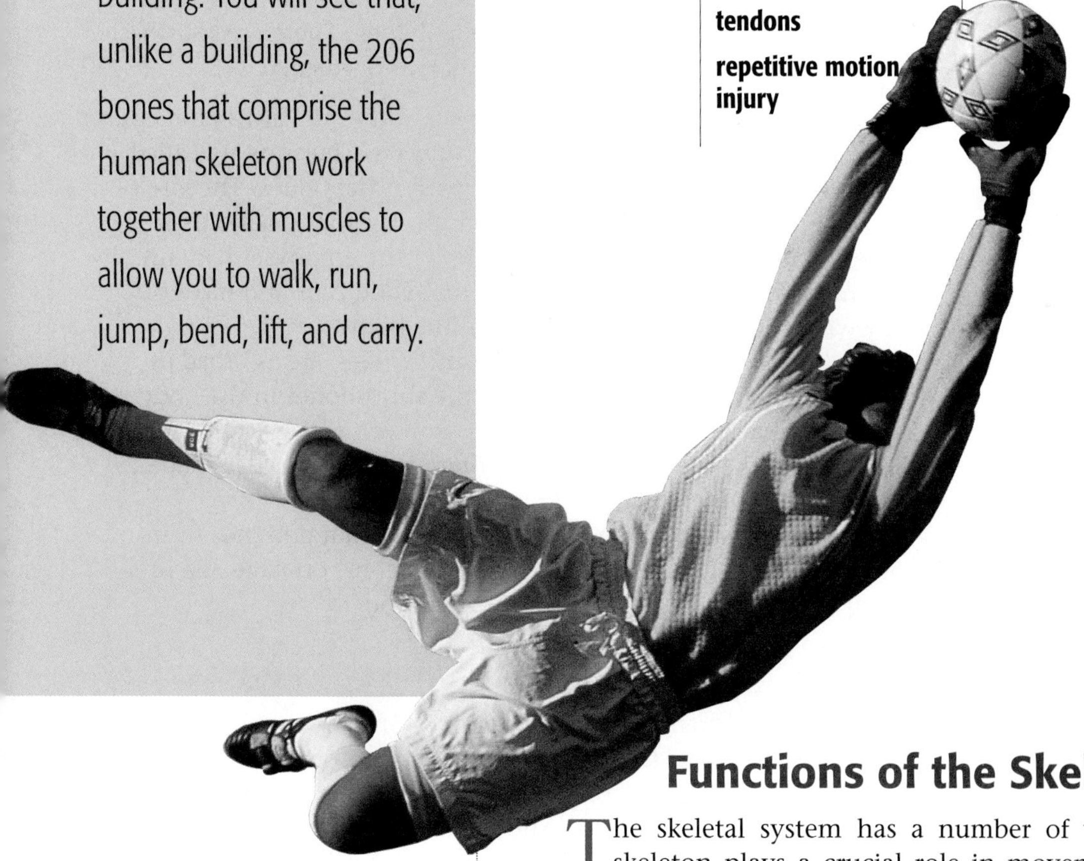

HEALTH TERMS

axial skeleton

appendicular skeleton

cartilage

ossification

ligaments

tendons

repetitive motion injury

HEALTH CONCEPTS

- Bones have four primary functions.
- The skeleton gives structure and stability to the body.
- Eating well is one of the keys to maintaining the health of the skeletal system.

Functions of the Skeletal System

The skeletal system has a number of vital functions. The skeleton plays a crucial role in movement by providing a strong, stable, and mobile framework on which muscles can act. It also supports and protects your delicate internal organs.

The bones that make up your skeleton have functions of their own. These living structures are the principal storage centers for essential body minerals, such as calcium and phosphorus. They are also the manufacturing center of the body's blood cells. Red bone marrow produces millions of blood cells each day.

TYPES OF BONES

Long bone (femur)

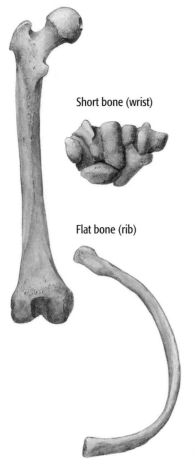

Short bone (wrist)

Flat bone (rib)

Structure of the Skeleton

The skeleton provides support and protection for tissues and organs of your body. The skeletal system is divided into two main parts:

■ **Axial** (AK-see-uhl) **skeleton.** The **axial skeleton** includes *the 80 bones of the skull, spine, ribs, and sternum, or breastbone.* The vertebrae—the small bones that make up your spine—protect your spinal cord. The ribs, most of which are attached to the sternum in your chest and to the vertebrae of your spine, protect your lungs and heart.

■ **Appendicular** (ah-pen-DIHK-yoo-lar) **skeleton.** The **appendicular skeleton** includes *the 126 bones of the shoulders, arms, hands, hips, legs, and feet.* It helps you perform a wide range of movement.

Types of Bones

Bones are grouped according to their shapes. There are four basic types in the human body: long, short, flat, and irregular.

■ Strong long bones, like the femur, are found in the arms and legs. The shafts of long bones are called *diaphyses*. The ends are called *epiphyses*. The epiphyses form joints with other bones. The enlarged ends, which are composed mainly of spongy bone tissue, give stability to joints. The inner parts of the epiphyses contain red marrow, which produces all the red blood cells and most of the white blood cells and platelets in the body.

■ Short bones, like those in the wrists and ankles, are as broad as they are long. More than half of all the short bones in the body are in the hands and feet.

■ Flat bones, like the ribs and skull bones, have a thin, flat shape. These bones generally serve to protect vital organs.

■ Irregular bones, like vertebrae, have a shape that does not fit into any of the other three categories. The vertebrae on page 366 in Chapter 16 is an example of an irregular bone.

Cartilage

Your skeletal system is made up not only of bones but of **cartilage**, a *strong, flexible connective tissue.* Different types of cartilage line the surfaces of joints and enable them to move smoothly, cushion adjoining vertebrae, and support the nose and ears. A baby's skeleton is mostly cartilage. As the body grows, most cartilage cells are replaced by bone cells and minerals through **ossification** (os-suh-fuh-KAY-shun), *the process by which bone is formed, renewed, and repaired.* Bone renewal occurs as part of the body's normal process in which old cells are replaced by new cells. Bone repair fuses broken bones after a fracture.

THE SKELETAL SYSTEM

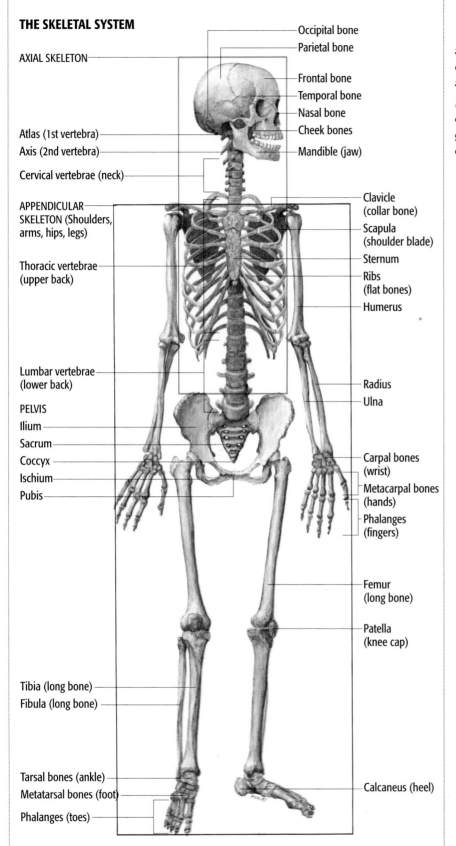

AXIAL SKELETON

Occipital bone
Parietal bone
Frontal bone
Temporal bone
Nasal bone
Cheek bones
Mandible (jaw)

Atlas (1st vertebra)
Axis (2nd vertebra)
Cervical vertebrae (neck)

APPENDICULAR
SKELETON (Shoulders,
arms, hips, legs)

Clavicle
(collar bone)
Scapula
(shoulder blade)
Sternum
Ribs
(flat bones)
Humerus

Thoracic vertebrae
(upper back)

Lumbar vertebrae
(lower back)

Radius
Ulna

PELVIS
Ilium
Sacrum
Coccyx
Ischium
Pubis

Carpal bones
(wrist)
Metacarpal bones
(hands)
Phalanges
(fingers)

Femur
(long bone)

Patella
(knee cap)

Tibia (long bone)
Fibula (long bone)

Tarsal bones (ankle)
Metatarsal bones (foot)

Phalanges (toes)

Calcaneus (heel)

> The axial skeleton is shown here in blue. The appendicular skeleton is shown in pink.

ACTIVITY Tell how the axial and appendicular systems got their names. Consult a dictionary if necessary.

Joints

The point at which two bones meet is called a *joint.* Some joints are fixed, such as those between the bones of the skull. Some joints, such as those between the vertebrae, allow only a small amount of movement. Most joints, however, allow a wide range of movement. Imagine you did not have a joint where your arm bones meet at your elbow. What kinds of activities would you be able to perform?

There are several types of mobile joints:

■ **Ball-and-socket joint.** This type of joint allows the widest range of movement: backward, forward, sideways, and in a circle. Examples are the shoulder and hip joints.

■ **Pivot joint.** In a pivot joint, a bony projection allows rotation. An example is the joint between the first two vertebrae in the neck that allows your head to rotate.

■ **Ellipsoidal joint.** In a joint like the one in your wrist, an oval-shaped part fits into a curved space. This allows all types of movement except pivotal.

■ **Hinge joint.** A hinge joint allows bending and straightening, as in the fingers. The knee and elbow are hinge joints that also allow some degree of rotation.

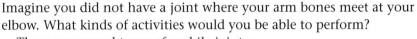

Different kinds of body movement are made possible by joints that move in several different ways.

ACTIVITY *Name another example of a ball-and-socket joint.*

At joints where movement occurs, the surfaces of the bones are coated with smooth, slippery cartilage to reduce friction during movement. **Ligaments** are *tough bands of fibrous, slightly elastic tissue that bind the bone ends at the joint.* In addition to binding the bones together, ligaments prevent excessive movement of the joint. **Tendons** are *fibrous cords that join muscle to bone or to other muscles.* Drum your fingers on your desk. The movements you see in the back of your hand are your tendons in action.

JOINTS

Skull (immovable joint)

Shoulder (ball-and-socket joint)

Elbow (hinge joint)

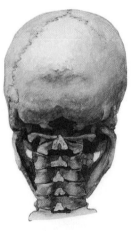

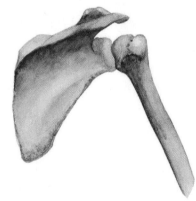

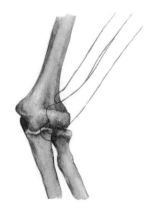

Head and neck (pivot joint)

Care of the Skeletal System

Your habits and decisions you make concerning nutrition and exercise can affect the health of your skeletal system now and later in life. Did you have milk or another dairy product for breakfast today? If you didn't, you should plan to tomorrow. Calcium, one of several **minerals** found in dairy products, is essential for building strong bones. It is especially important during the teen years, when the body builds most of its bone mass. Phosphorus, another vital mineral, combines with calcium to give bones their rigidity. Phosphorus can be found in milk, peas, beans, liver, cottage cheese, broccoli, and whole grains. Regular physical activity, especially weight-bearing exercise, increases bone mass. Exercise also promotes better circulation of the blood, increasing nourishment to your bones.

h⚬t link

minerals For more information on minerals and their role in bone growth and health, see Chapter 5, page 109.

BONE STRUCTURE

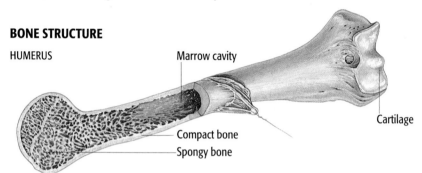

HUMERUS

Marrow cavity

Cartilage

Compact bone

Spongy bone

◀ *A bone is made up of three types of tissue—compact bone, spongy bone, and marrow.*
ACTIVITY *Explain how nutrition and exercise are important to healthy bones.*

Problems of the Skeletal System

Skeletal system disorders and injuries to bones can be the result of many factors. These include poor nutrition, infections, sports and recreational mishaps, accidents, and poor posture. The skeletal system is also affected by degenerative disorders such as osteoporosis.

Fractures

Fractures are any type of break in a bone. Fractures are divided into two main types, simple and compound. In a simple, or "closed," fracture, the broken bone does not protrude, or stick out, through the skin. In a compound, or "open," fracture, one or both bone ends project through the skin.

Fractures may also be classified according to the shape or pattern of the break:

- **Hairline fracture.** The fracture is incomplete, and the two parts of the bones do not separate.

- **Transverse fracture.** The fracture is completely across the bone. This may result from a sharp, direct blow or stress caused, for example, by prolonged running on an already damaged bone.

- **Comminuted fracture.** The bone shatters into more than two pieces, usually from severe force as in an auto accident.

▼ *Eating enough foods rich in calcium and phosphorus can prolong the life and health of your bones.*

ACTIVITY *Name two foods that are good sources of calcium and phosphorus.*

Osteoporosis

Loss of bone mass is a natural part of the aging process. In severe cases, osteoporosis—a condition in which bone density decreases, causing bones to become brittle and easily fractured—develops. Women are especially vulnerable to osteoporosis after menopause. Their bodies no longer produce estrogen, which helps maintain bone mass. You have the opportunity now in your teen years to prevent osteoporosis in later life. You can do this by getting ample physical activity and by eating enough foods that are sources of calcium, such as milk, cheese, and yogurt.

Scoliosis

Scoliosis is a lateral, or side-to-side, curvature of the spine. Scoliosis usually starts in childhood or adolescence and becomes more marked until the age at which growth stops. Most schools have scoliosis screening programs, usually conducted by the school nurse. Depending on the severity of the curvature, treatment may include exercise, a special brace, or surgery.

Injuries to the Joints

Common joint injuries include the following:

- **Dislocation.** A dislocation results when a bone slips from its normal position at a joint. Dislocation is usually accompanied by tearing of the joint ligaments. Never attempt to replace a dislocated bone. This condition requires the care of a physician to put the bone back in place and immobilize the joint so that the tissue can heal.

- **Torn cartilage.** Torn cartilage is a serious joint injury. It can result from a sharp blow or a severe twisting of a joint. Doctors can now repair some cartilage tears with arthroscopic surgery.

- **Bunion.** A bunion is a painful swelling of the bursa in the first joint of the big toe. Bunions are caused by wearing tight or high-heeled shoes, which cram the toes and cause them to bend in an abnormal way. To prevent this condition, it is important to wear well-fitting shoes. Large bunions may require surgery to remove the swollen tissue.

- **Bursitis.** Bursitis is a painful condition that occurs when the bursa in a joint becomes inflamed. It is common in the shoulder and knee joints. Bursitis is usually the result of pressure, friction, or slight injury to the membrane surrounding the joint.

- **Arthritis. Arthritis** is inflammation of a joint, characterized by pain, swelling, stiffness, and redness. The most common type, osteoarthritis, results from wear and tear on the joints and most commonly troubles older adults.

hotlink

arthritis For more information on arthritis and methods of treatment, see Chapter 31, page 692.

◄ *Exercise is important throughout life. Warming up before exercising can help prevent injuries to bones and joints.*

ACTIVITY *Name two other ways to avoid injury to bones while exercising.*

update
► Looking at Technology

Artificial Limbs: Skin and All

Artificial legs with a "skin-like" covering and even real-looking hair are now possible thanks to advances in the field of *prosthetics*—the making of artificial limbs and other body parts. These days, *prostheses*, or artificial limbs, are more high-tech than ever before.

Artificial limbs are nothing new. Prostheses were in use as early as 300 B.C., when crude limbs were made from wood and metal. Today, the drive to improve prostheses is in part due to increased awareness of the many great abilities of the physically challenged. David Barr, a double amputee, uses his high-tech artificial legs to walk miles a day and even ride a motorcycle!

Present-day prostheses fit better than ever. New materials have made limbs lighter and more comfortable for wearers. Even more exciting are new attempts to design prostheses that "feel." For example, two pressure sensors placed in the heel and ball of an artificial foot send signals to electrodes that touch the skin of the ends of the real, or residual, limb. These signals are carried through wires to a battery-operated device that not only signals the wearer's skin but sends messages to the brain, where they are interpreted as sensations.

A *The risk of repetitive motion injury can be reduced by proper placement of equipment and hand and arm positions that reduce strain.*

ACTIVITY *Describe four ways in which this teen can reduce the risk of repetitive motion injury.*

Repetitive Motion Injury

Technology has brought great things that improve our lives in many ways. Unfortunately, it has also introduced a new class of injuries to the skeletal system. Lumped together under the name **repetitive motion injury**, these result from *damage to tissues caused by prolonged, repeated movements*. Repetitive motion injury occurs when the same motions are performed for hours at a time. It is predominantly related to computer use. However, workers in industries where repetitive motions are common are affected as well.

One of the most common types of repetitive motion injury is carpal tunnel syndrome. It results from pressure on the median nerve where it passes into the hand through a gap known as the "carpal tunnel" under a ligament at the front of the wrist. Symptoms may include numbness, weakness, tingling, or burning in the fingers or hands and pain extending outward from the wrist. Treatment includes wearing a splint, resting the joint, and medication. Surgery to correct carpal tunnel syndrome has had limited success. Research is under way into how to prevent and correct this condition.

Repetitive motion injuries are turning up increasingly among students of college age. You can help prevent yourself from joining the ranks by taking steps such as these when you use a computer:

1. Keep your wrists relaxed and straight. Use only finger movements to strike the keys.
2. Press keys with the least pressure necessary. If possible, use an ergonomically designed keyboard. These specially made keyboards are designed to put less strain on the ligaments of the wrist.
3. Move your entire hand to press hard-to-reach keys.
4. Take frequent breaks, which is also good for your eyes.

LESSON 2 *Review*

Reviewing Facts and Vocabulary

1. What are the two main divisions of the skeletal system?
2. Name three functions of bones.
3. Describe two injuries or diseases of the skeletal system.

Thinking Critically

4. *Comparing and Contrasting.* How are ligaments and tendons alike? How are they different?
5. *Synthesizing.* Blanca wants to get enough phosphorus through the foods she eats, but she is allergic to milk products and dislikes beans, liver, and broccoli. What suggestions can you make that might help Blanca?

Applying Health Skills

6. *In Your Home and School.* At the grocery store, ask the butcher for soup bones. Try to get a long bone. Ask the butcher to saw it in half lengthwise so that you can look inside. With a family member at home or a partner in school, identify the periosteum, yellow marrow and epiphyses, spongy bone tissue, and red marrow. Find the hole where a blood vessel enters the bone.

The Muscular System

The action of a sling-shot is the result of two inter-dependent parts—a forked stick and a rubber band or other elastic material. The same is true of the human body. The role of the stick is taken by the skeleton. The role of the rubber band is taken by the muscular system. Muscles are elastic, stretching to allow a wide range of motions.

HEALTH TERMS

smooth muscles

skeletal muscles

flexors

extensors

cardiac muscle

muscle tone

tendinitis

hernia

HEALTH CONCEPTS

- Muscles are responsible for or involved in many body functions.
- Exercise is the main key to the health of the muscular system.
- In mass, muscle is the most abundant tissue in the body.

Functions of the Muscular System

When you hear the term *muscle*, does it bring to mind the image of a bodybuilder? Without muscles, nothing in your body would work. All body movements depend on muscles. Muscles pump blood throughout your body, move food through your digestive system, and control the movement of air in and out of your lungs.

Muscles work by means of two *complementary*—or opposing— actions. These are contraction, the shortening of a muscle, and extension, the stretching of a muscle. Muscle contraction is triggered by nerve impulses. At the point where a nerve enters a muscle, it breaks up into numerous nerve endings. Nerve impulses stimulate muscle fibers by means of tiny, buttonlike endings called *motor end plates*. A nerve may branch out to supply many muscle fibers.

Structure of the Muscular System

A muscle is composed of bundles of fibers. The major muscles in the body are made up of hundreds of bundles. A muscle fiber is made up of even smaller units called *myofibrils*. Each myofibril is in turn made up of microscopic filaments called *actin* and *myosin*. These are proteins that control muscle contraction.

Types of Muscles

Your body has three basic types of muscle tissue: smooth muscle, skeletal muscle, and cardiac muscle.

SMOOTH MUSCLES

Smooth muscles are *the type of muscle concerned with the movements of internal organs.* Many parts of the body, such as the intestines, the bronchi of the lungs, the bladder, and the walls of the blood vessels contain smooth muscle. Smooth muscles are also called involuntary muscles because they work without a person's conscious control.

SKELETAL MUSCLES

Skeletal muscles are *the striped, or striated, muscles attached to bones that cause body movements.* Skeletal muscles form the largest part of the body's muscular system. There are more than 600 such muscles. Skeletal muscles are voluntary. They are under conscious control.

Two or more skeletal muscles may oppose each other's actions. While one contracts, the other relaxes. Skeletal muscles are classified according to the type of action each muscle performs. *Muscles that close a joint* are called **flexors.** *Muscles that open out a joint* are called **extensors.**

CARDIAC MUSCLE

Cardiac muscle is *a special type of striated tissue that forms the walls of the heart.* Your heart is the most important muscle in your body. Its unique properties enable it to contract rhythmically about 100,000 times a day to pump blood throughout the body. Cardiac muscle is involuntary muscle.

Care of the Muscular System

Have you ever heard the expression "Use it or lose it"? It certainly holds true for muscles. An unused muscle will *atrophy,* or waste

THE SKELETAL MUSCLES

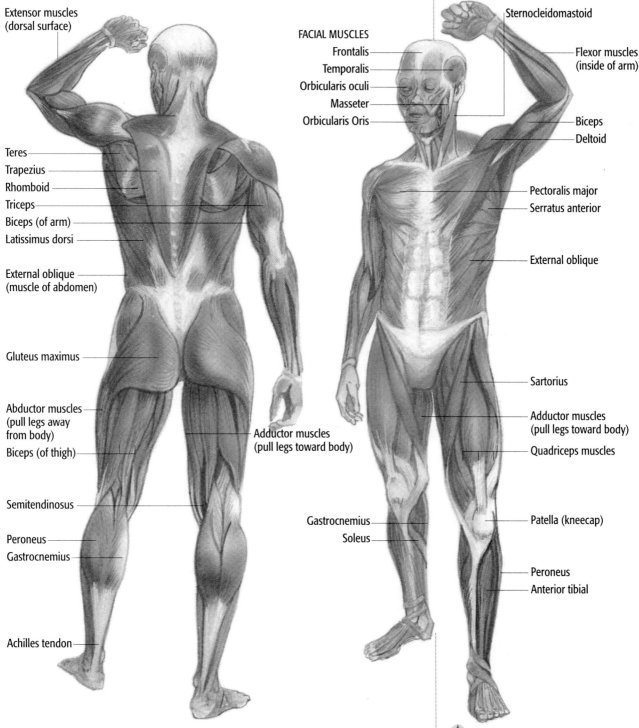

Extensor muscles (dorsal surface)

Teres

Trapezius

Rhomboid

Triceps

Biceps (of arm)

Latissimus dorsi

External oblique (muscle of abdomen)

Gluteus maximus

Abductor muscles (pull legs away from body)

Biceps (of thigh)

Semitendinosus

Peroneus

Gastrocnemius

Achilles tendon

Adductor muscles (pull legs toward body)

FACIAL MUSCLES

Frontalis

Temporalis

Orbicularis oculi

Masseter

Orbicularis Oris

Sternocleidomastoid

Flexor muscles (inside of arm)

Biceps

Deltoid

Pectoralis major

Serratus anterior

External oblique

Sartorius

Adductor muscles (pull legs toward body)

Quadriceps muscles

Gastrocnemius

Soleus

Patella (kneecap)

Peroneus

Anterior tibial

away. To maintain **muscle tone**—*the natural tension in the fibers of a muscle*—you need to keep active and eat balanced, nutritious meals. This should be a lifelong goal. Activity that maintains muscle tone is especially important for older adults to prevent loss of mobility, balance, and the risk of falls.

▲ *Skeletal muscles are essential in performing physical movements.*

ACTIVITY *Identify and describe the largest muscle shown.*

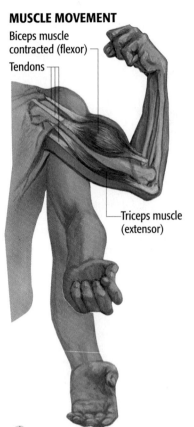

MUSCLE MOVEMENT

Biceps muscle
contracted (flexor)

Tendons

Triceps muscle
(extensor)

The biceps and triceps work together to move bones upward and downward.

ACTIVITY *What happens when your biceps muscle contracts?*

The more you use your muscles, the more efficient and strong they will become. Remember, the heart is a muscle, too. Regular exercise strengthens the heart and makes it work more efficiently by increasing the amount of blood pumped in a single beat. As a result, the heart can pump less rapidly and has more time to rest between beats.

A program of regular exercise with stretching, warm-up, and cool down increases muscular strength and flexibility and stamina in general. Activities that promote balance and coordination can reduce the risk of falls. Practicing good posture can help strengthen back muscles. Using the proper equipment and wearing appropriate clothing can help protect muscles during exercise.

Problems of the Muscular System

How many times have your muscles ached during strenuous exercise or a tough competition? This is due to lactic acid buildup. As the lactic acid dissipates, the ache goes away. Sore muscles and bruises are a temporary condition. Some other muscular system problems, however, have a lasting impact on a person's health and lifestyle.

- **Myasthenia Gravis.** Myasthenia gravis is a disorder in which the muscles become weak and easily fatigued. The muscles most commonly affected are the eye muscles, which may result in drooping eyelids and double vision.

- **Muscular Dystrophy.** Muscular dystrophy is an inherited disorder characterized by a progressive wasting away of skeletal muscles. Early detection of muscular dystrophy is crucial because even though there is no cure, muscle weakening can be delayed by regular exercise.

Making Responsible Decisions

Who Should Benefit?

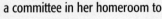

Della has had close family members who suffered from muscular dystrophy. She feels very strongly about raising funds for an upcoming muscular dystrophy telethon. She is forming a committee in her homeroom to organize a dance at her school to benefit the charity. Some of her classmates have opposed her plans, saying that any fundraising dance should benefit the students of their school, not people they don't even know. How should Della respond to her classmates?

What Would You Do?

Apply the six steps of the decision-making process to Della's problem.

1. **State the situation.**
2. **List the options.**
3. **Weigh the possible outcomes.**
4. **Consider your values.**
5. **Make a decision and act.**
6. **Evaluate the decision.**

Injury-Related Muscular Problems

Even when you take care of your muscles, accidents can happen. Injury-related muscle problems can be painful, but most are temporary.

▼ *Healthy skeletal muscles are strong and flexible and allow an athlete to perform at his or her peak.*

- **Muscle strain.** A strain, or a "pulled muscle," is a tearing or stretching of muscle fibers as a result of suddenly pulling them too far. Strains usually occur in large muscles and are a result of overexertion. They are most common in athletes. Treatment consists of applying an ice pack to the affected area to reduce swelling, wrapping it with a compression bandage, and resting the limb in a raised position.

- **Bruise.** A bruise is a discolored area under the skin caused by leakage of blood after an injury. Ice or a cold pack can reduce the pain and swelling of a large bruise.

- **Tendinitis.** Tendinitis is *the inflammation of a tendon,* usually caused by overuse. Symptoms include pain, tenderness, and restricted movement of the muscle attached to the affected tendon. Treatment may include anti-inflammatory medications, ultrasound, or injection of corticosteroids.

- **Hernia.** One of the more serious muscle injuries is a **hernia,** which is *protrusion of an organ or tissue through a weak area in the muscle.* In abdominal hernias, the intestine protrudes through a weak area in the abdominal wall. Abdominal hernias may appear after a person lifts a heavy object. Surgery is usually required to repair a hernia.

LESSON **3** *Review*

Reviewing Facts and Vocabulary

1. Name and describe the two types of muscle movement.
2. Describe two injuries or diseases related to the muscular system.

Thinking Critically

3. **Synthesizing.** What possible benefits to muscles may be derived from warming up and stretching before exercise? What about stretching after exercise?
4. **Synthesizing.** Suggest ways that a person can prevent injury to skeletal muscles.

Applying Health Skills

5. ***In Your Home and School.*** Interview family members and several classmates to find out what physical activities, particularly sports, they enjoy and are good at. Ask which activities they do not enjoy or find difficult. Use your findings to draw conclusions about the types of muscles that are used most often during these activities. Share your findings with the people you interviewed.

Health Skills Activities

Activity 1 — Training Safety Checklist

Weight-bearing exercise throughout a person's life is important both to maintain muscle tone and to keep bones strong and healthy. As with any physical activity, however, safety comes first.

Directions

1. Create a safety checklist for teens doing weight or resistance training.
2. Begin by forming groups to work on safety aspects of various topics, such as the proper use of equipment, appropriate clothing, and when and where to work out.
3. Use information from your book as well as outside sources.
4. If your classroom has a computer, input the guide and print out copies for the gymnasium and other prominent places around the school and community.

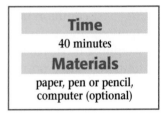

Time
40 minutes

Materials
paper, pen or pencil, computer (optional)

Self-Assessment

✓ Listed at least five tips for practicing weight training safely.
✓ Identified safe exercise procedures and proper use of exercise equipment for each weight-bearing exercise.

Activity 2 — Report to Congress

You have been asked to write and present a report to Congress on a disease affecting the integumentary, skeletal or muscular system. Your report must be informative. It must also convince Congress to fund additional research to find a cure.

Directions

1. With a group, locate a disease or disorder of the integumentary, skeletal, or muscular system that can be treated but not cured.
2. Research the disease, including symptoms, and how it affects the individual. Tell what medical treatments are currently available.
3. Each group will present an oral report to the class (Congress) on its disease. The report must convince "Congress" that additional funding is needed for further research.

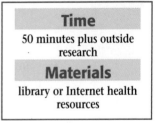

Time
50 minutes plus outside research

Materials
library or Internet health resources

Self-Assessment

✓ Reported correctly on a disease, noting symptoms, effects, and treatments.
✓ Presented facts on importance of a cure in a persuasive and convincing manner.

HEALTH NEWS

VIDEO

Extreme Sports Arthritis Warning

Snowboarders fly through the air, seeming to defy gravity. Of course, sometimes they crash into icy banks of snow. Inline-skaters slide gracefully along narrow rails. But not all slides end gracefully—some end in hard falls.

Extreme athletes put stress on their skeletal and muscular systems. It's hardly surprising that they sometimes break bones. However, it might surprise you that those injuries can have lasting effects. Long after a major joint injury has healed, extreme athletes may develop painful arthritis.

Every athlete—from amateur to pro—can apply rules of caution and safety to prevent injuries today. This prevention may pay off years from now in an increased resistance to diseases like arthritis.

Play the Video

Think About It

- How are the skeletal and muscular systems involved during inline skating? During mountain biking?
- What precautions can athletes use to take care of their skeletal and muscular systems?

Using Health Terms

On a separate sheet of paper, write the term that best matches each definition below.

LESSON 1

1. The pigment that gives skin, hair, and the iris of the eyes their coloring.
2. The inner, thicker layer of skin.
3. A fungal infection of the skin between the toes.
4. The outer, thinner layer of skin.

LESSON 2

5. Strong, flexible connective tissue.
6. The process by which bone is formed, renewed, and repaired.
7. The 80 bones of the skull, spine, ribs, and sternum, or breastbone.
8. Fibrous cords that join muscle to bone or to other muscles.

9. Tough bands of fibrous, slightly elastic tissue that bind the bone ends at the joint.
10. The 126 bones of the shoulders, arms, hands, hips, legs, and feet.
11. Damage to tissues caused by prolonged, repeated movements.

LESSON 3

12. Natural tension in the fibers of muscle.
13. The striped, or striated, muscles attached to bones that cause body movements.
14. The inflammation of a tendon.
15. Muscles that open out a joint.
16. Protrusion of an organ or tissue through a weak area in the muscle.
17. The type of muscle concerned with the movements of internal organs.
18. Muscles that close a joint.

Recalling the Facts

Using complete sentences, answer the following questions.

LESSON 1

1. What is the largest organ in the body?
2. Explain the process by which your skin helps regulate body temperature.
3. What eventually happens to dead cells in the epidermis?
4. In what part of the skin are new cells formed?
5. What causes athlete's foot, and how can it be avoided?

LESSON 2

6. Name the four kinds of bones in the human body and give an example of each.
7. In what part of the population is osteoporosis most common?

8. What two minerals are important for your bones to grow, harden, and repair?
9. What happens during the process of ossification?

LESSON 3

10. Name the three types of muscles and describe their functions.
11. What is the most important muscle in the body?
12. What is the best way to keep your muscles strong and working efficiently?
13. What is the difference between a voluntary muscle and an involuntary muscle?

Thinking Critically

LESSON 1

1. **Analyzing.** Compare the functions of the dermis and epidermis in terms of their importance to the body.
2. **Analyzing.** Review this statement: *Sweating a lot is good for you.* Do you agree with this statement? Tell why or why not?

LESSON 2

3. **Synthesizing.** Devise and write out a plan for a person who has a deficiency in calcium and phosphorus.

4. **Synthesizing.** Which player on a baseball team is most likely to develop a repetitive motion injury and why?

LESSON 3

5. **Analyzing.** Compare the functions of flexor and extensor muscles.
6. **Comparing and Contrasting.** Compare and contrast the three basic types of muscles. Explain the function of each type.

Making the Connection

1. **Science.** Place a chicken bone from which the meat has been removed in a jar with a tight-fitting lid. Fill the jar with white vinegar to cover the bone by several inches. Then close the lid. Let the jar sit for a week. Remove the bone and observe how the removal of its calcium by the acid in the vinegar has affected it.

2. **Language Arts.** Numerous advertisements appear in the media for suntanning products that profess to protect the skin from the sun's harmful UV rays. Find television and print ads geared toward teens. Investigate the truth of claims by consulting reputable on-line sources. Share your findings in an oral report.

BEYOND THE CLASSROOM

PARENTAL INVOLVEMENT Make a list of food sources for the vitamins and minerals that promote healthy skin, bones, and muscles. Share the list with family members and discuss ways of incorporating more of these foods into family meals. Write about your experiences in improving your family's awareness of the nutritional needs of these systems.

COMMUNITY INVOLVEMENT Contact the local chapter of an organization such as the Arthritis Foundation, the National Psoriasis Foundation, the Muscular Dystrophy Association, or the Myasthenia Gravis Foundation. Find out what the organization provides in terms of education and support, and what it is doing to help people who have the disease or disorder. Inquire about volunteer opportunities with the group.

SCHOOL-TO-CAREER

Exploring Careers. Interview several people who work in the field of sports or exercise. Examples include a physical therapist, a coach, a trainer, or an aerobics instructor. Describe the academic preparation necessary for that career and the personal characteristics that would be necessary to be successful in that field.

CHAPTER 16

Your Nervous and Endocrine Systems

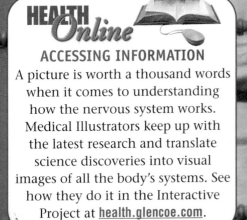

HEALTH Online

ACCESSING INFORMATION

A picture is worth a thousand words when it comes to understanding how the nervous system works. Medical Illustrators keep up with the latest research and translate science discoveries into visual images of all the body's systems. See how they do it in the Interactive Project at **health.glencoe.com**.

> ## The brain's task is to make sense of the world.... "

—Nicholas Wade
Contemporary writer

Self-Inventory Write the numbers 1–10 on a sheet of paper. Read each statement below and respond by writing *yes*, *no*, or *sometimes* for each item. Write a *yes* only for items that you practice regularly. Save your responses.

1	I wear a seat belt when traveling by car.
2	I wear a helmet when riding a bicycle, a skateboard, or a motorcycle, and when skating.
3	I wear protective headgear whenever I participate in a contact sport.
4	I get at least eight hours of sleep each night.
5	I exercise regularly.
6	I avoid alcohol and other drugs.
7	I determine the depth of water in a pool or lake before diving in.
8	I wear safety goggles when required for class or sports.
9	I avoid injuries to the spinal cord by lifting and carrying objects properly.
10	I include sources of iodine as part of my eating pattern.

Follow-up After completing the chapter, retake this self-inventory. Pick two items that you need to work on and set a goal to improve your health behaviors.

Quick Write How much do you really know about the workings of your brain? List three facts about its structure and three about its functions. Share this knowledge with your classmates.

The Nervous System

Computers are remarkable machines, capable of performing complex calculations in seconds. Yet even the fastest, most sophisticated computer is unable to compose a symphony or write a play. Only the human brain is capable of such achievements. In fact, if not for the human brain, there would be no computers.

Functions of the Nervous System

Your brain is just one part, but an important part, of your nervous system—your body's communication network and control center. Your nervous system controls all of your body's actions and functions. It senses changes not only within your body but also outside of it in your environment and enables you to respond within fractions of a second.

Structure of the Nervous System

There are two main divisions of the nervous system, the *central nervous system* (CNS) and the *peripheral nervous system* (PNS). The PNS gathers information from inside and outside your body. The CNS receives and analyzes this information and initiates responses. The

PNS then picks up and carries the response signals. This information is transmitted throughout your body by means of electrical charges—or *impulses*—that travel at speeds of up to 248 miles per hour (399 kmph). The messengers and receivers of these transmissions are **neurons,** or *nerve cells.*

Functions of Neurons

Neurons are classified according to their functions. There are three main types of neurons: sensory neurons, motor neurons, and interneurons. Sensory neurons carry signals from sense receptors into the CNS. Motor neurons carry signals from the CNS to muscles or glands. Interneurons form all the electrical connections within the CNS itself.

Unlike other cells, neurons cannot replace themselves. If the cell body of a neuron is damaged or degenerates, the cell dies. Each neuron is made up of three basic parts:

- **Cell body.** The cell body consists of a nucleus—the control center of the cell—in a sack of fluid contained within an outer skin called the *cell membrane.* The nucleus receives and sends nerve impulses. It also regulates the amount and types of proteins made in the cell.

- **Dendrites.** Dendrites are branching projections of the cell body. They receive and carry impulses toward the cell body.

- **Axons.** Every neuron has one threadlike extension called an *axon* that carries impulses away from the cell body. An axon branches at its end to form terminals through which signals are sent to target cells, such as the dendrites of other neurons, muscle cells, or glands. Axons vary in length from a fraction of an inch (a few mm) to several feet (more than 1 m). Most axons have a coating or sheath of fatty material called *myelin.* The myelin sheath insulates the nerve fiber and speeds the transmission of impulses.

A nerve impulse travels from the receptors of a sensory neuron, across an interneuron to a motor neuron, then to muscle fibers.

ACTIVITY *Describe the nerve actions that take place when you accidentally touch something that is very sharp.*

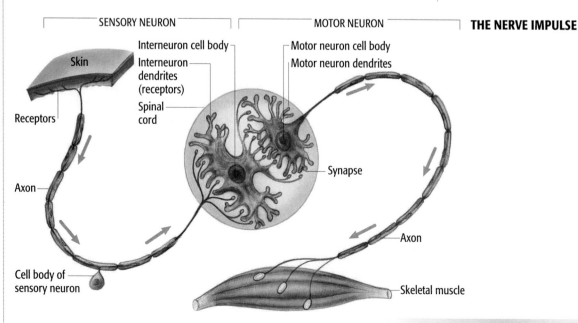

SENSORY NEURON | MOTOR NEURON

THE NERVE IMPULSE

Skin

Interneuron cell body

Interneuron dendrites (receptors)

Spinal cord

Receptors

Motor neuron cell body

Motor neuron dendrites

Synapse

Axon

Axon

Cell body of sensory neuron

Skeletal muscle

The Central Nervous System

In one way or another, every body function involves the CNS. The CNS is made up of two main parts, the spinal cord and the brain.

The Spinal Cord

The spinal cord is a cylinder of nerve tissue about 18 inches (45.7 cm) long and about as thick as your index finger. It is a downward extension of the brain. The spinal cord runs down the central canal in the spine and is protected by the vertebrae, the bones that make up your spine. It is also protected by cerebrospinal fluid that acts like a shock absorber and by three layers of connective membranes called the *spinal meninges.*

At the center of the spinal cord is a region called the *gray matter.* It contains the cell bodies of neurons along with supporting cells. Some of the neurons are interneurons. Others are motor neurons whose axons pass out of the spinal cord in bundles and extend to muscles and glands. The axons of sensory neurons enter the gray matter and connect with the motor neurons and interneurons. The gray matter is surrounded with areas of white matter that consist of nerve cell axons running lengthwise through the spinal cord.

NERVOUS SYSTEM

12 pairs of cranial nerves

Cerebrum

Cerebellum

8 pairs of cervical nerves

Spinal cord

Vertebra

12 pairs of thoracic nerves

5 pairs of lumbar nerves

5 pairs of sacral nerves

1 pair of coccygeal nerves

➤ *The CNS consists of the brain and spinal cord. The PNS is made up of the cranial and spinal nerves that branch from the brain and spinal cord.*

ACTIVITY *Use the illustration to locate cervical (neck), thoracic (chest), and lumbar (lower back) vertebrae which are the origin of nerves.*

CROSS SECTION OF SPINAL CORD

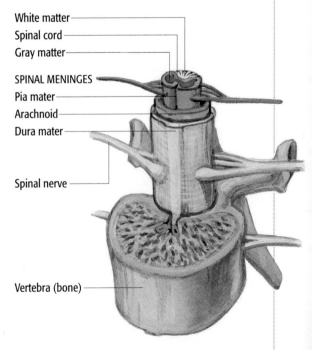

White matter

Spinal cord

Gray matter

SPINAL MENINGES

Pia mater

Arachnoid

Dura mater

Spinal nerve

Vertebra (bone)

The Brain

Your brain is the largest, most complex part of your nervous system. Your brain helps you receive and process messages—to think, remember, and reason—and coordinates your muscular movement. Your brain is involved in your emotions and everything you sense.

The brain weighs about three pounds (1.4 kg) and contains almost 100 billion neurons. At birth, the brain weighs about one pound (0.5 kg). In humans, it reaches full size by age six. Although the brain makes up only about 2 percent of your total body weight, it uses more than 20 percent of the oxygen you inhale. Without oxygen, the brain can last for only four to five minutes before suffering serious and irreversible damage.

The brain is protected by eight cranial bones that form the skull and three layers of membranes called *cranial meninges*. Cerebrospinal fluid between the meninges cushions the brain from injury.

The function of the brain is similar, on the one hand, to that of a computer and, on the other hand, to that of a chemical plant. Brain cells produce electrical signals and send them along pathways called *circuits*. These circuits receive, process, store, and retrieve information much as a computer does. Unlike a computer, however, the brain creates its electrical signals by chemical means. The proper functioning of the brain depends on the many complicated chemical substances that brain cells produce.

The brain has three main divisions: the cerebrum, the cerebellum, and the brain stem.

THE CEREBRUM

The largest, most complex part of the brain is the **cerebrum**. The cerebrum is the site of most conscious and intelligent activities. Its outer layer, or cortex, is where conscious thought takes place.

The cerebrum is divided into two halves called the *cerebral hemispheres*. These hemispheres are connected to the rest of the CNS in a crossed-over fashion. The right hemisphere controls the muscular activity of and receives sensory input from the left half of the body. The left hemisphere does the same for the right half of the body.

In the brains of animals, the cerebral hemispheres are essentially alike in function. In the brains of humans, however, they have developed different functions. The left hemisphere is mainly responsible for language, logic, arithmetic calculation, analysis, and critical thinking. The right hemisphere is concerned with imagination and

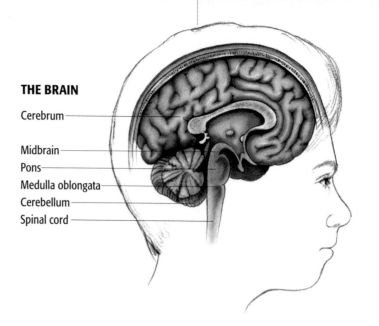

THE BRAIN

Cerebrum

Midbrain
Pons
Medulla oblongata
Cerebellum
Spinal cord

▲ *Your brain is an incredibly complex, responsive, and powerful structure.*

ACTIVITY *Describe the functions of each part of the brain shown in the diagram.*

▼ *Each hemisphere of the brain is responsible for a different range of mental activities.*

ACTIVITY *Explain why playing music requires left hemisphere activity and why painting uses the right hemisphere.*

BRAIN LOBES

Sensory information

Voluntary movements

Parietal lobe

Frontal lobe

Hearing and smell

Temporal lobe

Occipital lobe

Vision

Brain stem

Cerebellum

visual thinking—spatial relationships, form, artistic activities, and emotional responses such as color appreciation.

Each hemisphere has four lobes. Each lobe is named after the bone in the skull that protects it:

- The frontal lobe controls voluntary movements and also has a role in the use of language. The prefrontal areas of this lobe are believed to be involved with intellect and personality.
- The parietal lobe is involved with a wide variety of sensory information—heat, cold, pain, touch, and body position in space.
- The occipital lobe contains the sense of vision.
- The temporal lobe contains the senses of hearing and smell as well as memory, thought, and judgment.

THE CEREBELLUM

The **cerebellum** is *the second largest part of the brain.* It is a rounded structure located beneath the occipital lobes of the cerebrum. Like the cerebrum, the cerebellum is divided into two hemispheres.

The cerebellum is concerned mainly with maintaining posture and balance and coordinating skeletal muscle movement. It receives impulses from the balance organs of the inner ear and from muscles. After receiving this information, the cerebellum refines the orders

sent to muscles from the motor cortex in the cerebrum to ensure smooth, coordinated movements and balance. It also maintains equilibrium during movements as it receives information from the sensory organs.

THE BRAIN STEM

The **brain stem** is *a 3-inch-long (7.6-cm-long) stalk of nerve cells and fibers that connects the spinal cord to the rest of the brain.* It acts partly as a pathway for messages traveling between other parts of the brain and the spinal cord. The brain stem also connects with 10 of the 12 pairs of cranial nerves and controls basic functions such as breathing, heartbeat, and eye reflexes. The activities of the brain stem are not under conscious control.

The brain stem consists of three main parts—the medulla oblongata, pons, and midbrain.

- **Medulla oblongata.** The medulla oblongata is the lowest part of the brain stem. It contains vital control centers that regulate heartbeat, breathing, blood pressure, and digestion as well as control centers for swallowing, vomiting, sneezing, and coughing. The medulla also receives and relays taste sensations from the tongue and is involved in speech and in tongue movements.

- **Pons.** Just above the medulla, the brain stem enlarges to form the pons. The pons serves mainly as a pathway for nerve impulses passing to and from the cerebrum. The pons also contains the nuclei for four pairs of cranial nerves. It relays sensory information from the ear, face, and teeth as well as the signals that move the jaw and adjust facial expressions.

- **Midbrain.** The shortest part of the brain stem is the midbrain, which lies just above the pons. It contains the nuclei of the two pairs of cranial nerves that control eye movements and the size and reactions of the pupils. Closely associated with the brain stem are the thalamus and hypothalamus.

- **Thalamus.** Located above the midbrain are the two egg-shaped lobes of the thalamus. Each lobe is about the size of a walnut. The thalamus is an important relay center for incoming sensory impulses. Different clusters of nerve cells within the thalamus receive information from different sense organs such as the eyes and ears. Through the spine, the thalamus also receives information from touch and pressure receptors in the skin.

- **Hypothalamus.** Behind the eyes and under the thalamus is a tiny region of the brain called the *hypothalamus.* The hypothalamus has nerve centers that control various body processes and keep body conditions balanced. For example, different groups of nerve cells regulate body temperature, stimulate appetite for food and drink, and regulate sleep. The hypothalamus also controls secretions from the pituitary gland that control many processes such as metabolism and sexual development and emotional responses.

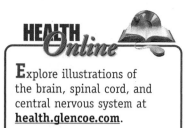

HEALTH *Online*

Explore illustrations of the brain, spinal cord, and central nervous system at **health.glencoe.com**.

▲ *Pediatric neurosurgeon Dr. Ben Carson is world-renowned for his achievements in medicine. As a student he was motivated to earn scholarships to attend medical school. He encourages all young people to develop their potential and reach their goals.*

ACTIVITY *Find out what classes you should take now to prepare for a career in the medical profession.*

The Peripheral Nervous System

Peripheral means "located away from the center." The peripheral nervous system (PNS) consists of nerves that fan out from the central nervous system to the muscles, skin, internal organs, and glands. The PNS carries messages between the CNS and the rest of the body. The PNS consists of 12 pairs of cranial nerves that branch from the brain and 31 pairs of spinal nerves that branch from the spinal cord.

The PNS is composed of two subdivisions: the autonomic nervous system and the somatic nervous system.

The Autonomic Nervous System

The autonomic nervous system (ANS) is responsible for controlling the involuntary functions of the body, such as sweating, digestion, and heart rate. The ANS consists of a network of nerves divided into two parts: the sympathetic nervous system and the parasympathetic nervous system. These two systems have opposing effects on the same organs. They act in conjunction and normally balance each other. The balance of activity between the sympathetic and parasympathetic systems is controlled by the CNS.

THE SYMPATHETIC NERVOUS SYSTEM

The sympathetic nervous system responds to the body's needs during increased activity and in emergencies. It prepares the body for a **"fight or flight" response**—the readiness to stand your ground and "fight" a stressor or "take flight" and escape. During such reactions, the heartbeat and breathing rate quicken as blood flow to the muscles increases. Nerves from the sympathetic system lead to all of the body's vital organs and glands, including the liver, heart, kidneys, pancreas, stomach, and salivary, sweat, and adrenal glands.

THE PARASYMPATHETIC NERVOUS SYSTEM

The parasympathetic system opposes the actions of the sympathetic system by slowing body functions. It slows down the heartbeat, opens blood vessels, and lowers blood pressure.

h⊙t link

"fight or flight" response For more information on the "fight or flight" response and its role in stress, see Chapter 9, page 216.

The Somatic Nervous System

The somatic nervous system includes cranial and spinal nerves that transmit impulses from the CNS to skeletal muscles. This involves voluntary responses—responses that are under your control.

Reflex Action

A **reflex** is *a spontaneous response of the body to a stimulus.* It occurs automatically, without conscious thought or effort. In simple reflexes such as the sudden jerk that occurs when the doctor taps the ligament below the knee, a sensory and motor neuron interact. The doctor's tap initiates the nerve impulse, which travels along sensory neurons to the spinal cord, then on to a motor neuron. The impulse travels back to the leg muscles, causing them to contract and the knee to jerk.

In other reflexes, when a receptor is stimulated—for example, when your hand touches a hot stove—the axon of the sensory neuron makes contact with a connecting neuron in the spinal cord. This neuron, in turn, contacts a motor neuron that sends an impulse down its axon to the muscles. The muscles respond by pulling the hand away from the stove. All of this happens in a split second, before the pain is even felt.

◄ *The nervous system plays an important part in coordination and reflexes during sports activities.*

ACTIVITY *Tell which part of the PNS works to transmit messages to the muscles when you want to swing a tennis racquet to return a serve.*

LESSON 1 *Review*

Reviewing Facts and Vocabulary

1. Describe the three types of neurons.
2. Name the two main parts of the central nervous system.
3. What is the difference between the sympathetic and parasympathetic divisions of the autonomic nervous system?

Thinking Critically

4. *Comparing and Contrasting.* How does the central nervous system compare with the peripheral nervous system?

Applying Health Skills

5. *In Your School.* Ask your teacher to obtain an MRI or CT scan from a teaching hospital. In a small group, examine the image. Attempt to identify the different parts of the brain. Discuss your observations and findings with other groups.

LESSON 2

Care and Problems of the Nervous System

When your computer crashes, you can just start it up again. When your nervous system goes "down," however, the solution is not so simple. Damage to the nervous system is far-reaching and often permanent. Proper care and preventive behaviors can help maintain the health of your body's control center.

HEALTH TERMS

epilepsy

cerebral palsy

HEALTH CONCEPTS

- By following rules of safety, you will prevent many head and spinal injuries.
- The nervous system can be damaged by degenerative diseases, infectious diseases, and genetic disorders.

Care of the Nervous System

To keep your nervous system functioning well, you need regular exercise, proper nutrition, and adequate rest and sleep. Avoid using alcohol and other drugs, which can cause permanent damage to the nervous system.

Many head and spinal cord injuries can be prevented by following basic safety rules. Wearing a seat belt in a car gives you added protection in case of an accident. Before diving into a pool or lake, you should always check the depth of the water and for the presence of underwater

obstacles, such as rocks. You can protect your head from injuries by wearing a helmet whenever you ride a bike, motorcycle, or other vehicle; use in-line skates; or play contact sports.

Problems of the Nervous System

The normal functioning of the nervous system can be disturbed in a number of ways. Accidents can damage or destroy nerve tissue. Degenerative diseases, such as Parkinson's disease, can destroy nerve tissue in the brain or spinal column. Illegal drug use and alcohol abuse can destroy brain cells and lead to nervous system disorders.

Head and Spinal Cord Injuries

Each year more than a half million Americans are hospitalized with brain or spinal cord injuries resulting from motor vehicle accidents, falls, sports, and physical abuse. Some 20 percent suffer lifelong mental or physical impairment.

Head Injuries

Although the brain is protected by the skull bones and the fluid that surrounds it, any direct blow to the head can lead to possible brain injury. Concussion, a temporary disturbance of the brain's ability to function, is the most common and mildest kind of brain injury. A more serious injury to the brain is a contusion. A contusion of the brain is a bruise, which may cause swelling of the brain. A severe contusion can result in a coma, a state of unconsciousness.

Making Responsible Decisions

Use Your Head

Nick is caught in a downpour on the way home from school one afternoon. Just then, his friend Greg drives by on his motorcycle. When Greg sees Nick, he stops and offers him a ride. The only problem is that

Greg is not carrying a spare helmet on his cycle, and riding without a helmet in the state the teens live in is against the law. Nick is getting soaked. He would love to get home quickly. However, accepting a ride could get him and his friend in trouble or, worse, lead to a serious injury. What should Nick do?

What Would You Do?

Apply the six steps of the decision-making process to Nick's problem.

1. **State the situation.**
2. **List the options.**
3. **Weigh the possible outcomes.**
4. **Consider your values.**
5. **Make a decision and act.**
6. **Evaluate the decision.**

Spinal Cord Injuries

The spinal cord is surrounded by protective membranes, shock-absorbing fluid, and the vertebrae of the spine. These defenses protect it from the bumps and falls common in everyday life. However, they often are not enough to protect the spinal cord from more serious accidents. Injury anywhere on the spinal cord can cause paralysis.

In general, injury to the upper part of the cord causes more extensive damage. An injury at the neck level, for example, may result in *quadriplegia*—paralysis in both the arms and the legs. Injury at the chest level or lower affects the legs and lower body. Paralysis of the lower body is called *paraplegia*.

Degenerative Diseases

Degenerative means causing a breakdown or deterioration of function or structure. Three common degenerative diseases of the nervous system are:

- **Parkinson's disease.** This is a progressive disorder, meaning that it gradually involves more and more nerves. Parkinson's disease is caused by degeneration of the nerve cells within the brain that modify nerve impulses transmitted from the motor areas of the brain. The result is uncoordinated muscular movement.

Building Health Skills

Setting Goals: Getting the Rest You Need

ARE YOU GIVING your body the rest it needs? If not, there are steps you can take to improve your sleep habits. These include the following:

1. **Maintain a regular schedule seven days a week.** People who follow routines find it easier to fall–and stay–asleep.

2. **Go to bed when you feel sleepy.** Don't force yourself to stay up. Tiredness is your body's way of letting you know it's time to turn in.

3. **Avoid caffeine in the evening.** Coffee, chocolate, and some soft-drinks contain this stimulant drug.

4. **Avoid vigorous physical activity just before bedtime.** Contrary to what some people think, exercising before bed will not tire you out. Rather, it stimulates areas of the brain that keep you awake.

5. **Avoid noise at bedtime.** Listening to music can relax you as long as you keep the volume on the radio, TV, or stereo player down. Turn down the energy in your body as you would turn down the volume on your radio.

- **Multiple sclerosis.** Multiple sclerosis (MS) is a progressive disease of the CNS. It involves the destruction of the myelin sheath that surrounds nerve fibers in the brain and spinal cord. MS is thought to be an autoimmune disease in which the body's defense system begins to treat the myelin as a foreign invader and attacks it. Scar tissue replaces the destroyed myelin. The underlying nerve fibers are damaged, and voluntary control of muscles gradually decreases.

- **Alzheimer's disease.** Alzheimer's disease causes general mental deterioration. Patients gradually lose their memory and powers of judgment. Speech and body coordination may also be affected. Although there is no cure, researchers continue to search for the causes of the disease and ways of preventing it. It is the fourth leading cause of death in adults.

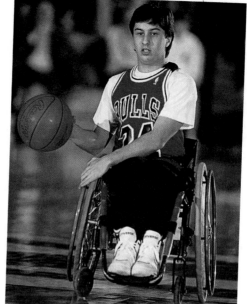

Specially designed wheelchairs enable persons with spinal cord injuries to lead full, active lives.

ACTIVITY *Explain why being able to participate in sports is important to the well-being of persons with spinal cord injuries.*

up date
▶ Looking at Technology

How a CT Scan Works

Computerized tomography, or CT, scanning is a technique that can produce clear pictures of the brain. X rays are passed through the brain at different angles. Computer screens then display cross-sectional slices of the brain viewed from any desired angle.

Before the scan is carried out, the patient may be injected with a dye to make blood vessels or abnormalities show up more clearly. To perform a CT scan, the patient lies on a table that can be moved to allow accurate positioning within the machine. The machine itself can be tilted to allow precise areas to be X-rayed. Numbers of X-ray beams are passed through the brain at different angles as the scanner rotates around the patient. These beams are of very low dosages and last only a fraction of a second. Detectors in the scanner record the amount of X rays absorbed by different tissues. A computer then transforms this information into a detailed image. CT scans are a valuable tool in diagnosing brain abnormalities. They have proved even more invaluable in determining which parts of the brain do what.

When it comes to physical activity of any sort, you can demonstrate responsibility and prevent injury to yourself and others by using **good judgment**. That means planning carefully and considering the consequences of your actions *before* you head out the door.

Character Check Before you begin any physical activity, consider the following carefully:

➤ proper equipment

➤ proper use of equipment

➤ safety precautions

➤ equipment maintenance

➤ weather and temperature

➤ visibility

➤ hydration and ventilation

Other Disorders and Problems

Although many disorders of the nervous system have known causes, some may have many possible causes. In some cases, the cause is unknown.

■ **Epilepsy.** The term *epilepsy* comes from a Greek word meaning "seizure." **Epilepsy** is *a disorder of the nervous system that is characterized by recurrent seizures—sudden episodes of uncontrolled electrical activity in the brain*. Epilepsy is not a disease but, rather, a symptom of an underlying problem. Seizures may result from chemical imbalance in the brain, head injury, tumor, injury to the brain before or during birth, brain infection, stroke, or withdrawal from drugs or alcohol, among other possible causes. Different types of seizures can affect people with epilepsy. A physician can identify the seizure type and prescribe proper medication to control the seizures and help the person lead a normal, healthy life.

■ **Cerebral Palsy.** **Cerebral palsy** refers to *a group of nonprogressive neurological disorders that are the result of damage to the brain before birth, during birth, in the newborn period, or in early childhood*. It was once thought that lack of oxygen during birth was the primary cause of cerebral palsy. In truth, only a minority of cases result from oxygen deficiency. Accidental injury, radiation, certain drugs, and diseases such as encephalitis and meningitis are among the causes. In the majority of cases, the cause is unknown. Physical therapy programs, braces, and walking aids all help cerebral palsy patients to lead full, active lives.

LESSON 2 *Review*

Reviewing Facts and Vocabulary

1. Describe injuries that might result from a sharp blow to the head.
2. What is the effect of multiple sclerosis on the body?

Thinking Critically

3. *Evaluating.* Some states have enacted laws requiring that children under certain ages be restrained by seat belts or, for very young children, car seats. Do you think parents should be required by law to use such devices? Why or why not?

Applying Health Skills

4. *In Your Home and School.* Fold a sheet of paper lengthwise to form two columns. Label the first column *Risks* and the second, *Prevention*. In the first column, write risks of possible head or spinal cord injury that exist in your home (for example, stairway with no handrail). In the second column, identify preventive measures your family has taken or might take to diminish each risk (for example, installed grab bars in shower stall). Do a second risk survey for your school.

The Endocrine System

You already know that the nervous system coordinates and regulates the functions of the body. It is aided in these tasks by the endocrine system. Unlike the nervous system, which sends messages in the form of electrical impulses, the endocrine system uses chemical messengers called hormones.

HEALTH TERMS

endocrine glands

hormones

pituitary gland

gonads

thyroid gland

parathyroid glands

adrenal glands

pancreas

HEALTH CONCEPTS

- The endocrine system works with the nervous system to coordinate and regulate body functions.
- Endocrine glands send messages to organs and systems of the body via chemical messengers called *hormones.*

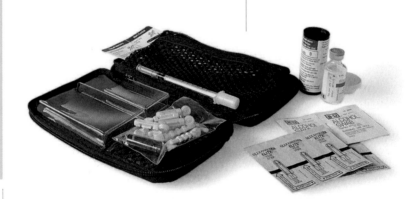

Insulin medication

Structure of the Endocrine System

The principal structures of the endocrine system are the **endocrine glands.** These are *ductless, or tubeless, structures that secrete hormones.* **Hormones** are *chemical substances produced by ductless glands that regulate the activities of different body cells.* They are secreted by the endocrine glands and carried to their destinations in the body via the bloodstream. This distinguishes endocrine glands from exocrine glands, which secrete substances into ducts, or tubes, to be carried to a specific area of the body.

Endocrine glands are scattered throughout the body. They work independently of one another, but they interact in well-defined ways. Major glands of the endocrine system include the pituitary, the thyroid, the parathyroid, the adrenals, the pancreas, and the gonads.

The Pituitary Gland

The **pituitary gland** *regulates and controls the activities of all other endocrine glands*. It is known, therefore, as the "master gland." This pea-sized gland is located at the midpoint of the skull, roughly behind the eyes. It has three sections, or lobes—anterior, intermediate, and posterior.

ANTERIOR LOBE

Anterior means "front." The hormones produced by this lobe control a range of body functions. They regulate metabolic activities of cells and stimulate other endocrine glands. The anterior lobe produces six hormones. These are as follows:

- Somatotropic, or growth, hormone stimulates normal body growth and development by altering chemical activity in body cells. It especially influences growth of the skeleton and skeletal muscles.
- Thyroid-stimulating hormone (TSH) stimulates hormone production by the thyroid gland.
- Adrenocorticotropic hormone (ACTH) stimulates hormone production by the adrenal glands.
- Two gonadotropic hormones—follicle-stimulating hormone (FSH) and luteinizing hormone (LH)—control the growth, development, and functions of the **gonads**, which is another name for *the ovaries* and *testes*. In females, FSH triggers the development of egg cells, or ova, in the ovary and stimulates cells in the ovary to produce estrogen, a female sex hormone. In males, FSH stimulates the testes to produce sperm cells. In females, LH is responsible for ovulation, or the release of a mature ovum from the ovary, and stimulates cells in the ovaries to produce progesterone, a female sex hormone. In males, LH stimulates cells in the testes to produce testosterone, a male sex hormone.
- Prolactin stimulates the production of milk in females who have given birth.

INTERMEDIATE LOBE

This lobe secretes melanocyte-stimulating hormone (MSH). MSH controls the darkening of the skin by stimulating pigment cells in the skin.

POSTERIOR LOBE

The posterior lobe secretes two hormones, antidiuretic hormone (ADH) and oxytocin. ADH's principal function is to regulate the balance of water in the body. It stimulates the kidneys to return water to the blood, which decreases water loss in the urine. Oxytocin stimulates the smooth muscles in the uterus of a pregnant female, causing contractions during the birth of a baby.

▼ *The glands of the endocrine system are situated at different locations throughout the body.*

ACTIVITY *Identify the glands that are different in males and females.*

THE ENDOCRINE SYSTEM

Pineal body
Pituitary gland

Thyroid gland
Parathyroid glands

Thymus gland

Adrenal glands
Pancreas

Ovaries (in female)

Testes (in male)

The Thyroid Gland

The **thyroid gland** *produces hormones that regulate metabolism—the use of nutrients by the body's cells—body heat production, and bone growth.* One of the largest glands of the endocrine system, the thyroid gland is located in the front of the neck, just below the larynx. It consists of two lobes, one on either side of the trachea, or windpipe.

The principal hormone produced by the thyroid gland is thyroxine, which regulates the way cells release energy from nutrients or use energy to create other substances, such as proteins. Overproduction of thyroxine causes symptoms that include tiredness, anxiety, weight loss, diarrhea, and inability to tolerate heat. Low thyroxine production causes symptoms that include tiredness, dry skin, hair loss, weight gain, constipation, and sensitivity to cold.

▲ *The demands of school, family, and extra-curricular activities require you to maintain energy throughout the day.*

ACTIVITY *Explain why the thyroid gland is important in regulating your energy level.*

The Parathyroid Glands

The **parathyroid glands** are *structures that produce parathyroid hormone, which regulates the body's calcium and phosphorus balance.* They are the smallest glands of the endocrine system and are situated on the lobes of the thyroid gland.

The Adrenal Glands

The **adrenal glands** are *two glands located on the top of the kidneys.* The adrenal glands consist of two parts—an outer region called the adrenal cortex and a smaller inner region called the adrenal medulla.

THE ADRENAL CORTEX

The adrenal cortex, which is absolutely essential for life, secretes a mixture of hormones that affect numerous body functions. It is made up of three distinct zones.

The outermost zone produces the hormone aldosterone. Its function is to inhibit the amount of sodium excreted in the urine. This serves to maintain blood volume and blood pressure.

Together, the inner and middle zones produce the hormones hydrocortisone and corticosterone as well as small amounts of androgen hormones. Hydrocortisone affects the metabolism of fats, proteins, and carbohydrates. It also helps the body recover from stress. The rate of hydrocortisone secretion is controlled by the release of ACTH by the pituitary gland. Both hydrocortisone and corticosterone play a role in stopping inflammation.

Growth Opportunity

Human beings come in a wide range of heights. Some of your classmates are probably taller than you, and some are probably shorter. Height differences are most obvious during the teenage years when the body is still growing and changing.

There is a great difference in the rates at which teens develop and grow. Some teens experience early growth spurts that make them taller than peers the same age. Other teens grow more slowly and take longer to achieve their full height.

Whatever a person's height, it is important to recognize and accept the uniqueness of individuals. A person's true value is not related to his or her size.

h t link

reproduction For more information on the role of the gonads in the process of reproduction, see Chapter 19, page 434.

THE ADRENAL MEDULLA

The adrenal medulla is highly dependent on the hypothalamus and the autonomic nervous system for regulation. It secretes the hormones epinephrine (more commonly called adrenaline) and norepinephrine. Epinephrine increases heart action, raises blood pressure, increases respiration, and suppresses the digestive process. This hormone is also known as the emergency hormone because it is released into the blood in greater amounts during highly emotional states, such as when a person experiences fear or anger.

The Pancreas

The **pancreas** is *a gland that serves two systems—the digestive and the endocrine.* This elongated, tapered gland lies behind the stomach, attached to the first section of the small intestine by a duct that transports its digestive juice to the intestine. It is the largest gland in the endocrine system.

Most of the pancreas consists of exocrine tissue, which secretes digestive enzymes into a network of ducts that meet to form the main pancreatic duct. Scattered throughout the pancreas are small clusters of endocrine cells. These are called the islets of Langerhans, named after Paul Langerhans, a German scientist who first noticed them in 1869. The endocrine cells in the islets of Langerhans secrete two hormones—glucagon and insulin—that regulate the level of glucose (blood sugar) in the blood.

One hormone, glucagon, helps maintain the sugar level in the blood by stimulating the liver to convert glycogen to glucose, thus raising the blood sugar level. Glycogen is a storage form of glucose, found mainly in the liver and muscle cells. The other hormone, insulin, tends to decrease blood sugar levels. Insulin stimulates the liver to form glycogen from glucose.

The Gonads

Of all the endocrine glands, only the gonads are different in males and females. The ovaries in the female and the testes in the male are part of the reproductive system. The ovaries produce and release ova, and the testes produce and release sperm.

Hormones secreted by these glands are responsible for the development and maintenance of the secondary sex characteristics that begin to appear during adolescence, such as breasts in females and facial hair in males. Gonads also play a key role in the process of **reproduction**. This will be discussed at greater length in Chapter 19.

Endocrine System Problems

Most disorders of the endocrine system are related to the production of too much or too little of a hormone. Following is a description of some problems associated with endocrine glands.

- **Diabetes Mellitus.** Diabetes mellitus is a disorder in which the pancreas produces too little or no insulin. As a result, the glucose level in the blood becomes very high. Symptoms include excessive urination, constant thirst, weight loss, and fatigue.
- **Graves' Disease.** Graves' disease, or hyperthyroidism, is an auto-immune disorder in which the thyroid gland becomes overactive and enlarged, producing excessive amounts of thyroid hormones.
- **Cushing's Disease.** Overproduction of adrenal hormones can result in Cushing's disease. People with Cushing's disease develop round faces, humped upper backs, weak limbs, thin and easily bruised skin, and fragile bones. Treatment depends on whether the cause is overuse of corticosteroid drugs, a tumor or overgrowth of an adrenal gland, or a tumor on the pituitary gland.
- **Goiter.** A goiter is an enlargement of the thyroid gland. It can be seen as a swelling on the neck. In many parts of the world, the main cause of a goiter is lack of iodine in the diet. The condition has virtually disappeared in the United States since the introduction of iodized salt.

Growth Disorders

If, during the growing years, the anterior lobe of the pituitary gland does not produce enough of the growth hormone, a person does not grow. The person's stature is short because of delayed bone growth. The bones are usually normal in shape, however. If this condition is diagnosed early, proper treatment can be prescribed. With early treatment, a child may reach full height.

LESSON 3 *Review*

Reviewing Facts and Vocabulary

1. Why is the pituitary gland called the master gland?
2. Make a chart showing the hormones produced by the pituitary gland. Include what they do.

Thinking Critically

3. *Synthesizing.* For each of the following conditions, identify the endocrine gland that probably is not functioning properly: (a) impaired growth, causing a person to be abnormally small for his or her age; (b) lowered metabolic rate accompanied by mental and physical sluggishness; (c) loss of salt through the kidneys and a drop in blood pressure. What general statement can be made about all three conditions that would characterize them?

Applying Health Skills

4. *In Your Home and School.* Does anyone in your family or among your classmates have diabetes? Ask the person to explain what symptoms were first experienced, how the disease was diagnosed, and what treatment was prescribed. Encourage the person to evaluate the results of the treatment.

Health Skills Activities

Activity 1 — Understanding Problems of the Nervous System

Millions of Americans are affected by diseases and disorders of the nervous system. Create an informational pamphlet to help the general public be more understanding of persons afflicted with such diseases.

Directions

1. In a group, locate a disease or disorder of the nervous system and/or brain. Create a pamphlet that describes the disease, how a person develops it, and its effect on the individual (e.g., loss of muscular control).
2. In a separate section, discuss current medical treatments for this disease and how to help a person who has this disease.
3. Make your pamphlet available to students in your school.

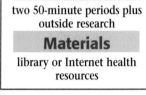

Time
two 50-minute periods plus outside research

Materials
library or Internet health resources

Self-Assessment

✓ Selected a disease or disorder of the nervous system.
✓ Included all the information requested.
✓ Produced an eye-catching pamphlet.

Activity 2 — Injury Prevention

Although skating and similar activities can be fun, they can also pose a risk of injuries to the head and spine. Find out how you can increase sports safety?

Directions

1. Choose a sport that is popular among teens.
2. Using library, Internet, or other resources, research this sport. Determine what safety measures need to be taken (such as equipment, avoiding "hot-dogging") and the types of head and spine injuries that arise when safety measures are not followed.
3. If possible, download pictures of appropriate sports equipment from the Internet (or people safely practicing the sport) and, using a color computer printer, print these pictures.
4. Present your sports safety information to the class.

Time
50 minutes plus outside research

Materials
library or Internet health resources, poster board, colored markers, paper, pen or pencil, word processor with printer (optional)

Self-Assessment

✓ Presented safety information that was both clear and complete.
✓ Included visual images of appropriate sports equipment.

Heads Up!

Use your head usually means "think about it." In some sports, however, the meaning is much more literal. Players really do use their heads—and sometimes they get hurt. Football tops the list of sports that lead to head injuries, but the list doesn't stop there. Soccer players might score an important goal by hitting the ball with their heads. They could also injure their brains with these repeated blows to the head.

Researchers are studying the effects of sports head injuries on players' ability to think. Even a mild concussion can lead to slower or confused thought processes for up to five days. They also discovered that returning to a sport before an injury is fully healed could lead to critical new injuries.

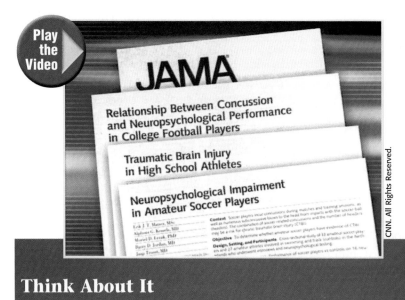

Play the Video

JAMA

Relationship Between Concussion and Neuropsychological Performance in College Football Players

Traumatic Brain Injury in High School Athletes

Neuropsychological Impairment in Amateur Soccer Players

Think About It

▶ Why do you think head injuries are more common during games than in practice?

▶ How can head injuries affect a player's ability to make decisions?

▶ What safety precautions will help protect the nervous system? Why aren't these precautions always effective?

Using Health Terms

On a separate sheet of paper, write the term that best matches each definition below.

LESSON 1

1. The second largest part of the brain.
2. Nerve cells.
3. A spontaneous response of the body to a stimulus.
4. A 3-inch-long (7.6-cm-long) stalk of nerve cells and fibers that connects the spinal cord to the rest of the brain.
5. The largest, most complex part of the brain.

LESSON 2

6. A group of nonprogressive neurological disorders that are the result of damage to the brain before birth, during birth, in the newborn period, or in early childhood.

7. A disorder of the nervous system that is characterized by recurrent seizures—sudden episodes of uncontrolled electrical activity in the brain.

LESSON 3

8. Produces hormones that regulate metabolism, body heat production, and bone growth.
9. A gland that serves two systems—the digestive and the endocrine.
10. Chemical substances produced by ductless glands that regulate the activities of different body cells.
11. Two glands located on the top of the kidneys.
12. Regulates and controls the activities of all other endocrine glands.
13. The ovaries and testes.

Recalling the Facts

Using complete sentences, answer the following questions.

LESSON 1

1. What does the peripheral nervous system consist of?
2. List the three main divisions of the brain.
3. What is the function of the autonomic nervous system?
4. What division of the autonomic nervous system responds to the body's needs during increased activities?
5. Give two examples of the opposing actions of the sympathetic and parasympathetic divisions of the autonomic nervous system.

LESSON 2

6. Name two degenerative diseases of the nervous system and describe the symptoms of each.

7. Tell what a concussion is and what the results of a concussion might be.
8. Tell what a contusion is and what the results of a contusion might be.
9. Name three ways of preventing head and spinal cord injuries.
10. What is a possible effect of injury to the spinal cord at the level of the neck?

LESSON 3

11. What are hormones and what is their function?
12. What is the difference between endocrine glands and exocrine glands?
13. Describe why the ovaries and testes are regarded as endocrine glands.
14. What does the principle hormone produced by the thyroid do?
15. What is the largest gland in the endocrine system, and what does it do?

Thinking Critically

LESSON 1

1. ***Synthesizing.*** Suppose that your frontal lobe was injured and you began to suffer from mood swings. How do you think your life might change?
2. ***Synthesizing.*** How might a person's ability to speak be affected by a stroke that damages the left hemisphere of the brain?

LESSON 2

3. ***Synthesizing.*** Summarize reasons for the stigma that has historically been attached to epilepsy.

4. ***Analyzing.*** Think of the different tasks you perform in a day. Which tasks do you think a paraplegic could perform? Which tasks would require retraining?
5. ***Evaluating.*** If you were to have an impairment on one side of the brain, which side would be hardest for you to live without? Why?

LESSON 3

6. ***Comparing and Contrasting.*** Compare the functions of the gonadotropic hormones FSH and LH in males and females.

Making the Connection

1. ***Science.*** Research scientific discoveries about how the left brain and right brain work. Of special interest are "split brain" studies—research done with individuals who underwent surgery that involved severing the connections between the two cerebral hemispheres.

2. ***Social Studies.*** Sometimes, a disease is named for a famous person who has been affected by it. Other times, a disease is named for the person who first describes its effects. Choose one of the diseases discussed in this chapter and find out the facts behind how it got its name.

BEYOND THE CLASSROOM

PARENTAL INVOLVEMENT Ask your parents whether any family members or close relatives—present and past—have ever suffered from disorders of the endocrine glands. With them, draw a family tree that includes all persons with any such disorders. Try to determine whether there seems to be a genetic component to the disorder(s).

COMMUNITY INVOLVEMENT With a small group of classmates, find out whether there is a helmet law and/or a seat belt law in your state. If there is, find out how the number of head injuries has changed since the law was enacted. If there is no law, find out what steps might be taken to enact such a law and how you can help.

SCHOOL-TO-CAREER
Technology. There are many exciting new medical and technological advances that offer new hope and improved quality of life for people with brain and spinal cord diseases and injuries. These range from experiments with repairing damaged spinal cords, to surgical implants that restore control to paralyzed limbs, to vastly improved wheelchairs. Find out about the latest technology in this field. Report your findings to the class.

CHAPTER 17

Your Circulatory and Respiratory Systems

HEALTH Online

ADVOCACY

What better way to promote the health of others than to become an advocate for healthy lungs? A career in the medical field as a Respiratory Therapist offers the chance to work with infants with breathing difficulties or adults fighting respiratory disease. Visit health.glencoe.com and check the Career Corner.

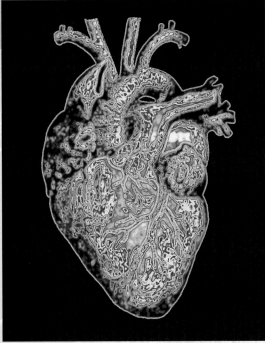
Scan of heart

Self-Inventory Write the numbers 1–10 on a sheet of paper. Read each statement below and respond by writing *yes*, *no*, or *sometimes* for each item. Write a *yes* only for items that you practice regularly. Save your responses.

1	I try to maintain the appropriate weight for my height.
2	I avoid foods that are high in fat, cholesterol, and salt.
3	I eat foods that are rich in iron (leafy green vegetables, dried fruits, enriched cereals) daily.
4	I get at least 20 minutes of aerobic exercise at least three times a week.
5	I sleep at least seven to eight hours every night.
6	I have a regular physical checkup that includes checking my blood pressure.
7	I do not smoke.
8	I avoid breathing other people's smoke.
9	I study, work, or exercise in a well-ventilated area.
10	I avoid breathing polluted air or car fumes.

Follow-up After completing the chapter, retake this self-inventory. Pick two items that you need to work on and set a goal to improve your health behaviors.

> ❝ *Many a man who would not dream of putting too much pressure in his automobile tires lays a constant overstrain on his heart and arteries.* ❞

—BRUCE BARTON
CONTEMPORARY WRITER, (1886–1967)

Quick Write Fold a paper in half. Write on one half words associated with the health of the circulatory system, on the other half words you associate with the respiratory system. Do any words fit both categories?

The Circulatory System

When you examine a road map of a city, you see an intricate, interconnecting network of roads over which goods are transported to and from a central hub. Without this network, the city could not function and thrive.

The same may be said of the circulatory system. It is the main transportation system for blood and other essential body fluids.

HEALTH TERMS

plasma
hemoglobin
platelets
arteries
capillaries
veins
lymph
lymphocytes

HEALTH CONCEPTS

- The heart is a pump that moves the body's blood supply through two major networks of pathways.
- Never resting, the heart continuously pumps blood throughout the body by means of the circulatory system.
- The lymphatic system works with the circulatory system to help the body maintain its fluid balance and helps the body fight infection.

Climbing equipment

hotlink

kidneys For more information on waste removal by the kidneys, see Chapter 18, page 425.

Functions of the Circulatory System

Your circulatory system maintains an internal environment in which all the cells of your body are nourished. As your heart pumps blood, blood vessels carry oxygen and nutrients to body cells. At the same time, another gas, carbon dioxide, is carried along with waste matter from your cells and delivered to your lungs and **kidneys** for removal from the body.

Structure of the Circulatory System

The main parts of the circulatory system are your heart, blood, and a network of branching vessels—arteries, veins, and capillaries— that carry fluids throughout your body.

The Heart

Along with your brain, your heart is the most important part of your body's vital organs. It never rests, even when you do. This muscular pump beats continuously to send blood to the lungs and the rest of the body.

Much of the heart consists of a special type of muscle called *myocardium*. Given sufficient oxygen and nutrients, the myocardium contracts rhythmically and automatically.

CHAMBERS OF THE HEART

A thick central muscular wall called the *septum* divides the interior of the heart into right and left halves. Each half has two chambers— an upper chamber called an *atrium* and a larger lower chamber called a *ventricle*. One-way valves at the exits from each heart chamber guarantee that blood can flow in only one direction.

A small area of the right atrium serves as a natural pacemaker, controlling the rate at which the heart beats. In response to impulses from the brain, this area sends an electrical impulse through the heart that causes both atria to contract. The contraction forces blood forward into the ventricles. Within milliseconds, this electric "charge" reaches a second piece of specialized tissue made of slow-conducting muscle cells. This tissue relays the charge to the muscles of the ventricles. The ventricles contract, increasing the pressure of blood in the heart. The increased pressure causes the valves to close, preventing backflow. The natural sound of the heart is related to the movements of these muscles and valves.

CIRCULATION IN THE HEART

Blood that has been depleted of oxygen but contains carbon dioxide and waste matter is carried to the heart by two large blood vessels called the *vena cava*. This blood enters the right atrium, is transferred to the right ventricle, and is then pumped to the lungs. In the lungs, the blood picks up oxygen from inhaled air and releases carbon dioxide. The newly oxygenated blood is returned to the heart. It enters the left atrium, is transferred to the left ventricle, and is then pumped to all the tissues of the body.

Blood

Blood is the fluid that transports all of the substances that your body needs to sustain life. Blood delivers oxygen, hormones, and nutrients to the cells and carries away wastes that the cells produce.

Rock climbing, backpacking, and other physical activities will keep your heart in good condition.

ACTIVITY *What physical activities do you enjoy?*

Ho you know why your heart beats faster during physical activity? Take the Healthy Heart I.Q. Test online to check your knowledge in Web Links at **health.glencoe.com**.

▼ *Blood flows into the right and left atria of the heart and leaves the heart via the right and left ventricles.*

ACTIVITY *Identify the blood vessels that carry blood from the lungs to the heart and the vessels that carry blood from the heart to the lungs.*

Blood also plays an important role in your body's defense against infection.

About 55 percent of the total volume of blood is made up of **plasma**, *the fluid in which the other parts of blood are suspended.* Plasma, which is about 92 percent water, contains many important nutrients, salts, proteins, other chemicals, and blood cells. Blood cells include red blood cells, which make up about 40 percent of normal blood, and white blood cells and platelets, which together make up less than 5 percent of your blood's volume.

RED BLOOD CELLS

Red blood cells carry oxygen from the lungs to the body tissues, where the oxygen is exchanged for carbon dioxide. Each red blood cell contains **hemoglobin**, *the oxygen-carrying part of blood.* Hemoglobin is a protein compound that is rich in iron. It binds with oxygen in the lungs and releases the oxygen in the tissues. Hemoglobin is the pigment that gives blood its red color.

WHITE BLOOD CELLS

The principal role of white blood cells is to protect the body against infection and to fight infection when it occurs. White blood cells are larger than red blood cells, but there are far fewer of them. Production of these cells increases when there is infection in the body. Some types of white blood cells surround invading pathogens and ingest them. Others form the antibodies that make you immune to second attacks of diseases such as measles.

PULMONARY CIRCULATION

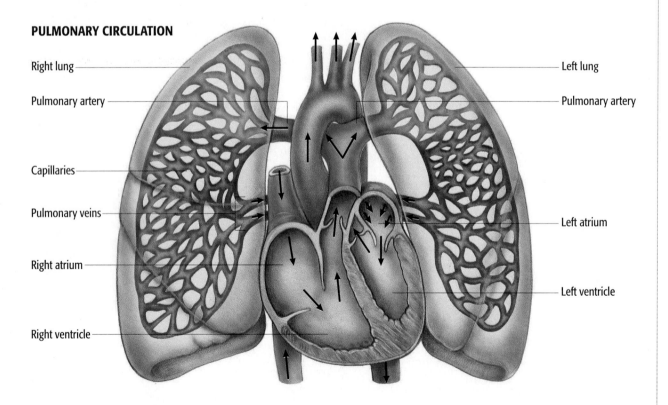

Right lung — Left lung
Pulmonary artery — Pulmonary artery
Capillaries —
Pulmonary veins — Left atrium
Right atrium —
— Left ventricle
Right ventricle —

Building Health Skills

Becoming Health Literate: Evaluating Sources

EVERY DAY you are subjected to a barrage of health information from various sources. Lately there has been much publicity about *psychoimmunology*—"thinking yourself well." "CANCER CURED BY THOUGHTS," shrieks a tabloid headline. "RESEARCHERS EVALUATE RELATIONSHIP BETWEEN EMOTIONS AND IMMUNE RESPONSE," a newspaper headline announces. In order for you to decide how valid the information provided by a news medium is, it is important to consider the source.

1. **Primary sources.** A primary source, such as a research report published in a scholarly journal, presents the findings of a scientific investigation reported by the researchers themselves.

2. **Newspaper articles.** These and articles in newsmagazines are secondhand reports written by reporters who have either interviewed researchers and/or patients. They may have also picked up information from another source, such as a wire service. News items generally identify the source of the information, give the credentials of people quoted, and provide background information.

3. **Television programs.** Whether specials or daily news shows, these may include interviews with researchers or with people claiming to have had personal experience on a subject.

4. **Tabloid articles.** These are usually sensationalistic. Sources may not be identified and generally cannot be checked or verified.

PLATELETS

Blood **platelets**, the smallest type of blood cell, are *the cells that prevent the body's loss of blood.* (Their name means "little plates.") Platelets initiate a chain reaction that causes blood to clot. When platelets come in contact with damaged blood vessel walls, they become sticky and clump at the site of the injury. Chemicals released by the platelets cause the blood to produce small fibers, called *fibrin.* The fibrin filaments trap the platelets along with red and white blood cells. The mass of fibrin, platelets, and red and white blood cells plug the injury and form a solid clot. The scab you see on a healing cut is evidence that a clot has formed.

Blood Vessels

Blood is distributed throughout the body through a network of vessels. There are more than 60,000 miles (96,540 km) of blood vessels in your body. They are divided mainly into three types.

THE CIRCULATORY SYSTEM

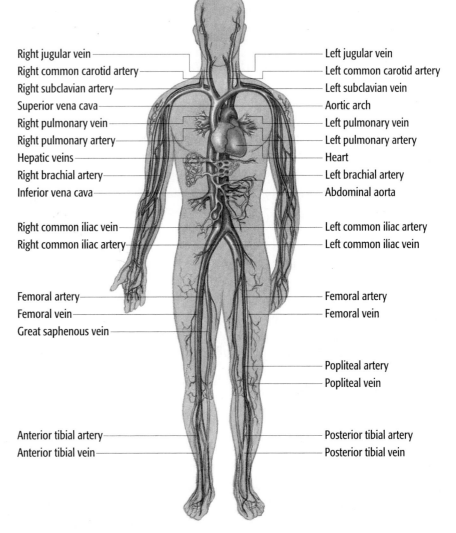

Right jugular vein — — Left jugular vein
Right common carotid artery — — Left common carotid artery
Right subclavian artery — — Left subclavian vein
Superior vena cava — — Aortic arch
Right pulmonary vein — — Left pulmonary vein
Right pulmonary artery — — Left pulmonary artery
Hepatic veins — — Heart
Right brachial artery — — Left brachial artery
Inferior vena cava — — Abdominal aorta

Right common iliac vein — — Left common iliac artery
Right common iliac artery — — Left common iliac vein

Femoral artery — — Femoral artery
Femoral vein — — Femoral vein
Great saphenous vein —

— Popliteal artery
— Popliteal vein

Anterior tibial artery — — Posterior tibial artery
Anterior tibial vein — — Posterior tibial vein

▶ *The circulatory system pumps blood from the heart to the body's cells to provide oxygen and nutrients and to remove waste products.*

ACTIVITY *Explain the functions of arteries, capillaries, and veins.*

ARTERIES

The largest blood vessels, the **arteries**, are *the vessels that carry blood away from the heart.* Pulmonary arteries carry blood from the right ventricle of the heart to the lungs. Systemic arteries carry blood from the left ventricle of the heart through the aorta (the largest artery in the body) to all parts of the body except the lungs.

Arteries are flexible tubes with a smooth inner lining, a thick, muscular middle layer, and a tough, fibrous outer covering. An artery's thick walls enable it to withstand the high blood pressure it is subjected to every time the heart beats.

Smaller vessels called *arterioles* branch directly off an artery. The arterioles connect to even smaller blood vessels called capillaries.

CAPILLARIES

The smallest blood vessels, the **capillaries** (KAP-uh-lair-eez), are *the vessels that carry blood between arterioles and small vessels called* *venules.* They form a fine network throughout the body's organs and tissues. Some capillaries are 50 times thinner than a strand of hair. It is through the thin capillary walls that nutrients and oxygen pass from the blood to body cells, and waste products move from the cells into the blood.

Capillaries are not always open to blood flow. They open and close in response to the body's need for oxygen and nutrients. The opening and closing of capillaries in the skin plays an important role in regulating the body's **temperature**.

VEINS

The system of capillaries leads into tiny vessels called *venules.* The venules join to form **veins**, *the vessels that return deoxygenated blood toward the heart from the body's organs and tissues.* There are two main exceptions to this definition: The pulmonary veins in the chest carry oxygenated blood from the lungs to the left side of the heart, and the portal vein carries nutrient-rich blood from the intestines to the liver.

Like arteries, veins have a smooth inner lining, a muscular middle layer, and a fibrous outer covering. However, blood pressure in veins is much lower than it is in arteries. The walls of veins are thinner, less flexible, less muscular, and weaker than the walls of arteries. The inner lining of many veins forms valves that help direct the flow of blood. These valves prevent blood from flowing back into the capillaries. Blood is helped on its way by pressure on the vessel walls from the contraction of surrounding muscles.

The Lymphatic System

Your body's circulatory system is supported by a second network known as the *lymphatic system.* This system serves two functions. It drains tissue fluid back into the bloodstream, and it fights **infection**. All body tissues are bathed in a watery fluid that comes from the blood. Much of this fluid returns to the blood through the walls of the capillaries. The remainder is carried to the heart through the lymphatic system. In a sense, the lymphatic system is your body's *second* circulatory system. It does not, however, have a central pump like the heart. Lymphatic fluid is circulated by movement of the body's muscles.

Lymph

The fluid that the lymphatic system transports is **lymph**, *a clear yellow fluid that fills the spaces around body cells.* Lymph is made up of proteins, fats, and **lymphocytes**, *white blood cells*

h⬤t link

temperature For more information on the role of the skin in regulating temperature, see Chapter 15, page 341.

infection For more information on the process by which the body fights infection, see Chapter 28, page 621.

THE LYMPHATIC SYSTEM

Tonsils

Thymus gland
Lymphatic duct

Lymphatic vessel
Spleen

Lymph node

Lymphatic vessel

▲ *Two separate systems transport fluids throughout your body.*

ACTIVITY *Name two similarities and two differences between the circulatory and lymphatic systems.*

that protect the body against pathogens—disease-carrying agents. There are two main types of lymphocytes, B cells and T cells.

B CELLS

About 10 percent of lymphocytes are B cells. When B cells encounter pathogens, they are stimulated to enlarge and multiply. The B cells turn into cells called *plasma cells*. Plasma cells produce antibodies that destroy or neutralize invading pathogens.

T CELLS

There are two main groups of T cells, killer cells and helper cells. Killer T cells are stimulated to multiply when abnormal body cells are present. They attach to these cells and release toxins that help destroy the abnormal cells. **Helper T cells** aid the activity of the B cells and killer T cells and control other aspects of the body's immune system.

Structure of the Lymphatic System

Lymphatic vessels are distributed throughout the body much the same as blood vessels are. They form a network that carries lymph to two lymph ducts, one in the neck area and the other in the chest area. These ducts empty into veins. At certain places along the lymphatic vessels, lymph passes through lymph nodes. These are masses of tissue that filter lymph before it returns to the blood. The nodes act as a barrier to the spread of infection, destroying or filtering out bacteria before they can pass into the blood.

h⊙t link

helper T cells For more information on the relationship between helper T cells and HIV infection, see Chapter 30, page 658.

LESSON 1 *Review*

Reviewing Facts and Vocabulary

1. What are the chambers of the human heart, and how do they function?
2. What is the function of blood?
3. What substances are carried through the body in plasma?
4. Describe the functions of lymphocytes.

Thinking Critically

5. *Analyzing.* Why do you think the body has more red blood cells than white blood cells?
6. *Comparing and Contrasting.* Compare the functions of the circulatory system with those of the lymphatic system.

Applying Health Skills

7. *In Your School.* With several classmates, purchase a beef, calf, or lamb heart and a chicken heart from a local butcher or supermarket meat department. Looking down from the top, try to identify the main blood vessels. Carefully cut the beef heart in half lengthwise. See whether you can find the four chambers, the valves, and the main arteries and veins. Do the same with the chicken heart. What is the main difference between the two hearts? Share your findings with classmates.

Care and Problems of the Circulatory System

Some highway problems, such as rush-hour congestion, are unavoidable. Measures such as carpooling can be taken to reduce or control these situations. In the case of your circulatory system, some problems may be inherited. Most problems of the circulatory system however, can be controlled through behavior.

HEALTH TERM

congenital

HEALTH CONCEPTS

- Eating right, exercising regularly, and getting adequate rest are steps you can take to care for your circulatory and lymphatic systems.
- Taking good care of your circulatory system can help reduce risk factors related to environment and heredity.

Blood pressure cuff

hotlink

smoking For more information on the dangers of smoking and other forms of tobacco use, see Chapter 24, page 533.

weight For more information on managing your weight, see Chapter 6, page 133.

Care of the Circulatory and Lymphatic Systems

Most of the risk factors related to problems with your circulatory system are within your control. Your health choices and behaviors affect its health. You probably know that **smoking** puts added stress on your circulatory system. Nicotine in cigarettes increases blood pressure and heart rate by narrowing the arteries. Not smoking—as well as avoiding secondhand smoke from smokers—is a healthy choice for you. It is also important for you to maintain an appropriate **weight**. Being overweight is linked to high blood pressure and coronary heart disease.

hotlink

aerobic exercise For more information on aerobic exercise and its contribution to total fitness, see Chapter 3, page 57.

▼ *Aerobic exercise increases your heart rate and promotes the health of your heart and blood vessels.*

ACTIVITY *Make a list of aerobic activities you enjoy that increase your pulse rate.*

Care is the same for both the circulatory and lymphatic systems. This means making sure that you care for your total health by exercising regularly, eating healthfully, and getting enough sleep—at least seven to eight hours a night during the teen years. A program of regular exercise—especially **aerobic exercise** for at least 20 minutes three times a week—will strengthen your heart, making it work more efficiently, and improve your circulation. Limiting your intake of fried foods and other foods high in fat, cholesterol, and salt will protect your heart and blood vessels. Finally, having regular medical checkups enables your physician to monitor the health of your circulatory system, keep you up to date on your immunizations, and encourage healthy behaviors.

Blood Pressure

Blood pressure is the force of the blood in the main arteries. It rises and falls as the heart and muscles of your body cope with varying demands, including stress, exercise, and sleep.

Each time the ventricles contract, blood surges through the arteries with so much force that the artery walls bulge. At this point, arterial pressure is at its greatest and is called *systolic pressure.* As the ventricles relax and refill with blood, arterial pressure is at its lowest and is called *diastolic pressure.*

As part of a regular checkup for people over age 50, an electrocardiogram (ECG or EKG) may be taken to detect signs of heart disease. During the teen years, one way that a health care professional can monitor the health of your heart is to check your blood pressure.

To measure blood pressure, a health care professional wraps a soft cuff around your upper arm and inflates it until it is tight enough to stop the flow of blood. As air is slowly released from the cuff, the health professional uses a stethoscope to listen for the sound of blood as it moves through the main artery again. This is recorded as the systolic pressure. It is the upper number of the fraction representing your blood pressure and is usually between 110 and 140. He or she then deflates the cuff further and listens until the beat disappears and the blood flows steadily through the now open artery. This is the diastolic pressure. It is the lower number of the fraction and is usually between 70 and 90.

Circulatory System Problems

With proper care, some problems of the heart and circulatory system can be avoided. Some of these avoidable conditions are covered in Chapter 31. Other problems are explained below.

Congenital Heart Disease

Before birth, the heart begins as a single tube. It enlarges and divides into chambers as the fetus grows. This process involves a progression of developmental steps. A disruption in the process can result in a defect in the heart. Such a defect is called **congenital**, which means *occurring at birth.*

Congenital heart disease covers a wide range of conditions. There may be a hole between two chambers of the heart. The valves may not function properly, or there may be a blockage of the blood flow. The defect may be in the blood vessels leading into or away from the heart. Most cases can be treated with surgery.

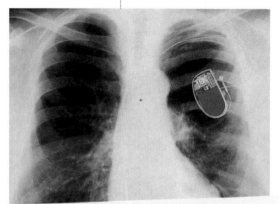

An artificial pacemaker, shown in this X ray, can stimulate an irregular heart to maintain a regular beat.

ACTIVITY *Locate the tiny wire leading from the pacemaker to the heart.*

up date
▶ *Looking at Technology*

Internal Cardiac Defibrillator and Pacemaker Module

When the heart's natural pacemaker is faulty, a surgeon can implant an artificial pacemaker that supplies electrical impulses to the heart to maintain a regular heartbeat. The device may be implanted below the collarbone or into a pocket created under the skin of the abdomen. A wire from the pacemaker goes down through the vena cava into the part of the heart muscle to be stimulated. Alternatively, an electrode may be attached to the outer surface of the part of the heart muscle to be stimulated. Modern microelectronic circuits require little power, and the lithium batteries that power them have a long life. Battery replacement, when required, involves a minor operation.

Disruption of the nerve impulses through the muscle wall of a heart chamber can cause fibrillation of the heart—rapid contractions of individual muscle fibers. As a result, the chamber no longer contracts as a single unit and produces a rapid, irregular rhythm. An implanted defibrillator sends bursts of electricity through the heart to convert fibrillation back into a normal, regular heartbeat.

Combined into a single unit, defibrillator-pacemaker modules can enable a person with life-threatening heart rhythm disturbances to lead a normal life.

Heart Murmur

Have you ever used a stethoscope to listen to your heart? Blood passing through a healthy heart makes a strong, clear *lub-dub* sound. A heart murmur is an abnormal sound. The major cause is a defective valve that is too narrow causing blood to be pushed through the restricted opening with more force than normal. A valve that does not close properly allows blood to leak back through it. Both situations cause the sound labeled a "murmur." Most murmurs are slight and do not need correction. Others may require surgical treatment.

Varicose Veins

Varicose veins are swollen and enlarged veins, especially in the legs. They develop when the valves in the veins are weakened and cannot close tightly to prevent the backflow of blood. Blood then collects in the veins. This condition may affect men and women of all ages. Exercise is a means of both preventing and treating varicose veins. In severe cases, surgical removal of the veins may be necessary.

Anemia

Anemia is a condition in which the concentration of hemoglobin in the blood is below normal levels. With a low level of hemoglobin, body cells do not receive a sufficient amount of oxygen. The most common cause of anemia is a deficiency of iron in the diet. This can be corrected by eating foods that are rich in iron, such as leafy green vegetables, dried fruits, or enriched cereals, or by taking iron supplements.

Green, leafy vegetables such as spinach, cabbage, and kale are rich in iron.

ACTIVITY *What other iron-rich foods can you eat to avoid getting anemia?*

Leukemia

Leukemia is any of several types of cancer resulting from abnormal production of white blood cells in the bone marrow. The abnormal cells may spill into the blood, enter other organs, and interfere with their function. Far worse, the abnormal cells prevent the bone marrow from producing red blood cells, platelets, and normal white blood cells. There is a risk of death from overwhelming infection or blood loss. Bone marrow transplants have been successful in treating some types of leukemia. Chemotherapy and radiation are also used to slow down the disease process.

Hemophilia

Hemophilia is an inherited bleeding disorder caused by a deficiency of a blood protein (called *factor VIII*) that is essential to the process of blood clotting. This causes the blood to clot very slowly or not at all. Persons with hemophilia suffer recurrent bleeding, most often into their joints. Bleeding may occur after injury or spontaneously with no apparent cause.

Lymphatic System Problems

Several problems can affect the lymphatic system. Some can usually be cured. Others have no cure.

Immune Deficiency

Normally, your body protects itself against anything that might enter it and cause it harm. Sometimes, however, the immune system's defenses fail to fight infection. Such an immune deficiency disorder may be the result of a congenital or inherited defect. Often it is the result of an acquired disease that damages the immune system's function. For example, HIV, the virus that causes AIDS, destroys the T cells that fight pathogens. The result of an immune deficiency disorder is infections that recur and are hard to treat.

Hodgkin's Disease

Hodgkin's disease, also known as Hodgkin's lymphoma, is cancer of lymph tissue, which is found mainly in the lymph nodes and spleen. The cancer cells spread quickly throughout the lymphatic system. Radiation therapy can usually successfully treat early stages.

Tonsillitis

The function of your tonsils is to help protect the upper respiratory tract against infection. However, sometimes the tonsils themselves become infected by the organisms they are fighting. Tonsillitis occurs mainly in childhood but sometimes affects teens. The tonsils become inflamed and tender, and symptoms include a sore throat and fever. Tonsillitis may be treated with antibiotics. Once common, surgical removal of the tonsils is rarely done today.

LESSON  *Review*

Reviewing Facts and Vocabulary

1. Name and define two problems of the circulatory system.
2. Explain how a defective valve in the heart could affect blood flow.
3. What makes an immune deficiency disorder so dangerous?

Thinking Critically

4. *Analyzing.* How might a heart or circulatory disorder affect your life?
5. *Evaluating.* Categorize the following food items as being generally healthy or unhealthy for your heart: potato chips, broccoli, cheeseburgers, donuts, coffee, fish, carrots, butter.

Applying Health Skills

6. *In Your School.* Have your blood pressure checked in class by the school nurse. What is the average blood pressure for the class? How does the blood pressure of students who exercise regularly differ from that of students who do not?

The Respiratory System

While reading this paragraph, you will inhale and exhale four or five times. This will happen without your even thinking about it. Your body's respiratory system, whose principal organ is the lungs, takes care of this for you. Understanding how the lungs function will help you to keep your respiratory system healthy.

HEALTH TERMS

respiration

diaphragm

pharynx

trachea

bronchi

larynx

pleurisy

asthma

HEALTH CONCEPTS

- Respiration—the exchange of gases between your body and your environment—is essential to life.
- Regular exercise and avoidance of pollutants, especially the smoke from tobacco products, help keep the respiratory system healthy.

Functions of the Respiratory System

As its name implies, the main function of the respiratory system is **respiration**—*the exchange of gases between your body and your environment.* There are two major parts to respiration, external and internal. External respiration is the exchange of oxygen and carbon dioxide between the blood and the air in the lungs. As you breathe, you inhale air that contains oxygen into your lungs. Oxygen moves from your lungs to your blood, and carbon dioxide moves from your blood to your lungs. Internal respiration is the exchange of gases between the blood and the cells of the body. Oxygen moves from your blood to your cells, and carbon dioxide moves from your cells to your blood. Without oxygen you could live only a few minutes.

Structure of the Respiratory System

The main structures within the respiratory system are the lungs and structures within the nose and mouth. These are supported by the **diaphragm,** *a muscle that separates the chest and abdominal cavities.* Without the diaphragm, respiration would be impossible.

The Lungs

The principal organ of your respiratory system is your lungs. They take in oxygen from the air you inhale and return carbon dioxide to the air when you exhale. Every day your lungs take in enough air to fill a fairly large room.

In a real sense, your lungs are like the bellows used to fan the flames of fires in days of old. Like a bellows, lungs rely on external muscle power to do their job. Whereas arm muscles provided the muscle power for bellows, lungs get their power from the diaphragm.

THE BREATHING PROCESS

When you inhale, your rib muscles and diaphragm contract. The diaphragm moves downward, and the ribs are pulled upward and outward. This action enlarges the chest cavity, creating lower pressure in the lungs. Air rushes into the lungs to equalize the pressure between the lungs and the outside environment. The reverse happens when you exhale. The diaphragm relaxes, moving upward, and the ribs move inward, increasing the pressure within the lungs. Air moves from the higher pressure in the lungs to the lower pressure of the outside environment.

STRUCTURE OF THE LUNGS

Each lung is divided into sections called *lobes.* There are three lobes in the right lung and two lobes in the left lung. The airways that lead into the lungs divide and subdivide to form a network of tubes called *bronchioles.* At the end of each bronchiole is a cluster of thin-walled air sacs called *alveoli,* covered with a vast network of capillaries. Thin capillary walls and equally thin alveolar walls allow the exchange of air and carbon dioxide to take place.

▼ *The alveoli in the lungs are surrounded by a network of capillaries. External respiration takes place in the alveoli.*

ACTIVITY *Make a flowchart showing the movement of air into and out of the lungs.*

THE LUNGS

Branch of pulmonary artery

Branch of pulmonary vein

Bronchiole

Capillary

Alveolus

Bronchus

UPPER RESPIRATORY SYSTEM

➤ *The air you breathe is cleaned, moistened, and warmed as it moves through the upper respiratory system.*

ACTIVITY *Create a drawing that shows, without using words, what makes the upper respiratory system so vulnerable to infection.*

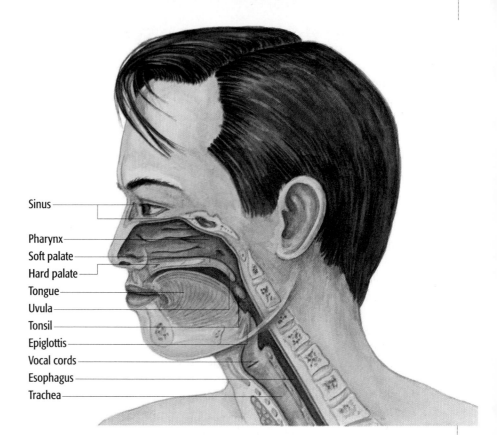

Sinus
Pharynx
Soft palate
Hard palate
Tongue
Uvula
Tonsil
Epiglottis
Vocal cords
Esophagus
Trachea

keeping
Fit

Posture and Breathing

"Stand up straight! Don't slouch!" You may have felt annoyed if you were ever told this, yet it is good advice when it comes to breathing. When you stand erect, sit erect, or walk erect, you give the breathing mechanisms in your body the best opportunity to do their work. In order to work properly, your lungs need room to expand. This means that your ribs must be free to move upward and outward and your diaphragm downward as you inhale. By slouching, you hinder effective breathing.

Practice sitting with your back straight in a chair that supports your head and back. Stand with your head up, neck straight, shoulders down and back, and stomach and buttocks in, but hold yourself naturally, not stiffly. Do you notice how much more air you can take in than when you slouch?

Other Respiratory Structures

Air needs a way to get into your lungs in the first place. Two points of entry are your nose and your mouth. From a biological standpoint, the nose is better suited to this purpose. Whereas air entering the mouth goes directly to the lungs, air that enters through the nose is filtered and cleaned by mucous membranes and tiny hairs called cilia.

From your nose, air moves through the **pharynx** (FAIR-inks), or *throat,* and into the **trachea** (TRAY-kee-uh), or *windpipe.* Like the nose, the trachea is also lined with a mucous membrane and cilia. These form a second line of defense to trap foreign particles and keep them from entering the lungs. Air completes its journey to the lungs through the **bronchi** (BRAHN-kye), *the airways that connect the trachea to the lungs.*

The Larynx and the Epiglottis

On its journey to your lungs, air passes over two structures that are not directly related to inspiration—the part of respiration in which oxygen is taken in—but that are nonetheless important. One of these is the **larynx** (LAIR-inks), or *voice box.* The larynx contains two fibrous sheets of tissue known as the vocal cords. As air passes over these cords, the cords vibrate and produce sound. Without them, speech is not possible.

Air also passes over the epiglottis, a flap of cartilage in front of the entrance to the larynx. At rest, the epiglottis is open to allow air to pass into the lungs. When you swallow, it closes to prevent food and liquid from being inhaled. Have you ever swallowed something that "went down the wrong pipe"? That is exactly what it did! Your epiglottis failed to close properly, allowing food or drink to enter your trachea.

Care of the Respiratory System

The respiratory system is highly susceptible to infection from both bacteria and viruses. Your hands are a carrier of disease organisms. To reduce the risk of infection—such as from the common cold—avoid putting your hands up to your nose and mouth, something people often do without thinking. It is vital to develop an awareness of this habit and to do it less. Remember also that washing your hands often is important.

The respiratory system is sensitive to pollutants such as tobacco smoke. Avoiding polluted air—as well as never smoking yourself—helps promote the health of your respiratory system.

A regular program of exercise helps keep the lungs working efficiently. Exercise strengthens the lungs and helps keep the other parts of the respiratory system clear.

Bicycling in fresh air is a good way to strengthen the lungs.

ACTIVITY *Name two other steps you can take to care for your respiratory system.*

Respiratory System Problems

As you have learned, the respiratory system is a common site of infection. Pathogens have easy access into the body through the mouth and nose. Colds and sore throats are common problems with the upper respiratory tract. More serious respiratory infections are those that affect the lower respiratory tract, such as those described below.

Bronchitis

Bronchitis is an inflammation of the bronchi. The main symptoms are wheezing, shortness of breath, and coughing. Bronchitis can be either acute or chronic. Both types are more common in smokers and in areas with high pollution.

Acute bronchitis comes on suddenly and usually clears up within a short time. It is usually a complication of a viral infection such as a cold or the flu.

Chronic bronchitis is a longer-lasting, recurring disease that can get progressively worse. Most important in the treatment of chronic

Whose Lungs Are They?

Leah's boyfriend smokes. She dislikes the fact that his clothes, his hair, and his breath smell of cigarette smoke. She has noticed that he coughs a lot and seems to be short of breath. He's even stopped playing softball on weekends because he can't run bases fast enough anymore. Leah had an uncle who died of emphysema, and she remembers that his symptoms began with shortness of breath and coughing. Leah worries about the health risks to both her and her boyfriend, but she is afraid that he will break up with her if she tries to get him to quit. When she brought the issue up before, he said to her, "They're my lungs." What should Leah do?

What Would You Do?

Apply the six steps of the decision-making process to Leah's problem.

1. **State the situation.**
2. **List the options.**
3. **Weigh the possible outcomes.**
4. **Consider your values.**
5. **Make a decision and act.**
6. **Evaluate the decision.**

▲ *A bronchiodilator from an inhaler helps relax the muscles that have tightened around the airways during an asthma attack.*

ACTIVITY *Name situations that can trigger an asthma attack.*

bronchitis is avoiding respiratory irritants such as cigarette smoke, dust, fumes, or other air pollutants.

Asthma

Asthma (AZ-muh) is *an inflammatory condition in which the small airways in the lungs called bronchioles become narrowed, causing difficulty in breathing.* The mucous lining swells and secretions build up, making breathing even more difficult. The condition may be triggered by any number of causes, such as exertion, emotion, infection, allergens, even changes in the weather. About 1 in 20 people—1 in 10 children—are asthmatic.

Asthma attacks are treated with bronchodilators—medications that relax and widen the airways. Most people with asthma administer the medications themselves with a hand-held inhaler. Prophylactic (preventive) medications, taken several times daily through an inhaler, have been successful in preventing attacks.

Pneumonia

Pneumonia is an inflammation of the lungs. Pneumonia is not a single disease but the name for several types of lung inflammation caused by infectious organisms, such as bacteria and viruses. The two main types of pneumonia are lobar pneumonia and bronchial pneumonia. In lobar pneumonia, one lobe of one lung is affected at first. In bronchial pneumonia, inflammation starts in the bronchi and then spreads to tissue in one or both lungs. Symptoms of pneumonia include fever, chills, shortness of breath, and a severe cough. Chest pain that is worse when breathing in may occur because of **pleurisy** (PLUR-uh-see), *an inflammation of the membrane lining the lungs and chest cavity.*

Tuberculosis

Tuberculosis is an infectious bacterial disease of the lungs. Symptoms include fever and sweating, weakness, poor appetite, shortness of breath, and severe coughing. Tuberculosis is now rare in developed nations because of the use of modern antibiotic medicines. However, resistant forms of the disease have become more prevalent recently.

Emphysema

Emphysema is a disease in which the alveoli in the lungs burst and blend to form fewer, larger sacs with less surface area. The normal exchange of carbon dioxide and oxygen in the alveoli is disrupted. Symptoms include difficulty in breathing and a chronic cough. Emphysema is caused by breathing in foreign matter such as smoke and other air pollutants over a long period of time. In almost all cases, emphysema is caused by cigarette smoking. The condition cannot be reversed.

Sinusitis

Sinusitis is an inflammation of the membrane lining the facial sinuses, the air-filled cavities in the bones that surround the nose. Most sinusitis is caused by infection that spreads to the sinuses from the nose. Symptoms include fever, a stuffy nose, and a throbbing ache in the affected area. Antibiotic medications, decongestant drops or spray, and steam inhalation are used to treat sinusitis.

LESSON 3 *Review*

Reviewing Facts and Vocabulary

1. Why is it better to breathe through your nose than through your mouth?
2. What is the difference between chronic and acute bronchitis?
3. Describe how emphysema affects the alveoli.

Thinking Critically

4. *Comparing and Contrasting.* Compare external and internal respiration.

5. *Analyzing.* Explain the relationship between oxygen and carbon dioxide in the body.

Applying Health Skills

6. *In Your Home and School.* Interview three smokers and three nonsmokers. Ask them how often they experience respiratory infections, sore throats, and colds. Draw conclusions from your findings and share them with the class.

Health Skills Activities

Activity 1 — Keeping Body Systems Healthy

How much do you know about your circulatory, respiratory, muscular, or skeletal system? You and a group of classmates are about to become an expert on one of these systems.

Directions

1. Find a drawing or photo of a person and, using a grid for accurate proportions, transfer a full-length outline drawing of the person onto a large sheet of bulletin board paper. All group members are then to fill in and label the body system organs designated by your teacher. Use your textbook as a guide.
2. Around the border of your poster, identify lifestyle factors (for example, physical activity, low-fat diet) that promotes the health of the system.
3. Display your diagram along with those of other groups.

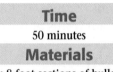

Time
50 minutes

Materials
6-x-8-foot sections of bulletin board paper, colored markers, index cards, scissors, masking tape, colored sheets of paper

Self-Assessment

✓ Labeled all structures of the body system accurately.
✓ Identified lifestyle-related factors for the body system.

Activity 2 — Health Is a Heartbeat Away

Any physical activity that raises your heart rate to between 60 and 85 percent of its maximum rate and keeps it there for 15 to 20 minutes is good for your heart. Do you get enough of this type of activity?

Directions

1. Name an exercise or vigorous physical activity that you enjoy—or might enjoy—doing.
2. Create a chart listing these benefits as well as disadvantages (such as the stress that jogging places on the joints). You may need to do some research.
3. With a partner, perform your activity twice in the following week. Time your sessions to make sure you are active between 15 to 20 minutes. Your partner should record your heart rate before and after the activity.
4. What changes if any did you notice? Did the activity offer aerobic benefits?

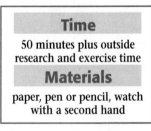

Time
50 minutes plus outside research and exercise time

Materials
paper, pen or pencil, watch with a second hand

Self-Assessment

✓ Organized chart clearly and with all information requested.
✓ Recorded heart rate for an exercise or activity tried during the week.

HEALTH NEWS

Nothing to Sneeze At

A beautiful spring brings fresh new flowers and bright green leaves. For people who suffer from pollen allergies, this beauty can be hard to see. They're too busy sneezing and wiping their watery eyes.

Every spring, plants create pollen, a spore that helps plants reproduce. Since plants can't move, they release pollen into the air. Some of it lands on other plants, but people inhale a lot of pollen, too.

When pollen enters your respiratory system, your immune system identifies it as a foreign object. To get rid of these spores, your body begins to sneeze and your eyes begin to water.

You can avoid the problems of pollen by staying inside. Medicines and treatments can help you enjoy the beauty of spring without tears.

Play the Video

CNN. All Rights Reserved.

Think About It

- What happens when people inhale pollen? Why do some people respond more dramatically to pollen than others?
- What parts of your respiratory system are involved in pollen allergies?
- What can you do to avoid the effects of pollen?

Using Health Terms

On a separate sheet of paper, write the term that best matches each definition below.

LESSON 1

1. The vessels that return deoxygenated blood toward the heart from the body's organs and tissues.
2. The oxygen-carrying part of blood.
3. A clear yellow fluid that fills the spaces around body cells.
4. The fluid in which the other parts of blood are suspended.
5. A type of white blood cell that protects the body against pathogens.
6. The cells that prevent the body's loss of blood.
7. The vessels that carry blood between arterioles and small vessels called venules.
8. The vessels that carry blood away from the heart.

LESSON 2

9. Occurring at birth.

LESSON 3

10. An inflammation of the membrane lining the lungs and chest cavity.
11. Windpipe.
12. The airways that connect the trachea to the lungs.
13. An inflammatory condition in which the small airways in the lungs called bronchioles become narrowed, causing difficulty in breathing.
14. The exchange of gases between your body and your environment.
15. Throat.
16. A muscle that separates the chest and abdominal cavities.
17. Voice box.

Recalling the Facts

Using complete sentences, answer the following questions.

LESSON 1

1. What is plasma?
2. What are the functions of the blood?
3. Why are platelets important to your health?
4. Explain the functions of the lymphatic system.
5. What is the function of the lymph nodes?

LESSON 2

6. Describe two conditions that are examples of congenital heart disease.
7. What causes varicose veins?
8. What is anemia and what is its main cause?

9. Name and briefly describe three problems of the lymphatic system.
10. How can you care for your lymphatic system?

LESSON 3

11. What are the main parts of the respiratory system?
12. What are the functions of the mucous membranes and cilia in the nose?
13. Name and briefly describe three serious respiratory diseases.
14. What regulates the movement of air in and out of the lungs?
15. Explain why food and drink do not usually get into the trachea.

Thinking Critically

LESSON 1

1. ***Analyzing.*** Discuss ways in which the circulatory and lymphatic systems are mutually supportive.
2. ***Comparing and Contrasting.*** Discuss ways in which the circulatory and lymphatic systems are alike and different.

LESSON 2

3. ***Analyzing.*** How do nutrition and exercise contribute to the health of your circulatory and lymphatic systems?

4. ***Synthesizing.*** Summarize the major contributions of the lymphatic system to your health.

LESSON 3

5. ***Evaluating.*** Some workplaces are smoke-free. What are some advantages and disadvantages of this policy? Judge the appropriateness of such a policy.
6. ***Synthesizing.*** How might suffering from asthma affect your life?

Making the Connection

1. ***Math.*** Compare the survival rates for people with cardiovascular diseases 40 years ago and today. Prepare a bar graph or a line graph that shows your findings. Interpret these statistics and suggest reasons for the changes.
2. ***Science.*** Vitamin E is being credited with many health benefits including lowering heart disease, warding off cancer, preventing infection, even preserving youth. Investigate the claims made for this vitamin. Determine what evidence supports the claims, how vitamin E works, and how much of the vitamin is needed. Prepare a written report of your findings.

BEYOND THE CLASSROOM

PARENTAL INVOLVEMENT Ask your parents to tell you about any problems with the circulatory or respiratory system they have experienced. Find out what their symptoms were, what actions they took to correct the problem, and how they evaluated the effectiveness of their actions.

COMMUNITY INVOLVEMENT Just about all communities today have laws and ordinances identifying certain areas and types of retail establishments as smoke-free. Some communities, in fact, are entirely smoke-free. Unfortunately, not all individuals or retailers uphold these laws. Learn about the rulings in your own community and about the penalties for violating them. Share your findings in the form of a public service announcement, if possible, to be broadcast over a public access cable station in your locality.

SCHOOL-TO-CAREER
Technology. With multiplying advances in technology, health care professionals in the field of cardiology are able to diagnose and treat heart problems in ways they were not capable of just a few years ago. Learn more about technological advances in this important area of medicine.

CHAPTER 18

Your Digestive and Urinary Systems

HEALTH *Online*

DECISION MAKING

You're hungry, and you head to your favorite restaurant for a quick bite to satisfy that hunger. Will your meal also satisfy the nutritional needs to keep your digestive and urinary systems healthy? Check out the "Fast-Food Dining Guide" in the Interactive Projects at **health.glencoe.com** to see whether your meal meets the Dietary Guidelines for Americans.

Personal Health Inventory

Self-Inventory Write the numbers 1–10 on a sheet of paper. Read each statement below and respond by writing *yes*, *no*, or *sometimes* for each item. Write a *yes* only for items that you practice regularly. Save your responses.

1	I eat a variety of healthful foods that are high in fiber every day.
2	I eat salty snacks and fried foods in moderation.
3	I chew each bite of food throughly before swallowing.
4	I do not eat as a way of coping with stress or when I am emotionally upset.
5	I drink at least six to eight glasses of water a day.
6	I brush my teeth after every meal and floss my teeth daily.
7	I use laxatives only when recommended by a health care professional.
8	I have regular bowel movements.
9	I seek medical attention when diarrhea persists for more than 48 hours.
10	I discuss any changes in urine color, odor, or frequency with a health care professional.

Follow-up After completing the chapter, retake this self-inventory. Pick two items that you need to work on and set a goal to improve your health behaviors.

> ❝ *Now good digestion wait on appetite, And health on both!* ❞

—WILLIAM SHAKESPEARE
ENGLISH PLAYWRIGHT AND POET, (1564–1616)

Quick Write Create a short paragraph in which you tie together the key words in the quote above: *digestion*, *appetite*, and *health*.

The Digestive System

Digestion is the breaking down of food into simpler substances to be carried in the blood to body cells. This process is both mechanical and chemical. The mechanical portion involves chewing, mashing, and breaking food into smaller pieces. The chemical portion involves changing food into simpler substances.

HEALTH TERMS

digestion

absorption

elimination

ingestion

mastication

peristalsis

gastric juices

chyme

bile

HEALTH CONCEPTS

- Food is the body's fuel.
- Digestion is both a mechanical and a chemical process.
- Digestion begins with ingestion, the taking in of food, and ends with the elimination of wastes.
- Each organ of the gastrointestinal tract has a specific function.

Functions of the Digestive System

The digestive system performs three different functions that are essential to provide nutrition:

- **Digestion**—*the mechanical and chemical breakdown of foods for use by the body's cells.*
- **Absorption**—*the passage of digested food from the digestive tract into the circulatory system.*
- **Elimination**—*the expulsion of undigested food or body wastes.*

Once food is broken down, nutrients from it are absorbed through the small intestine. The nutrients are then passed along to the circulatory system. Any food that is not broken down in this process is eliminated in the form of wastes.

Structure of the Digestive System

You might assume that the process of digestion begins in your stomach or intestines. In truth, it begins before you take a bite of food when the aroma of food activates the salivary glands.

The Mouth and Teeth

A number of different structures are involved in **ingestion**, *the taking of food into the body,* which is the earliest stage of digestion. These structures include the teeth, the salivary glands, and the tongue.

THE TEETH

The primary function of your teeth is to break the food you eat into smaller pieces. **Mastication (MAS-tuh-KAY-shuhn)**—*the process of chewing*—prepares the food to be swallowed.

THE SALIVARY GLANDS

As food moves through your digestive system, various secretions are added to it. This process starts in your mouth, where three pairs of salivary glands secrete saliva. Saliva is a watery solution containing an enzyme that starts the digestion of carbohydrates by converting them to a soluble form of sugar. It also lubricates your food, making it easier to swallow.

THE TONGUE

Your tongue forms food into a ball to prepare for swallowing. As you begin to swallow, a wave of muscular contractions passes over your tongue, forcing food into the pharynx. At the same time, the uvula, a small, muscular flap of tissue suspended at the back of your mouth, closes over the opening to the nasal passages. The epiglottis, the flap of tissue covering the trachea, closes to keep food from entering the respiratory system. If you talk or laugh while swallowing, the epiglottis will open and food may enter the windpipe. A reflex response causes you to cough to force food out of the windpipe.

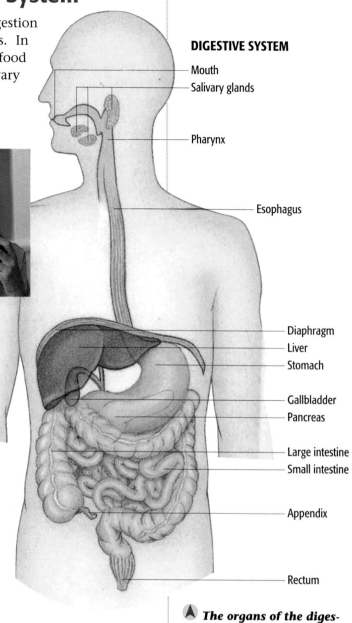

DIGESTIVE SYSTEM

- Mouth
- Salivary glands
- Pharynx
- Esophagus
- Diaphragm
- Liver
- Stomach
- Gallbladder
- Pancreas
- Large intestine
- Small intestine
- Appendix
- Rectum

▲ *The organs of the digestive system form a continuous passageway for the movement of food through your body.*

ACTIVITY *Locate the stomach and tell whether it is where you expected to find it.*

The Esophagus

When you swallow, food enters the esophagus. This is a muscular tube that extends from the pharynx to the stomach and is situated behind the trachea and the heart. It is about 10 inches (25 cm) long. A process called **peristalsis** (PER-uh-STAWL-suhs)—*a series of involuntary muscular contractions*—moves food through the esophagus. Solid food takes about nine seconds to complete this brief journey. Food moves through the entire digestive tract as the result of peristalsis.

A sphincter muscle—a circular muscle at the entrance to the stomach—allows food to move from the esophagus into the stomach. When the muscle is relaxed, it forms an opening. When it contracts, the opening closes. Sphincter muscles located along the digestive tract prevent food from backing up as it moves through the digestive process.

The Stomach

The stomach is a hollow, saclike organ enclosed in a muscular wall. This wall consists of three layers of muscles. The stomach is flexible, allowing it to expand when you eat. The main activities of the stomach are to:

- continue the breakdown of food.
- serve as a storage organ for food until it is ready to enter the small intestine.
- mix together food and **gastric juices**—*secretions from the stomach lining that contain pepsin and hydrochloric acid.* Pepsin is an enzyme that breaks down protein. Hydrochloric acid kills bacteria taken in with the food and creates the best environment for the pepsin to do its work. The hydrochloric acid your stomach produces is

▼ *The stomach's role in digestion is both physical: churning food; and chemical: producing gastric juices that begin the digestion of proteins.*

ACTIVITY *Explain why the three layers of muscles move in three different directions.*

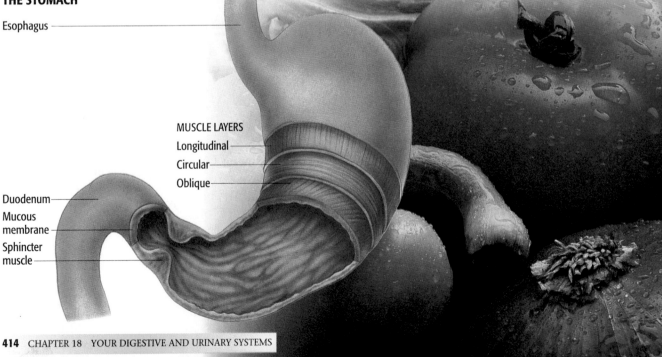

THE STOMACH

Esophagus

MUSCLE LAYERS
Longitudinal
Circular
Oblique

Duodenum
Mucous membrane
Sphincter muscle

strong enough to dissolve metal. In fact, if it were not for the mucus your stomach produces to form a protective lining, your stomach would digest itself!

■ control the rate at which food enters the small intestine.

As the stomach fills, the layers of muscle produce rhythmic contractions that churn the food and gastric juices together. This action produces a substance called **chyme** (kym), *a creamy, fluid mixture of food and gastric juices.* Peristalsis moves the chyme into the small intestine.

The Small Intestine

The major part of digestion and absorption occurs in the small intestine, which is 20 to 23 feet (6 to 7 m) in length and 1 inch (2.5 cm) in diameter. (The small intestine gets its name from its diameter, not its length.) It consists of three parts: the duodenum, the jejunum, and the ileum. Chyme enters the duodenum from the stomach. The ileum opens into the large intestine.

Peristalsis moves chyme through the small intestine at a relatively slow rate for approximately three to five hours. Chyme that enters the small intestine includes partially digested carbohydrates and proteins and undigested fats. Intestinal juices produced by glands in the lining of the small intestine, along with secretions from the liver and the pancreas, complete the chemical breakdown of all food. You will learn about the liver and pancreas later in this lesson.

The small intestine is lined with millions of fingerlike projections called villi (VIL-eye). Each villus has a network of capillaries. These capillaries absorb digested food particles from the small intestine. Villi, especially those in the jejunum, increase the surface area for the absorption of digested food particles about 600 times. Once food particles enter the capillaries in the villi, they are carried throughout the body by the blood. Unabsorbed material leaves the small intestine in the form of liquid and fiber, moving by peristalsis into the large intestine.

The Large Intestine

The large intestine, or colon, forms the lower part of the digestive tract. The large intestine is 5 to 6 feet (1.5 to 1.8 m) long and about 2½ inches (6 cm) in diameter. Movement of undigested food materials through the large intestine is very slow. The main functions of the large intestine are to absorb water and eliminate undigested food.

As unabsorbed material from the small intestine passes through the large intestine, water, vitamins, and mineral salts are absorbed into the bloodstream. This action is important in maintaining the water balance in your body.

Many harmless bacteria normally live in the large intestine, changing the consistency of undigested food to a semisolid waste, called feces. Feces pass from the body through the anus and is excreted as a bowel movement.

Organs That Aid Digestion

Three other organs play key roles in digestion.

■ **The Liver.** The second-largest organ in your body (your skin is the largest), your liver functions as your body's chemical factory and regulates the levels of most of the main chemicals in your blood.

The liver acts to clear the blood of drugs and poisonous substances. The liver absorbs the substances, changes their chemical structure, and makes them water soluble. It then excretes them in the **bile**, *a yellowish-green, bitter fluid important in the breakdown of fats*. Bile flows through the hepatic duct to the gallbladder, where it is stored.

■ **The Gallbladder.** The gallbladder is a small, pear-shaped sac 3 to 4 inches (7 to 10 cm) long and located underneath the liver. The neck of the gallbladder forms a duct leading to the duodenum, the first section of the small intestine. The gallbladder stores bile until food moves into the duodenum from the stomach. A hormone produced in the small intestine stimulates the release of bile through the bile duct into the duodenum, where the bile breaks down fats contained in the food.

■ **The Pancreas.** The pancreas, as part of the endocrine system, produces the hormone insulin. As part of the digestive system, the pancreas produces three digestive enzymes: trypsin, which digests proteins; amylase, which digests carbohydrates; and lipase, which digests fats.

LESSON 1 *Review*

Reviewing Facts and Vocabulary

1. Trace the path a bite of pizza follows until it is absorbed into the bloodstream.
2. Describe the three different functions of the digestive system.
3. Define the following terms and use each in a sentence: *mastication, peristalsis, saliva, bile.*

Thinking Critically

4. **Analyzing.** Support the following statement: *The real work of the digestive system is done in the small intestine.*
5. **Synthesizing.** Explain in what way chewing food well contributes to the health of the digestive system.

6. **Synthesizing.** Based on their actions, change the names of the different parts of the digestive system to parts of machines. Draw a diagram of the digestive system and label it with the new names.

Applying Health Skills

7. **In Your Home and School.** Prepare a chart that shows what happens to food once it leaves the stomach. Describe the function of each organ involved in the digestive process. Share the chart with classmates and with your family.

Care and Problems of the Digestive System

There are many parts to your digestive system, all vital to the process of digestion. Some parts of this system, such as your teeth and tongue, are essential to a second process—speech production. It is, therefore, critical to take care of your digestive system.

HEALTH TERMS

indigestion

hiatal hernia

appendicitis

peptic ulcer

HEALTH CONCEPTS

- The health of the digestive system depends in large part on healthful eating habits.
- The more you chew your food, the easier it is on your digestive system.

Fiber-rich foods: kale, bran, fruits, oatmeal

h⊙tlink

fiber For more information on the importance of fiber, see Chapter 5, page 103.

Care of the Digestive System

Good eating habits are the best way to avoid or minimize digestive system problems. The reward for maintaining good eating habits may well be a lifetime free of the kinds of problems that lead drugstores to stock their shelves with antacids, laxatives, and other such products. Make the following suggestions part of your lifestyle habits:

- Eat a variety of foods.
- Avoid an overabundance of fried foods. Choose foods that are low in fat and high in **fiber**.
- Do not hurry through your meals—eat slowly while sitting down. Relax and enjoy your meal!
- Do not wash food down with liquid. Wait until you are finished chewing—swallow, and then take a sip of liquid.
- Drink plenty of water. Your digestive system needs a lot of water to do its job properly.

hotlink

stress For more information on managing stress in your life, see Chapter 9, page 214.

keeping Fit

Improving Digestion

Americans spend millions of dollars a year on medications to aid in the digestive process. Much of this money is wasted. Promoting healthy digestion is a simple matter when you:

➤ Chew your food thoroughly.

➤ Eat slowly.

➤ Eat a balanced assortment of foods.

➤ Try to swallow your food without drinking liquids.

➤ Drink six to eight glasses of water daily.

➤ Limit your intake of carbonated, acidic beverages.

➤ Avoid eating fried foods or other greasy foods.

➤ Avoid eating as a way of dealing with problems, or when under extreme stress.

By choosing a variety of foods that are high in fiber, you will promote the health of your digestive system.

ACTIVITY *Name foods other than fruits and vegetables that are good sources of fiber.*

■ Do not eat when you are under **stress**. Avoid using food as a way of coping with stress.

Problems of the Digestive System

Your complex digestive system usually functions normally, digesting and absorbing food and eliminating undigested material. However, problems can occur, some of them functional and some of them structural.

Functional Digestive System Problems

Even with care, on occasion problems with the digestive system arise for most people. These include indigestion, heartburn, gas, nausea, diarrhea, and constipation.

■ **Indigestion.** Indigestion refers to *a burning discomfort in the upper abdomen.* It may be accompanied by a buildup of gas and nausea. Indigestion can result from eating too much, eating too quickly, eating certain foods, stomach disorders, or stress. To prevent food-related indigestion, avoid eating foods that in the past have caused you discomfort, eat slowly, and avoid eating when under stress.

- **Heartburn.** Heartburn is a burning pain in the center of the chest that may travel from the tip of the breastbone to the throat. This condition has nothing to do with your heart. It is caused by *acid reflux*—a backflow of stomach acid into the esophagus. Acid reflux can occur if the sphincter muscle between the esophagus and stomach does not close tightly. The irritating stomach acids are responsible for the burning sensation of heartburn and can cause inflammation of the esophagus.

  Heartburn may also be a symptom of a **hiatal hernia,** *a condition in which part of the stomach pushes through an opening in the diaphragm.* If heartburn continues or recurs, it is important to consult a health care professional.

- **Gas.** A certain amount of gas in the stomach or the intestines is normal. An excess amount of gas, however, can cause a great deal of discomfort. Certain foods, including cooked onions and heavily spiced dishes, seem to be gas-producing for some people.

- **Nausea.** Nausea is a feeling of distress, fullness, and weakness and often precedes vomiting. It can be caused by motion (such as that on a boat or in a car), pathogens, medicines, drugs, or other substances in the stomach. Vomiting is a reflex response that provides a kind of built-in protection if you swallow a foreign substance. Vomiting is the result of reverse peristalsis, or waves of muscular contractions, in the stomach and esophagus.

HEALTH Online

Adding fiber to your diet helps decrease the risk of some cancers that affect the digestive system. Learn how cancers could be prevented by better health and eating habits at **health.glencoe.com**.

Building Health Skills

Adding Sources of Fiber

ADDING FIBER to your daily intake of food during your teenage years can provide benefits that will last throughout your lifetime. There are two forms of fiber, soluble and insoluble. Soluble fiber, which dissolves in water, may lower cholesterol. Insoluble fiber, which does not dissolve in water, may help protect you against colon cancer and other bowel problems. To get more fiber from the foods you eat:

1. **Start the day with a good breakfast.** If you don't eat breakfast already, now is the time to start. Breakfast cereals made with oats or bran are excellent sources of soluble fiber. So are whole-grain muffins.

2. **Eat meatless meals several times a week.** Try a bean burrito with cheese at lunch or dinner. The legumes in it will give you a fiber boost, and the cheese will convert the beans—an incomplete protein by themselves—into a complete protein.

3. **Choose high-fiber snacks.** It's easy. Popcorn is a great source of fiber, and so are nuts. Reach for a piece of fruit, especially the kind with edible skin, such as apples and pears.

COMPARING ANTACIDS

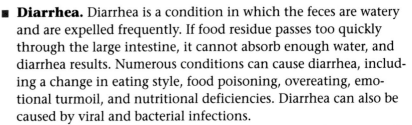

Magazine ads and TV commercials for over-the-counter medicines, which relieve the discomfort of indigestion and heartburn, share claims to be "better" or to "go to work faster." Are these claims true? A simple test can help you find out.

- **Diarrhea.** Diarrhea is a condition in which the feces are watery and are expelled frequently. If food residue passes too quickly through the large intestine, it cannot absorb enough water, and diarrhea results. Numerous conditions can cause diarrhea, including a change in eating style, food poisoning, overeating, emotional turmoil, and nutritional deficiencies. Diarrhea can also be caused by viral and bacterial infections.

  To avoid dehydration, it is important to replace the water and electrolytes lost during an attack of diarrhea by drinking plenty of liquids, especially water. Diarrhea usually clears up when the cause is eliminated. Medical help may be necessary.

- **Constipation.** Constipation is a condition in which feces become dry and hard, and bowel movements are difficult. Feces that stay in the large intestine too long will have too much water absorbed from them. Constipation can be caused by a lack of fiber, erratic eating habits, drinking too little water, or lack of exercise. Healthful eating—especially of foods high in fiber—drinking plenty of water, and exercising regularly are the best ways to avoid constipation. It is rare for teenagers to suffer from chronic constipation.

  When recommended by a health care professional, laxative drugs may be useful in clearing up constipation. However, continued use of laxatives should be avoided. Laxatives can cause diarrhea, abdominal cramps, gas, and a chemical imbalance in the blood. Some types may coat the intestine and prevent vitamin absorption. The body may also become dependent on laxatives and fail to function normally on its own.

What you will need

- 8-ounce cups (250 ml) of water
- Self-stick labels
- Marking pen
- Samples of several commercial over-the-counter antacid remedies
- Stopwatch or watch with second hand
- Vinegar
- Eye dropper
- Litmus paper

What you will do

1. Label each cup of water with the name of the antacid remedy to be tested. Then dissolve a standard dose of the product in each cup.

2. Test one product at a time. Set the stopwatch or make note of the time in seconds. Add vinegar to the container, an eye-dropperful at a time. After each addition, test the acidity of the solution with litmus paper. Keep track of how much vinegar you add. Stop when the solution tests acidic. You will know this because the litmus paper will turn red.

3. For each container, note how much vinegar it took to make the solution acidic and how long it took.

In conclusion

1. Did one antacid neutralize the acid more quickly than the others?

2. Did one antacid neutralize more acid than the others?

3. Which antacid, if any, seemed to be the most effective?

4. What ingredient or ingredients listed on the product's label do you think contributed to the antacid's effectiveness?

5. What conclusions, if any, can you draw about the advertising of health products as a whole? about the comparative costs of the products?

Structural Digestive System Problems

Structural problems of the digestive system vary in seriousness. Most problems are temporary and not serious. However, if any problem persists for a long period of time or is accompanied by fever or other symptoms of illness, a health care professional should be consulted.

GALLSTONES

Gallstones are small crystals that form in the gallbladder when an upset occurs in the chemical composition of the bile. They may block the bile duct between the gallbladder and the duodenum, causing pain. Stones that do not cause symptoms may be left alone. Gallstones can be treated with medicines that dissolve them, or they can be shattered by ultrasound-guided shock waves. When symptoms are severe, the gallbladder may be surgically removed.

APPENDICITIS

Appendicitis is *the inflammation of the appendix,* which is a 3- to 4-inch (8- to 10-cm) extension at one end of the large intestine. When bacteria or other foreign matter lodges in the appendix, the closed end beyond the blockage becomes swollen and fills with pus. If the appendix ruptures, the infection spreads into the abdomen, which is an extremely serious condition. The symptoms of appendicitis include pain and cramps in the lower right portion of the abdomen, fever, loss of appetite, nausea, and vomiting. Medical care is essential. The usual treatment is surgical removal of the appendix.

GASTRITIS

One of the most common disorders of the digestive system is gastritis, an inflammation of the mucous membrane that lines the stomach. Gastritis can be caused by irritation of the stomach lining from foods, aspirin, tobacco smoke, or alcohol or by bacterial infection. Symptoms include pain in the upper abdomen, nausea, and vomiting. A person with gastritis should avoid irritating substances. Antibiotics can cure the condition if bacteria are the cause. A health professional may also prescribe or recommend an acid controller or medication that "coats" the stomach lining.

LACTOSE INTOLERANCE

Lactose is one of the sugars present in milk. For the body to digest lactose, it must be broken down by lactase, an enzyme released by the lining of the small intestine. Some people have a deficiency of lactase, resulting in lactose **intolerance**—the inability to digest lactose. Undigested lactose ferments in the intestine and causes severe abdominal cramps, bloating, gas, and diarrhea. People with lactose intolerance should drink only lactase-reduced milk or use enzyme replacements that help break down lactose. Fermented milk products such as yogurt can be eaten without a problem.

PEPTIC ULCER

A **peptic ulcer** is *a sore in the lining of the digestive tract.* A peptic ulcer may occur in the esophagus, stomach (gastric ulcer), or duodenum. The lining of the stomach is constantly at risk from acid produced by the stomach wall. Gastric ulcers develop when something damages the protective lining and allows stomach acid to eat away at

h t l nk

intolerance For more information on other food intolerances and food allergies, see Chapter 6, page 155.

Making Responsible Decisions

A Milk Dilemma

Rashid is over at his friend Curt's house. The teens have just returned from a softball game in the park and are feeling hot and thirsty. Upon examining the contents of the refrigerator, Curt announces that the only cold beverage is milk. This poses a

problem for Rashid, who is lactose intolerant. Even though Rashid recalls how ill he felt the last time he consumed a dairy product, right now the thought of an ice-cold glass of milk is tempting. Besides, he knows the importance of restoring body fluids after vigorous physical activity. What should Rashid do?

What Would You Do?

Apply the six steps of the decision-making process to Rashid's problem.

1. **State the situation.**
2. **List the options.**
3. **Weigh the possible outcomes.**
4. **Consider your values.**
5. **Make a decision and act.**
6. **Evaluate the decision.**

it. Factors that increase the risk of ulcers include regular use of aspirin, ibuprofen, and other anti-inflammatory drugs, smoking, and infection with the bacterium *Helicobacter pylori (H. pylori).*

The typical symptom of a gastric ulcer is a gnawing pain in the abdomen when the stomach is empty. Ulcers can cause bleeding in the stomach. Without treatment, ulcers may perforate, or break through, the stomach wall. Ulcers may be treated with medicines that neutralize or reduce stomach acids or with antibiotics.

COLITIS

Colitis is inflammation of the colon. It may be caused by a virus, an amoeba, a bacterium such as the one that causes peptic ulcers, or stress. Symptoms include diarrhea (usually with blood and mucus), abdominal pain, and sometimes fever. The cause of ulcerative colitis is unknown. In most cases, medical treatment controls the disease.

HEMORRHOIDS

Hemorrhoids are swollen veins in the lower rectum and anus and are the result of increased pressure in the veins of the anus. They are most common in people with constipation or who sit a lot, in pregnant women, and following childbirth. Itching, pain, and bleeding are signs of hemorrhoids. Regular exercise and eating fiber-rich foods can help reduce your risk of developing hemorrhoids.

TOOTH DECAY

It may surprise you to find **tooth decay** listed as a digestive system problem. Your teeth are part of your digestive system. Tooth decay weakens a tooth and affects the way a person bites and chews food. This is one more reason to care for your teeth.

hotlink
tooth decay For more information on tooth decay and strategies for maintaining healthy teeth, see Chapter 7, page 167.

LESSON 2 *Review*

Reviewing Facts and Vocabulary

1. Why is fiber so important to the health of your digestive system?
2. What are some of the causes of indigestion?
3. What makes tooth decay a problem of the digestive system?

Thinking Critically

4. *Analyzing.* How do nutrition and exercise contribute to the prevention of many common digestive system disorders?
5. *Synthesizing.* Review the digestive disorders detailed in the chapter.

Summarize what you have learned by stating one or two concepts that apply to digestive disorders in general.

Applying Health Skills

6. *In Your Home and School.* Visit a drugstore or the health care aisle of a supermarket. Make a list of over-the-counter medicines for common digestive disorders that are available. Make notes on what each product can be used for. Then suggest a behavior that might eliminate the problem without the need for medicine. Share your list with your family and classmates.

The Urinary System

J ust as your city or community has a fleet of sanitation trucks that systematically remove waste and prevent its accumulation, so your body has its own waste removal systems. One of these systems, the digestive system, was covered in Lesson 1. Another such system is the urinary system.

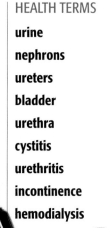

HEALTH TERMS

urine

nephrons

ureters

bladder

urethra

cystitis

urethritis

incontinence

hemodialysis

HEALTH CONCEPTS

- Filtering waste from the circulatory system is essential to maintaining life.

- The urinary system regulates the concentration and volume of blood by removing and restoring selected amounts of water and chemicals.

- Any change in the normal functioning of the urinary system represents a health threat and should be reported to a health care professional.

Functions of the Urinary System

The chief function of the urinary system is removal of water-soluble waste products that result from chemical changes to cells. This *liquid waste material*—**urine**—contains nitrogen and, therefore, would become toxic if allowed to remain in your body. Urination, the process whereby this waste is removed, is thus essential to life.

Structure of the Urinary System

The urinary system consists of several organs that are linked together, forming the urinary tract. These include the kidneys, the ureters, the bladder, and the urethra.

Drinking six to eight glasses of water a day will help keep your urinary system functioning efficiently.

ACTIVITY *Explain why other liquids, such as coffee or cola drinks, should not be counted as part of the six to eight glasses of water.*

The Kidneys

Your kidneys are your body's master chemists. Shaped like beans and each about the size of a fist, the kidneys lie on either side of the spine in the small of the back. They are embedded in a protective mass of fatty tissue. Within each kidney are as many as one million highly specialized, microscopic units called **nephrons** (NEH-frahnz), *the functional units of the kidneys.* Each nephron consists of a tubule and a cluster of capillaries, called a glomerulus, that functions as a filtering funnel. Your kidneys filter about 50 gallons (189.2 l) of blood each day.

Your kidneys filter waste products from your blood and modify the amount of salts and water excreted in the urine according to your body's needs. Your kidneys are miraculous organs, monitoring and maintaining your body's acid-base and water balances automatically. When your blood and body fluids become too acid or too alkaline, your kidneys alter the acidity of the urine to restore the balance. When your body is dehydrated, your kidneys release a hormone that signals your brain. In turn, your brain sends a message you recognize as "I'm thirsty," and you are stimulated to take a drink.

The urine that your kidneys excrete is carried along to the next step in its journey by **ureters**—*tubes that connect the kidneys with the bladder.*

The Bladder and the Urethra

Your **bladder** is *a hollow, muscular organ that acts as a reservoir for urine*. It is like a holding tank, but it has walls that can expand. The bladder in males is somewhat larger than the bladder in females. The average bladder may hold as much as a pint (500–600 ml) of urine. The need to urinate is stimulated as the bladder becomes full. Sphincter muscles under your voluntary control relax and allow urine to flow through the **urethra**, *the tube that leads from the bladder to the outside of the body*. The urethra is different, both structurally and functionally, for males and females. The male urethra is much longer than the female urethra: 9 inches (23 cm) versus 1½ inches (4 cm). Whereas the female urethra has the sole function of emptying waste products from the body, the male urethra has a second function—the release of semen, a fluid necessary for the process of reproduction. More information about this process can be found in Chapter 19.

Care of the Urinary System

Waste products that are not removed from your body can be toxic to your body's organs and tissues. Care of your urinary system can assure the regular movement of these wastes out of your body and keep you healthy.

The main way to care for your urinary system is to drink plenty of fluids—at least six to eight glasses of water every day and more in hot weather. A well-balanced eating style also plays a part in the care of the urinary system. Practicing good personal health care will help prevent the risk of bacterial infection to the organs of your urinary system. Regular physical checkups are necessary to detect changes in urine content.

▶ *Your urinary system removes waste products and excess water or chemical substances from your body.*

ACTIVITY *Describe the process by which your urinary system removes body wastes.*

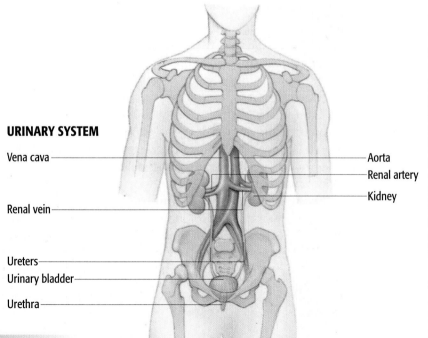

URINARY SYSTEM

Vena cava
Renal vein
Ureters
Urinary bladder
Urethra

Aorta
Renal artery
Kidney

Teens Making a Difference

...COMPASSION...CARING ...EMPATHY

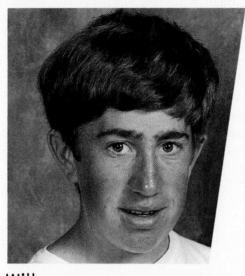

Will, 17, likes to play lacrosse and basketball, listen to music, and hang out with friends. He doesn't take any of these activities for granted because, as a kidney transplant recipient, he knows how lucky he is to simply be alive. In turn, he feels a responsibility to help others receive the gift of life as well, and he has made organ donation one of his causes.

RECEIVING THE GIFT "I was born with a kidney disorder called Post Urethral Valve Syndrome," he begins. "That pretty much means my kidneys didn't work right. I was sick from the time I was born. I had to be fed by a tube for a while, and I couldn't run or be as active as other kids. I was on the waiting list for the kidney for a long time," he says. Will speaks of the organ donor to whom he owes so much. "I know that the donor was a young teacher who died in a car accident. We met her parents last year for the first time. I told them how much it meant for me to meet them. They had to give their okay for the donation, so they played a part in saving my life, too.

EDUCATING OTHERS I try to do things for Gift of Life, an organ transplant organization, and for St. Christopher's Hospital for Children, where I had my transplant. The Phillies had an Organ Donation Day, and I got involved. They had organ donor cards at the baseball stadium, and I talked to people from the radio station about it and taped a message. I even got to throw out the first pitch," he adds. "That was really fun. Last year I gave a talk at my high school about the importance of organ donation. I talk to kids at the hospital who are going through transplantation. I take part in the Transplant Olympics, an event where organ recipients from all over come together to compete in athletic contests. I've also done interviews for articles because education about organ donation is so important."

WHAT YOU CAN DO "I think it's incredible to be an organ donor. One person donating organs can save not just one life but many lives. The waiting lists are huge. People die waiting. You never know who is going to need a transplant," Will concludes. "It could be you or someone you love."

WILL'S STORY
1. How does Will's story demonstrate the importance of both giving and receiving?
2. What work does he do to educate others?

YOUR STORY
1. What values will you be demonstrating by signing an organ donor card or discussing willingness to be an organ donor with your parents?
2. How can you educate others about the importance of organ donation? What might the benefit be to yourself and others?

Problems of the Urinary System

Because of the shortness of the urethra in females, it is prone to allowing infectious bacteria to reach the bladder. Urinary tract infections are therefore more common in females than in males. Any changes in urine color, odor, or frequency should be discussed with a health care professional; so should any discomfort or pain during urination. These symptoms might signal one of the following conditions:

- **Cystitis** is *a bacterial infection of the bladder* that occurs most frequently in females. Symptoms include a burning sensation and a high frequency of urination. Fever may be present as well as blood in the urine. If left untreated, the infection can move to the ureter and kidneys.

- **Urethritis** is *an inflammation of the urethra*. It is usually caused by an infection. The passage of urine becomes painful and difficult.

Another urinary system problem is urinary **incontinence**, *the inability of the body to control the bladder and the elimination of waste*. Urinary incontinence may occur if the sphincter muscle that closes the urethra is weak or damaged. This condition is more common in older adults.

Kidney Problems

Because the function of the kidneys is so essential to maintaining the balance of fluids in the body, any disruption of their function is potentially serious. However, only one normal kidney is needed for good health. Kidney problems are rarely life-threatening unless both kidneys are affected. Some problems include the following:

NEPHRITIS

Nephritis is an inflammation of the nephrons in the kidneys. Symptoms may include high blood pressure, weakness, fatigue, and swelling of body tissues.

KIDNEY STONES

Kidney stones are small, hard crystals formed from substances in the urine. Small stones may pass out of the body in the urine. With larger stones, or if an infection is present or the urinary tract is blocked, medical treatment is necessary.

In the past, surgery was necessary to remove a kidney stone. Now, however, a procedure called lithotripsy has largely replaced surgery. High-intensity sound waves are focused on the area where the stones are located. The sound waves pass through the body and literally disintegrate the stones. The process is painless, and the resulting fragments pass out of the body in urine.

UREMIA

When the kidneys are unable to rid wastes from the body, poisonous substances build up. The presence of excess urea and other chemical waste products in the blood is called uremia. Uremia develops as a result of kidney failure.

KIDNEY FAILURE

Kidney failure can be acute, meaning of sudden onset, or chronic, meaning it develops gradually. It may be caused by blockage of urine, a serious case of nephritis, loss of blood, or any disease that causes damage to the kidneys. Treatment of acute kidney failure varies depending on the cause. Three techniques are in use today to help people who suffer from chronic kidney failure.

- **Hemodialysis** (HEE-moh-dy-AL-uh-suhs) is *a technique in which an artificial kidney machine removes waste products from the blood.* A needle connected to plastic tubing passes blood from the patient to the kidney machine and the cleansed blood back to the patient. The process takes two to six hours and is usually carried out three times a week. This kind of dialysis usually takes place in a hospital or clinic setting, although it may also be carried out in the patient's home.
- Peritoneal dialysis involves insertion of a catheter—a tube that provides a passageway for fluids—through an abdominal incision into the peritoneal cavity. It uses the peritoneum, a thin membrane that surrounds the digestive organs, to filter the blood and remove waste products. Peritoneal dialysis allows the patient to be treated at home.
- In the third technique, kidney transplant, the diseased kidney is surgically replaced with a healthy kidney from a donor. Kidney transplants are successful in more than 80 percent of cases when the donor is not related to the patient and 90 percent if the donor is a close blood relative.

Medical technology has made it possible to treat kidney failure by filtering blood artificially.

ACTIVITY **List the steps you should take to maintain the health of your urinary system.**

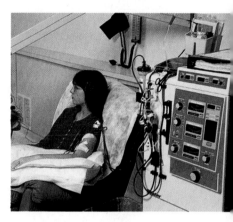

LESSON 3 *Review*

Reviewing Facts and Vocabulary
1. Describe the function of the kidneys.
2. Define the terms *urine, nephrons,* and *hemodialysis.*

Thinking Critically
3. *Analyzing.* How does drinking plenty of water each day promote a healthy urinary system?
4. *Analyzing.* How might kidney dialysis affect a person's lifestyle?

Applying Health Skills
5. *In Your Home and School.* Ask the butcher for lambs' kidneys, which are similar in size and shape to your own. Split the kidney in half lengthwise (you may want to ask the butcher to do this for you) and make a crosscut to see the inside. Use a magnifying glass to locate the tiny, threadlike nephrons. Find the tubes that collect liquid from the nephrons and drain it from the kidney through the ureter. Share your findings with your family and classmates.

Health Skills Activities

Digestive System—What's Your Function?

The digestive system is composed of many different organs that work together. Do you know all these organs and how to maintain the health of each? As a class, you will write an informational booklet about digestion.

Directions

1. With a group, select an organ of the digestive system.
2. Using information from the chapter, determine the functions of the organ you have selected. Describe the best ways to maintain the health of this organ and what problems when care is not taken in choosing foods, rate of speed in eating, and so on.
3. Include photos, illustrations, or other visual aids if possible.
4. Combine your findings with those of other groups. Arrange your booklet in the order in which digestion (mouth first, then esophagus, and so on.).

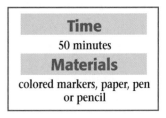

Time

50 minutes

Materials

colored markers, paper, pen or pencil

Self-Assessment

✓ Correctly described the functions of the organ selected and identified ways to maintain its health.
✓ Listed at least two problems that can occur when care is not taken.

Water, Water Everywhere

You have learned that one of the keys to a healthy urinary system is drinking plenty of fluids. Many people find it difficult, however, to drink 8 glasses of water in a day. Is there an alternative?

Directions

1. With a group, think about and list fruits, vegetables, and other foods you would describe as juicy (for example, oranges, tomatoes, and watermelon).
2. Compare your list with that of other groups. Investigate the actual water content of these and other foods by speaking with a family and consumer science teacher in the school or visiting the Web site your teacher recommended.
3. Use the information to create a pamphlet explaining how people can meet their daily water requirement through "solid" foods.

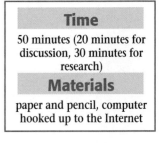

Time

50 minutes (20 minutes for discussion, 30 minutes for research)

Materials

paper and pencil, computer hooked up to the Internet

Self-Assessment

✓ Identified at least three foods with high water content.
✓ Created a persuasive and eye-catching health pamphlet.

Camera in a Capsule

Soon doctors might prescribe a pill to view the inside of their patients' intestines.

In the past, doctors diagnosed digestive problems by using X rays or endoscopy, which involves sedating a person and guiding a tube with a camera attached down the throat into the stomach and intestinal tract.

Now physicians are developing a less invasive device. Called pill endoscopy, the device uses a dime-size capsule that contains a miniature camera. A patient swallows the capsule. As the tablet moves through the digestive system, it transmits signals that are downloaded as images on a computer.

On his 1998 trip into outer space, former U.S. Sen. John Glenn swallowed a device similar to a pill endoscopy capsule to measure his core body temperature. The device offers several advantages over endoscopy.

"It's relatively painless," said Dr. Paul Swain. Second, the pill's camera would provide images of the intestine that before now have been too difficult to reach with an endoscope camera.

But there also are drawbacks. Physicians can use endoscopies to perform biopsies, which means collecting tissue samples, to test for cancer. They also can use the endoscopy device to stop bleeding.

The biggest disadvantage of the pill is the inability to direct the device. Physicians performing traditional endoscopy can aim the camera at areas to examine more closely. But the free-floating nature of the pill makes that impossible.

Think About It

1. How is a pill endoscopy different from a traditional endoscopy?
2. What are the advantages of this new technology? What are the drawbacks?
3. How do you think promising new devices and techniques become accepted medical practice?

Using Health Terms

On a separate sheet of paper, write the term that best matches each definition below.

LESSON 1

1. Secretions from the stomach lining that contain pepsin and hydrochloric acid.
2. A yellowish-green, bitter fluid important in the breakdown of fats.
3. The taking of food into the body.
4. A creamy, fluid mixture of food and gastric juices.
5. A series of involuntary muscular contractions.
6. The mechanical and chemical breakdown of foods for use by the body's cells.
7. The process of chewing.
8. The passage of digested food from the digestive tract into the circulatory system.
9. The expulsion of undigested food or body wastes.

LESSON 2

10. A burning discomfort in the upper abdomen.
11. A condition in which part of the stomach pushes through an opening in the diaphragm.
12. The inflammation of the appendix.
13. A sore in the lining of the digestive tract.

LESSON 3

14. The tube that leads from the bladder to the outside of the body.
15. Use of artificial kidney machine to remove waste products from the blood.
16. A hollow, muscular organ that acts as a reservoir for urine.
17. An inflammation of the urethra.
18. Liquid waste material.
19. The functional units of the kidneys.
20. Tubes that connect the kidneys with the bladder.

Recalling the Facts

Using complete sentences, answer the following questions.

LESSON 1

1. What are the mechanical processes that take place during digestion?
2. What are the chemical processes that take place during digestion?
3. What is the role of the sphincter muscles located along the digestive tract?
4. In what part of the digestive system does most of the chemical breakdown of food take place?
5. What are the two main functions of the large intestine?

LESSON 2

6. What causes heartburn?
7. What is a hiatal hernia?
8. List three symptoms that may be present in a person suffering from appendicitis.
9. What is lactose intolerance?
10. List three ways to prevent tooth decay.

LESSON 3

11. Name the four parts of the urinary system.
12. In what body organ is urine stored?
13. Why are the kidneys important?
14. Name and define four problems that may be associated with the urinary system.
15. Describe the process of hemodialysis.

Review

Thinking Critically

LESSON 1

1. **Synthesizing.** Explain why the teeth should be included in any discussion of the digestive system.
2. **Analyzing.** Summarize the work of gastric juices.
3. **Analyzing.** What makes the liver, gallbladder, and pancreas important to the digestive system even though they are not part of it?

LESSON 2

4. **Analyzing.** In what ways are smoking, stress, and digestive problems related?

5. **Synthesizing.** Develop a plan that would help young people prevent gastrointestinal problems.

LESSON 3

6. **Synthesizing.** Make a diagram or chart of the urinary system of the human body to show how this system works. Name and label the parts of the system and tell how each part functions.
7. **Evaluating.** Think of some ways in which you could determine whether your urinary system is healthy.

Making the Connection

1. **Science.** Research one of the digestive problems described in Lesson 2. Write a short paper on its causes, symptoms, and cures.
2. **Math.** Calculate the cost to an individual of kidney dialysis for one year based on average costs of treatment in your local area. A hospital billing office or a medical insurer can assist by providing current figures. Share your findings with the class.

BEYOND THE CLASSROOM

PARENTAL INVOLVEMENT Ask your parents to share with you any problems they have experienced with their digestive or urinary systems. Ask them to describe their symptoms, to tell what actions they took to correct the problem, and to evaluate the effectiveness of the treatment. Work together at devising a plan that reduces the risk of future problems of the digestive or urinary system.

COMMUNITY INVOLVEMENT Find out what support groups are available in your community for people suffering from digestive and urinary system problems. There may, for example, be groups for people with colitis or irritable bowel syndrome. Prepare a pamphlet listing the name of each group, its contact person and telephone number, meeting location, and when the group meets. In addition, indicate the types of medical specialists who treat these problems. Make the pamphlet available through your school health office.

SCHOOL-TO-CAREER
Technology. Find out what is involved in kidney transplants. How do physicians match a donor and a recipient? How long is the average wait for a donor organ? What advancements have been made in the procedure? What is the success rate for this type of surgery?

CHAPTER 19

Your Body's Reproductive System

HEALTH *Online*

ACCESSING INFORMATION
This chapter will give you an understanding of important reproductive system terms. Tackle these terms and definitions with a plan to learn the correct meanings and spellings. Find out how to use a Word Processing program to make study notes and flash cards. See health.glencoe.com, *Technology Projects.

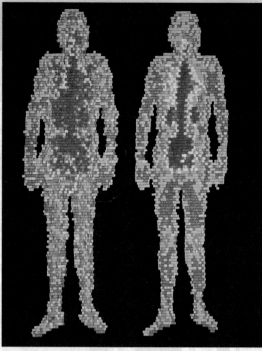
Gamma scans of male and female

Personal Health Inventory

Self-Inventory Write the numbers 1–10 on a sheet of paper. Read each statement below and respond by writing *yes, no,* or *sometimes* for each item. Write a *yes* only for items that you practice regularly. Save your responses.

1	I eat a well-balanced diet.
2	I exercise regularly.
3	I manage the stress in my life.
4	I practice daily health care.
5	I avoid situations that might put me at risk of contracting an STD or HIV/AIDS.
6	I have regular physical checkups.
7	For males only: I do a monthly testicular self-exam.
8	For males only: I wear a protector or supporter if I am participating in strenuous activity.
9	For females only: I do a monthly breast self-exam.
10	For females only: I avoid using feminine hygiene products, such as sprays or douches.

Follow-up After completing the chapter, retake this self-inventory. Pick two items that you need to work on and set a goal to improve your health behaviors.

> " *Pay attention to the most important thing of all, the care of your health.* "
>
> —CATO THE ELDER
> ROMAN STATESMAN, (234–149 B.C.)

Quick Write Write five different sentences in which the phrase *reproductive system* and the words *responsibility* and *health* all appear. Share these sentences with your classmates.

The Male Reproductive System

Reproduction is one of the essential functions of living organisms. It is as necessary for the preservation of the species as getting food is for the preservation of the individual. In humans, as in many other animal species, reproduction occurs by means of a system of organs known as the *reproductive system.*

HEALTH TERMS

testosterone

sperm

testes

penis

semen

fertilization

circumcision

sterility

HEALTH CONCEPTS

- The male reproductive system produces sperm, male reproductive cells.
- Regular hygiene and self-examinations are important components of male reproductive system care.

Sperm cells magnified

Functions and Structure of the Male Reproductive System

During the early teen years, the male reproductive system reaches maturity. Hormones released by the pituitary gland stimulate the testes to begin producing the *male sex hormone* **testosterone.** Testosterone initiates physical changes, including broadening of the shoulders, development of muscles, facial and other body hair, and deepening of the voice.

Testosterone also causes the production of **sperm,** *male reproductive cells.* Once a male is physically mature, he is capable of manufacturing sperm for the rest of his life. The production of sperm and the transfer of it to the female's body during sexual intercourse are the two main biological functions of the male reproductive system.

External Male Reproductive Organs

Some of the organs involved in the process of reproduction are internal to the male's body; others are external. The main external organs are the testes and penis.

Also known as the *testicles,* the **testes** are *two small glands that produce sperm* at the rate of 100 million per day. The sperm resemble tadpoles and are so tiny that 500 of them lined up would measure only an inch.

The testes hang outside the body in a sac called the *scrotum.* This sac protects sperm by keeping the testes at a temperature slightly below the normal body temperature of 98.6°F (37°C). If body temperature rises, the muscles of the scrotum relax, lowering the testes away from the body. If body temperature drops, the muscles contract, pulling the testes closer to the body. Any clothing or other restraint that holds the testicles too close to the body can interfere with sperm production. Even wearing pants that are too tight is believed to interfere with the natural cooling of the testicles.

The **penis** is *a tube-shaped organ attached to the trunk of the body just above the testes.* The penis is composed of spongy tissue that contains many blood vessels. As a result of increased blood flow, the penis becomes enlarged and erect. Males of every age experience erections, and these can occur for no reason at all. Sometimes an erection results from friction of the clothing a male is wearing.

THE MALE REPRODUCTIVE SYSTEM

▼ *The male reproductive system produces sperm in the testes.*

ACTIVITY *Name the other main function of the male reproductive system.*

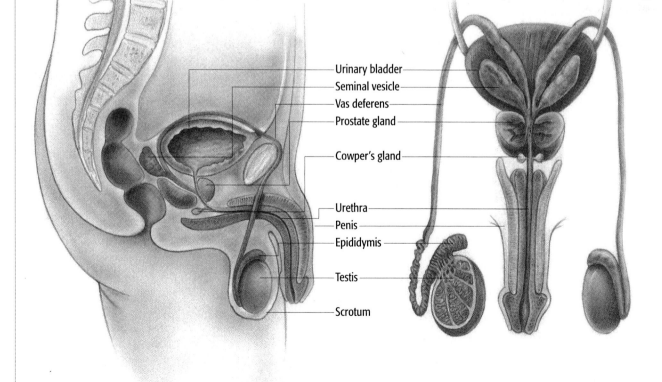

Urinary bladder
Seminal vesicle
Vas deferens
Prostate gland

Cowper's gland

Urethra
Penis
Epididymis

Testis

Scrotum

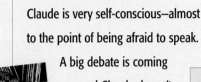
The Voice of Reason

Claude is the star of his school's debating team. The problem is that his voice is changing, causing it to "crack." Although

no one has said anything to him, Claude is very self-conscious—almost to the point of being afraid to speak. A big debate is coming up, and Claude doesn't know what to do. One thing he *does* know is that his team is counting on him!

What Would You Do?

Apply the six steps of the decision-making process to Claude's problem.

1. **State the situation.**
2. **List the options.**
3. **Weigh the possible outcomes.**
4. **Consider your values.**
5. **Make a decision and act.**
6. **Evaluate the decision.**

keeping Fit

Steps to Performing a Testicular Exam

Once a month, males should examine themselves for testicular cancer. Although the majority of testicular lumps do not signify cancer, it is wise to seek a doctor's advice if you do find a lump.

➤ Examine the testicles after a warm bath or shower, and lying down.

➤ Cup the scrotum in the palms of both hands. Note any changes from the last examination.

➤ With thumb and fingers, gently roll each testicle around.

➤ Squeeze the testicles gently to note the firm, not hard, consistency.

➤ Examine the epididymis. It feels softer than the testicles and it may be spongy and a little tender.

➤ A hard, painless pea-sized nodule and any swelling on the testicle should be reported to a doctor.

Erections also occur as the result of becoming sexually aroused. At the height of sexual arousal, a series of muscular contractions known as *ejaculation* may occur. During ejaculation, **semen**—*a thick fluid containing sperm and other secretions from the male reproductive organs*—is propelled from the penis. If this happens during sexual intercourse, fertilization may be initiated. **Fertilization** is *the union of a reproductive cell from a male and one from a female.*

When a male begins to produce sperm, he may experience a nocturnal emission, or "wet dream," in which he becomes erect and ejaculates during sleep. This is a normal occurrence.

At birth, the tip of the penis is covered with a fold of skin called *foreskin.* Some parents choose **circumcision**—*surgical removal of the foreskin of the penis*—for their male child. It is important to remember that a male child is normal whether he is circumcised or not.

Internal Male Reproductive Organs

The internal structures of the male reproductive system play a role in the delivery of sperm. These include the epididymis, the vas deferens, the seminal vesicles, the prostate gland, the Cowper's glands, and the urethra. The urethra is also involved in the removal of liquid wastes from the body.

The tubes in each testis join a larger coiled tube, which is called the *epididymis.* Located at the outer surface of the testes, the epididymis is a temporary storage facility for sperm. Sperm mature in the epididymis.

The vas deferens are a pair of connecting tubes, each about 18 inches (46 cm) long, that lead up into the male's body toward two other internal organs, the seminal vesicles and the prostate gland. The thick muscle walls of the vas deferens propel the sperm forward in powerful spurts just before ejaculation.

As sperm move through the vas deferens, they are combined with a fluid produced by the seminal vesicles. These are glands that are about 2 inches (5 cm) long and attached to the vas deferens near the base of the bladder. The fluid contains nutrients and mixes with sperm to make them more mobile and to provide nourishment. The seminal vesicles and vas deferens meet to form the ejaculatory duct.

As sperm continue on their journey through the ejaculatory duct, they are next mixed with fluids secreted from the prostate gland—a small gland that surrounds the urethra—and from Cowper's glands, which are located below the prostate gland. Semen, or seminal fluid, is now fully formed. The secretion from the Cowper's glands also neutralizes the acid content before semen is ejaculated.

The urethra is the passageway through which both semen and urine leave the body. Semen and urine do not pass through the body at the same time. A muscle near the bladder contracts, preventing urine from entering the urethra when semen is present.

▼ *The groin area should be protected from possible injury when playing sports.*

ACTIVITY *List sports that you play and name the protective equipment you wear during these sports.*

Care of the Male Reproductive System

Caring for the male reproductive system involves cleanliness, protection, and self-examination. To stay healthy, males should shower daily, completely cleansing the penis and scrotum. A male who is uncircumcised must practice extra hygiene, taking care to wash underneath the foreskin.

Another aspect of male reproductive care is avoiding clothing that is too tight and wearing a protector or supporter during strenuous activity to help shield the groin area and the external reproductive organs.

In addition, once a male is physically mature, he should perform a monthly self-examination of his testes for signs of cancer. Any lumps, thickenings, or change in texture or size of the testes should be reported to a doctor, even though such signs do not always mean cancer has developed. If cancer is present, however, early detection usually leads to successful treatment.

► **Talk to a school nurse, doctor, or other health professional to get accurate health information.**

ACTIVITY *List questions you may have that can be answered by a health professional.*

h t l nk

sexually transmitted diseases (STDs) For more information on sexually transmitted diseases (STDs) and ways to avoid them, see Chapter 29, page 640.

Steps to Becoming a Responsible Young Male

The ability to produce sperm is a major responsibility. Yet, in truth, it has nothing to do with becoming a responsible man. Here are some ways to show you are responsible:

➤ Respect yourself and other people.

➤ Control your sexual feelings and never impose them on others.

➤ Distinguish between sexual information that is designed to excite and "sell" and sexual information that is designed to inform.

Problems of the Male Reproductive System

The organs of the male reproductive system can be affected by both functional and structural problems. The effect of **sexually transmitted diseases (STDs)** on these organs will be discussed in Chapter 29.

Hernia

A hernia occurs when part of an organ pushes through an opening of a membrane or muscle that usually contains the organ. Hernias occur in various parts of the body. A common hernia of the male reproductive system is an inguinal hernia. This is a weak spot in the abdominal wall in the lowest lateral regions of the abdomen near the top of the scrotum. Sometimes straining the abdominal muscles can cause a tear in this spot. A part of the intestine can then push through into the abdominal area. Surgery is usually necessary to correct such a hernia.

Sterility

Sterility is *a condition in which a person is unable to reproduce.* In a male, this can be the result of producing too few sperm—less than 20 million sperm per milliliter (ml) of seminal fluid—or sperm of poor quality. Environmental hazards that damage the sperm-making process include exposure to X rays, radiation, and lead from motor exhaust. Sterility can arise as a result of temperature change, exposure to certain chemicals, smoking, contracting mumps as an adult, complications of an STD, or malfunction of one of the internal male reproductive organs.

Enlarged Prostate Gland

The prostate gland can enlarge for reasons such as infection, a tumor, or old age. When the gland enlarges, it tends to squeeze the urethra, resulting in frequent or difficult urination. Treatments for enlarged prostate include special exercises to improve bladder control, medications that shrink an enlarged prostate or relax the prostatic muscle, and surgery to remove excess tissue.

Cancer of the Prostate Gland

Cancer is an uncontrolled growth of cells. The prostate gland is often a cancer site in older males. Prostate cancer is the second highest incidence of cancer in males. Only a doctor can diagnose prostate cancer. Early detection is important because prostate cancer can be treated if it is localized in the gland. Surgical removal of the prostate or radiation therapy and hormone therapy are current treatments.

Cancer of the Testes

Cancer of the testes occurs most frequently in males between the ages of 15 and 35 in the United States. The first sign of testicular cancer is usually a slight enlargement of one of the testes. The male may not experience any pain at all, or he might have a dull ache in the lower abdomen and groin. Hard lumps, or nodules, on the testes may be a sign of cancer. Testicular cancer can be cured in 90 percent of cases if it is caught early.

h t link

cancer For more information on cancers and their treatment, see Chapter 31, page 683.

LESSON **1** *Review*

Reviewing Facts and Vocabulary

1. Trace the path that sperm follow from the testes to the urethra.
2. Name two problems that can affect the male reproductive system and describe them.

Thinking Critically

3. **Analyzing.** Why would it be important for a male to get a medical checkup if he experienced difficulty urinating?
4. **Synthesizing.** Contact the American Cancer Society for information about testicular and prostate cancers. Make a list that shows how a male can increase his chances of surviving both cancers.

Applying Health Skills

5. **In Your Home.** Increasing evidence suggests that toxic chemicals are responsible for decreased sperm counts in men. Find out what chemicals may be at fault. Research if any of these chemicals exist in your neighborhood. Write letters to your local government to ask what can be done to limit or remove any such harmful substances uncovered in your investigation.

The Female Reproductive System

Like the male repro- ductive system, the female reproductive system matures during the early teen years. Like the male body, the female body goes through a number of changes. These include the devel- opment of breasts and widening of the hips. Other changes that occur are treated in the paragraphs that follow.

HEALTH TERMS

ova

vagina

ovaries

ovulation

fallopian tubes

zygote

uterus

cervix

menstrual cycle

infertility

HEALTH CONCEPTS

- The female reproductive system produces ova, or egg cells.
- The menstrual flow rids the body of tissue when fertilization does not take place.
- In order to keep the female reproductive system in good health, it is important to practice regular hygiene and breast self-examination.
- Females should have a Pap test done by age 18 to help prevent cervical cancer.

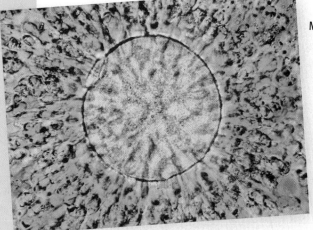

Magnified ovum

Functions and Structure of the Female Reproductive System

As with the male, the primary biological functions of the female reproductive system are related to the process of reproduction. The female reproductive system stores *female reproductive cells,* or **ova.** It also nourishes and protects each fertilized ovum from the begin- ning of pregnancy through birth. Sperm from the male enter the female reproductive system through the **vagina,** *a muscular, elastic passageway that extends from the uterus to the outside of the body.*

Female Reproductive Organs

Ova are stored in the **ovaries,** *the female sex glands that house the ova and produce female sex hormones.* The two ovaries are almond-shaped and located on each side of the body in the lower abdominal area. At birth, a female has over 400,000 immature ova in her ovaries.

During the early teen years, hormones cause the immature ova to mature. The ovaries begin *the process of releasing one mature ovum each month.* This process is called **ovulation.** Usually, one ovary releases a mature ovum one month, and the other ovary releases a mature ovum the next month.

When a mature ovum is released from an ovary, it moves into one of the **fallopian tubes.** These are *a pair of tubes with fingerlike projections that draw the ovum in.* Each fallopian tube is about 4 inches (10 cm) long and about ⅓ inch (0.8 cm) in diameter. Tiny hairlike structures and muscular contractions move the ovum along.

If a sperm cell introduced during intercourse is present in the fallopian tubes, it may unite with an ovum and fertilization occurs. *The cell that results from the union of sperm and ovum* is a **zygote.**

The **uterus** is *a small, muscular, pear-shaped organ, about the size of a fist.* Once a zygote has been formed, it leaves the fallopian tube, travels to the uterus, and attaches itself to the uterine wall.

▼ *The female reproductive system produces ova to unite with sperm in the process of reproduction.*

ACTIVITY *Name another function of the female reproductive system.*

THE FEMALE REPRODUCTIVE SYSTEM

- Fallopian tube
- Maturing ovum
- Mature ovum
- Ovary
- Uterus
- Endometrium
- Cervix
- Urinary bladder
- Vagina
- Urethra
- Labia minora
- Labia majora

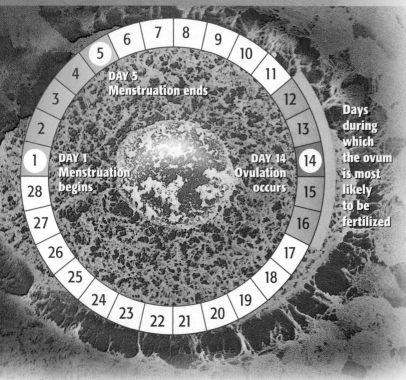

On the diagram:
- 1 — DAY 1 Menstruation begins
- 5 — DAY 5 Menstruation ends
- 14 — DAY 14 Ovulation occurs
- Days during which the ovum is most likely to be fertilized

▲ *On average, the menstrual cycle is 28 days.*

ACTIVITY *Name the days during which the ovum is most likely to be fertilized.*

Menstruation

If the ovum does not become fertilized, the lining of the uterus breaks down into blood, tissue, and fluids which pass through the **cervix**, or *neck of the uterus,* and out of the vagina. This process of shedding the lining of the uterus is called *menstruation,* from the Latin word *mensis,* meaning "month."

The menstrual flow usually lasts about three to five days. Women wear either sanitary pads or tampons to absorb the blood flow from menstruation. After the menstrual period ends, the entire cycle begins again. The lining of the uterus thickens again, preparing for the possibility of receiving a fertilized egg. Although there can be great variations, the **menstrual cycle**—*the time from the beginning of one menstrual period to the onset of the next*—is usually 28 days. The menstrual cycle is regulated by endocrine hormones.

Most females begin menstruating between the ages of 10 and 15. The menstrual cycle may be irregular at first. Although hormones control the menstrual cycle, poor nutrition, stress, and illness can influence the cycle. Irregularity of the menstrual cycle is caused not only by these factors but also by physical maturity. Growth and time usually result in more predictable onset and duration of the cycle.

Care of the Female Reproductive System

Cleanliness is an important part of keeping the reproductive system healthy. The vagina is a self-cleansing organ. Once a female matures, the cells in the lining of the vagina are constantly being shed, causing a slight vaginal discharge. This is normal. Cleanliness is especially important during the menstrual period, when menstrual flow may cause a slight odor. Sanitary napkins and tampons should be changed every few hours. Feminine hygiene products such as deodorant sprays and douches should not be necessary and may, in fact, cause irritation to the sensitive tissues around the vagina.

Breast Self-Examination

Breast self-examination (BSE) is an important habit for females to develop. It is one way that they can take charge of their bodies and maintain good health. BSE should be done once a month, about a week after the start of their menstrual period, when the breasts are usually not tender or swollen.

There are three ways to examine the breasts: in the shower, in front of a mirror, and lying down. In all cases, a thorough BSE includes the following steps:

- Inspect both breasts for anything unusual, such as any discharge from the nipples or puckering, dimpling, or scaling of the skin. If standing in front of a mirror, clasp your hands behind your head and press your hands forward. Then, press your hands firmly on your hips and bow slightly toward the mirror as you pull your shoulders and elbows forward. Get to know the shape of your breasts and note any changes.

- Raise your left arm. Use three or four fingers of your right hand to explore your left breast firmly, carefully, and thoroughly. Beginning at the outer edge, press the flat part of your fingers in small circles, moving the circles slowly around the breast. Gradually work toward the nipple. Finally, squeeze the nipple gently. Look for any discharge.

- Pay special attention to the area between the breast and the armpit, including the armpit itself. Feel for any unusual lump or mass under the skin. Using the left hand, repeat the process for the right breast. If you find anything unusual, contact your doctor at once. Only a doctor can make a diagnosis.

▼ *Physical activity, good nutrition, and regular check-ups can contribute to a healthy reproductive system.*

Problems of the Female Reproductive System

Problems with the female reproductive system can be functional or structural. Some of the problems that can occur are related to menstruation. Others are related to **infertility,** *the inability of a woman to become pregnant.*

Problems Related to Menstruation

Problems related to menstruation can range from minor discomfort to life-threatening illness. Problems include:

- **Menstrual Cramps.** A female may experience abdominal cramps at the beginning of the menstrual period. Menstrual cramps are usually mild, lasting several hours. Light exercise can help relieve cramps. A heating pad might also help relax the muscles. If cramps are severe, the doctor may recommend an over-the-counter medication that contains antiprostaglandins, or the doctor may prescribe medication for pain relief. Severe or persistent cramping may be an indication that medical attention is necessary.

Expressing Concerns About Sexual Maturity

THE CHANGES THAT OCCUR to your body and your emotions during the teen years can be exciting. Yet, they can also be a source of concern. Fortunately, there are people who can put some of your worries to rest. In seeking help, remember:

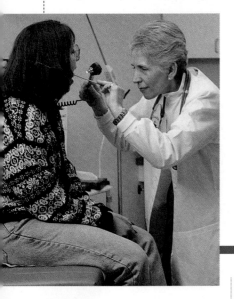

1. Different people possess different strengths and skills. Choose a "consultant" based on your needs. If your concerns are of a physical or medical nature, you might speak with the school nurse or your family's health care provider. For problems of a general nature, remember that parents were once teens themselves and often have good answers.

2. Choose someone who will listen. This can be a parent, teacher, counselor, or even a mature older brother or sister. The only qualification is that the person should have time to give you his or her undivided attention.

3. Make sure the information you get is reliable. Discussing your concerns with a peer might only deepen them. The same is true of "popular" print materials, such as supermarket tabloids, which often contain misinformation.

keeping Fit

TSS and Tampons

TSS risk increases with tampon absorbency. If you use tampons, it is important to use the products with the lowest absorbency that meets your needs. There is usually less need for high-absorbency tampons at the end of a menstrual period.

Also, it is important to follow the manufacturer's instructions. Remember to:

➤ Store tampons in a clean, dry place.

➤ Wash your hands with soap and water before and after inserting or removing a tampon.

➤ Seek medical attention if you have symptoms of TSS.

- **Premenstrual Syndrome (PMS).** Although many females do not experience PMS, others may have a variety of symptoms they experience several days to two weeks before the menstrual period. The symptoms of PMS include nervous tension, anxiety, irritability, bloating, weight gain, depression, mood swings, and fatigue. The causes of PMS are not completely understood. Some doctors believe that PMS is related to a hormonal imbalance.

- **Toxic Shock Syndrome (TSS).** Young women ages 15–19 are the most frequent victims of TSS, but there is a risk of TSS to all women using tampons during their menstrual period. TSS is a rare but serious disease that may be fatal. Scientists believe that TSS requires the presence of the bacterium *Staphylococcus aureus* that causes infection. Signs of TSS include aching muscles, bloodshot eyes, a sore throat, a sudden high fever, vomiting, diarrhea, dizziness, fainting, and a rash that looks like a sunburn.

Problems that Can Cause Infertility

Infertility can affect as many as 8 percent of women of childbearing age. Some of the more common causes are:

- **Blocked Fallopian Tube.** A blocked fallopian tube is the leading cause of female infertility. Some of the causes of a blocked fallopian tube include pelvic inflammatory disease (PID) or abdominal surgery.

- **Endometriosis.** Endometriosis is the second leading cause of infertility. In this disease, uterine tissue grows outside the uterus, often appearing on the ovaries, fallopian tubes, and in the abdominal cavity.
- **Pelvic Inflammatory Disease (PID).** Pelvic inflammatory disease is an infection of the fallopian tubes, ovaries, and surrounding areas in a woman's pelvis. It can damage the reproductive organs and is usually caused by sexually transmitted diseases.

Other Reproductive Disorders

Other reproductive disorders include ovarian cysts and cancers of the reproductive system. An ovarian cyst is a fluid-filled sac on the ovary. Small, noncancerous cysts can develop often but usually dissolve on their own. Large cysts may have to be surgically removed.

About one out of eight females develop cancer at some time. Most breast lumps are found during breast self-examination. About 80 percent of these lumps are not cancerous, but should be checked.

The cervix, uterus, and ovaries are common sites of cancer in females. Cervical cancer is detected through a Pap test, a test in which samples of cells are taken from the cervix by a doctor and viewed under a microscope. Early detection contributes to successful treatment. Early sexual activity, as well as a family history of cervical cancer and other factors, is related to an increased incidence of cervical cancer. A Pap test should be done every one or two years after a woman has reached 18 years of age or has become sexually active.

keeping Fit

Why Have a Pelvic Exam?

A pelvic exam is one in which a gynecologist checks a female's pelvic area, first with an instrument called a speculum and then by hand. The American College of Obstetricians and Gynecologists (ACOG) recommends that young females have pelvic exams by the time they are 18. The following are reasons having a pelvic exam is important:

➤ During a pelvic exam, the doctor can check the shape, size, and position of pelvic organs.

➤ The doctor can check for any tumors or cysts.

➤ If a female has unusual vaginal discharge, the doctor can check to find the possible cause.

LESSON 2 *Review*

Reviewing Facts and Vocabulary

1. What is menstruation?
2. What is PMS?
3. Name two causes of infertility in females.
4. Name at least two ways to lessen menstrual cramps.

Thinking Critically

5. *Analyzing.* What is the relationship between ovulation, fertilization, and menstruation?
6. *Comparing and Contrasting.* Compare and contrast the male and female reproductive systems.
7. *Synthesizing.* While the causes of PMS are still being researched, some medicine companies are producing over-the-counter medications to treat PMS. From what you have learned, how effective do you think the medicines might be? What symptoms do you think the medicines might help alleviate?

Applying Health Skills

8. *In Your Home.* Make a list of some of the myths you have heard about menstruation. Discuss these myths with a parent or an adult female relative. Why do you think there is so much misinformation? Talk about some ways to clarify and correct some of these myths.

Health Skills Activities

Activity 1 — Cancer Awareness Day

Cancer claims numerous lives each year. As with so many other diseases, education can be the key to reducing the risks of various cancers. Plan your own Cancer Awareness Day to educate others about cancers that affect the reproductive system.

Directions

1. With a group, gather information about the reproductive cancers detailed in your book.
2. From the American Cancer Society and other health organizations, learn about lifestyle behaviors and choices that can reduce a person's risk of one of these cancers.
3. Using the information that you have gathered, create promotional and informational literature in the form of bumper stickers, badges, and leaflets to be passed out to other students on a day designated as Cancer Awareness Day.

Self-Assessment

✓ Described prevention strategies associated with primary health care (e.g., BSE, testicular self-exam, Pap smear, etc.).
✓ Presented a clear message promoting healthful behaviors that reduce risk of disease.

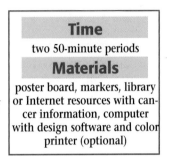

Time
two 50-minute periods

Materials
poster board, markers, library or Internet resources with cancer information, computer with design software and color printer (optional)

Activity 2 — Be a Health Reporter

Care of the reproductive system is important, but it is also a topic that many people are embarrassed to talk about. Be a health reporter. Write an article that will provide the public with the information they need.

Directions

1. Choose a reproductive health topic that would make a good health article (such as diseases of the reproductive system, proper care, or advancements in reproductive health).
2. Write a feature article or editorial. Include information such as how to screen for a disease or recognize a problem, how to prevent problems from occurring, and so on.
3. Share your health articles with your classmates. You may want to submit your article to the school or local newspaper.

Self-Assessment

✓ Selected a topic concerning reproductive health.
✓ Included adequate information about the topic selected.

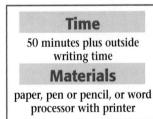

Time
50 minutes plus outside writing time

Materials
paper, pen or pencil, or word processor with printer

Fitness and Gender

Many people think that men are naturally stronger than women. Scientists studying athletes have discovered that's simply not true.

Men have more upper body strength, but women's lower body muscles can be as strong as a man's. These strengths may explain why men are drawn to upper-body activities like baseball and weight lifting. Women favor activities like tennis and gymnastics because they use lower body strength.

Men also experience more sports injuries, partly because they participate in more events. However, men are also less flexible than women. For both genders, the keys to avoiding injury are stretching, warming-up, and building endurance.

Think About It

▸ What are the differences between men's and women's body strength? Name three sports that focus on each type of strength.

▸ What types of injuries are women more vulnerable to?

▸ What strategies can you use to avoid injury? Are these strategies the same for men and women? Explain.

Using Health Terms

On a separate sheet of paper, write the term that best matches each definition below.

LESSON 1

1. The union of a reproductive cell from a male and one from a female.
2. A condition in which a person is unable to reproduce.
3. Male sex hormone.
4. A thick fluid containing sperm and other secretions from the male reproductive organs.
5. Two small glands that produce sperm.
6. Surgical removal of the foreskin of the penis.
7. A tube-shaped organ attached to the trunk of the body just above the testes.
8. Male reproductive cells.

LESSON 2

9. The inability of a woman to become pregnant.

10. A muscular, elastic passageway that extends from the uterus to the outside of the body.
11. The time from the beginning of one menstrual period to the onset of the next.
12. Female reproductive cells.
13. A pair of tubes with fingerlike projections that draw the ovum in.
14. Neck of the uterus.
15. The process of releasing one mature ovum each month.
16. The cell that results from the union of sperm and ovum.
17. A small, muscular, pear-shaped organ, about the size of a fist.
18. The female sex glands that house the ova and produce female sex hormones.

Recalling the Facts

Using complete sentences, answer the following questions.

LESSON 1

1. What is the function of testosterone? Name three physical changes initiated by testosterone in the male.
2. What are the functions of the male reproductive system?
3. Explain how the scrotum keeps the testes at a temperature that is slightly below normal body temperature.
4. Explain what is involved in caring for the male reproductive system.
5. Why is it important for a male to examine his testes regularly? How often should this be done?

LESSON 2

6. What functions does the female reproductive system serve?
7. What can relieve menstrual cramps?
8. What functions do the ovaries serve?
9. What are the internal reproductive organs in females?
10. How does a mature ovum travel through the fallopian tube?
11. What is one suspected cause of PMS?
12. What is the purpose of performing a breast self-examination (BSE)? How often should it be done? What is the best time to do it and why?
13. What is a Pap test? What does it detect?
14. What is toxic shock syndrome?

Thinking Critically

LESSON 1

1. *Evaluating.* Compare testicular cancer and prostate cancer.
2. *Synthesizing.* What advice might you have for individuals who say they would not go to the doctor if they found a suspicious lump after a testicular self-examination for fear that the lump might be cancer?

LESSON 2

3. *Analyzing.* What factors do you think may have prompted people to make up myths about menstruation? Suggest ways to clear up these types of myths.
4. *Synthesizing.* What information would you include in an accurate and persuasive advertisement to encourage women to have an annual mammogram and Pap test?
5. *Evaluating.* Kim, who is 13, is about to have her first appointment with a gyne-cologist. What questions should she pre-pare to ask before she sees the doctor? Explain your answer.

Making the Connection

1. *Language Arts.* Read an article about one of the following issues or problems concerning the reproductive system: the spread of STDs, multiple births, or effec-tiveness of feminine hygiene products. Create an outline for the article that sum-marizes its key and supporting points.

2. *Mathematics.* Contact the American Cancer Society for current statistics on cancers that affect people in the United States today. Compare the number of people who had breast or prostate cancer in 1980 with those in more recent years. Learn about medical breakthroughs. Present your findings in a report.

BEYOND THE CLASSROOM

PARENTAL INVOLVEMENT With your parents' help, make a family tree. Find out what diseases members of the family tree had. Discuss with your parents why it is important for you to be aware of a history of cancer and other diseases in your family.

COMMUNITY INVOLVEMENT The "Race for the Cure" is an annual foot race that benefits breast can-cer research and is held in many communities. Find out if your community sponsors this race and, if so, when the next race is to be held. If possible, participate in this worthwhile event with other classmates and the community. In your private Health Journal, write a brief ac-count of your experiences, summarizing any comments made by organizers of the race.

SCHOOL-TO-CAREER
Exploring Careers. Interview a gynecologist or a urologist. Find out how a gynecologist helps keep women in good health and how a urologist helps keep men in good health. Determine requirements for this career, including school-ing and types of interpersonal skills. Learn in what settings these doctors work. Share your findings with the class in the form of a brief oral report.

CHAPTER 20

The Beginning of the Life Cycle

HEALTH Online

ADVOCACY
You can make learning fun for younger students, and share what you know about healthy behaviors. Visit **health.glencoe.com** and find the Interactive Project on how to "Create a Health Lesson Plan" for an elementary class or a younger brother or sister.

Personal Health Inventory

Self-Inventory Write the numbers 1–10 on a sheet of paper. Read each statement below and respond by writing *yes, no,* or *sometimes* for each item. Write a *yes* only for items that you practice regularly. Save your responses.

1	A pregnant female has a responsibility to make healthy choices for her unborn child.
2	I come to children's assistance if they are in trouble.
3	I have taken care of younger brothers, sisters, cousins, or neighbors.
4	Children with special needs can experience a healthy development.
5	I treat children with respect.
6	I intervene if I see a child is being mistreated.
7	Children make a valuable contribution to society.
8	The way I treat a younger child has a positive impact on that child's self-concept.
9	I avoid picking on or teasing younger children.
10	I occasionally enjoy fun-filled, quality time with younger children.

Follow-up After completing the chapter, retake this self-inventory. Pick two items that you need to work on and set a goal to improve your health behaviors.

> ❝ *You had better live your best and act your best and think your best today; for today is the sure preparation for tomorrow and all the other tomorrows that follow.* ❞

—HARRIET MARTINEAU
ENGLISH WRITER, (1802–1876)

Quick Write Write down one example of a healthful behavior that you can practice now to prepare for a healthful tomorrow.

Prenatal Development and Care

You and everyone you know began as a single microscopic cell smaller than the head of a pin. Within a nine-month period, this cell divided again and again, millions of times. Ultimately, it formed tissues, organs, and systems that made up your body, your characteristics, and the person you are today.

HEALTH TERMS

embryo

placenta

umbilical cord

fetus

Apgar test

miscarriage

stillbirth

HEALTH CONCEPTS

- Every individual starts off as a single microscopic cell.
- The health of a developing child is dependent on a number of factors, many of which are controlled by the mother-to-be.
- Eating healthfully, getting enough rest, and avoiding harmful substances, including tobacco, alcohol, and other drugs are all essential steps in sound prenatal care.

Cell division

Prenatal Development

The entire complex human body begins as one cell that is formed by the union of an egg cell, or ovum, from a female and a sperm cell from a male. These two cells are microscopic in size. The union of these cells is called *fertilization*. As soon as the ovum is fertilized, it is called a *zygote*. Once the zygote has been formed, a protective membrane around it prevents more sperm from entering the ovum. By the time the zygote reaches the uterus, it has divided many times to form a cluster of cells that has a hollow space in the center. It is now called a *blastocyst*.

Implantation

As the cells of the blastocyst divide, they begin to implant, or attach, to the lining of the uterus. This process is called *implantation*.

The lining of the uterus is made up of layers of tissue that will protect and nourish the fertilized egg throughout pregnancy. The *cluster of developing cells following implantation* is called an **embryo.** At this time, the embryo is about the size of the dot over the letter *i*.

Embryonic Development

The cells of the embryo continue to divide, forming three layers of tissue. One layer becomes the respiratory and digestive systems. Another layer develops into muscles, bones, blood vessels, and skin. The third layer becomes the nervous system, sense organs, and mouth.

At the same time, a thin membrane called the *amniotic sac* forms and surrounds the developing embryo. Fluid in this sac acts as a shock absorber that protects the embryo when it is jarred or bumped. The fluid also helps insulate the embryo from temperature changes.

A blood-rich tissue developed from an outer layer of cells from the embryo and tissue from the mother develops into the **placenta.** The embryo is connected to the placenta by the **umbilical cord,** *a tube through which nutrients and oxygen pass from the mother's blood into the embryo's blood.* The blood vessels of the umbilical cord also carry waste products from the embryo, where they diffuse into the mother's blood. These wastes are then excreted from the mother's body along with other body wastes.

Fetal Development

During the first six weeks of pregnancy, the embryo grows rapidly in length and gains weight. At the start of the third week, it is about one-half to one inch long (2 to 2.5 cm), or 10,000 times the size of the original egg cell! At eight weeks the embryo measures about 1½ inches in length (3.5 to 4 cm). *The name by which the embryo is known from the end of the eighth week until birth* is **fetus.** The skin of the fetus is clear and hairless and covered with a waxy protective coating. The fetus contains millions of cells that will arrange themselves into tissues and organs.

TWINS

In most cases of twins, a female's ovaries release two mature ova instead of one. If a separate sperm fertilizes each ovum, two embryos develop. The two embryos, called *fraternal twins*, have different genetic makeup and therefore do not look any more alike than brothers and sisters normally do. Fraternal twins can be the same gender or different gender.

In about one-third of these cases of twins, *identical twins* result. In this situation, a single ovum that has been fertilized divides and two embryos develop. These embryos have the same genetic information. These twins will be the same gender and look almost exactly the same. They are identical twins.

▲ *Identical twins have the same genetic makeup.*

ACTIVITY *How is genetic research with twins helpful in finding health cures?*

The brain is one of the first organs to develop. The nervous system grows rapidly, and at nine weeks the head develops. All the body systems are now present.

Growth of the fetus is rapid during the fourth month, but it slows down in the fifth month. During this time, the mother can feel the fetus move. It may begin to suck its thumb. By the end of the sixth month, the fetus is about 14 inches (36 cm) long.

During the last three months of pregnancy, the weight of the fetus more than triples. The fetus moves freely within the amniotic sac. The eyes open during the seventh month. During the ninth month, the fetus usually moves into a head-down position and is ready for birth. The fetus is now 18 to 20 inches (46 to 51 cm) long and weighs about 7 to 9 pounds (3 to 4 kg).

Prenatal Care

The health of a developing baby is not totally within the control of the mother-to-be. Heredity, which will be addressed in the next lesson, is one unavoidable factor that can affect the developing baby. Yet, there is much the mother can do to improve the chances of having a healthy baby.

Building Health Skills

Obtaining Help: Choosing a Health Professional

THE HEALTH PROFESSIONAL whom the mother-to-be chooses is a partner in the health care of the baby and mother. When selecting a professional, whether it be an obstetrician or certified nurse midwife, a female should address the following considerations and questions:

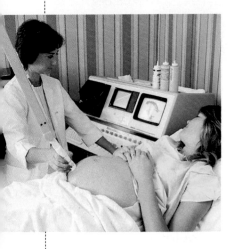

1. **Qualifications.** What professional training has the person received? Do I know anyone who has made use of his or her services? Am I able to obtain reliable references?

2. **Cost.** Can I afford this professional? Is this type of service covered by my health insurance or health plan? If not, can I set up a payment schedule?

3. **Interpersonal Skills.** What kind of "bedside manner" does the person have? Am I comfortable talking to this professional? Am I encouraged to call if I have questions?

4. **Location.** Is the office located nearby? What are the office hours? Will I have to wait long? Is the professional associated with a hospital or a birthing center?

Other issues that need to be taken into account are the professional's views on natural childbirth and whether he or she is able to administer pain relief during labor, if desired.

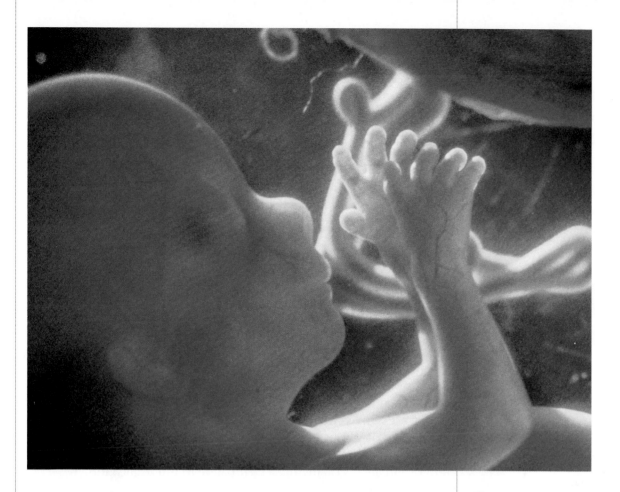

As soon as a female confirms her pregnancy, she should begin prenatal care. This includes having regular visits with either an obstetrician or a certified nurse midwife. An obstetrician is a doctor who specializes in the care of a female and her developing baby. A certified nurse midwife is an advanced practice nurse who, in addition to providing prenatal care, specializes in the delivery of healthy babies. Either professional will give the pregnant female a complete physical, including blood tests and a pelvic examination. Possible problems may be identified and corrected early.

Prenatal care gives the mother-to-be a chance to ask questions about pregnancy and the birth process, and it helps educate her with respect to important health behaviors. Nutrition is a special concern. The mother-to-be needs increased amounts of many micronutrients, especially calcium, vitamin E, and iron. Without sufficient iron, the fetus will draw its supply of iron from the mother, leaving her exhausted and possibly anemic. Eating foods rich in folic acid, such as whole grains and fish, reduces the chance of certain birth defects such as spina bifida, a neural tube defect that affects the baby's spine.

During prenatal care, the obstetrician or certified nurse midwife will also monitor the female's weight and discuss the importance of physical activity. An exercise program will be recommended depending on the female's health and level of fitness.

By the fourth month the fetus is 8 to 10 inches long and weighs about 6 ounces.

ACTIVITY *Compare the size of a fetus at 4 months and at 9 months.*

The March of Dimes works to reduce the rate of infant deaths due to birth defects. Visit **health.glencoe.com** and gather material to create a booklet for couples expecting their first child.

hotlink

medicines For more information on medicines and procedures for using them safely and correctly, see Chapter 23, page 518.

hotlink

fetal alcohol syndrome (FAS) For more information on fetal alcohol syndrome (FAS) and its dangers to the developing child, see Chapter 25, page 561.

Medicines, Drugs, and Pregnancy

A pregnant female must be very careful about what substances she takes into her body. Any medicines, even natural supplements, should be taken only with her health professional's approval. Even prescription and over-the-counter **medicines** pose a potential danger to the fetus.

No illegal drugs should be taken. Illegal drugs present a serious threat to the mother and her baby. Babies can be born physically dependent on the drugs their mothers used while pregnant. Use of certain drugs during pregnancy can cause serious birth defects, including mental retardation.

Caffeine, which is present in coffee, tea, chocolate, and cola drinks, is another potential hazard to the fetus. A high caffeine intake has been associated with an increased risk of birth defects and other problems.

ALCOHOL AND PREGNANCY

Females who drink alcohol during pregnancy may cause permanent damage to the developing baby. Alcohol use by females during pregnancy has been associated with many defects in their children, because the alcohol passes from the mother's body into the baby's bloodstream. Consumption of alcohol is associated with a risk of **fetal alcohol syndrome (FAS)** and other neurodevelopmental effects. Fetal alcohol syndrome consists of three main features: mental retardation, slow growth before and after birth; and a wide range of physical defects ranging from cleft palate to hip dislocation.

The tragedy of FAS is that the unborn baby has no control over what enters the body. The decision to drink alcohol or not is the

Making Responsible
Decisions

When Saying No Counts Double

Sheila is seven months pregnant, which has her and her husband Tom very excited. Both are also eager that their baby be healthy—a point Tom's parents don't seem to understand. Tonight, Sheila and Tom are out to dinner with Tom's parents to celebrate his mother's birthday. When Sheila declined the waiter's offer of something from the bar, Tom's father insisted. "It's a doubly joyous occasion," he said loudly and ordered Sheila a glass of wine.

What Would You Do?

Apply the six steps of the decision-making process to Sheila's problem:

1. **State the situation.**
2. **List the options.**
3. **Weigh the possible outcomes.**
4. **Consider your values.**
5. **Make a decision and act.**
6. **Evaluate the decision.**

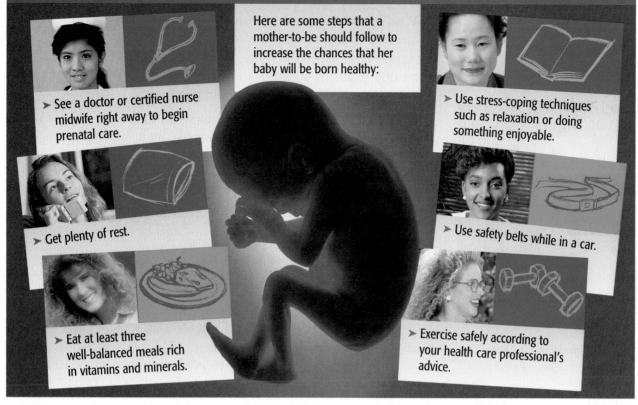

Here are some steps that a mother-to-be should follow to increase the chances that her baby will be born healthy:

➤ See a doctor or certified nurse midwife right away to begin prenatal care.

➤ Get plenty of rest.

➤ Eat at least three well-balanced meals rich in vitamins and minerals.

➤ Use stress-coping techniques such as relaxation or doing something enjoyable.

➤ Use safety belts while in a car.

➤ Exercise safely according to your health care professional's advice.

mother's. Because even small amounts of alcohol may be harmful, the safe decision for a pregnant woman is not to drink any alcoholic beverages. FAS is entirely preventable.

TOBACCO AND PREGNANCY

A pregnant female also must avoid using tobacco. Babies born to females who use tobacco have a greater chance of being born prematurely with low birth weights. Babies weighing 5½ pounds (2.5 kg) or less at birth often develop serious health problems early in life. Low birth weight is a leading cause of death in a baby's first year of life.

Studies have found that smoking during pregnancy may affect the growth, mental development, and behavior of children at least up to the age of 11. Children whose parents smoke have a higher incidence of respiratory problems, such as bronchitis and pneumonia, than do children whose parents do not smoke.

Stages of Birth

Babies usually are born headfirst. In the last few weeks of pregnancy, the baby's head moves to the lower part of the uterus. During the birth process, the baby is pushed out of the uterus and passes out of the mother's body. There are three stages in the birth process:

keeping Fit

Do's and Don'ts During Pregnancy

A mother-to-be should follow the guidelines above, and to protect the health of her baby she should:

➤ Never use tobacco, alcohol, or other drugs.

➤ Never take any drugs without your health care provider's permission.

➤ Limit or avoid products that contain caffeine such as tea, coffee, and cola drinks.

1. **Dilation,** or stretching of the cervix. This results from mild contractions, which are known as *labor.*
2. **Passage of the baby through the birth canal.** This is caused by continuing contractions that shorten the uterus.
3. **Afterbirth.** Once the baby is born, contractions continue for another 10 to 15 minutes, ultimately pushing the placenta, now called the *afterbirth,* out of the mother's body.

Immediately after birth, most hospitals administer an **Apgar test.** This is *a routine diagnostic test that determines an infant's physical condition at birth.* The Apgar test measures the baby's condition in five significant areas: appearance or coloring; pulse; grimace or reflex irritability; activity; and respiration. Any significant difference from the normal response in each of these areas may require further testing and observation.

Complications During Pregnancy

Although pregnancy is not an illness, complications can occur, among these miscarriage and stillbirth. A **miscarriage** is *a spontaneous abortion,* in which the female expels the embryo or fetus. A **stillbirth** is *the birth of a dead fetus.* Females who use tobacco or drugs during pregnancy are more likely to have a miscarriage or stillbirth than those who abstain from their use. As with FAS, the problems associated with tobacco and drug use during pregnancy are completely preventable.

▲ *Both mother and baby are checked for signs of problems after the birth.*

ACTIVITY *List areas checked with the Apgar test.*

LESSON 1 *Review*

Reviewing Facts and Vocabulary

1. Use the terms *embryo* and *fetus* in a paragraph about prenatal development.
2. Identify factors over which the mother-to-be has control when she is planning for the health of her developing child.

Thinking Critically

3. *Evaluating.* Consider how the use of alcohol, tobacco, and drugs is both an irresponsible act of the mother-to-be and also harmful to the unborn child. What are the consequences to both mother and child?
4. *Synthesizing.* Contact a local hospital or clinic for educational materials for mothers-to-be. Identify the health benefits of each step in prenatal care to the developing fetus.

Applying Health Skills

5. *In Your Home.* When a female becomes pregnant, her body changes. Ask your mother or the mother of a friend about the changes she experienced while she was pregnant. Discuss how these changes helped her body to nourish a fetus until birth. Discuss the other responsibilities that a pregnant woman must consider while preparing for the birth of a child.

From Generation to Generation

What color eyes do you have? What color is your hair? Would you describe yourself as tall, short, or medium compared with other people your age? These and related questions are determined by heredity, the passing on of traits from parents to offspring.

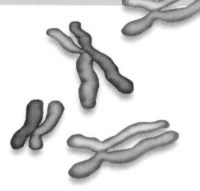

Chromosome pairs, magnified

Chromosomes

Heredity is determined by **chromosomes,** *tiny structures within the nuclei of cells that carry information about hereditary traits.* Most cells in the body contain 46 chromosomes—23 pairs each.

At the foundation of chromosomes is the chemical compound *deoxyribonucleic acid,* or *DNA.* All living things are made of DNA. The DNA molecule resembles a twisted ladder, or helix, the rungs of which are made up of more chemical compounds, called *bases.* There are four kinds of bases that can be paired only in certain combinations, much like pieces of a jigsaw puzzle.

Genes

Specific information about hereditary traits are carried within sections of chromosomes called *genes.* **Genes** are *segments of DNA molecules* and, like chromosomes, are paired. A pair of genes—one from each parent—contributes to a single genetic trait such as hair color or hair straightness.

You have thousands of genes in every cell, and they each contain the same four bases. The variation among genes—which is the reason no two people are exactly alike—is a result of the arrangement of the bases along the DNA molecule. Because several hundred pairs of bases are in each gene, a countless number of arrangements is possible.

Cells make proteins when they interpret the order of these bases, or DNA code. Proteins help build and maintain body tissues. Cells make different proteins when they interpret different arrangements of bases. Different kinds of proteins will result in individual traits.

Dominant and Recessive Genes

As the chromosomes divide and separate, the two genes for a particular trait line up next to each other. Some genes will be *dominant,* while others will be *recessive.* Dominant genes are genes that generally show up in the offspring whenever they are present. Recessive genes are genes that usually show up only when dominant genes are not present. Suppose, for example, one parent has one of the genes that contributes to brown eyes (B), which is dominant, and the other parent has a gene that contributes to blue eyes (b), which is recessive. The likelihood that their child will have brown eyes is greater than that of his or her having blue eyes.

In actuality, the situation is slightly more complex than in the previous example. That is because traits that express a quantity or extent—such as height, weight, or degree of color—usually depend on many gene pairs, not just one.

Genes and Gender

Every living organism has a certain number of chromosomes. Human body cells, with the exception of sperm and ova, contain 46 chromosomes each. Ova and sperm have half that amount—23 chromosomes each. After fertilization, the zygote has 46 chromosomes (23 from each parent) that carry the hereditary traits of the mother and the father. The traits are passed on to another generation.

As you have learned, the zygote divides, eventually producing trillions of cells that make up the human body. Between each cell division, each chromosome in the cell nucleus duplicates itself. As the cell divides, the two sets of 46 chromosomes separate and each new cell contains one set of 46 chromosomes, identical to those in the first cell. This process continues throughout life.

Of the 46 chromosomes in a zygote, two are specialized sex chromosomes. In females, these two chromosomes look exactly alike and are called X chromosomes. In males, one chromosome is shorter and does not match the other. This shorter one is the Y chromosome. The longer one is the X chromosome.

A *All living cells contain the genetic material DNA.*

ACTIVITY *Give an example of a physical trait determined by dominant genes.*

Teens Making a Difference

...RESPONSIBILITY...COURAGE ...PERSEVERANCE

Nicole is 16 and has a genetic disease called Osteogenesis Imperfecta, also known as "Brittle Bone Disease." The disease causes her bones to break easily, and she has had over one hundred bone breaks. "I have pain in my bones," she says matter-of-factly. "I'm in a wheel-chair. I've had major surgeries, and I have rods in my arms, three of them for support." Despite these hardships, she turns the situation around, showing compassion to other young people who are chronically ill.

REACHING OUT Nicole participates in a support group in the hospital school that she attends. "We talk about our illnesses. If the kids are having a bad time, we will talk about that." Nicole has been made an informal group co-leader. "I'm like everybody's psychia-trist," she says with a smile in her voice. "I've become a leader because they see how much pain I go through and how I'm treated in public, and yet I just keep going. I'm a role model to them, I guess. They can give me sup-port when I need it, and I can give it to them." The support group works on projects to help others in need. "We do things for the Salvation Army. We col-lected stuffed animals for young people who don't have a lot. Next, we are going to make quilts for AIDS babies. I also try to raise money for medicines or to find a cure for cancer. I want somebody to find a cure for my disease, so I want to help people with other diseases."

BECOMING AN ADVOCATE

Nicole is outspoken about her condition. Small for her age, people often mistake her for a child and say insensitive things. "I understand that they don't understand. Sometimes people even pet me on the head or treat me like a baby. I just want to be treated with respect. I tell them, too." But Nicole doesn't let this stand in her way. She is a strong advocate both for her own needs and those in her support group. "It's taken a lot of courage," she adds, speaking of her condition. "It's scary, but I know I just have to get through it. I don't depend on everyone to do everything for me. Listen," she says, "You've got to believe in yourself to reach to the level you want to reach, and there is help available. You can give it; you can get it."

NICOLE'S STORY
1. What values has Nicole put into action in facing her disease?
2. How is she reaching out to help others?

YOUR STORY
1. What strategies for facing your own dif-ficulties can you take from Nicole's story?
2. How can you turn your difficult experi-ences into positive actions to help others and help you build strong character along the way?

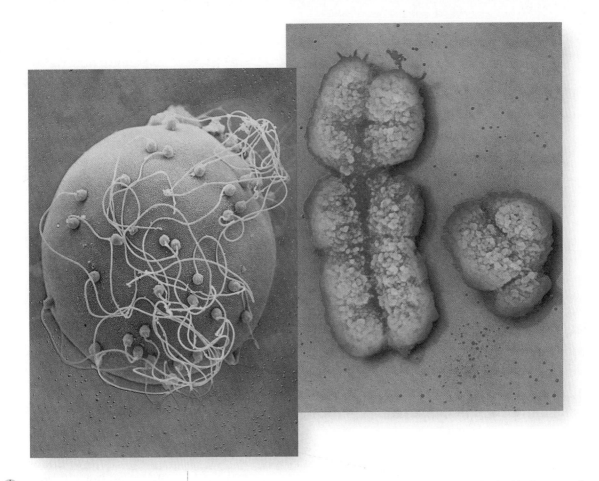

Left: Only one sperm cell will penetrate the ovum for fertilization. Right: Human X and Y chromosomes determine gender.

Remember that sperm and ova contain only half the number of chromosomes as other cells. This means that these cells contain only one sex chromosome, not two. Sperm may contain either an *X* or a *Y* chromosome. The ovum can have only an *X* chromosome. If an ovum is fertilized with a like chromosome, the combination is *XX*, resulting in a girl. If the sperm is carrying a *Y* chromosome, the pairing forms an *XY* combination, resulting in a boy. Thus, the determination of the gender of a child is based on which type of sperm finds the egg, an *X* or a *Y*.

Genetic Disorders

Sometimes the genes children inherit contain mutations, or abnormalities, in the genetic code. The resulting health problems and diseases, which can be severe, are known as *genetic disorders*. Some genetic disorders are observable at birth—in the form of birth defects such as cleft lip and cleft palate—whereas others tend to show up in childhood or adult life. In addition to a genetic cause, some disorders may also be affected by environmental factors, such as the lifestyle habits of one or both parents. There is an especially high rate of birth defects among children born to teenage girls, largely due to ignorance about proper prenatal care.

Types of Genetic Disorders

There are more than 4,000 hereditary disorders. A number of these disorders are recessive—caused by two defective genes, one from each parent. Others result from chromosomal abnormalities. The following are among the more common genetic disorders:

- **Sickle cell anemia.** This disease occurs when a child inherits the hemoglobin "Hbs" gene from both parents. The red blood cells develop a sickle shape and clump together, obstructing blood

up date
Looking at the Issues

Genetic Testing, Genetic Discrimination?

In the past few years, researchers have begun to link specific genes or gene mutations with various diseases. Soon, access to even a tiny sample of a person's DNA will enable trained professionals to run a battery of genetic tests. As the number of genetic tests—and of people tested—increases, a great many legal and ethical questions are being raised. Perhaps the most troubling is the question of how these test results will be used and whether or not they may lead to certain kinds of discrimination, for example, in trying to get a job or health insurance.

ANALYZING DIFFERENT VIEWPOINTS

▶ Viewpoint One

Those who favor genetic testing say that having the knowledge of whether a gene has been carried on can better prepare people for the future. Results of genetic tests, they add, can help decrease the risk of developing certain diseases, such as breast, ovarian, or colon cancer. Frequent screenings or even preventive surgeries can increase the potential for longer lives.

▶ Viewpoint Two

Critics of genetic testing say that having such test results only adds to a person's fear. They point out that just because a person is genetically predisposed to a disease such as cancer doesn't mean that the person will necessarily develop it. They also point out that people who undergo genetic testing are at great risk of being discriminated against both by insurance companies, who won't insure people at risk for these diseases, and by employers, who may not want to hire those at increased risk because of large medical bills and lost productivity.

EXPLORING YOUR VIEWS

1. If there were a test that could alert you to the possibility of developing a life-threatening illness later in life, would you want to be tested? Why or why not?

2. Do you think genetic test information should be released only with a person's consent? Why or why not?

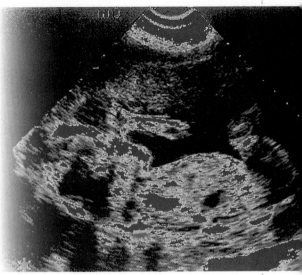

> **Ultrasound images allow doctors to see an image of the fetus.**

ACTIVITY *Identify the head and hand in this ultrasound image.*

What do genetic counselors do? What educational background do they have? Find the answers to these questions at **health.glencoe.com**. Compile information presented into a career profile for students interested in genetic counseling.

flow and oxygen to the tissues. The symptoms of sickle cell anemia are severe joint and abdominal pain, weakness, and kidney disease.

- **Phenylketonuria.** In Phenylketonuria (FEE-nuhl-kee-toh-NOOR-ee-uh)—or *PKU*—a protein called *phenylalanine* accumulates in the body, interfering with the development of brain cells and causing mental retardation. In many states, babies are screened at birth for PKU by a blood test. If results are positive, treatment can begin before mental retardation sets in. Diet can stop the retardation from happening.

- **Tay-Sachs disease.** Tay-Sachs disease affects 1 in 3,600 Americans of Eastern European Jewish ancestry. Tay-Sachs disease causes the destruction of the nervous system, blindness, paralysis, and death during early childhood. A blood test can detect carriers, and a test can diagnose the disease prenatally.

- **Cystic fibrosis.** One in every 2,000 infants is born with cystic fibrosis. The disease, which makes breathing and digestion difficult, is caused by two abnormal genes, one coming from each parent. If both parents are carriers, their offspring have a 25 percent chance of having the disease.

- **Down syndrome.** Down syndrome is primarily caused by a chromosomal abnormality known as *trisomy-21,* the presence of three copies of the twenty-first chromosome. As a result, the affected individual has an extra forty-seventh chromosome in all body cells. Down syndrome affects approximately 1 in 700 births, but the risk varies with the mother's age. By the time a woman reaches 40, the chances are about 1 in 40 that her child will be affected by Down syndrome. Children with Down syndrome share certain characteristics such as mental retardation, which can range from severe to moderate.

Identifying Genetic Disorders

There are several methods used to investigate the health of the fetus. These include the following:

- **Amniocentesis.** Amniocentesis (am-nee-oh-sen-TEE-sis) is *a procedure in which a syringe is inserted through the pregnant female's abdominal wall into the amniotic fluid surrounding the developing fetus.* The physician removes a small amount of the fluid to examine the chromosomes, study the body chemistry, and determine the sex of the fetus. Amniocentesis is performed usually 16 to 20 weeks after fertilization.

- **Ultrasound.** Ultrasound is *a test in which sound waves are used to project light images on a screen.* The sound waves are directed at the pregnant female's abdomen and reflected onto a screen. The reflected waves act like an echo and form an image of the fetus. Ultrasound is used to determine the position of a fetus, and if there is more than one fetus in the uterus.
- **Chorionic villi sampling.** Also known as *CVS,* **chorionic villi** (kor-ee-ON-ik VIL-eye) **sampling** is *a test in which a small piece of membrane is removed from the chorion, a layer of tissue that develops into the placenta.* This material is examined for possible genetic defects. The procedure takes place around the eighth week of fetal development, so it is a procedure that can be done earlier than amniocentesis.

Genetic Counseling

Knowledge about genetically related diseases and about new research for diagnosing, preventing, and treating them has produced a wide variety of programs to deal with genetic disorders and birth defects. One way to help prevent genetically caused birth defects is to identify carriers. Genetic counselors can advise families about the probability of having a child with a genetically related disease. They also can guide families of children with genetic disorders about possible treatment options.

LESSON 2 *Review*

Reviewing Facts and Vocabulary

1. Define *chromosomes* and *genes,* and identify the role each plays in heredity.
2. List two means of identifying genetic disorders, and describe the processes involved.

Thinking Critically

3. *Evaluating.* Do you think it is a good idea to know the sex of a baby before birth? Explain your answer.

Applying Health Skills

4. *In Your Community.* Visit a local garden center or greenhouse. Ask those who raise the flowers or plants how many different varieties of several particular plants there are. Read about the works of Gregor Mendel, and discuss how his work with pea plant varieties led to the science of genetics.

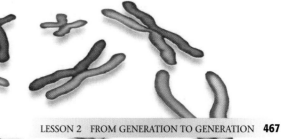

Birth Through Late Childhood

Throughout life you grow and develop physically, socially, emotionally, intellectually, and culturally. Your growth and development are predictable, following certain general patterns. However, you will grow and develop at a rate that is unique to you. Your growth and development are affected by your heredity, your environment, and your health decisions.

HEALTH TERMS

developmental task

autonomy

HEALTH CONCEPTS

- The period from birth through late childhood is marked by four developmental stages.
- How well a person adapts to changes and events that occur within each stage will affect his or her growth and development.

Developmental Stages

Several noted scientists have identified certain basic stages of growth and development. For each stage, developmental tasks are identified. A **developmental task** is *something that needs to occur during a particular stage for a person to continue his or her growth toward becoming a healthy, mature adult.* Developmental tasks in adolescence, for example, include forming more mature relationships with peers and achieving emotional independence from parents.

One of the most widely accepted theories of development is that of psychologist Erik Erikson. Erikson describes stages of development from birth through old age. Our success in each stage has much to do with our experiences during that stage. Erikson believes, however, that failure at one stage can be overcome by successes in following stages.

Infancy

From birth to one and one-half years, you experienced the fastest period of growth in your life. Your weight tripled and your height doubled. The developmental tasks of an infant include learning to eat solid food, beginning to walk and explore the environment, perceiving objects and people, and learning to talk.

In the first year of life, according to Erikson, one of a child's main tasks is that of developing trust. The child of parents who play with and talk to the baby and pick him or her up when crying learns to view the world as a safe place and people as being dependable. If a child's needs are inadequately met or rejected—for example, if parents ignore or do not tend promptly or lovingly to the child's needs—he or she learns to be fearful of the world and people.

Early Childhood

Early childhood refers to the second and third years of life. During this period, children develop many new physical and mental skills. They master walking, learn to climb, and can push and pull. They increase their vocabulary and even begin talking in sentences. Among other important developmental tasks at this age is learning to control the elimination of body wastes.

Children at this age are proud of these accomplishments and try to do as many things as possible on their own. Have you ever been around a 2- or 3-year-old who insisted on putting on his or her own shoes or clothes? This behavior is very typical of a child's increasing desire for independence.

If parents accept the child's need to do whatever he or she is capable of, then the child will develop a sense of **autonomy**, *the confidence that one can control one's own body, impulses, and environment.* However, if parents insist on doing everything for the child or are critical when the child attempts something and fails, then the child will develop doubts about his or her abilities.

As children go through developmental stages of infancy, early childhood, and childhood, they become more independent and capable of doing things for themselves.

TV AND CHILD DEVELOPMENT

Because children of all ages spend so much time in front of the television, TV producers have begun developing shows that they claim to be "developmentally appropriate." Do these shows communicate information that will help young children master developmental tasks?

What you will need

- Annotated list of local television shows
- Several televisions
- Videocassette recorder (VCR)
- Notepads and pencils

What you will do

1. With two classmates, examine an annotated list of TV programs in your area. Find six shows that are supposedly geared toward children ages three to five. Choose three shows that are broadcast on network TV and three that are shown on public TV.

2. Each group member is to watch two programs, one network broadcast and one public TV broadcast. If the shows are aired only during school hours, use a videocassette recorder (VCR) to tape them and view them at a more convenient time.

3. As you view each show, pay close attention to its theme and content and to whether it encourages a young child to achieve or fail at a particular developmental task. Take detailed notes as you view the show. Compile your findings as a group. Use your notes to answer the questions that follow.

In conclusion

1. Did any shows encourage a young child to achieve at a particular developmental task? Which shows and which tasks? Was the task appropriate to the age?

2. Which show most surprised you? Why?

3. Do you think TV can be valuable in helping a young child achieve particular developmental tasks sooner than if the child did not watch television? Why or why not?

4. If one show did not encourage a young child to achieve a particular developmental task, what do you feel is the purpose of the show?

Childhood

During the fourth and fifth years of life, physical abilities develop. Children can initiate play activities rather than merely follow other children. They often play make-believe, imagining themselves in a variety of adult roles. They copy what they see adults doing and begin to ask many questions, a sign of intelligence.

If parents show approval of these new abilities and activities and encourage questions, children learn *initiative*, the ability to start something on their own. They also learn to be creative and explore new ideas. If, however, the parent is impatient with all of the child's questions or makes the child think the activities are wrong, the child will likely develop a sense of guilt about self-initiated activities.

Late Childhood

Between the ages of 6 and 11, children experience a major part of their social development—school. The developmental tasks at this age reflect social, emotional, intellectual, physical, and cultural growth.

Children learn physical skills necessary for games and activities. They develop basic skills in reading, writing, and calculating. An important task during this stage is building wholesome attitudes toward themselves. Children learn to get along with peers and learn appropriate roles in society. During this stage, children develop a conscience. They learn right from wrong and develop attitudes toward social groups and institutions.

As children in this stage begin to acquire new skills, they develop a sense of industry. They begin to make things—cookies, model planes, and the like. The child's sense of industry is reinforced if parents and teachers praise and reward these creative efforts. If, however, an adult constantly scolds a child for making a mess, getting in the way, or not following directions, the child may develop feelings of inferiority and self-doubt.

CHARACTER
IN ACTION

Modeling Moral Behavior

Remember that you can be a **positive role model** to the children in your life.

Character Check Try these strategies for being a role model to someone younger than yourself.

➤ Talk to him or her about the importance of core values such as honesty, caring, and respect.

➤ Read books to him or her or make up stories that illustrate these highest values.

➤ Share with him or her healthful ways to resolve conflicts other than through violence or the use of bad language.

➤ Steer him or her away from violent television programs or Web sites.

◄ *Children develop social skills and expand their knowledge and curiosity.*

ACTIVITY *How can praise and encouragement help a child succeed?*

LESSON 3 *Review*

Reviewing Facts and Vocabulary

1. Define the term *developmental task,* and give two examples.
2. What are the main developmental tasks during a child's first year?

Thinking Critically

3. *Comparing and Contrasting.* Compare and contrast development during the first year of life with development from 2 to 3 years of age.

Applying Health Skills

4. *In Your Community.* Observe parents of a 3-year-old whom you know. Make a list of all the things they say or do to encourage a sense of autonomy in their child.

Health Skills Activities

Activity 1 — Healthful Nutrition During Pregnancy

Following sound nutrition and exer- cise guide- lines benefits not only the health of a pregnant female but also of her unborn baby. Sadly, this is a reality some pregnant females do not practice.

Directions

1. In a group, review information in your book on the health needs of pregnant females and their unborn babies.

2. Compose a 60-second script on this topic for a pub- lic service announcement. As preparation, think about how best to reach the intended audience.

3. Videotape or record the announcement and share it with the class. Afterward, analyze which messages had the most influence and why.

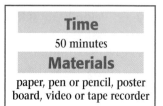

Time

50 minutes

Materials

paper, pen or pencil, poster board, video or tape recorder

Self-Assessment

✓ Described proper nutrition and health care for pregnant females and their unborn babies.

✓ Analyzed how media messages can influence behaviors.

Activity 2 — Stages of Development

A human baby goes through a number of stages both before and after birth. Proper health care and nutri- tion are critical at every stage of the child's development.

Directions

1. As a class, create a detailed chart of the different stages of prenatal and child development. Begin by forming groups. Each group is to investigate a different developmental stage, determine what changes occur, the care that is needed, and any risks associated with this stage.

2. Each group is to share its findings on a sheet of poster board that has been arranged in a grid. Columns should be labeled *Growth and Development*, *Health Care*, and *Risks*. Rows are to correspond to stages.

3. Display your poster in the classroom.

Time

50 minutes plus outside research

Materials

poster board, colored markers, photos of the different stages of prenatal and child develop- ment, library or Internet health resources

Self-Assessment

✓ Identified factors that can influence the growth and development of a healthy baby.

✓ Described the types of growth that occurs at different stages of development.

Fighting Cancer, One Cell at a Time

Cancers grow uncontrollably without treatment. Today, doctors use radiation, surgery, and chemotherapy to try to halt growing cancers. A promising new treatment uses genetic cancer-fighters to help cells resist cancer's invasion.

Researchers inject patients with a virus. But this virus won't make people sick. It delivers a new gene, called P-53, into the patient's cells.

P-53 acts as a cell guardian. If the cell becomes damaged by a cancer, P-53 helps the cell repair the damage. However, the gene also contains an important sensor. If the sensor discovers that too much of the cell is damaged, P-53 triggers the cell to self-destruct. Through these controls, genetic therapy may help prevent cancers from spreading.

Play the Video

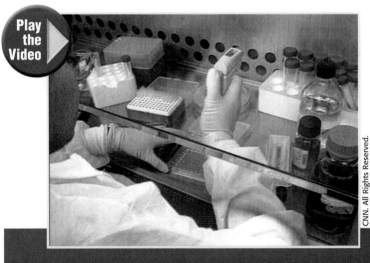

Think About It

▶ What is gene therapy? How is it different from other types of cancer treatments?

▶ Describe what researchers mean by "programmed cell death"? How can this process help cancer treatment?

▶ What other diseases do you think might be treated with gene therapy? Name three diseases and tell why you think this type of treatment might be effective against them.

Using Health Terms

On a separate sheet of paper, write the term that best matches each definition below.

LESSON 1

1. A tube through which nutrients and oxygen pass from the mother's blood into the embryo's blood.
2. A spontaneous abortion.
3. The birth of a dead fetus.
4. Cluster of developing cells following implantation.
5. The name by which the embryo is known from the end of the eighth week until birth.
6. An outer layer of cells of the embryo with blood-rich tissue from the mother.
7. A routine diagnostic test which determines an infant's physical condition at birth.

LESSON 2

8. A procedure in which a syringe is inserted through the pregnant female's abdominal wall into the amniotic fluid surrounding the developing fetus.
9. Segments of DNA molecules.
10. A test in which a small piece of membrane is removed from the chorion, a layer of tissue that develops into the placenta.
11. Tiny structures within the nuclei of cells that carry information about hereditary traits.
12. A test in which sound waves are used to project light images on a screen.

LESSON 3

13. Something that needs to occur during a particular stage for a person to continue his or her growth toward becoming a healthy, mature adult.
14. The confidence that one can control one's own body, impulses, and his or her environment.

Recalling the Facts

Using complete sentences, answer the following questions.

LESSON 1

1. What is the function of the umbilical cord?
2. In what ways do a female's health choices affect the health of her developing baby?
3. What is the leading cause of death in an infant's first year of life in the U.S.?
4. Identify and describe each of the three stages of birth.

LESSON 2

5. How does the male determine the gender of the baby?

6. What is the relationship between dominant and recessive genes?
7. What are the causes of genetic disorders?
8. Name two tests that can be used to determine the health of a developing fetus. Explain each.

LESSON 3

9. State two developmental tasks for each of Erik Erikson's first four stages of development.
10. What causes an infant to learn mistrust?
11. What leads to autonomy in childhood?

Thinking Critically

LESSON 1

1. ***Evaluating.*** If a pregnant female goes into a bar or restaurant and orders an alcoholic beverage, how do you feel about a server who serves it to her? Support your answer.

2. ***Synthesizing.*** What advice might you give a pregnant female who says that smoking relaxes her?

LESSON 2

3. ***Synthesizing.*** Mei, who is 41, is pregnant with her first child. Mei's obstetrician has advised her to have an amniocentesis, but Mei has responded that she "wants to be surprised" about her baby's gender. What information should Mei discuss with her doctor?

LESSON 3

4. ***Synthesizing.*** For each of Erikson's first four stages of development, write two comments parents could make to their child to help him or her progress successfully through that stage.

Making the Connection

1. ***Science.*** Research in greater detail one of Erik Erikson's stages of development. Prepare a report on how an individual might develop healthy or unhealthy characteristics based on experiences in the stage you are studying. You may wish to interview parents of young children to determine if they are aware of these stages. Draw conclusions on what people do to promote healthy development.

2. ***Math.*** A Punnett square is a mathematical diagram consisting of a grid, or array, and is often used to help determine the likelihood of a child inheriting or failing to inherit a specific trait from his or her parents. Learn more about Punnett squares and their use in this regard. Then create a Punnett square that shows the chances of giving birth to a female (XX) or a male (XY) child.

BEYOND THE CLASSROOM

PARENTAL INVOLVEMENT Discuss with parents or other adult family members memories they have of you during various early developmental stages. Looking at a family photo album together may help elicit memories.

COMMUNITY INVOLVEMENT Find out what public health services your community provides for pregnant women. Share this information in the form of a pamphlet you create using computer art or desktop publishing software, if available.

SCHOOL-TO-CAREER
Exploring Careers. Interview a genetic counselor. Find out how a genetic counselor helps parents-to-be deal with the possibility of having a baby with a genetic defect. What educational background does the genetic counselor need to do this job well? Share your findings with the class in the form of a brief oral report.

CHAPTER 21

Adolescence— A Time of Change

ACCESSING INFORMATION

What new challenges and issues do teens face today? Stay informed on important health issues by checking the Health Updates section of **health.glencoe.com**.

Personal Health Inventory

> " *I think what is happening to me is so wonderful, and not only what can be seen on my body, but all that is taking place inside.* "

—ANNE FRANK
GERMAN DIARIST, HOLOCAUST VICTIM, (1929–1945)

Quick Write Make two lists: one stating the ways adolescence is exciting to you and one stating the ways this time of life is sometimes frustrating.

Changes During Adolescence

Duthe first year of life. The second spurt occurs near the beginning of **adolescence,** *the stage between childhood and adulthood.* Growth is rapid and uneven at this time—a sign of puberty and its changes.

HEALTH TERMS

adolescence

puberty

sex characteristics

gametes

cognition

personal identity

HEALTH CONCEPTS

- Adolescence is a time of physical, mental, emotional, and social changes.
- Mastering the developmental tasks of adolescence is an important step toward achieving maturity.

h t link

developmental stages For more information on psychologist Erik Erikson's developmental stages of life, see Chapter 20, page 468.

hormones For more on the chemical substances called hormones and their role in growth, see Chapter 16, page 377.

Puberty

Between the ages of 9 and 13, children go through puberty—the fifth of Erikson's **developmental stages**. **Puberty,** which marks the beginning of adolescence, is *the period of time when males and females become physically able to reproduce.* Puberty occurs as a result of the release of **hormones**. The male hormone, testosterone, and the female hormones, estrogen and progesterone, are responsible for the physical, emotional, and social changes that occur.

Physical Changes

Perhaps the most important of the physical changes that take place during puberty is the development of **sex characteristics,** *those traits related to one's gender.* There are two kinds of sex characteristics:

- **Primary sex characteristics** are directly related to the production of **gametes,** *reproductive cells produced by the gonads.* In males, the gamete takes the form of sperm, and in females the ovum. As noted in Chapter 19, all of a female's ova are present at birth but do not mature until puberty, which is also when ovulation begins. For males, puberty marks the time when the testes begin to produce sperm.

- **Secondary sex characteristics** include body hair and the development of breasts in the female and muscle development in the male. These cover a wide range of characteristics, from broadening of the chest and deepening of the voice in males to an increase in breast size for females.

Concerns Over Physical Changes

As individuals reach puberty, and for the next four to five years that follow, there is great variation in the size and shape of people approximately the same age. This variation can be a source of concern among individual teens, who tend to compare themselves with others. Girls who are much taller than classmates, for example, may feel self-conscious about their height. An increase in the size of the larynx in males may cause the voice to "crack"—or switch abruptly from a low to high pitch—which can be a source of embarrassment. In members of either gender, the feet and hands grow and may appear large and awkward in proportion to the rest of the body.

It is important for teens to remember that changes such as these are normal. Most of these experiences are temporary and resolve themselves as time passes.

Mental Changes

During adolescence, the brain reaches its adult size and weight. **Cognition**—*the act or process of knowing, including both awareness and judgment*—and memory both increase. At this age, males and females are able to predict the outcomes of many situations. Whereas during

Acting on Acne

Acne, a condition usually accompanied by unsightly pimples or blemishes, is a common problem among adolescents. Acne is caused by androgens, male hormones that are present in both males and females. If you have acne, consider these tips:

➤ Avoid oil-based makeup and greasy lotions.

➤ Keep your face and hair clean.

➤ Change washcloths and towels often.

➤ Don't squeeze or scratch pimples.

In cases of severe acne, you may need to consult your family health care professional or a dermatologist, a doctor who specializes in problems of the skin.

Graduating from high school is one way in which teens grow into maturity.

ACTIVITY *Explain what other steps in a teen's life lead to becoming a mature adult.*

childhood they saw only one solution to a problem, during adolescence they begin to look at different ways of solving problems and making decisions. Adolescents' ability to think logically, or reason things out, increases. They start becoming able to solve more complicated problems.

As they begin to mature, many adolescents discover that they are able to look beyond themselves to understand someone else's point of view. Many teens will develop new interests and hobbies. Career goals begin to come into focus.

Emotional Changes

Along with spurts of physical and mental change come spurts of energy and strong emotional feelings. Many teens feel that puberty is like being on a roller coaster, with emotions and feelings that go up and down quickly. It is common for teens to feel on top of the world one day and down in the dumps the next. Friendships and the love and support of family are important, yet adolescents may feel unable to let others know what they are feeling and thinking. This difficulty in communicating is a normal part of development.

Social Changes

Social change is another important aspect of the development that occurs during puberty and the rest of adolescence. For instance, friendships and peer acceptance become very important. Peers may occasionally challenge what you stand for, what you believe, and what you think is right or wrong. Good friends, however, will not challenge you to do something that goes against what you believe. A growing ability to feel more deeply and to consider others' needs is also part of social development.

Developmental Tasks

Adolescence has been studied by psychologists and sociologists for more than 50 years. They have identified certain developmental tasks that can be considered basic to adolescence. Robert Havighurst, a well-known sociologist in the field, suggests these tasks are:

- forming more mature relationships with people your age and of both genders
- achieving a masculine or feminine social role
- accepting one's physique
- achieving emotional independence from parents and other adults
- preparing for marriage and family life and career
- acquiring a set of personal standards as a guide to behavior
- developing social intelligence, which includes becoming aware of human needs and becoming motivated to help others attain their goals

Building Health Skills

Self-Inventory: My Developmental Rate

HOW MANY OF THE DEVELOPMENTAL tasks of adolescence have you accomplished so far? This survey will help you find out. Copy the following statements into your private Health Journal. After each, write *true* or *false.* Answer the questions again every six months or so to see how far you've come—and how far you have to go.

1. I strive to be a health-literate person and to make choices that promote my overall health and well-being.

2. I have set long-term goals for myself.

3. I have more adult discussions and fewer confrontations with my parents or other adults than I used to have.

4. I am able to identify my four most important beliefs and values and act in ways that support them.

5. I am successful most of the time at maintaining relationships with friends of both genders.

6. I am aware of and able to accept my physical strengths and weaknesses.

7. I listen to other people's ideas even when they are different from mine.

8. I try to think through problems, looking at all possible solutions before arriving at a decision.

- being able to cope with success and failure
- developing conceptual and problem-solving skills

Each of these tasks is important and must be achieved before reaching maturity. As you can see, there is quite a lot involved in growing up.

Personal Identity

Some researchers group a number of the developmental tasks into a general task of achieving a personal identity. A **personal identity** consists of *the factors you believe make you unique, or unlike anyone else.* Establishing your own personal identity has a great impact on all the other developmental tasks and is centered on your self-concept. Here are some questions you can ask yourself as you work toward forming your own personal identity:

- Am I carrying out my responsibilities on my own, such as getting schoolwork done on time, without needing someone to remind me of them?
- Can I make independent decisions and accept the consequences of my actions?
- Am I thinking about what I want to do after high school?
- Have I examined my beliefs about what types of behavior are appropriate for young adult males and females?
- Does my behavior reflect a personal set of values and standards by which I live?
- Do I expect to work for what I want, rather than just having things done for me or given to me?

Volunteering to clean up your environment is one way to demonstrate social responsibility.

ACTIVITY *Name other developmental tasks that assist adolescents in forming a personal identity.*

LESSON **1** *Review*

Reviewing Facts and Vocabulary

1. What is the name of the stage of life between childhood and adulthood?
2. What are traits called that are related to one's gender?
3. Identify two physical changes, two mental changes, two emotional changes, and two social changes that occur during puberty.

Thinking Critically

4. *Analyzing.* In your private Health Journal, answer the six questions relating to personal identity. Write a short explanation of each answer, giving examples for the questions you answered *yes* and telling what changes you can make for the questions you answered *no.*

Applying Health Skills

5. *In Your Home.* Talk with parents or other adults in your home about any changes they have noticed in you since you became an adolescent. Have them list these changes in four areas— physical, mental, emotional, and social. Discuss your reactions with your family, telling how you feel about these changes.

Practicing Abstinence

A nother aspect of the emotional changes that occur during adolescence is an awakening of feelings of sexual attraction toward others. These feelings are a normal and healthful response and are part of becoming a healthy adult.

HEALTH TERMS

abstinence

priorities

self-control

sexually transmitted disease (STD)

HEALTH CONCEPTS

■ Sexual activity before marriage carries a number of serious health risks, particularly for teens.

■ Abstinence from sexual intercourse before marriage is the only safe and responsible choice.

Decisions and Peers

The emotional awakening during adolescence is accompanied by a number of physical responses that can be a source of concern and even confusion among teens who are experiencing them for the first time. The face gets hot and flushed, the heart beats faster, the hands get clammy, and there is a fluttery feeling inside. You cannot keep these feelings from happening. They are normal and healthful. At the same time, sexual attraction is not the same as love. Sexual feelings do not have to be acted on. They can be controlled and dealt with in responsible ways.

Decisions About Sexual Activity

In our society, physical attraction and sexual activity are portrayed in movies, on television, and in advertisements. Perfume commercials describe their products as *sexy* or *alluring*. Some TV programs

Responsibility and Commitment

When it comes to issues of sexuality, truly responsible behavior for teens means making a **responsible commitment** to abstinence. It also means:

➤ learning to control sexual feelings or diverting them into positive activities like sports

➤ never imposing sexual impulses on others

➤ speaking up for your own highest values when others pressure you to have sexual contact

➤ taking care of reproductive organs through self-exams and doctor's exams

➤ getting and staying informed about the dangers of STDs, HIV, and teen pregnancies, keeping these real risks in mind as you continue to commit to abstinence

Character Check List all the reasons why you will make the commitment to abstinence to ensure your long-term health.

now carry warnings about containing "partial nudity" and "explicit sexual content." Whether out of curiosity, a desire to be an adult, or pressure by others, some teens are tempted to be sexually active. However, there are many consequences of these actions.

One of the biggest decisions any teen can make is whether or not to become sexually active. Being sexually active can have implications for life—not just for a moment. Because people do not think clearly when faced with sexual feelings, it is much easier and a lot smarter to think through a decision about sexual behavior before getting into the situation in the first place.

Abstinence Until Marriage

More teens are examining the risks of sexual behavior and deciding that the only safe and responsible choice is abstinence from sexual intercourse. **Abstinence** is *the conscious decision to avoid harmful behaviors, including sexual activity before marriage and the use of tobacco, alcohol, and other drugs.* Abstinence is the only healthful and safe choice for teenagers. By postponing sexual activity until marriage, teens avoid the many risks of sexual behavior such as unplanned pregnancy, sexually transmitted diseases, and loss of self-respect.

Making a Commitment to Abstinence

Practicing abstinence takes planning, preparation, and self-control. Here are the steps you can follow to help you practice abstinence:

■ **Establish your priorities in life. Priorities** are *those things that are first in importance.* To set priorities, give some thought to your plans for the future. Think about the goals you have set for yourself, such as going to college or pursuing a particular career. Also think about such personal values as respect, honesty, and morality. Consider the effects of an unplanned pregnancy or an STD on your life, and what it might do to your plans.

■ **Set personal limits on the ways in which you are willing to express affection.** Base these limits on your priorities for your life. Make sure you set limits in advance, not when in a situation where your sexual feelings are beginning to build.

■ **Share your feelings with your boyfriend or girlfriend.** Tell your partner about your priorities and what your limits are. Be honest about your feelings and values. If you are unable to talk openly and honestly with your partner, you are not in a mature, responsible relationship.

■ **Discuss your feelings and concerns with a trusted adult.** Talking with a parent, teacher, or other trusted adult can be a release valve for pent-up fears or frustrations you may have. Remember, your parents and other adults have lived through adolescence themselves. They may offer suggestions for demonstrating affection in safe and healthful ways.

- **Steer clear of high-pressure situations.** When possible, go out on dates in a group. Avoid dark rooms and unsupervised parties. If you are in a car, avoid parking in a secluded spot. Do not use alcohol or other drugs, which can interfere with your ability to think clearly and make rational judgments.

- **If you are currently sexually active, re-evaluate.** One way of doing this is to avoid those places and situations that led you to being sexually active in the past.

Using Refusal Skills

Once you have decided to practice abstinence, you must communicate that decision clearly. This is another area where verbal and nonverbal messages may cloud the issue. One person may give a convincing no, but the nonverbal actions send a conflicting message. This confusion, added to the tension of the moment, makes communication difficult.

Before finding yourself in this situation, talk to your partner about your decisions. After stating your position simply but firmly, you may be relieved to find that your partner agrees with you. Having discussed the matter, you will find it easier to exercise **self-control,** *a person's ability to use responsibility to override emotions.* First, insist on stopping. Then back away from your partner and explain why you want to stop.

If your partner persists, you will need to become more assertive. Say no, and make sure your body language supports your verbal message.

Consequences of Sexual Activity

Sexual involvement has a number of negative consequences for which teens are not prepared—physically, mentally, emotionally, socially, and financially. These include an unplanned pregnancy, **sexually transmitted diseases,** loss of self-respect, and negative effects on social relationships.

UNPLANNED PREGNANCY

Adolescence is a full-time job. Add pregnancy—and the birth and care of an infant—and life becomes very complicated. Becoming a parent is a serious responsibility that changes a person's life. Teens are not ready for parenthood. For many teens, pregnancy is a consequence they did not plan for.

h⊙t link

sexually transmitted diseases (STD) For more information on avoiding sexually transmitted diseases (STD), see Chapter 29, page 642.

▼ *Make decisions based on your own values, even if your peers disagree.*

ACTIVITY *Practice some effective refusal skills both males and females can use to say no.*

Eighty percent of teen pregnancies are unplanned pregnancies. Having a child at a young age risks the health of the teen mother and her child. It also limits a teen's future. Many teen parents have had to drop out of school to support a child, or give up plans for college or job training.

SEXUALLY TRANSMITTED DISEASES (STDs)

A **sexually transmitted disease** is *an infectious disease that is spread from person to person through sexual contact.* People in the 15–19 age group have the greatest risk of getting STDs. Nearly 3 million adolescents contract an STD each year. One in four sexually active adolescents will become infected before graduating from high school. STDs require medical treatment. Some STDs, such as **acquired immune deficiency syndrome (AIDS)**, which is caused by the human immunodeficiency virus (HIV), are fatal. STDs can also render a person sterile, making it impossible for her or him to ever conceive a child.

h⊙t link

AIDS For more information on the problems associated with the AIDS epidemic, see Chapter 30, page 656.

up date
▶ Looking at the Issues

"Hanging Out" On-Line: Is It Safe?

These days, an increasing number of teens are turning to on-line connections as part of their social life. Some use their computers to meet and "hang out" with other teens in forums and chat rooms. Other teens even "date" in cyberspace. The growth of these trends has raised questions about their safety and healthfulness.

ANALYZING DIFFERENT VIEWPOINTS

▶ **Viewpoint One**
In one national teen survey, 7 out of 10 teens opposed any attempts to limit their access to the Internet. They believe that they are old enough to choose and judge responsibly whom they meet and talk to—including people they meet on-line.

▶ **Viewpoint Two**
Many teens, adults, and experts alike voice the opinion that there is no substitute for conventional in-person introductions, talking, and hanging out. They contend that you can tell more about a person by looking into his or her eyes than by the way he or she constructs a sentence. Another problem is that some people who meet and "date" on-line are not who they say they are at all.

EXPLORING YOUR VIEWS

1. What are the pros and cons of communicating with other teens in cyberspace? What safeguards can teens take when logging on?

2. What advice would you give to a peer about how to have responsible relationships?

LOSS OF SELF-RESPECT

Engaging in sexual activity goes against many people's values and religious beliefs. A teen may find himself or herself sneaking around or lying to parents or other adult family members about his or her whereabouts. Coupled with the constant fear of being caught, such actions and feelings can lead to guilt and regret, which can be emotionally harmful to a teen. Having and following clear values leads teens to healthy feelings of self-respect. You build character and feel good about yourself when you follow your values.

NEGATIVE EFFECTS ON SOCIAL RELATIONSHIPS

Sexually active teens also risk developing a reputation among peers as someone who is "sexually easy" and may find it difficult to build new and healthy relationships in the future.

Choosing to become sexually active can even complicate the relationship with one's partner. When sexual activity is involved, expectations in relationships often change. Many teens have found that, instead of bringing them closer together, sexual activity actually tears the relationship apart.

FAMILY DISAPPROVAL

As **protective factors** in a teen's environment, most parents and guardians show their love and concern for their children by setting limits and establishing guidelines. Because parents want to protect their teens' self-respect, values, and safety, they do not want their teens to be sexually active. Going against such values can lead to feelings of parental disillusionment, disappointment, and even betrayal.

Did You Know?

➤ 1 in 4 teens in the United States who is sexually active gets a sexually transmitted disease.

➤ 1 in 5 girls who are sexually active gets pregnant.

➤ Up to 20 million Americans are infected with genital herpes.

➤ Around the world, maternal mortality rates for mothers ages 15–19 are double the rates for mothers ages 20–24.

hotlink

protective factors For more information on protective factors and their effect on the risk-taking behavior of teens, see Chapter 1, page 20.

LESSON 2 *Review*

Reviewing Facts and Vocabulary

1. Name three risks of sexual activity during the teen years.
2. Why might the choice to become sexually active cause a teen to lose self-respect?
3. What is self-control?
4. Name three benefits gained from not being sexually active during the teen years.

Thinking Critically

5. *Evaluating.* In speaking of teen parenthood, adults sometimes say, "A child is raising a child." Analyze this statement.

6. *Synthesizing.* Tara's boyfriend is putting pressure on her to become sexually active. "After all," he argues, "We've been going out for a long time now." What factors will come into play in determining how Tara responds?

Applying Health Skills

7. *In Your Home.* Talk with your parents or other adults in your home about the goals and priorities they had when they were your age. Have them explain what things, if any, they would do differently if they could live their lives over again. Summarize what you can learn from your parents' experiences.

Health Skills Activities

Activity 1 — Resisting Peer Pressure

For every line commonly used to persuade another person to practice a risky behavior, there is an equally powerful response. Practicing refusal skills can help you be prepared in a pressure situation.

Directions

1. In a group, list common high-pressure lines that might be used to convince someone to engage in high-risk behavior.
2. For each line, brainstorm several snappy and effective responses that can be used to defuse the situation. Your teacher will share several responses to start your thinking.
3. Share the results by creating a poster of high-pressure lines and assertive refusal responses that can be displayed in the school or community.

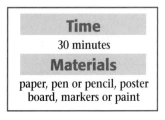

Time
30 minutes

Materials
paper, pen or pencil, poster board, markers or paint

Self-Assessment

✓ Listed at least three common high-pressure lines that teens may use to persuade others to practice high-risk behavior.
✓ Illustrated at least three strategies to combat each peer pressure statement.

Activity 2 — Setting Life Goals

Knowing your long-term goals and values can help you make healthful decisions today that will help you achieve those goals and maintain your values. What are your goals for the future? What short-term goals will help you reach those goals?

Directions

1. Working independently, make a list of goals for your life. Include eductation, job, and career goals you would like to have.
2. List your values, those principles that you consider important and will use to guide your life.
3. Using your lists, create a "road map" for your short-term goals that will help you reach your lifetime goals.
4. In a short essay, identify what you learned from this activity. Store your essay in your private Health Journal. Reread your essay from time to time.

Time
30 minutes

Materials
paper, pen or pencil

Self-Assessment

✓ Identified at least three goals that one can work toward to achieve.
✓ Listed personal values and developed goals that are consistent with those values.

HEALTH NEWS

Please, Get Your ZZZs

High school student Naomi Freeman is busy, like many of her peers. She juggles academic, extracurricular, and work responsibilities–and, when there's time, she sleeps.

Freeman's six hours of sleep a night is not unusual among teenagers. It's also not healthy according to experts, who say millions of young people may be risking their health and education by not making sleep a higher priority.

"Kids are too sleepy to learn well. They're too sleepy to be happy. And they're at great risk for such things as traffic accidents," said Dr. Mary Carskadon of the National Sleep Foundation.

Most adolescents need at least 8½ hours of sleep each night according to the National Sleep Foundation. But it estimates that only 15 percent of young people get that much, with 25 percent of teens getting less than seven hours.

The foundation, in what it calls a "wake-up call" to teens, parents, and educators, released a report warning of the consequences of sleep deprivation. It also suggests lifestyle changes to ensure adolescents get adequate rest.

"Teenagers don't need less sleep the older they get. They still need as much sleep as they did when they were pre-teens," Carskadon said. Her research shows that adolescents tend to fall asleep and awaken later than adults and often experience an increase in daytime sleepiness, even when they get enough rest.

The NSF recommends the creation of "sleep-smart schools" that adopt sleep education curricula and offer school starting times that adequately respond to a teen's biological need for sleep.

Think About It

1. Summarize the findings of this report on sleep and teenagers. Do observations of your peers match the report's conclusions?

2. What strategies can your school adopt to encourage healthy sleep patterns? What strategies can help at home?

Using Health Terms

On a separate sheet of paper, write the term that best matches each definition below.

LESSON 1

1. The period of time when males and females become physically able to reproduce.
2. Reproductive cells produced by the gonads.
3. The act or process of knowing, including both awareness and judgment.
4. The stage between childhood and adulthood.
5. Those traits related to one's gender.
6. The factors you believe make you unique, or unlike anyone else.

LESSON 2

7. A person's ability to use responsibility to override emotions.
8. An infectious disease that is spread from person to person through sexual contact.
9. Those things that are first in importance.
10. The conscious decision to avoid harmful behaviors, including sexual activity during the teen years and the use of tobacco, alcohol, and other drugs.

Recalling the Facts

Using complete sentences, answer the following questions.

LESSON 1

1. Which sex characteristics are directly related to the production of gametes?
2. Name some secondary sex characteristics that appear at puberty.
3. Name three physical changes that occur at puberty for boys.
4. What is another term for the reproductive cell?
5. How is increased memory skill helpful to adolescents?
6. Name three developmental tasks during adolescence.
7. What is a personal identity?

LESSON 2

8. How do sexual feelings come about?
9. In what ways does an unplanned pregnancy compromise a teen's future?
10. How does becoming sexually active change relationships with family? How does it change relationships with friends and dating partners?
11. How can setting priorities help teens remain sexually abstinent?
12. How does talking about sexual feelings openly with a partner help teens use self-control?
13. What are steps you can follow to help you choose sexual abstinence before marriage?

Thinking Critically

LESSON 1

1. ***Analyzing.*** Although most of Candi's peers have grown several inches since reaching puberty, Candi has not. She is one of the shortest persons in her class and wonders if she will ever grow tall. Candi's mother and most of her relatives on her mother's side of the family are short. On which developmental task is Candi working on, and what can she do to complete that task?

LESSON 2

2. ***Comparing and Contrasting.*** Gwen likes to go with the feelings of the moment. She prefers dancing to having serious conversations. Sam brought up the issue of sexual activity as soon as he and Maddy began to see each other regularly. He explained that, even though he liked her, he had made a choice for abstinence and planned to remain abstinent until he was married. Which teen is better prepared to say no when pressured? Why?

Making the Connection

1. ***Science.*** Choose one of the following topics to research: acne; vocal changes in males; the sex hormones testosterone, progesterone, and estrogen. Report your findings to the class in an oral report.
2. ***Social Studies.*** Compare adolescence in the 1960s with adolescence today by interviewing people who were teens dating then. What were their concerns? What were their favorite songs? Who were their role models?

BEYOND THE CLASSROOM

PARENTAL INVOLVEMENT Ask your parents to share with you recollections from their adolescence. Prepare several questions you might like to ask, such as "How old were you when you reached adult height?" "What kinds of things did you worry about as a teenager?" "What responsibilities did you have?" After you finish your interview, write in your private Health Journal, telling how your experiences are similar or different from those of your parents.

COMMUNITY INVOLVEMENT Interview an employer who hires teenagers, such as the manager of a fast-food restaurant. Ask the person to describe the responsibilities of a teen employee and the responsibilities of the employer. Take notes while conducting the interview. Afterward, make two lists in your private Health Journal to describe the responsibilities of an employer and those of an employee. Tell how the responsibilities differ.

SCHOOL-TO-CAREER

Resources. Investigate a career as a sociologist. Research the educational requirements, including the time and costs of attending school. Find out the various careers a sociologist might pursue, and the responsibilities of each position.

CHAPTER 22

The Life Cycle Continues

HEALTH Online

PRACTICING HEALTHFUL BEHAVIORS

Combine the technologies of Spreadsheet and Database technologies to track lifestyle behaviors that promote long life. See health.glencoe.com Technology Projects for help on collecting and graphing information on your everyday health behaviors.

Personal Health Inventory

Self-Inventory Write the numbers 1–10 on a sheet of paper. Read each statement below and respond by writing *yes*, *no*, or *sometimes* for each item. Write a *yes* only for items that you practice regularly. Save your responses.

1	I have caring, loving relationships with other people.
2	I look to older adults for insights about adult life.
3	I have my own political ideas, religious views, and sense of community responsibility.
4	I have a close friend or family member with whom I can share my innermost feelings.
5	I have younger brothers or sisters, cousins, or neighbors that I have taken care of.
6	I am beginning to understand the responsibilities of caring for children.
7	I have a general understanding of the emotional and physical changes of aging.
8	I have close relationships with older adults with whom I spend time.
9	I enjoy talking to older adults.
10	I avoid making hurtful comments that stereotype the elderly.

Follow-up After completing the chapter, retake this self-inventory. Pick two items that you need to work on and set a goal to improve your health behaviors.

> **Our todays and yesterdays are the blocks with which we build.**
>
> —HENRY WADSWORTH LONGFELLOW
> AMERICAN POET, (1807–1882)

Quick Write Imagine that you are building a structure called "Total Health." List some of the building blocks that you are using today to build a healthful tomorrow.

Growth for a Lifetime

When compared with the entire life cycle, the stages of infancy, childhood, and adolescence last only a short time. You and your friends may feel that the years of growing up will never end, but these years are only a small part of the rest of your life. With an average life expectancy of 78 years, you truly do have a lifetime of activity ahead of you.

HEALTH TERMS

physical maturity
emotional maturity
emotional intimacy

HEALTH CONCEPTS

- During adulthood, a person's growth and development continue.
- Developmental tasks of adulthood include developing intimate relationships, establishing a career, and establishing a place in society.

Considering the Entire Life Cycle

The study of all the years of the life cycle, from birth to death, is relatively new. In the past, few scientists studied life as a whole, focusing instead on the early years, when development is so rapid. In fact, some researchers believed human development ended with childhood or early adolescence. They viewed the progression from birth to death as much like hiking up a hill to adulthood, then walking across a level plateau that finally headed downward toward the end of life's journey.

Today, it is clear that life is more dynamic than depicted in this earlier view. Human growth and development do not end at age 6 or 16. Instead, they continue through every stage of life.

Adulthood

What does it mean to be an adult, and what steps do you take to become one? Is adulthood merely a function of age? Do you simply awake one day and find that you have become an adult?

One term often used in conjunction with adulthood is *maturity*. However, like the notion of adulthood itself, maturity can mean different things:

- **Physical maturity** is *the state at which the physical body and all its organs are fully developed.* Once your body reaches physical maturity, you will not grow any taller. By late adolescence or the early twenties, most people will have achieved maturity as it is defined in this sense.

- **Emotional maturity** is *the state at which the mental and emotional capabilities of an individual are fully developed.* Emotional maturity is a more important component of adulthood than physical maturity. It includes achieving independence but, at the same time, cultivating close relationships. Being emotionally mature means having a strong personal identity and an acceptance of self. It also means having strong values and goals. Many people reach emotional maturity after they have already matured physically—in some cases long after.

Developmental Tasks of Adulthood

Whereas physical maturity occurs automatically, emotional maturity does not. A person needs to satisfy certain well-defined developmental tasks of adulthood in order to reach this emotional plateau. The developmental tasks of adulthood focus on four major aspects of people's lives:

- occupational role
- individual identity and personal independence
- intimate relationships
- place in society

Each of these developmental tasks represents lessons that adults must learn to adjust to the world around them.

⬆ *Decisions you make now can help prepare you for a career that is satisfying.*

ACTIVITY *Name several jobs you think you might enjoy doing as a young adult.*

Establishing an Occupational Role

During adolescence many people start to form ideas about the kind of life they want as adults. An occupation or career is usually a large part of that idea or dream of the future. As they become young adults, people begin to see themselves more clearly in an occupational role. This view of their role may occur through on-the-job training or through education beyond high school as preparation for a career. Making an occupational choice, even though it may not be the final one, is one of the major developmental tasks that must be achieved on the way to adulthood.

Establishing an Individual Identity and Personal Independence

The desire for independence during adolescence is preparation for establishing an individual identity as an adult. It is also part of the continuing process of **self-actualization**, which includes developing one's capabilities to their fullest.

Leaving home or starting to work full-time are ways in which young adults can begin to achieve self-actualization. At first, they

hot link

self-actualization For more information on self-actualization and its place in the hierarchy of human needs, see Chapter 8, page 193.

Building Health Skills

Conflict Resolution: Strengthening Relationships Through TALK

WHETHER RELATIONSHIPS ARE intimate or merely casual, conflicts are inevitable. When conflicts or disagreements occur, relying on the TALK strategy will help both parties reach a peaceful resolution. The TALK strategy is named for the first letters of each of its four steps:

1. **T–Take time out.** Set aside at least 30 minutes, especially when tempers have flared. Go into another room, or go for a walk.

2. **A–Allow each person to express opinions uninterrupted.** Use active listening skills. Permit the other person to express his or her entire opinion on the subject.

3. **L–Let each person ask questions** as a means of clarifying any statement that was unclear.

4. **K–Keep brainstorming to find a good compromise.** Compromise, or give-and-take, is essential to every healthy relationship. Yet finding a common ground is not always easy. Invest the time searching for it. You will both be happier in the end.

may substitute the emotional support of friends for the support they once received from parents. As their development continues, however, young adults will become more self-sufficient. In so doing, they will be continuing on the developmental path that will lead to the establishment of an individual identity and personal independence.

Establishing Intimate Relationships

This developmental task involves the ability to build close relationships with people of both genders while still maintaining a sense of self. It involves developing **emotional intimacy**, *the ability to experience a caring, loving relationship with another person with whom you can share your innermost feelings.* During this time there may be several successive romantic relationships. Some people give a sense of permanence to romantic relationships through marriage. Others develop romantic relationships but prefer to remain single. Still others are occupied with establishing a career or defining their own identity, and intimate relationships come later or not at all.

Establishing a Place in Society

Another task of adulthood includes determining where and how a person fits into society. Political ideas, religious views, and a sense of community responsibility contribute to finding a place in society. They may, for example, do volunteer work, promote recycling, or join a neighborhood sports team.

LESSON 1 *Review*

Reviewing Facts and Vocabulary

1. What is the difference between emotional maturity and emotional intimacy?
2. How does forming ideas about a career help an individual meet developmental tasks as an adult?
3. Name three ways an adult determines where and how he or she fits into society.

Thinking Critically

4. *Analyzing.* James is 22 years old and married, with a child. He does not have a high school diploma or a steady job. He works odd jobs, but dreams of someday becoming a manager of a store or an artist. What task does James need to work on to reach adulthood? What can he do to complete this task?

5. *Evaluating.* Make a list of criteria based on the information in this lesson that you can use to determine when you have left adolescence and entered adulthood. Then list what tasks you need to complete to become an adult.

Applying Health Skills

6. *In Your Home and School.* Write a letter to yourself at age 30 or 35. In it, describe where you expect to be in regard to relationships, career, and place in society. Ask your parents for their input and feedback on your plans and goals for the future.

Marriage and Parenthood

Marriage and having children are two major components of young adulthood for many individuals. Marriage plays an important role in meeting the task of developing intimate relationships, especially the emotional intimacy you learned about in Lesson 1. Marriage and parenting bring on new experiences and additional responsibilities.

HEALTH TERMS

commitment

marital adjustment

planned pregnancy

self-directed

HEALTH CONCEPTS

- Marriage is an agreement between two people to face the realities of life as a couple.
- Teen marriages suffer a high rate of failure.
- Responsibilities of parenthood include maintaining discipline and providing love.

Marriage

Ninety-five percent of Americans who marry do so before the age of 40. Their steps down the aisle are among the most important steps they will ever take. Yet, of the millions of people who say "I do" each year, 68 percent will divorce. The primary reason for these failed marriages is that couples are not prepared to make a commitment. A **commitment** is *a promise or a pledge*. Marriage is a long-term, ongoing commitment. Getting married is deciding to spend the rest of your life with someone else.

Reasons for Marrying

Most people say they are marrying because they are "in love." Often, however, there are other motives hidden deep inside. People may decide to marry because they are lonely or they want to escape an unpleasant situation at home. They also may marry because a pregnancy is involved or because they seek financial security. Without close self-examination, couples may not even be aware of the motives driving them. If there are any doubts or questions about reasons for marrying or about the intended spouse, the best time to face them and reconsider is before the marriage.

Factors Affecting Marital Adjustment

Sociologists have conducted extensive research to develop measures of **marital adjustment**—*how well people adjust and adapt to marriage and to each other.* Researchers have concluded that a well-adjusted marriage is one in which the husband and wife

- agree on critical issues in their relationship.
- share common interests and activities.
- demonstrate affections and shared confidences.
- have few complaints about the marriage.
- do not have feelings of loneliness or irritability.
- had a close association before marriage.

Researchers have also found that some factors related to social background were also associated with successful marital adjustment. A similarity in family backgrounds and the domestic happiness of parents are positive factors.

Teen Marriages

Statistics show that teen marriage is not a good idea. Teen marriages often deteriorate as the excitement wears off and the responsibilities increase. Teens who marry, or feel forced to marry because of unplanned pregnancies, often choose their mates before they have any idea who they themselves are or what they want. The results can be disastrous. Consider:

- Females between the ages of 14 and 17 who marry are twice as likely to divorce as females who wait until they are older.
- About three-quarters of all teen couples who marry because of pregnancy divorce within six years.

Conflict in Marriage

A successful marriage requires both partners to demonstrate respect, trust, and care for one another. It also requires individuals to resolve conflicts fairly and without damaging one's own or one's partner's self-esteem. Among the issues that sometimes cause problems in marriages are:

- differences in spending and saving habits
- conflicting loyalties involving friends and families
- intimacy or sexual problems

Maturity and Marriage

Maturity means being ready to accept responsibility for your actions, including responsibility for your part in a long-term relationship. A successful marriage requires emotional and social maturity. Marriage partners should make a commitment to building a life of shared values that are based on ethics and their highest principles.

Character Check Consider a couple you know or have read about who seems to have a mature marriage. Ask yourself whether they demonstrate the following signs of maturity in a marriage, that each partner

➤ has the ability to give as well as receive.

➤ can compromise and accept not always getting his or her own way.

➤ accepts responsibility for his or her feelings and actions and does not blame the other.

➤ supports the growth of the partner as an individual and respects his or her partner's highest values.

➤ *Children bring many changes and responsibilities to a couple's life.*

ACTIVITY *Name some of the responsibilities parents have when raising children.*

- jealousy, infidelity, or lack of attention
- housework
- decisions about having children and child care

Developing skills in communication and resolving conflicts before they escalate, or get out of hand, are essential in dealing with the issues and conflicts in any marriage.

Parenthood

Having a child can be a wonderful experience. It can be rewarding to provide a nurturing environment for a child and watch that child grow and develop within it. However, parenting is a huge, ongoing responsibility.

The decision to have a child can be a very complex and private decision for a couple. It is often affected by religious, economic, career, emotional, cultural, and social considerations. Many couples wait until their marriage, careers, or finances are established. They may even put off having babies for years, waiting until they are in a financial and psychological position to parent. A carefully planned pregnancy between two people ready to nurture and support a child to adulthood remains the route with the best chance of success for both the parents and the child. **Planned pregnancy** is *making a decision to get pregnant before the baby is conceived.*

Responsibilities of Parenthood

Parents must provide food, clothing, shelter, education, medical care, and protection from harm for their children. They are responsible also for the emotional, social, and intellectual upbringing of their offspring. Parenting involves setting limits, providing guidance, and instilling values. Perhaps most important, it means giving unconditional love.

Setting Limits

Parents need to set limits and establish a clearly defined set of rules. When children learn limits, they become self-directed. Being **self-directed** means *making correct decisions* *about behavior when adults are not there to enforce rules.* Parents should follow these guidelines when disciplining their children:

- Act quickly so that children understand the link between misbehavior and consequences.
- Be consistent so that children expect that certain behaviors will result in certain consequences.
- Distinguish between the behavior (action) and the child so that children think of themselves as people who occasionally do bad things, rather than as bad children.
- Praise positive behavior.

Providing Guidance and Instilling Values

Parents can guide children by setting good examples. They can teach children skills for getting along with others and handling problems. Children need to develop a sense of pride in their studies or work and to recognize that they, more than anyone else, are responsible for their success or failure in life. One of a parent's greatest challenges is to instill **values** in his or her children.

Giving Unconditional Love

Children cannot prosper without love, attention, and guidance. Parents need to express their delight in their children and their existence whenever possible. They should praise their children for their efforts. Parents can give encouragement through words, letters, hugs, and facial expressions. They can show they care by giving their time.

h⬦t link

values For more information on values and their function in the health of the individual and society, see Chapter 1, page 20.

LESSON 2 *Review*

Reviewing Facts and Vocabulary

1. In what way can marriage be said to be a commitment?
2. Name three components of good marital adjustment.
3. Name several unsound reasons for having children.

Thinking Critically

4. *Comparing and Contrasting.* Imagine that two of your friends, Monica and Pedro, are thinking about marriage. At 18, what problems would they face that probably would not be problems if they decided to wait five years before getting married?

5. *Analyzing.* Explain why parenthood is one of the most serious decisions a person can make. Then list criteria people can use to determine whether they are ready to have children.

Applying Health Skills

6. *In Your Home.* Analyze and describe your parents' child-rearing beliefs and practices by writing about them in your private Health Journal. Have your parents review what you wrote to see whether they agree with your observations. Then tell what changes, if any, you will make if you raise children in the future.

The Aging Experience

F or most of human history, only a tiny segment of the population has lived beyond age 40, and this is still true in many developing parts of the world today. In American society today, however, 40–the onset of middle adulthood–marks more or less a midpoint in life. This lesson will examine how people respond to the experience of aging.

HEALTH TERMS

transitions

generativity

menopause

empty-nest syndrome

integrity

HEALTH CONCEPTS

- People of every age have the same needs but different ways of meeting them.
- Aging is a normal process.
- Important changes occur during middle adulthood.
- Every person has some control over the way he or she ages.

Middle Adulthood

L ife is filled with transitions. **Transitions** are *critical changes that occur at all stages of life.* One important transition you will face soon, for example, is graduating from high school and going out to make your place in the world.

During middle adulthood, people go through a number of transitions, all relating to yet another of Erik Erikson's developmental tasks. This task, **generativity**, marks *a shift of attention away from oneself in the present to concerns for future generations.* Generativity includes active concern for young people and for the society in which young people will live and work as adults. Refusal to accept and deal with changes during middle adulthood can result in self-absorption, or preoccupation with meeting only one's own needs.

Physical Transitions

As adults turn 40, their bodies begin to show signs of aging. Wrinkles and dry skin may appear, and hearing and eyesight start to decline. The hair may thin and turn gray. Adults of middle age may also experience muscle loss. It is best that adults exercise throughout life so that they can remain physically active well into late adulthood.

Around ages 45 to 55, women go through menopause. **Menopause** is *the stopping of ovulation and menstruation* that results from hormonal changes. During menopause, some women experience rapid changes in body temperature, hot flashes, and night sweats as the levels of estrogen in the body drop. After menopause, a woman cannot get pregnant.

Mental and Emotional Transitions

Middle adulthood is a time for looking both back at where you have come from and ahead to where you are going. Most people by this time have experienced many of life's greatest joys, including children, pride in their personal accomplishments as well as some disappointments, such as the death of a friend or loved one. In contrast to early adulthood, in which one's orientation tends to be focused on relationships with others, the middle years are marked by self-evaluation.

For some middle-aged adults, the emotional transitions of middle age are much like the growing pains of adolescence. People experiencing this "midlife crisis," as it is often called, may be caught up with questions and concerns about whether they have met their goals, feel loved and valued, or have made a positive difference in the lives of others.

Some middle-aged adults find it difficult to accept the passage of time and make drastic changes in their behavior and way of life. People experiencing these difficulties may imitate youthful or immature ways of living. Since these middle-aged adults have not recognized and dealt with changes within themselves, they often find they still are not happy.

Most people, however, progress through middle adulthood without serious problems. They adjust their hopes and dreams and adapt their lifestyles to their newly experienced feelings of being in touch with themselves.

▼ Continuing to be physically active throughout life is a healthy decision.

ACTIVITY *Name three other ways to promote overall health.*

CHARACTER IN ACTION

Sages and Ages: Valuing Wisdom

Older adults often have lots of information—insights, knowledge, and good judgment based on many and varied experiences. Be **considerate** and listen to the ideas of others.

Character Check You may benefit from the wisdom of an older adult by

➤ corresponding with a grandparent or an older relative.

➤ getting to know an older adult in your neighborhood.

➤ volunteering in an organization that pairs teens with older adults.

➤ discussing the importance that ethical values have made in shaping his or her life.

Social Transitions

Social transitions during middle adulthood focus on the family. Middle-aged adults may have to adjust to the death of their parents. They also must adapt to their children's growing up and leaving home to establish independent lives. Some adults experience *feelings of despair or loneliness that accompany children's leaving home and entering adulthood*. The **empty-nest syndrome**, as this reaction is called, prompts some couples to establish a closer, more loving relationship, often similar to the one they had during their courtship. Other middle-aged adults adjust by realizing that they have more time for themselves and their interests.

Late Adulthood

Erikson's eighth and final stage of development is late adulthood. This stage is accompanied by another transition—retirement from the workforce. For the first time since early childhood, the individual is free for the most part of pressures and daily responsibilities. Retirement can occur as early as age 50 or well into one's eighties.

Physical Changes

Older adults continue to experience physical changes. As cells grow older, age pigment collects in them, prompting the appearance of so-called "liver spots." Skin loses its elasticity, the functioning of the body's organs slows, and the body's immune system becomes less

Making Responsible Decisions

Balancing Reponsibilities

Krista has made a commitment to visit her grandparents in another city over the weekend. She has always been the "apple of their eye" and has enjoyed doing things with them throughout the years. This time they are house-bound, because her grandmother is recovering from surgery. They hope Krista's visit will cheer them up. Today the boy Krista has been dating for a few months asked her to take part in a series of fun activities his family is planning for the weekend. This is appealing, not only for the fun, but because she has been trying to get to know his parents better. What should Krista do?

What Would You Do?

Apply the six steps of the decision-making process to Krista's problem.

1. **State the situation.**
2. **List the options.**
3. **Weigh the possible outcomes.**
4. **Consider your values.**
5. **Make a decision and act.**
6. **Evaluate the decision.**

effective. When older people continue to be active, maintain good nutrition, and take good care of themselves, however, body functions remain more efficient.

Many diseases can occur in older adulthood, including cancer and heart disease. Osteoporosis occurs as the bones of older people become weak and easily breakable due to bone loss. Arthritis may cause crippling swelling and pain in joints, especially fingers. Parkinson's disease causes loss of muscle function. Alzheimer's disease is a condition that causes mental deterioration.

Although body functions decrease with older age, negative stereotypes about older people are not true. Many persons flourish in old age. Some individuals even reenter the job force through the American Association of Retired Persons (AARP) or volunteer groups.

Emotional and Social Changes

Erik Erikson's eighth and final developmental task occurs during late adulthood. This task, **integrity**, is *a feeling of wholeness and contentment*. Integrity is achieved by keeping intimate relationships and remaining committed to a cause, including family or religion. Older adults who achieve integrity can look back on life with contentment and no regrets. They are able to enjoy the time they have left and accept the approach of death.

Family and other social relationships are a very important factor in helping individuals adjust successfully to aging. In some families, grandparents not only care for young children but also do household tasks to contribute to the household.

Older adults may have social opportunities in their communities as well. Many older adults belong to groups where they enjoy such activities as playing cards, painting, or doing other hobbies such as gardening or traveling.

▲ *Many middle-aged adults find they have additional time to pursue recreational activities.*

ACTIVITY *Explain why decisions you make as a teen are important to your later years.*

LESSON **3** *Review*

Reviewing Facts and Vocabulary

1. What transitions do middle-aged adults face?
2. Describe the developmental tasks of generativity and integrity.
3. What causes empty-nest syndrome?

Thinking Critically

4. *Comparing and Contrasting.* Make a chart in which you compare and contrast the concerns you might have in middle adulthood with those of late adulthood.

Applying Health Skills

5. *In Your Home.* Interview your parents or an aunt, uncle, or other relative in middle age to find out their plans for retirement. Ask them what steps they have taken for retirement, such as having a retirement savings account. Also find out what they want to do, including hobbies and travel, and where they want to live.

Health Skills Activities

Activity 1 — Windows of Your Life

Have you ever wondered what your life will be like 10, 20, or even 30 years from now? Create a "window" to your future, showing the different phases of your future adult life.

Directions

1. Divide a large sheet of newsprint into four equal sections. Label the sections *Early Adulthood* (25-35), *Middle Adulthood* (35-50), *Older Adulthood* (50-65), and *Late Adulthood* (65 and on).
2. Decorate each window with magazine pictures or original art showing what your life will be at that stage. Describe two goals you will have had to achieve.
3. Present your "windows of life" to the class. Identify which phase of life will be your favorite. Dress up as if you were actually in that particular phase of life.

Time

two 50-minute periods

Materials

newsprint, magazines, colored markers, masking tape, glue

Self-Assessment

✓ Listed at least two goals related to the achievements suggested.
✓ Provided meaningful reasons for the choices made.

Activity 2 — True Love Songs

The songs you hear on the radio do not always depict an accurate or positive view of love and marriage. Compose your own "true love" song describing a healthy, lifelong relationship.

Directions

1. Think about characteristics you would like in a future spouse. What words would describe the kind of marriage you hope to have?
2. Express these ideals in a "true love" song. Create at least three verses and a refrain. Use music from an existing song, or compose your own melody.
3. Read or sing your song for the class. Afterward, lead them in a discussion of the kinds of qualities you would look for in a mate. Ask whether class members feel these qualities were communicated in your song.

Time

50 minutes

Materials

paper, pen or pencil

Self-Assessment

✓ Identified characteristics and values that contribute to a healthful long-term relationship.
✓ Effectively communicated those ideals in song or verse.

HEALTH NEWS ARTICLE

Living Longer and Better!

"I was 16 and working summers as an orderly in a nursing home. I was seeing older adults in really bad conditions. Even at my age then, I could tell that half of them didn't even need to be there."

Still in his teens, Thomas Perls, M.D., M.P.H., was discovering what would become a career concentration. He and his research team are studying centenarians—people who live to be 100. They hope to discover the genetic reasons for their striking longevity.

Dr. Perls calls the goal of his studies the exploration of "an ideal genome." A genome is the total genetic makeup of one organism. Every person has a unique genome. Dr. Perls' study suggests that centenarians may share a genetic makeup in which most age-related illnesses are postponed or deflected.

Perls hopes that his research will "debunk the myth that the older you get, the sicker you get. Instead, the older get, the healthier you've been–that's what we're seeing with the centenarians. To live to older ages, you can't have been sick for a period of time. You have to age slowly or escape these age-related diseases.

"I'd like to think we can go on to discover some disease-resistance genes, understand how they work and find the biochemical pathways they affect. These discoveries could lead to drugs that could make people more like centenarians."

He and study co-authors Lou M. Kunkel, Ph.D. and Annibale A. Puca, M.D., believe they now can proceed to locate the precise genes responsible for such longevity—that is, for the delay or deflection of age-related diseases. The search is on.

Think About It

1. How did Dr. Perls' experiences as a teenager contribute to his profession and field of study?
2. What does Dr. Perls mean when he says, "The older you get, the healthier you've been"?

Using Health Terms

On a separate sheet of paper, write the term that best matches each definition below.

LESSON 1

1. State at which the physical body and all its organs are fully developed.
2. State at which the mental and emotional capabilities of an individual are fully developed.
3. Ability to experience a caring, loving relationship with another person with whom you can share your innermost feelings.

LESSON 2

4. Making correct decisions about behavior when adults are not there to enforce rules.
5. Making a decision to get pregnant before the baby is conceived.

6. How well people adjust and adapt to marriage and to each other.
7. A promise or a pledge.

LESSON 3

8. A feeling of wholeness and contentment.
9. A shift of attention away from oneself in the present to concerns for future generations.
10. Feelings of despair or loneliness that accompany children's leaving home and entering adulthood.
11. Critical changes that occur at all stages of life.
12. The stopping of ovulation and menstruation.

Recalling the Facts

Using complete sentences, answer the following questions.

LESSON 1

1. Name three developmental tasks of adulthood.
2. Why does emotional maturity take longer to achieve than physical maturity?
3. How does becoming involved in community help adults find their place in society?

LESSON 2

4. Name several unsound reasons for getting married.
5. Why do married teens often feel like social outcasts?
6. What kinds of conflicts do married couples often face?

7. In what way is the ability to resolve conflicts necessary to establishing and maintaining a solid marriage?
8. Name several considerations a couple may make before deciding to have a child.
9. Name several guidelines for disciplining children.
10. How can parents show their children that they are loved?
11. What values should parents teach their children?

LESSON 3

12. What transitions do older adults face?
13. Why do some middle-aged adults experience a midlife crisis?
14. Describe an adult who has successfully completed the stage of integrity.

Thinking Critically

LESSON 1

1. ***Comparing and Contrasting.*** Make a chart in which you compare adolescence with young adulthood in the areas of relationships, jobs, and place in society.

LESSON 2

2. ***Analyzing.*** Is "getting out of the house" a valid reason for teens to get married? Explain your answer.

3. ***Comparing and Contrasting.*** At one time, marriages were arranged by the parents. Using information in this lesson, determine what might be some advantages and disadvantages of arranged marriages.

LESSON 3

4. ***Evaluating.*** What advice would you give someone who is suffering from empty-nest syndrome? What advice would you give someone experiencing the cluttered-nest syndrome?

5. ***Analyzing.*** Taking into account some of the ways your body changes as you approach old age, tell what you can be doing now to help slow down your body's aging process.

6. ***Synthesizing.*** Explain what needs individuals from all age groups share.

Making the Connection

1. ***Social Studies.*** Many famous artists, including Michelangelo, Pablo Picasso, and Georgia O'Keeffe lived to an old age. Choose an artist to research, and write an essay explaining how the person's passion for art may have led to a longer life. Then explain a passion you have or wish to develop through the years.

2. ***Math.*** Estimate the cost of taking care of an infant or toddler for a year. Figure out costs for food, clothing, and medical care. Include purchases of such items as a crib, car seat, and high chair. Remember to include diapers, which cost about $25 a week, and child care, which averages about $100 per week.

BEYOND THE CLASSROOM

PARENTAL INVOLVEMENT Ask your parents to draw from their own experiences to give you some advice about marriage. Ask them what they have learned about marriage over the years and what, if anything, they would do differently. Comment about their answers in your private Health Journal.

COMMUNITY INVOLVEMENT Visit a senior citizen center in your community and meet some of the older adults who use the center. Find out about the various programs they offer for older adults. If possible, become a volunteer at the center.

SCHOOL-TO-CAREER
Interpersonal. Visit a child-care center to observe the skills needed to be a child-care assistant. Also interview the workers to find out what skills they think are necessary for working with young children. Make a list in your private Health Journal of the interpersonal abilities you would need to pursue a career in this area.

CHAPTER 23

Understanding Medicines

HEALTH Online

ACCESSING INFORMATION

What's the safest way to use the Internet for specific and accurate health information? Learn more about how to find exactly what you're looking for in the Technology Project "Searching on the Internet" at health.glencoe.com.

Personal Health Inventory

Self-Inventory Write the numbers 1–10 on a sheet of paper. Read each statement below and respond by writing *yes*, *no*, or *sometimes* for each item. Write a *yes* only for items that you practice regularly. Save your responses.

1	I use over-the-counter medicines only when necessary.
2	I use only one kind of medicine at a time, unless otherwise instructed by my physician.
3	I take prescription medicine only with my physician's advice.
4	I ask my physician for information before using prescriptions.
5	If I am not sure about a medicine, I ask my parent, physician, or pharmacist.
6	I read all the enclosed information and follow the directions carefully when taking medicines.
7	I never take someone else's prescription medicines.
8	I keep myself informed about types of medicines, their effects on the body, and their proper use.
9	I alert my parents or physician immediately if side effects occur.
10	I do not take over-the-counter medicines for an extended period without my physician's knowledge.

Follow-up After completing the chapter, retake this self-inventory. Pick two items that you need to work on and set a goal to improve your health behaviors.

> ❝ *It takes a wise doctor to know when not to prescribe.* ❞

—Baltasar Gracián
Spanish Jesuit scholar, (1601–1658)

Quick Write Imagine talking to an elementary school student about the proper use of medicines. Write down five guidelines that you would give to the youth.

The Role of Medicines

Sometimes, even the healthiest person becomes sick. A person may sustain a painful injury while playing sports or may develop a chest cold accompanied by a hacking cough. To help overcome these ailments, some people turn to medicines. **Medicines** are *substances that, when taken internally or applied to the body, help prevent or cure a disease or other medical problem.*

HEALTH TERMS

medicines

vaccine

analgesics

side effects

additive interaction

synergistic effect

antagonistic interaction

tolerance

withdrawal

HEALTH CONCEPTS

- A medicine helps prevent or cure a disease or medical problem.
- Medicines are classified according to their effect on the body.
- Safe and healthful use of medicines includes knowing how different substances behave when present in the body at the same time.

Classification of Medicines

Although there are countless medicines that treat a wide range of health problems, all may be classified into four broad categories—medicines that

- prevent disease,
- fight pathogens (microorganisms that enter the body and attack its cells and tissues),
- relieve pain,
- help the heart and regulate blood pressure.

Medicines That Prevent Disease

The first line of defense in modern medicine is to prevent diseases before they ever occur in an individual. There are two main types of preventive medicines:

- **Vaccines.** Your **immunization** schedule shows a record of what shots or vaccines you were given as an infant, child, and teen. A **vaccine** is *a preparation, containing weakened or dead pathogens that cause a particular disease, given to prevent one from contracting that disease.* Vaccines stimulate your body to produce specific antibodies against those pathogens. Once the antibodies are produced, they give your body long-lasting protection against these specific pathogens, should these enter your body in the future. Current vaccine research is geared toward developing a safer, less painful vaccine against **rabies** and vaccines against hepatitis B and pneumonia-causing bacteria. A major effort, as noted in Chapter 30, is being conducted toward isolating a vaccine to combat **HIV**.

- **Antitoxins.** Antitoxins are extracts of blood fluids that contain antibodies and act more quickly than vaccines. Antitoxins are produced by inoculating animals—such as horses, sheep, or rabbits—with specific toxins that stimulate the animal's immune system to produce antibodies against the toxins. When antitoxins are injected into a human being, they neutralize the effect of toxins, such as those that cause tetanus and diphtheria.

Medicines That Fight Pathogens

Virtually unknown before the twentieth century, antibiotics are a class of chemical agents that destroy disease-causing microorganisms while leaving the patient unharmed. The best known and earliest antibiotic—penicillin—was discovered by accident in 1928 by the British scientist Sir Alexander Fleming. Depending on the type of medicine and the dosage, antibiotics either kill harmful bacteria in the body or prevent them from reproducing. Each antibiotic has a different chemical composition and is effective against a particular range of bacteria, though none is effective against viral infections.

h⚬t link

immunization For more on immunization and its role in disease prevention, see Chapter 28, page 633.

rabies For more information on rabies and actions to take when someone is bitten by a suspected rabid animal, see Chapter 35, page 786.

HIV For more information on HIV and ways of reducing the risk of infection, see Chapter 30, page 656.

◄ *Immunization against once common diseases such as measles and tetanus has made instances of these diseases rare.*

ACTIVITY *Explain why it is important to adhere to the immunization schedule your physician has set for you.*

In recent years, strains of bacteria have emerged that are resistant to penicillin and other commonly prescribed antibiotics. This resistance occurs when a bacterial strain undergoes a change in genetic structure as a result of overexposure to an antibiotic, making the bacterium essentially "immune" to the medicine. This development has prompted a new generation of antibiotics, including cephalosporins (sef-uh-luh-SPOHR-unz)—broad-spectrum antibiotics that kill a wide variety of bacteria, including penicillin-resistant strains.

Originally derived from molds and fungi, antibiotics today are largely made synthetically, in laboratories. This has blurred somewhat the distinction between antibiotics and a second class of antibacterial medicines that was always derived through synthetic means. This class includes the sulfa family, still used to treat some urinary tract infections, and the quinolones, still used to some extent to combat hospital-derived infections.

In one acre of rain forest there can be more than 250 species of trees and 20,000 different kinds of insects.

ACTIVITY *Explain how this biodiversity can be important in the search for new medicines.*

up|date
Our Changing World

Medical Treatment for Biological Threats

In recent years, the United States has been faced with increasing concern over the threat of bioterrorism. In this type of warfare, terrorists use biological agents, such as anthrax, as weapons. Anthrax is an infection caused by a type of bacteria called Bacillus anthracis. With bioterrorism, anthrax or other biological agents may be used to intentionally spread disease.

Although the potential for bioterrorism does exist, there is little cause for panic. Anthrax and other diseases can be prevented or successfully treated with common antibiotics, including penicillin and ciprofloxacin. In some cases, vaccines are available to prevent infection. Most often, however, these vaccines are given only to military personnel who may be more likely to encounter biological agents.

1. How might public panic over bioterrorism negatively affect the availability of medical treatment for bacterial infections?

2. Research new developments in the search for more effective antibiotics.

Cardiovascular Medicines

There are five main kinds of medicines that help the heart and regulate blood pressure:

- Beta blockers block the action of nerves that constrict blood vessels. This helps slow heartbeat and lower blood pressure.
- Diuretics (dy-uh-RET-iks) increase urine production to reduce the amount of water and sodium in a person's body. Removing water from the blood vessels helps reduce blood fluid volume. This is especially important after heart failure.
- Vasodilators (VAH-zo-DY-layt-uhr) dilate the veins and arteries to increase blood and oxygen flow.
- Antiarrhythmics (AN-tee-uh-RITH-miks) are used to treat arrhythmia—any disturbance in the rhythm of the heart.
- Clot-dissolving medicines lower high blood pressure and help prevent blood clots.

Medicines That Relieve Pain

"What do you take for a headache?" This advertising slogan has been answered again and again over the years as researchers look for new *pain relievers,* or **analgesics.** This class of medicines ranges from narcotics, such as the opium derivatives morphine and codeine, to comparatively mild medicines such as aspirin.

Aspirin is by far the most widely used non-prescription analgesic medicine in the United States. In common use since 1899, aspirin contains a chemical, acetylsalicylic (uh-SEE-tuh-sal-uh-SIL-ik) acid, that relieves pain and reduces fever. One of the most effective anti-inflammatory medicines, aspirin is widely used in treating arthritis. Because of its widespread use, many people do not realize that aspirin can be dangerous. Even small amounts can irritate the stomach, especially when empty. Aspirin can interfere with blood clotting, and large doses can cause dizziness and ringing in the ears. Children who take aspirin are at risk of developing Reye's syndrome, a potentially life-threatening illness of the brain and liver. Aspirin, therefore, should not be given to children when illness with fever is present and undiagnosed.

Some people who are sensitive to aspirin take acetaminophen or ibuprofen instead. Like aspirin, both these substances serve as analgesics. Ibuprofen is an anti-inflammatory agent, but acetaminophen is not.

▼ *Medicines are available in a variety of forms to prevent diseases, fight pathogens, and relieve pain.*

   ACTIVITY *Name two important considerations when choosing a pain relief medication.*

Medicines and the Body

Medicines can have different effects on or cause different reactions in different people. A person's reaction to a given medicine depends on how the medicine mixes with the chemicals in his or her body. Most medicines cause some **side effects**—*reactions to medicine other than the one intended.* It is important to be aware of your reactions to medicines and report these to your physician.

When two different medicines are taken together or when a medicine is taken in combination with certain foods, the combination may produce effects different from those produced when the medicine is taken alone. In many cases, interactions are beneficial. Physicians often make use of interactions to increase the effectiveness of a treatment. Other interactions, however, are unwanted and may be harmful.

- **Additive interaction** occurs when *medicines work together in a positive way.* For example, both an anti-inflammatory and a muscle relaxant may be prescribed to treat someone with joint pain.
- **Synergistic effect** is *the interaction of two or more medicines that results in a greater effect than when the medicines are taken*

Building Health Skills

Being Health-Literate: Using Medicines Safely

CERTAIN PRECAUTIONS should be taken with all medicines. Keep in mind the following guidelines for safe use of medicines:

1. **Ask questions.** Ask your physician or pharmacist about any possible side effects or precautions to take when using a medicine. Before taking two or more medicines at the same time, ask whether they can be taken together safely. Do not take *any* medicine that contains aspirin if you are allergic to aspirin or have ulcers or a bleeding problem.

2. **Read the label.** The label on the container in which the medicine is packaged will tell you how much medicine to take and when and how to take it. Check the expiration date on medicines and discard any that have passed this date.

3. **Practice safety.** Make sure a medicine is used only by the person for whom it is prescribed. Keep medicines out of the reach of children. If anyone, particularly a child, takes a large dose, get medical help immediately.

4. **Become a partner in your health care.** As a health-literate person, it is your responsibility not to use any medicine for an extended period of time without medical supervision. If symptoms persist or unexpected symptoms develop, see your physician right away.

independently. It occurs when one medicine increases the strength of the other. For example, one medicine may speed the rate at which the stomach empties and thereby increase the rate at which another medicine is absorbed and takes effect.

■ **Antagonistic interaction** occurs when *the effect of a medicine is canceled or reduced when taken with another medicine.* For example, someone who receives an organ transplant must take anti-rejection medicines. If this person is diabetic and takes insulin, the effectiveness of the insulin may be decreased.

Other Problems

Sometimes people develop a dependence on a particular medicine. Physiological dependence is a chemical need for a medicine. Physiological dependence is determined when a person experiences tolerance and withdrawal.

■ **Tolerance** is *a condition in which the body becomes used to the effect of a medicine.* The body then requires increasingly larger doses of the medicine to produce the same effect. In the case of some substances and individuals' chemical makeups, a person will experience "reverse tolerance." In this condition, less of the substance is required to be effective.

■ **Withdrawal** is *the process that occurs when a person stops using a medicine or other substance to which he or she has a physiological dependence.* Withdrawal symptoms include nervousness, insomnia, severe nausea, headaches, vomiting, chills, and cramps. Symptoms gradually ease after a period of time off the medicine. Withdrawal from certain medicines may require medical attention.

LESSON 1 *Review*

Reviewing Facts and Vocabulary

1. Name two types of medicines that prevent disease, and tell how they work.
2. Define the term *antibiotic*.
3. Describe problems related to the use of aspirin.

Thinking Critically

4. *Comparing and Contrasting.* What is the difference between an additive interaction and an antagonistic interaction?
5. *Synthesizing.* Why might two people have different reactions to the same medicine?

Applying Health Skills

6. *In Your Home.* If a member of your family is taking one or more medicines for a health problem, ask the person to share information about the type of medicine, how the medicines interact if more than one is being taken, and how successful the medicine has been in treating the problem. Ask whether there have been any problems related to the medicine and, if so, how the problems were dealt with.

LESSON 2

Using Medicines Wisely

Medicines can do a great deal of good. You may be familiar with some positive effects medicines can have. They can also cause harm if they are used unwisely. In this lesson, you will examine ways of getting the greatest benefit from medicines and minimizing risks in their use.

HEALTH TERMS

prescription medicines

over-the-counter (OTC) medicines

medicine misuse

HEALTH CONCEPTS

- Using medicines wisely includes learning how to read medicine labels and using medicines as prescribed or intended by the manufacturer.

- Medicine misuse is using medicine in a way other than that for which it was intended.

Medicine Safety

To minimize risks from medicines for the American public, the federal government has established a system for testing and approving new medicines. In the United States all medicines must meet standards set by the Food and Drug Administration (FDA) before being approved and made available to the public.

Testing and Approving New Medicines

The FDA requires a manufacturer of medicines to supply information about a medicine's chemical composition, intended use, effects, and possible side effects. Before a medicine is approved by the FDA, it undergoes a step-by-step testing process that can last from six to ten years. By federal law, a medicine must be both safe and medically effective. Safety is usually established through tests. The effectiveness of a medicine is proved through tests on groups of healthy and ill patients.

Release to the Public

One function of the FDA is to determine how medicine should be released to the public. There are two ways in which this can be done:

■ **Prescription medicines.** Because of their strength and potential for harm, the FDA has ruled that there are some *medicines that cannot be used safely without the written approval of a licensed physician.* These **prescription medicines** are available only by means of a doctor's written instructions to a pharmacist to give specific amounts of a certain medicine to a patient. Only a physician can prescribe such medicines, and only a licensed pharmacist can dispense them.

THE CONTROLLED SUBSTANCES ACT

The Comprehensive Drug Abuse Prevention and Control Act of 1970—commonly called the Controlled Substances Act—classifies medicines for use in the United States into five categories, or schedules, according to their use and potential for abuse.

SCHEDULE	USE OF MEDICINE
I	**Illegal and not prescribable** No current accepted medical use in United States Improper use may lead to severe physiological and psychological dependence
II	**Written prescription required** No prescription refills allowed Severe restrictions on medical use Improper use may lead to serious physiological and/or psychological dependence
III	**Written or oral prescription required** Refill up to five times in six months Has accepted medical uses Improper use may lead to moderate/low physiological and high psychological dependence
IV	**Written or oral prescription required** Refill up to five times in six months Has accepted medical uses Improper use may lead to limited physiological or psychological dependence
V	**OTC or by prescription depending on state law** Has accepted medical uses Improper use may lead to limited physiological or psychological dependence

▼ *When choosing OTC medicines, be certain to read and follow package directions.*

keeping Fit

Medicine Safety at Home

All medicines can be dangerous if misused. These guidelines can help make the medicines in your home safer:

➤ Never place medicine in an un-labeled vial or other container. Keep it in the container in which it was originally packaged.

➤ Store medicines in a safe place out of the reach of children.

➤ If there is a child in the house, never disable or tamper with the child-resistant cap on a medicine container.

➤ Throw away any medicines that have passed their expiration date. Some medicines merely lose their effectiveness with age. Others can become dangerous.

■ **Over-the-counter (OTC) medicines.** Over-the-counter (OTC) **medicines** include a wide variety of *medicines you can buy without a doctor's prescription.* These medicines can be purchased in pharmacies, supermarkets, and other stores that sell medicines. Although the FDA considers it safe to use these medicines without medical supervision, they still have the potential of being harmful if not used as directed.

Medicine Misuse

There are many controls—both federal and state—on medicines, but there are still risks and responsibilities when it comes to their use. **Medicine misuse** is *using a medicine in a way other than the one intended.* Examples of medicine misuse include:

■ giving your prescription medicine to someone else.
■ taking too much or too little of a medicine.
■ taking someone else's medicine.
■ discontinuing use of a medicine without informing one's doctor.
■ taking medicine for a longer period of time than was prescribed.
■ mixing medicines.

If you suspect that someone you know is guilty of medicine misuse, urge that person to speak immediately with his or her health care professional or pharmacist. If the person refuses to seek help, discuss the situation with a responsible adult.

Making Responsible Decisions

Should I Quit This Medicine?

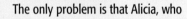

Alicia, who suffers with asthma, recently experienced a flare-up of the disease. Six days ago, her doctor prescribed a 10-day course of pred-nisone, a steroid medication, to reduce the inflammation in her lungs and help her breathe more easily.

The only problem is that Alicia, who plays for her school's field hockey team when healthy, knows that a big game is coming up in a few days and that her teammates are counting on her. Since her morning dose of medicine, she is feeling much better and is now thinking about not taking any more before the game. What do you think she should do?

What Would You Do?

Apply the six steps of the decision-making process to Alicia's problem.

1. **State the situation.**
2. **List the options.**
3. **Weigh the possible outcomes.**
4. **Consider your values.**
5. **Make a decision and act.**
6. **Evaluate the decision.**

Labeling

When the FDA approves a medicine, it is saying that the medicine is safe when used as directed. FDA approval also means that a medicine is effective in treating the illness or condition for which it was prescribed. The FDA requires manufacturers to include certain information on every prescription label, including the name of the prescribing doctor, patient's name, name and address of the pharmacy, date prescription was filled, prescription number, whether refills are allowed, and any special instructions. The illustration below shows basic information that must appear on every OTC medicine label.

▼ *The FDA governs the advertising and labeling of OTC medicines.*

ACTIVITY *Analyze why FDA officials might feel that regulation of advertising and package labels is necessary.*

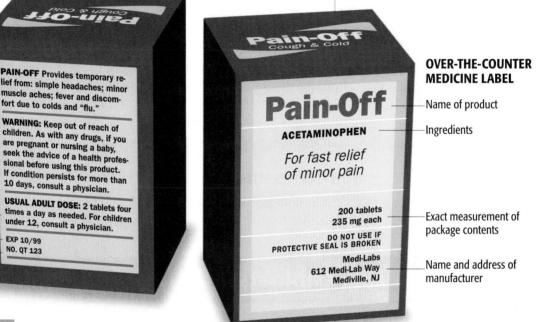

Purpose of medicine

PAIN-OFF Provides temporary relief from: simple headaches; minor muscle aches; fever and discomfort due to colds and "flu."

Cautions on use

WARNING: Keep out of reach of children. As with any drugs, if you are pregnant or nursing a baby, seek the advice of a health professional before using this product. If condition persists for more than 10 days, consult a physician.

Directions for safe use

USUAL ADULT DOSE: 2 tablets four times a day as needed. For children under 12, consult a physician.

Expiration date — EXP 10/99
Control number — NO. QT 123

OVER-THE-COUNTER MEDICINE LABEL

Pain-Off
Cough & Cold

Pain-Off — Name of product
ACETAMINOPHEN — Ingredients
For fast relief of minor pain

200 tablets
235 mg each — Exact measurement of package contents

DO NOT USE IF PROTECTIVE SEAL IS BROKEN

Medi-Labs
612 Medi-Lab Way
Mediville, NJ — Name and address of manufacturer

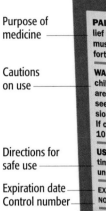

LESSON 2 *Review*

Reviewing Facts and Vocabulary

1. What is the role of the Food and Drug Administration in approving new medicines?
2. List actions that are examples of medicine misuse.

Thinking Critically

3. *Synthesizing.* Suggest possible reasons why a physician, not a pharmacist, is licensed to write prescriptions.
4. *Evaluating.* Do you think it is better to have a government agency or a privately owned company regulating approval of medicines? Support your answer.

Applying Health Skills

5. *In Your Home and School.* Ask your parents or guardians what questions they customarily ask a pharmacist when having a prescription filled. Interview a pharmacist to determine what questions consumers ask most often about their medicines. Draw conclusions about how active consumers are in their own health care. Share your findings with the class.

Health Skills Activities

Activity 1 — Patient's Desk Reference

The Physician's Desk Reference—or "PDR"— is a book that lists and describes all prescription medications currently on the market. Your class will create a medical resource to help you use OTC medicines wisely.

Directions

1. Split up into groups. Each group will work with one of the OTC medicine labels handed out by the teacher.
2. For your group's medicine, note the active ingredient, the price, the price of the generic version if available, the medical problems it is used to treat, the dosages, and any warnings about side effects and other interactions. Share your findings.
3. Decide on a mode of organization for your PDR (e.g., by body system, by ailment). Publish your PDR on the classroom computer.

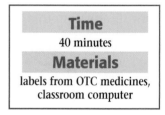

Time
40 minutes

Materials
labels from OTC medicines, classroom computer

Self-Assessment

✓ Included information called for with regard to each medicine.
✓ Described the best way to safely use each medicine.

Activity 2 — Medicine Cabinets That Make the Grade

Are you and your family prepared to meet the health situations that might occur in your home? Part of the answer to this question depends on how well-stocked and up-to-date your home medicine cabinet is.

Directions

1. Work in groups to develop a Medicine Cabinet Checklist.
2. One group is to brainstorm minor health problems (e.g., minor cuts, colds, and headaches) and corresponding remedies. Another will summarize useful information from the chapter.
3. Compile your findings into a checklist that includes names of essential remedies, expiration date of all medicines, etc.
4. Print out copies of the checklist to be posted on the door of home medicine cabinets. Urge family members to review the checklist periodically.

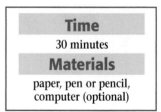

Time
30 minutes

Materials
paper, pen or pencil, computer (optional)

Self-Assessment

✓ Listed at least five common health situations that might arise.
✓ Described safe use of medicines in your checklist.

Natural Cures for the Common Cold?

We've all felt the symptoms: sniffling, sneezing, coughing, congestion.

The average American suffers two to six colds a year, and as yet, there's no known cure. Nevertheless, stores are stocked with products claiming to be natural remedies for the common cold.

Herbal industry experts say Americans spend about $400 million yearly on cold treatments such as zinc. But natural remedies are only loosely regulated by the Food and Drug Administration and are available despite conflicting evidence about whether they work.

Devona Beard got hit with a cold. "I came down with a headache, sniffles, nasal congestion, nasal drip and sneezing," she explained. She took zinc lozenges and felt better within a few days.

Her physician, Dr. Ananda Prasad of Wayne State University, evaluated how 48 patients with colds responded to using zinc lozenges.

"Using zinc lozenges shortened the duration of the cold by almost 50 percent. The severity also decreased," Prasad said.

Prasad's study is just one of at least 10 careful studies evaluating zinc. Half the studies showed zinc shortens the duration of cold symptoms; the other half showed it did not.

Dr. Ron Turner, a noted cold remedy researcher, said his studies of zinc have found no benefit. What works for one patient may not work for another. The FDA will require strong evidence for any remedies containing drugs that they are safe and effective before they can be sold.

Think About It

1. What is the difference between a natural remedy and a drug?

2. What evidence suggests whether or not natural remedies are effective against the common cold? Are there any drawbacks to these natural remedies?

3. Why do you think similar studies have such different results?

Using Health Terms

On a separate sheet of paper, write the term that best matches each definition below.

LESSON 1

1. The effect of a medicine is canceled or reduced when taken with another medicine.
2. The process that occurs when a person stops using a medicine or other substance to which he or she has a physiological dependence.
3. Pain relievers.
4. Medicines work together in a positive way.
5. Substances that when taken internally or applied to the body help prevent or cure a disease or other medical problem.
6. A preparation, containing weakened or dead pathogens that cause a particular disease, given to prevent one from contracting that disease.

7. The interaction of two or more medicines that results in a greater effect than when the medicines are taken independently.
8. A condition in which the body becomes used to the effect of a medicine.
9. Reactions to medicine other than the one intended.

LESSON 2

10. Medicines you can buy without a doctor's prescription.
11. Medicines that cannot be used safely without the written approval of a licensed physician.
12. Using medicine in a way that is not intended.

Recalling the Facts

Using complete sentences, answer the following questions.

LESSON 1

1. What problem has arisen with the use of antibiotics?
2. What is the active ingredient in aspirin? What is aspirin used for?
3. What factors affect how one's body will interact with medicine?
4. Name and describe three types of medicine interactions.
5. Define *physiological dependence*.
6. When does withdrawal take place, and what are its symptoms?

LESSON 2

7. What information must a manufacturer of medicines provide to the FDA?

8. What does FDA approval of a medicine mean?
9. How do OTC medicines differ from prescription medicines?
10. Medicines are classified into five schedules. Describe the legal basis for categorization.
11. What information is always given on prescription medicine labels?
12. List four ways in which a medicine might be misused.

Thinking Critically

LESSON 1

1. **Synthesizing.** What is a person really saying when he or she says that vaccines are dangerous substances because they contain pathogens?
2. **Evaluating.** The FDA regulates what manufacturers can say in advertisements for both prescription and OTC medicines. Do you feel that such regulation is necessary? Support your answer.
3. **Evaluating.** Sometimes insurance companies will not pay for a prescription if a generic equivalent was available but not dispensed. Do you feel this practice is justified? Support your answer.

LESSON 2

4. **Analyzing.** In later stages of development, experimental medicines are often tested on groups of people. Where do you think these groups of people come from? What would be the possible consequences of being in such an experimental group?
5. **Synthesizing.** What are some appropriate questions to ask a physician before he or she writes a prescription?
6. **Synthesizing.** What are some questions that your physician should ask you before prescribing a drug?

Making the Connection

1. **Math.** Study the advertisements in a magazine. Determine what percentage of the total number of ads is for medicines. Display this information in a circle, or pie, graph.
2. **Science.** At your school or local library, research one of the following scientists who discovered an important medicine or a scientist of your own choosing: Sir Frederick Banting, Sir Alexander Fleming, Edward Jenner, Jonas Salk. Write a one-page paper on your findings.

BEYOND THE CLASSROOM

PARENTAL INVOLVEMENT With your parents, conduct a home safety check by determining whether all medicines at home are safely stored. Consider questions such as these: Is the cabinet difficult for small children to reach? Do medicines have childproof caps? Have out-dated medicines been discarded? Summarize your findings and recommendations in writing.

COMMUNITY INVOLVEMENT Invite a health department official to class to speak about problems connected with immunization. Write a two-page paper on what steps can be taken to remedy the situation. Work out a plan to increase community awareness of the need for immunization.

SCHOOL-TO-CAREER
Interpersonal. Invite a pharmacist to speak to the class about career possibilities and requirements in the field of pharmacy. Before the visit, prepare questions designed to elicit information about educational requirements, special training and skills, and responsibilities of the position.

CHAPTER 24

Tobacco

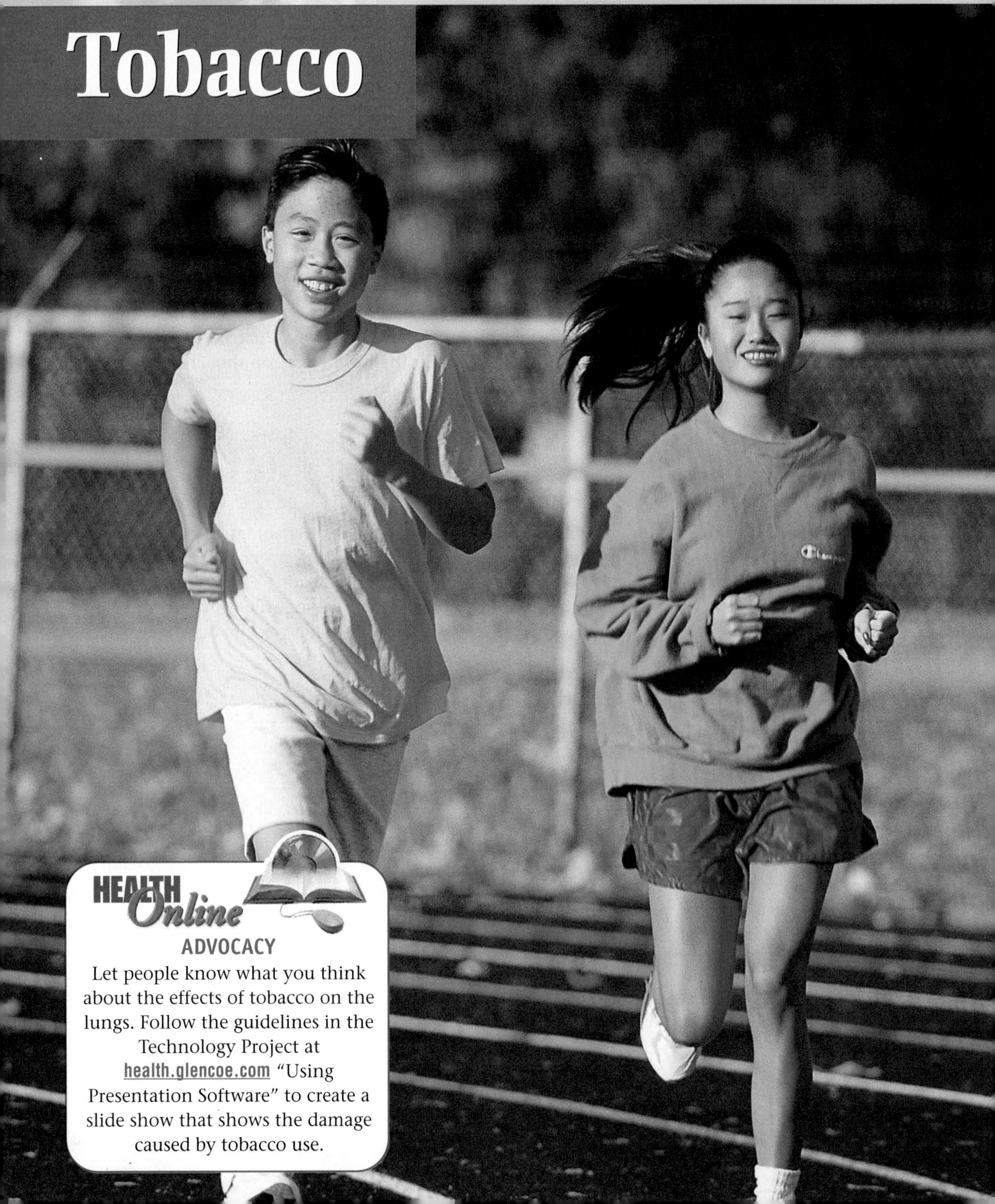

HEALTH Online

ADVOCACY

Let people know what you think about the effects of tobacco on the lungs. Follow the guidelines in the Technology Project at health.glencoe.com "Using Presentation Software" to create a slide show that shows the damage caused by tobacco use.

> ## " Cigarettes cause lung cancer. It's as simple as that. "

—Dr. Dan Sullivan
Radiologist, National Cancer Institute

Quick Write Jot down some other harmful and dangerous effects you know that are caused by tobacco use.

Personal Health Inventory

Self-Inventory Write the numbers 1–10 on a sheet of paper. Read each statement below and respond by writing *yes*, *no*, or *sometimes* for each item. Write a *yes* only for items that you practice regularly. Save your responses.

1	I don't smoke cigarettes, cigars, or pipes.
2	I don't use smokeless tobacco.
3	I let my friends and family know that I mind when they light up around me.
4	When someone offers me a cigarette or other tobacco product, I feel comfortable refusing it.
5	I try to avoid smoke-filled places.
6	When people around me are smoking, I ask them to stop or I walk away.
7	I don't "buy into" ads that try to make smoking seem attractive or cool.
8	If I'm in a car or other enclosed space and someone is smoking, I ask him or her to stop.
9	I am knowledgeable about the dangers of tobacco use.
10	I practice stress management so that I'm not tempted to try unhealthful ways of relieving tension such as smoking.

Follow-up After completing the chapter, retake this self-inventory. Pick two items that you need to work on and set a goal to improve your health behaviors.

Tobacco Use—A High-Risk Behavior

Cigarette-smoking is the leading cause of avoidable death in the United States, accounting for more deaths than AIDS, car crashes, suicides, homicides, fires, and illegal drugs combined. Fifty million Americans still smoke. Even worse is that teens are the nation's fastest-growing group of smokers.

HEALTH TERMS

addiction

nicotine

stimulant

tar

carcinogens

carbon monoxide

smokeless tobacco

HEALTH CONCEPTS

- Tobacco use is a high-risk behavior that can have serious health consequences.
- A number of factors affect young people's decisions to begin using tobacco.
- The only sure way to avoid getting addicted to nicotine is to never start using any tobacco product.

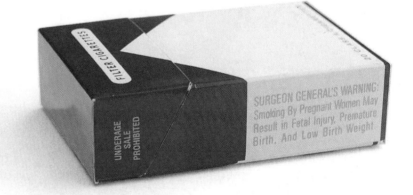

Why Young People Start Smoking

An estimated one in five American teens smokes, and about one million young people start smoking every year. Even though the message from the health community underscores the hazards of tobacco use to health, teens continue to smoke, chew, and dip tobacco in large numbers. Consider these troubling facts:

- Every day in the United States, 6,000 teens light up their first cigarette and another 3,000 teens become regular smokers.
- Approximately nine in ten adult smokers began smoking as teens and continue to smoke into adulthood, unable to stop.
- Of those who begin smoking as teens, one-third will eventually die from some smoke-related causes.
- About 2.6 million packs of cigarettes are sold illegally to minors in this country every day.

Statistics like these might leave you wondering why teens ever start to smoke. One major reason is that many feel insecure in social situations. Before they begin smoking, some teens believe that puffing on a cigarette will somehow remove their fears or insecurities, something a cigarette simply cannot do. They may also mistakenly believe smoking will make them seem older or more sophisticated than they are.

Many teens report that they start smoking because of **peer pressure** or because advertising on billboards and in magazines has made smoking seem attractive. They may associate specific brands with good-looking models, exciting settings such as the beach, or enjoyable activities such as parties, all of which may be portrayed in these ads.

Teens may smoke because they think the bad effects of smoking on health occur only after many years of smoking. They may not realize that health risks begin from the moment the cigarette smoke from the first cigarette enters the body.

Perhaps the greatest reason young people smoke is that they believe they can drop the habit at any time. They do not realize that for many smokers, smoking is no habit. Rather, it is an **addiction**—*a physiological or psychological dependence on a substance or activity*—that is difficult to shake. Still, some teens who realize that people sometimes get addicted to cigarettes feel certain that they are the exception and can stop at any time.

In a large survey of teens who smoke, half claimed they either definitely or probably would not be smoking after five years. They viewed it as a passing habit. The problem is that after five years of smoking, many of these same teens found that they had an addiction to cigarettes. Many adult smokers who began smoking as teens are still smoking—not because they want to be but because they are addicted.

What Is in Cigarettes?

Many forms of tobacco products are on the market, but cigarettes are still the most used product. With each puff of a cigarette, the smoker comes in contact with at least 43 chemicals known to cause cancer, among these cyanide, formaldehyde, and arsenic. The chemicals in tobacco can cause ailments other than cancer. Tobacco contains **nicotine**, *the addictive drug in cigarettes.* People smoke to

hotlink

peer pressure For more information on peer pressure and ways of resisting pressure that is negative, see Chapter 13, page 304.

▼ *Even though more segments of society seem to be saying "Don't smoke," millions of Americans continue to light up.*

ACTIVITY *Discuss why you think smoking continues to be a leading cause of death.*

DEATHS FROM SMOKING

Smoking kills more Americans than all other causes shown below combined.

Smoking	420,000
Alcohol	105,000
Car accidents	46,000
Suicide	31,000
AIDS	30,000
Homicides	25,000
Illicit drugs	9,000
Fires	4,000

SOURCES: Centers for Disease Control and Prevention, Institute for Social Research

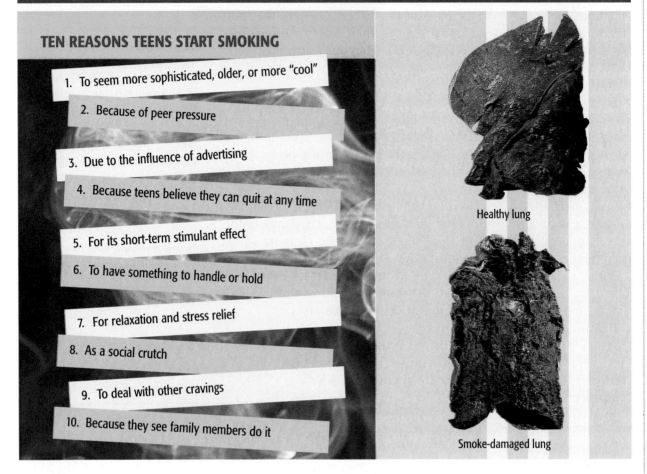

TEN REASONS TEENS START SMOKING

1. To seem more sophisticated, older, or more "cool"
2. Because of peer pressure
3. Due to the influence of advertising
4. Because teens believe they can quit at any time
5. For its short-term stimulant effect
6. To have something to handle or hold
7. For relaxation and stress relief
8. As a social crutch
9. To deal with other cravings
10. Because they see family members do it

Healthy lung

Smoke-damaged lung

There has been a steady increase in the rate of teens who smoke.

Did You Know?

➤ Nicotine is a deadly poison that is used as an insecticide.

➤ Cigarettes contain formaldehyde, the same chemical used to preserve dead animals in biology class.

➤ Cigarettes also contain many of the same chemicals that make paint, toilet cleaner, and car antifreeze poisonous.

➤ Cigarette use has been tied to a common cause of blindness in the elderly, and a pack a day doubles that risk.

reduce the craving for nicotine, which is a poisonous stimulant. A **stimulant** is *a drug that increases the action of the central nervous system, the heart, and other organs.* Nicotine raises blood pressure and increases heart rate.

The flavor of a cigarette is due mostly to the tar in tobacco. **Tar** is *a thick, sticky, dark fluid produced when tobacco burns.* Tar penetrates the smoker's airways and lungs. Combined with the drying effect of cigarette smoke, tar paralyzes or destroys cilia, the waving hairlike projections that work to keep the respiratory tract clear. Several substances in tar are known as **carcinogens**, *cancer-causing substances.*

Low-tar, low-nicotine cigarettes, once advertised as safer than their standard counterparts, actually encourage the smoker to inhale more deeply and to smoke more cigarettes to maintain the body's accustomed nicotine levels.

Carbon monoxide is *a colorless, odorless, poisonous gas in cigarette smoke that passes through the lungs into the blood.* This is the same gas in automobile exhaust fumes that, if inhaled, could prove fatal. It unites with the hemoglobin in red blood cells, preventing them from carrying the oxygen needed for energy to the body's cells.

Smokeless Tobacco

Smokeless tobacco is *tobacco that is sniffed through the nose or chewed.* Over 12 million Americans are regular smokeless tobacco users, and the use of these products continues to increase, especially among teenagers, many of whom start chewing tobacco or dipping snuff between the ages of 13 and 15. Advertisements featuring famous people, especially athletes, give the false impression that smokeless products contribute to an image of being "macho" or "cool." There is nothing cool, however, about the brown-stained teeth or unsightly spitting of tobacco juice that are part of this habit. Many teens also wrongly believe that smokeless tobacco is safer than cigarettes because it does not involve taking in smoke or putting it back into the air. In truth, smokeless tobacco carries many of the same health risks as smoking cigarettes, including addiction to nicotine. Other health risks associated with chewing or dipping include mouth sores that can turn into cancer of the lip, mouth or throat; damage to teeth and gums; and damage to the digestive system.

Other Forms of Tobacco

Like smoking cigarettes, smoking pipes or cigars also presents major health risks. Although pipe and cigar smokers usually inhale less smoke, they are more likely to develop cancers of the lip, mouth, and throat because more tar and other chemicals are generated by pipes and cigars. If the pipe or cigar smoker makes it a habit to inhale the smoke, his or her chances of developing lung cancer also increase.

connections Social Studies

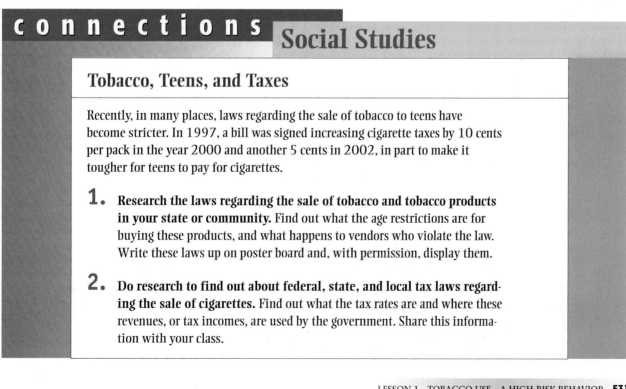

Tobacco, Teens, and Taxes

Recently, in many places, laws regarding the sale of tobacco to teens have become stricter. In 1997, a bill was signed increasing cigarette taxes by 10 cents per pack in the year 2000 and another 5 cents in 2002, in part to make it tougher for teens to pay for cigarettes.

1. **Research the laws regarding the sale of tobacco and tobacco products in your state or community.** Find out what the age restrictions are for buying these products, and what happens to vendors who violate the law. Write these laws up on poster board and, with permission, display them.

2. **Do research to find out about federal, state, and local tax laws regarding the sale of cigarettes.** Find out what the tax rates are and where these revenues, or tax incomes, are used by the government. Share this information with your class.

Specialty Cigarettes

Specialty cigarettes are those prepared with tobacco and other ingredients. They are often made with strong tobacco and contain spices that make them taste and smell sweet. However, the effects they can have on the body of the user are anything but sweet. Experts say that specialty cigarettes contain more cancer-causing tars than standard cigarettes. Clove cigarettes, one such specialty product, have been linked to lung problems and possible deaths and may have as much as two times the tar and nicotine as regular cigarettes.

SHEDDING LIGHT ON LIGHTING UP

The use of cigars is a growing fad and addiction among many Americans, including teens. From 1993 to 1996, the sales of larger cigars grew 45 percent to 4.5 billion. One national sample taken by the CDC showed that 27 percent of students had tried at least one cigar within the past year. However, cigars are not the safe alternative to cigarettes that many teens mistakenly assume they are. In fact, cigar smokers are 34 percent more likely to die from some form of cancer than nonsmokers and four to ten times more likely than are nonsmokers to die of cancer of the throat, mouth, or larynx. Though many states ban cigar sales to those under age, their sales to minors continue to increase.

LESSON 1 *Review*

Reviewing Facts and Vocabulary

1. Name at least three factors that influence teens to start smoking.
2. What is one major misconception, or mistaken idea, that many teens have about tobacco products and the health risks associated with them?

Thinking Critically

3. *Analyzing.* Bring in three print advertisements for tobacco products. Analyze the pictures that accompany them, what the ads say, and what messages concerning tobacco use these advertisements suggest. Discuss the accuracy and ethics of these sales approaches.
4. *Synthesizing.* Write a public service announcement titled "Ten Reasons for Teens Not to Smoke."

Applying Health Skills

5. *In Your Home.* Discuss with adults at home the use of tobacco among members of your immediate family as well as among aunts, uncles, grandparents, and so on. Then working as a group, compose, copy, and send a letter to all family members, sharing what you have learned about the dangers of tobacco use and the ways in which individuals and groups can become tobacco-free. Challenge the whole family to become tobacco-free. Set up a buddy system whereby those who are tobacco-free help those who are tobacco users to become tobacco-free.

What Tobacco Does to the Body

Every day in the United States over 8,000 people die from diseases caused from using tobacco. Cigarette smoking is responsible for respiratory and circulatory diseases, and this impacts a person's level of fitness, performance, and overall health.

HEALTH TERMS

leukoplakia

passive smoke

mainstream smoke

sidestream smoke

HEALTH CONCEPTS

- Smoking causes diseases of the respiratory and circulatory systems.
- Tobacco smoke can harm a fetus and lead to low birth weight and other health complications.
- Being in the presence of cigarette smoke puts a person's health in jeopardy.

Effects of Smoking on the Smoker

Cigarettes impair the health of the smoker in two ways—through short-term effects that occur immediately after the smoker lights up and long-term effects that occur as the smoking continues. Over time, the tar and pollutants in tobacco smoke take their toll on several body systems. Some of the deadliest problems are those affecting the respiratory and circulatory systems.

hotlink

chronic bronchitis For more information on chronic bronchitis and other health measures that can help prevent you from developing this disease, see Chapter 17, page 403.

emphysema For more information on emphysema and its symptoms, see Chapter 17, page 405.

lung cancer For more on lung cancer and habits that can decrease your risks, see Chapter 31, page 686.

Diseases of the Respiratory System

Cigarette smoking is associated with the two principal diseases that make up chronic obstructive pulmonary disease, or COPD. These are chronic bronchitis and emphysema, which are ten times more likely to occur among smokers than among people who do not smoke.

Chronic bronchitis is a condition in which the bronchi are irritated. As cilia become useless, tar from cigarette smoke builds up, which results in chronic coughing and excessive mucus secretion.

Emphysema is a condition that involves the destruction of the tiny air sacs in the lungs through which oxygen is absorbed into the body. As the walls between the sacs are destroyed, they lose their elasticity and provide less total surface from which oxygen can be absorbed. More breaths are required, and instead of using 5 percent of one's energy in breathing, a person with advanced emphysema uses up to 80 percent of his or her energy just to breathe.

Lung cancer, directly linked to cigarette smoking, is the leading cause of cancer deaths among males. With the increase in female smokers, lung cancer is becoming a more significant cause of cancer

TEENS, TOBACCO, PERFORMANCE, AND HEALTH

The next time you are tempted to use tobacco, consider these hazardous effects reported in the CDC's *Facts of Youth Smoking, Health and Performance:*

- Smoking hurts your physical fitness both in endurance and performance.
- The resting heart rates of young adult smokers beat two to three beats per minute faster than the hearts of nonsmokers.
- Regular smoking in teens leads to coughing and respiratory illnesses.
- Smoking teens are twice as likely as nonsmoking teens to cough with phlegm or blood.
- They are three times more likely to report shortness of breath when exercising than nonsmoking teens.
- Teens who smoke are three times more likely as nonsmokers to drink alcohol, eight times more likely to use marijuana, and 22 times more likely to use cocaine.
- Smoking is also associated with other high-risk behaviors such as fighting.

death among females, too. Lung cancer begins as the bronchi are irritated by cigarette smoke. Cilia are destroyed and extra mucus cannot be expelled. The smoker develops a cough. Cancerous cells can grow in these conditions, block the bronchi, and move to the lungs. In advanced stages, cancerous cells can travel to other organs through the lymphatic system. Unless caught early, lung cancer causes death.

Diseases of the Circulatory System

Nicotine makes the heart work harder and speeds up the pulse. Smoking constricts the blood vessels, which cuts down on the circulation, or blood flow, to the limbs. This can result in a tingling feeling in a smoker's hands and feet. Nicotine contributes to plaque buildup in the blood vessels. The formation of these fatty deposits in the arteries increases the chance of arteriosclerosis, or hardening of the arteries, and gradually clogs the blood vessels to the heart. This condition increases the risk of heart attack. In fact, the risk of sudden death from heart disease is three times greater for smokers than for nonsmokers. This risk increases for those who smoke more than a pack a day.

Smoking raises blood pressure and leads to increased risk of stroke. If a smoker has high blood pressure and high cholesterol, the risks of coronary heart disease are even greater. Experts estimate that if all Americans stopped smoking, deaths from heart disease could be cut by almost a third, saving more than 30,000 lives a year.

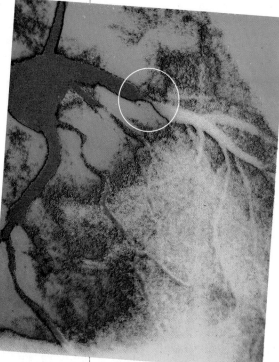

▲ *The blockage of this artery has stopped the flow of blood to surrounding tissue.*

The Dangers of Smokeless Tobacco

Although smoke does not get into the lungs when using smokeless tobacco, other health problems exist, some of which can be serious and even life-threatening. The nicotine in smokeless tobacco is as addictive as that in cigarettes. Once a person starts chewing and dipping, it can become very difficult to stop.

People who use smokeless tobacco secrete more saliva. Although the chewers usually spit this excess out, some of it is unconsciously swallowed, introducing tar and other harmful chemicals into the digestive and urinary systems. Tobacco juices also contain chemicals that may delay healing of wounds.

Tobacco and its by-products are extremely irritating to the sensitive tissues in the mouth. Irritation from direct contact with tobacco juices is responsible for **leukoplakia,** *thickened, white, leathery-appearing spots on the inside of a smokeless tobacco user's mouth that can develop into cancer of the mouth.* Oral cancer strikes about 30,000 Americans annually. Because this form of cancer is often discovered late, only 50 percent of its victims survive longer than five years.

Should All Tobacco Advertising Be Banned?

Up to $6 billion is spent annually on advertising by tobacco firms, much of it on targeting teen markets. As awareness about the dangers of smoking among teens grows, so does the commitment on the part of government and health officials to try to stop teens from smoking. One solution that has met with a mixed reaction is to ban all advertising of tobacco products.

ANALYZING DIFFERENT VIEWPOINTS

▶ **Viewpoint One**

Though cigarette ads have been banned from TV since 1971, print advertising remains. Those opposed to allowing tobacco ads to exist in any form point out that teens are three times as likely to be influenced by these ads as adults.

▶ **Viewpoint Two**

Other critics of tobacco-product advertising complain about tobacco companies' public image promotion and their continued aggressive marketing targeted to teen audiences.

▶ **Viewpoint Three**

Representatives of the tobacco industry counter that their ads do not target teens specifically and that the right to buy or not buy a product is the right and responsibility of each consumer. Others in this industry add that tobacco manufacturers are doing their part by investing large sums of money in anti-smoking education programs for teens.

EXPLORING YOUR VIEWS

1. Do you think tobacco-product advertising should be banned at all? Explain your views.

2. Do you think tobacco companies should be able to advertise indirectly but in large-scale ways by sponsoring sporting and cultural events aimed at teen audiences? Why or why not?

Smokeless tobacco users also tend to show greater tooth wear than nonusers. Their gums tend to be pushed away from their teeth where the tobacco is held. The roots of the teeth become exposed and more susceptible to decay, causing early loss of teeth. Users of smokeless tobacco also develop bad breath and discolored teeth. Tobacco products decrease the user's ability to smell and taste, especially salty and sweet foods.

Effects of Smoke on the Nonsmoker

People who breathe passive smoke receive the same unhealthy effects as smokers. **Passive smoke** is *cigarette, cigar, or pipe smoke inhaled by nonsmokers as well as smoke that remains in a closed environment after the smoker is through smoking.* Passive smoke includes **mainstream smoke,** *the smoke that a smoker blows off,* as well as **sidestream smoke,** *the smoke that comes from burning tobacco.* Passive smoke causes eye irritation, headaches, and coughing. It causes more frequent ear infections, asthma attacks and other respiratory problems and aggravates existing heart and lung diseases. It can also cause lung cancer. At least 3,000 people die annually from lung cancer because of exposure to others' smoke. Lengthy exposure to sidestream smoke can, in fact, result in the same kinds of life-threatening health problems that the smoker may experience.

A smoke-filled room may contain levels of carbon monoxide and other pollutants as high as those that occur during an air pollution emergency. A nonsmoker could inhale enough nicotine and carbon monoxide in an hour to have the same effect as having smoked a whole cigarette.

Smoking During and After Pregnancy

A 1997 study in *the Archives of Pediatrics and Adolescent Medicine* maintained that parents who smoke contribute to the deaths of at least 6,200 children in this country every year. According to the study, at least 2,800 deaths of low birth weight babies are caused by mothers who smoked while pregnant, with another 1,100 resulting from respiratory infections.

As noted in Chapter 20, cigarette smoking during pregnancy is also associated with small fetal growth, an increased chance of spontaneous abortion and prenatal death, and increased stillbirths, as well as growth and developmental problems during early childhood. Babies born to mothers who smoked during pregnancy may be adversely affected in intellectual development and behavioral characteristics.

Nicotine passes through the placenta, constricting the blood vessels of the fetus in the mother's uterus. Carbon monoxide reduces the oxygen levels in the mother's and fetus's blood. Smoking is especially harmful during the second half of pregnancy. After the baby is born, nicotine can be transferred during breast-feeding.

Most people would not give an infant or small child a cigarette, but people who smoke around children are doing the same damage to these youngsters that they would if they were helping them to light up. Children of cigarette smokers are nearly twice as likely to be in poor or fair health as those of nonsmokers. Such children are more likely to suffer from respiratory problems, including poorer lung function and more wheezing. Their risk of developing lung cancer, moreover, is double that of children of nonsmokers.

Rights of the Nonsmoker

Despite the growing awareness of the dangers of passive smoke, nearly half of all smokers light up without asking those around them

▲ *When pregnant women smoke, their unborn babies are affected, too.*

ACTIVITY *Name three negative effects on the unborn when mothers-to-be smoke.*

if they mind. According to one medical report, even though at least 80 percent of nonsmokers report that they are bothered by passive smoke, only about 4 percent actually ask smokers to stop. Because of the dangers of passive smoke, that fact has to change. You can help to change it.

You have a right to express your preference that people not smoke around you. By doing so, you protect the air you breathe and the air of those around you. If you are allergic to smoke or if the smell of it makes you sick, you may be more inclined to speak up. Everyone has a right to ask that the air they breathe remain smoke-free.

If you are in a restaurant or public place that has a nonsmoking section, ask to be seated there. Choosing places that are altogether smoke-free may be the answer. Increasingly, smoke-free establishments are easier to find. Also, be sure to ask that no one smoke in your home or at public meetings or events that you attend.

It is considerate of smokers to ask others in an enclosed area if they mind their smoking. For the sake of your health, you should always say yes. Smokers should take responsibility to smoke where there are no nonsmokers around. When they do not, nonsmokers also should take responsibility for their own health by asking smokers to extinguish their cigarettes or by moving to a smoke-free space.

▲ *A smoke-free environment benefits your health and the health of others.*

LESSON 2 *Review*

Reviewing Facts and Vocabulary

1. Describe the dangers of smokeless tobacco.
2. Explain in your own words the meaning of the terms *passive smoke, mainstream smoke,* and *sidestream smoke.*
3. What are some of the effects that smoking has on a fetus or newborn?

Thinking Critically

4. *Evaluating.* Health insurance companies increase premium rates for those who smoke and cut the rates of those who do not. Do you feel this a fair practice? Explain your answer.
5. *Analyzing.* Look through magazine ads aimed at teens and analyze the kinds of physical characteristics of models, expressions, emotions, activities, and settings that are used by advertisers to try to sell tobacco products. In what ways do these ads paint a false picture?

Applying Health Skills

6. *In Your School.* Have a physician from the community visit your class and discuss what percentage of his or her patients present problems related to tobacco use. Prior to the visit, brainstorm ten questions to pose to the expert. Afterward, write an entry in your private Health Journal noting how this visit has increased your awareness of the health risks of tobacco use.

Choosing to Be Tobacco-Free

M ore and more people are taking responsibility for their health and the health of others by giving up the use of tobacco. Quitting can be tough, but it is the way of the future. There are many ways to stop and many places that offer support and help with the process.

HEALTH TERMS

nicotine withdrawal

nicotine substitutes

HEALTH CONCEPTS

■ There are many successful approaches to stopping smoking.

■ The keys to success for a smoker are recognizing the need to quit, making the commitment, and taking the steps to do so.

■ For the addicted tobacco user, if one technique does not work, others should be tried, including medical help and short-term nicotine-replacement therapy.

Strategies for Quitting

A person who wants to quit using tobacco should be reminded that he or she will probably go through a period of **nicotine withdrawal.** This is *the process that occurs when nicotine, an addictive drug, is no longer used.* During this period the person may feel nervous or moody or have difficulty sleeping. These symptoms of withdrawal do not last long, however.

There are many techniques for quitting smoking. One involves using a series of filters over several weeks. Each filter reduces the tar and nicotine levels so that withdrawal is gradual. An increasingly popular method is the use of **nicotine substitutes.** These are *manufactured forms of nicotine that deliver small amounts of the drug into the user's system while he or she is trying to give up the tobacco habit.* Nicotine gum is one such substitute which can now be purchased as an over-the-counter product. Another technique, the nicotine patch, requires a prescription. The patch, placed on the body, gives off decreasing amounts of nicotine.

Many people combine several of these approaches and techniques to become tobacco-free. In 1996, a prescription nicotine nasal spray was approved by the FDA, allowing nicotine to get into the bloodstream faster than gum or patches. Patients using the spray inhale it once or twice an hour, but can use it up to five times an hour. As with other nicotine substitutes, the ultimate goal is gradually to cut doses until no nicotine at all is used.

Benefits of Quitting

The benefits of quitting tobacco are both immediate and long-term. Benefits to physical health can be measured in improved cardiorespiratory endurance. Physical fitness increases as a person is able to breathe easier and has reduced chances of heart disease and stroke. Quitting not only improves a person's health physically, it also affords emotional and social benefits. Former smokers often experience a sense of freedom and a renewed vigor, as though a burden has been lifted. Constant concern over finding a place to light up or over disapproving glances from nonsmokers vanishes. The money saved from kicking an expensive habit can be spent on more healthful forms of recreation.

Building Health Skills

Goal Setting: Quitting Smoking

IF YOU ARE TRYING to give up smoking or other tobacco use, the following tips might help you to reach your goal.

1. **Begin by deciding once and for all that you want to quit.** Although it seems obvious, many smokers never take this first step.

2. **Set a target date for quitting.** This date might be associated with a joyous event, such as the smoker's birthday.

3. **Take intermediate steps to help you reach your goal.** This might take the form of setting checkpoints at which the smoker cuts down on the number of cigarettes.

4. **Get help meeting your goal.** Many smokers find that quitting with a friend makes the experience easier. Each is there as a daily—and even hourly—source of support for the other.

5. **Plan a healthy way to reward yourself once you have kicked the habit.**

Teens Making a
Difference

**...INITIATIVE...RESPONSIBILITY
...CIVIC DUTY**

Mike (back row, center) is a tobacco-free teen. A junior at McNeil High School in Austin, Texas, he and his friends are active members of TATU, Teens Against Tobacco Use, a nationally-known peer education program sponsored by the American Lung Association. Their goal is to help themselves and others understand the dangers of tobacco and prevent its use. The group even welcomes teen smokers, and often what they learn there inspires them to quit. "In one of our groups, three smokers decided to quit," Mike says proudly.

GETTING INVOLVED "I got involved," Mike begins, "because, with TATU, you get to teach young people about smoking—a big health issue. We went to an elementary school and taught the facts, the consequences, and the statistics about people who die because of smoking. We used a metal bowl and a bunch of metal BBs to teach our lesson. Each BB represented a certain number of people who had died of a specific condition, such as AIDS, car crashes... etc. When dropped, the BBs made a

pretty loud sound. But when we dropped the BBs representing the 450 thousand people a year who die of smoking related diseases—more than all the others causes combined—the kids were totally amazed! "Next, we made a cigarette out of household chemicals. We took simple household ingredients that are in cigarettes like nail polish remover, rubbing alcohol, and battery acid, and used maple syrup to represent tar, lawn grass to represent tobacco, other products to represent the rat poison and arsenic in cigarettes. We also put on a skit, teaching ways to say no when someone offers you cigarettes. Other TATU members made an anti-smoking video." TATU groups write letters to legislators and will hold a rally at the state capital.

STRENGTH IN NUMBERS "It's hard to have just one person teach a large group of people," Mike says. "With a lot of volunteers, everyone has a different approach, and those approaches are interesting and unique. You can also reach many more people." He continues, "If you care about others, you help them to choose a positive environment that will be good for them, including one in which people don't smoke."

MIKE'S STORY
1. What strategies have Mike and his group used to teach people about the dangers of tobacco use?
2. What values have they demonstrated in the process?

YOUR STORY
1. What steps can you take with your peers to make a difference on the issue of tobacco use?
2. What benefits of health and character might all of you gain in taking these actions not alone but together?

Fresh-Air Friends

Mike has been carpooling with Ashley for the past three months. Having a ride to school has made Mike's life easier, but there is a problem: Ashley smokes. After riding in her car, he feels tightness in his chest and even coughs. He also can't stand the way his clothes and hair smell when he gets out of the car. When he opens the window, Ashley complains that the wind messes up her hair. Mike doesn't want to seem ungrateful or lose his ride. He just wants to be "fresh-air friends." What should Mike do?

What Would You Do?

Apply the six steps of the decision-making process to Mike's problem.

1. **State the situation.**
2. **List the options.**
3. **Weigh the possible outcomes.**
4. **Consider your values.**
5. **Make a decision and act.**
6. **Evaluate the decision.**

---

hotlink

stress management For more information on stress and stress management, see Chapter 9, page 224.

▼ *More and more public places are becoming smoke-free.*

ACTIVITY *List those places in your community that you know are smoke-free.*

SMOKE-FREE ENVIRONMENT

PACIFIC FINANCIAL COMPANIES
PROVIDE A SMOKE FREE ENVIRONMENT.
PLEASE RESPECT OUR NON SMOKING POLICY
BY REFRAINING FROM SMOKING
WITHIN THIS BUILDING AND
CENTER ATRIUM AREA.

THANK YOU.

Tips for Quitting

Although each person might approach quitting tobacco use in his or her own way, certain general tips apply. For example, those thinking about quitting might first observe how much they smoke, when and where they smoke, what triggers the desire for a cigarette, and how those needs might be addressed in other, more healthful ways. They might also begin to think of and even write down the costs of smoking, in dollars spent, health concerns, and negative reactions from family, friends, and others. They might make a list of the reasons they want to quit smoking, post the list around the house, and read it whenever the urge to smoke arises. Sometimes learning **stress management** techniques can help someone through the withdrawal process. Among the basic steps a person should take when quitting tobacco use are:

- Setting a specific date for when the person will quit and sticking to this date.
- Setting short-terms goals to reinforce one's decision.
- Deciding which approach or combination of approaches will be used to become tobacco-free.
- Getting one's environment ready for a new smoke-free life.
- Setting up a support system whereby the person is helped through the process and later helped to stay smoke-free.

Toward a Smoke-Free Society

Increasingly, the American public is working toward becoming smoke-free. As people realize that the decision to smoke can affect not only their own health but also the health of loved ones, the drive to become a smoke-free society increases. Evidence of this can be seen in public places across the country.

Whole towns are now banding together to restrict smoking. Once-lax laws prohibiting the sale of tobacco products to minors are being more strictly enforced. Tobacco licenses are being revoked when stores and store chains sell cigarettes to minors. Vending machines are being moved out of unsupervised areas. Many cities are passing laws that restrict smoking in public places, such as restaurants, civic buildings, business offices, and lobbies. Airlines now prohibit smoking on commercial flights. Hotels have whole floors for nonsmokers. Laws are being proposed to ban smoking in all enclosed public spaces. Increasingly, the law is taking into consideration the rights of the nonsmoker.

Smoking is less common in private social settings, too. Meetings of all kinds are now often designated as smoke-free. Even people giving parties no longer put out ash trays, and they ask guests who smoke to do so outside. With continued commitment to health, the remaining bad news about tobacco can be turned into good news about non-use as Americans head into the future. You, too, can do your part in helping to make this society increasingly smoke-free.

keeping Fit

Weight Gain: A Common Concern

A common concern of smokers is the risk of weight gain if they quit. Although statistics vary, only approximately one-third of quitters gain weight because they substitute eating for smoking; one-third lose weight because they start a fitness program at the same time; and one-third find that their weight stays the same. If you quit smoking or using other tobacco products:

➤ Exercise vigorously and regularly.

➤ Replace the oral stimulation of using tobacco with carrot sticks or other low-calorie snacks.

➤ Don't pay attention to the scale while you're trying to stop smoking. Even if you gain a few pounds, that's much less health risk than continuing to smoke.

LESSON 3 *Review*

Reviewing Facts and Vocabulary

1. Define the word *withdrawal* and describe the process of withdrawal from nicotine.
2. Compare and contrast methods of quitting smoking, citing pros and cons of each.

Thinking Critically

3. ***Analyzing.*** What are some of the reasons that teens sometimes do not speak up when their peers smoke around them?
4. ***Evaluating.*** What positive steps have you seen taken in your home, school, community, or country in terms of becoming increasingly smoke-free?

In which of these areas does the most progress seem to have been made?

Applying Health Skills

5. ***In Your School.*** Take a position on your school's tobacco policies. Find out what the policies are now. Along with other class members, write individual letters to the school board about your feelings on the matter. Make suggestions where appropriate to change the policies.

Health Skills Activities

Activity 1 — Not Allowing the Future to Go Up in Smoke

Choosing to be tobacco-free shows you care about your future. What about the future of young, impressionable children in your home and community? What steps can you take to help them avoid becoming hooked on tobacco?

Directions

1. In groups, using poster board and markers, create "anti-tobacco advertisements" that counter the claims made in typical tobacco ads.
2. Design your poster in a way that would capture the attention of elementary school-age students. One possibility would be to focus on a popular TV or video game character that appeals to students that age.
3. If possible, post the completed posters in a local elementary school.

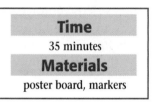

Time
35 minutes
Materials
poster board, markers

Self-Assessment

✓ Indicated at least three reasons why young people should not start smoking.
✓ Presented a persuasive, convincing message written for a young audience.

Activity 2 — Communicating Personal Attitudes about Tobacco Use

Despite the growing awareness of the health dangers of tobacco use, there are still those who choose to smoke. What's the best way to communicate the health risks of tobacco smoke to smokers and non-smokers alike?

Directions

1. Form small groups. Read the three situations handed out by your teacher.
2. Choose one of the situations. Think about how you could effectively communicate your knowledge of the dangers of tobacco smoke to the smoker and to those in the smoker's immediate environment. Look for a non-confrontational approach.
3. Share your group's response with the class. Discuss which approaches would be most likely to encourage a smoker to put out a cigarette.

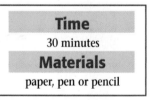

Time
30 minutes
Materials
paper, pen or pencil

Self-Assessment

✓ Included at least five negative effects of tobacco smoke on health.
✓ Used a respectful tone of voice and made use of "I" statements in your group's response.

Targeting Teens

A recent study shows that the number of women smoking in high school is increasing. Critics of tobacco say that teens are vulnerable targets of big business.

Almost all smokers begin the deadly habit when they are teenagers. That's why tobacco companies target male and female teens with powerful ads that identify smoking with independence, rebellion, and weight loss.

Of course, the ads don't mention the conditions that are really linked with smoking: heart disease, lung cancer, reduced fertility, and premature menopause.

Although companies deny that they target teens, the statistics show that many teens are listening to tobacco ads and ignoring their health.

Play the Video

Think About It

⊙ Do you think tobacco companies target teenagers—both males and females? Or do you believe the companies' claims that they target only older smokers?

⊙ "Ad placement" refers to the specific magazines or newspapers where advertisements are printed. How can ad placement target a teen audience without using teen magazines?

Using Health Terms

On a separate sheet of paper, write the term that best matches each definition below.

LESSON 1

1. A drug that increases the action of the central nervous system, the heart, and other organs.
2. Cancer-causing substances.
3. A physiological or psychological dependence on a substance or activity.
4. The addictive drug in cigarettes.
5. A colorless, odorless, poisonous gas in cigarette smoke that passes through the lungs into the blood.
6. A thick, sticky, dark fluid produced when tobacco burns.
7. Tobacco that is sniffed through the nose or chewed.

LESSON 2

8. Thickened, white, leathery-appearing spots on the inside of a smokeless tobacco user's mouth that can develop into cancer of the mouth.
9. The smoke that comes from burning tobacco.
10. The smoke that the smoker blows off.
11. Destruction of the tiny air sacs in the lungs through which oxygen is absorbed into the body.

LESSON 3

12. Manufactured forms of nicotine that deliver small amounts of the drug into the user's system while he or she is trying to give up the tobacco habit.
13. The process that occurs when nicotine, an addictive drug, is no longer used.

Recalling the Facts

Using complete sentences, answer the following questions.

LESSON 1

1. Give three reasons why teens smoke.
2. Define the words *nicotine, carcinogens,* and *carbon monoxide,* and use them in a paragraph identifying some of the dangers of smoking.
3. What kinds of cancers are more likely to occur in pipe and cigar smokers than cigarette smokers?
4. How are specialty cigarettes generally more or less harmful than standard cigarettes?
5. What are three dangers of using smokeless tobacco, and why do some teens mistakenly think it is safe to use?

LESSON 2

6. How serious is the threat of developing cancer from breathing passive cigarette smoke? The risk of heart disease?
7. List five risks associated with smoking during pregnancy.
8. What is the difference between mainstream and sidestream smoke?
9. Name three effects that cigarette smoking can have on the respiratory system.
10. List five rights of the nonsmoker.

LESSON 3

11. Describe what happens during the withdrawal process.
12. Offer five tips for quitting smoking.
13. What steps have federal, state, and local governments taken in recent years to discourage teen smoking?

Thinking Critically

LESSON 1

1. *Evaluating.* Evaluate three strategies for reducing smoking rates. Consider their effectiveness with teen groups.
2. *Evaluating.* How effective do you think laws forbidding the sale of cigarettes to minors are?
3. *Synthesizing.* What other measures might effectively decrease the use of cigarettes by teens, considering what is known about what has not worked?

LESSON 2

4. *Evaluating.* Should people who smoke be denied jobs because they are at greater risk for many serious illnesses? Why or why not?

LESSON 3

5. *Comparing and Contrasting.* Interview a former smoker. Ask him or her what his or her life and health were like while smoking and after giving it up. Ask what methods he or she used to get smoke-free.

Making the Connection

1. *Science.* Investigate the most common kind of tobacco plant used in tobacco products. Make a poster showing an example of this plant type. Include information about its classification, growing conditions and season, flowers, plant size, common diseases, growing regions, and standard human uses.

2. *Social Studies.* In your local library, look through popular magazines from the 1930s, 1940s, and 1950s. Evaluate all ads that show people smoking cigarettes. Write three paragraphs, one for each decade, summarizing what each decade's attitude about cigarette smoking seemed to be.

BEYOND THE CLASSROOM

PARENTAL INVOLVEMENT As a family, brainstorm ways that you can work together to become a smoke-free household if there are smokers in the family. Help others outside the family who smoke to learn about the dangers of tobacco use. Together, make and post no-smoking signs in your home. Create a no-tobacco-use pledge and have all family members sign it. Post this, too, within your home.

COMMUNITY INVOLVEMENT Conduct a survey of your neighborhood or local business center, recording data on the places where smoking is allowed and those where it is not. Compile this data with your observations, and write a series of articles for your local paper about what you have observed.

SCHOOL-TO-CAREER
Exploring Careers. Interview a pulmonary specialist or a respiratory therapist. Ask the person what education is needed for his or her career, what training in the field, and what kinds of practice or facility he or she is part of. In particular, ask about the effects of smoking that he or she sees in patients under his or her care.

Alcohol

Personal Health Inventory

1	I have made a decision not to drink any alcohol.
2	I don't buy alcoholic beverages or ask anyone to buy them for me.
3	I don't use alcohol to escape from my problems, relieve stress, or help me to feel more comfortable with others.
4	When other teens are drinking and offer me alcohol, I say no.
5	I don't attend parties where I know there will be a lot of drinking, and I don't take part in drinking contests or dares.
6	I never drink and drive or ride in a car with a driver who has been drinking.
7	Because I don't drink, I can stay in control of my behavior.
8	I don't rescue or cover for friends who drink or get drunk.
9	I don't organize my thinking, my day, my friendships, or my social life around alcohol.
10	I know and practice stress-reducing techniques.

Follow-up After completing the chapter, retake this self-inventory. Pick two items that you need to work on and set a goal to improve your health behaviors.

> **" *Drunkenness is nothing but voluntary madness.* "**
>
> —SENECA
> ROMAN STATESMAN AND WRITER, (C. 4 B.C.–65 A.D.)

Quick Write Use the word *responsibility* in a sentence describing some of the reasons why teens should not drink alcohol.

Alcohol Use: A High-Risk Behavior

HEALTH TERMS

ethanol

fermentation

intoxication

HEALTH CONCEPTS

- Alcohol is a drug that has great potential for abuse.
- Drinking is against the law for minors, and it can have serious legal consequences.
- Drinking alcohol can be a high-risk behavior at any age, and it can damage or even ruin one's health, one's life, and the lives of others.
- Teens who drink alcohol do so for a variety of reasons.

Imagine turning on your TV or opening a newspaper and seeing a large, splashy ad promoting the sale and use of a dangerous drug such as cocaine or heroin. Most people would be outraged and shocked. Yet, ads of this kind appear every day. The drug's name is *alcohol.* It can cause accidents and other serious problems.

h t link

depressant For more information on depressants and their effects on the body, see Chapter 26, page 582.

What Is Alcohol?

Alcohol, or more properly speaking, **ethanol**—*the type of alcohol found in alcoholic beverages*—is a powerful drug. Ethanol can be made synthetically, or it can be produced naturally by fermentation of fruits, vegetables, or grains. **Fermentation** is *the chemical action of yeast on sugars.* Water, flavoring, and minerals are added to ethanol to form one of several beverages, including beer and wine. Alcohol can also be processed to create spirits—or liquors—such as whiskey, rye, gin, and vodka. All have the potential to do serious harm.

At first, alcohol may give the drinker a certain energy and "buzz." Soon, however, its true nature as a **depressant** takes over, causing the central nervous system to slow down. At some point in the consumption of alcohol, a state of intoxication sets in. **Intoxication** is *physical and mental impairment resulting from the use of alcohol* and can range from an inability to walk to unconsciousness. Because the amount of alcohol needed for intoxication varies from person to person and because alcohol impairs judgment, driving a car or using heavy machinery when under its influence can have deadly consequences. Alcohol, moreover, robs the body of its ability to absorb key nutrients and, with long-term overuse of the drug, may lead to malnutrition.

MYTHS ABOUT ALCOHOL

MYTH

Drinking alcohol through a straw "filters out" the alcoholic content of the beverage.

FACT

The alcohol content remains the same no matter how the drug is delivered into the body.

MYTH

Someone who doesn't seem drunk can't be drunk.

FACT

Many people, particularly those with alcohol problems, can drink a lot without showing the obvious signs of drunkenness.

MYTH

Beer and wine are safer drinks than "hard" liquors like whiskey.

FACT

One standard serving of beer, wine, or spirits contains the same amount of alcohol.

MYTH

Using alcohol on weekends or only once in a while is harmless.

FACT

People can get into serious health, legal, and social situations *anytime* they use alcohol.

MYTH

When a person has a hangover, coffee, a cold shower, or fresh air will sober him or her up.

FACT

These practices do not speed up the liver's ability to break down the alcohol, so they don't help to sober a person up.

Alcohol and Teens

In recent years, as evidence of the harm drinking can do has increased, alcohol consumption among adults has declined. Yet, among teens it has not. According to the CDC's 1998 *Youth Risk Behavior Survey,* about 80 percent of teens nationwide have had at least one alcoholic drink during their lifetime.

At any age, alcohol use can become a high-risk behavior that affects the lives and health of drinkers and of those around them. For teens in particular, alcohol can have a negative impact on schoolwork, athletic performance, friendships, family relationships, and career goals. For many, it leads to health problems and, for some, even to death. Consider these facts:

- Half of all teens who die each year die as a direct result of alcohol or other drug use, and many of these deaths happen in accidents.

▲ *Misconceptions about alcohol use and effects can lead you into dangerous situations.*

ACTIVITY *Investigate the truth about some myths you have heard about alcohol.*

"SEEING THROUGH" ALCOHOL ADVERTISING

One way not to fall prey to alcohol advertising is to learn to spot and understand its sales strategies.

hot link

sexually transmitted diseases For more information on the relationship between alcohol use and sexually transmitted diseases, see Chapter 29, page 640.

dating violence For more information on alcohol as a contributing factor in dating violence, see Chapter 14, page 331.

homicides For more information on homicides and factors that trigger these violent crimes, see Chapter 14, page 324.

- Alcohol is a factor in many unplanned pregnancies as well as in cases of **sexually transmitted diseases**, **dating violence**, rapes, suicides, and **homicides**.
- Nearly 5 million problem drinkers in this country are between the ages of 14 and 17.

Consider these facts, and then consider that it is against the law for people under 21 years of age to buy, possess, or drink alcohol in the United States. Being caught drinking or drinking and driving can have serious legal consequences.

Why Young People Drink

If alcohol causes so much trouble, why do so many teens choose to drink? The reasons that teenagers give for drinking often are not very different from the reasons that adults give. Many claim that they drink

- to escape pressures or problems,
- to feel better or get over being sad or lonely,
- to deal with stress and relax,
- to feel more self-confident in social situations,
- for excitement,
- because their friends are doing it,
- to deal with boredom,
- to get away with something they are not supposed to do, and
- to fit in.

What you will need

- a notebook and pencil
- a television
- video camera (optional)
- poster board, crayons, colored pencils, or markers

What you will do

1. Divide a sheet of notebook paper into two columns. Label the first column *Images,* and the second *Messages.*

2. Tune in to one or more TV events, such as a professional sports event, in which alcohol products are likely to be advertised. Carefully watch one such commercial. In the first column, list the kinds of images used—including settings, people, and activities—as well as music. Describe the overall mood or tone of the commercial. In the second column, write down the implied messages about the use of alcohol.

3. Using techniques similar to those in the commercial, make either a short video ad or a poster showing teens in a healthful and happy recreational setting. Your ad is to "sell" healthful, alcohol-free products.

4. Present your findings and your video or poster to the class.

In conclusion

1. In what ways was the ad you examined inaccurate and deceptive?

2. Do you think alcohol products should be advertised on television? On billboards? In magazines and newspapers? Why or why not?

3. Do you understand what kind of advertising appeals to you and attracts you, and what kind doesn't? What do you think would be the most effective means of getting teens who drink to understand the dangers of drinking and to become alcohol free?

Factors that Affect Teen Alcohol Use

Friends are often an important, although unconscious, influence on a teenager's choice to drink. There is pressure to drink, and it can be very difficult to say no, especially when you want to be accepted as part of the group.

The family is another major influence on a teen's attitudes and behavior with respect to drinking. If a teen sees his or her parents use alcohol when they have problems or when they want to socialize or celebrate, there is a greater likelihood the teen will do the same.

Yet another factor in the decision of many teens to drink is the portrayal of alcohol in advertisements. Advertisers spend over $1 billion a year promoting alcoholic beverages. These advertisers try to keep their product names prominent so that people remember them and are influenced when making a decision. By the time teens reach ninth grade, most will have seen more ads for wine and beer than for any other product. Many of these ads, moreover, are aimed at a teen audience and include one or more of the following:

- young people who are handsome, attractive, fit, and healthy-looking.
- a partylike atmosphere with upbeat music.
- an otherwise healthful environment, often in the beauty of the outdoors.
- problem-free drinking.
- a verbal message that really does not say anything about the risks of using the product.

Did You Know?

- ➤ Approximately 100 million Americans use alcohol.
- ➤ Ten teenagers a day die in alcohol-related crashes.
- ➤ About half of all fatal car crashes in this country involve alcohol.
- ➤ According to the National Safe Boating Council, alcohol is involved in more than 50 percent of the boating accidents in the United States.
- ➤ New efforts are being made to pass and enforce convictions for drunk boaters.

Steering Clear of Trouble

Choosing to stay alcohol-free demonstrates personal **responsibility** and helps to ensure your own and others' well-being. Consider these facts from national studies.

➤ Driving under the influence of alcohol may also diminish driving ability by as much as 20 percent.

➤ At low doses, alcohol has some of the effects of a stimulant; at higher doses, it acts as a depressant. Both impair driving ability.

➤ Even small amounts of alcohol can reduce your vision.

➤ Alcohol decreases fear, affects judgment, and increases one's likelihood of taking dangerous risks.

Character Check Create a short booklet that offers tips on why teens should not combine drinking and driving.

EFFECTS OF ADVERTISING

The hidden message advertisers are sending through these images is that alcohol is an aid to successful, romantic, and problem-free relationships, working situations, and recreational opportunities. Advertisers would not spend the large sums of money they do if these ads did not accomplish their purpose. It is rare to see a sporting event these days that is not sponsored in part by a liquor or beer company. Car races, boat races, and tennis events are just a few examples. The brand names of alcohol are in abundance on college campuses where basketball and football scoreboards are sometimes donated to a school just to make the name of the company or product visible.

One of the most effective advertising gimmicks is having the consumer buy products with the name of the company on them. T-shirts and hats are examples of this type of promotion. By wearing the product, a person actually provides free advertising for the company.

You and Your Decisions About Drinking

Everyone has the need to belong, to feel loved, and to feel important. It is possible to meet these needs in many ways. Drinking does not have to be one of them.

Using alcohol in any form has no place in your life. It is unhealthful, unsafe, and in most places illegal. As you apply your decision-making skills to the question of whether to drink, you will see that the negative consequences greatly outweigh any imagined benefits. In the remainder of this chapter, you will learn more about these consequences, and you will learn strategies for saying no to alcohol.

LESSON **1** *Review*

Reviewing Facts and Vocabulary

1. What is the name of the drug contained in alcoholic beverages?
2. Identify five reasons why many teens drink alcohol.
3. Name three techniques that advertisers use to get people to buy alcohol products.

Thinking Critically

4. *Evaluating.* Some teens use alcohol to deal with their emotional distress. Is this an effective approach to solving their problems? Why or why not?
5. *Synthesizing.* Summarize the reasons why so many adults use alcohol in spite of all the potential harmful consequences.
6. *Evaluating.* Why do you think older Americans usually are not featured as models or actors in ads selling alcohol products?

Applying Health Skills

7. *In Your Home.* Interview a parent and grandparent (or people from each of those generations) to find out what attitudes, practices, laws, and penalties existed regarding alcohol sale and use when they were teens.

What Alcohol Does to the Body

When someone has a drink, the alcohol follows the same path that food does as it travels through the digestive system. Once in the blood, alcohol affects every system in the body. Some of these effects are short-term. Others are not apparent for some time, perhaps even years. In either case, alcohol can do damage.

HEALTH TERMS

blood alcohol concentration

designated drivers

fatty liver

cirrhosis

fetal alcohol syndrome

HEALTH CONCEPTS

- Alcohol can quickly impair a person's judgment and, over time, cause permanent and serious health problems.
- Being in the presence of someone under the influence of alcohol can place a person's health and safety in jeopardy.
- Alcohol consumed by a pregnant female can damage the health of her fetus for life.
- Drinking and driving or riding with a drinking driver is taking a foolish, unnecessary, and sometimes deadly risk.

Short-Term Effects of Drinking

The short-term effects alcohol has on the body depend on several factors. These include the amount of alcohol consumed, the person's gender and size, and whether or not there is food in the person's stomach.

- **Brain.** Alcohol reaches the brain almost as soon as it is consumed. It depresses the activity of the brain, slowing the work of the **central nervous system**. Thought processes are disorganized, and memory and concentration are dulled. Decision making can be badly affected.

- **Liver.** The **liver**, in a process called *oxidation,* changes alcohol to water, carbon dioxide, and energy. The liver can oxidize only about one-third to one-half of an ounce (10 to 15 ml) of alcohol an hour. There is no way to speed up this process. Until the liver

hotlink

central nervous system For more information on the central nervous system and its functions, see Chapter 16, page 364.

liver For more information on the functions of the liver and ways of caring for this vital organ, see Chapter 18, page 416.

SHORT-TERM EFFECTS OF ALCOHOL

BRAIN
Alcohol reaches the brain within minutes, and the brain becomes less able to control the body. Movement, speech, and vision may be affected.

LIVER
The liver changes alcohol into water and carbon dioxide. When a person drinks alcohol faster than the liver can break it down, the person becomes intoxicated.

LUNGS
The carbon dioxide is released from the body through the lungs. The water passes out of the body in the form of urine, perspiration, and breath vapor.

SMALL INTESTINE
The rest of the alcohol moves to the small intestine, where it enters the bloodstream more slowly.

MOUTH AND THROAT
Chemicals affect mucosal lining, tongue, gums, and throat.

HEART
Alcohol causes the heart to beat faster and the blood vessels to widen. The increased blood flow to the surface gradually allows body heat to escape and body temperature to drop.

STOMACH
About 20 percent of the alcohol consumed passes through the lining of the stomach and into the bloodstream. Too much alcohol in the stomach may cause vomiting.

Alcohol has many negative effects on the drinker's body and behavior. The short-term effects are those that occur within minutes of drinking an alcoholic beverage.

has time to oxidize all the alcohol, the alcohol keeps circulating through all body parts. Contrary to popular myth, neither a cold shower nor black coffee can counter these effects and sober up a person who has been drinking.

- **Blood Vessels.** The blood carries the alcohol to all parts of the body, including the heart, liver, and brain. When alcohol enters the blood, it causes the blood vessels to dilate, or widen. The result is an increased flow of blood, especially to the skin. This makes the skin feel flush and warm. However, it is an artificial warmth. The increase of blood flow near the surface of the skin causes the body to lose heat by radiation. Body temperature actually decreases. People who drink and then go out into cold weather are at increased risk for **hypothermia**.

- **Heart.** Alcohol causes an increase in heart rate and an increase in blood pressure. It can lead to arrhythmias, or abnormal heartbeats.

hotlink

hypothermia For more information on the condition known as hypothermia and ways of protecting yourself against it, see Chapter 4, page 87.

It can cause scar tissue to build up in the muscle fibers of the heart. The risk of heart attack and stroke also increases.

- **Kidneys.** Alcohol affects the pituitary gland, which, in turn, acts on the **kidneys**, causing them to produce more urine. It is for this reason that a person feels dehydrated the day after he or she has been drinking heavily.

- **Stomach.** Because the alcohol molecule is very small and water-soluble, it does not have to be digested. It can be immediately absorbed from the stomach into the blood. Having food in the stomach slows the absorption process. Even so, food will not keep a person from getting drunk if he or she drinks too much. Alcohol increases the flow of gastric juices from the stomach lining. Larger amounts of alcohol cause a larger flow of these high-acid juices, irritating the stomach lining. Repeated irritation can cause internal bleeding.

Driving Under the Influence

Among the problems related to the short-term effects of drinking, one of the deadliest and most widespread is that of driving while intoxicated (DWI), also known as *driving under the influence* (DUI). A person is said to be driving while intoxicated when his or her blood alcohol concentration exceeds the limit allowed by law in that state. **Blood alcohol concentration**, or BAC, is *the amount of alcohol in a person's blood expressed as a percentage.* Signs of being intoxicated can begin to appear at blood alcohol concentrations as low as .02. Factors that affect the amount of alcohol in a person's blood include gender, weight, **metabolism**, the amount of alcohol (not the number of drinks) consumed, whether the person ate before or while drinking, and the time that elapsed between drinks or after drinking stopped.

What effect does alcohol have on an individual's ability to operate a car or other heavy machinery? Driving experts and medical researchers have found that drinking on any level

- reduces the ability to judge distances, speeds, and turns.
- reduces the ability to judge accurately one's own capabilities and limitations.
- increases the tendency to take risks.
- slows reflexes.
- adds to forgetfulness to take precautions such as using signals when turning.
- reduces the ability to concentrate.

CONSEQUENCES OF DWI

Driving while intoxicated is the leading cause of death among teenagers. Each day in the United States, 11 teenagers are killed and over 350 are injured in alcohol-related motor vehicle crashes.

Driving under the influence is a problem not only for the drinker but also for the nondrinker, who can easily become a victim in a crash caused by an alcohol-impaired driver. Almost 50 percent of the

hot link

kidneys For more information on the functions and problems of the kidneys, see Chapter 18, page 425.

hot link

metabolism For more information on metabolism and its role in fitness, see Chapter 3, page 54.

Did You Know?

➤ For years, police have asked drunk drivers to perform such tests as touch their nose with their fingers or walk a straight lines, heel to toe. Now, a test called the Horizontal Gaze Nystagmus test is being used to see if further breath or blood testing is needed. This test is based on the theory that people high on alcohol or other drugs can't prevent the jerking motions of their eyes when they try to track, or follow, moving objects.

Did You Know?

➤ About 85 percent of all car crashes involving teens are linked to alcohol.

➤ In the past decade, a quarter of a million Americans have died in car crashes in this country due to the use of alcohol.

➤ Alcohol and marijuana in combination have greatly increased sedative effects. They impair manual dexterity, psychomotor skills, and the ability to process information, and they cause visual disturbances.

crashes in which the passenger dies occur because the drivers were legally drunk. Although traffic deaths caused by drunken driving have declined in recent years, 38 percent of all traffic deaths in 1999 were alcohol-related.

OTHER COSTS OF DWI

Even when fatal traffic accidents are averted, numerous problems exist for the individual who is stopped for driving while intoxicated. Here are some:

- immediate confiscation of driver's license
- arrest, a trip to jail, court appearance, and fine
- possible suspension of driver's license
- possible mandatory jail sentence
- cost of bail to get out of jail
- higher insurance rates
- possible lawsuits

EFFORTS TO REDUCE DWIs

Each state has determined the legal acceptable limit of alcohol in the blood. In most states, driving while intoxicated is defined as having a 0.1 percent BAC, though other states have pushed and are pushing for lower concentrations such as 0.08. In all states, driving while intoxicated is against the law. There are also laws in some

Building Health Skills

Using Refusal Skills: Ways to Turn Down a Drink

EVEN WHEN THE PRESSURE to use alcohol is intense, saying no becomes much easier when you're prepared. Copy the following responses into your private Health Journal. Add any other responses that work as well or better for you, and practice them in front of a mirror. Make sure your body language backs up your words.

1. **Refuse politely but firmly.** No, thanks. I've already got a drink (such as bottled water, juice, etc.).

2. **Give a personal reason.** I'm watching my weight; I'm allergic to it; I hate the taste; It gives me a headache.

3. **Explain that you have more important goals.** I've got a game in the morning. It affects my schoolwork. I want to be in control of my life.

4. **State your values and responsibilities.** I wouldn't consider it. It's against the law for people my age.

states that make it illegal to have an open alcohol container inside the car. Mandatory chemical tests for blood, breath, or urine exist in some states. Refusal to submit to a test can mean automatic suspension of the person's driver's license. In some states, anyone caught driving while intoxicated may go to jail immediately.

Organizations such as MADD, Mothers Against Drunk Driving, and SADD, Students Against Destructive Decisions, have been powerful forces in making the public and state legislators aware of the problem of drunk driving. Stricter enforcement of existing laws, tougher new laws, the banning of open containers in cars, and abolishment of drive-through liquor stores are a few of the contributions that these organizations have made in trying to reduce the problem of driving while intoxicated.

A response to the problem is also beginning to come from individual concerned citizens. Increasingly, the idea of identifying **designated drivers**—*people in social settings who choose not to drink so that they can safely drive themselves and others*—is becoming a popular trend in a drinking society. Such people recognize the importance of *never* riding with anyone who has had *any* alcohol to drink.

Long-Term Effects of Drinking

Long-term effects of alcohol on the body can include vitamin deficiencies, stomach and skin problems, and loss of appetite. Prolonged alcohol use can also do permanent damage to the liver and central nervous system.

Brain Damage

Long-term, excessive use of alcohol invariably leads to major brain damage. It may even lead to a decrease in brain size. People have been hospitalized in mental institutions for severe brain damage caused by excessive alcohol use. Even moderate drinking can destroy brain cells. There can be a loss of intellectual abilities, such as memory and problem solving. These losses can seriously interfere with everyday functions.

Chronic Liver Problems

Alcohol interferes with the liver's ability to break down fats. **Fatty liver,** *a condition in which fats build up in the liver and cannot be broken down,* develops. This increased amount of fat prevents the liver from functioning normally. It also interferes with the growth of new liver

◣ *In 1981, SADD began work to reduce alcohol-related traffic deaths. Their efforts were so successful they have since launched programs to address more issues affecting teens.*

ACTIVITY *List issues that students in your school might work on to solve through programs like SADD.*

**Top: A healthy liver.
Bottom: A liver damaged by
alcohol use.**

ACTIVITY *Explain the function
and importance of a healthy
liver.*

h⊙tlink

hepatitis For more information
on hepatitis and modes of treatment, see Chapter 28, page 630.

tolerance For more information
on tolerance to substances, see
Chapter 23, page 517.

withdrawal For more information on withdrawal from substances, see Chapter 23, page 517.

synergistic effect For more
information on the synergistic
effect that occurs when two or
more medicines are combined,
see Chapter 23, page 516.

cells. As a result, old liver cells are not replaced as quickly as
they normally would be. The excess fat in the liver blocks
the flow of blood in the liver cells, resulting in reduced oxygen and eventually cell death. This condition has been
found in both moderate and heavy drinkers. It can be reversed when drinking stops.

Prolonged heavy alcohol use can cause **cirrhosis** (sir-ROH-
sis) of the liver, *a condition in which liver tissue is destroyed and
then replaced with useless scar tissue. Cirrhosis* means "scarring."
There is no blood flow in the scarred area because there are no
blood vessels, so the work of the liver is greatly reduced.

Alcohol abuse can also lead to **hepatitis**, an inflammation
or infection of the liver that can cause weakness, jaundice,
fever, and sometimes death. Also referred to as *alcoholic hepatitis,* it is caused by the toxic effects of the drug. Recovery can
be slow, and liver failure sometimes results.

Tolerance and Dependence

Because alcohol is a drug, people who use it regularly
may develop a **tolerance**, making it necessary to drink
more and more in order to produce the same effects. As tolerance develops, a person may drink an increasing amount
without appearing to be intoxicated. The person may continue to
function reasonably well until some severe physical damage results
or until he or she is hospitalized for some other reason. Then the individual will experience symptoms of **withdrawal** that range from
jumpiness, sleeplessness, sweating, and poor appetite to severe
tremors, convulsions, and hallucinations.

Some people become physiologically dependent on alcohol. The
body develops a chemical need for alcohol. Physiological dependence
is marked by tolerance and withdrawal. The symptoms of withdrawal
are so unpleasant, a person tends to drink more alcohol in order to
avoid the symptoms. As a result, the level of tolerance increases.

The Multiplier Effect

Similar to the **synergistic effect** that occurs when two or more
medicines are taken simultaneously, alcohol combined with other
drugs or medicines produces an interaction known as the *multiplier
effect.* When alcohol is mixed with another depressant such as a tran-
quilizer, the effects can be particularly devastating. Impairment of
both mental and physical abilities results. Many accidental deaths result from combining alcohol with other drugs or medicines. What is
especially dangerous is that these effects are often not predictable.

Both over-the-counter medicines, such as aspirin and prescription
medicines, can alter the way alcohol affects the body. Medicines that
might cause reactions with alcohol have labels that warn against
drinking any alcoholic beverages while using the medicine.

Alcohol and Pregnancy

In recent years, scientists have found that heavy drinking by pregnant females carries a risk not only to themselves but to their unborn child. **Fetal alcohol syndrome** (FAS) is *a condition in which a fetus has been adversely affected mentally and physically by its mother's heavy alcohol use during pregnancy.* FAS babies may exhibit some or all of the following problems: low birth weight, impaired speech, cleft palate, general weakness, slow body growth, facial abnormalities, poor coordination, and heart defects. Mental retardation, poor attention span, nervousness, and hyperactivity are also common in children born with FAS. FAS is, in fact, the leading cause of mental retardation in the United States.

The alcohol the pregnant female drinks moves into her blood, then across the placenta and through the umbilical cord into the blood of the unborn child. Any effects felt by the pregnant female as a result of drinking are also experienced by the unborn child. The alcohol remains in the baby's body much longer. If the pregnant female drinks three or four times a week, chances are the fetus *never* rids itself of alcohol.

The most sobering fact about FAS is that it is 100 percent preventable. It does not occur in babies of nondrinking pregnant females. Yet each year, some 5,000 FAS babies are born in this country. Many more cases go undiagnosed. The public is becoming increasingly aware of the dangers of FAS, but now every woman who is pregnant must make the choice not to drink any alcohol at all.

In 1988, the U.S. Senate passed a bill that, in part, approved a label that warned of the dangers of drinking during pregnancy. The warning reads:

> "ACCORDING TO THE SURGEON GENERAL, WOMEN SHOULD NOT DRINK ALCOHOLIC BEVERAGES DURING PREGNANCY BECAUSE OF THE RISK OF BIRTH DEFECTS."

LESSON 2 *Review*

Reviewing Facts and Vocabulary

1. List three short-term and three long-term effects of using alcohol.
2. Identify four ways that drinking impairs driving.
3. What are some of the characteristics of children suffering from fetal alcohol syndrome?

Thinking Critically

4. *Synthesizing.* In what ways can the short-term effects of alcohol sometimes become deadly?

5. *Analyzing.* Imagine that you are an alcohol molecule entering a human body. Describe your journey through the brain, liver, bloodstream, kidneys, lung, stomach, and small intestine.

Applying Health Skills

6. *In Your Home and Community.* Interview parents and other adults as to their feelings about checkpoints for drunk drivers. Summarize your findings and share them in a general class discussion.

Alcohol and Society

F or some adults, alcohol used occasionally and with moderation has pleasurable effects and few, if any, damaging ones. For others who drink, alcohol becomes a serious problem—one that negatively affects their lives and the lives of those around them. Healthy social gatherings do not include alcohol.

HEALTH TERMS

binge drinking

alcohol poisoning

alcoholism

delirium tremens (DTs)

HEALTH CONCEPTS

- You do not have to be an alcoholic to get in trouble with alcohol.
- Alcoholism is a chronic disease that can be treated with total abstinence.
- Alcoholism imposes heavy costs on the family of the alcoholic and on society.
- Not drinking is the only responsible choice.
- There are many effective ways to say no to alcohol.

Patterns of Alcohol Abuse

A lthough most people equate problem drinking with the disease of alcoholism, there are other troubled patterns of alcohol use whose effects can be every bit as devastating. Some of these patterns can even be life-threatening.

Binge drinking, one such pattern, is *periodic excessive drinking*. This type of drinking, which is popular among some high school and college students, can take the form of a social event or a contest to see who can drink the most in the shortest time. Binge drinking can lead to serious difficulties. Some binge drinkers mistakenly believe that they are not really in trouble with alcohol because they do not drink every day. However, even alcoholics can go days on end without drinks until later stages of their disease.

A danger associated more with binge drinking than with any other pattern of alcohol abuse is **alcohol poisoning.** This is *a dangerous toxic condition that occurs when a person drinks a large amount of alcohol in a short period of time.* Generally, when a person's blood alcohol level reaches about 400 milligrams per deciliter—four times the legal limit for driving under the influence—the brain's ability to control breathing can be interrupted. Death can result.

Alcoholism

Many myths and misconceptions surround the pattern of alcohol abuse called *alcoholism.* Many people, for example, erroneously believe it is just a passing state when in fact **alcoholism**—*a physical and psychological dependence on the drug ethanol*—is a disease. Another myth is that all alcoholics are "falling down" drunk and, hence, easily recognized. Although it is true that some people reach this extreme, a great many alcoholics appear clean, orderly, and well groomed. One common denominator that does exist among alcoholics is this: They all need help.

Traits of the Alcoholic

Alcoholics are unable to stop drinking despite the toll it takes on their health and their lives. People with alcoholism may exhibit one or a combination of these behaviors or traits:

- They are preoccupied in one way or another with alcohol.
- Once they pick up the first drink, they cannot promise or predict what they will say or do or how much they will drink.
- They cannot manage tension without drinking.
- They may have personality changes or memory lapses due to drinking.

Stages of Alcoholism

There are three clearly defined stages of alcoholism that happen over a period of time. The time span can be long or short, depending on the individual and the age at which he or she started drinking. The American Medical Association states that alcoholism develops in three phases: abuse, dependence, and addiction.

STAGE ONE

Alcoholism typically begins with social drinking, often to relax or to relieve stress or depression. Gradually, this kind of drinking becomes necessary to manage stress. A physical and psychological dependency on alcohol develops. The person begins to drink and become intoxicated regularly. The drinker may have short-term memory loss and blackouts—times when he or she cannot remember with whom he or she was drinking or what was said or done after each drinking episode. Often, at this stage, the drinker makes excuses

HEALTH Online

From **health.glencoe.com**, link to the M.A.D.D. home page to learn about alcohol myths and facts, the negative effects of alcohol, and advice for teens about avoiding alcohol. How can you inform people about the dangers of drinking and driving?

CHARACTER
IN ACTION

Signs of Trouble, Signs of Caring

One of the ways to be a **caring** friend is to notice the signs that a friend may be heading for trouble with alcohol. Look for the signs:

➤ odor on the breath

➤ trouble remembering or concentrating

➤ sudden emotional outbursts

➤ changes in choice of friends

➤ absences from school

➤ falling grades

➤ irritability

➤ poor coordination

➤ slow reflexes

➤ slurred speech

Character Check Write a fictitious "letter to a friend" showing caring ways you would encourage someone to stop drinking.

and tries to rationalize his or her drinking behavior. His or her tolerance to alcohol increases, meaning more is needed to feel the same effects. He or she may be called a problem drinker by others.

STAGE TWO

Gradually, the person reaches a point where he or she cannot stop drinking. In other words, the person is now physically dependent on the drug. He or she may drink alone and may drink every day, and the craving for a drink may occur earlier and earlier in the day. Physical and mental problems may become evident. More excuses are made for drinking, and often, others are blamed for what happens. At this stage of the disease, defensive behavior is evident. The drinker denies or tries to hide the problem. The body has developed a tolerance, and more alcohol is necessary. Drinking becomes the central event in the person's life. Performance on the job, at school, or at home decreases. Frequent absences from school, work, or other commitments occur.

STAGE THREE

In the final and worst stage of the disease, drinking is more important in the person's life than everything else. The problem can no longer be denied, and it is also uncontrolled. There may be hallucinations. Alcohol becomes a constant companion. The alcoholic becomes aggressive and is isolated from friends and family. Malnutrition results because the drinker overlooks his or her nutritional needs. The body is addicted to the drug. At this stage, the person has fallen apart physically, mentally, emotionally, and socially. He or she also now has decreased or reverse tolerance, meaning that it takes less alcohol

Making Responsible
Decisions

Saying No to a Drinking Driver

Lenny, who won't be 16 for another three months, is at a party with his friend Rod and some of Rod's friends, whom he's never met before. A little while ago, when Lenny looked over at Rod, he

saw Rod and one of his friends drinking a beer. Lenny has to be home in half an hour, and it doesn't look like Rod is ready to leave—or in any shape to drive.

Lenny could call home for a ride, but he's afraid of how the other teens at the party might react. He's even more afraid,

however—and rightfully so—about getting into Rod's car.

What Would You Do?

Apply the six steps of the decision-making process to Lenny's problem.

1. **State the situation.**
2. **List the options.**
3. **Weigh the possible outcomes.**
4. **Consider your values.**
5. **Make a decision and act.**
6. **Evaluate the decision.**

to cause drunkenness. If the alcoholic stopped drinking, he or she would experience the withdrawal symptoms associated with alcoholism, called **delirium tremens** (DTs), *the dramatic physical and psychological effects of alcohol withdrawal.* These consist of hot and cold flashes, severe tremors, nightmares, hallucinations, and having fear of people and animals. People with DTs need prompt medical attention.

Although alcoholism cannot be cured, it definitely can be treated. As many as two-thirds of all alcoholics recover with proper treatment. The goal of the various programs to treat alcoholism is to stop or control the intake of alcohol. Several sources are available to help people who have a drinking problem. Help is also available for the families and friends of people who have a drinking problem. These programs, such as Alcoholics Anonymous and Alateen, are discussed in Chapter 27.

▲ *The heavy use of alcohol is often a cause of serious family problems, including child abuse, abuse of the elderly, and domestic violence.*

ACTIVITY *Name three steps that a person who lives in a family with active alcoholism might take to get help for himself or herself.*

Costs to the Family

It is estimated that there are more than 3 million teen alcoholics. Up to 5 million young people in this country are considered to be alcoholics or problem drinkers. In addition, alcohol use, abuse, and alcoholism are major factors in the four leading causes of accidental death: car crashes, falls, drownings, and burns caused by fire. They are also factors in 20 to 35 percent of all suicides and play a major part in **domestic violence**, spousal and child abuse, abuse of the elderly, and marital separation and divorce. Alcoholism is one of the leading stressors and factors in troubled families. People who are involved with alcoholics and whose lives are enmeshed in the alcoholic's problems are called *co-alcoholics* or *codependents* and suffer from **codependency**. By living with chronic alcoholism, they learn to ignore their own needs and center all of their energy on the alcoholic, losing trust and self-esteem, and sometimes damaging their own health in the process. Their suffering, like that of the alcoholic, is enormous.

h⊙t link

domestic violence For more information on domestic violence, including spousal abuse, child abuse, and elderly abuse, see Chapter 12, page 286.

codependency For more information on codependency and help for the codependent, see Chapter 27, page 608.

Costs to Society

Alcohol is a major factor in the three leading causes of death for 16- to 24-year-olds. These are traffic crashes, homicides, and suicides. In all, alcohol claims about 100,000 Americans a year. Off the highway, alcohol contributes to about 6 million nonfatal and 15,000 fatal injuries per year. In the workplace, up to 40 percent of industrial fatalities and 47 percent of industrial injuries can be linked to alcohol.

A You have a choice in the kind of life you wish to lead.

ACTIVITY Think of the priorities in your life and list the choices that will allow you to fulfill your dreams.

The estimated cost to society for drug abuse is up to $110 billion and for alcoholism, $167 billion. According to the National Council on Alcoholism and Drug Dependence, alcohol abuse costs employers an estimated $30 billion every year in lost revenue. In addition, about half of all hospitalizations, excluding those related to childbirth, are linked to alcohol.

However, when it comes to alcoholism, there is good news and a lot of hope. More people than ever before are joining self-help support groups to get sober, and more young people than ever before are entering treatment centers and programs for their alcohol-related problems. The best news of all is that many people, including many teens, are deciding never to drink at all. During one recent spring, almost 3 million students in 3,500 high schools across the country registered in a program to abstain from using drugs and alcohol on prom night. This is just one of many efforts across the country in which teens themselves have come forward to declare that they intend to stay alcohol free and drug free.

Choosing to Be Alcohol-Free

Despite the rise in teen drinking, many teens are deciding to remain or become alcohol-free. The most common reason given for not drinking is: "I do not need it." Some teens who choose not to drink seem to be saying, "I don't have to drink to be popular," or "I don't need to drink to be accepted, to have fun, or to act in some way that I usually wouldn't."

Saying No to Alcohol

Saying no to drinking takes a firm mental commitment from you before you go to a party or other social situation where alcohol may be served. Practicing what you are going to say in such situations can help prepare you for the event. Whatever you do to turn down a drink, keep it brief, polite, confident, and to the point. Sometimes humor or the unexpected, creative comment can do the trick.

Alcohol and Sexual Activity

Alcohol affects a person's judgment and may interfere with self-control over one's emotions, decisions, and behavior. It may cause a person to do or say things he or she otherwise would not normally do, including engaging in sexual activity. Some people who are shy or otherwise socially uncomfortable may use alcohol as an "ice-breaker" only to find themselves in a place or situation that they later regret. This behavior is extremely unhealthful. HIV/AIDS, sexually transmitted diseases, unplanned pregnancies, ruined reputations, date rape, and other violence can result from mixing alcohol with social relationships. Remember that making the decision to practice **abstinence** from all risk behaviors, including alcohol use, is the best way to avoid injury and illness and to maintain good health.

hotlink

abstinence For more information on abstinence and its importance during the teen years, see Chapter 21, page 484.

Which Life Do You Choose?

Picture a car being driven by a sober, careful, respectful driver. It goes at a reasonable pace, moves carefully, and makes turns only when necessary. With a destination in mind, the driver steers the car in the desired direction until it reaches its goal. Now picture a car being driven by a drunk driver. It rambles, weaves, stops and starts, and perhaps even crashes.

So it is with your life. You can choose to live an alcohol-free life in which you pursue your goals and work steadily at reaching them, or you can get sidetracked and thrown off course altogether by using alcohol. When you come right down to it, there's only one healthful choice to make: to be alcohol-free.

LESSON **3** *Review*

Reviewing Facts and Vocabulary

1. Define the terms *binge drinking* and *alcohol poisoning,* and use them in a single paragraph.
2. Describe the three stages of alcoholism.
3. List three of the costs of alcoholism to society at large.
4. Identify four reasons why young people choose not to drink.

Thinking Critically

5. *Synthesizing.* What makes drinking contests particularly dangerous? For what reasons do you think teens sometimes engage in them? What advice would you give to a teen about to take part in such a contest?

6. *Evaluating.* Do you think the Surgeon General and the U.S. Senate were justified in passing the bill to require a warning label on alcoholic beverages? Defend your answer.
7. *Analyzing.* Why do you think teens who have problems with alcohol might pressure others to drink?

Applying Health Skills

8. *In Your School.* Write a 30-second radio announcement about teen alcoholism and where teens in trouble with drinking can get help.

Health Skills Activities

Activity 1 — Redesigning Warning Labels

Warning labels on alcohol products in this country advise pregnant women to avoid drinking because of the risk of birth defects. How could a message about alcohol's other dangers be communicated to the public?

Directions

1. Think about the many health risks alcohol poses to the drinker and to those around him or her. What kinds of information would most likely influence a potential user to think twice? Think about the best visual design to communicate your message.
2. Working with a group, design a new warning label for alcohol. The label should warn the public in words and pictures.
3. Make copies of your warning label, if possible, on the classroom computer. Place these in highly visible locations in the school or community.

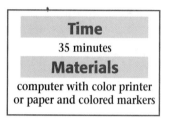

Time
35 minutes

Materials
computer with color printer or paper and colored markers

Self-Assessment

✓ Included at least three examples of the risks of alcohol use.
✓ Created a persuasive message that convinces others to avoid alcohol.

Activity 2 — How Alcohol Affects the Body

Many people associate fun-filled images with alcohol when, in fact, it is a lethal drug. Knowing exactly how alcohol can negatively affect the body can help you make the responsible choice to be alcohol-free.

Directions

1. Review the long-term effect of alcohol on different parts of the body, including brain damage, cirrhosis of the liver, and hepatitis.
2. As a group, investigate one effect in depth, noting how the disease or condition develops, typical effects or symptoms, and types of treatment. Combine your findings with those of other groups.
3. Present these findings, in the form of a documentary, to members of other classes in the school.

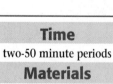

Time
two-50 minute periods

Materials
health resources found on the Internet, in the library, or in the textbook, paper, pen or pencil

Self-Assessment

✓ Included accurate and complete information.
✓ Demonstrated clarity and sound organization.

HEALTH NEWS VIDEO

Home Safe from the Prom

On prom night in Glen Rock, New Jersey, teens are proving that they can be safe and responsible drivers. Some teens like Rebecca Carvalho decide to wait before they get their driving license. By the time she learned to drive, she knew that she was really ready for the responsibility.

Others are taking unusual steps to alert classmates to the dangers. George Peña staged a frighteningly realistic car crash. Why? He wanted to drive home the possible consequences of drunk driving.

Teens in New Jersey, and around the country, are getting the message that drinking and driving don't mix. The number of teen drivers involved in automobile deaths has begun to decrease.

Play the Video ▶

Think About It

❍ Do you think that staging a mock car accident would successfully draw attention to the problem of drinking and driving in your community? Why or why not?

❍ Why is prom night a particularly dangerous night for some teens? How can you make sure you will make wise choices during special events like this?

❍ Do you think students in your school respect the message that drinking and driving don't mix? Explain your response.

Using Health Terms

On a separate sheet of paper, write the term that best matches each definition below.

LESSON 1

1. Physical and mental impairment resulting from the use of alcohol.
2. The type of alcohol found in alcoholic beverages.
3. The chemical action of yeast on sugars.

LESSON 2

4. A condition in which liver tissue is destroyed and then replaced with useless scar tissue.
5. People in social settings who choose not to drink so that they can safely drive themselves and others.

6. The amount of alcohol in a person's blood expressed as a percentage.
7. A condition in which fats build up in the liver and cannot be broken down.
8. A condition in which a fetus has been adversely affected mentally and physically by its mother's heavy alcohol use during pregnancy.

LESSON 3

9. A physical and psychological dependence on the drug ethanol.
10. The dramatic physical and psychological effects of alcohol withdrawal.
11. A dangerous toxic condition that occurs when a person drinks a large amount of alcohol in a short period of time.

Recalling the Facts

Using complete sentences, answer the following questions.

LESSON 1

1. Name three ways in which alcohol can negatively affect or even destroy a teen's future.
2. What are some of the dangers of being intoxicated?
3. What are some of the techniques that advertisers use to get young adults to buy and use alcohol products?

LESSON 2

4. What is the legal definition of *driving while intoxicated,* or a DWI?
5. Name five problems that someone stopped for driving while intoxicated may face.
6. What happens when a person has cirrhosis of the liver, and what is one of its primary causes?

7. Explain the multiplier effect, also known as the synergistic effect.
8. Describe three defects or problems of children with fetal alcohol syndrome.

LESSON 3

9. What are some of the dangers of binge drinking?
10. What are the three stages of alcoholism?
11. What are some of the symptoms of withdrawal from alcohol?
12. Where can a teen alcoholic get help? Where can the teen child of an alcoholic get help?
13. What is the relationship between alcohol and self-control?
14. Write a sentence or two using the word *abstinence* in which you relate it to your personal habits.
15. For what reasons is not using alcohol the only responsible choice?

Thinking Critically

LESSON 1

1. ***Analyzing.*** Which, in your opinion, has a greater influence on a teen's decision to drink alcohol: the influence of family, friends, or advertisements? Why?

LESSON 2

2. ***Synthesizing.*** *It is especially hazardous to use alcohol in cold climates.* Give some reasons why this statement might be accurate.

LESSON 3

3. ***Analyzing.*** For what reasons do you think alcoholism is considered a disease? Why do you think some people believe, mistakenly, that it is simply a matter of having little or no willpower?

4. ***Evaluating.*** What strategies or arguments seem to work best with teens in trying to convince them not to drink at all?

Making the Connection

1. ***Social Studies.*** In 1920, the Eighteenth Amendment to the Constitution was passed, prohibiting the manufacture, sale, and transportation of alcohol products. Find out what social forces led up to the signing and passing of this amendment, what its effects were, and when and why it was repealed. Share your findings with the class.

2. ***Language Arts.*** Interview a police officer in your community. What is being done to reduce the number of accidents caused by people who drive while intoxicated? Have the efforts worked? What age group presents the most serious problem? How can teenage drivers help fight this problem? Prepare your questions in advance, then summarize your interview.

BEYOND THE CLASSROOM

PARENTAL INVOLVEMENT With your parents or guardians, learn more about MADD. Learn when, where, and why it was founded, what its mission is, and how you and your family can get involved. Draw up a contract for all family members to sign that includes a commitment never to drink and drive and never to ride with any driver who has been drinking—even a family member.

COMMUNITY INVOLVEMENT Find out what your state's laws are regarding the purchase, possession, and consumption of alcohol by minors and the sale or delivery of alcohol to minors.

With school and community leaders and the police, organize a school assembly in which the legal consequences of underage alcohol use and purchase are made clear.

SCHOOL-TO-CAREER

Exploring Careers. Invite a family physician to speak to the class about his or her profession. Ask how much time in medical school was spent discussing the effects of alcohol and alcoholism. Ask what kinds of medical effects he or she sees among heavy drinkers, particularly young people.

CHAPTER 26

Illegal Drugs

HEALTH Online

ACCESSING INFORMATION
Get the facts and learn the best
ways to avoid the dangers of
"Club Drugs and Ecstasy" in the
Health Update article at
health.glencoe.com.

Self-Inventory Write the numbers 1–10 on a sheet of paper. Read each statement below and respond by writing *yes*, *no*, or *sometimes* for each item. Write a *yes* only for items that you practice regularly. Save your responses.

1	I avoid any type of illegal or improper drug use.
2	I choose friends who avoid drug use.
3	I feel comfortable saying no to peers who offer me drugs.
4	I take only medicines that are prescribed by a doctor and never abuse or combine them.
5	I do not abuse over-the-counter drugs for any reason.
6	I stay away from areas and events where I know drugs are likely to be used or sold.
7	I never cover for a friend or peer who uses drugs.
8	I don't attend parties where I know there will be drug use.
9	I know where to get help for drug problems and would feel comfortable passing the information along to someone who needed it.
10	I understand the dangers of drugs, avoid high risks, and know healthier ways to relax.

Follow-up After completing the chapter, retake this self-inventory. Pick two items that you need to work on and set a goal to improve your health behaviors.

66 *The unexpected consequence of drug use is what I have called 'the oops phenomenon.' Why oops? Because the harmful outcome is in no way intentional.* 99

—ALAN I. LESHNER, PH.D.
DIRECTOR, NATIONAL INSTITUTE ON DRUG ABUSE
NATIONAL INSTITUTES OF HEALTH

Quick Write The word *oops* implies a small, unintentional mistake. Write in one or two sentences why experimentation with drugs is not a small mistake, but is irresponsible and leads to dangerous outcomes.

Drug Use—A High-Risk Behavior

W hat is a prime contributing factor in many homicides, suicides, domestic abuse, absenteeism, and accidents? The answer is substance abuse. Substance abuse has effects on individuals and on society as a whole. You will learn strategies for avoiding and preventing substance abuse. Staying drug-free will help you to reach your goals.

HEALTH TERMS

substance abuse

illegal drugs

synthetic drugs

illicit drug use

gateway drugs

overdose

HEALTH CONCEPTS

- Substance abuse is a high-risk behavior that includes misusing legal drugs or using illegal drugs or other chemicals.
- People abuse drugs for a variety of reasons, none of them healthful.
- Substance abuse can harm a person's physical, mental, emotional, and social health and even lead to death.
- Substance abuse has far-reaching consequences for the abuser, for others in the abuser's life, and for society at large.

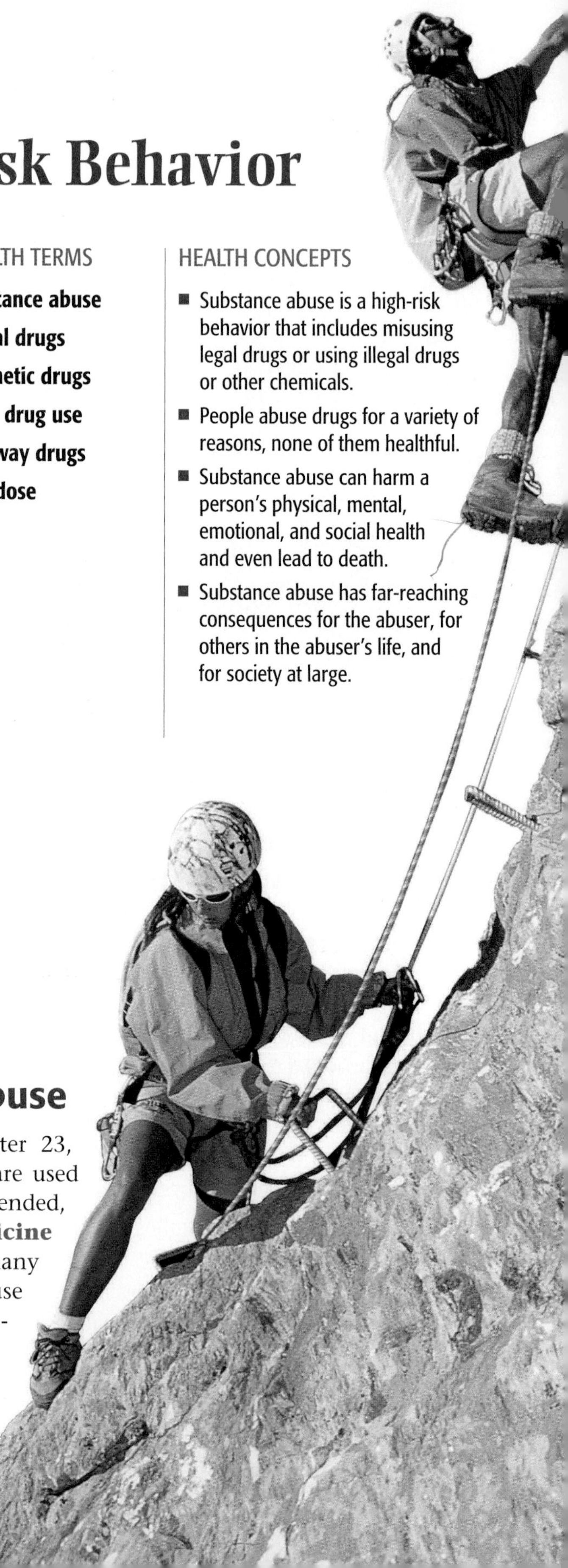

h⊙tlink

medicine misuse For more information on medicine misuse and its dangers, see Chapter 23, page 520.

Substance Abuse

A s noted in Chapter 23, when medicines are used in ways other than intended, a problem called **medicine misuse** exists. In many cases, medicine misuse results from carelessness. Sometimes, however, medicines are misused intentionally. People will take them deliberately to achieve a "high" from one or more of the known effects or reactions. In such cases, the user is guilty not only of *mis-use* but of *abuse*. **Substance abuse** is *any unnecessary or improper use of chemical substances for nonmedical purposes*. Substance abuse includes overuse or multiple use of a drug, including alcohol taken in combination with other drugs.

Not all substances that are abused are medicines. Many are *drugs*, chemical substances that serve no medical purpose and are simply used for recreational or other unhealthful purposes. Also known as **illegal drugs**, or *street drugs*, these substances are against the law for people of any age to manufacture, possess, buy, or sell. Their potential for harm is great.

Some drugs occur naturally, taking the form of extracts from plants, animals, or minerals. Others, called **synthetic drugs**, are *chemical substances produced artificially in a laboratory*. Regardless of their source or how they are taken, the effects of these drugs are deadly.

People who use illegal drugs are guilty of a crime called **illicit drug use.** This is *the use or sale of any substances that are illegal or otherwise not permitted.* Illicit drug use includes the selling of prescription medicines on the street. Even some drugs that are legal for adults, such as alcohol, are illegal for teens and can cause major health, safety, and social problems. For teens, alcohol and nicotine are also considered **gateway drugs**, or *drugs that often lead to other serious and dangerous drug use.*

Trends in Teen Drug Use

Even though in recent years abuse of drugs by teens has begun to level off, other drug trends suggest increases in use of some illegal substances. Consider these facts:

- Teens in the United States are now using drugs at younger ages than ever before.
- According to the National Household Survey on Drug Abuse, drug use among 12- to 17-year-olds began to decline in 1997 and has continued to stay level.
- In 1999, drug use among Americans age 12 and up fell to 6.7 percent.
- More teens are trying heroin than ever before, and more teen heroin users are showing up in hospital emergency rooms.
- Marijuana is the most commonly used illicit drug, used by 75 percent of all illegal drug users.
- More teens than ever mistakenly consider marijuana to be a safe drug.

During the 1990s, these substance abuse statistics prompted the Secretary of Health and Human Services to call this generation of teens "a generation at risk." The good news is that trends can be changed. By choosing to stay away from drugs, you can become part of a generation newly committed to getting and staying drug-free.

◀ *You will protect your health by being physically active and avoiding substance abuse.*

You know that drugs can be dangerous, but do you know how they alter the body and the mind? Find out the short-term and long-term physical and mental effects of illegal drugs at **health.glencoe.com**.

h⊙t link

side effects For more information on the nature and types of side effects, see Chapter 23, page 516.

synergistic effect For more information on the synergistic effect and other interactions that result when medicines are combined, see Chapter 23, page 516.

h⊙t link

HIV For more information on HIV, the virus that causes AIDS, see Chapter 30, page 656.

STDs For more information on STDs and measures you can take to avoid them, see Chapter 29, page 640.

tolerance For more information on tolerance to substances, see Chapter 23, page 517.

Why People Begin Using Drugs

If people know of the dangers of drugs, then why do so many try them? This question has different answers for different people. Many teens try drugs for one or more of the following reasons:

- They see their friends, parents, or older siblings using them.
- They feel pressured to use drugs and don't know how to say no.
- They want to fit in, relax, or seem mature.
- They see drugs glamorized on TV, in videos, in the movies, or in song lyrics.
- They seek a solution to boredom or are searching for new thrills.
- They are trying to escape from their problems.

Dangers of Substance Abuse

Like medicines, some drugs have serious **side effects**, which can range from minor to deadly. When taken in conjunction with one or more medicines or other drugs, including alcohol, they can also result in a **synergistic effect**. Illegal drugs may prove especially dangerous because, unlike medicines, there are no controls or means of monitoring these substances for quality, purity, or strength. Anyone who abuses drugs is also at risk for overdosing. An **overdose** is *a strong or even fatal reaction to taking a large amount of a drug.* Many overdoses are accidental. Often, overdoses occur when alcohol and other drugs are combined.

When drug use involves injecting substances through a needle, there may be added risks of contracting diseases such as hepatitis B, a serious and sometimes fatal liver ailment, and **HIV**, the virus that causes AIDS. Intravenous drug users often share needles, and traces of viruses in body fluids from infected people are easily spread to others who use the same needles.

People who experiment with drugs tend to lose control more readily than those who do not. This can lead to unwanted sexual encounters, **STDs**, or pregnancies. Substance abuse is also a major factor in many crimes, suicides, and both accidental and intentional deaths.

Substance abuse is like riding a "down" escalator. Taking that first step onto the moving stairway may seem harmless, but the consequences are enormous. These include the following:

- **Tolerance.** The body of the substance abuser begins to develop **tolerance** to the drug, needing more and more of it to get the same effects, and eventually needing it just to function.

- **Physiological dependence.** The body develops a chemical need for a drug. A person who has developed tolerance and experiences severe effects when the drug is taken away is said to be physiologically dependent on that drug.

- **Withdrawal. Withdrawal** occurs when a person stops using a drug on which he or she is physiologically dependent. The symptoms of this process can include nervousness, insomnia, severe nausea, headaches, vomiting, chills, cramps, and, in some instances, even death.

- **Psychological dependence.** With psychological dependence, a person believes a drug is needed in order to feel good or to function normally. He or she has a continual desire to take the drug for its effect.

- **Addiction.** Addiction involves physiological and psychological dependence on a drug.

h⊙t link

withdrawal For more information on withdrawal from substances, see Chapter 23, page 517.

▼ *Helping people to understand the risks involved with drug use is one way to combat substance abuse.*

ACTIVITY *With classmates, brainstorm a list of reasons teens should avoid drug use.*

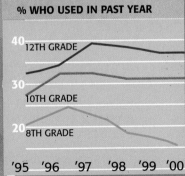

Teen Marijuana Use

% WHO USED IN PAST YEAR

12TH GRADE
10TH GRADE
8TH GRADE

40
30
20

'95 '96 '97 '98 '99 '00

SOURCE: University of Michigan Monitoring the Future Study, 2000.

Why Teens Use Drugs

	AGE 12	AGE 17
To be cool	49%	11%
Friends are doing it	24%	25%
To feel good	9%	23%
Substance abuse in family	7%	4%
To relieve stress	6%	22%
To escape problems	3%	7%
To rebel	1%	6%

SOURCE: National Center on Addiction and Drug Abuse.

Costs of Substance Abuse

In a teen's life, substance abuse can negatively affect performance in school, in sports, in relationships with peers, and in family life. It can affect a teen's emotional, social, and physical health. It can add undue pressure and stress to a period of life that is already filled with both. Furthermore, experimenting even once with a drug can get a teen in trouble with the law or even ruin his or her life. Educational goals may be interrupted and substance abuse can slow the progress toward becoming a mature adult.

up|date
▶ *Looking at the Issues*

Drug Testing: Yes or No?

It is estimated that substance abuse costs employers $90 billion a year in decreased productivity, absenteeism, and accidents. In the interest of health, safety, and economics, many companies are now testing employees for drug use. This has triggered a debate over whether people should be tested, who should do the testing, and whether the results are reliable.

ANALYZING DIFFERENT VIEWPOINTS

▶ **Viewpoint One**
Some groups claim that randomly testing people for drug use without just cause is an invasion of their rights, including their right to privacy.

▶ **Viewpoint Two**
Others believe that drug testing should be restricted to those who are in jobs where public safety is involved—such as pilots or bus drivers—or to cases where there is reason to suspect substance abuse, such as after a workplace accident.

▶ **Viewpoint Three**
Still other people argue that drug tests are not always accurate. They point out that people sometimes have others give drug-free urine samples in their place. Such situations can have severe consequences for the person being tested and for those in his or her life. The consequences for those incorrectly testing positive include job loss or damaged reputations.

EXPLORING YOUR VIEWS

1. Who, if anyone, do you think should be tested for drugs in the workplace? Why? In what kinds of situations?

2. When people do test positive for drugs, what do you think should happen to them? Why?

3. What do you think about schools testing students for drugs? What about testing for athletes?

4. What other means of identifying and getting help for students who are in trouble with drugs can you suggest?

COSTS TO OTHERS

Substance abuse affects not just the abuser but others in his or her life. Think about the number of drug-related crimes and deaths you read or hear about. According to the National Clearinghouse for Alcohol and Drug Information, illegal drugs burden American society with an estimated $67 billion in health, social, and criminal costs every year.

DRUGS AND PREGNANCY

Substance abuse can do serious harm to developing fetuses and to babies who ingest the substance through breast milk from nursing mothers who use drugs. Despite this, nearly 7 percent of babies born each year in this country have been exposed to one or more illegal drugs passed along through the mother's blood supply. Babies born to mothers who used depressants during pregnancy may be physically dependent on them and show withdrawal symptoms at birth. Birth defects and behavioral problems among these infants are common. Babies born to women who drink too much suffer from fetal alcohol syndrome. In addition, babies are often born addicted to the drugs their mothers have ingested. Those whose mothers used cocaine, heroin, or other narcotics go into severe withdrawal a few days after birth. Hearing the cries of a newborn going through withdrawal is a graphic reminder of the high and sometimes tragic costs of substance abuse.

Using illegal drugs can lead to serious trouble.

ACTIVITY *Make a list of warnings about the dangers of substance abuse.*

LESSON 1

Review

Reviewing Facts and Vocabulary

1. Define the terms *substance abuse, illegal drugs,* and *gateway drugs,* and use them in a single paragraph.
2. Describe three trends in teen drug use in recent years.
3. Identify five different reasons why a teen might start using drugs.

Thinking Critically

4. **Synthesizing.** List three costs of drug use in society, and give examples of how each of these costs might affect you.
5. **Evaluating.** Find examples of drug-related crimes and deaths in the newspaper and magazine articles. List some of the types of victims involved, such as family, friends, innocent bystanders, business owners, taxpayers, or health care workers. Evaluate the way in which each crime was handled by the criminal justice system. Do you think this strategy was effective in preventing further drug-related crimes? Why or why not?

Applying Health Skills

6. *In Your Home.* Write down three of your personal goals. Next to each goal, write a statement about how substance abuse would interfere with your ability to reach that goal. Post this list somewhere in your home where you will read it frequently.

Psychoactive Drugs

Like drugs used as medicines, drugs of abuse are grouped according to their effects on the body. Psychoactive drugs are one such group. **Psychoactive drugs** are *chemicals that affect the central nervous system and interfere with the normal functioning of the brain*. The use of psychoactive drugs among teens has increased alarmingly.

HEALTH TERMS

psychoactive drugs
stimulants
paranoia
euphoria
depressants
narcotics
hallucinogens

HEALTH CONCEPTS

- Psychoactive drugs affect the central nervous system and interfere with the normal functioning of the brain.
- Some psychoactive drugs have medicinal value whereas others do not, though all can be misused and abused.
- Misused or abused psychoactive drugs can have dangerous effects on the health and lives of their users.

Types of Psychoactive Drugs

There are four main groups of psychoactive drugs: stimulants, depressants, narcotics, and hallucinogens (huh-LOOS-ih-nuh-juhns). The first three groups have medicinal value when properly used. Hallucinogens, however, have no medical use. It is important to note that, when abused, *any* of these drugs can lead to serious health problems and even death.

Stimulants

Stimulants are *drugs that speed up the central nervous system.* Commonly abused stimulants are amphetamines (am-FET-uh-meens), methamphetamine (meth-uhm-FET-uh-meen), and cocaine. The **nicotine** in tobacco products is also a well-known stimulant, as is the caffeine in coffee, colas, tea, and chocolate.

Stimulants cause increased heart and respiratory rates, high blood pressure, dilated pupils, and decreased appetite. In addition, users may experience sweating, headaches, blurred vision, dizziness, and sleeplessness. Extremely high doses can cause irregular heartbeat, shaking or trembling, loss of coordination, and even physical collapse. Inhalation or injection of stimulants can cause a sudden increase in blood pressure that can result in stroke, high fever, or heart failure.

The psychological effects of stimulant use include moodiness, restlessness, and anxiety. Chronic users can experience hallucinations, delusions, and paranoia. **Paranoia** is *irrational suspiciousness or distrust of others.* These symptoms disappear when drug use ceases.

Amphetamines

Amphetamines are stimulants that have an effect similar to that of the **sympathetic nervous system**. Medical use of amphetamines has declined greatly in recent years. Some people use amphetamines illegally to stay awake and alert, to improve athletic performance, to lose weight, and to offset the effects of depressant drugs. Some use them for a temporary high and for **euphoria** (yoo-FOR-ee-uh), *a feeling of intense well-being or elation that may be followed by a complete "crash" or letdown.* These temporary highs, however, come at great cost to a person's physical and mental well-being, because once the craving begins, it may not go away. Tolerance to amphetamines can easily develop. Psychological dependence also can result. The user can experience exhaustion and depression as the effect of the drug wears off.

h⚫t link

nicotine For more information on nicotine, the addictive drug found in tobacco, see Chapter 24, page 529.

h⚫t link

sympathetic nervous system For more information on the sympathetic nervous system and its function, see Chapter 16, page 370.

◄ *What do you and your peers think can be done to stop the increase of drug use among teens?*

ACTIVITY *List some ideas you think of that could convince teens that drugs are dangerous.*

h⊙t link

Parkinson's disease For more information on Parkinson's disease and its symptoms, see Chapter 16, page 374.

obesity For more information on the problem of obesity, see Chapter 6, page 133.

Did You Know?

➤ Passive smoke, smoke harmful to those around a smoker, does not involve just tobacco; it also applies to cocaine.

➤ About six out of every 100 children treated in emergency rooms have cocaine in their systems from breathing in the smoke from adult crack-cocaine smokers.

Methamphetamine

Methamphetamine is a stimulant that has been used medically in treating certain diseases, including **Parkinson's disease** and **obesity**. When used illegally, this drug, which is also called *crank, speed,* or *ice,* may cause a person to turn paranoid or even violent. Because crank is made in labs, it is readily available. Crank can be smoked, "snorted"—sniffed up the nostrils—injected, or swallowed. The effects of this drug are long-lasting. Food and water become unimportant after taking crank and often just the fumes alone prove deadly.

Cocaine

Cocaine is a white powder made from the coca bush, which grows in parts of South America. Cocaine use and possession is now illegal under state and federal laws.

Cocaine is a rapid-acting, powerful stimulant. Its effects can last from 20 minutes to several hours. The feelings of confidence that come from cocaine use are often followed by a letdown. Regular use can lead to depression, edginess, weight loss, and physiological dependence. Repeated cocaine use can cause tissue damage in the nose and even holes in the nasal septum, the wall dividing the two halves of the nose.

Cocaine use can cause malnutrition and, especially among those with cardiac problems, an increase in the risk of heart attack. Even in healthy individuals who are not heavy users, the drug may disturb the electrical impulses of the heart and cause death. An additional risk of cocaine use is the possibility of being infected with HIV when injecting cocaine with a shared needle.

CRACK

Crack is a form of cocaine that can be smoked. Processing converts cocaine into lumps or rocks—a form of the drug known as *freebase.* Preparing freebase may involve the use of dangerous solvents and can result in injury or death from an explosion or fire.

Crack is extremely addictive. Because it is smoked, its stimulant effects are felt within seconds. Crack users may develop a sore throat, hoarseness, and lung damage. Using crack can cause death by cardiac or respiratory failure. The drug is considered both extremely addictive and extremely dangerous.

Depressants

Depressants, or sedatives, are *drugs that tend to slow down the central nervous system.* As noted in Chapter 25, alcohol is a depressant. It is also the most commonly used psychoactive drug. Other commonly abused depressants are barbiturates (bar-BICH-uh-ruhts), tranquilizers, and methaqualone (muh-THA-kwuh-lohn).

Depressants relax muscles, relieve feelings of tension and worry, and bring on sleep. They slow down the heart and breathing rates and reduce blood pressure. Depressants can easily cause physical and psychological dependence.

Barbiturates

Barbiturates belong to the family of sedative-hypnotic drugs—drugs that induce sleepiness. Barbiturate use can result in mood changes, more sleep than normal, or even a coma. Barbiturates are rarely used for medical purposes. They are used illegally to produce a feeling similar to that of intoxication and to counteract the effects of stimulants. Combined with alcohol, they sometimes prove fatal.

Tranquilizers

Tranquilizers are depressants that reduce muscular activity, coordination, and attention span. Anti-anxiety tranquilizers, such as diazepam, are used medically to relieve anxiety, muscle spasms, sleeplessness, and nervousness. However, when tranquilizers are used in excess, physiological and psychological dependence occurs.

Methaqualone

The form of depressant known as methaqualone was originally prescribed to reduce anxiety and to help with insomnia. Known for producing temporary euphoria, the feeling does not last, and withdrawal from the drug is extremely unpleasant. Serious effects of using the drug include rapid dependence, headaches, diarrhea, dizziness, convulsions, and coma. Many people die by combining this depressant with alcohol.

▲ *Turning to drugs is never a solution when you feel pressured or overwhelmed. Substance abuse only leads to more complex problems.*

ACTIVITY *List positive ways you can respond to stress.*

Narcotics

Narcotics are *drugs derived from the opium plant that have a sedative effect.* The most commonly abused narcotics are morphine, heroin, opium itself, and codeine. Formerly, the term *narcotic* referred only to drugs made from the opium poppy flower. These drugs are called *opiates.* Narcotics now also include medicines used to relieve pain. Narcotics cause drowsiness and can result in physiological dependence. Drugs made from opium can cause stupor or sleep so deep that they depress respiration and can result in coma or death.

Morphine

Morphine is a natural narcotic compound that is contained in opium. It is sometimes used to reduce severe pain, for example, in terminal cancer patients. It can act as an appetite suppressant, cause severe constipation, and lead to addiction.

Codeine

A weaker cousin to morphine, codeine is also a narcotic compound derived from opium. Codeine is sometimes used in cough medications to stop coughing, and, like morphine, it can lead to dependence and abuse.

Heroin

Heroin is made from morphine and has no accepted medical use in the United States. It is an illegal drug. Heroin depresses the central nervous system and slows breathing and pulse rate. Coma or death may occur with large doses. Tolerance develops very quickly. Pregnant females who use heroin risk having babies who are born addicted. Retardation and delayed growth of these babies' muscular and nervous systems can result. Withdrawal from this drug is very painful. As with any drug that is injected, there are risks of HIV infection from using contaminated needles.

Until recent years, heroin was thought to be a drug of the inner city, used by hard-core drug addicts. According to the Drug Enforcement Administration, or DEA, its use is higher in the United States now than it has ever been, and it is moving to the suburbs and to rural areas. In fact, in 1997, the reported heroin use among American teens was approximately two to three times higher than in 1991. The dangers now are greater than ever in part because the drug's purity is now sometimes 10 times higher than it was in the 1980s.

Hallucinogens

Some people who have suffered from mental disorders such as schizophrenia suffer from hallucinations and other distorted perceptions of the world around them. They may see and hear things that are not really there. People who use hallucinogenic drugs may have similar experiences. **Hallucinogens** are *drugs that alter moods, thoughts, and sense perceptions, including vision, hearing, smell, and touch.* The most commonly abused narcotics are PCP, LSD, and mescaline.

PCP

Phencyclidine, also known as *PCP* or *angel dust,* is a powerful and dangerous hallucinogen. It is prepared synthetically. PCP is considered to be one of the most dangerous of all drugs. Users report that PCP makes them feel distant and detached from their surroundings. Time seems to pass slowly; body movements slow down. Muscle coordination is impaired, and the sensations of touch and pain are dulled. PCP can make the user feel strong and powerful. This feeling has resulted in tragic deaths, serious accidents, and terrible acts of violence.

Even though overdoses of PCP can cause death, most PCP-related deaths are caused by the strange, destructive behavior that the drug produces in the user. PCP users have drowned in shallow water because they were so disoriented they could not tell where they were or which direction was up. Others have died in fires because they were disoriented and had no sensitivity to the pain of burning.

LSD

LSD is the shortened name for lysergic acid diethylamide. Commonly referred to as *acid,* it is one of the most potent of all mood-altering chemicals. A hallucinogen, LSD comes in tablet, capsule, and sometimes liquid form and is colorless, tasteless, and odorless. LSD's effects are wildly unpredictable. It can cause a false sense of security and power that has resulted in the deaths of users who, for example, believed they could fly or could stop a train by standing on the train tracks. Hallucinations may lead to panic, anxiety, or accidental suicide. Use of hallucinogens is illegal.

Mescaline

Mescaline is the psychoactive ingredient of the peyote cactus. Like LSD, it can lead to "bad trips," or frightening imagined phenomena and may lead to vicious stomach cramps and vomiting.

LESSON 2 *Review*

Reviewing Facts and Vocabulary

1. Define the term *psychoactive drugs* and use it in a well-developed paragraph about this class of drugs.
2. What are some legitimate medical uses for narcotics? What are their dangers to those who abuse them?
3. What unusual effects do hallucinogens have on their users?
4. In what ways may these effects be long-lasting?

Thinking Critically

5. *Synthesizing.* Some teens use amphetamines to lose weight. This is not an effective weight management technique. Give some of the reasons why and tell what, in addition to weight, a person might lose by using amphetamines.
6. *Comparing and Contrasting.* How do the effects of stimulants differ from those of narcotics? For what reasons do you think each has had some of its legal medical uses removed?
7. *Analyzing.* Street drugs such as LSD and heroin are often mixed with other chemicals. How does that differ from what you can expect when you buy aspirin, acetaminophen, or a prescription in a pharmacy?

Applying Health Skills

8. *In Your School.* Drug users often start experimenting occasionally with drugs and then become dependent on them. With classmates, brainstorm ways to teach preteens how to live drug-free and all of the benefits to be derived from doing so. Put your ideas in the form of a video, public service announcement, or comic book that will speak to children of that age.

Steroids and Other Dangerous Drugs

A number of misconceptions surround illegal drugs and their use. Many of these are created by drug pushers whose unsuspecting victims, all too often, are teens. This lesson will examine three other drug groups—anabolic steroids, cannabis (KAN-uh-bus) derivatives, inhalants, and designer drugs.

HEALTH TERMS

marijuana

hashish

inhalants

designer drugs

look-alike drugs

HEALTH CONCEPTS

- The damaging effects of anabolic steroids far outweigh their perceived athletic benefits.

- Marijuana and other psychoactive drugs have the properties and risks of hallucinogens, stimulants, and depressants.

- Inhalants are not meant for human consumption and can be deadly the first time they are abused.

hotlink

anabolic steroids For more information on other risks associated with the use of anabolic steroids, see Chapter 4, page 80.

Anabolic Steroids

The first stories about steroid abuse made news some two decades ago and involved professional athletes. Nowadays, sadly, some of these stories are unfolding in school locker rooms. What are **anabolic steroids**, and what is all the fuss about?

As noted in Chapter 4, anabolic steroids are synthetic derivatives of the male hormone testosterone. When used as medicine, these substances help build muscles in patients with chronic diseases. When used as an illegal drug, as they are by some athletes, anabolic steroids can exact a terrible price on the user in terms of both health and behavior. Steroid use causes mood swings and abnormally violent and aggressive behavior, sometimes referred to as "roid rage." Other serious side effects include **high blood pressure**, acne, baldness, increased risk of liver damage, heart disease, increased growth of body hair and facial hair, and stroke resulting from clogged arteries. In addition, males can experience depression, a decrease in sperm production and testicle size, and an increase in breast size; females can experience breast shrinkage.

One of the most tragic aspects of steroid abuse among teens is that their use is often based on the misguided belief that they make a person stronger. Although these drugs do cause muscles to look bigger, added strength comes only from working the muscles. In the meantime, the risks the drugs pose to life and limb are great.

Cannabis Derivatives

*C*annabis is the scientific name for the hemp plant, which is used as an illegal drug in two forms. **Marijuana**, the more widely used form, is *cannabis that is smoked, eaten, or drunk for intoxicating effects.* **Hashish** (hah-SHEESH), or "hash," is *the dark brown resin collected from the tops of the cannabis plant.* Hashish is usually sold in small brown chunks that are smoked in a pipe. It is sometimes boiled to make hashish oil, which is then combined with tobacco and smoked for even stronger effects.

h⊙t link

high blood pressure For more information on high blood pressure and ways of reducing its risk, see Chapter 31, page 678.

HEALTH Online

Visit **health.glencoe.com** to learn about the health effects of crack and cocaine, heroin, marijuana, and other drugs. Review the hazards of steroid abuse in athletes and teens.

Making Responsible Decisions

Running Scared

Today after practice, Jared, a new member of the school track team, was approached by Hank, one of the team's co-captains. Hank told Jared that he thought Jared had great potential, but he needed a little "help."

At this point, Hank held open his hand to reveal some pills. "Take them just before the all-city meet," Hank instructed, "and remember, the team is counting on you." Jared, who doesn't "do drugs," is worried about letting down his team.

What Would You Do?

Apply the six steps of the decision-making process to Jared's problem.

1. **State the situation.**
2. **List the options.**
3. **Weigh the possible outcomes.**
4. **Consider your values.**
5. **Make a decision and act.**
6. **Evaluate the decision.**

> *When you get behind the wheel you take on added responsibility to yourself and others to be safe and alert at all times.*

keeping Fit

Driving and Marijuana

Driving under the influence of marijuana can be as dangerous as driving under the influence of alcohol. Marijuana puts added "blindfolds" on a driver by:

➤ interfering with the perception of distance,

➤ interfering with the perception of depth,

➤ impairing thinking and judgment skills,

➤ slowing reflexes, thus affecting one's ability to brake and negotiate curves, and

➤ impairing the ability to stay in the proper lane.

Physical and Psychological Effects of Cannabis

Cannabis is a hallucinogen that also has the effects of both a depressant and a stimulant. Despite a widespread misconception that people can use marijuana or hashish and still seem and act normal, cannabis used in any form alters your senses, coordination, and reaction time and can interrupt your ability to make rational and healthful decisions. The drug lowers body temperature but increases the heart rate and blood pressure. It stimulates the appetite. Some people may become talkative and giddy, others quiet and withdrawn. The effects vary from person to person and can be influenced by a person's mood and surroundings. Regular marijuana and hashish users tend to have personality problems that include loss of willpower and motivation, lack of energy, and paranoia.

Studies have shown that cannabis affects memory, making it more difficult to recall things and to pay attention. Drivers under the influence of marijuana or hashish react slower and make more accident-causing mistakes than drivers who are not under the influence.

Cannabis smoke contains more cancer-causing chemicals than cigarette smoke. Because marijuana users often inhale unfiltered smoke deeply and hold it in the lungs, it is damaging to the respiratory system, making breathing difficult. Smoking cannabis also interferes with the immune system and may cause permanent damage, making the user more highly susceptible than normal to infections from bacteria.

Regular use of marijuana or hashish lowers levels in the blood of the male hormone testosterone and decreases sperm production. Females of childbearing age should avoid cannabis use, since the drug can result in stillbirths, decreased birth weight, and a condition in the infant similar to fetal alcohol syndrome.

Inhalants

Inhalants are *substances with breathable fumes that are sniffed and inhaled to give a hallucinogenic or mind-altering high.* Included among the inhalants are glue, spray paints, aerosols, lighter fluid, and gasoline. Most inhalants depress the central nervous system and produce effects similar to those of alcohol. Immediate effects of inhalants include nausea, sneezing, coughing, nosebleeds, fatigue, lack of coordination, and loss of appetite. Heavy use of inhalants can result in liver and kidney damage, changes in bone marrow, and permanent brain damage. Inhalant use can also lead to hearing loss, limb spasms, and blood oxygen depletion. A person can go into a coma from a single use and be in a vegetative state, on a respirator, the rest of his or her life. High concentrations of inhalants can cause suffocation.

Did You Know?

➤ Every year in this country, an estimated 1,000 teens die from breathing fumes from such products as glues, gases, and household sprays.

➤ According to the Monitoring the Future Survey, in 2000, 9 percent of eighth graders and 7 percent of tenth graders had used inhalants at least one time in the previous year.

HEALTH Online

Link to the National Inhalant Prevention Coalition at **health.glencoe.com** to learn about the damaging effects of inhaling common substances.

Building Health Skills

Refusal Skills: Saying No to Drugs

LEARNING TO SAY NO effectively to drugs can be an important component in maintaining a drug-free life. Here are some effective ways to help you in your efforts to refuse drugs.

1. **Make a firm commitment to stay drug-free.** You may even want to write it down in contract or pledge form or make a drug-free pact with a close friend.

2. **Learn and practice effective lines to use in refusing drugs.** Possibilities include: "No thanks, I don't do drugs"; "That stuff makes me sick"; or "I'm on medication." Once you have said no, stick to your guns.

3. **Avoid being around drugs and people who use them.** If you are at a party or other gathering where drugs are being used, leave. Stick with friends who support your drug-free commitment. Create a life that is active, full, and contrary to a life of drug use.

Behavior while under the influence of an inhalant has been the cause of many accidental deaths. Inhalants have also been shown to be gateway drugs, and teens often used them first before moving on to "hard" drugs such as heroin. The peak age for inhalant use is about 14.

Designer and Look-Alike Drugs

To avoid using illegal substances, underground or street chemists make **designer drugs**, *synthetic substances meant to imitate the effects of narcotics and hallucinogens.* One of the most well-known designer drugs is called *ecstasy,* or *MDMA,* which has a chemical composition similar to that of methamphetamine and mescaline. A combination stimulant and hallucinogen, ecstasy may give a short-term feeling of euphoria but can result in confusion, depression, paranoia, psychosis, increases in heart rate and blood pressure, and even long-term damage to brain cells.

These drugs can be several hundred times stronger than the drugs they are meant to imitate. Symptoms of designer drug use include uncontrollable tremors, drooling, impaired speech, paralysis, and irreversible brain damage.

An equally dangerous group of street drugs is **look-alike drugs**, *drugs made so as to physically resemble specific illegal drugs.* With these drugs, the user never knows exactly what he or she is getting. Look-alike "speed," for example, might contain high doses of caffeine plus cold medicines. Such mixtures can cause dangerously fast heart rates, changes in blood pressure, strange behavior, nervousness, and breathing problems. Using these kinds of drugs or mixing them with other drugs is very dangerous. Sometimes a sugar substitute is put in a capsule and sold as an illegal drug—at a huge profit.

The use of look-alikes is hard to diagnose. This makes treatment very difficult. If look-alikes are taken with other drugs, such as alcohol, serious reactions can occur. If a user is admitted to an emergency room, the medical staff may not be able to treat the patient successfully because no one can know for sure what drugs the user took.

LESSON 3 *Review*

Reviewing Facts and Vocabulary

1. Identify some short-term and long-term risks of using marijuana or hashish.
2. Explain why designer and look-alike drugs are dangerous.

Thinking Critically

3. *Analyzing.* Analyze and discuss some of the reasons why teens are using more marijuana these days, and how this trend might be effectively reversed.

Applying Health Skills

4. *In Your Home.* Share with your family information from this lesson about the dangers of inhalants. Then, working as a team, survey your home for all household products with a potential for inhalant abuse.

Strategies for Preventing Substance Abuse

When a person gets caught in the web of drug abuse, it becomes extremely difficult to get out. The best course of action therefore, is to identify the problem before it begins. This is true not only for yourself but for other people in your life whom you care about.

HEALTH TERMS

therapeutic communities

Drug-Free School Zones

drug watches

HEALTH CONCEPTS

- The decision to abstain from drug use is one of the most important a person can make.
- Programs and facilities are available nationwide for people who want to become drug-free.
- School and community drug watches help curb substance abuse.

Drugs and Peer Pressure

As a teenager, you may already have been confronted with situations where drugs were involved. You may even have been pressured to try, buy, or sell drugs. **Peer pressure** can be intense during the teen years, particularly in settings where using drugs and drinking seem "the norm."

hotlink

peer pressure For more information on peer pressure and ways to avoid negative influence, see Chapter 2, page 29.

CHARACTER
IN ACTION

Asking for Help

Asking for help with a drug problem demonstrates **courage** and strength of character.

Character Check To get help for a drug problem:

➤ Talk to a trusted adult.

➤ Look in the Yellow or Blue Pages under headings such as *Drug Abuse and Addiction* or *Alcoholism Information*.

▼ *A healthful lifestyle includes staying drug-free.*
ACTIVITY *Name ways you show you are committed to a drug-free lifestyle.*

You may hear that "everyone's doing it." The fact of the matter is that for most teens, illegal drugs never become a part of their lives. The National Clearinghouse for Alcohol and Drug Information reports that over 96 percent of 12- to 17-year-olds in this country have never tried marijuana, and over 80 percent have never tried cocaine. So the claim that "everyone's doing it" is simply not true.

The Commitment to Be Drug-Free

The first step in staying free of drugs is to make a clear and deliberate decision to stay drug-free. The only way to avoid the pitfalls and dangers of substance abuse and addiction is to be firmly committed to the idea of not using them *before* they are offered. In many cases, that also means steering clear of people who use drugs and of where drugs are likely to be used or offered.

Making the commitment to abstain from drugs is a positive, life-enhancing decision. It does not mean, as some teens fear, that you will be deprived of friends or fun. Quite the opposite, being drug-free means being able to savor life's true pleasures and deal with its problems. Living a drug-free life means:

- Finding healthful ways to have fun and enjoy your life.
- Sticking with people who know how to have fun without chemicals and who make you feel good about yourself.
- Figuring out what else makes you feel good about yourself and doing more of it.
- Thinking about your true purpose and how you can put your life and talents to good use.
- Tapping into your creativity.

- Learning healthful ways to relax and to manage stress.
- Staying connected socially and reaching out to others.
- Learning new skills, hobbies, and crafts, developing your talents, and expanding your mind.
- Connecting to the world and its many needs and issues.
- Getting lots of physical exercise.
- Caring for your body in other ways, including healthful nutrition and adequate rest.

Remember that no one's life is completely problem-free or full of natural "highs." Accept the ups and downs of life without chemicals, and live your life with kindness, attention, and a clear head. You won't be sorry.

How to Become Drug-Free

For those teens already in trouble with drugs, it is never too late to get help. The first thing to do is to talk with a trusted adult. Self-help programs, support groups, and treatment facilities exist across the country that can help a teen in trouble with drugs to get and stay drug-free. There are facilities that provide medical supervision while a person goes through withdrawal and detoxification, getting the drug out of his or her system. These include both **therapeutic communities,** or *residential treatment centers,* and outpatient programs. In addition, there are support groups such as Cocaine Anonymous, Marijuana Anonymous, Narcotics Anonymous, and Alcoholics Anonymous. With the increase in public awareness that addiction is indeed a disease, more and more people are willing to admit to and get help for their drug-related problems and chemical dependencies.

School Efforts to Stop Drugs

All over America there are now **Drug-Free School Zones.** These are *areas within 1,000 feet of schools and designated by signs, within which people caught selling drugs receive especially tough penalties.* Sometimes the penalties are even double what they might otherwise be for the same drug offense elsewhere. Among other efforts in and around schools to cut down on drugs are classes in drug education,

▲ *Taking a wrong turn at any moment can derail your plans for the future.*

ACTIVITY *List three places a teen can turn to for help with a drug problem.*

Teens Making a Difference

...CARING...RESPONSIBILITY ...CITIZENSHIP

Bobbie Jo's passion right now is her involvement in YELL—Youth to Eliminate Lost Lives—a group dedicated to helping teens make healthful decisions and prevent accidents and deaths due to drug and alcohol use. A high school senior, she is currently president of her school's YELL chapter and an example of a teen putting her highest values into practice.

TEACHING AND REACHING Bobbie Jo puts caring into action by reaching out to educate other teens. "At YELL," she begins, "we do programs like Prom Promise to get students to think about ways to have fun that don't involve drugs or alcohol. We also do a program in the elementary school called Milk Mustaches, where we talk about the dangers of drugs and alcohol. We sponsor a White-Out Day, in the high school, when we pull students out of class at the same rate that students are killed in our country due to drug or alcohol related crashes. Once they have their faces painted—these students can't speak for the rest of the day. At the end of the day, YELL announces the total number of deaths these students represent."

AGAINST DRUGGED DRIVING Bobbie Jo works to heighten others' awareness that drugged driving can be just as dangerous as drinking and driving. The dangers of impaired driving are close to home for her: her stepmother was pregnant and lost her baby when hit by an impaired driver; the former president of YELL at her school was also killed in the same way. "Kids who drive and use drugs or alcohol don't realize what's happening until after the fact when it's too late," she says. "Driving and using drugs or alcohol can hurt not only you but everyone around you, and the people in the other car, their family, their friends. If you want to be responsible, you can't use drugs."

She has taken her message to the community, speaking at a university conference on drug and alcohol abuse and addiction. Recently, she went to a national conference about drugs, alcohol, and driving where teens made policy suggestions to the United States Congress. Among the suggestions made were to have more sobriety checks—not just for alcohol but for other drugs as well.

BOBBIE JO'S STORY

1. What are some of the ways Bobbie Jo has demonstrated the values of caring and responsibility?
2. How has she reached out to the community to advocate against drugged driving?

YOUR STORY

1. What values are you exercising when avoiding drug and alcohol use?
2. What steps can you take to teach others about the dangers of drugs and the negative effects they have on one's values, goals, and health?

suspensions and expulsions for drug use, police or security guards in halls, drug and alcohol counselors on the premises, locker searches, school uniforms, the banning of beepers and certain kinds of clothing, and more. Of course, the best way to keep any school drug-free is for each person attending the school to make a personal pledge to be drug-abstinent. Have you done your part?

Community Efforts to Stop Drugs

Communities across the nation are taking positive action. **Drug watches,** *organized community efforts by neighborhood residents to patrol, monitor, report, and otherwise help try to stop drug deals and drug use,* utilize volunteers with noisemakers, megaphones, civilian street patrols, and cellular phones to report drug deals and drug-related problems. Taking an interest in the welfare of your environment is both an indicator of a health-literate person and a **developmental task** of adolescence. Becoming involved in stopping drug use by instituting a drug watch in your community is one way to meet both these goals. Making and keeping your own personal commitment to staying drug-free is a healthful place to start.

h⊙t link

developmental task For more information on meeting the developmental tasks of adolescence, see Chapter 21, page 482.

▼ *There are many ways to get involved in your school or community's efforts to stop substance abuse.*

ACTIVITY *With a partner, make a list of five ways teens can help to promote and build drug-free environments.*

LESSON 4 *Review*

Reviewing Facts and Vocabulary

1. What steps can a teen take to increase his or her chances of staying drug-free?
2. Identify some of the strategies schools and communities have taken to decrease the availability of drugs.

Thinking Critically

3. **Synthesizing.** With classmates, brainstorm a list of "boredom busters," or exciting and pleasurable ways for teens to socialize without having to rely on drugs.
4. **Synthesizing.** Develop a list of strategies that might help to reduce drug use in your school. Write these up in the form of a formal proposal, and submit it to the school principal or school board.

Applying Health Skills

5. **In Your School.** Prepare a pamphlet or article for your school newspaper entitled "Marijuana: Weeding Out the Problem" about the dangers of marijuana use and how teens in your school might join together in an anti-marijuana campaign.

Health Skills Activities

Activity 1 — Getting Help

It is often difficult for young persons to reach out to others when they have a serious problem. How can people with drug problems overcome these communication barriers and get the help and support they need?

Directions

1. Working in small groups, brainstorm reasons why an addicted person might not seek help.
2. Using markers and newsprint divided into two columns, list your reasons in the left-hand column. Then, in the right-hand column, list all the reasons why a teen with a drug problem might finally reach out for help.
3. Share your findings with the class. Examine and compare your list with other group's lists.

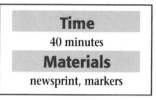

Time
40 minutes
Materials
newsprint, markers

Self-Assessment

✓ Highlighted the difficulty of asking for help for drug-related problems.
✓ Demonstrated that young people can overcome communication barriers and get help with their problems.

Activity 2 — Dangers of Steroids

Middle school students are often worried they are not going to fit in at high school. They might at times consider high-risk behavior in an effort to impress peers. How could you persuade a younger relative or friend that this thinking is harmful?

Directions

1. Read the letter your teacher hands out.
2. Review the effects of steroids on the body, as noted in the chapter. Then write a letter to your cousin advising him of these dangers. Suggest healthful ways he could fit in with his peers.
3. Share and compare your letter with those of classmates. Compile all of your letters, along with the fictional letter by Marcus, into an original book titled *Dear Cousin* to be printed on the classroom computer.

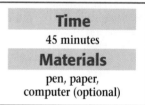

Time
45 minutes
Materials
pen, paper,
computer (optional)

Self-Assessment

✓ Demonstrated knowledge of health risks related to anabolic steroids.
✓ Described alternative ways to have fun with peers and fit in that do not involve drugs.

596 CHAPTER 26 ILLEGAL DRUGS

HEALTH NEWS
VIDEO

No Joy in Ecstasy

Some of the dangerous effects of illegal drugs occur right away. Disorientation, impaired speech, and clouded thinking can lead to immediate and critical problems. Some effects, however, build up over time. The full impact of taking a drug can take years, or even decades, to become apparent. Scientists have conducted the first human study of the drug Ecstasy. The results show that people who use Ecstasy are taking huge risks. The consequence can be permanent brain damage.

Ecstasy is an amphetamine that affects the way the brain handles a chemical called serotonin. Researchers know that this chemical is linked to mood and thinking ability. They predict that using Ecstasy could lead to devastating anxiety and depression.

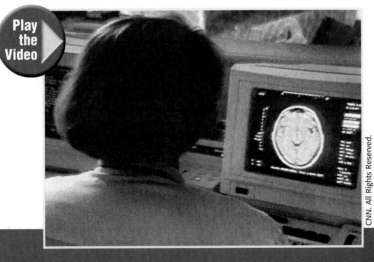

Play the Video

Think About It

- What is an amphetamine? Why is Ecstasy classified in this category?
- This study is the first one that analyzes the use of Ecstasy in humans. Why is this an important step?
- How can the results of this study be used to persuade teens not to use this dangerous drug?

Using Health Terms

On a separate sheet of paper, write the term that best matches each definition below.

LESSON 1

1. Drugs that often lead to other serious and dangerous drug use.
2. Chemical substances produced artificially in a laboratory.
3. Street drugs.
4. Any unnecessary or improper use of chemical substances for nonmedical purposes.

LESSON 2

5. Drugs that alter moods, thoughts, and sense perceptions, including vision, hearing, smell, and touch.
6. Chemicals that affect the central nervous system and interfere with the normal functioning of the brain.

7. Drugs that tend to slow down the central nervous system.
8. Drugs derived from the opium plant that have a sedative effect.

LESSON 3

9. Drugs made so as to physically resemble specific illegal drugs.
10. The dark brown resin collected from the tops of the cannabis plant.
11. Synthetic substances meant to imitate the effects of narcotics and hallucinogens.

LESSON 4

12. Areas within 1,000 feet of schools and designated by signs, within which people caught selling drugs receive especially tough penalties.
13. Residential treatment centers.

Recalling the Facts

Using complete sentences, answer the following questions.

LESSON 1

1. What are some of the reasons why teens begin using drugs?
2. Distinguish between physiological dependence and psychological dependence.
3. What are three of the signs of physical dependence?

LESSON 2

4. What are psychoactive drugs?
5. Define the word *stimulants* and give three different examples.
6. What is crack, and what makes it so dangerous?
7. What problems can result from regular cocaine use?
8. Define *depressants* and give two examples.

9. Define *narcotics* and *hallucinogens* and give two examples of each.

LESSON 3

10. What are the risks of using anabolic steroids?
11. Why does hashish affect a user more strongly than marijuana does?
12. Why is it dangerous to ride in a car with a driver who has been smoking marijuana?
13. What health problems do look-alike drugs present?

LESSON 4

14. What is a drug watch?
15. What are some of the steps schools and communities are taking to stop substance abuse?

Thinking Critically

LESSON 1

1. ***Analyzing.*** Drug use takes an enormous toll on society as well as on the individual. Explain this statement and provide several illustrations of the costs to both the individual and society.

LESSON 2

2. ***Analyzing.*** Some parents who used drugs feel conflicted about whether or not to tell their own children about their drug histories. Analyze the pros and cons of talking about past drug use with one's offspring.

LESSON 3

3. ***Evaluating.*** Research more of the harmful effects of steroid use to the body. List the serious, long-term, potentially fatal consequences. Then write a one-page report describing the symptoms that may indicate the presence of steroid use.

LESSON 4

4. ***Synthesizing.*** One way to stop the spread of drugs in your school is to recognize the signs of drug use. Write, edit, design, and print an informational leaflet called "Signs of Possible Drug Use."

Making the Connection

1. ***Social Studies.*** Investigate several important laws passed in the twentieth century regarding control of the sale and possession of psychoactive sustances, including the 1906 Pure Food and Drug Act and the United States Controlled Substances Act of 1970. Report on the content of these laws to the class.

2. ***Language Arts.*** Write a fictional, first-person story in which you imagine that you are the victim of a drug-related crime. Set the stage of the crime. Then in a dramatic court scene, through a Victim's Rights program, face the criminal who made you a victim and tell him or her what the crime has done to you.

BEYOND THE CLASSROOM

PARENTAL INVOLVEMENT With a parent or guardian, visit a hospital emergency room on a Saturday night. Observe what kinds of injuries people have. Talk with emergency room workers when there is a lull, or a break in the action. Find out how many and which kinds of injuries seem to be drug- and alcohol-related.

COMMUNITY INVOLVEMENT Learn more about Neighborhood Watch or a drug-watch effort in your neighborhood or community. Become involved in civilian patrols, anti-drug marches, and other efforts to rid your area of drugs.

SCHOOL-TO-CAREER
Exploring Careers. Invite a pharmacist to speak to your class. Ask him or her to tell you about the education and training required to become a pharmacist, and what kinds of licensing and updating of training are required. Ask about the kinds of abuses or misuses he or she has seen regarding prescribed and over-the-counter medications.

CHAPTER 27

Recovering from Addiction and Codependency

COMMUNICATION SKILLS
Use Word Processing skills outlined in Technology Projects at **health.glencoe.com** to compose a letter to someone who needs encouragement and support while fighting an addiction.

" *Just as no one starts out to have lung cancer when they smoke, or no one starts out to have clogged arteries when they eat fried foods...no one starts out to become a drug addict when they use drugs.* "

—ALAN I. LESHNER, PH.D.
DIRECTOR, NATIONAL INSTITUTE ON DRUG ABUSE
NATIONAL INSTITUTES OF HEALTH

Quick Write Quickly jot down what you might say to a friend who is in trouble with drugs and needs to get help.

Personal Health Inventory

Self-Inventory Write the numbers 1–10 on a sheet of paper. Read each statement below and respond by writing *yes*, *no*, or *sometimes* for each item. Write a *yes* only for items that you practice regularly. Save your responses.

1	I do not live with a person who suffers from an addiction.
2	I do not have a close friend who is an alcoholic or addict.
3	My life and emotions are not totally wrapped up in the addiction of a person I care about.
4	I do not spend a great deal of time, energy, or money trying to fix the person's problems.
5	My involvement with this person is not affecting my sleep habits, appetite, or mental or physical health.
6	I never lie or cover up for the person about his or her smoking, drinking, or drug use.
7	I don't feel overly responsible for other people's behavior.
8	I don't feel comfortable or useful only when I'm trying to rescue someone in trouble.
9	I do not try to control other people or situations.
10	I do not feel as if I have to please everyone all the time.

Follow-up After completing the chapter, retake this self-inventory. Pick two items that you need to work on and set a goal to improve your health behaviors.

Recovering from Addiction

Addiction is a disease that knows no limits. Anyone can become addicted, and the source of the addiction can vary. A person can become addicted to alcohol, nicotine, drugs, gambling, or even food. Yet, of all possible addictions, none is more serious—or has more devastating consequences—than a dependence on alcohol or another drug.

HEALTH TERMS

intervention

recovery

detoxification

relapse

inpatient treatment

outpatient treatment

halfway house

HEALTH CONCEPTS

■ A number of clear warning signs indicate that a substance abuse problem exists.

■ You can help someone you care about recover from drug addiction by seeking help on the person's behalf.

■ Recovery from addiction occurs gradually in a series of steps.

The Addiction Continuum

Addiction is a process—a series of gradual changes that happen over time. This process happens more quickly to some than to others. Some people get hooked on a drug from the first time they take a drink, a pill, or an injection. For other people, an addiction develops more slowly, perhaps over a period of many years. Others do not become addicted at all. For this reason, it is difficult to predict exactly when the use of an addictive substance—or how much of it— might lead to a problem.

This much is clear, however. Once an addiction to alcohol or some other drug sets in, the person needs help if he or she is to have any hope of returning to a normal, drug-free life.

Addiction: Recognizing the Problem

The first step in getting help with an addiction is to recognize that a problem exists. Sometimes it is the people close to the addict or alcoholic who first recognize and point to the problem. Sometimes, it is the addict himself or herself. In either case, there are clear-cut warning signs of possible addiction. These include:

- continual concern about where the next "fix"—drink or pill, for example—will come from.
- choosing friends who can supply the addictive substance.
- changes in appearance or personal habits.
- irritability, nervousness, personality changes, or mood swings.

up|date
▶ Looking at the Issues

Teen Gambling: Addiction, Compulsion, or Bad Habit?

Teen gambling is now a major problem in the United States, with an estimated 40 to 70 percent of teens under 18 having gambled at one time or another. Whether flipping quarters or betting on football games, teens bet an estimated $500 million to $1 billion a year. Are these teens addicted? Opinions on the subject are divided.

ANALYZING DIFFERENT VIEWPOINTS

▶ **Viewpoint One**

Studies sponsored by the National Institutes of Health, using positron emission tomography (PET) scans, are attempting to establish a link between brain chemistry and compulsive gambling. Those who support the claim that gambling is an addictive disease note that gamblers experience an adrenaline rush and a "high" much as drug addicts do when their craving is temporarily satisfied by a drug.

▶ **Viewpoint Two**

Some experts now make a distinction between problem gamblers and compulsive gamblers just as they do between problem drinkers and alcoholics. The *problem gambler* is someone whose gambling is no longer just recreation. He or she might have difficulty controlling the money spent or the time gambling. The *compulsive gambler's* life is completely taken over by the need to gamble.

EXPLORING YOUR VIEWS

1. Do you believe that gambling for some can be an addiction, just like being hooked on other substances? Why or why not?

2. Do you gamble or know other teens who do? If you gamble, has it caused any trouble in your life? If you know teens who gamble, has it caused trouble in their lives? What kinds of additional trouble might it cause down the road?

Dangerous to the Core

A person who uses alcohol, marijuana, or other illegal drugs is not living up to his or her **core ethical values**. Losing sight of the highest values can lead a person to cheat, lie, steal, and head for all kinds of danger to obtain the drug. By considering the highest values, a person can more easily make the right decision to stay drug-free.

Character Check Write a short script or develop a comic strip showing how a person battles the temptation to use drugs. Depict your character upholding his or her highest values as a defense against the dangers of illegal drugs.

- violent behavior.
- black-outs.
- needing increasing amounts of a substance to feel "normal."

Intervention

In the past, it was believed that the alcoholic or addict had to "reach bottom" before he or she would be willing to accept help. Recently, that thinking has changed, and nowadays many families—recognizing that a problem exists—stop the downward slide through a process called **intervention**. This is *interruption of the addiction continuum before the addict or alcoholic hits bottom.* Intervention begins with meetings between family members or other significant people involved in the life of the chemically dependent person and a certified drug or alcohol counselor. These meetings take place without the addicted person's knowledge. At the meetings, family members learn about addiction and the ways in which they have become affected by it. They make a list of all the episodes they can remember involving the person's drinking and drug use and how it made them feel.

The next step in the process is a surprise meeting with the addict that forces the person to face the seriousness of his or her addiction and how unmanageable his or her life has become because of it. The group then presents the addict with a plan for immediate treatment.

connections Math

The High Costs of Addiction

The costs of addiction are staggering. For example, illicit drug and alcohol use in the workplace in this country costs businesses an estimated $140 billion a year in lost productivity, accidents, and medical claims. Sadly, that is just a fraction of the overall cost in the lives of the addicted, in the lives of their families, and in society at large.

1. **With classmates or in small groups, brainstorm some of the costs of addiction to individuals and society.** List these costs in two columns, one under *Cost in Dollars*, the other under *Other Kinds of Costs*.

2. **Using print or on-line resources, gather statistics relating to some of the costs in dollars.** Reputable sources of such information include the National Institute on Alcohol Abuse and Alcoholism, the NIH National Institute on Drug Abuse, and SAMSA National Clearinghouse for Alcohol and Drug Information.

3. **Use the statistics you gather to create a bar graph showing the costs of alcohol and drug use to society.** Share and compare your graph with those of other groups.

If the person refuses to get this needed help, the family, boss, or others taking part in the intervention process tell the person what steps they plan to take in response to the refusal. For example, a wife might say, "If you won't get help, I'll move out." Such ultimatums let the chemically dependent person know that he or she must now face the consequences of his or her addiction. It is only when the person has decided to do so that recovery is possible. **Recovery** means *learning to live an alcohol-free or drug-free life.*

The Recovery Continuum

Like addiction, recovery is a process that happens over time. In fact, a recovering person never says, "I am cured," but rather, "I am recovering." This is because recovery is an ongoing, lifelong process. This process happens at different rates and in different ways for different people. Yet, there are certain characteristics common to most recovery stories.

The first step in the recovery process is **detoxification,** *the removal of all drugs from the body.* This process should take place under medical supervision. In addition to the addict's regaining physical health, recovery also involves restoring one's mental health by learning to build healthy relationships and by taking responsibility for one's own life. It is generally recognized that people can begin the recovery process at any point on the downward slide into addiction—even before they suffer major losses.

Most experts in the field of addiction recommend total **abstinence** from any mood-altering drugs, including alcohol, for the recovering alcoholic or addict. Long-term studies show that attempts at controlled drinking and drug use usually fail. Even small amounts of alcohol or other drugs can send an addict back into addiction.

Many people in recovery manage to stay drug-free for the rest of their lives. Others may have **relapses,** *slips from recovery, or periodic returns to drinking and drug use.* Yet, despite how far down the addiction continuum a person goes or how many times that person relapses, the choice of and chance for recovery are always there.

Treatment Options

Where can a person with an addiction problem turn for help? As with any problem, a good starting point is to talk with someone the person trusts and who can point him or her in the direction of professional help. For a teen, this might be a parent, teacher, school counselor, or peer counselor. He or she might also directly contact a drug and alcohol treatment center. Such facilities specialize in drug and alcohol counseling. Depending at which point the person is along the addiction continuum and his or her previous experience with addictive problems, the person may be directed to a **support group** or an alcohol and drug treatment center.

A *Teens with addiction in the family often suffer in silence.*

ACTIVITY *Give three reasons why it is very important that children of alcoholics or other addicts get help for themselves.*

h t l nk

abstinence For more information on abstinence and strategies for abstaining from harmful behaviors, see Chapter 21, page 484.

h t l nk

support group For more information on the benefits of a support group, see Chapter 9, page 227.

Support Groups

A support group is a group of people who share a common problem and work together to help one another and themselves cope with and recover from that problem. Regular attendance at such support groups is the most popular form of ongoing treatment for addictions. Support groups such as Alcoholics Anonymous (AA) have played a major role in helping people to become and stay alcohol- and drug-free. At meetings, which are held frequently all over the world, members provide support and help one another stay sober or otherwise drug-free. Such meetings are confidential—members can remain anonymous because no one has to give his or her last name—and also free of charge. Each AA office can direct people to local AA meetings or to other support groups such as Narcotics Anonymous or Cocaine Anonymous.

Alcohol and Drug Treatment Centers

Alcohol and drug treatment centers offer a wide range of services to addicts who want to recover. Many centers specialize in treating teens with addictions or have special units solely for adolescents.

Some treatment centers are privately owned, but there are also state and community alcoholism and mental health clinics that offer professional care at little or no cost. Since drug and alcohol dependence are considered diseases, some health insurance plans may cover at least some of the costs.

DETOX UNITS

In some hospitals or treatment centers, there are medical detox units for alcoholics and addicts undergoing the detoxification process. During this process, the person is under a doctor's care and may be given some medication to ease the symptoms of withdrawal. Some people go directly from detox to ongoing involvement in a support group.

INPATIENT OR RESIDENTIAL TREATMENT CENTERS

Inpatient treatment is *medical and psychological care during which a person stays at a medical or rehabilitation facility.* Inpatient centers offer peaceful time and attractive surroundings away from the person's usual environment so that full concentration on recovery can take place. The first

▼ *Recovery from addiction can mean new hope and happiness for every member of the family.*

ACTIVITY *List some of the short-term and long-term effects of recovery on the family.*

few days are spent in detox. After that, people spend a month or more taking part in drug and alcohol education, individual and group counseling, and support group meetings.

OUTPATIENT TREATMENT CENTERS

Outpatient treatment is *on-site medical and psychological care for a person trying to become alcohol-free and drug-free.* Outpatient programs often allow the recovering person to go to work or school and to live at home during the treatment process. It is less expensive than inpatient treatment, but it takes place over a longer period of time.

CONTINUING PROGRAMS

Many rehabilitation centers have long-term programs of counseling and support for people in recovery who have gone through their standard short-term treatment programs. These programs usually involve follow-up sessions, individual and group counseling, and counseling that involves the entire family in the recovery process.

HALFWAY HOUSES

Halfway houses are *continuing care facilities that offer people housing, counseling, and support meetings as they are recovering from a severe addiction.* People are generally admitted to halfway houses only after having completed at least a 28-day program of recovery at a treatment center. They stay for six months to a year as they learn coping and living skills they will need when they return to society. Residents are also sometimes channeled into vocational rehabilitation or job training programs.

Did You Know?

➤ People in recovery sometimes develop transfer addictions. That means they go from being addicted to one substance to being addicted to another substance or behavior. For example, recovering alcoholics sometimes develop eating disorders or become compulsive gamblers.

➤ People in recovery do not concentrate on the fact that they will have to live a lifetime without drugs. Instead, they talk about staying sober or clean one day at a time.

LESSON 1 *Review*

Reviewing Facts and Vocabulary

1. In what ways is addiction both a physical and psychological disease?
2. For what reasons do people in recovery describe themselves as *recovering* instead of *recovered?*
3. Outline some of the treatment choices for an alcoholic who wants to recover.

Thinking Critically

4. *Synthesizing.* What explanations can you give for why some people become addicts and some people do not?
5. *Comparing and Contrasting.* Explore the similarities and differences between inpatient and outpatient treatment centers.

6. *Evaluating.* What would be your impression of a recovery program that focused only on physical detoxification?

Applying Health Skills

7. *In Your School.* Evaluate the current services available for someone with a smoking, drinking, or other drug problem in your school. Consider such factors as accessibility, confidentiality, the competency of providers, types of services, and cost. Share the above, along with any other information you can gather, in a brochure to be distributed to students in your school.

Recovering from Codependency

 Addiction is like a fire raging out of control. It extends beyond the addict, sometimes spreading to those in his or her life. In many cases, these people fan the flames of addiction, ultimately becoming part of the problem rather than part of the solution.

HEALTH TERMS

codependent

enabling

Al-Anon

detachment

Alateen

HEALTH CONCEPTS

- Codependency is a problem that occurs when those in an addict's life become part of the problem rather than part of the solution.
- In efforts to help the addict, codependents actually make the problem worse.
- The codependent did not cause the addiction and cannot cure it, but he or she can get help whether or not the addict decides to get well.

Common Traits of Codependents

*P*eople who become overly concerned with another's addiction problem and feel driven to fix or control it are called **codependents**, or "co-addicts." Though each person who exhibits codependent behavior does so in a unique way, codependents have many traits in common. Typically such people:

- feel lost, bored, or bad about themselves when not rescuing someone in trouble.
- feel responsible for other people's feelings, actions, and happiness.
- have difficulty having fun, relaxing, or taking good care of themselves.

- constantly seek others' approval.
- do not meet their own needs and may not even know what their own needs are.

This much is for sure. Whatever behaviors or emotions they may exhibit on the outside, the spouses, children, and close friends of the addict suffer terribly and often in silence.

What Codependency Is Not

Codependent people are not physically addicted to a drug the way an addict is. Though codependency is often referred to as an addiction, it is neither an addiction nor a disease in the physical sense. It is, instead, a very damaging emotional and social preoccupation, or obsession, which often can have physical consequences. This type of obsession is different from drug addiction.

Codependents can suffer from a variety of stress-related mental or physical disorders, from depression and eating disorders to high blood pressure and digestive disorders. They may also be at increased risk for addictions.

Enabling: Hurting by Helping

One of the most common traits of codependency is enabling. **Enabling** means *trying to protect the person having trouble with alcohol or drugs from facing the consequences of his or her drug-related problems.* Codependent people enable an addict in many ways, including lying or covering up for the addict's mistakes; lending money, which may be used to purchase more drugs or alcohol; making excuses for him or her being late, absent, or irresponsible; doing the person's homework or other work for the addict; or trying to deflect attention from the person's addiction or bad behavior through humor, understatement, diverting attention, or denial.

What many people do not realize is that enabling is not healthful caring. Such actions do not help the addict. They just make it more comfortable and possible for the alcoholic or addict to keep on drinking or using drugs. In this way, enabling may actually help the addict to become more sick.

▲ *Individuals who care about one another sometimes find themselves caught in the circle of codependency.*

Addiction as a Family Problem

In a family where there is alcoholism or other drug dependence, both addicts and codependent family members are hurting and need help. That is why alcoholism and drug dependence are sometimes referred to as *family diseases*. They affect everyone in the family.

People in a family with drug or alcohol dependency may experience shame, fear, disappointment, guilt, and anger. They are embarrassed to admit these feelings, not realizing that millions of other families suffer from the effects of drug dependency.

Families Dealing with Addiction

In a healthful **family system**, rules are flexible and members play many roles based on changing situations and needs. When someone in a family has a drug dependency, other members of the family must learn to cope with the addict's problems. Some individuals tend to act out roles to deal with the situation.

Different people react in different ways. They adjust their needs, emotions, and behaviors to the unhealthy demands, behaviors, and emotions of the addicted person. In the process they also become unhealthy.

The Codependency Continuum

As a family member's alcoholism or addiction progresses, his or her family's codependency becomes more complex. Some family members may become overly involved in others' problems, taking the

h⬤tl⬤nk

family system For more information on the family system and ways of maintaining its health, see Chapter 12, page 276.

Making Responsible Decisions

When Help Is Needed

Lately, Pete's best friend Carmine has been unusually quiet and withdrawn. At first Carmine refused to tell Pete what was wrong, but yesterday he finally blurted out, "It's my dad. He lost his job and has been drinking a lot." Pete really cares about Carmine and would like to help his friend get his life straightened out. Yet, when he asked Carmine what he could do, his friend angrily snapped, "Nothing! It's none of your business!" Pete has never seen Carmine act like this. What can he do to help?

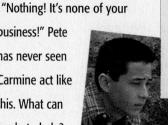

What Would You Do?

Apply the six steps of the decision-making process to Pete's problem.

1. **State the situation.**
2. **List the options.**
3. **Weigh the possible outcomes.**
4. **Consider your values.**
5. **Make a decision and act.**
6. **Evaluate the decision.**

focus off themselves. Other family members may simply withdraw. In either case, family members put their lives on hold hoping the addiction will go away, but it does not. In turn, they may demonstrate unhealthful behaviors. Like the alcoholic or addict, they may also be in denial, not realizing or being able to admit just how bad things at home have become.

However, there is good news and hope for all families with addiction. There are many ways for families with chemical dependency to get help.

Recovering from Codependency

Just as addiction is not hopeless, neither is codependency. The downward slide into codependency can be turned around and changed into a process of recovery. Like recovery from chemical dependency, recovery from codependency takes time and effort. Different people may recover at different speeds and in different ways. Regardless of the timetable for recovery, the personal and family rewards can be great.

Recovery from Codependency

THE UPWARD CLIMB

A codependent's recovery might progress like this as the person:

- Hits an emotional bottom as a result of involvement with someone else's addiction
- Desires and goes for help
- Gets educated about the diseases of addiction
- Accepts the disease concept and his or her part in the disease
- Stops trying to control others, including the addict
- Focuses on self instead of the addict
- Begins to pay attention to personal appearance
- Experiences improvement in own physical, mental, and social health
- Rebuilds self-esteem
- Helps family become more flexible; aids in the process of redefining roles
- Continues to attend support group meetings, helping other codependents and self
- Takes full responsibility for his or her own life

Strategies for Getting Well

There are many ways that a person from a family with addiction as well as the addicted family member can get help. The first step is to admit that there is a problem. The next step is to reach outside the family system for help. This can seem like an impossibility to many people, since families of active alcoholics and drug addicts usually have lived by three unspoken rules: "Don't talk, don't trust, don't feel."

Reaching outside the family for the first time can feel like a betrayal. However, it is a healthy step to take, and a sense of relief often results. Whatever the risks are in seeking outside help, not seeking it holds greater risks. Continuing to adapt to an unhealthy family system can be far more damaging to everyone involved.

Sometimes only one person in a chemically dependent family seeks and gets outside help. Because of this, that person may feel very lonely. When everyone in the family seeks help and assumes responsibility for his or her own role in the family, recovery can occur more quickly.

hotlink

psychiatrist For more information on the services provided by the mental health care professionals known as psychiatrists, see Chapter 10, page 249.

psychologist For more information on the services provided by the mental health care professionals known as psychologists, see Chapter 10, page 250.

social worker For more information on the services provided by the mental health care professionals known as social workers, see Chapter 10, page 251.

Counseling

Many codependents need professional care. Individual and group counseling may be available with a **psychiatrist**, **psychologist**, **social worker**, or therapist trained in chemical dependency and codependency. Family therapy is often recommended and may help the family even if the alcoholic or addict refuses to participate.

Support Groups

There are many support groups for people involved in the lives of alcoholics and other drug addicts. The most widely known of these groups is Al-Anon. Structured similarly to Alcoholics Anonymous, **Al-Anon** is *a worldwide self-help organization for people who are close to alcoholics.* It welcomes family members and friends of alcoholics. It is open to the codependent whether or not the chemically dependent person decides to get well. Like AA meetings, Al-Anon meetings offer a support system for coping and a structured program for regaining emotional and social health. The program encourages **detachment—** *the process of pulling back or separating from involvement with someone else's addiction and refusing to let that addiction rule one's life any longer.* Al-Anon meetings are free, and what is said at the meetings remains confidential.

Building Health Skills

Obtaining Help: Helping Someone Who Needs Help

SOMETIMES, GETTING A PERSON you care about to make that first call for help can be the most important step you can take to aid in the recovery process. If someone you know needs help, consider guiding them to the following resources:

1. Talk to people. Encourage the person to talk with a parent, teacher, coach, clergy person, or a trusted adult.

2. Locate support groups. Look in the phone book under Alcoholics Anonymous, Cocaine Anonymous, or Narcotics Anonymous. The local AA office or volunteer phone counselor can help you or your friend find help.

3. Investigate medical facilities. Have the person call his or her family physician or a local hospital or medical center. If there is no drug or alcohol treatment program on-site, they may be able to direct you to the nearest facility.

4. Contact information-giving organizations. If all other efforts fail, you or the person you're trying to help can contact a reputable information source, such as the National Council on Alcoholism and Drug Dependence; the National Clearinghouse for Alcohol and Drug Information; or Partnership for a Drug-Free America.

Other support groups such as Codependents Anonymous, the National Association for Adult Children of Alcoholics, the National Association for Children of Alcoholics, and Children of Alcoholics offer information and support at both national and local levels.

An offshoot of Al-Anon, **Alateen** is *a support program for people ages 12 to 20 whose parents, other family members, or friends have drinking problems.* Like Al-Anon, Alateen's members come together to share their experiences and discuss how the addiction of someone close to them has affected their lives and how they can cope and recover. Information about Al-Anon and Alateen can be found by calling the local Al-Anon office listed in the phone book. Other similar programs such as Nar-Anon and Coc-Anon are available to help families and close friends of narcotics and cocaine addicts.

◄ *Teens do not have to face problems alone when dealing with a friend or family member who has an addiction.*

ACTIVITY *List people you can turn to and support groups such as Alateen where teens can go for support.*

LESSON 2 *Review*

Reviewing Facts and Vocabulary

1. Define *codependent* and list some of the common traits of codependents.
2. Give three examples of enabling behavior.
3. List three places where the family of an addict or alcoholic might turn to get treatment information for the addict and help for themselves.

Thinking Critically

4. *Comparing and Contrasting.* In what ways are addiction and codependency similar? In what ways are they different?

5. *Analyzing.* What factors make it possible for the codependent person to recover even if the alcoholic or addict in his or her life does not?

Applying Health Skills

6. *In Your Home and School.* Think about times in your life you have enabled a family member or friend in an unhealthful way. List three other, more healthful ways that you might have dealt with the situation and how these alternative behaviors might have benefited both you and the other person.

Health Skills Activities

Activity 1 — Helping a Friend Overcome Addiction

Convincing someone you know to seek assistance for drug use can be tough. Yet, it could also save this person's life. What would you say and do to help a friend overcome addition?

Directions

1. Working in a group of at least five, list ways to approach an individual who has an addictive problem with a drug. Think of as many strategies as you can to help this person change his or her behavior and get help.
2. Write down the potential negative consequences of each strategy.
3. Decide what would be the best strategy to employ. Write down why you believe this would be the best method.
4. Write a brief report detailing your group's recommendations and reasons. Present your report to the class.

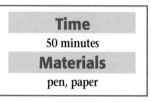

Time
50 minutes
Materials
pen, paper

Self-Assessment

✓ Showed evidence that several realistic strategies and negative consequences were considered.
✓ Gave support of intervention strategy chosen.

Activity 2 — Intervention Public Service Announcement (PSA)

Structured interventions are often a first step toward convincing a drug-addicted individual to seek help. Unfortunately, many people do not know what an intervention is or how effective it can be. How would you describe an intervention?

Directions

1. In a group, review the information on interventions on pages 604-605.
2. Try to reach an agreement on what the essential elements of an intervention are. For example, the more key people who are involved, the less likely it is that the drug-addicted person can make excuses for his or her actions.
3. Discuss how this information could be woven into a 1- or 2-minute PSA for the general public.
4. Compose your intervention PSA.
5. Read your group's PSA to the class.

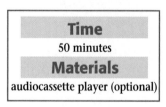

Time
50 minutes
Materials
audiocassette player (optional)

Self-Assessment

✓ Accurately described elements of an intervention.
✓ Indicated at least three benefits of an intervention and persuasively communicated this in PSA.

Your Brain and Drugs

How do drugs actually work in the brain? Why do some people become addicts? These are just two of the questions researchers hope to answer using complex new technology.

A scanning camera and a cyclotron are the essential components of the brain imaging center. The cyclotron produces radioactive tracers that can follow brain activity. Scientists can use this device to gain a clear picture of which parts of the brain are active.

Researchers hope that this new center will help them understand how drug use damages and changes people's brains. They already know that drugs like cocaine and heroin reduce brain activity. Soon they will have more answers about the terrible toll of drug use.

Play the Video

DRUG ABUSER GREATER ACT ORBITOFRONTA

Control

Think About It

- Do you think the brains of people who are addicted to drugs have anything in common? Why or why not?

- How does this research emphasize the dangers of using illegal drugs? Tell how you could use information from this report to persuade a friend not to use drugs.

Using Health Terms

On a separate sheet of paper, write the term that best matches each definition below.

LESSON 1

1. Slips from recovery, or periodic returns to drinking and drug use.
2. Learning to live an alcohol-free or drug-free life.
3. Interruption of the addiction continuum before the addict or alcoholic hits bottom.
4. The removal of all drugs from the body.
5. Medical and psychological care during which a person stays at a medical or rehabilitation facility.
6. On-site medical and psychological care for a person trying to become alcohol-free and drug-free.
7. Continuing care facilities that offer people housing, counseling, and support meetings.

LESSON 2

8. A worldwide self-help organization for people who are close to alcoholics.
9. The process of pulling back or separating from involvement with someone else's addiction and refusing to let that addiction rule one's life any longer.
10. Trying to protect the person having trouble with alcohol or drugs from facing the consequences of his or her drug-related problems.
11. People who become overly concerned with another's addiction problem and feel driven to fix or control it.
12. A support program for people ages 12 to 20 whose parents, other family members, or friends have drinking problems.

Recalling the Facts

Using complete sentences, answer the following questions.

LESSON 1

1. Describe the addiction continuum and how it varies for different people.
2. How long does it take for one to become addicted?
3. What factors might contribute to addiction?
4. What is intervention, and how does it work?
5. What is meant by the statement "Recovery is a process"?
6. Why do experts on addiction recommend total abstinence for the alcoholic or drug addict?
7. What happens at a detoxification unit?

8. Besides regaining physical health, what factors are involved in an addict's recovery?
9. What is a halfway house? How does the facility help in the treatment of the addict?

LESSON 2

10. Name and describe three roles a codependent might play in a family with addiction.
11. List some emotions people in a family living with an addict might experience.
12. How might being a codependent adversely affect a person's physical and mental health?
13. What part might a family play in an addict's recovery program?
14. Describe some of the functions of Al-Anon and Alateen.

Thinking Critically

LESSON 1

1. ***Comparing and Contrasting.*** What factors might be responsible for one person becoming an addict and another not?
2. ***Evaluating.*** Cigarette ads were banned from television in the 1970s. Do you think ads for alcohol should be banned? Support your answer.
3. ***Analyzing.*** Some say that addiction is a social disease. What is the thinking behind this statement?

LESSON 2

4. ***Evaluating.*** Years ago, people often hid the problem of addiction within a family and suffered in silence. How are things beginning to change? What do you think is causing the change? How is this change for the better?
5. ***Comparing and Contrasting.*** Describe similarities and differences in the recovery process from alcoholism and from codependency.

Making the Connection

1. ***Language Arts.*** In the past, newspaper obituaries often did not specify, or point out specifically, that a person died from drug addiction, drug or alcohol overdose, or alcoholism. Often just the phrase "heart failure" was given as the cause of death. Write an editorial column expressing your viewpoint on this practice.

2. ***Social Studies.*** Using library resources, learn about residential treatment centers and their origins in the 1950s. Investigate the types of health professionals who staffed such facilities in the early days and what methods they used. Explain changes that have been made since, as well as factors that have prompted reforms.

BEYOND THE CLASSROOM

PARENTAL INVOLVEMENT In recent years, programs have been developed encouraging young people not to get started using alcohol or drugs. Make some collective judgments about the effectiveness of these programs, emphasizing how your parents feel about them.

COMMUNITY INVOLVEMENT Research two support groups for addicts and codependents within your community. Interview a facilitator or member from each group to learn all you can about the program. If no group presently exists, research the need for such a group in your area and ways to go about getting one started.

SCHOOL-TO-CAREER

Exploring Careers. Invite a certified drug or alcoholism counselor to your class. In advance, prepare questions asking about kinds of education and training required. Ask about how a person gets certified and what he or she must do to keep that certification up to date. Ask what drew the person to this field of work in the first place and what its rewards and frustrations are. Ask him or her to tell one anonymous and unidentifiable story of hope about an addict, alcoholic, or codependent with whom he or she has successfully worked.

CHAPTER 28

Infectious Diseases

HEALTH Online

PRACTICING HEALTHFUL BEHAVIORS

Get information on "Hepatitis B on the Rise." Find out how this infectious disease can be avoided and how you can protect yourself in the article in Health Updates at **health.glencoe.com**.

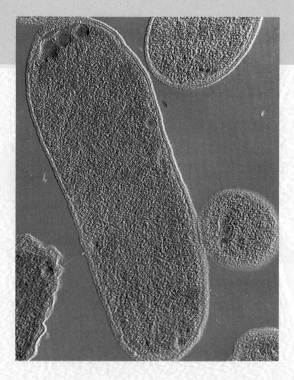

Personal Health Inventory

Self-Inventory Write the numbers 1–10 on a sheet of paper. Read each statement below and respond by writing *yes*, *no*, or *sometimes* for each item. Write a *yes* only for items that you practice regularly. Save your responses.

1	I keep my immunizations up to date.
2	I avoid contact with people who currently have a cold or the flu.
3	I bathe or shower every day.
4	I wash my hands after using the bathroom, before preparing or serving food, and before meals.
5	I practice good nutrition.
6	I get at least eight hours of sleep each night.
7	I do not share eating utensils or glasses with other people.
8	I avoid eating foods—especially dairy products and poultry—that might not have been refrigerated.
9	I cover my mouth when I cough or sneeze.
10	I stay home at least the first day that I have the symptoms of an illness.

Follow-up After completing the chapter, retake this self-inventory. Pick two items that you need to work on and set a goal to improve your health behaviors.

> 66 ***Prosperous nations must work in partnership with developing nations to help remove the cloud of disease from our world's future.*** 99

—GEORGE W. BUSH
PRESIDENT OF THE UNITED STATES, 2001

Quick Write List three health behaviors you practice to protect yourself against infections or to prevent spreading infections to others.

What Causes Infectious Diseases?

When you catch a cold, you may sneeze, cough, and run a fever. You probably feel discomfort but do not think of yourself as having a disease. Yet, the common cold is a type of disease. More specifically, it is an **infectious disease,** *a disease caused by organisms that enter and multiply within the human body.*

HEALTH TERMS

infectious disease

parasites

virus

transmission

immunity

mucous membranes

phagocytosis

neutrophils

antibodies

HEALTH CONCEPTS

- Infectious diseases are caused by tiny organisms called *pathogens.*
- Infectious diseases are transmitted, or spread, through contact with a person, an animal, a contaminated object, or the environment at large.
- The body offers several layers of protection against infection by pathogens.
- You can take measures to maintain the health of your immune system.

Protozoan

Causes of Infectious Diseases

Every infectious disease is caused by one of several types of small, microscopic organisms (microorganisms) known as *pathogens.* Pathogens invade the body and attack its cells and tissues. Most pathogens are **parasites,** *organisms that live in or on another organism and derive nourishment from it.* Among the forms pathogens can take are bacteria, viruses, rickettsias (rik-ET-see-uhs), protozoans, and fungi.

Bacteria

A bacterium is a single-celled microorganism. Bacteria can live almost anywhere. They are abundant in the air, soil, and water. Some bacteria produce poisons that are harmful to human cells. If there are enough bacteria and the person is not immune, disease results.

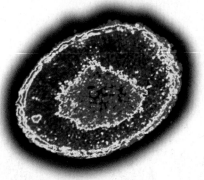

E. coli bacterium

Most diseases caused by bacteria begin when microorganisms not usually present in the body invade it. When bacteria enter the body, they multiply at a rapid rate through cell division. If conditions are perfect—the right temperature and sufficient nourishment—division can take place every 20 minutes. After just 15½ hours, one bacterium can have multiplied into more than 4 billion bacteria! This rarely happens, however. In a healthy individual, the body's immune system destroys the invading bacteria. Also, perfect conditions rarely occur.

Viruses

A **virus** is *the smallest known type of infectious agent.* Viruses are about one-half to one-hundredth the size of the smallest bacterium. These organisms are also one of our worst enemies. One of the deadliest viruses known today is **HIV**, the virus that causes AIDS.

Viruses are not living cells. They consist of an inner core of genetic material surrounded by a protective protein shell and are entirely dependent on living cells for survival and reproduction. Viruses invade all known forms of life—mammals, birds, reptiles, insects, plants, and even bacteria. Viruses are highly specific in the kinds of cells they invade. Only certain viruses invade animal cells, and these viruses can attack only specific types of cells.

When a virus enters the body, it attaches itself to a cell—called the *host*—and injects its genetic material into that cell. The virus then makes copies of itself, using materials within the host cell. The copies then spread to other body cells, where the process is repeated. Viruses usually run their course and are eventually killed by the immune system.

Rickettsias

Rickettsias are organisms that resemble small bacteria but, like viruses, are able to multiply only by invading the cells of another life form. Most rickettsias are found in the intestinal tracts of insects—notably fleas—as well as in mice, ticks, and mites. Rickettsias are passed on to human and animal hosts through bites or through feces deposited on the skin. Human diseases caused by rickettsias include typhus, mentioned in the chapter-opening paragraph, and Rocky Mountain spotted fever.

Protozoans

Protozoans are single-celled organisms that are larger than bacteria and have a more complex cell structure. Most protozoans are harmless, but about 30 different types cause disease in humans. Disease-producing protozoans are most common in tropical areas that have poor sanitation.

h⊙t link

HIV For more information on HIV, the virus that causes AIDS, see Chapter 30, page 656.

▼ *The smallest forms of life on earth, these microorganisms can be the most threatening to your health.*

ACTIVITY *Describe the differences that you see among the microorganisms on these pages.*

Ebola Zaire virus

Protozoan

Fungi

Fungi are simple organisms that cannot make their own food. Many are *saprophytes* (SAP-ruh-fyts)—organisms that feed off dead animals, insects, and leaves. Fungi prefer dark, damp environments. The most common disease-causing fungi invade mainly deep tissues of the hair, nails, and skin and cause infections of the scalp or feet, such as ringworm and athlete's foot.

How Infectious Diseases Are Spread

There are several well-defined means of **transmission**, or *spread,* of infectious pathogens. Transmission can occur through direct contact with an infected person, an animal, or a contaminated object. Some pathogens can also reside in the environment at large.

People

Many infectious diseases are spread as a result of direct or indirect contact with an infected person.

■ **Direct Contact.** Pathogens may be spread when an uninfected person comes into physical contact with an infected person. Sexually transmitted diseases are spread in this way. The human

Building Health Skills

Goal Setting: Reducing Infectious Disease Risk

SOME OF THE COMMON bacteria associated with food poisoning are *Salmonella, Staphylococcus aureus,* and *Clostridium perfringens.* Although home kitchens are breeding grounds for these potentially life-threatening microorganisms, the risk of infection exists outside the home as well. There are precautions you as a health-literate consumer can take to protect yourself. Exercise care when:

1. **Eating out.** Avoid restaurants that do not look clean or that you think might not practice safe cooking and food storage procedures. Refuse any food that does not smell right or tastes bad.

2. **Cooking out.** If you are camping or planning a cookout at the beach or park, remember to keep all perishable foods chilled. Cook meats thoroughly and place them on a clean platter, not one that held raw meat.

3. **Buying prepared foods.** Although you might expect fresh-cut deli meats, mayonnaise-based salads, and other such foods to be free of bacteria, they are not always. Many local newspapers publish lists of food sellers that fail to pass periodic health inspections. Learn to consult such lists from time to time, and avoid establishments that "make the list."

bite is another, and especially dangerous, mode of transmission. A pregnant woman may also transmit an infection to her unborn child.

- **Indirect Contact.** Both bacteria and viruses can enter the body through the lungs if droplets—exhaled, coughed, or sneezed out by an infected person—are inhaled. The common cold, influenza, and tuberculosis are spread in this way.

Animals

Animals, including insects, spread many infectious diseases. The bite of an infected dog or other animal can spread rabies, a disease that can be fatal. When a bloodsucking insect, such as a mosquito, ingests blood from an infected person or animal, the insect may take pathogens into its own body. When the insect later takes blood from an uninfected person, it injects some of the pathogens into that person's body, thus spreading the disease. Malaria and dengue fever, infectious diseases common to tropical regions, are spread in this fashion.

Contaminated Objects

Certain pathogens are spread when an uninfected person touches objects that an infected person has used. These objects can include eating utensils, glasses, or toothbrushes. They also include needles used to inject drugs that are shared with another person.

The Environment

Food, water, soil, and even the air we breathe contain potentially harmful pathogens. Some forms of infectious disease are the direct result of human negligence, such as the careless disposal of infectious waste materials from hospitals, which constitutes a form of toxic dumping. This form of pollution can be deadly. Yet another way in which pathogens in the environment are spread is through the careless handling of food, which is a main source of food poisoning.

▲ *Diseases are often spread through contact with contaminated objects such as eating utensils and even pens and pencils.*

ACTIVITY *Name ways the items pictured should be handled to prevent the spread of diseases.*

Common (Cold) Sense

Colds, though they are minor inconveniences for most people other than those with chronic respiratory conditions, are nothing to sneeze at. Colds are caused by any number of viruses, all of which, like the deadly HIV, continue to change their genetic "fingerprint" as they move from host to host. This is why a cure for the common cold has never been discovered.

When you experience symptoms of a cold—mild fever, sneezing, runny nose—treat it as the disease it is. Be sure to

➤ get plenty of rest.

➤ drink plenty of fluids.

➤ maintain proper nutrition.

Keeping your body healthy will also make it more resistant to infection, possibly reducing the number of colds you get. Again, good nutrition, combined with regular physical activity and adequate rest, is the cornerstone of a prevention plan. Controlling stress levels and not smoking are other steps a person can take.

hot link

cilia For more information on the role cilia play in resisting infection, see Chapter 17, page 402.

How Your Body Defends Against Infectious Disease

Pathogens are everywhere in numbers beyond comprehension. If they are so widespread, why are we not constantly sick? This question can be answered in one word: *immunity*. **Immunity** is *the body's natural defenses against infection.*

The Immune Response

Although you cannot see them, your body is exposed each day to millions of pathogens. Pathogens are in the air you breathe, and they cling to the surfaces you touch. Your body is constantly fighting pathogens that enter it. When they enter your body, pathogens attack your body cells and use these cells to grow and multiply. The end result of such an attack is an infection.

Most of the time, your body manages to stay free of infection because of your immune system. Your immune system includes two main types of defenses. The *innate immune system*—your inborn defenses—provides nonspecific resistance. The *adaptive immune system* provides specific resistance. Both types work together to protect your body against pathogens that could harm you.

Nonspecific Resistance

Each of us has lines of inborn, nonspecific—or "general"—defenses against infection. Body defenses that are nonspecific respond in the same way each time your body is invaded by a foreign substance. Your body's nonspecific defenses include physical and chemical barriers, body cells, and the inflammatory response.

■ **Physical Barriers.** Your body's first line of defense against invading pathogens consists of physical barriers, the main barrier being your skin. Unbroken skin helps prevent pathogens from entering body tissues. The tough dead cells that make up the outer layer of skin form an effective barrier. **Mucous membranes**—*the soft, skinlike lining of many parts of the body*—in your mouth, nose, and bronchial tubes produce a sticky substance called *mucus* that traps pathogens. Some mucous membranes have **cilia**, tiny hairs, that also trap pathogens, which are then expelled when you cough or sneeze.

■ **Chemical Barriers.** Enzymes in tears and saliva are chemical barriers that can destroy bacteria. The acidic digestive juices of the stomach are also chemical barriers. These juices destroy pathogens that are swallowed with food. Other chemicals cause body changes that help cells inside the body fight pathogens.

■ **Body Cells.** Once pathogens reach your bloodstream, certain types of white blood cells, called *phagocytes,* travel through the blood and group together to destroy them. *The process by which* *phagocytes engulf and destroy pathogens* is called **phagocytosis** (FAG-uh-suh-TOH-suhs). **Neutrophils** (NOO-truh-filz) are *the chief type of phagocyte involved in the process of phagocytosis.*

■ **Inflammatory Response.** If pathogens break through the body's outermost barriers, your body then goes into a "red alert" stage known as the *inflammatory response.* Chemical mediators are released that cause the blood vessels to dilate and allow increased blood flow. This permits phagocytes to leave the blood and enter the body tissues. This process continues until the pathogens are destroyed. Once the pathogens are destroyed, tissues can be repaired. Symptoms of inflammation confined to a specific area include heat, redness, and swelling, which result from increased blood flow.

Specific Resistance

The general response of your nonspecific defenses is not always enough to protect your body from disease. The adaptive immune system mounts specific attacks against particular types of pathogens. When this happens, another body defense goes to work in the form of cells called *lymphocytes.*

Health
Online

Examine microscopic images and learn about the cell activities of streptococcus and other infectious diseases. At **health.glencoe.com** link to animations that show how the body defends itself against infectious diseases.

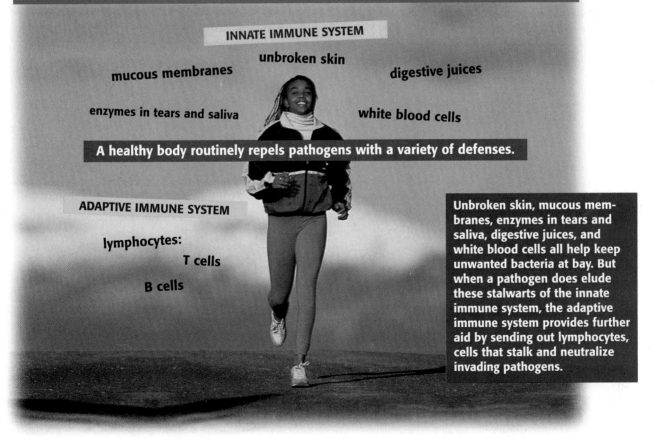

THE BODY'S BARRIERS AGAINST DISEASE

INNATE IMMUNE SYSTEM

unbroken skin

mucous membranes

digestive juices

enzymes in tears and saliva

white blood cells

A healthy body routinely repels pathogens with a variety of defenses.

ADAPTIVE IMMUNE SYSTEM

lymphocytes:

T cells

B cells

Unbroken skin, mucous membranes, enzymes in tears and saliva, digestive juices, and white blood cells all help keep unwanted bacteria at bay. But when a pathogen does elude these stalwarts of the innate immune system, the adaptive immune system provides further aid by sending out lymphocytes, cells that stalk and neutralize invading pathogens.

hot link

lymphatic system For more information on the lymphatic system and its other functions, see Chapter 17, page 394.

LYMPHOCYTES

Lymphocytes are a type of white blood cell that fights pathogens. Lymphocytes travel through your body along two networks of vessels. One of these networks is your blood vessels. The other network is your lymph vessels, which are a part of your **lymphatic system**. There are two main types of lymphocytes—B cells and T cells.

- **B Cells.** When B cells encounter pathogens, they are stimulated to enlarge and multiply. The B cells turn into cells called *plasma cells,* which in turn produce **antibodies**—*proteins that destroy or neutralize invading pathogens.* The antibodies for a particular pathogen remain in your blood to become active if you encounter the specific pathogen again.

- **T Cells.** There are two main groups of T cells—killer cells and helper cells. Killer T cells are stimulated to multiply by the presence of abnormal body cells. They attach to these cells and release toxins that help destroy the abnormal cells. Helper T cells aid the activity of the B cells and killer T cells and control other aspects of the body's immune system.

Care of the Immune Response

The ability of your immune system to fight off invading pathogens varies, depending on a number of preventive factors. Perhaps the most important is good nutrition. When you fail to take in adequate nutrients, you can jeopardize your immune system. This is one reason poorly planned weight-loss programs can make a person ill. Overexposure to **ultraviolet rays** also affects your immune response.

hot link

ultraviolet rays For more information on protecting yourself against the sun's ultraviolet rays, see Chapter 7, page 163.

LESSON 1 Review

Reviewing Facts and Vocabulary

1. Use the terms *infectious disease* and *antibodies* in a paragraph.
2. In what ways can direct contact with an animal spread disease?
3. List the body's nonspecific defenses.

Thinking Critically

4. ***Comparing and Contrasting.*** Tell how viruses are different and more difficult to deal with than other pathogens.
5. ***Analyzing.*** Explain why the presence of antibodies is often used to determine whether an individual has an infectious disease.

6. ***Synthesizing.*** Explain the factors that would cause one person to have a healthy immune system and another person not to have one.

Applying Health Skills

7. ***In Your Home and School.*** Contact a local veterinarian to find out about parasites such as fleas and ticks that affect pets. How do these insects function? What problems or illnesses can they cause to pets or people? What steps can a pet owner take to prevent problems associated with fleas and ticks? Share your findings with your class and your family.

Common Infectious Diseases

Some 40 types of infectious disease, including the common cold and the flu, commonly occur in the United States. Many of them are preventable or can be treated with medication. In this lesson, you will learn about some of these diseases, their causes and symptoms, and how to treat them.

HEALTH TERMS

pneumonia
tuberculosis (TB)
strep throat
vaccine
immunization
rubella

HEALTH CONCEPTS

- New cases of infectious diseases once believed to be stamped out are recurring.
- Although some infectious diseases are better understood than others, all have a well-defined course of treatment that includes rest.

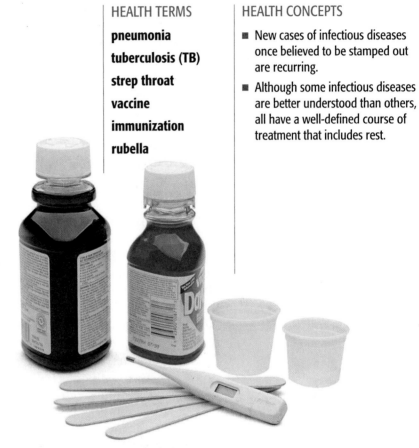

Respiratory Infections

Respiratory tract infections are infections of the breathing passages, which range from the nose to the alveoli of the lungs. Most of these illnesses are caused by viruses or bacteria.

Common Cold

The common cold is a viral infection that causes inflammation of the mucous membranes lining the nose and throat. Its symptoms include a stuffy, runny nose, sneezing, and sometimes a sore throat and headache. Most colds are contracted by breathing in virus-containing droplets that have been sneezed or coughed out by an infected person. Another method of transmission is rubbing the eyes or nose with fingers that have picked up the virus by hand-to-hand contact or by handling contaminated objects.

HEALTH Online

"I've got the flu" is a commonly heard complaint, especially during the winter. Links at **health.glencoe.com** provide detailed influenza information, including symptoms and treatments. Identify the three types of influenza viruses.

Most colds clear up within a week or so. There is no cure. The best treatment for a cold is rest, maintaining proper nutrition, and drinking plenty of fluids.

Influenza

Influenza is a viral infection of the respiratory tract. Symptoms of the flu include chills, fever, headache, muscle ache, and weakness. Like the common cold, flu is spread by virus-infected droplets coughed or sneezed into the air by an infected person. Major outbreaks of the flu tend to occur every few years, usually in the winter. Treatment for the flu is the same as for the common cold—rest, proper nutrition, and drinking plenty of fluids. Secondary bacterial infection may accompany the flu, particularly in the elderly and people with lung or heart problems. Flu may then develop into **pneumonia** (noo-MOHN-yuh), *a serious inflammation of the lungs.* Many people die each year from pneumonia. Secondary infections need **antibiotic** treatment.

Tuberculosis

h t link

antibiotic For more information on the antibiotic medicines and their uses, see Chapter 23, page 513.

Tuberculosis (TB) is *a highly contagious bacterial infection that most often affects the lungs.* TB is spread by airborne droplets produced by coughing or sneezing. The bacteria breathed into the lungs then multiply. In the majority of cases, the body's immune system stops the infection and healing takes place. When this does not happen, the infection spreads through the lymphatic system to the lymph nodes. Bacteria may then enter the bloodstream and spread to other parts of the body. In some people, the bacteria become inactive and may stay that way for years. When they are reactivated, damage may occur.

Because TB usually affects the lungs, the main symptoms include coughing (sometimes bringing up blood), chest pain, shortness of breath, fever, sweating, poor appetite, and weight loss. Before the development of antibiotics, TB was a major cause of death in the United States. Modern medicines have proved highly effective in treating the disease. During the 1980s, however, antibiotic-resistant strains of the bacterium that causes TB appeared. This made the standard treatment ineffective, and the incidence of TB began to rise.

Strep Throat

Strep throat is *a bacterial infection of the throat.* It is spread by droplets coughed

▶ **Infections caused by bacteria can be treated with antibiotic medications.**

ACTIVITY *Name as many diseases as you can that are commonly treated with antibiotics.*

or breathed into the air. Symptoms may include a sore throat, fever, a general feeling of illness, and enlarged lymph nodes in the neck. An untreated strep throat infection may lead to serious complications, such as inflammation of the kidneys or rheumatic fever, which can cause permanent heart damage. Strep throat can be cured with antibiotics.

Infectious Diseases of the Nervous System

The nervous system is subject to a variety of infectious diseases. Some of these can have serious consequences if not caught and treated at an early stage.

Encephalitis

Encephalitis is an inflammation of the brain, usually caused by a virus carried by mosquitoes. Encephalitis often starts with a headache and fever. Untreated, it can progress to hallucinations, confusion, paralysis, and disturbances of speech, memory, behavior, and eye movement. There is a gradual loss of consciousness and sometimes coma. If encephalitis is caused by the herpes simplex virus, the antiviral medicine acyclovir may be effective. When the disease is caused by other viral infections, there is no known treatment.

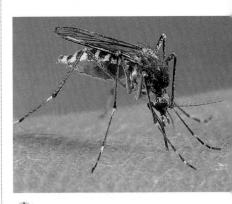

▲ *Certain diseases can be spread through the bite of insects such as a mosquito.*

ACTIVITY *Tell why the protective barrier of your skin is not effective against diseases carried by mosquitos.*

Meningitis

Meningitis is an inflammation of the meninges, the membranes that cover the brain and spinal cord. Viral meningitis is relatively mild, but meningitis caused by bacterial infection is life-threatening. The organisms that cause meningitis usually reach the meninges through the bloodstream from an infection elsewhere in the body. The main symptoms are fever, severe headache, nausea and vomiting, sensitivity to light, and a stiff neck. In viral meningitis, the symptoms may resemble those of the flu. Viral meningitis requires no treatment. Bacterial meningitis is treated with antibiotics.

Poliomyelitis

Poliomyelitis (POHL-ee-oh-my-uh-LY-tuhs), more commonly known as *polio,* is an infectious disease of the central nervous system caused by a virus. In serious cases, the disease may lead to extensive paralysis, including paralysis of the muscles used in breathing, and death. During the mid-1950s, medical researchers Jonas Salk and Albert Sabin, working independently, each developed a polio **vaccine**—*a preparation based on a weakened or dead pathogen that provides immunity by causing the body to produce antibodies to the pathogen.* These new wonder medicines all but eliminated the disease from the United States and Europe. However, the disease has begun to reemerge among people who have not been vaccinated against it.

Measles

Measles is a highly contagious viral disease characterized by fever and a rash that covers the entire body. Measles mainly affects children but can occur at any age. The illness starts with a fever, runny nose, sore eyes, and cough. After three to four days, a red rash appears. The most common complications of measles are ear and chest infections. Prevention of the disease is important, because measles can have rare but serious complications. One of these is encephalitis, which was discussed earlier in this lesson.

Measles was largely eliminated through widespread **immunization,** *a program whereby communities or other large populations are systematically made immune to a disease.* During the 1990s, however, there was a brief rise in incidence of the disease because of a drop in Federal funding for immunization programs.

A viral disease with similar symptoms, **rubella,** or *German measles,* causes only a minor infection in children. However, the disease has serious consequences when it affects a woman in the early months of pregnancy. The virus may infect the fetus and cause a range of severe birth defects.

Mononucleosis

Mononucleosis (mon-oh-noo-klee-OH-sis)—or *mono*—is a viral infection common among young people in their teens. Its symptoms include chills, fever, sore throat, fatigue, and swollen lymph nodes. Mononucleosis spreads primarily through direct contact, which has given it its popular name, "the kissing disease." Once in the body, the virus multiplies in the lymphocytes. When infected with the virus, the lymphocytes change in appearance. Complete bed rest is needed in the care of mono. Treatment and recovery can take three to six weeks.

Hepatitis

Hepatitis is an inflammation of the liver. Toxic hepatitis may be caused by certain drugs, chemicals, or poisons. The most frequent cause of hepatitis is viral infection. The most obvious symptom is jaundice—yellowing of the skin and the whites of the eyes. Other symptoms include fever, nausea, loss of appetite, pain in the abdomen, aching muscles, and sometimes joint pain. In severe cases, hepatitis can result in permanent liver damage. Symptoms usually appear three to four weeks after exposure to the virus and last from two to six weeks. There are three main types of viral hepatitis.

- **Hepatitis A.** Hepatitis A results from eating food or drinking water that has been contaminated with the virus from an infected person's feces. Many cases occur among people who have traveled to areas where standards of hygiene are low.

- **Hepatitis B.** Hepatitis B is found in all body fluids of an infected person, especially blood. Hepatitis B used to be spread mainly by contaminated blood transfusions and blood products. However, tests that detect the virus in the blood have helped eliminate transfusion as a means of transmission. Contaminated medical instruments, sexual contact with an infected person, and hypodermic needles shared by infected drug users are the main ways hepatitis B is spread. Hepatitis B is more serious than hepatitis A. In some cases, the virus may lead to a chronic infection and eventually to liver damage.

- **Hepatitis C.** Like hepatitis B, hepatitis C is spread through infected blood. Discovered in 1989, hepatitis C can cause liver cancer. The virus can be detected in the blood, and blood is now screened before transfusion.

As with most other viral infections, there is no cure for hepatitis, although a vaccine for hepatitis B is now available. The treatment for hepatitis is rest, proper nutrition, and ingesting plenty of fluids.

The best way to treat a cold is also the best way to prevent it—rest, good nutrition, and drinking lots of fluids.

ACTIVITY *Explain why drinking fluids is important when you have a cold or other infectious disease.*

LESSON 2 *Review*

Reviewing Facts and Vocabulary

1. Name four common infectious diseases and the type of pathogen that causes each.
2. In what ways might a person contract viral hepatitis?

Thinking Critically

3. *Analyzing.* How do you think bacteria become resistant to antibiotics?

Applying Health Skills

4. *In Your Home and School.* Take a survey of family members and classmates to determine favorite ways of treating a cold. Use the results to create a bar graph to share at home and in school. What treatments are the most popular? Why?

Preventing Infectious Diseases

Between the years 1347 and 1351, bubonic plague raged through western Europe, killing nearly half the population. In 1918, an outbreak of influenza affected 2 billion people worldwide and killed more than 22 million of them! Medical science has come a long way toward preventing such disasters.

HEALTH TERMS

active immunity

passive immunity

HEALTH CONCEPTS

- Science has developed strategies to help combat infectious diseases.
- Some common sense measures can be used to help prevent the spread of infectious diseases.

Immunity

As noted in Lesson 2, your body creates lines of defenses against disease. Immunity is the body's natural resistance to many pathogens. Certain pathogens cannot live in the body, whereas others are quickly destroyed when they enter the body.

Active Immunity

One important feature of the body's immune system is that it remembers the pathogens it meets. This gives the body long-term protection—immunity—against many infectious diseases. For example, if you had chicken pox, your immune system remembers the chicken pox virus. If the virus enters your system again, cells designed specifically to combat the chicken pox virus will attack it immediately. In most cases, the virus does not get a chance to make you sick again.

This *immunity your body develops to protect you from disease* is called **active immunity.** Some types of immunity last a lifetime. Others last only a short period of time. A single virus causes chicken pox, so once a person has had the disease, the body is usually protected against chicken pox for life. Many different kinds of virus cause the common cold. Because the body is continually exposed to different pathogens, immunity to colds is limited.

Passive Immunity

At birth, babies carry in their blood small amounts of the antibodies that protected their mothers. Babies are thus protected from the same diseases as their mothers. This immunity lasts for a few months after birth until the baby can produce antibodies of its own. *The temporary immunity that an infant acquires from its mother* is called **passive immunity.**

Immunization

Sometimes the body needs help to establish immunity against specific pathogens. This help can come in the form of immunization to give the body the ability to fight off the disease. There are two main types of immunization: passive and active.

Passive Immunization

Passive immunization provides immediate, short-lived protection against specific disease-causing pathogens. Blood is taken from a person (or sometimes an animal) that has been exposed to a specific microorganism. The blood contains antibodies that work against that organism. An extract of the blood is then injected into the person to be protected. If the pathogen is present in the person's blood or enters it within a few days, the antibodies help destroy it.

Active Immunization

Also known as *vaccination,* active immunization involves the introduction into the body of a vaccine. Vaccines provide immunity by causing the body to produce antibodies against the pathogen. Each vaccine contains substances that are strong enough to cause the production of the desired antibodies but not strong enough to cause the disease.

◀ *Researchers are constantly at work to find ways to fight infectious disease. You can also play a role in this.*

ACTIVITY *How can healthy habits and physical activity help you to win the race against the spread of infectious diseases?*

There are three major types of vaccines:

■ **Live-virus vaccines.** These are made from weakened viruses. Scientists develop live-virus vaccines by artificially altering the genetic material of the virus or by infecting laboratory animals over and over until the organisms can no longer cause the disease but can still stimulate the production of antibodies. Measles, rubella, and oral polio vaccines all contain live viruses.

■ **Killed-virus vaccines.** These contain viruses that have been killed. The killed-virus vaccine causes the body to produce antibodies, but it is not as powerful as a live-virus vaccine. Because the vaccine is less powerful, people need booster shots from time to time. Booster shots are follow-up injections given to reinforce the effect of the first injection. Cholera, typhoid fever, rabies, and Salk injected polio vaccines contain killed viruses.

■ **Toxoids.** Some diseases are caused by bacteria that release a toxin. Scientists have discovered that by chemically treating bacteria toxins, they can make very effective vaccines. The treated toxins, called toxoids, stimulate the production of antibodies and establish active immunity against these diseases.

Immunization for All

Immunization is more than just a good idea—the law often requires it. Each state has its own laws governing immunizations and school attendance. In most states, students cannot enter kindergarten without up-to-date immunizations. Several states now enforce laws that prevent teenagers from attending school without complete

Although vaccination may cause reactions ranging from a mild fever or rash to more serious responses, the risks from vaccines are far less than the risks from the diseases themselves.

ACTIVITY *Name as many diseases as you can that children are commonly vaccinated against.*

Making Responsible Decisions

Letting the Team Down

Enrique woke up this morning with a bad cold. He is heavily congested, has a runny nose, and keeps coughing. He knows he should stay home and rest, both for his own sake and to avoid infecting other students.

However, Enrique is a key member of the school's wrestling team. There is an important meet this afternoon with one of their toughest opponents. If Enrique does not compete, his team will lose by default in his weight class. Enrique does not want to let the team down. What should he do?

What Would You Do?

Apply the six steps of the decision-making process to Enrique's problem.

1. **State the situation.**
2. **List the options.**
3. **Weigh the possible outcomes.**
4. **Consider your values.**
5. **Make a decision and act.**
6. **Evaluate the decision.**

immunization. Why do you think immunizations are important in the school setting?

Some infectious diseases are more common than others. Diseases that once were dreaded can now be controlled through immunization, and some have been totally eradicated. However, because some diseases are no longer the threat they used to be, people have become lax in obtaining immunization. Isolated cases of some diseases, such as polio, are being reported. An immunization program is essential to prevent the kinds of plagues and pestilences that wiped out entire populations in the past.

Common Sense Measures

What can you do to protect yourself from being infected by disease? You have several choices. You can avoid contact with pathogens and you can avoid spreading pathogens to others. Follow these common sense guidelines to reduce the spread of infection.

- Keep your body healthy so that it can better resist infection. Good nutrition, regular exercise, adequate sleep, and good health care all contribute to prevention.
- Bathe or shower every day to keep your skin, hair, and nails clean.
- Avoid sharing eating or drinking utensils.
- Store and prepare food in a safe way to prevent food poisoning.
- Wash your hands after using the bathroom, after changing diapers, and before preparing, serving, or eating food.
- If you know you are sick, avoid giving your illness to someone else. Get medical treatment for your illness. Cover your mouth when you cough or sneeze to prevent spreading the pathogens. Use tissues only once and dispose of them in a waste container.
- If you are well, avoid contact with people who are sick.

▲ *Pathogens are expelled into the air when a person coughs or sneezes.*

ACTIVITY *Tell what this person should do to prevent the spread of pathogens.*

Review

Reviewing Facts and Vocabulary

1. Define *active immunity* and *passive immunity.*
2. Name three major types of vaccines.
3. What is the difference between active immunization and passive immunization?

Thinking Critically

4. *Analyzing.* Each year, as flu season approaches, a flu vaccine is made available. Elderly people and people with weakened immune systems are advised to receive this vaccine. Why do you suppose this is recommended?

Applying Health Skills

5. *In Your Home and School.* Make an informational poster listing ways to protect yourself from infectious disease. Post copies of the poster in your home and school.

Health Skills Activities

Activity 1 — Infectious Disease Handbook

Despite progress in the war on infectious diseases, millions of people become ill every year. Building knowledge about the causes, modes of transmission, and prevention of these diseases is the key to an all-out victory.

Directions

1. In groups, gather information on one of the infectious diseases discussed in this chapter.
2. Do research to identify the following: pathogen, means of transmission, symptoms, and treatment. Record your findings.
3. Using either markers or computer design software, develop a poster identifying ways to prevent contracting this disease as well as steps to take in the event of symptoms.
4. Brainstorm places in the school where your posters might be displayed.

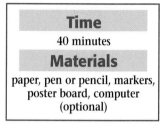

Time
40 minutes

Materials
paper, pen or pencil, markers, poster board, computer (optional)

Self-Assessment

✓ Described routes of transmission, signs, and symptoms of the infectious disease selected.
✓ Identified prevention strategies and treatments for the disease.

Activity 2 — Art and Diseases Through the Ages

Quilts for remembering people who have died of AIDS are considered an art form that reflects the problems of a society. What art forms could best convey a message about other infectious diseases?

Directions

1. In small groups, investigate infectious diseases of the past, such as bubonic plague. Learn about the causes as well as early myths and superstitions about the disease.
2. Locate and obtain a depiction of this disease in the visual arts, music, or literature. The bubonic plague, for example, was described in medieval songs, artwork, and poems. You might contact a local archive or museum or download a sound or image file from a Web site.
3. Share the artwork in a class discussion of diseases then and now.

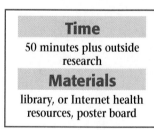

Time
50 minutes plus outside research

Materials
library, or Internet health resources, poster board

Self-Assessment

✓ Highlighted a disease of the past and explained beliefs and superstitions.
✓ Identified art forms that depicted the illness.
✓ Showed advances in diagnosis and treatment of disease.

Disease Detectives

Every person has unique fingerprints. Detectives use these fingerprints to solve mysteries. A new tool called PFGE helps scientists use a bacteria's "fingerprints" to solve medical mysteries.

PFGE can analyze the genetic pattern of a bacteria. Every strain of bacteria has its own unique genetic "fingerprint."

Public health officials read these fingerprints to track infectious disease. In Atlanta, Georgia, a toxic strain of the E. coli bacteria infected 26 young people. PFGE showed that all of them carried exactly the same E. coli strain. These results helped pinpoint the site of this epidemic: a popular local water park.

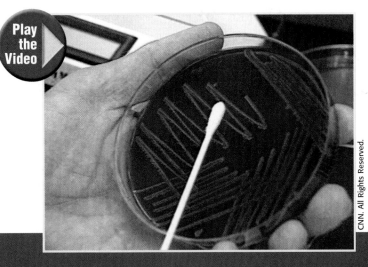

Play the Video

CNN. All Rights Reserved.

Think About It

◗ What are the steps in the PFGE process?

◗ Why can't genetic fingerprinting identify the first source of an outbreak? Could this limitation restrict the value of PFGE?

◗ How will Pulse Net, the electronic database of genetic fingerprints, help public health officials track diseases?

Using Health Terms

On a separate sheet of paper, write the term that best matches each definition below.

LESSON 1

1. The body's natural defenses against infection.
2. Spread.
3. A disease caused by organisms that enter and multiply within the human body.
4. The smallest known type of infectious agent.
5. Organisms that live in or on another organism and derive nourishment from it.
6. The process by which phagocytes engulf and destroy pathogens.
7. The soft, skinlike lining of many parts of the body.
8. The chief type of phagocyte involved in the process of phagocytosis.
9. Proteins that destroy or neutralize invading pathogens.

LESSON 2

10. A highly contagious bacterial infection that most often affects the lungs.
11. A bacterial infection of the throat.
12. A serious inflammation of the lungs.
13. German measles.
14. A program whereby communities or other large populations are systematically made immune to a disease.
15. A preparation based on a weakened or dead pathogen that provides immunity by causing the body to produce antibodies to the pathogen.

LESSON 3

16. The temporary immunity that an infant acquires from its mother.
17. Immunity your body develops to protect you from disease.

Recalling the Facts

Using complete sentences, answer the following questions.

LESSON 1

1. Bacteria can multiply rapidly enough to take over one's body in a short time. What usually prevents this from happening?
2. How does a virus work?
3. Explain nonspecific resistance.
4. Explain specific resistance.
5. Describe how antibodies are made and their role in the blood.

LESSON 2

6. Name four diseases caused by viruses and two diseases caused by bacteria.
7. What disease is a possible complication of measles, and what part of the body does it affect?

8. Name two possible complications of an untreated strep throat.

LESSON 3

9. What are some behaviors that will help a person avoid infectious diseases?
10. In what two ways can a person become immune to an infectious disease?
11. Name and briefly describe the three types of vaccines.

Thinking Critically

LESSON 1

1. ***Comparing and Contrasting.*** Make a chart that reflects similarities and differences among the five types of pathogens discussed in this lesson.

2. ***Comparing and Contrasting.*** Compare and contrast the function of phagocytes during nonspecific resistance and lymphocytes during specific resistance.

LESSON 2

3. ***Analyzing.*** Many people think they can catch a cold by becoming chilled, getting caught in the rain, or not dressing warmly enough in cold weather. Why might people think this way?

LESSON 3

4. ***Synthesizing.*** Why is it important to have a child immunized?

5. ***Synthesizing.*** What are some of the major reasons that there is now more of a focus on wellness?

Making the Connection

1. ***Social Studies.*** Write a one-page report about a protozoan-caused infectious disease, such as malaria or dysentery. How did the disease affect people in the past? What measures were taken to prevent or control it? Is it still affecting people today? What conditions contribute to the disease's decreased or increased incidence?

2. ***Science.*** The chapter mentioned several notable "microbe hunters," people whose pioneering work has combated the spread of infectious disease. Learn about another, Louis Pasteur, founder of the science of microbiology. Learn about Pasteur's specific contributions to this field, and report your findings.

BEYOND THE CLASSROOM

PARENTAL INVOLVEMENT Ask your parents to share with you the immunization records for yourself, other family members, and any family pets. Determine whether these are complete and up to date. Share any suggestions you may have about improving your family's disease-prevention efforts.

COMMUNITY INVOLVEMENT Tuberculosis is a disease that is on the rise again in the United States. Groups with the highest incidence of TB include the homeless, people who are in prison, and people infected with HIV. Interview a local public health official about cases of TB in your community. Find out about testing and treatment programs for persons who are most at risk. If there are homeless shelters in your community, ask how TB is tracked among the transient population.

SCHOOL-TO-CAREER

Interpersonal. Invite someone in or knowledgeable about the field of epidemiology—the branch of medical science that deals with the incidence, distribution, and control of disease in a population—to speak with the class about career possibilities and requirements, such as educational background and skills required.

CHAPTER 29

Sexually Transmitted Diseases

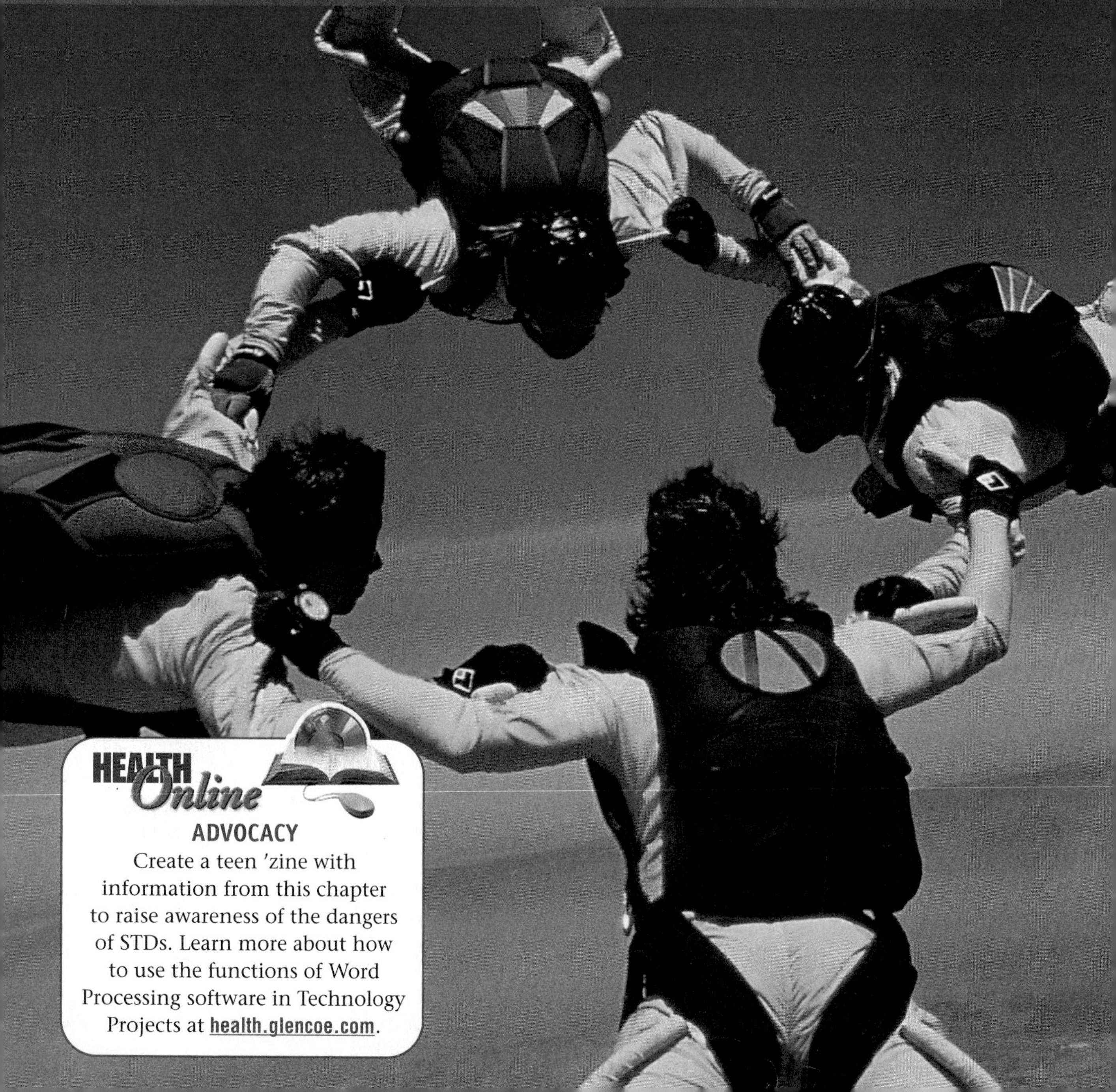

HEALTH Online

ADVOCACY

Create a teen 'zine with information from this chapter to raise awareness of the dangers of STDs. Learn more about how to use the functions of Word Processing software in Technology Projects at **health.glencoe.com**.

Personal Health Inventory

1	I know the facts about sexually transmitted diseases.
2	I can recognize the symptoms of a sexually transmitted disease.
3	I practice abstinence from sexual activity to reduce my risk of contracting an STD.
4	I am able to use assertive refusal to say no to sex.
5	I know and use alternatives to sexual intimacy in relationships.
6	I know the medical names for sexually transmitted diseases.
7	I know the medical symptoms of sexually transmitted diseases.
8	I know how to avoid getting a sexually transmitted disease.
9	I know how to advise someone infected with a sexually transmitted disease on where and how to seek medical help immediately.
10	I am aware of the responsibilities a person infected with a sexually transmitted disease has to his or her partner.

Follow-up After completing the chapter, retake this self-inventory. Pick two items that you need to work on and set a goal to improve your health behaviors.

66 *Only one in five teens recognizes that a person puts him or herself at risk for STD infection with just one sexual encounter.* 99

—SEXUALLY TRANSMITTED DISEASE INFORMATION CENTER
CENTERS FOR DISEASE CONTROL AND PREVENTION

Quick Write List five ways you can remind yourself, your friends, and other teens that taking risks even once during your teen years can have lifelong negative consequences.

Preventing STDs

Some infectious diseases such as the flu or a virus can be transmitted through actions as simple as sharing a fork. Other infectious diseases, however, are not so easily spread. Sexually transmitted diseases, or STDs, are 100 percent avoidable. **Sexually transmitted diseases** are *infectious diseases spread from person to person through sexual contact.*

HEALTH TERMS

sexually transmitted diseases (STDs)

epidemic

HEALTH CONCEPTS

- Sexually transmitted diseases (STDs) are spread from person to person, primarily by means of sexual contact.

- Although the rate of transmission of STDs has been steadily declining, the problem remains an epidemic in this country.

- The only sure way to avoid contracting or spreading an STD is by abstaining from sexual activity and other high-risk behaviors.

STDs: The Silent Epidemic

At the turn of the twentieth century, this country was faced with an epidemic of typhoid fever, an infectious disease caused by bacteria acquired through infected water. An **epidemic** is *an outbreak of an infectious disease that affects a large population.* With intervention on the part of health officials at the state and county level, the typhoid epidemic was wiped out.

Today our country faces another epidemic. This one is an epidemic of STDs. About 13 million new cases of STDs are reported each year in the United States. What is perhaps even more alarming is that numerous other cases go unreported. This is because STDs carry a social stigma, or mark of shame. Many people are embarrassed to talk about them, especially those who become infected. For

this reason, STDs are often referred to as the "silent" epidemic. Partly because of this silence, a number of myths and misconceptions have arisen around STDs and how they are spread.

STDs and Adolescents

One common myth surrounding STDs is that they are not a problem among teenagers, when in reality two-thirds of all STD cases occur in adolescents and young adults. The Centers for Disease Control and Prevention has noted that one in four sexually active teens will contract an STD before graduating from high school.

Why are teens as a group at particularly high risk for infection from STDs? One reason is that teens who are sexually active are likely to exhibit one or more of the following behaviors:

- Having more than one sexual partner rather than committing to a single, long-term relationship.
- Engaging in unprotected sex.
- Selecting partners at higher risk, such as those with a history of multiple sex partners or intravenous drug use. An additional risk for teen females is that they lack an **immunity** to some of the pathogens that cause STDs.

These risk factors are magnified by the fact that when teens do contract an STD, they are less likely than adults to seek medical attention. Some teens are simply unaware of what action to take, though in many cases the reluctance to seek help stems from a fear of disapproval by parents or other adults at home. Other teens refuse to believe that they could have an STD. Through denial and rationalization, they ignore the signs and symptoms of infection.

Partly because of this silence, a number of myths and misconceptions have arisen around STDs and how they are spread.

hotlink

immunity For more information on immunity and how it protects the body from pathogens, see Chapter 28, page 631.

MORE MYTHS ABOUT STDs

MYTH You can get STDs only if you have lots of sexual partners.
FACT You can get an STD from your first sexual experience.

MYTH STDs can easily be cleared up with antibiotics.
FACT Some types of STDs are incurable and last a lifetime.

MYTH If you have an STD, you would have symptoms of the disease.
FACT In some cases, especially early in the disease, no symptoms are present.

MYTH Once the symptoms of an STD go away, the disease is cured.
FACT You can still have an STD, even if the symptoms go away.

MYTH You can have only one type of STD at a time.
FACT It is possible to have more than one kind of STD infection.

MYTH Once infected with an STD, you cannot get it again.
FACT No one can become immune to STDs. Anyone can be reinfected.

MYTH A vaccine can prevent the spread of STDs.
FACT No vaccine exists for STDs, except for hepatitis B.

MYTH Having a Pap test is one way a female can find out if she has an STD.
FACT A Pap test detects cancer cells, not the presence of an STD.

The Silent Killer

sterility For more information on sterility and other conditions that can cause it, see Chapter 19, page 440.

AIDS For more information on AIDS and the virus that causes it, see Chapter 30, page 656.

hotlink

hotlink

STDs and Your Future

Contracting an STD can dramatically change the course of your life. Consider:

- Some STDs can cause **sterility**, the inability to reproduce.
- Infants born to mothers with STDs can be infected at birth and suffer consequences such as blindness and deformities.
- Some STDs are incurable, meaning that the individual must live with the reoccurrence of painful genital sores for the rest of his or her life.
- Individuals with STDs are at a greater risk for cancer, and some STDs such as **AIDS** are fatal.

Being informed with facts about STDs can help you avoid behaviors that lead to infection. In the pages that follow, you will learn critical facts about STDs. For now, it is enough to be aware of the most important fact: *The primary means of transmission of STDs is sexual contact.* A person who practices abstinence from sexual activity reduces his or her risk of contracting an STD.

Building Health Skills

Communication Skills: Setting Limits for Expressing Physical Attraction

THERE ARE MANY WAYS of expressing positive feelings for another person. When affection turns physical, however, there is a danger of acting impulsively—or "on the spur of the moment." Casual kissing and hugging may intensify sexual feelings when dating couples express physical affection.

How can you set limits on mutual displays of affection with someone you are dating? Here is a plan of action:

1. **Recognize that there are degrees of "liking."** Wanting to be liked is one of life's basic needs. One form liking can take is affection; another is respect. When a date respects you, he or she will act in your best interests. This includes *never* asking you to do something you are not ready to do.

2. **Discuss your limits.** Let your partner know in advance that sexual intimacy is not in your plans. Back up your words with your actions.

3. **Keep your brain in charge of your actions.** Express your affection in ways that will allow you to remain in control of your actions and your decisions.

4. **Avoid alcohol and other drugs.** Insist that your date do the same. The last thing either of you needs when emotions are running high is a substance that can cloud your judgment.

Practicing Abstinence

Y ou have probably learned about cause-and-effect relationships. Touching a hot iron, for example, can be a *cause* of sustaining a burn, which is the *effect*.

A clear cause-and-effect relationship exists between sexual intercourse and sexually transmitted diseases. If you have sexual contact with an infected person, you will be at high risk of contracting an STD. Sexual activity is the cause; an STD is the effect.

Having sexual relations during the teen years can lead to other unwanted consequences as well, including an unplanned or unintentional pregnancy and the responsibility of becoming a parent. Having sexual contact can complicate relationships with family members and friends. Remaining abstinent will allow teenagers to focus more clearly on their goals for the future.

Fortunately, more and more teens are learning about the realities of STDs and practicing **abstinence**. Their actions have resulted in a decrease in the rates of STD infection over the past several years. The recent decline in the most prevalent STD of them all, chlamydia, is one example of this positive trend.

h t link

abstinence For more information on abstinence from sexual activity before marriage and other high-risk behaviors, see Chapter 21, page 484.

LESSON 1 *Review*

Reviewing Facts and Vocabulary

1. What is an epidemic?
2. How do STDs differ from the infectious diseases discussed in Chapter 28?
3. What high-risk behaviors can lead teens to become infected with an STD?
4. What is the best way to avoid getting an STD?

Thinking Critically

5. *Analyzing.* Determine whether the following statements are myths or facts. Rewrite any myths to make them factual statements: (a) The body builds immunities to certain STDs. (b) A person could have an STD and not know it. (c) Having a Pap test is one way a female can find out if she has an STD. (d) Once the symptoms of an STD go away, the disease is cured.
6. *Synthesizing.* Explain what steps public health agencies can take to prevent

the further spread of STDs in the United States.

7. *Evaluating.* Some say that those who are sexually active before marriage have poor self-esteem. Is this a fair statement? Explain your answer.

Applying Health Skills

8. *In Your Home.* Share what you are learning about sexually transmitted diseases with your parents. You might want to show them what you are reading and tell them how you feel about learning the facts about sexually transmitted diseases. Ask them to share any additional information they know about STDs.

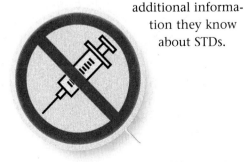

Common STDs and Their Treatments

You have probably heard the saying, "An ounce of prevention is worth a pound of cure." This saying certainly holds true when it comes to sexually transmitted diseases. This lesson will provide the facts about common STDs, including their symptoms and treatment. Chapter 30 will contain information on the most deadly STD of them all, AIDS.

HEALTH TERMS

chlamydia

nongonococcal urethritis

gonorrhea

trichomoniasis

vaginitis

genital warts

genital herpes

syphilis

HEALTH CONCEPTS

- Knowing the risk and symptoms of common STDs is an important first step toward prevention for sexually active people.
- Learning to identify the symptoms of STDs can help infected individuals seek appropriate treatment.
- People who discover that they have been infected with an STD have a responsibility to seek treatment and to inform any and all past sexual partners.
- Common sense, positive values, and good decision-making skills all contribute to the prevention of STDs.

Chlamydia

Chlamydia (kluh-MID-ee-uh) is *an infection caused by a bacterium that affects the vagina in females and the urethra in males.* The U.S. Centers for Disease Control and Prevention estimates that more than 4 million new cases of chlamydia infection occur each year. Chlamydia is a common cause of sterility and, if untreated, can lead to **nongonococcal urethritis** (non-gon-uh-KOK-uhl yur-ih-THRYT-uhs). Also known as *NGU,* this is *an infection caused by several different kinds of bacteria-like organisms that infect the urethra in males and the cervix in females.*

In males, the symptoms of chlamydia include pain and burning during urination and an unusual discharge from the penis. In females, the symptoms are not always obvious. If symptoms do occur, they may include an unusual discharge from the vagina, pain in the pelvic region, and painful urination. Untreated chlamydia in females can cause **pelvic inflammatory disease** (PID), a painful infection of the ovaries, fallopian tubes, and/or uterus. A pregnant female who has chlamydia can transmit it to her baby during delivery. In infants, the disease can cause eye infection, blindness, and sometimes even pneumonia.

Chlamydia is diagnosed through a laboratory test. Certain antibiotics can cure chlamydia. However, if scar tissue has already formed, treatment cannot undo that damage. Chances of sterility in the male and the female will remain.

Gonorrhea

Gonorrhea (gon-uh-REE-uh) is *an STD caused by bacteria that affect the genital mucous membrane, primarily in the lining of the urethra of the male and in the cervix and vagina of the female.* The bacteria are transmitted during sexual contact. A person cannot pick up the pathogens from towels or toilet seats because the bacteria cannot live outside the body. A pregnant female can, however, transmit the infection to her unborn child.

Symptoms of gonorrhea are not always obvious, especially in females. In the female, symptoms may include a slight discharge from the vagina, a burning sensation during urination, abnormal menstruation, and abdominal pain or tenderness. In the male, symptoms may include a whitish discharge from the penis and a burning sensation during urination. The lymph nodes in the groin may also become enlarged and tender. These symptoms usually appear between three days and three weeks after sexual contact with an infected person. These symptoms may go away on their own, but the disease is still present in the body.

Gonorrhea can be confirmed only by a medical diagnosis. In a male, gonorrhea is diagnosed by examining discharge from the penis under a microscope. In a female, a culture test of the vagina is done to make the diagnosis. This involves taking a sample of cells from the vagina and examining them under a microscope. Gonorrhea can be treated with antibiotics.

h ot link

pelvic inflammatory disease For more information on pelvic inflammatory disease, see Chapter 19, page 447.

▼ *Your family physician, school nurse, your parents, and other health-care professionals can give you accurate health information.*

Trichomoniasis

Trichomoniasis (trik-uh-muhn-EYE-uh-suhs) is *a vaginal infection that can lead to urethra and bladder infections.* Males are rarely infected with trichomoniasis, but they can be carriers. Like chlamydia, this STD can lead to nongonococcal urethritis. In females, symptoms of trichomoniasis include burning and itching in the vagina, a yellowish-green discharge, and pain upon urination. In males, symptoms include itching of the penis, a clear discharge, and pain upon urination. Trichomoniasis can be cured with a medicine that can be prescribed only by a physician.

Trichomoniasis can also cause vaginitis, another secondary infection, in females. **Vaginitis** is *a common inflammation of the female genitals* that can be carried by males. Vaginitis is rare in young women who are not yet sexually active. In more than 90 percent of all cases, vaginitis is caused by a bacterium, protozoan, or virus transmitted through semen and certain other body secretions. Medication is now available that can be taken in a single dose and that cures vaginitis within 24 hours.

Genital Warts

Genital warts are *pink or reddish warts with cauliflowerlike tops that appear on the genitals.* Genital warts are caused by a virus called the human papilloma virus (HPV). Once infected, a person has the virus for the rest of her or his life. The warts appear on the genitals one to three months after infection. A physician can remove the warts, but they may reappear. Medical treatment may also include

Making Responsible Decisions

Getting Treatment for an STD

One of Angel's friends has just confided in Angel that she has herpes. She was dating a boy that Angel has known for several years, but Angel heard that they have recently stopped seeing each

other. The friend told Angel that she is embarrassed and does not want her reputation to suffer by having people find out that she has a sexually transmitted disease. She is also afraid to discuss it with her old boyfriend. What should Angel do?

What Would You Do?

Apply the six steps of the decision-making process to Angel's problem.

1. **State the situation.**
2. **List the options.**
3. **Weigh the possible outcomes.**
4. **Consider your values.**
5. **Make a decision and act.**
6. **Evaluate the decision.**

application of a prescription skin medication. This STD is known to be one of the causes of cervical cancer in women.

Genital Herpes

Genital herpes appears as *blisterlike sores in the genital area* that are caused by the herpes simplex type 2 virus. Like genital warts, genital herpes cannot be cured. The virus remains in the body for a lifetime. The sores usually appear two to twenty days after contact with an infected person and may last as long as three weeks. Other symptoms include fever and a burning sensation during urination. With the help of moisture and friction, the virus can spread to other areas of the body. This is why a person with herpes is told not to rub the skin and to keep the skin dry. The blisters can break out at any time and often occur during periods of stress.

Herpes is diagnosed by a medical examination of genital sores and verified by lab tests. Medications are used to treat the symptoms. To avoid spreading genital herpes, an infected person should avoid having sexual contact when blisters are present and right after they disappear.

Syphilis

Syphilis (SIH-fuh-luhs) is *an STD that attacks many parts of the body and is caused by a small bacterium called a spirochete.* When left untreated, it can damage vital organs, such as the heart, the liver, the kidneys, and the central nervous system, including the brain. It can cause heart disease, blindness, paralysis, and insanity.

Syphilis is different from other STDs in that it develops in stages. Symptoms appear and then go away on their own. However, if treated in the early stages, the disease can be cured.

- **Primary Stage.** The first sign of syphilis is a *chancre* (SHAN-kuhr), a painless, reddish sore at the place where the pathogen enters the body, usually the genitals. It appears within 10 to 90 days after contact with an infected person. The chancre lasts one to five weeks and will then go away, even if untreated. However, the disease remains in the body.

- **Secondary Stage.** If not treated, the pathogen will be circulated in the blood. Within one to six months after contact, the highly contagious second stage of syphilis appears. This stage is commonly characterized by a non-itching rash on the chest, backs of the arms, and legs. In females, the rash is most often found on the outer edges of the vagina. Sores may develop from the rash. These sores will likely give off a clear liquid filled with infectious spirochetes. Swelling may occur in the lymph nodes under the arms and around the groin. Fever, sore throat, and a general sick feeling are common symptoms. Without treatment, these symptoms will disappear, but the disease continues to develop.

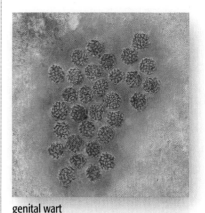
genital wart

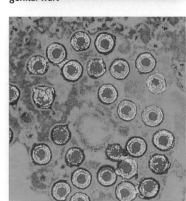
herpes blister

▲ *Genital warts (top) and genital herpes (bottom) are caused by virus.*

ACTIVITY *Tell how genital warts are different from genital herpes.*

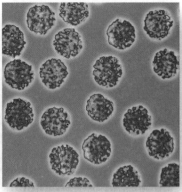
Hepatitis B

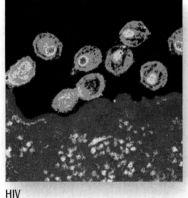
HIV

▲ *Hepatitis B and HIV are caused by viruses carried in the bloodstream.*

h⊙t link

hepatitis B For more information on hepatitis B and other forms of this infectious disease, see Chapter 28, page 629.

■ **Latent Stage.** The third stage of syphilis usually begins about two or more years after the initial infection. All signs disappear, leading the individual to think that he or she is cured or perhaps never had the disease. However, it is in this stage that syphilis begins to attack the heart and blood vessels and the central nervous system. The damage to these areas is slow and steady. Even though people have reached the latent stage, they can relapse into the second stage, and sores will reappear.

■ **Neurosyphilis Stage** (NOOR-uh-SIH-fuh-luhs). If untreated, syphilis moves into the neurosyphilis stage within 10 to 30 years, and the heart, skin, brain, and spinal cord are affected. A person loses the ability to coordinate muscular movements and may experience blindness or insanity. The central nervous system is affected, resulting in a loss of mental abilities. A person in this stage of syphilis may experience paralysis and convulsions. Syphilis in this stage can be treated but not cured.

The medical test for syphilis is a blood test. The presence of the spirochete bacteria in the blood or in sores indicates the presence of the disease. Penicillin is the main drug used in the treatment of syphilis. No matter how effective the treatment is, it cannot undo any harm that has already been done. Early treatment is crucial.

Other STDs

Several other problematic infectious diseases are spread through sexual contact:

■ Chancroid (SHAN-kroyd) is a bacterial infection with many similarities to the primary stage of syphilis. Deep sores show up near the genitals. Contact with these sores will spread the disease. Chancroid is treated with antibiotics.

■ Candidiasis (kan-duh-DY-uh-suhs) is a yeast infection of the vagina. This condition usually occurs without sexual contact, but is often passed to a partner during sexual contact. Symptoms include a yellowish discharge, strong odor, and itching. It can be cured through medicated creams and tablets sold over the counter.

■ Pubic lice are tiny insects that attach themselves to skin and hair in the pubic area. The lice feed on blood and cause intense itching. Treatment consists of using a special medicated shampoo.

■ Scabies is an infestation of the skin by mites that cause red, swollen, itchy bumps similar to those found during the primary stage of syphilis. Itching begins four to six weeks after infection. Treatment includes hot baths and medicated creams.

■ **Hepatitis B** is caused by a virus that attacks the liver. It also can be spread through contact with infected blood. Symptoms do not show up for six months, during which time a person may not know that he or she is infected. Treatment includes bed rest and a healthy diet. A **vaccine** is available.

■ Human immunodeficiency virus (HIV) is the virus that causes AIDS. **HIV** also can be spread through contact with infected blood. Once the virus is contracted, it remains in the body. At this time there is no cure for HIV or AIDS, and the disorder is considered fatal.

h⚬t link

vaccine For more information on vaccines and their role in combating infectious diseases, see Chapter 28, page 632.

HIV For more information on HIV/AIDS, see Chapter 30, page 656.

Responsibilities of Infected Individuals

Treatment for sexually transmitted diseases is an important personal as well as social responsibility. Having an STD is not like having a cold. It will not simply go away if a person waits long enough. The individual must take action to have the disease treated. Although a person may feel embarrassed about having an STD, he or she should seek treatment from a private doctor or a public health clinic immediately. By law, it is guaranteed that all information will remain confidential.

It is also important for a person infected with an STD to notify all people with whom he or she has had sexual contact. The infected person has a responsibility to educate partners about the symptoms and risks of the STD and encourage them to have a medical checkup. Informing someone else about the possibility of having an STD could save that person's life. A doctor or a public health clinic can help an infected person take these steps.

LESSON 2 *Review*

Reviewing Facts and Vocabulary

1. Which STD is characterized by reddish cauliflowerlike warts? Which STD, if left untreated, can affect the brain?
2. Why is it important for someone who suspects he or she is infected with an STD to seek treatment?
3. Identify two responsibilities of an individual who suspects he or she is infected with an STD.

Thinking Critically

4. *Comparing and Contrasting.* Divide the STDs in this lesson into two lists—one for STDs that can be cured if immediate treatment is sought, the other for STDs that cannot be cured. Describe the treatment for each.

5. *Synthesizing.* Tell how you would advise a friend who confides that he or she is experiencing pain during urination and itching in the genital area.

Applying Health Skills

6. *In Your Home and School.* Invite your school nurse or a community health official to speak to your class about STDs in your community. Find out if any of the STDs are more common than others. Ask the speaker to explain what occurs when a teenager comes forward to seek help with a possible STD.

Health Skills Activities

Evaluating STD Information

Teens who fear they have an STD can benefit from knowing what steps to take. The most effective way to reach an audience is to speak to them in their own language. What would you say to other teens about the dangers of STDs?

Directions

1. In a group, evaluate one of the STD brochures provided by your teacher. Is the approach as effective as it could be? In what ways might the language or other aspects appeal more to teens?
2. Use your ideas to create a more effective, persuasive brochure by hand or on the classroom computer.
3. Exchange a first draft of your brochure with another group. Share and implement useful criticism. Distribute the finalized brochures around the school.

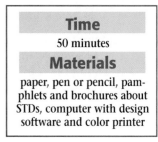

Time

50 minutes

Materials

paper, pen or pencil, pamphlets and brochures about STDs, computer with design software and color printer

Self-Assessment

✓ Analyzed health information for effective communication and appeal to specific audience.
✓ Included accurate information about the prevention of STDs.

Helping a Friend Choose Abstinence

The most effective way to prevent contracting a sexually transmitted disease is to practice abstinence. Fortunately, more and more teens are choosing to abstain from sexual activity before marriage. You can help promote this trend.

Directions

1. Imagine that your best friend, who is usually talkative and lively, has been quiet and withdrawn lately. Since the beginning of the school year your friend has been dating a classmate. When you ask your friend what's wrong, your friend explains that he or she is being pressured to engage in sexual activity.
2. Write a letter to your friend explaining the importance of practicing abstinence. Convince your friend to resist the pressure and make the healthy decision. Point out the risks involved in making the wrong choice, and mention the positive things you want for your friend's future.

Time

30 minutes

Materials

paper, pen or pencil

Self-Assessment

✓ Explained the benefits of practicing abstinence from sexual activity before marriage.
✓ Identified persuasively the risks involved in engaging in sexual activity before marriage.

Study Rates STDs in U.S.

A new study shows that the United States has an "astronomical number" of new cases of sexually transmitted diseases, or STDs, per year.

Experts say the study, done by the American Social Health Association and Kaiser Family Foundation, indicates it's time the nation confront the issue–particularly because everyone who is sexually active is at risk.

"There are about 15 million new cases of STDs in the U.S. each year," said Linda Alexander of the American Social Health Association. "That's an astronomical number. It's one of the highest rates of all industrialized countries in the world."

Having any STD greatly increases a person's risk of developing a disease that cannot be cured. Alexander explains this dangerous connection: "If you have a sexually transmitted disease, you're more likely to acquire HIV if you're exposed to it and you're more likely to transmit HIV if you have it."

According to the study, STDs affect one in four U.S. citizens over a lifetime. The risks associated with STDs range from sterility to cancer to death. The top STDs include these four that can be treated with antibiotics: Chlamydia, gonorrhea, syphilis and trichomoniasis. They also include viral infections that have no cure: genital herpes, genital warts (also known as human papilloma virus), hepatitis B, and HIV, which causes AIDS.

Experts say a national discussion on the issue could help change social attitudes toward STDs.

Experts also say some major challenges must be overcome to beat back the high rate of STDs. Those challenges include getting doctors to talk about STDs with their patients and convincing both men and women to get tested.

Think About It

1. Summarize the findings of the recent study on sexually transmitted diseases in the United States.
2. What are some of the strategies that might effectively limit the trend identified by this study?

Using Health Terms

On a separate sheet of paper, write the term that best matches each definition below.

LESSON 1

1. An outbreak of an infectious disease that affects a large population.
2. Infectious diseases spread from person to person through sexual contact.

LESSON 2

3. A vaginal infection that can lead to urethra and bladder infections.
4. Pink or reddish warts with cauliflowerlike tops that appear on the genitals.
5. An infection caused by a bacterium that affects the vagina in females and the urethra in males.

6. Blisterlike sores in the genital area.
7. An infection caused by several different kinds of bacterialike organisms that infect the urethra in males and the cervix in females.
8. An STD that attacks many parts of the body and is caused by a small bacterium called a spirochete.
9. An STD caused by bacteria that affect the genital mucous membrane, primarily in the lining of the urethra of the male and in the cervix and vagina of the female.
10. A common inflammation of the female genitals.

Recalling the Facts

Using complete sentences, answer the following questions.

LESSON 1

1. Why are STDs considered an epidemic?
2. Why are teens less likely than adults to seek medical attention for an STD?
3. Why is it important for teens to say no to sexual activity?

LESSON 2

4. Which STD is the most prevalent in the United States today?
5. How is gonorrhea treated?
6. How are the symptoms of chancroid similar to those of the primary stage of syphilis?
7. Which STDs also can be contracted through another means of contact?
8. What two infections can result from untreated chlamydia?
9. Why is it possible for a female not to know that she has an STD?
10. How is trichomoniasis treated?
11. How is genital herpes diagnosed?

Thinking Critically

LESSON 1

1. ***Comparing and Contrasting.*** Which of the following teens is more likely to get an STD? Explain your answer. (a) Robert loves the thrills of taking risks. He is usually the one who takes on a dare given by members of his clique, even when it involves dangerous behaviors. (b) Tim is a member of Students Against Destructive Decisions (SADD) at school. He often gives talks about abstaining from alcohol. He socializes with other members of SADD and with family friends.

2. ***Comparing and Contrasting.*** Compare and contrast assertive and aggressive styles in letting others know that you don't want to be part of a situation where sexual activity is practiced openly.

LESSON 2

3. ***Evaluating.*** Some states have a law requiring couples who apply for marriage licenses to be tested for syphilis. Explain the purpose of this law. Then develop a law of your own that you think would be effective in the control of STDs. Explain your thinking.

4. ***Synthesizing.*** Prepare a chart that explains the stages of syphilis. Include symptoms for each stage of the disease. Do additional research to fill in any information not provided in the text.

Making the Connection

1. ***Math.*** Use current, up-to-date resources to research the number of cases of gonorrhea during five-year intervals from 1950 to the present. Present your findings in a bar graph. Develop a comparable bar graph for population increases during the same period. Compare the two graphs.

2. ***Language Arts.*** Use a dictionary to find the etymology, or origin, of the words *gonorrhea, syphilis,* and *herpes*. Which of these words has an alternate spelling, and what is it?

BEYOND THE CLASSROOM

PARENTAL INVOLVEMENT Ask your parents or other adults at home how they learned about STDs. Ask about the quality of that information. Talk with them about the best ways for young people to learn about STDs.

COMMUNITY INVOLVEMENT Find out what kinds of assistance are available to help people who have STDs in your community. Prepare a report to share your findings with your classmates.

SCHOOL-TO-CAREER

Interpersonal. Some artists build a career as a medical illustrator, one who draws illustrations used in medical writings, such as brochures or textbooks. Determine what kinds of preparation and experience are required in both art and science for a career as a medical illustrator. Share your findings with the class in a brief oral report.

CHAPTER 30

HIV and AIDS

ACCESSING INFORMATION
Where would you find the most up-to-date, accurate research on treatment and cures for HIV/AIDS? Learn about finding reliable sources on the Internet in the Technology Project "Searching the Internet" at <u>health.glencoe.com</u>.

Personal Health Inventory

Self-Inventory Write the numbers 1–10 on a sheet of paper. Read each statement below and respond by writing *yes*, *no*, or *sometimes* for each item. Write a *yes* only for items that you practice regularly. Save your responses.

1	I keep informed about HIV infection and AIDS.
2	I know which behaviors pose the highest risk for infection from HIV.
3	I know with whom to talk and where to get information when I have questions about HIV infection and AIDS.
4	I avoid all behaviors that can transmit HIV.
5	I can say no to something I do not want to do or do not feel ready for.
6	I do not use illegal drugs.
7	I abstain from sexual activity.
8	I do not use needles, including tattoo needles, razors, or other items that have been used by someone else.
9	I am not easily influenced by peer pressure.
10	I know the relationship between HIV and AIDS.

Follow-up After completing the chapter, retake this self-inventory. Pick two items that you need to work on and set a goal to improve your health behaviors.

> **"** *The underlying reality... is that the HIV epidemic in our country is far from over.* **"**

—DIVISIONS OF HIV/AIDS PROTECTION
CENTERS FOR DISEASE CONTROL AND PREVENTION

Quick Write List five myths or misconceptions about HIV or AIDS that you think teens often mistakenly believe to be true. Discuss these with your teacher and classmates.

HIV Infection

O f all STDs, none has received more attention—and deservedly so—than AIDS. The costs of this deadly affliction—in both monetary cost and the loss of human potential—have been enormous. AIDS is now the leading cause of death in people between the ages of 25 and 44.

HEALTH TERMS

acquired immune deficiency syndrome (AIDS)

human immunodeficiency virus (HIV)

intravenous (IV) drugs

HEALTH CONCEPTS

- AIDS is a disorder that interferes with the body's ability to fight off infections.
- Viruses are the simplest form of life.
- HIV plays a central role in the AIDS epidemic.
- The human immunodeficiency virus (HIV) is transmitted mainly through semen, secretions from the female's vagina, blood, and breast milk, sharing needles, and transfusions.

hotlink

immune system For more information on the immune system and how it protects the body from infection, see Chapter 28, page 624.

AIDS and HIV

A cquired immune deficiency syndrome (AIDS)—defined formally as *HIV infection combined with severe immune deficiency*—is the final stage of infection with HIV. Short for **human immunodeficiency (im-myuh-noh-duh-FIH-shuhn-see) virus**, HIV is *a virus that attacks the body's immune system*. This lesson will look at how people become infected with HIV—and how they do not.

HIV and the Human Body

I n order to understand how HIV attacks the body's **immune system**, it is necessary to review the function of lymphocytes—white blood cells made in bone marrow. The human body contains billions of lymphocytes, found in the blood, spleen, lymph nodes, appendix, tonsils, and adenoids.

Lymphocytes help your body fight disease-causing organisms, or pathogens. There are two major types of lymphocytes: B cells, which mature in bone marrow, and T cells, which mature in the thymus gland. T-helper cells, a type of T cell, stimulate B cells to produce antibodies. Antibodies are proteins that help destroy pathogens that enter the body.

When HIV enters the bloodstream, it enters certain cells, including T-helper cells. Here HIV reproduces its genetic material. More T-helper cells become infected and are destroyed. This decrease in the number of T-helper cells reduces the ability of the immune system to fight pathogens, making the body vulnerable to certain illnesses.

HIV can be present anywhere in the body—the bloodstream, lymph nodes, even brain cells.

How HIV Is Transmitted

There are many myths about how HIV is or is not spread. The fact is, HIV must enter a person's bloodstream in order to infect the person. HIV has been found in body fluids such as blood, semen, and vaginal secretions of infected persons. Small concentrations have also been found in saliva, sweat, tears, feces, urine, and breast milk. To date, HIV is known to be transmitted only through semen, blood, vaginal secretions, and breast milk. Certain behaviors and situations are known to transmit HIV from an infected person to an uninfected person because the exchange of body fluids is involved.

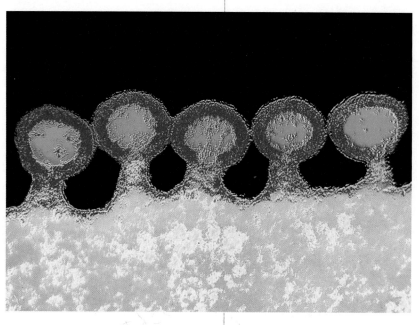

▲ *This microscopic photograph shows HIV reproducing from a host cell.*

ACTIVITY *Describe the process by which HIV invades the immune system.*

Risk Behaviors Known to Transmit HIV

About 93 percent of adults and teenagers revealed through testing to be infected with HIV have acquired the virus through sexual intercourse or the use of **intravenous (IV) drugs**—*drugs that are injected into the veins*. These two actions are high-risk behaviors for HIV infection.

■ **Sexual Intercourse.** HIV can be transmitted during any form of sexual intercourse. During intercourse, secretions containing HIV can enter a partner's blood through tiny cuts in the body. The risks of HIV infection increase with the number of sexual partners a person has or by having sexual contact with someone who has had many sexual partners. Having an STD that results in sores and bleeding or discharge also increases the risk of HIV entering the blood.

- **Sharing Needles.** If a person who is infected with HIV injects drugs into his or her veins with a syringe, drops of that person's blood are left on the needle. If another person uses the same needle, it is very likely that the infected blood will be passed to this person's blood. Sharing any needle, including one used to inject steroids, make tattoos, or pierce ears, puts a person at risk of becoming infected with HIV.

MYTHS ABOUT HIV TRANSMISSION

MYTH

You can get HIV from a mosquito bite if that mosquito has bitten an HIV-infected person.

FACT

Although mosquitoes can spread diseases such as malaria and yellow fever, HIV is not spread through a mosquito's salivary glands.

MYTH

You can get HIV by touching a glass from which a person infected with HIV has drunk.

FACT

HIV is spread primarily through blood, semen, and vaginal secretions.

MYTH

You can get HIV from swimming in a pool with someone who is infected.

FACT

Even if an HIV-infected person bled into a swimming pool, the blood would be so diluted it would be harmless.

MYTH

You can get HIV from being sneezed on by someone who is infected.

FACT

HIV is not spread through airborne droplets.

Is Honesty the Best Policy?

Stuart, a high school freshman, found out that he is infected with HIV. He contracted the virus through a blood transfusion years ago. Because Stuart has hemophilia, his blood does not clot properly. As a result, he may bleed excessively from a minor injury. Stuart has been receiving a clotting factor through injections and transfusions. Stuart is aware from other cases like his that there is a great deal of fear and misunderstanding related to HIV infection. If people know he is infected, there may be a negative reaction to his being on the school team. Yet he wants to lead as normal a life as possible, and he wants to be honest. He is uncertain how to handle the situation.

What Would You Do?

Apply the six steps of the decision-making process to Stuart's problem.

1. **State the situation.**
2. **List the options.**
3. **Weigh the possible outcomes.**
4. **Consider your values.**
5. **Make a decision and act.**
6. **Evaluate the decision.**

OTHER MODES OF TRANSMISSION

Two other modes of HIV transmissions are blood transfusions and mother-to-child transfer during birth. Combined, however, these modes account ultimately for less than 3 percent of all cases of AIDS. Since March of 1985, all blood donated in the United States has been tested for the presence of HIV antibodies. This testing has greatly reduced—although not eliminated—the risk of receiving contaminated blood or blood products from a transfusion. There is no risk when donating blood because disposable needles are used. These needles are used only one time.

A pregnant female who is infected with HIV can pass the virus to the fetus in blood exchanged through the umbilical cord. This occurs between 20 and 35 percent of the time when the mother is infected with HIV. There is a treatment available that can reduce the risk of HIV being transmitted from an infected woman to her unborn child. Therefore, it is important for all pregnant women to get early prenatal care to protect their infants. A baby also could be infected with HIV during birth if the virus enters through a cut on the baby's body. A nursing baby could receive HIV while breast-feeding.

Teenagers at Risk

Unlike other STDs whose rates are decreasing among adolescents, the incidence of HIV infection among teenagers is on the rise, especially among African Americans, Hispanic Americans, and females. The Centers for Disease Control and Prevention (CDC) reports the following:

- AIDS is now the leading cause of death in the 25- to 44-year-old age group. Many of those in their 20s probably became infected with HIV as teenagers.
- As of June 1997, the CDC reported 3,359 cases of HIV infection among people 13–19 years old. Considering that many cases go unreported, the numbers may be substantially higher.
- AIDS is now the leading cause of death for women in 15 of the largest cities in the United States.

HIV infection can be prevented, as will be seen in the lesson that follows. A teen who chooses to abstain from sexual intercourse and who does not use IV drugs greatly reduces the risk of HIV infection. In addition, abstaining from the use of alcohol and other drugs, which can impair a person's judgment in regard to sexual activity and drug use, can also reduce the risk of HIV infection. Making responsible decisions about your own activities and behaviors is your most valuable tool for protecting yourself against HIV infection. As scientists continue to search for a cure for this disease, you have a responsibility to yourself and to others to avoid any behaviors that could put you at risk of infection.

LESSON 1 *Review*

Reviewing Facts and Vocabulary

1. What is AIDS?
2. What is the function of T-helper cells?
3. Explain the ways HIV is known to be transmitted.

Thinking Critically

4. **Evaluating.** Do you think it is wrong for an individual who is infected with HIV to remain silent about her or his condition while being sexually active with another person?
5. **Synthesizing.** Why are there so many myths surrounding AIDS?
6. **Analyzing.** We live in a society that does not encourage open discussion of sex. How does this contribute, if at all, to the misunderstandings surrounding AIDS and how HIV is spread?

Applying Health Skills

7. **In Your Home and School.** Interview family members and five people in your school or neighborhood. Ask them what they think are the five primary causes of infection with HIV. Are their ideas based on fact or fiction? Share and discuss your findings with classmates.

Treatment for HIV-Related Illnesses and AIDS

F ollowing the initial outbreak of AIDS cases in the early 1980s, researchers set to work developing tests that would indicate infection with HIV. This lesson will describe the testing process. It will also examine what happens to an individual who tests **HIV-reactive,** or "positive"— that is, *infected with HIV.*

HEALTH TERMS

HIV-reactive

ELISA (EIA)

confirmatory test

asymptomatic stage

AIDS-opportunistic illnesses (AIDS-OIs)

HEALTH CONCEPTS

- A number of tests are used to detect the presence of HIV antibodies.
- AIDS interferes with the normal functioning of the immune system, making patients prey to a host of AIDS-opportunistic illnesses that seldom appear in people with healthy immune systems.
- AIDS education can help stem the AIDS pandemic.
- Choosing abstinence from high-risk behaviors is the 100 percent effective way to limit the spread of HIV infection.

Detecting HIV Antibodies

Just as there are misconceptions about how HIV is spread, there are also misunderstandings about the tests used to indicate whether a person is HIV-reactive. There are two phases of testing that may be done in suspected cases of HIV infection. Together, the tests have an accuracy level of greater than 99 percent.

HIV Testing

Persons who suspect they are infected with HIV due to high-risk behaviors are urged to seek testing. It takes anywhere from two weeks to six months for the body to produce antibodies following infection. Individuals are advised to see a health professional right away and to

CHARACTER
IN ACTION

Honesty and Responsibility

When it comes to HIV/AIDS and other STDs, **honesty** and responsibility are both critical, central, and ethical values that need to be upheld. Sexual activity outside of marriage is a high-risk behavior that has grave consequences. When a person has been sexually active or knows that he or she may have been infected with HIV/AIDS or another STD, withholding information is not only unethical for unsuspecting partners; it can prove deadly.

Staying abstinent is a decision that is based on the highest values, including self-respect and responsibility. It is the only reasonable and responsible decision for protecting your health and the health of others.

Character Check Fold a piece of paper into four columns. Then list respectively: Physical, Emotional, Social, and Ethical Benefits of remaining sexually abstinent.

---

avoid all behaviors known to transmit HIV. After six months, testing should indicate accurately whether infection is present in the body.

The first test performed, **ELISA**—or **EIA**—is *a test that screens for the presence of HIV antibodies in the blood,* not a test for HIV infection or AIDS. The ELISA (EIA) is very sensitive and will be reactive even if there are only one or two antibodies in the blood sample. Because certain health conditions such as hemophilia, hepatitis, and pregnancy can cause "false" reactive readings, the ELISA (EIA) may be repeated if the first test proves reactive. A reactive ELISA (EIA) will be followed up by a second **confirmatory test**, *a highly accurate test used to confirm the results of a reactive ELISA (EIA).* One of three different tests—the Western blot test, the IFA, or the RIA—will be administered for this purpose. A reactive confirmatory test result means that the person has HIV antibodies in his or her blood. This person is infected with HIV, although he or she may show no signs of infection at the time of the test. A non-reactive test means that there were no HIV antibodies in the sample of blood and that the person is not infected. If, however, a person subsequently becomes exposed to HIV through a risk behavior—or if the test was done within six months of the suspected risk incident—he or she will need to be retested.

Symptoms of HIV Infection

A person infected with HIV may or may not experience illness. In fact, a person infected with HIV can feel and look healthy. However, this individual can still infect others when practicing behaviors known to transmit HIV. A person can be infected with HIV for years before showing signs of infection. The earliest phase of HIV infection is the **asymptomatic** (AY-sim-tuh-MAT-ik) **stage.** This is *a period of months or years during which the virus is present in the blood but there are no symptoms or signs of disease.*

Although symptoms of HIV infection may not appear for six months to 10–12 years, a person infected with HIV will almost always develop AIDS. During that period, a person infected with HIV will go through a number of stages, each accompanied by different signs and symptoms. In the symptomatic stage, symptoms—which include fever, rash, headache, body aches, and swollen glands—may be mistaken for those of flu. Although these symptoms may pass over time, the person's ability to fight pathogens decreases, along with his or her T-helper cell count.

Diagnosis of AIDS

Yet another misconception is that AIDS itself is a disease. In point of fact, AIDS is a disorder associated with the last stage in the course of HIV infection. Once the immune system fails, the person's body is open to a host of infections that can attack other systems and create serious illness.

HIV Testing Through In-Home Collection Kits

In May of 1996, the FDA approved the first in-home collection kit for HIV testing. An individual draws a small amount of his or her own blood. The dried blood spot is mailed to a laboratory where it is tested for the presence of HIV antibodies through standard tests such as ELISA and Western blot. To get the results of the test, the person calls a toll-free number. Telephone counseling services are provided when the test result is positive. Issues surrounding in-home collection kits include questions related to counseling services and the quality, accuracy, and reliability of testing.

ANALYZING DIFFERENT **VIEWPOINTS**

▶ Viewpoint One

According to the National Center for Health Statistics, less than 15 percent of adults in the United States have been tested for HIV. Findings from surveys showed that, of people who have not taken HIV tests, 24 percent would undergo testing if it could be done at home. Clearly, in-home access to testing would increase the number of people tested for HIV who would not otherwise seek testing.

▶ Viewpoint Two

Some people feel that to assure proper collection and treatment of blood samples, the samples should be collected only by a health care professional. The laboratory doing the testing has no control over the conditions under which samples are collected in the home. Individuals may fail to follow accurately the instructions that come with the kit. They may delay mailing the sample to the laboratory for a period of time, which could affect test results.

▶ Viewpoint Three

Of major concern to some people is the issue of pretest and posttest counseling. Quality in-person counseling services can decrease anxiety over test results, can link individuals to other services, and may reduce high-risk behaviors. Counseling over the telephone with no face-to-face contact, however, may not provide intervention support or address risk-reduction activities, which in some cases could be dangerous for the consumer.

▶ Viewpoint Four

Other people recognize that for some, remaining anonymous is extremely important. For such people, in-home collection and phone counseling provide an easily accessible, highly private, and confidential form of testing.

EXPLORING YOUR **VIEWS**

1. If you feared you were at risk for HIV infection, what would be the advantages and disadvantages of being tested by your physician, being tested at a public clinic or other site, or using an in-home collection kit?

2. What do you think the advantages and disadvantages would be in receiving counseling on the phone or in person about a positive HIV test?

3. How careful do you think people would be about taking their own blood sample and mailing it to a laboratory in a timely manner? Explain your answer.

Good News, Bad News

It is true that some people with HIV/AIDS are living healthier and longer lives than a few years ago. This is in large part due to new potent medicines and combinations of medicines. However, the news about HIV/AIDS is definitely not all good. No one should be fooled into thinking HIV/AIDS is no longer a terrible and deadly threat. Consider these facts:

➤ Potent new medicines and combinations of medicines do not work for everyone.

➤ Many of these cause terrible side effects—so terrible that some infected people stop using them.

➤ Many of these new medicines are too expensive for some people.

➤ Medicine therapies often involve complex schedules of pill-taking, including large numbers of pills to take throughout the day and night and at exact times.

AIDS-opportunistic illnesses (AIDS-OIs) are *infections and other diseases caused by organisms that do not usually produce illness in healthy people with unimpaired immune systems.* Several infectious diseases, as well as a number of cancers and diseases that damage the heart and nervous system, are typically associated with AIDS. In addition to a reactive test result for HIV antibodies and a T-helper cell count of under 200, diagnosis of AIDS is based on the presence of one or more AIDS-OIs. AIDS-OIs are the eventual cause of death in AIDS patients.

Common AIDS-OIs

Some of the more common AIDS-OIs are diseases that have been discussed in other chapters, or variations of such diseases. These include tuberculosis as well as the following:

■ **Mycobacterium Avium Complex (MAC or MAI).** MAC is a bacterial infection. Its symptoms include persistent fever, night sweats, fatigue, weight loss, chronic diarrhea, anemia, abdominal pain, weakness, dizziness, and nausea.

■ **Cryptococcosis (Cryptoccal Disease).** Cryptococcosis (krip-tuh-kaw-KOK-sis) is a fungal infection that may cause meningitis—inflammation of the coverings of the brain—or a form of pneumonia. The symptoms of meningitis include headache, stiffness in the neck, fever, blurred vision, a staggering gait, and fatigue. Untreated, the infection may end in coma and death.

■ **Pneumocystis Carinii Pneumonia (PCP).** PCP is a protozoal infection that causes a form of pneumonia. Its symptoms include difficulty in breathing, fever, and persistent cough.

■ **Toxoplasmosis Gondii (Toxo).** Toxo is a protozoal infection that can cause encephalitis. It is characterized by an altered mental state—confusion, lethargy, and delusional behavior—as well as paralysis on one side of the body, seizures, severe headaches, fever, and coma.

■ **Cytomegalovirus (CMV).** CMV is a viral infection with symptoms that include blurry vision, blindness, pain and difficulty swallowing, lesions in the esophagus, fever, diarrhea, abdominal pain, wasting, and eventual blindness.

■ **AIDS-Related Cognitive Motor Dysfunction.** Formerly known as AIDS dementia complex, this condition is a progressive disorder in which brain tissue is destroyed. Symptoms range from mild confusion to inability to control one's muscular movement.

■ **Peripheral Nerve/Spinal Cord Dysfunction.** This is an inflammation of the nerves connecting the central nervous system to the sensory organs, muscles, glands, and internal organs. Symptoms include numbness, tingling, pain, and muscle weakness.

Many of these illnesses are accompanied by wasting syndrome, an infection of the cells lining the intestine. The symptoms include extreme weight loss, weakness, fever, diarrhea, nausea, and inability to absorb food.

Research and Treatment

The search for a vaccine to prevent HIV infection is ongoing. Research is also being done on medical treatments to prolong the life of persons infected with HIV and even reverse symptoms of HIV-related illnesses and AIDS. Scientists have isolated chemicals that need to be present in a person's body in order for HIV to infect that person's cells. Understanding how the virus works is a key to finding out how to stop it from reproducing.

Once HIV enters the body, it begins producing copies of itself at a rate of about one billion a day. Every day the body produces new immune cells to fight the virus, and eventually the immune system becomes exhausted and overwhelmed by the virus. To prevent this from occurring, researchers have geared their treatment efforts toward attacking the virus as soon as possible after the initial infection.

The U.S. Food and Drug Administration has approved several new medications that interfere with HIV's ability to reproduce. A new class of medications, *protease inhibitors* (PROH-tee-ayz in-HIB-uh-tuhrs), when used in combination with other antiviral medications such as zidovudine (zih-DOH-vyoo-deen) (AZT) and 3TC, has considerably reduced the amount of HIV in infected individuals. A recently completed clinical trial has determined that giving AZT to a pregnant woman significantly reduces the rate of maternal-fetal transmission of HIV. Effective treatments for AIDS-OIs are prolonging the lives—and improving the quality of life—of people with HIV.

Trace the reaction of HIV as it is blocked by medications used in treatment of the virus.

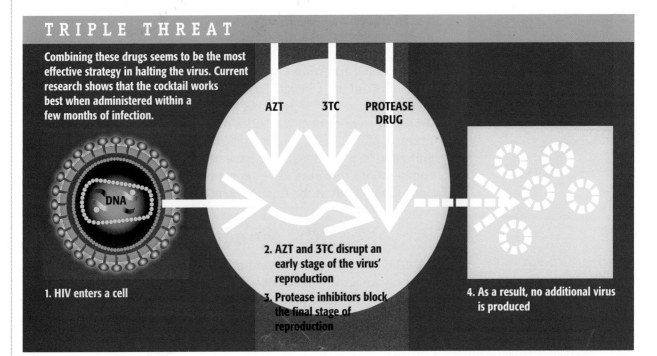

TRIPLE THREAT

Combining these drugs seems to be the most effective strategy in halting the virus. Current research shows that the cocktail works best when administered within a few months of infection.

AZT   3TC   PROTEASE DRUG

DNA

1. HIV enters a cell

2. AZT and 3TC disrupt an early stage of the virus' reproduction

3. Protease inhibitors block the final stage of reproduction

4. As a result, no additional virus is produced

Assessing Health Information: Classroom Resource Folder for AIDS Information

INFORMATION ABOUT HIV, AIDS, and the number of people they affect is being revised almost constantly. Having information that is up-to-the-minute is critical in preventing the spread of this dreaded virus and educating the public at large. One way of doing so is by maintaining an AIDS information resource folder on your classroom computer. Here are some guidelines for getting started:

1. **Contact reputable sources.** These include organizations such as the Centers for Disease Control and Prevention and the National Institutes of Health.

2. **Communicate your needs.** In requesting information, remember that much of the literature published by scientific organizations is intended for health professionals and may, therefore, be beyond your level of comprehension. Specify fact sheets, press releases, and other print materials intended for a non-scientist audience.

3. **Update the contents of your file regularly.** In the world of HIV/AIDS research, nothing stays the same for long. The CDC updates statistics at 6-month intervals. Make sure to do the same with your resource folder.

Obstacles to Research and Treatment

Despite the supposed promise of cutting-edge research and treatment, a number of obstacles remain in the fight against HIV and AIDS. One is the nature of the virus itself. HIV belongs to a family of viruses called *retroviruses*, which reproduce in a manner that makes them difficult to combat. Since HIV was first detected, moreover, several new strains of the virus have emerged, further complicating the already enormous difficulties of developing an effective vaccine. Another obstacle to research is lack of appropriate animal models. Still another roadblock is the issue of affordability of treatment. The combination therapies cost tens of thousands of dollars a year, putting them out of the financial reach of many patients.

Preventing the Spread of HIV

Although the hopes of ever finding a cure or vaccine for HIV infection are uncertain at this point, there is some cause for optimism. HIV is, for the most part, preventable. By avoiding high-risk behaviors, staying informed, and making responsible decisions, you can protect yourself and others from infection.

AIDS Education

As opposed to a mere epidemic, AIDS is a *pandemic*—an outbreak of infectious disease of global proportions. The first step toward altering the picture is educating the public. As Dr. C. Everett Koop, former U.S. Surgeon General, has said, "It is important that we all understand this disease, but it is particularly important for young people who are more often involved in behaviors that put them at risk for getting AIDS."

Abstinence and HIV/AIDS

As noted earlier, a person infected with HIV can look and feel healthy for months or years. As a result, a person can be lured into a false sense of security regarding physical intimacy. The only solution is **abstinence.** You need to say no not only to sexual activity but also to drugs. The following tips can help you practice abstinence from sexual activity and drugs:

- Avoid situations and events where drug use or the pressure to have sexual activity is likely to occur. If you are at a party where things are getting out of control, leave immediately.
- Choose your relationships carefully. Avoid forming a dating relationship with someone whom you know to be sexually active. Avoid known drug users or people who approve of drug use.
- Learn and practice **refusal skills.** Information on strategies for saying no may be found in Chapter 13.

▲ *The AIDS quilt, spread over 24 acres in Washington, D.C.*

h⊙t link

abstinence For more information on abstinence and its importance, see Chapter 21, page 484.

refusal skills For more information on refusal skills and ways of saying no, see Chapter 13, page 304.

LESSON 2 *Review*

Reviewing Facts and Vocabulary

1. What tests are used to determine if a person is HIV-reactive?
2. List two medicines currently being used to treat AIDS.
3. Why is confidentiality an important aspect of HIV testing?

Thinking Critically

4. **Analyzing.** HIV/AIDS is not treated like other infectious diseases in the United States. What aspects of the disorder account for its unique status?
5. **Evaluating.** Should information about HIV and AIDS be part of the regular health education curriculum in public schools? Why or why not?

6. **Synthesizing.** Why might someone armed with knowledge about HIV/AIDS choose to continue to engage in high-risk behaviors?

Applying Health Skills

7. **In Your School.** Develop a one-minute public service announcement (PSA) to inform others about the importance of avoiding the spread of HIV by never doing drugs and remaining abstinent at this time in their lives. Submit the PSA to your school office to be read over the intercom during announcements.

Health Skills Activities

Activity 1 — HIV/AIDS in the United States

The United States is among the world's most advanced nations, yet we continue to see new cases of HIV/AIDS reported.

Directions

1. With several classmates, create a live documentary presentation on the problem of HIV/AIDS. Use information in the chapter and gathered through research.
2. Note the problem's extent, how it is being dealt with, and your evaluation of the costs associated with ongoing research, caring for the sick, and loss in productivity.
3. Perform your documentary for the class.
4. Offer time for a question-and-answer session.

Time
50 minutes

Materials
paper, pen or pencil, library or Internet information

Self-Assessment

✓ Identified at least three risks of contracting HIV/AIDS in your documentary.
✓ Frankly evaluated the HIV/AIDS problem.
✓ Listed at least two prevention strategies.

Activity 2 — Lines of Defense

Abstaining from sexual intercourse is the only 100-percent effective way to protect yourself from HIV/AIDS. Yet, standing your ground under intense peer pressure can be difficult. The board game you are about to create may help.

Directions

1. Write each of 15 or so high-pressure come-ons on one side of an index card. Brainstorm responses for each. Write these on a sheet of paper.
2. Rule off squares around the outside of a sheet of poster board. Label some squares "Pick a card." Others should have to do with navigating the board (e.g., "Lose a turn," "Advance 3 spaces").
3. Place the cards face-down at the center. Two players take turns rolling dice and answering come-ons. A third student compares each response with the answer sheet. First to circle the board wins.

Time
50 minutes

Materials
poster board, pair of dice, colored markers, ruler, index cards, buttons

Self-Assessment

✓ Suggested responses that support the decision to practice abstinence for each high-pressure come-on presented.
✓ Created a colorful and interesting board game.

A New Image of HIV

How can you fight something if you don't know what it looks like? That's the problem scientists face when they treat a new disease. Now scientists have developed a computer model that presents a close-up of a deadly virus.

A recent experimental lab has created the first three-dimensional image of HIV, the virus that causes AIDS. The image can be rotated, color-coded, and analyzed to find weaknesses in the structure of the virus. Researchers hope this model will help them develop medicines that will take advantage of these once-invisible weaknesses.

Play the Video

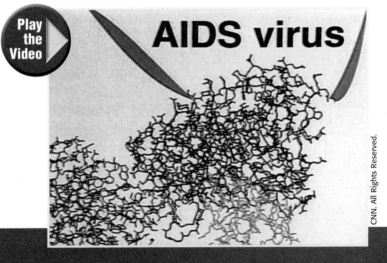

AIDS virus

Think About It

- How can this imaging technology contribute to preventing and curing AIDS?
- Researchers explain that the HIV virus wears an outer layer of sugar molecules. Why do they compare this strategy to "a criminal wearing a disguise"?
- What is an "Achilles heel"? What do researchers at the Dana-Farber Cancer Institute believe might be the Achilles heel of HIV?

Using Health Terms

On a separate sheet of paper, write the term that best matches each definition below.

LESSON 1

1. A virus that attacks the body's immune system.
2. Drugs that are injected into the veins.
3. HIV infection combined with severe immune deficiency.

LESSON 2

4. A period of months or years during which the virus is present in the blood but there are no symptoms or signs of disease.

5. Infected with HIV.
6. A highly accurate test used to confirm the results of a reactive ELISA.
7. Infections and other diseases caused by organisms that do not usually produce illness in healthy people with unimpaired immune systems.
8. A test that screens for the presence of HIV antibodies in the blood.

Recalling the Facts

Using complete sentences, answer the following questions.

LESSON 1

1. What is the connection between HIV infection and AIDS?
2. How does HIV attack the body's immune system?
3. Through which body fluids is HIV known to be transmitted?
4. What happens when T-helper cells become infected and are destroyed?

LESSON 2

5. What is the first test used for detecting HIV? What happens if the results of this test are reactive?
6. How long may the body take to develop antibodies to HIV after being infected?
7. How long can HIV stay in the body before a person shows signs of infection?
8. What are some of the obstacles that stand in the way of research and treatment for AIDS patients?

9. AIDS is not curable, but it is preventable. What are the best methods of prevention?
10. Name two ways teens can reduce their risk of HIV infection.
11. How can using alcohol and illegal drugs increase a person's risk of HIV infection?
12. What role does sexual intercourse play in the spread of HIV?
13. What are two suggestions for practicing abstinence when pressure to engage in sexual activity arises? For practicing abstinence when it comes to drugs?

Thinking Critically

LESSON 1

1. ***Analyzing.*** Indicate which of the following behaviors are known to transmit HIV from an infected person to an uninfected person.
   a. sexual intercourse
   b. kissing with the mouth closed
   c. sharing contaminated needles
   d. sharing bathroom facilities
   e. receiving a blood transfusion
   f. being stung by a wasp
   g. donating blood
   h. breast-feeding a baby

2. ***Evaluating.*** Why do you think many people are uninformed about HIV infection and AIDS?

LESSON 2

3. ***Analyzing.*** What makes opportunistic infections more dangerous for individuals who are HIV-reactive than for persons who are not infected with HIV?

4. ***Synthesizing.*** Outline an HIV-prevention program aimed at teens entering high school, emphasizing not doing drugs, ever, and not becoming sexually active before marriage.

Making the Connection

1. ***Math.*** Through June of 1997, the CDC had received reports of 612,078 cases of AIDS. By exposure category, 84 percent were adult or adolescent males, 15 percent were adult or adolescent females, and 1 percent were children under 13 years of age. Create a pie graph that reflects this information.

2. ***Science.*** Find out about the important discoveries made by one or more of the following researchers: Dr. David Ho, Dr. Robert Gallo, Flossie Wong-Staal, Irving Sigal, or Dr. Peter Piot. Report your findings to the class.

BEYOND THE CLASSROOM

PARENTAL INVOLVEMENT Ask your parents or other adults at home how they learned about HIV and AIDS. Ask them to discuss the quality of the information they were given. Talk with them about the best ways for young people to learn about HIV and AIDS.

COMMUNITY INVOLVEMENT Find out what organizations in your community are helping people with HIV infection and AIDS. Make a list of these organizations and include information about the services each provides. Use the information you have gathered to produce a pamphlet on the classroom computer that can be made available through the school health office.

SCHOOL-TO-CAREER
Resources. Investigate the educational requirements, special skills—including interpersonal skills—time, experience, and other important information about the work of an epidemiologist specializing in HIV and AIDS research. You might start by contacting the American Medical Association, 515 North State Street, Chicago, IL 60610.

CHAPTER 31

Noninfectious Diseases and Disabilities

HEALTH Online

ACCESSING INFORMATION

What can a piece of clothing do to help a person suffering from a disease? An exciting new technology incorporates medical technology into a Lifesaving Vest. Read the facts in "Dressed to Live" in Health Updates at health.glencoe.com.

Personal Health Inventory

Self-Inventory Write the numbers 1–10 on a sheet of paper. Read each statement below and respond by writing *yes*, *no*, or *sometimes* for each item. Write a *yes* only for items that you practice regularly. Save your responses.

1	I avoid being around people who are smoking.
2	I abstain from using tobacco products myself.
3	I avoid adding salt to my food without first tasting it.
4	I eat foods high in fiber, including fruits and vegetables.
5	I keep my weight at an acceptable level.
6	I use some effective ways to relax.
7	I use a sunscreen when participating in activities out of doors.
8	I exercise aerobically at least three times a week.
9	I can identify some of the special challenges that people with disabilities face.
10	I am aware of ways in which my community has met or failed to meet the needs of people with special challenges.

Follow-up After completing the chapter, retake this self-inventory. Pick two items that you need to work on and set a goal to improve your health behaviors.

> " *The more serious the illness, the more important it is for you to fight back, mobilizing all your resources— spiritual, emotional, intellectual, and physical.* "

—NORMAN COUSINS
WRITER, HUMANITARIAN, (1915-1990)

Quick Write Jot down five steps you can take regularly to increase the chances you will stay healthy and avoid the risks of preventable diseases. How many of these steps are you already taking each day?

Lifestyle Diseases

When people hear the word *disease,* they often think of a condition that is contagious, or "catching." Yet, one of the greatest threats today is a group of *diseases that are not transmitted by means of a pathogen.* While you cannot "catch" a heart attack or "come down" with a stroke, these and other **noninfectious diseases** are linked to real risk factors.

HEALTH TERMS

noninfectious diseases

cardiovascular diseases (CVDs)

hypertension

arteriosclerosis

angina pectoris

fibrillation

congestive heart failure

stroke

HEALTH CONCEPTS

- Many cardiovascular diseases relate to a person's habits and lifestyle.
- Adopting positive habits now, while you are young, can help set you on the road to good health for life.

hot link

circulatory system For more information on the circulatory system and its functions, see Chapter 17, page 388.

What Is Cardiovascular Disease?

What do you think is the number one killer in the United States today? It is cardiovascular disease, or *CVD.* **Cardiovascular diseases** are *medical disorders that affect the heart and blood vessels.* The heart and blood vessels are two key parts of the **circulatory system**.

According to the Centers for Disease Control and Prevention, CVDs account for over 45 percent of all deaths among persons in the United States aged 45 years or over. The lifestyle choices and health habits you adopt now can have a direct influence on whether you will be a candidate for a CVD in the future.

Risk Factors for Cardiovascular Disease

A number of risk factors have been identified that increase a person's chances of developing a CVD. Five of these risk factors—heredity, ethnicity, gender, age, and environment—are beyond a person's control.

- **Heredity.** A tendency toward heart disease runs in families. If one or both parents had a CVD, one's chances of developing it are higher. Children of parents with **hypertension**, or *high blood pressure*, are also more likely to develop this CVD.

- **Ethnicity.** Some ethnic groups are at greater risk than others for developing CVDs. For example, African Americans are twice as likely as whites to develop high blood pressure. The reasons for this remain unknown at present.

- **Gender.** Males have a greater risk of heart disease and stroke than females. At the same time, the latest studies indicate that heart attack is the number one killer among American women and that their chances of survival are lower than those of men.

- **Age.** Risk of CVDs increases with age. Heart attack death rates increase markedly after the age of 45, with 55 percent of all heart attack victims being 65 or older. Risk of stroke also increases dramatically with age.

- **Environment.** Environmental factors such as smog are beyond your control, another form of air pollution—tobacco smoke from another person's cigar, pipe, or cigarette—is often avoidable. Stress, likewise, is a controllable environmental risk factor.

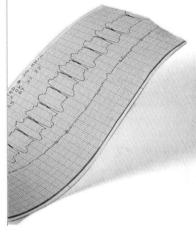

Behavior

Although the factors identified in the previous section are beyond the individual's ability to control, a fifth risk factor is not. That factor is behavior. Making the right healthful choices now, while you are young, can reduce your risk of developing a CVD later in life. These choices include ample physical activity, electing not to smoke, and moderation and balance in your food selections. Because of the link between lifestyle and CVDs, these diseases are sometimes referred to as "lifestyle diseases."

HOW MUCH IS ENOUGH?

When it comes to food, a problem for many Americans is not only *what* they eat but *how much.* Learning to identify healthful portions can be a first step in controlling the tendency to overeat–not to mention the risk of CVDs in the future.

What you will need

- Large bowls of the following foods: applesauce, cooked rice or pasta, unsalted pretzels, and shelled nuts.
- A 1-cup measuring cup
- Paper plate, pad and pencil

What you will do

1. Begin by consulting the Food Guide Pyramid on page 114 for suggested single servings of each of the foods you have assembled.

2. Transfer what you imagine to be a single serving of one of the foods onto a paper plate. Let your eyes alone judge quantity.

3. Using the measuring cup, measure out a 1-cup portion of the same food onto a second paper plate. Record any differences you observe between the two portions.

4. Repeat the procedure with the other three foods. Again, note any differences.

5. After several days, repeat the entire experiment again.

In conclusion

1. How close were you at estimating correct serving sizes? Did you become more proficient at "eye-balling" correct amounts when you repeated the experiment?

2. Were the recommended serving sizes less or more of each food than you normally eat?

Types of Cardiovascular Diseases

The heart, blood, and arteries are the principal parts of the circulatory system. When these parts work together properly, the circulatory system runs efficiently. When a problem affects one part, the entire system is threatened.

Hypertension

Blood pressure is the force of blood against the walls of blood vessels as blood flows through the circulatory system. The force is created by the contraction of the heart muscle and the resistance of the vessel walls. Normal blood pressure varies with age, height, weight, and other factors. If a person's blood pressure stays above his or her normal pressure, the person is said to have hypertension. An estimated 60 million Americans suffer from hypertension, which is both a disease and a causative factor in other CVDs. Because an individual may show no symptoms in the early stages, hypertension often goes undetected. Hypertension is, therefore, known as the "silent killer."

In many cases, the exact cause of hypertension is not known. However, many factors have been identified as being related to it, including the uncontrollable risk factors noted earlier. Controllable factors include obesity, alcohol use, inactivity, smoking, and excessive intake of salt or sodium.

Hypertension cannot be cured but can be controlled through basic lifestyle changes, such as eating well, losing excess weight, and exercise. In more extreme cases, medications are sometimes prescribed.

Diseases of the Arteries

At birth, the lining of the blood vessels is smooth. Over the years, fatty deposits, called *plaque,* build up along the inner lining of the arteries. This buildup is due mainly to food choices. If this buildup is permitted to continue, **arteriosclerosis** (ahr-tir-ee-oh-skluh-ROH-suhs), or *hardening of the arteries,* occurs. Arteriosclerosis is a condition in which the walls of the arteries become thick and lose their elasticity. It is the most common cause of death in the United States. Hypertension is a factor that contributes to arteriosclerosis.

As fatty deposits accumulate, blood vessels narrow. This condition, called *atherosclerosis* (ath-uh-roh-skluh-ROH-suhs), can result in blockage of the arteries. Foods high in fat and **cholesterol** are key contributing factors to atherosclerosis.

Diseases of the Heart

When atherosclerosis becomes severe enough, the blood vessels leading to the heart become blocked. Normal oxygen supply is cut off. The heart sends out a warning in the form of **angina pectoris** (AN-juh-nuh PEK-tuh-ris), or *pain and tightness in the chest caused by the lack of oxygen to the heart.* Angina is like an SOS from the body warning that the heart is in distress. Angina pain usually lasts a few minutes. Treatment includes medications that relax the blood vessels.

HEART ATTACK

If the distress of angina continues over time, eventually heart attack occurs. A heart attack is caused by insufficient oxygen and nutrients to the heart muscle cells. One and a half million people in the United States each year suffer heart attacks.

A heart attack can occur at any time and usually happens without warning. However, immediate response to the early signs, which include discomfort in the center of the chest, can mean the difference between life and death. The sensation of a heart attack may be one of pressure, fullness, squeezing, or aching. This distress may extend into one or both arms, the neck, jaw, upper abdomen, and even the back.

Are you "heart smart"? Visit **health.glencoe.com** to learn how to lower your risk of heart disease and recognize warning signs of heart attack and stroke. Take an online quiz to see how much you have learned.

h t l nk

cholesterol For more information on the risks associated with elevated cholesterol levels, see Chapter 5, page 106.

hotlink

cardiopulmonary resuscitation (CPR) For more information on the lifesaving technique of cardiopulmonary resuscitation (CPR), see Chapter 35, page 781.

▼ *Early signs of a heart attack can include a tightness in the chest, sensation in the arms or back, and shortness of breath.*

ACTIVITY *List the causes of heart attack and of congestive heart failure.*

Nausea, vomiting, sweating, and shortness of breath may accompany the attack. A person with these symptoms should seek medical attention immediately.

Depending on the amount of tissue death, a heart attack can cause death or a decrease in heart function. An immediate cause of death in many heart attacks is **fibrillation**—*the rapid ineffective beating of the heart in one of two chambers called ventricles.* Ventricular fibrillation is also known as "cardiac arrest." When this occurs, **cardiopulmonary resuscitation (CPR)** should be initiated as soon as possible.

Heart attack is related to many risk factors, such as high levels of cholesterol in the blood. Cholesterol builds up inside the scarred arteries, which can lead to fatal blockages. Studies also link excess levels in the blood of *homocysteine* (hoh-moh-SIS-teen), a potentially deadly amino acid, to heart disease. Stress, another major risk factor, can increase other existing risk factors, such as overeating, smoking, and hypertension. People with Type A personalities may also be at higher risk.

CONGESTIVE HEART FAILURE

Heart attack is an immediate event in response to stress on the heart. Sometimes the result of years of arteriosclerosis and hypertension result not in heart attack but in **congestive heart failure**, *a slow, gradual weakening of the heart muscle from overwork.* Congestive heart failure can also be brought about by the use of certain illegal drugs.

Stroke

Sometimes arterial blockage affects the blood supply to the brain. When the blockage is severe, **stroke**—*an interruption of the flow of blood to any part of the brain*—may occur. Stroke can affect different parts of the body. The warning signs of stroke are:

- sudden weakness or numbness of the face, arm, and leg on one side of the body
- loss of speech, or trouble in speaking or understanding people
- sudden dimness or loss of vision, particularly in only one eye
- unexplained dizziness, unsteadiness, or sudden falls

There are various causes of stroke. One of the most common is the blocking of a cerebral artery by a blood clot, or *thrombus,* that forms inside the artery. Sometimes a diseased artery in the brain can burst and flood the surrounding brain tissue with blood. This damaging condition, called a *cerebral hemorrhage* (suh-REE-bruhl HEM-uh-rihj), is more likely to occur when a person suffers from a combination of atherosclerosis and hypertension.

Treating Cardiovascular Diseases

In recent decades there have been amazing advances in treating heart disease. These include new instruments and techniques for measuring electrical activity of the heart and the extent of the disease, as well as new surgical procedures.

- **Electrocardiogram.** An electrocardiogram (ih-lek-troh-KAR-dee-uh-gram)—or *EKG*—produces a graph of the electrical activity of the heart's rhythm. An EKG can help detect the nature of a heart attack and how the heart is behaving.

- **Radionuclide** (RAY-dee-oh-NOO-klyd) **imaging.** This process includes several tests that involve the injection of substances called *radionuclides* into the blood. Following the progress of the radionuclides on a computer screen, technicians are able to determine how much blood is being supplied to the heart, how well its chambers are functioning, and whether any part of the heart has been damaged by heart attack.

- **Phonocardiography** (FOHN-uh-kar-dee-OG-ruh-fee). This process involves placing a microphone on a person's chest to record heart sounds and signals, which are transferred through photography to graph paper. A professional can then examine the tracings for heartbeat irregularities.

- **Coronary angiography** (KOR-uh-nayr-ee an-jee-OG-ruh-fee). This procedure is used to help evaluate the extent of coronary artery disease. This procedure uses a *catheter,* a thin, flexible tube that can be guided through blood vessels to the heart. When dye is injected into the catheter, motion X rays can be taken, by which narrow or obstructed areas of the heart can be detected.

- **Artificial pacemaker.** If the heart's natural pacemaker fails, an artificial one is implanted in the chest and wired to the heart. The pacemaker can be set to work on demand when the natural heartbeat is too slow or at a fixed rate to work all the time.

- **Magnetic resonance imaging (MRI).** This test uses powerful magnets to look inside the body. Images of the heart muscle are transferred to a computer, allowing technicians to identify damage from a heart attack and diagnose certain congenital heart defects.

Surgical Procedures

Many surgical procedures have saved the lives of people with heart problems. Only since the middle of the twentieth century, however, have these procedures been available. Some, such as the implantation of artificial hearts and blood vessels, are still on the cutting edge. Procedures currently in use include:

- **Heart transplant.** If a patient's heart is badly damaged by heart disease, doctors may remove the weak heart and replace it with a heart from a person who has recently died.

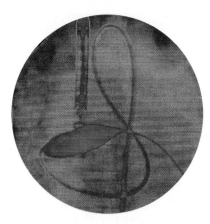

A *Balloon angioplasty inside a blocked artery will open a path for blood flow.*

ACTIVITY *What measures can you take to keep your arteries free of plaque buildup?*

- **Coronary bypass surgery.** Coronary bypass surgery creates detours around obstructed or narrowed coronary arteries so that more blood can reach the heart. In this operation a large vein from the patient's leg is grafted onto the heart. This allows blood to flow to the area that was not getting enough blood.

- **Balloon angioplasty.** Balloon angioplasty involves threading a balloon-tipped catheter through the body to the site of the blockage. As the balloon is inflated, it pushes the plaque against the artery wall, opening a path for the blood to flow through.

- **Heart valve surgery.** Valves control the proper flow of blood through the heart. Defective valves may be present at birth or develop later in life. A valve may be too tight, which can restrict the flow of blood, or it may not close tightly enough, which can cause blood to flow backward. A surgical procedure replaces a defective valve with an artificial one made of metal or plastic.

Prevention of Cardiovascular Disease

Adopting healthful habits now, while you are young, can help prevent your risk of heart disease in the future. Practice the following:

- Avoid the use of tobacco products, alcohol, and drugs.
- Reduce your intake of cholesterol. Choose an eating plan that has plenty of vegetables, fruits, and grain products.
- Maintain a weight that is healthful for you.
- Limit your intake of salty foods. Avoid adding salt to food.
- Get plenty of physical activity.
- Manage stress in your daily life.

LESSON 1 *Review*

Reviewing Facts and Vocabulary

1. What are the five uncontrollable risk factors associated with cardiovascular diseases?
2. Use the terms *hypertension, arteriosclerosis, atherosclerosis,* and *angina pectoris* in a paragraph that discusses the progression of heart disease.
3. List three techniques or procedures for treating heart disease.

Thinking Critically

4. *Analyzing.* Why do you think the noninfectious diseases have replaced the infectious diseases as the leading causes of death?

5. *Synthesizing.* Denial is the major reason why someone who is suffering the warning signs of a heart attack does not seek medical attention. Why would someone deny having a heart attack? How can denial of the warning signs of a heart attack cost someone his or her life?

Applying Health Knowledge

6. *In Your Home.* If you or someone in your home is in a high-risk group for heart disease, what lifestyle changes could you suggest to reduce the risks of heart attack?

Cancer

Human life begins as a single cell that divides millions of times. Cell division occurs throughout life as old dead cells are replaced by new ones. Sometimes the normal forces regulating cell growth are disrupted. Abnormal cells grow and spread to healthy cells. These *uncontrolled abnormal cell growths* are called **cancers.**

HEALTH TERMS

cancers

tumors

benign

malignant

metastasis

carcinogen

melanoma

biopsy

chemotherapy

HEALTH CONCEPTS

- Risk factors for cancer include heredity, environment, and lifestyle.
- There are seven warning signs of cancer.
- The earlier a cancer is diagnosed, the greater the range of treatment options that are available.

hotlink

lymph For more information on lymph and the role of the lymphatic system, see Chapter 17, page 393.

Tumors

All cancers are **tumors**, *masses of tissue*, but not all tumors are cancers. Some tumors are **benign**, or *noncancerous*. Noncancerous tumors are characterized by abnormal cells, but their growth is less aggressive than that of cancerous ones. Also, these tumors are surrounded by membranes that prevent them from spreading.

Malignant, or *cancerous*, tumors—by contrast—have no such membranes. Sometimes cancerous cells break away from a malignant tumor and move through **lymph** or blood vessels to other healthy tissues. This *spread of cancer from the point where it originated to other parts of the body* is known as **metastasis**.

ABCD of Skin Care

Catching melanoma early can mean the difference between life and death. An important part of cancer prevention, therefore, is to periodically check any skin moles for the "ABCDs":

➤ **A**symmetry–or unevenness;

➤ **B**order–look for telltale features such as notched, scalloped, or indistinct edges;

➤ **C**olor–be alert for the following colors and patterns: tan and brown, black, or red and white; and

➤ **D**iameter–a mole larger than 6 mm should be reported to a physician.

Lymphocytes attacking cancer cell

Causes of Cancer

A number of risk factors have been associated with cancer, among them heredity, environment, and lifestyle. Some cases of cancers are caused by exposure to a **carcinogen** (kar-SIN-uh-jihn), *a cancer-causing substance in the environment.* Carcinogens include chemicals found in tobacco smoke, asbestos, and toxic wastes. Exposure to certain forms of radiation, including X rays, radon, and the sun's ultra-violet rays, is another known cause of cancer. Some viruses and contaminated water have also been found to be carcinogenic.

Not everyone is equally susceptible to the same carcinogens. You can control your exposure to and ingestion of many carcinogens.

Types of Cancer

Cancers are classified in two ways: by the part of the body where the cancer cells first develop, and by the type of body tissue within which the cancer begins.

Cancers that develop in *epithelial tissue,* tissue that forms the skin and linings of body organs, are called carcinomas (KAR-suh-NOH-muhs). Sarcomas are cancers that develop in connective and

Different Types of Cancer

BODY-SITE TYPE	ORGAN(S) MOST OFTEN AFFECTED	OCCURRENCE
Skin cancer	Skin	Most common type in the United States
Digestive system	Colon (large intestine) and rectum (excreting tract)	Most common type in United States next to skin cancer
Respiratory system	Larynx and lungs	Mainly occurs in men: increase in incidence of lung cancer in women
Breast	Breast	Mostly women
Reproductive system	*Males*—prostate gland *Female*—cervix, ovaries, uterus	
Blood and lymph system	Bone marrow, lymph (cancer of the bone marrow is called *leukemia*)	Occurs in men and women

supportive tissues such as bones, muscles, and tendons. Lymphomas are cancers that develop in the lymphatic system. Hodgkin's disease is a type of lymphoma.

Skin Cancer

There are three types of skin cancer: **melanoma,** the *often deadly type of skin cancer,* the more curable basal cell, and squamous cell skin cancers. There are 100,000 new cases of melanoma every year. While there is an increased awareness about the dangers of exposure to the sun, people develop skin cancers because they fail to protect them-selves by using sunscreens.

▼ *When it is used correctly, sunscreen protects your skin from the sun's ultraviolet rays.*

ACTIVITY *Find which SPF (sun protection factor) found in sunscreen offers the greatest amount of protection from the sun's rays for the longest period of time. How often should you apply sunscreen while in the sun?*

Building Health Skills

Reducing the Risks of Cancer

SOME CANCER RISK FACTORS such as age and family history cannot be changed. However, other risk factors such as eating patterns and use of known carcinogens can be controlled. The following guidelines can help lower your chances of developing cancer.

1. Be physically active.

2. Achieve and maintain a healthful weight.

3. Eat plenty of fruits, vegetables, and whole grains.

4. Reduce the amount of fat in the foods you eat, particularly from animal sources, to no more than 30 percent of your total daily calorie intake.

5. Limit your time in the sun. Use sunscreen when exposed to the sun for any length of time.

6. Avoid using all forms of tobacco and alcohol.

7. Know your body and recognize the warning signs of cancer. Visit your doctor immediately if you suspect a problem.

Lung Cancer

The American Cancer Society reports that cigarette smoking is the single greatest cause of cancer in the United States today, accounting for 85 percent of lung cancer cases among males and 75 percent among females. Males who start smoking before the age of 15 are five times more likely to die of lung cancer than those who started after age 25. Among women, lung cancer has tripled in the last 20 years. This is a direct result of the increasing numbers of women who now smoke. Survival rate is only 13 percent.

Oral Cancer

Oral cancer affects the mouth and throat area. Risk factors for oral cancer include smoking of cigarettes, cigars, or a pipe, and the use of smokeless tobacco. These cancers form where tobacco has touched the person's lips, mouth, and throat tissues. Excessive use of alcohol is another risk factor for oral cancer.

Cancer of the Colon and Rectum

Cancer of the colon and rectum is the third most commonly occurring cancer in the United States today. This cancer usually develops in the lowest part of the colon, near the rectum. As the cancer grows larger, it either blocks the colon or causes bleeding, often during elimination. Cancers of this type are slow to spread. Seeking early medical help greatly increases a person's chance of survival. An eating plan low in fat and high in fiber decreases a person's risk of this cancer.

Reproductive Cancer

Most new cancer cases in the United States are found in the **reproductive system**—breast cancer in women and prostate cancer in men. In women, cancerous tumors can develop in the ovaries and uterus as well. Early detection through regular pelvic examinations and a Pap test has reduced the death rate from uterine and cervical cancers. **Breast self-examination (BSE),** regular medical checkups, and mammography are ways that breast cancer is detected.

Prostate cancer can often be detected during a rectal exam. Cancer in males can also develop in the testes. Testicular cancer, the leading type of cancer among males aged 15 to 34, can be detected during regular testicular self-examination. Any lumps or thickening detected by a male or female through a reproductive self-examination should be reported to a doctor.

htlink

reproductive system For more information on the reproductive system and its care, see Chapter 19, page 434.

breast self-examination (BSE) For more information on how to perform breast self-examination, see Chapter 19, page 444.

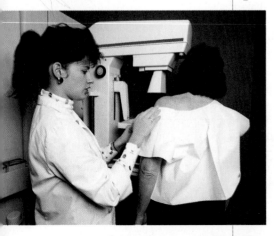

▼ *Regular mammogram checks provide early detection of breast cancer.*

Leukemia

Leukemia is cancer of the blood-forming tissue in the bone marrow. In leukemia, immature white blood cells multiply too rapidly and crowd out mature white cells. This weakens the body's immune system. Although often thought of as primarily a childhood disease, leukemia strikes people of all ages and both genders. Childhood leukemia is very curable, with a success rate of 95 percent.

Detecting Cancer

Early detection of cancer is the most critical factor in combating the disease. Many types of cancer can be detected during a routine physical examination. This is one reason why regular physical check-ups are important. If a tumor is found, a physician may do a **biopsy,** *a laboratory analysis of a section of tissue taken from a site where abnormal cell growth is suspected.* Ultrasound, which uses sound waves, can be used to locate abnormal growths when they are small and more easily treatable. This diagnostic procedure can also help determine the best method of treatment.

Treating Cancer

Treatment of cancers is directed at confining and killing the cancerous cells. At present, this is accomplished by three basic approaches: surgery, radiation, and chemotherapy.

▼ *Due to constant improvements in medicine and technology, today cancer patients experience a high rate of recovery.*

ACTIVITY *Explain ways you could support a friend or relative who is undergoing treatment for cancer.*

up date
▶ *Looking at Technology*

The Cyberknife

A new technological advancement in the war on cancer is the *cyberknife.* A blend of robotics, computers, and radiation therapy, the cyberknife is used to blast away cancerous tumors deep in the brain. A robotic arm is programmed to fire beams of low-level gamma rays toward specific targets—in this case, tumors. Much like a guided missile, the cyberknife is able to hit the tumor with maximum accuracy and without damaging surrounding tissue. The cyberknife compensates for any slight movement of the patient's head by automatically and constantly readjusting its fix on the target. This capability has rendered obsolete the bulky, uncomfortable metal devices that brain tumor patients were once forced to wear when undergoing gamma radiation. What is more, the cyberknife is lighter, faster, more flexible, and more powerful than past "gamma knife" treatments.

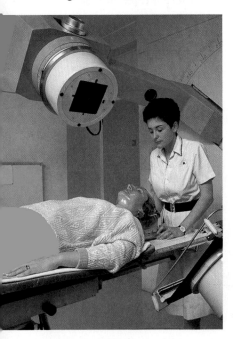

Surgery, radiation, and chemotherapy are techniques used to treat and control many types of cancers.

ACTIVITY *Describe how different treatments destroy or stop the growth of cancer cells.*

Surgery

Surgery has been a standard method in removing tumors and affected areas. Today, with improved surgical techniques, cancer patients have a longer life expectancy and an improved quality of life. Whereas amputation used to be standard practice for treating cancer of arm and leg bones, now doctors are able to treat many such cancers by removing only the diseased bone tissue and transplanting healthy tissue from another part of the patient's body.

Radiation

Radiation energy from cobalt or radium can penetrate a tumor. The energy destroys the tumor cells by damaging DNA in the nuclei. DNA is the genetic material responsible for cell division. Radiation therapy is very successful in arresting—or slowing the growth of—certain kinds of cancer, such as cervical cancer. It is also very helpful in areas of the body where surgery is difficult, such as the head and neck.

Chemotherapy

Chemotherapy is *the use of anti-cancer medications in the treatment of cancer.* Its goal is to destroy malignant cells without excessive destruction of normal cells.

Chemotherapy works by interfering with cell division of the cancer cells and, by doing so, preventing the cancer from spreading. Unfortunately, some unpleasant side effects such as nausea and vomiting may occur with the use of these strong medicines. However, new techniques are allowing doctors to administer chemotherapy more safely and with fewer complications and side effects.

LESSON 2 *Review*

Reviewing Facts and Vocabulary

1. What is the difference between a benign tumor and malignant tumor?
2. Why is early diagnosis and treatment of cancer so important?

Thinking Critically

3. *Synthesizing.* Find out if there is such a thing as a "safe" tan. Compare tanning that results from the sun's rays to tanning from a tanning salon. Share your findings in a report.
4. *Comparing and Contrasting.* Use information from the chapter as well as other current resources to make a three-column chart. The first column should note the body system or organ affected by the cancer, the second should note the number of people affected by it annually, and the third should describe the success rate of treatment.

Applying Health Knowledge

5. *In Your Home and School.* Interview someone at home or in your school or community who has successfully undergone cancer treatment. Get details about the treatment, any side effects, and time needed for recovery. Share your findings in a report.

Other Noninfectious Diseases

Some noninfectious diseases can seem to strike without warning. Others tend to "build" in the body over time, eventually leading to poor health. Regardless of the manner in which a disease presents itself, having information about these diseases is a first step toward prevention and recognition of their signs and symptoms.

HEALTH TERMS

diabetes

insulin

impaired glucose tolerance (IGT)

arthritis

rheumatoid arthritis

osteoarthritis

HEALTH CONCEPTS

- Knowing the differences between type 1 and type 2 diabetes is essential to treatment of the diseases.
- Arthritis can affect people of any age.
- Treatment programs to ease the discomfort of arthritis are available.

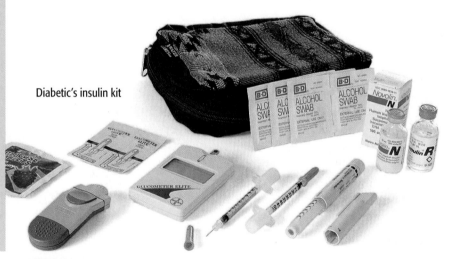

Diabetic's insulin kit

h⊙tlink

glucose For more information on glucose and its role in nutrition, see Chapter 5, page 102.

Diabetes

Diabetes is *a chronic disease that affects the way body cells convert food into energy.* It is the seventh leading cause of death by disease in the United States, affecting 16 million Americans. Each day approximately 2,200 new cases are diagnosed.

Diabetes can lead to a host of other major illnesses and health conditions, including blindness, kidney disease, nerve disease and amputations, and heart disease and stroke.

What Causes Diabetes

In the normal digestive process, carbohydrates are changed to the sugar **glucose**, then absorbed into the blood and delivered to body cells. **Insulin,** *a hormone that is produced in the pancreas and that helps the body convert glucose to energy,* is an essential link in this process. In the case of diabetes, sufficient insulin is not produced or is not used efficiently. When glucose is unable to enter the cells, it accumulates in the blood until the kidneys filter out some of the surplus, which is passed off in urine. High sugar content in urine and in the blood is one of the surest signs that a person has diabetes.

In Case of a Diabetic Emergency

TYPE I	TYPE II
SOURCE	**SOURCE**
■ Low blood sugar (Insulin reaction/*hypoglycemia* (high-poh-gly-**see**-mee-uh), an abnormal decrease of sugar in the blood)	■ High blood sugar
TIME SPAN	**TIME SPAN**
■ Sudden onset (minutes to hours)	■ Gradual onset (hours to days)
SIGNS	**SIGNS**
■ Staggering, poor coordination	■ Thirst
■ Irritability, belligerence, hostility	■ Very frequent urination
■ Pale color	■ Flushed skin
■ Sweating	■ Vomiting
■ Eventual stupor or unconsciousness	■ Fruity or winelike odor or breath
	■ Eventual stupor or unconsciousness
CAUSES	**CAUSES**
■ Delayed or missed meals	■ Undiagnosed diabetes
■ Too much insulin, by overdose or error	■ Insulin forgotten or omitted
■ Extreme exercise	■ Stress, such as illness or injury
	■ Overindulgence in food or drink
TREATMENT	**TREATMENT**
■ Provide sugar.	■ Get the person to a hospital.
■ If the person can swallow without choking, offer *any* food or drink containing sugar, such as soft drinks, fruit juice, candy.	■ If you are uncertain whether the person has high blood sugar or low blood sugar, give some food or drink containing sugar. If the person does not respond in 10 to 15 minutes, he or she needs a physician's help.
■ Do not use diet drinks!	■ Do not give food or drink if the person is unable to swallow. Take the person to a hospital if he or she has no response to treatments.
■ If the person does not respond in 10 to 15 minutes, take him or her to a hospital.	
■ Look for a diabetic identification bracelet or necklace.	
■ The diabetic may carry candy or special quick-sugar commercial preparations in plastic, soft-tipped containers. Squeeze the contents into the person's mouth.	

Types of Diabetes and Risk Factors

There are two main classifications of diabetes: type 1, or immune-mediated (formerly known as *insulin-dependent*) diabetes, and type 2 (formerly known as *non-insulin-dependent*) diabetes. Type 1 usually occurs during childhood or adolescence. Type 2, the most common form of the disease, usually occurs after age 40.

Like CVDs, some risk factors for diabetes are related to lifestyle, principally obesity and physical inactivity, while others are genetic. For reasons not entirely understood, whites are more likely than other groups to develop type 1 diabetes, while African Americans, Hispanics, and Native Americans are more likely to develop type 2. Yet another major risk factor for type 2 diabetes is **impaired glucose tolerance (IGT),** *a condition in which blood sugar levels are higher than normal but not high enough to be classified as diabetes.*

Type 1 Diabetes

Type 1 diabetes, which accounts for about 10 percent of all cases of the disease, appears abruptly and progresses rapidly. Most often, type 1 diabetes results from a malfunction of the **immune system**—the system that defends the body against invading pathogens. In an individual with type 1 diabetes, the immune system mistakenly attacks and destroys the insulin-producing cells of the pancreas. The body's cells become "starved" for insulin.

Symptoms of type 1 diabetes include frequent urination, abnormal thirst, unusual hunger, weight loss, weakness, fatigue, irritability, and nausea. Because the pancreas is unable to produce insulin,

h·t l·nk

immune system For more information on the functions of the immune system, see Chapter 28, page 624.

Making Responsible Decisions

Confronting Diabetes

Diabetes runs in Sylvie's family on her mother's side. Last month, her aunt was diagnosed as having type 2 diabetes. Sylvie has seen the effect the disease has had on other family members. Her grandfather lost a leg to the disease, and an uncle went blind. Now a new problem has arisen in the family, and it has Sylvie worried. Her mother, afraid of becoming the next victim of diabetes, has stopped eating. She has lost over 25 pounds. Sylvie's father is away much of the time on business, and Sylvie feels there is no one else she can turn to for help for her mother. What should she do?

What Would You Do?

Apply the six steps of the decision-making process to Sylvie's problem:

1. **State the situation.**
2. **List the options.**
3. **Weigh the possible outcomes.**
4. **Consider your values.**
5. **Make a decision and act.**
6. **Evaluate the decision.**

People with diabetes must pay close attention to the foods they eat and monitor the amount of sugar in their blood to avoid diabetic emergencies.

ACTIVITY *Find out what you would need to do for a friend with diabetes in case of emergency.*

patients must take daily doses of insulin either through injection or by means of a special pump that is attached to the body via tubing or surgically implanted. Today, because of advanced methods of treatment, many persons with diabetes live near-normal lives.

Emergencies can arise for people with diabetes that necessitate immediate medical attention. It is, therefore, important for a person with diabetes to wear an identification device, such as a bracelet or necklace, advising of this medical condition so that passersby can act quickly and get help that can be the difference between life and death.

Type 2 Diabetes

Type 2 diabetes is a metabolic disorder resulting from the body's inability to make enough, or properly use, insulin. In type 2 diabetes, the pancreas produces some insulin, but because of a cell receptor defect, the cells cannot use the insulin effectively. Symptoms of type 2 diabetes include excess weight, drowsiness, blurred vision, tingling or numbness in the hands and feet, slower than normal healing of cuts and bruises, itching, and recurring skin, gum, or bladder infections.

About 80 percent of all type 2 patients are overweight at the time of diagnosis. Type 2 diabetes can usually be controlled by eating patterns, exercise, and—when necessary—by losing excess weight. In some cases, oral medications or injections of insulin are also required. Problems related to circulation are common in this type of diabetes. Because the onset of type 2 diabetes is gradual, the disease often goes undetected for years. In fact, of the estimated 15.3 million Americans currently inflicted with the disease, roughly half are unaware they have it.

Arthritis

Arthritis covers *at least 100 different conditions that cause aching, pain, and swelling in joints and connective tissue throughout the body.* The term *arthritis* itself means "inflammation of a joint." Arthritis can and does occur at all ages, from infancy on. The National Center for Health Statistics estimates that over 40 million people have arthritis severe enough to require medical care.

The two most common types of arthritis are rheumatoid (ROOM-uh-toyd) arthritis and osteoarthritis. Like type 1 diabetes, these are *autoimmune diseases,* conditions in which the body's immune system turns on itself. Why this occurs is still a mystery.

Rheumatoid Arthritis

The most serious type of arthritis, **rheumatoid arthritis** is mainly *a destructive and disabling inflammation of the joints*. It affects primarily the joints of the hands and arms, the hips, and the feet and legs. Rheumatoid inflammation also attacks connective tissue, causing symptoms such as fever, fatigue, and swollen lymph glands. Rheumatoid arthritis causes the joints to stiffen, then swell and become tender. The inflammation can do progressive damage inside the joint if it is not diagnosed and properly treated.

Scientists do not know the cause of rheumatoid arthritis, and at present there is no cure. A full treatment program for rheumatoid arthritis depends on the physician and may include anti-inflammatory medicines such as aspirin and ibuprofen, rest, exercise, weight control, splints, walking aids, heat, surgery, and rehabilitation.

Osteoarthritis

Osteoarthritis is *a disease that affects primarily the weight-bearing joints of the knees and hips, causing aches and soreness especially when moving.* It is the most common type of arthritis, affecting about 16 million people. Osteoarthritis results from wear and tear in the mechanical parts of a joint. Inflammation is rarely a problem.

In osteoarthritis, the cartilage becomes pitted and frayed and, in time, may wear away completely. Bone ends then become thicker and bony spurs may develop. As a result, surrounding ligaments and membranes become thickened, changing the whole structure and shape of the joint. There is no cure for arthritis, but early detection and diagnosis is essential to managing the disease. The treatment program includes exercise, weight control, eating a balanced assortment of foods, and pain medications.

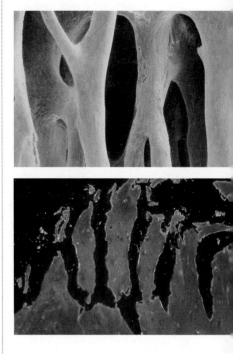

Compare the appearance of normal bone tissue (top) with tissue affected by osteoarthritis (bottom).

LESSON 3 *Review*

Reviewing Facts and Vocabulary

1. What is a sure sign that a person has diabetes?

2. What are the early signs of arthritis?

3. How is arthritis treated?

Thinking Critically

4. *Comparing and Contrasting.* Review the similarities and differences of type 1 and type 2 diabetes. Explain why type 2 diabetes is considered a lifestyle disease for most people.

5. *Analyzing.* Compare rheumatoid arthritis and osteoarthritis.

Applying Health Knowledge

6. *In Your School.* Invite to class an individual with diabetes. Find out how the disease has affected his or her life. What special precautions must he or she take to stay healthy? How are these precautions the same as and different from measures you take to stay healthy?

Physical and Mental Challenges

Does your school have ramps and special bathroom facilities to accommodate people in wheelchairs? Are there telephones for the hearing or vision impaired? Such aids for people with physical and mental challenges began to appear in recent decades.

HEALTH TERMS

disability

profound deafness

mental retardation

Americans with Disabilities Act

HEALTH CONCEPTS

- Depending on its nature and severity, a disability can interfere with an individual's performance of tasks that nondisabled people may take for granted.
- Understanding the realities of physical and mental challenges is important for all people.

Disabilities

A **disability** is *any physical or mental impairment that limits normal activities, including seeing, hearing, walking, or speaking.* It is estimated that between 9 and 10 percent of the population in this country has a disability.

People with a disability sometimes have difficulty doing things other people take for granted. They may have difficulty riding buses and subways, climbing stairs, or even using certain household appliances. However, the greatest challenge facing people with a disability is the misguided view society has long held. Historically, people with disabilities have been seen as a "breed apart." They have been pitied, ignored, and even placed in institutions that offered mere custodial care.

Physical Challenges

The most common types of physical challenges affect a primary sense or ability to move and get around easily. These include sight impairment, hearing impairment, and motor impairment.

Sight Impairment

As with other disabilities, sight impairment can be moderate, as is the case with the more than 5 million Americans who are vision-impaired, or it can be severe, as with the 1 million who are blind. About 10 percent of people fitting this description are under 20 years old.

The leading cause of blindness today is from complications due to diabetes. Whereas everyone must take care of their vision and have regular eye examinations, those with diabetes must take special care to have more frequent exams in addition to maintaining a special diet and taking medication. Other causes of blindness are macular degeneration, **glaucoma**, and **cataracts**. Early diagnosis means that treatment can begin sooner to prevent blindness.

Hearing Impairment

Hearing impairment affects 20 million Americans. Like blindness, hearing impairment can range from minor to severe. **Profound deafness** is *a hearing loss so severe that a person affected cannot benefit from mechanical amplification such as a hearing aid.*

Deafness can be inherited or caused by injury or disease. Most hearing impairments are caused by infections, obstructions, or nerve damage. Obstructions may block sound waves traveling to the inner ear. If obstruction is the cause of hearing impairment, the hearing loss may involve only one ear. Obstructions may be due to a buildup of wax, bone blockage, or something stuck in the ear.

A person born with abnormal bone growth in the inner ear may have inherited an obstruction that results in impaired hearing or deafness. Surgery can cure many of these cases.

Nerve damage usually distorts hearing in both ears. Exposure to loud noise can cause nerve damage. It may also occur with aging. Hearing impairments from nerve damage and obstruction may be gradual. If your hearing has changed, it may be time for a visit to your doctor or to an *audiologist,* a specialist in hearing problems.

HEALTH Online

Visit **health.glencoe.com** to learn about eye care, diseases, and the responsibilities of eye care professionals.

hot link

glaucoma For more information on glaucoma, a disease that damages the optic nerve of the eye, see Chapter 7, page 174.

cataracts For more information on cataracts, a clouding of the lens of the eye, see Chapter 7, page 174.

◀ *Learning sign language can give you the ability to communicate with the hearing impaired.*

ACTIVITY *List organizations in your area that offer special classes for sign language or for Braille, a system that allows blind people to read through the sense of touch.*

► *A visit to someone who is chronically ill can help make them feel better.*

ACTIVITY *Write the name of someone you know who is chronically ill, and next to the name write at least two things you can do to help that person feel better.*

Motor Impairment

An injury to the brain or a disorder of the nervous system can affect the body's range of movement and coordination, including that of the hand and eye. Sometimes, especially when there is trauma to the brain, motor impairment of this sort may be accompanied by mental impairment.

Advances have been made to assist people with motor impairments. For example, people with limb amputations are fitted with *prosthetic,* or artificial, limbs. Motorized wheelchairs also allow many people with motor impairment to get around without assistance.

Mental Challenges

Some challenges affect a person's ability to live independently in society. This is the case with some of the physical challenges mentioned above. It is also true of the mental challenge called *mental retardation.* **Mental retardation** is *below-average intellectual ability present from birth or early childhood and associated with difficulties in learning and social adaptation.* Mental retardation affects about 3 percent of the population. The four levels of mental retardation are mild, moderate, severe, and profound. Mildly affected individuals make up about 75 percent of the mentally retarded population and often cannot be outwardly distinguished from nonretarded people.

Several factors have been isolated as causes of mental retardation. One is heredity. Symptoms of **genetic disorders** such as Down syndrome, PKU, or Tay-Sachs disease include mental retardation. Lifestyle of the mother-to-be during pregnancy is another factor. Women who use alcohol or other addictive drugs greatly increase the risk that

hotlink

genetic disorders For more information on genetic disorders and health conditions associated with each, see Chapter 20, page 464.

their babies will be born with retardation. Yet another preventable risk factor is infection with rubella, or German measles, during pregnancy. Immunization against this disease either during a female's childhood or within three months of her becoming pregnant reduces this risk.

Eliminating Barriers

People with physical and mental challenges have the same needs and interests as the rest of the population. They also have many of the same abilities. In recent decades, strides have been made toward eliminating barriers of stereotyping and prejudices. These trends have been the result in part of lobbying efforts by people with physical and mental challenges themselves. In securing their rights, these individuals have worked to establish several important principles:

- that society make certain changes—such as wheelchair access to public transportation and building entrances—that allow people with physical or mental challenges to take part more readily in business and social activities;
- that people be evaluated on the basis of individual merit, not on stereotyped assumptions about disabilities; and
- that, to the extent each is able, these people be integrated among persons who do not have physical or mental challenges.

A major action toward achieving these goals was the passage by Congress in 1990 of the **Americans with Disabilities Act.** This is *a law prohibiting discrimination against people with physical or mental disabilities in the workplace, transportation, public accommodations, and telecommunications.*

LESSON 4 *Review*

Reviewing Facts and Vocabulary

1. Define *disability*.
2. Describe the possible causes of deafness.
3. Name one way a mother-to-be can decrease the risk of mental retardation in her baby.

Thinking Critically

4. *Analyzing.* Make a list of ways in which people use their eyes and ears each day. Next to each item, list the problems that might be associated with each task for persons with sight impairment or hearing impairment.

Applying Health Knowledge

5. *In Your Home.* Loud noise over a long period of time can cause permanent hearing loss. Loud noise also causes temporary hearing loss, but over the years a permanent high-tone hearing loss develops. Name some hobbies or activities that you and your friends participate in that include loud noise. What can you do to protect your hearing?

Health Skills Activities

Activity 1 — Community Report Card

Since passage of the Americans with Disabilities Act, many communities have instituted changes such as greater wheelchair accessibility. What does your community do to meet the special needs of its members?

Directions

1. With several classmates, develop a checklist of ways your community meets the special needs of the physically and mentally challenged.
2. Make an inspection tour of community buildings and facilities. Note ramps, Braille signage, and other features you find at a location.
3. Assign your community a grade based on the presence of helpful features. Devise a total grade based on the section grades. Suggest improvements, if any, your community could make.
4. Discuss your findings in class. You may also want to send your Community Report Card to a local legislator.

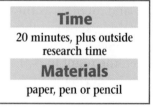

Time
20 minutes, plus outside research time

Materials
paper, pen or pencil

Self-Assessment

✓ Identified community services or features available to the physically and mentally challenged.
✓ Suggested improvements your community could undertake.

Activity 2 — Radio Broadcast to Stop Cancer

There are many different types of cancer. Each has warning signs and risk factors. You can help inform others of the risks and of the healthful behaviors that will reduce those risks.

Directions

1. As a class, review types of cancers most likely to affect teens. Appoint members to write a script for a two-minute radio broadcast about one type of cancer. Other members are to gather additional information about the disease, as needed. Include warning signs and steps that can be taken to reduce the risk of that cancer.
2. Still other group members should review the broadcast to make sure the language is powerful and effective.
3. If possible, broadcast your message over the school public address system.

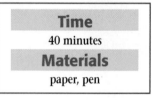

Time
40 minutes

Materials
paper, pen

Self-Assessment

✓ Identified cancer warning signs, risk factors, and prevention strategies.
✓ Created a broadcast that is clear and persuades the listener of the importance of practicing disease prevention.

HEALTH NEWS

Adult Diseases, Young Bodies

Many teens are eager to accept adult responsibilities. Unfortunately, poor lifestyle choices make some teens susceptible to adult diseases as well.

Type 2 diabetes is often called "adult-onset diabetes" because it usually occurs in people over 40. Because of an alarming new trend, doctors may need to change the name of this hazardous condition.

The number of teenagers who develop type 2 diabetes has increased dramatically. This rise is tied to risk factors such as high-fat diets, skipping breakfast, obesity, and lack of exercise.

Once diagnosed with diabetes, teens can manage their condition by adopting a balanced, healthy diet and limiting inactivity. Making these choices now can help everyone avoid this unwanted part of growing up.

Play the Video

Complications of Diabetes

Kidney Failure

Heart Disease

Eye Problems

Degeneration of the Nerves

Think About It

- Nigel was diagnosed with adult-onset diabetes when he was 15. What risk factors do you think made him vulnerable to this disease?

- What steps has Nigel taken to manage the disease?

Using Health Terms

On a separate sheet of paper, write the term that best matches each definition below.

LESSON 1

1. High blood pressure.
2. An interruption of the flow of blood to any part of the brain.
3. Medical disorders that affect the heart and blood vessels.
4. A slow, gradual weakening of the heart muscle from overwork.

LESSON 2

5. Noncancerous.
6. Often deadly type of skin cancer.
7. Uncontrolled abnormal cell growths.
8. A laboratory analysis of a section of tissue taken from a site where abnormal cell growth is suspected.

LESSON 3

9. A condition in which blood sugar levels are higher than normal but not high enough to be classified as diabetes.
10. A hormone that is produced in the pancreas and that helps the body convert glucose to energy.
11. A destructive and disabling inflammation of the joints.

LESSON 4

12. A law prohibiting discrimination against people with physical or mental disabilities in the workplace, transportation, public accommodations, and telecommunications.
13. Any physical or mental impairment that limits normal activities, including seeing, hearing, walking, or speaking.

Recalling the Facts

Using complete sentences, answer the following questions.

LESSON 1

1. What are the early signs of a heart attack?
2. What happens as a result of plaque building up in the arteries?
3. To what health problems does hypertension often lead?
4. What are the signals that indicate a stroke may be occurring?

LESSON 2

5. What factor is the leading cause of lung cancer?
6. What are the seven warning signs of cancer?
7. What is an advantage of chemotherapy over surgery or radiation in the treatment of cancer?

LESSON 3

8. Which groups are most likely to suffer from type 1 diabetes?
9. Why might a case of type 2 diabetes go undetected for years?
10. What are the goals of treatment of rheumatoid arthritis?

LESSON 4

11. Name two physical challenges a person might face.
12. What are some causes of mental retardation?
13. Explain what strides have been made toward eliminating barriers for the physically and mentally challenged.

Review

Thinking Critically

LESSON 1

1. ***Synthesizing.*** What lifestyle decisions are associated with the development of hypertension or heart disease?

LESSON 2

2. ***Synthesizing.*** How is early detection of cancer related to the likelihood of cure?

LESSON 3

3. ***Synthesizing.*** Although persons with diabetes can die because of too much or too little sugar in their blood, they are more likely to die from complications of heart or kidney disease that has progressed over the years. What is the connection between diabetes and these other life-threatening illnesses?

LESSON 4

4. ***Evaluating.*** Which of the following statements would you say is more appropriate: (a) The disabled are special people. (b) The disabled are normal people. Defend your selection.

Making the Connection

1. ***Language Arts.*** Using print or on-line newsmagazine or other sources, research the history of one of the treatments for heart disease. How did the treatment develop? How long did research continue before the treatment was tried on humans? How effective has this particular treatment proven?

2. ***Social Studies.*** Read about countries that have lower incidences of certain types of cancer—for example, the lower incidence of breast cancer in Japan and the higher incidence of colon cancer in Western nations. Chart how the types of foods people eat in these countries may contribute to these trends.

BEYOND THE CLASSROOM

PARENTAL INVOLVEMENT Encourage your family to participate in a "save your heart" week. Make a chart that lists at least four lifestyle behaviors family members can adopt during a seven-day period, such as taking a walk after dinner or eating fruit instead of a high-fat dessert. At the end of the week, report in your private Health Journal on the success of your experiment.

COMMUNITY INVOLVEMENT Speak with a public official or law enforcement officer in your community about the issue of handicapped parking spaces. Learn how the number of such spaces for a given facility is determined, what the fine or punishment is for abusing such a space, and whether fines are levied against nonchallenged individuals driving a car with handicapped license plates. Share your findings in an oral report.

SCHOOL-TO-CAREER
Exploring Careers. Interview an oncologist about the possibilities of a career in the area of oncology. Determine what preparation, including schooling, is necessary, the various settings in which oncologists work, and the types of interpersonal skills needed for the job. Share your findings with the class in an oral report.

CHAPTER 32

Consumer Choices and Public Health

HEALTH *Online*

GOAL SETTING
You can make a difference in someone's life, offer help in the community, or put your communication skills to work by choosing a health services profession. Browse the Career Corner at health.glencoe.com for ideas for your future.

Personal Health Inventory

Self-Inventory Write the numbers 1–10 on a sheet of paper. Read each statement below and respond by writing *yes*, *no*, or *sometimes* for each item. Write a *yes* only for items that you practice regularly. Save your responses.

1	I have a doctor that I see regularly for checkups.
2	I trust my physician and can communicate easily with him or her.
3	I understand the roles played by various health care professionals, such as therapists and laboratory technicians.
4	I know my medical history and keep a written record of it.
5	In case of a medical emergency, I know what action to take.
6	I have health insurance and know how to use it.
7	I pay attention to the effectiveness of the medical treatments I receive.
8	I avoid using unproven or useless over-the-counter remedies.
9	I follow instructions when taking over-the-counter or prescription medications.
10	I pay attention to side effects from taking medications and report these to my doctor.

Follow-up After completing the chapter, retake this self-inventory. Pick two items that you need to work on and set a goal to improve your health behaviors.

> ❝ *Our nation is strong, and our people resilient. We have a well-earned reputation for pulling together in the worst of times to help each other.* ❞

—LAURA BUSH
FIRST LADY, SEPTEMBER 12, 2001

Quick Write In the photo on the facing page, volunteers are lined up at the American Red Cross building in Washington, D.C., to donate blood for emergencies. Make a quick list of the ways you can contribute to the health and well-being of others.

Selecting Health Care and Services

A s you move toward your adult years, you will become increasingly responsible for making decisions about your health care. Knowing about the vast complex of services and institutions that make up our nation's health care system will better prepare you to make these decisions.

HEALTH TERMS

health care providers

primary care physician

specialist

health care facility

outpatient surgical facility

health insurance

Medicare

Medicaid

health maintenance organization (HMO)

preferred provider organization (PPO)

HEALTH CONCEPTS

- Health care providers offer many different types of health services.
- Health care facilities include medical offices, hospitals, and nursing homes.
- Health insurance is a participatory program that covers some of the costs of health care.

Ophthalmologist's equipment

Health Care Providers

The foundation of the nation's health care system is a group of *professionals trained in the health fields* called **health care providers.** This group includes physicians, nurses, and allied health care professionals. Each plays an important role in providing comprehensive health care for the American public.

Physicians

When you think of health care, perhaps the provider that most often comes to mind is the physician. The physician has traditionally been the backbone of the American health care system. *A medical professional who provides the first line of health care* is called a **primary care physician.** You see a primary care physician for checkups or when a health problem arises.

A primary care physician may refer you to a **specialist,** *a physician who has received additional training in a particular area of medicine.* Dermatologists, for example, specialize in treating diseases and problems of the skin. Oncologists specialize in treating cancer. The chart below lists other specialists.

Nurses

Nurses provide care for sick people. Their responsibilities vary according to the amount of training they have received. Licensed practical nurses (LPNs) assist physicians and provide direct care such as bathing or changing bandages. Registered nurses (RNs) take more responsibilities for patients and sometimes supervise LPNs. Nurse practitioners have advanced training that enables them to work independently of a physician. A nurse practitioner may specialize in a field such as childbirth or public education. Nurse practitioners can assume the role of a primary care physician in examining and treating patients.

Health Care Specialists

PHYSICIAN	SPECIALIZES IN...
Allergist	allergies
Dermatologist	skin diseases
Gynecologist	female reproductive system problems
Internist	internal, nonsurgical diseases
Neurologist	nervous system problems, such as strokes
Oncologist	cancer
Ophthalmologist	eye disease
Orthopedist	skeletal deformities or injuries
Pediatrician	primary care for children
Psychiatrist	mental health
Rheumatologist	pain and stiffness in muscles or joints
Urologist	urinary problems

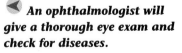

An ophthalmologist will give a thorough eye exam and check for diseases.

ACTIVITY *Describe the difference between a primary care physician and a specialist.*

Allied Medical Professionals

ALLIED MEDICAL PROFESSIONAL	SPECIALIZES IN...
Clinical psychologist	treating emotional or behavioral disorders
Dental hygienist	cleaning and polishing teeth
Dietitian	nutritional counseling; planning specialized menus
Emergency medical technician (EMT)	emergency treatment
Laboratory technician	lab tests, such as urine or blood workup
Nurse's aide	making beds, feeding and bathing patients
Occupational therapist	training persons with disabilities for daily activities and jobs
Optometrist	testing vision for eyeglasses
Pharmacist	dispensing medicines
Physical therapist	physical rehabilitation after injury, accidents, strokes, other disorders
Radiology technician	X rays
Social worker	counseling people with health problems
Speech therapist	helping people overcome speech problems

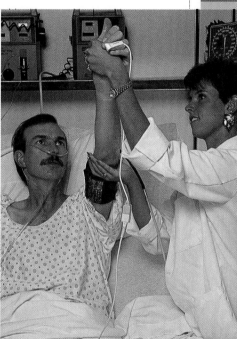

▲ *This registered nurse is giving the patient specialized, personal care.*

ACTIVITY *Name several duties of an RN and a nurse's aid.*

hotlink

clinical psychologist For more information on clinical psychologists and the health services they perform, see Chapter 10, page 250.

Allied Health Care Professionals

Other health care professionals cover a broad range of job descriptions from dentist to physical therapist to **clinical psychologist**. Some allied health professionals work closely with and under the supervision of physicians in medical settings.

Health Care Facilities

A **health care facility** is *any place staffed by health care professionals and equipped for delivery of health services.* A doctor's office is one type of health care facility. Generally speaking, however, the term is used to denote two main types of institutions—*short-term facilities,* such as hospitals, and *long-term facilities,* such as nursing homes.

Short-Term Health Care Facilities

The hospital is perhaps the most familiar type of short-term health facility in a community. Hospital stays are usually measured in days or weeks, although sometimes a patient must stay longer, depending on the condition.

Hospital care is provided on both an inpatient and outpatient basis. Inpatients are people who are admitted to a treatment facility and occupy a bed in it. Outpatients receive various services such as X rays or other diagnostic tests and return home the same day.

Various clinics may be part of a hospital setting. A clinic provides medical tests and treatment that does not require an overnight stay. Urgent care clinics provide emergency care on a walk-in basis. Due to breakthroughs in postsurgical treatment, which have shortened hospital stays, a new type of clinic has emerged. The **outpatient surgical facility** is *a place where surgery is performed on patients who are released the same day.*

Long-Term Health Care Facilities

Long-term health care facilities provide care for patients over an extended period of time. Persons recovering from serious accidents or crippling illnesses may spend time at a rehabilitation center. There they receive physical therapy and, where necessary, relearn basic living skills, such as feeding themselves and bathing. A hospice, another type of long-term health care facility, provides care for the terminally ill. Through a team effort of loved ones, hospice nurses, and a participating physician, a dying patient can live out the rest of his or her life in a homelike setting.

Nursing homes are facilities in which care is provided for medical and nonmedical needs. Though most residents are 65 years of age or older, these facilities are used by people of all ages. A person with a serious long-term illness or recovering from surgery may also live in a nursing home.

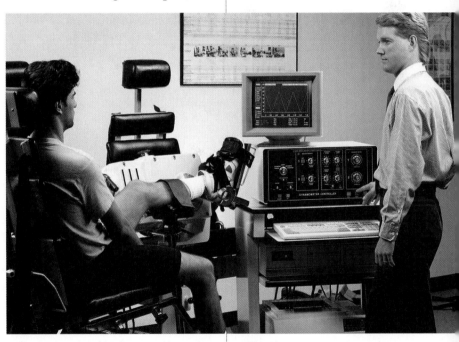

Health Insurance

Health insurance is *a plan to cover part or most costs of expenses and care associated with medical treatment.* To maintain membership in such a plan, the insured person pays a periodic *premium,* or fee, for his or her coverage. In conventional insurance plans, the insured person pays for doctor's visits and other forms of treatment out of pocket and is then reimbursed by the insurance company for a predetermined portion of the cost, often 80 percent.

Soaring costs of health care in this country in recent decades have driven up the costs of insurance and prompted some alternatives to

▲ *Often physical therapy can be provided in an outpatient facility.*

ACTIVITY *Name an injury or illness that might require physical therapy.*

conventional coverage. Two alternate programs are provided by the government. **Medicare** is *a health insurance program that is available to people who are 65 years of age or older and to people who receive Social Security disability benefits.* Some people who receive Medicare also are eligible for Medicaid. **Medicaid** is *an assistance program of medical aid for people of all ages who are unable to afford medical care.*

Other approaches to health insurance include *managed health care.* Under a managed care plan, a person must choose a physician affiliated with the plan. This physician, usually a primary care physician, "manages" the person's health care. If the primary care physician thinks the patient needs to see a specialist, a referral will be made.

Health maintenance organizations (HMOs) are the most common type of managed care. A **health maintenance organization (HMO)** is *a group of physicians of different specialties who work together to provide medical services to members.* Members pay a monthly fee but receive most or all medical services without paying an additional charge or by making a small *co-payment* fee at the time of an office visit.

Another kind of managed care is the **preferred provider organization (PPO)**, *a type of health insurance in which medical providers agree to charge less to members of the plan.* The patient, however, can still choose to see a physician outside the plan, but at a higher cost.

LESSON 1 *Review*

Reviewing Facts and Vocabulary

1. Which medical professional provides the first line of health care?
2. Give a definition for a health care facility.
3. How is a preferred provider organization different from a health maintenance organization?

Thinking Critically

4. *Analyzing.* Explain why it is important to have health insurance. What risks does one take by not having health insurance?
5. *Evaluating.* Conventional health care is expensive. In managed care or in programs where health care is free, patients may not choose their own doctors and may have to wait for care. Some specialized care may not be available to everyone. Is it better to have good care at high cost for some, or minimal care for everyone at low cost? Explain your response.

Applying Health Skills

6. *In Your Home.* Talk with your parents or other adults at home about the kind of health coverage your family has. What services are covered, and what restrictions apply, if any? Also, find out what costs are covered and what costs are paid by the patient. Determine, finally, whether the adults are pleased overall with this coverage, and if not, why.

Being an Alert Health Consumer

Have you ever taken cough medicine or a pain reliever? If so, you have experience as a **health consumer,** *a person who uses health products or services.* As a health consumer, you have a right to be informed about the products or services you buy. This is true whether you are shopping for medicine or a health plan.

HEALTH TERMS

health consumer
medical history
generic

HEALTH CONCEPTS

- A health consumer is anyone who shops for and purchases health products and services.
- Being an alert health consumer includes knowing and standing up for your rights.

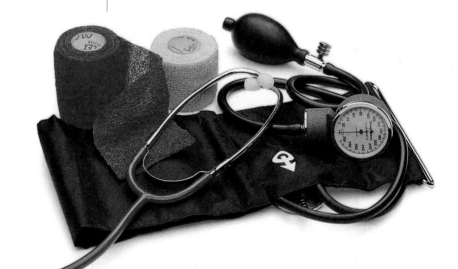

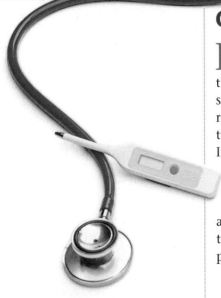

Choosing a Health Plan

In the past, the task of shopping for a health plan was one many Americans never needed to face. The decision was often made for them by their employer; health coverage in a group plan was often a standard job benefit. Today, however, with the cost of such coverage reaching unprecedented highs, many companies have cut back drastically on health benefits to employees or eliminated them altogether. Increasingly, in recent years, the responsibility for selecting and maintaining health coverage has fallen on the shoulders of the private health consumer.

Although this may seem like an awesome responsibility, an awareness of several key factors can help. These factors, which need to be taken into account when considering enrollment in any health plan, include:

- **Cost.** Some 46 million Americans have responded to the rising costs of health care by enrolling in HMOs. An advantage to HMOs is that the premiums are generally far lower than those associated with conventional coverage. A disadvantage is that such plans limit your choice of health care providers to doctors who are affiliated with the plans.

- **Special needs.** Certain health conditions and forms of treatment are not covered by some insurance policies. Most, for example, deny coverage for treatment with an experimental medication. Many, moreover, have "ceilings"—dollar amounts after which a condition, such as a catastrophic illness, will no longer be covered.

- **Eligibility.** Some health plans have attractive rates and coverage but are limited to people affiliated with a certain group. Religious and professional organizations are two examples. It is important to be aware of eligibility requirements when choosing a plan.

Choosing a Health Care Provider

When choosing a health care provider, the following guidelines will be helpful:

- Ask friends or relatives outside your immediate family for recommendations.
- Ask other health care professionals you know for a referral. These people know who can provide you with the best medical care.
- Call your local medical society. Most medical societies will provide three names, chosen in rotation from the society's membership roster.

Making Responsible
Decisions

Choosing a Health Plan

The plant at which Gilbert has worked for 12 years recently announced that they will be offering a limited health benefits package to its employees. For Gilbert and his wife, this is a special hardship, because their two-year-old daughter, Sara, was born with a heart valve defect, which has required ongoing treatment. What should Gilbert do to make sure his family has the health coverage they need?

What Would You Do?

Apply the six steps of the decision-making process to Gilbert's problem.

1. **State the situation.**
2. **List the options.**
3. **Weigh the possible outcomes.**
4. **Consider your values.**
5. **Make a decision and act.**
6. **Evaluate the decision.**

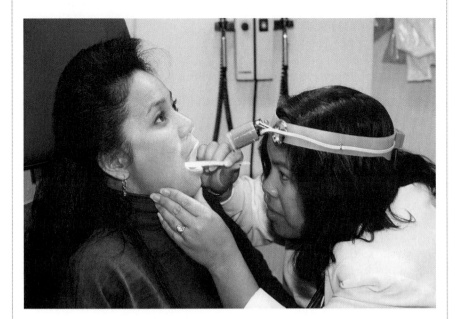

◄ *A health-literate consumer asks questions about medical procedures and treatments.*

keeping
Fit

For the Record: Your Rights

Your medical records are your doctor's property. What can you do if you need to get access to the health information your physician has on file?

➤ Remember that you have the right to get copies of all records.

➤ You also have the right to have copies of these records sent to another doctor of your choosing.

➤ If a person is under age or seen as incompetent, then a parent, legal guardian, or other authorized person may have to sign for the documents to be released.

➤ If a doctor can't find your records, mixes your records with someone else's, or has recorded very little information about you, you should be concerned.

➤ Check to see what the law is in your state regarding confidentiality. More than 50 percent of states now have laws requiring patient access.

➤ Ask who else can be given copies of your records, such as insurance companies, government agencies, and others.

■ Ask a local librarian or consumer protection agency if a directory of doctors has been compiled in your community, or use the *American Medical Directory* at your local library to get detailed information about specific doctors, including their professional credentials and areas of specialization.

In getting referrals, make any personal preferences and needs known. Some people feel more comfortable going to a physician of the same gender. Others prefer to start a relationship with a doctor who is relatively young and is likely to be practicing well into the future. Yet another consideration is personality—what kind of "bedside manner" does the person have? Is he or she easy to talk with?

Patient Skills

Many people choose a physician according to his or her level of skill, then place themselves in the hands of the physician, feeling that their job is done. As a health consumer, however, a patient continues to bear responsibility for his or her own care. Good health care requires an active partnership between the health care provider and the patient. It requires skills not only on the part of the health professional but also on the part of the patient. Good "patient skills" begin with an awareness of one's own **medical history.** This is *complete and comprehensive information about immunizations and any health problems to date.* A good patient is also one who:

■ *is prepared when visiting a physician.* Write down the reasons for your visit, including any specific health complaints such as pains or discomfort.
■ *asks questions of the doctor when necessary.* If the doctor explains a problem, make sure you understand what he or she is saying. Ask for a repetition of any points that are sources of confusion. If

medication is prescribed, make sure you understand how it is to be taken and why you are taking it.

- *follows up on a visit as needed.* If a problem for which you have been treated persists or recurs, inform the doctor.

h⊙t l⊙nk

medicines For more information on medicines and their role in health, see Chapter 23, page 512.

Although patients do not have a major role in choosing the **medicines** a doctor prescribes, there are some important consumer skills in this area. Be sure you understand the doctor's instructions regarding prescription medicines, and know why you are taking a particular medicine. It is also important to make sure you are taking a medicine as intended and to report any problems or side effects.

As a patient, it is also your right to inquire about taking a **generic** equivalent of a medicine. This is *a less-expensive version of a medicine that may be substituted for a brand-name medication.* In some cases, a doctor may insist on a patient's taking a nongeneric medicine because the generic equivalent lacks *buffers*—added ingredients that make the medicine easier to tolerate. As a patient, you have a right to this information as well.

Over-the-Counter Medicines

h⊙t l⊙nk

over-the-counter (OTC) medicines For more information on over-the-counter (OTC) medicines and their use, see Chapter 23, page 519.

When shopping for **over-the-counter (OTC) medicines**—those that can be bought without a doctor's prescription—it is important to use the same skills as when shopping for any other product. This includes a careful reading of the label to make sure you understand how the medicine is meant to be used. Another consideration when shopping for OTC medicines is price comparison.

LESSON 2 *Review*

Reviewing Facts and Vocabulary

1. What is a health consumer?
2. Identify three patient skills.
3. What is the difference between generic medicines and nongeneric medicines?

Thinking Critically

4. *Analyzing.* Interpret the following statement: The doctor *cannot* do what the patient *will* not do.
5. *Synthesizing.* Beth has had severe cramps for several days. John is seeing his doctor for a follow-up visit after suffering a concussion in a football game last Friday night. Write several questions that each teen might want to ask his or her physician.

Applying Health Skills

6. *In Your Home.* Find out about your own medical history. Ask your parents or other adults in your home to show you any records they have on doctor visits and health problems you have had. Also, check to see if t…ey have a list of your immunizations. If not, work with them and your family physician to compile a list of immunizations and health treatments, and keep these in a safe place where they are easily accessible.

Strategies for Dealing with Consumer Problems

Have you ever purchased a health-care product that did not fulfill its claim? When it comes to health care, receiving quality health care and products is important. Sometimes a consumer will receive poor, ineffective, or even harmful products and services. This lesson will tell you what steps a consumer can take when this happens.

HEALTH TERMS

quackery

advocate

HEALTH CONCEPTS

- Developing an awareness of the potential for fraud and deception in health care is one of the keys to being an alert consumer.
- A consumer who suspects fraud has several actions to choose from.

Medical Fraud

It is illegal to make false claims, promising that a medicine or medical treatment can do something that it cannot do. Yet, there are people looking to benefit from other people's misfortune. You may have heard such people referred to as "quacks." **Quackery** is *a type of medical fraud* that plays on human emotion, weakness, and fear. Quackery is used to extract money from people who want fast cures or relief from pain. Quacks may appeal to consumers' emotions by using techniques such as testimonials, personal stories from individuals who claim to have been cured by a particular product or treatment.

Fraudulent Products and Remedies

Among the many useless products sold over-the-counter to vulnerable consumers are anti-aging aids. In our youth-oriented society, many middle-aged adults are interested in stopping the processes of aging such as wrinkling or balding. However, no product can reverse the process of aging. The best way to stay healthy and fit is to exercise, avoid tobacco and other drugs, limit your hours in the sun, and eat a balance of foods from the different sections of the Food Guide Pyramid.

Another lucrative area for health quackery is weight-loss formulas. Popular weight-loss products claim that using them can cause weight loss without the hard work of exercising or reducing calories. Unlike most quack remedies, many of these products may, if faithfully followed, lead to an actual loss of weight. The real "secret," however, is not in the product itself but in the fact that most involve a cutback in the amount of food consumed.

Building Health Skills

Obtaining Help: When You're Unhappy with a Health Service or Product

EVEN THE MOST CAREFUL health consumers find themselves buying products or securing services that do not work right or serve them well. This is why it is necessary for you, as a health consumer, to know what to do and where to go for help. Here are some tips to follow:

1. **Identify the problem.** Decide on what you feel would be a fair way to resolve it.

2. **Have some documentation available to back up your complaint.** This might be an invoice or canceled check. Include a list of symptoms.

3. **Go back to the source.** Contact or visit the health care provider or, in the case of medication, the pharmacy or store that sold it to you. State the problem and how you would like to have it solved.

4. **Go to a higher authority.** If the first person you contact is not helpful, ask to speak to a supervisor or, in the case of medications, a store manager. Repeat your story. Most problems are resolved at this level.

5. **Write a letter.** If you are still not satisfied with the response at the higher level, do not give up. If the health facility operates nationally or the product is a national brand, write a letter to the president or the director of consumer affairs of the company.

Fraudulent Treatment

Among the people most susceptible to fraudulent treatments are those with chronic illnesses such as Alzheimer's disease and osteoporosis, for which there is no cure or instant relief. Because many older adults fall into this category, they are likely targets for fraud. Although some fraudulent treatments may not cause physical harm, they may be dangerous because the patient delays seeking sound medical advice and treatment until it is too late. Cancer and arthritis are two areas where many kinds of fraudulent and useless treatments are offered.

HEALTH Online

Locate articles on consumer protection and learn how to avoid product scams and to protect your consumer rights at **health.glencoe.com**.

Help for Consumer Problems

Several agencies and organizations exist to help consumers with complaints against health providers or products. These include licensing boards, consumer affairs bureaus, media action programs, private consumer groups, and government services.

- **Licensing Boards.** If you have a problem with a professional health care provider, you may be able to get help from a state licensing or regulatory board such as the American Medical Association (AMA), which licenses physicians and provides peer review when problems arise.

Government Services

AGENCY	PURPOSE	ADDRESS
Consumer Product Safety Commission (CPSC)	protects consumers against harmful products; can ban or recall a dangerous product	Director, Office of Communications Consumer Product Safety Commission Washington, DC 20207
Consumer Information Center (CIC)	distributes consumer information materials; provides free copies of the Catalog of Consumer Information	Consumer Information Center Pueblo, CO 81009
Food and Drug Administration (FDA)	ensures that medicines are properly labeled and safe and effective for their intended uses; determines whether a medicine should be prescription or over-the-counter	Director, Consumer Communications Food and Drug Administration 5600 Fishers Lane Rockville, MD 20857
Federal Trade Commission (FTC)	prevents unfair, false, or deceptive advertising of consumer products and services	Office of the Secretary Federal Trade Commission Washington, DC 20580

keeping Fit

Avoiding Quackery

Medical quackery can result in a waste of money. Even more serious, it can result in injury, illness, or death. Be on the lookout for the following "red flags":

➤ "secret formula"

➤ "miracle cure"

➤ "overnight results"

➤ "limited offer"

➤ endorsements by famous persons

➤ availability only through mail order

➤ foreign medicine not usually available in the United States

➤ passionate testimonials of those supposedly "cured"

➤ hard-sell approaches

If you contact a state board for help, it will usually bring your complaint to the attention of the person whom you filed against. The board will seek a satisfactory solution to your problem and can conduct an investigation if necessary.

■ **Consumer Affairs Bureaus.** Local consumer affairs offices are easy to contact by phone or in person, and they are usually familiar with local regulations and procedures. The Better Business Bureau (BBB) is a nonprofit organization sponsored by private businesses that provides general information on products and services, reliability reports, and background information on local businesses and organizations.

■ **Media Action Programs.** If you live in or near a large city, you may be aware of one of the more than 100 newspapers and 50 radio and TV stations that offer action groups or phone-in services for consumers who need help.

■ **Private Consumer Groups.** In addition to the many government and business organizations that can be of assistance to the consumer, private consumer groups exist in all 50 states. In almost all cases, these are made up of individual consumer members who join together to support consumer interests. They are called *advocates*. An **advocate** is *someone who speaks out for another person or a cause*.

■ **Government Services.** The federal government has established a number of specialized agencies that deal with health-related products and services. See the chart on page 715. You have a right as a citizen to make use of their services, and these agencies have a responsibility to help you.

LESSON 3 *Review*

Reviewing Facts and Vocabulary

1. What is quackery? Which products and treatments are often at the midst of quackery?
2. How can an advocate help a consumer with a complaint?
3. What does the Consumer Product Safety Commission (CPSC) do to help health care consumers?

Thinking Critically

4. *Evaluating.* List several criteria you could use to distinguish between an effective complaint against a health care provider or product and an ineffective complaint.

Applying Health Skills

5. *In Your School.* Prepare a survey on the kinds of over-the-counter medicines used by students in your school. Ask students to complete the survey on a confidential basis. Determine which medicines are most used by students you surveyed. Compile the results and share them with the class.

Community Health

People today are living longer than ever. This is due partly to the advent in this country in the late 1800s of a system of **public health,** *a community-wide effort to monitor and promote the welfare of the population.* Thanks to developments in public health, American citizens can be reasonably sure that their drinking water, food, and medicines are safe.

HEALTH TERMS

public health

epidemiology

famine

HEALTH CONCEPTS

- Public health is a community-wide effort to monitor and promote the welfare of the population.
- Organizations and agencies that promote the health of the public exist at the local, state, and national levels, as well as in the private sector.
- Every member of a society has a responsibility toward the health of the community at large.

Public Health Agencies

Although public health is defined as a community health effort, the term *community* may have a variety of connotations. You probably think of a neighborhood or an organized group of people when you hear this term. Yet, a community—especially with regard to health matters—may also include an entire city, a state, a nation, or even the world at large. As a result, many organizations and agencies have been formed for administering public health on all levels.

Public Health at the Local Level

You are undoubtedly familiar with the names of such organizations as the March of Dimes and the American Lung Association. These groups are private agencies usually devoted to a particular

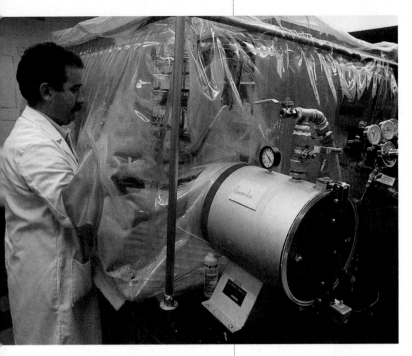

health concern—in these specific cases, to birth defects and lung disease. Although many of these groups are local chapters of a national organization, they are usually run by local volunteers and funded through donations. The goals of private groups range from educating the public about a health problem to raising funds for research and treatment of particular diseases.

Government public health agencies also exist on the local level. These groups include county and state health departments that set regulations affecting the local community. For example, they may pass regulations to set standards for sanitation in restaurants, compile health statistics, and control environmental pollution.

▲ *Hazardous or toxic materials need to be handled by a trained technician.*

ACTIVITY *Name the government agency responsible for controlling toxic substances.*

CHARACTER
IN ACTION

Civic Duty and Public Health

Civic duty means being a responsible citizen. You are fulfilling your civic duty when you follow the law, vote, and participate in community projects. By observing basic health practices you promote your own health and the health of those around you.

Character Check Be responsible when it comes to public health:

➤ Make certain your immunizations are up-to-date.

➤ Do not expose others when you have a contagious illness.

➤ Participate in a fund-raiser like a walk or race for a particular disease.

Public Health at the National Level

The Department of Health and Human Services is a federal agency whose responsibility is public health in the United States. A division of the Department of Health and Human Service is the Public Health Service. This division is in charge of promoting the prevention of disease and enforcing health and safety standards. It has several agencies through which this work is done:

■ **The National Institutes of Health (NIH).** This Public Health Service agency conducts medical research of all kinds. It also provides grants—or funding—for other medical research done at universities or other institutions.

■ **The Centers for Disease Control and Prevention (CDC).** The CDC conducts research and collects data that help control the spread of diseases. Part of the CDC's job involves **epidemiology** (ep-uh-deem-ee-OL-uh-jee), *the scientific study of epidemics.* An epidemic, as you learned in Chapter 24, is the sudden spread of disease among many people.

■ **The Agency for Health Care Policy and Research.** This agency sets policies to improve health care, including its organization and access. It also promotes improvements in the financing of health care in the United States.

■ **The Health Resources and Services Administration.** This agency provides health resources and services for those in need, such as persons with AIDS, migrant workers, and the homeless.

■ **The Agency for Toxic Substances and Disease Registry.** The task of this agency is to investigate hazardous materials and their effects on humans.

- **The Substance Abuse and Mental Health Service Administration.** This agency provides programs to serve substance abusers and people with mental and emotional disorders.

Public Health at the International Level

With such comprehensive and far-reaching public health policy, Americans often take public health for granted. In developing nations, however, these measures are not available. Many diseases that have all but disappeared in our society still exist in developing countries. In addition, these countries may still suffer from famines. A **famine** is *a widespread shortage of food* that results in nutritional deficiencies, starvation, and death. Several organizations work cooperatively among different sponsor nations to address world health. These include the World Health Organization, the Peace Corps, and the International Red Cross.

Public Health and You

One of the **developmental tasks** of adolescence involves developing a social intelligence, or concern for others and the environment. Being concerned about public health is part of this task. Reporting any suspected public health problems protects not only your own health but the health of your family, friends, and community members. Chapter 33 contains further information on ways of becoming an involved citizen in the interests of public health.

h⊙t l⊙nk

developmental tasks For more information on the developmental tasks of adolescence, see Chapter 21, page 482.

LESSON 4 *Review*

Reviewing Facts and Vocabulary

1. What is public health?
2. The Public Health Service is a division of which federal government department?
3. What is the role of the National Institutes of Health?

Thinking Critically

4. *Comparing and Contrasting.* Explain the differences in the way that a media action group might handle a consumer complaint and the way a government agency might handle the same complaint.

5. *Evaluating.* Better Business Bureaus are sponsored by private businesses. Is this a good or bad arrangement? How does the term *conflict of interests* come into play here?

Applying Health Skills

6. *In Your School.* Find out what steps your school takes to stop the spread of disease among students and staff. Think of other suggestions students can follow to stop the spread of disease at school. Make a list of these suggestions and post them or publish them in the school newspaper.

Health Skills Activities

Activity 1 — Letter of Complaint

When writing to a company to complain about a product or service, you need to include specific information. What would you include in such a letter?

Directions

1. With a partner, review the "Building Health Skills" activity on page 714. Then compose a complaint letter about a real or imaginary problem with a provider or product.
2. Be sure to state the problem clearly and include all necessary information.
3. Transfer your letter to poster board. Make the text large enough to be read at a distance.
4. If possible, teach a lesson on writing a complaint letter to a middle school class in your school or community. Use your enlargement as a model.

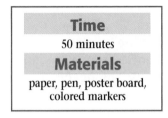

Time

50 minutes

Materials

paper, pen, poster board, colored markers

Self-Assessment

✓ Letter clearly stated the problem.
✓ Letter was respectful, yet assertive in tone.
✓ Lesson to middle school students clearly explained how to write a complaint letter.

Activity 2 — Medicine Pricing Guide

Determining the comparative costs of OTC medicines can be difficult, especially when two competing products are sold in varying sizes. You can help your family members compare and save on OTC medicines.

Directions

1. Visit a pharmacy to get information about the prices of competing brands of cough formulas, pain relievers, adhesive bandages, and other commonly used products in your home.
2. Note each type of product, the brand name, the net weight on the packaging, and the store price.
3. Determine the unit price of each product by dividing the price expressed in dollars and cents by the net weight in ounces.
4. Share your results in a pricing guide. Make copies available to family members and to classmates' families.

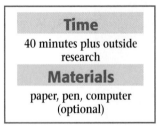

Time

40 minutes plus outside research

Materials

paper, pen, computer (optional)

Self-Assessment

✓ Pricing guide was well-organized and easy to read.
✓ Used mathematical equation to correctly calculate unit prices.

Internet Health Caution

Many people use the Internet to research health questions. The Net contains tons of health information. Some of it is clear, accurate, and helpful. Some of it is none of the above.

A recent study emphasizes the importance of reading Web pages cautiously and critically. When scientists studied Internet resources on one type of cancer, they found that more than half the pages had no peer review. This means the pages reflected the ideas of just one person. The study also found that 6 percent of the pages contained false information.

Surfers need to be critical of information on the Web. Look for reliable sites that have been created by more than one author. Check credentials of doctors at Web sites, and always ask your doctor about health information you find.

Play the Video

Think About It

● What are some of the advantages of using the Internet to research health questions? What are some disadvantages?

● What does Dr. J. Sybil Biermann mean when she says, "There really isn't gatekeeping on the Internet?"

Using Health Terms

On a separate sheet of paper, write the term that best matches each definition below.

LESSON 1

1. A plan to cover part or most costs of expenses and care associated with medical treatment.
2. Type of health insurance in which medical providers agree to charge less to members of the plan.
3. A physician who has received additional training in a particular area of medicine.

LESSON 2

4. A less-expensive version of a medicine that may be substituted for a brand-name medication.

5. Complete and comprehensive information about immunizations and any health problems to date.
6. A person who uses health products or services.

LESSON 3

7. A type of medical fraud.
8. Someone who speaks out for another person or a cause.

LESSON 4

9. The scientific study of epidemics.
10. A community-wide effort to monitor and promote the welfare of the population.
11. A widespread shortage of food.

Recalling the Facts

Using complete sentences, answer the following questions.

LESSON 1

1. Name three kinds of professionals who are health care workers.
2. How is a health maintenance organization (HMO) different from conventional health insurance?
3. How is a primary care physician different from a specialist?
4. What is the difference between a licensed practical nurse (LPN) and a registered nurse (RN)?
5. How does an outpatient surgical facility differ from a hospital?
6. What services does a hospice provide?

LESSON 2

7. What factors should you take into consideration when choosing a health plan?

8. What are some guidelines for choosing a health care provider?

LESSON 3

9. What kinds of techniques do quacks use to draw in unsuspecting patients?
10. Why might fraudulent treatments for cancer or arthritis be dangerous?
11. How could the Better Business Bureau (BBB) help a consumer with a complaint against a health care provider?
12. What does the Food and Drug Administration regulate in the field of health care?

LESSON 4

13. What is the role of county and state health departments?
14. How does the Centers for Disease Control and Prevention (CDC) help to control the spread of diseases?

Thinking Critically

LESSON 1

1. ***Comparing and Contrasting.*** To which specialist might a primary care physician refer a person who has: (1) acne; (2) scoliosis (curvature of the spine); (3) unrealistic fears about getting sick?

LESSON 2

2. ***Synthesizing.*** Write several criteria besides those listed in the lesson that you could use to choose a new primary care physician.

LESSON 3

3. ***Synthesizing.*** What conclusions might a person draw if he or she spent money on a weight-loss remedy and lost weight but gained it all back in a few months? Explain.

LESSON 4

4. ***Analyzing.*** Makers of name-brand products pay large sums of money to have their products used in movies. Do you feel this is fair advertising? Should it be permitted?

Making the Connection

Math. A conventional health insurance plan might offer the following coverage: 80 percent of expenses plus a $500 deductible—a dollar amount the insured person must pay out of pocket before health benefits begin. Under this plan, the member pays out-of-pocket the first $500 of medical expenses incurred each year. For the rest of medical expenses, if any, the member pays 20 percent and the plan pays 80 percent. What out-of-pocket expenses might a person incur if their total costs for medical expenses in one year totals $1500?

BEYOND THE CLASSROOM

PARENTAL INVOLVEMENT Interview your parents or other adults at home about their use of health insurance and health care during their adult years. Ask them what decisions they think they made wisely, as well as what they might have done differently as they look back on their lives. Write a private Health Journal entry telling what you have learned.

COMMUNITY INVOLVEMENT Ask a health clinic in your community for a brochure that describes the various health care professionals who work there. Determine whether each person listed is a physician or an allied health care professional, and tell what their specialty is or what job they perform. Share the information with your class.

SCHOOL-TO-CAREER
Interpersonal. Use a book about careers from your school's career center or from the library. Determine which interpersonal skills are needed to become a hospital administrator. Consider skills needed in both business and medicine.

CHAPTER 33

The Health of the Environment

HEALTH Online

ADVOCACY

Get involved in a project of your choice to help save the planet. Visit health.glencoe.com and choose the Interactive Project on "Impacting the Environment" to find out how to get involved.

Personal Health Inventory

Self-Inventory Write the numbers 1–10 on a sheet of paper. Read each statement below and respond by writing *yes*, *no*, or *sometimes* for each item. Write a *yes* only for items that you practice regularly. Save your responses.

1	I work at conserving water in my home.
2	I make a habit of turning out lights when I leave a room.
3	I try to make other people aware of the problem of littering.
4	I refuse packaging for products that already have a package.
5	I avoid buying disposable products when longer-lasting alternatives exist.
6	I read labels and buy the least toxic products available.
7	I reuse paper and plastic bags that are brought home from the store.
8	I buy recycled paper when I have the choice.
9	I actively participate in a recycling program in my community.
10	At home, I put on a second layer of clothing rather than turn up the heat when feeling cold.

Follow-up After completing the chapter, retake this self-inventory. Pick two items that you need to work on and set a goal to improve your health behaviors.

> ❝ *You look down at this planet and it's all one living system.* ❞

—RUSSELL SCHWEICKART
AMERICAN ASTRONAUT, (1935–)

Quick Write Imagine being out in space and looking down at the Earth. Write a message to the planet about your personal commitment to preserving its resources and health.

Air and Water

We live in a society fueled by modern technology. People once traveled by foot or on horseback. Today forms of high-speed transportation get us where we are going fast. Essential goods once made by hand are now mass-produced. These breakthroughs have not come without cost to the health of the environment. The name of this cost is *pollution.*

HEALTH TERMS

acid rain

greenhouse effect

chlorofluorocarbons (CFCs)

particulates

asbestos

biodegradable

HEALTH CONCEPTS

- Air pollution can result from gases or particles introduced into the atmosphere.
- Water pollution is largely the result of chemical wastes or poor sanitation.

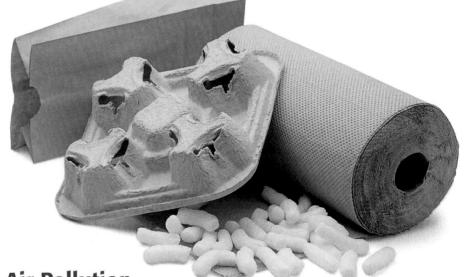

Recyclable paper products

Air Pollution

Air pollution is the contamination of the earth's atmosphere by substances that pose a health threat to humans, plants, and animals. Each year industrialized countries such as the United States generate billions of tons of air pollutants. The majority of these take one of two main forms—gases or particulates.

Gases

We survive by breathing in a mixture of gases, chiefly oxygen and nitrogen. During the last 50 years, other undesirable gases have begun to pollute the air we breathe. Most of these harmful gases are produced by the burning of fossil fuels such as coal, oil, wood, or natural gas. The evaporation of liquid solvents such as paint thinner is another source of air pollution.

CARBON MONOXIDE

Carbon monoxide, a colorless, odorless gas, results from the burning of most substances. Sources of carbon monoxide include tobacco smoke and the exhaust fumes from cars. A danger of carbon monoxide to humans is that it binds with hemoglobin, the oxygen-carrying part of blood, and prevents your body from receiving the oxygen it needs. When inhaled in sufficient quantities, carbon monoxide is fatal.

NITROGEN OXIDES AND SULFUR OXIDES

Produced by the burning of fossil fuels such as coal and oil, these gases can cause burning and tearing eyes. They can also lead to or trigger respiratory problems. Another serious environmental problem to which these gases are related is **acid rain.** *A by-product* of *nitrogen oxides or sulfur oxides mixed with rain,* acid rain can destroy plant life and corrode stone and metal.

CARBON DIOXIDE

As noted in Chapter 17, we produce carbon dioxide ourselves as part of the process of **respiration**. However, when large quantities of this gas are released into the atmosphere by the burning of petroleum, coal, or other fossil fuels, one possible result is *a slowdown of the rate at which the earth loses heat, causing an increase in the earth's temperature.* This condition, known as the **greenhouse effect**, has serious and far-reaching consequences. The "global warming" trends it threatens to bring about would negatively affect crop production and cause sea levels to rise significantly, leading to major flooding.

In addition to the burning of fossil fuels, the slash-and-burn method of clearing tropical forests has contributed in recent years to the 0.4-percent-a-year increase in atmospheric carbon dioxide.

HYDROCARBONS

When solvents such as turpentine evaporate or fossil fuels are incompletely burned, a combination of hydrogen and carbon called *hydrocarbons* escapes into the atmosphere. The reaction of hydrocarbons with nitric oxide in the presence of sunlight produces the form of pollution known as *smog*. Smog reduces visibility, in some parts of the country by as much as 70 percent, and causes the eyes to sting. By themselves, hydrocarbons are poisonous and have been linked to some cancers. Motor vehicle exhaust is a primary source of hydrocarbons.

▲ *Much of the air pollution in major cities comes from the burning of fuel by motor vehicles.*

ACTIVITY *World vehicle production is approaching 40 million units annually, and the total vehicle fleet is currently nearing 500 million. If this trend continues, how many cars and trucks will be on the road by the year 2020?*

h◉t l★nk

respiration For more information on respiration and the body organs involved in it, see Chapter 17, page 400.

In the early 1970s, researchers began to consider the effect on the atmosphere of a particular group of chemicals known as **chlorofluorocarbons** (KLOHR-uh-FLOHR-uh-kar-buhns). Known as *CFCs* for short, these *compounds of chlorine, fluorine, and carbon* are odorless and invisible. Although their main industrial use—as refrigerants and propellants in aerosol spray cans—was long viewed as harmless, the effect of CFCs on the atmosphere has proved to be anything but harmless. When these chemicals rise high into the upper atmosphere, they react with sunlight to produce chemicals that destroy ozone molecules. These molecules shield the earth's surface from the harmful **ultraviolet rays** of the sun. In 1984, researchers measured drastic reductions in ozone over Antarctica, which many have linked directly to the action of CFCs. Since 1987, more than 150 countries have signed a series of international agreements calling for an eventual end to the manufacture of CFCs.

Particulates

Another main source of air pollution besides gases is **particulates** (par-TIK-yuh-luhts), *tiny particles suspended and carried through air.* Particulates can take the form of dust, soot, and mold spores. They also occur suspended in some gases. The Environmental Protection Agency (EPA) estimates that some 60,000 people in the United States die each year from respiratory problems linked to particulate emissions such as from:

- **Lead.** Lead can poison the kidneys, liver, and nervous system and can cause mental retardation in babies and young children. Paint-related lead poisoning remains a problem in older, substandard dwellings.

- **Asbestos.** *A mineral occurring in the form of fibers,* **asbestos** (az-BES-tus) was once widely used on hot-water pipes and as an insulator because of its fireproof properties. Asbestos has been linked to lung cancer, especially in people who also smoke.

Water Pollution

Each year, industry, agriculture, and private citizens threaten the planet's rapidly dwindling freshwater resources through one form of pollution or another. Much of this pollution is a result of the dumping of raw sewage or industrial waste into rivers, lakes, and streams.

hotlink

ultraviolet rays For more information on the sun's ultraviolet rays and the damage they do, see Chapter 7, page 163.

▲ *Using a cloth bag to carry groceries eliminates the need for paper and plastic bags.*

ACTIVITY *What extra steps is this girl taking to reduce pollution?*

Raw Sewage and Industrial Wastes

When sewage is dumped in quantities too large to be **biodegradable** (BY-oh-duh-GRAYD-uh-buhl)—*able to be broken down by microorganisms in the environment*—the water is no longer safe for use. Disease-causing viruses and bacteria contained in the sewage become a serious health threat to humans and to aquatic life forms.

Wastes produced by industrial operations such as manufacturing and mining are another problem. Toxic, nonbiodegradable, or both, these wastes include acids, dyes, and metals such as mercury and lead.

Harmful Chemicals

Some of the pollution of our water resources happens indirectly through *runoff*, polluted groundwater that drains into streams. Pesticides and herbicides, chemicals used to kill crop pests and weeds, are toxic and contaminate drinking water. Some household cleaning products, such as bleaches and detergents, contain chlorine or phosphates, two other chemicals that are harmful to the environment.

Oil Spills

Millions of gallons of petroleum and crude oil are transported on the world's major waterways every day. There is always the risk of accidental spills. Oil pollution in ocean regions is caused by the discharging of tank flushings and the release of oil from offshore drilling rigs. By exploring alternative forms of energy, the world could greatly reduce the problem of ocean pollution.

▲ *The trash collecting on this riverbank contributes to water pollution.*

ACTIVITY *List alternative ways you would dispose of the objects pictured.*

Review

Reviewing Facts and Vocabulary

1. Write a public service announcement about air pollution using the terms *acid rain* and *greenhouse effect*.
2. Identify three causes of water pollution.

Thinking Critically

3. *Analyzing.* Find out the major sources of air pollution in your area. Determine whether current efforts to reduce the problem are sufficient.
4. *Synthesizing.* Investigate which water pollution problems appear to be most prevalent in today's world. Prepare an oral report describing the causes and effects of these threats.

Applying Health Skills

5. *In Your Home.* Check the labels of laundry and household products being used in your home. Note any that contain chlorine or phosphates. Share your findings with family members, noting any dangers that exist. Make recommendations that will remedy the problem.

Land

Ås a group of people, we are collectively making decisions about the way we use our natural resources. Our actions and attitudes toward the environment can make a difference in the health of future generations. In this lesson you will learn how the earth is impacted by our actions. You will learn how you can make decisions that will help preserve the land and its resources.

HEALTH TERMS

hazardous wastes

deforestation

desertification

HEALTH CONCEPTS

- Solid and toxic waste disposal are poisoning the land.
- Worldwide population living in concentrated areas has upset the natural balance of our planet.

Toxic Dumping

Each year, billions of tons of solid waste are dumped, burned, and buried in the United States alone. Much of this waste is deposited in landfills or canyons, a trend that has created a twofold environmental problem. The first problem is the availability of landfill space—many landfills are at or nearing full capacity. A second and perhaps more compelling problem is the nature of the wastes themselves. The Environmental Protection Agency has coined a term—**hazardous wastes**—for *any substances that are explosive, corrosive, flammable, or toxic to human or other life forms.* Some hazardous wastes are generated by the military or private industry. Other toxic wastes are produced by hospitals. Once dumped into landfills, these wastes release gases and other toxins that seep into the soil, polluting underground and surface water. Measures have been taken to line landfills and place them in sites not subject to flooding or high groundwater levels. Despite such measures, experts agree that more reliable means of solid waste disposal need to be explored.

Nuclear Waste Disposal

Another outcome of modern technology is nuclear energy. Today, nuclear energy power plants dot the world's landscape. Industrialized nations that are poor in energy resources rely heavily on nuclear power. Unfortunately, the widespread use of this energy has led to a new problem—the disposal of a special form of hazardous wastes called *nuclear wastes*. Nuclear wastes are a radioactive, extremely dangerous collection of materials. The decay rates of some nuclear materials is such that they must be isolated for 10,000 years or more.

Expansion and Development

Throughout history, population growth has been accelerating. Whereas it took half a million years for humankind to reach a population size of 1 billion, the next billion people were born in a span of only 80 years, and close to 1½ billion more have been born since 1975.

Too many people living in concentrated areas continues to have a dramatic impact on the land. As new cities are built to accommodate the growing masses, room for them must be cleared. This clearing has been at the expense of wilderness areas and rain forests.

Disappearing Forests

Developing nations in Central America, Africa, and Southeast Asia are rapidly expanding in agriculture and industry. These nations have been clearing tropical forests on a massive scale to make way for farms, ranch land, and fuel. This **deforestation**, or *destruction of forests,* has upset the fragile balance of nature.

Aside from providing a home to countless plant and animal species, the world's great forests play a vital part in controlling soil erosion, flooding, and sediment buildup in rivers, lakes, and reservoirs. Deforestation interferes with these processes. It can also change regional patterns of rainfall as a result of altered rates of evaporation, transpiration (vapor exhaled from the surface of green plants), and runoff. Without trees, precipitation declines and the region grows hotter and drier. Ultimately, desertlike conditions prevail where there had once been a rich tropical grassland.

up date
Looking at Technology

Jason, the Sludge-Detecting Robot

Toxic dumping is a problem not only on land but at sea. After years of chemical dumping by industries and individuals, many waterways in the United States now have thick black sludge on their bottom, sometimes referred to as "black mayonnaise." Originally, it was assumed that such sludge buildup would occur only in shallow or landlocked waterways, but now evidence is mounting that sludge is even accumulating on the ocean floor.

Now scientists studying the problem are getting some help from Jason. Who is Jason? He is a sludge-detecting robot working on the ocean floor off the coasts of New Jersey and New York. The robot, attached by fiber-optic cables, is operated by a scientist on a research ship who maneuvers Jason by means of a joystick. Using a variety of monitors and video screens, scientists are able to watch as the remote-controlled robot moves across the ocean floor, scooping up sediment and water samples 9,000 feet below the water's surface. The samples will be studied to determine the long-term damage of the millions of tons of sewage and other pollutants that have been dumped into the ocean.

Jason is just the beginning of a high-tech trend. Increasingly, robots are being used to study and to clean up wastes, chemicals, and other hazardous materials that might prove unhealthful for humans to handle directly.

Clearing large tracts of tropical forest may also have global repercussions because the trees help maintain the cycling of carbon and oxygen. When the trees are harvested or burned, carbon is released into the atmosphere in the form of carbon dioxide, which may play a role in the greenhouse effect.

Expanding Deserts

The world has always had deserts. One-third of the earth's surface is now believed to be affected by **desertification**, *the conversion of grasslands, rain-fed cropland, or irrigated cropland to desertlike conditions.* Desertification worldwide has prompted a drop in agricultural productivity.

Today, large-scale desertification is occurring mainly as a result of overgrazing. With world population on the rise and the growing demand for food supplies, scientists believe that food production must be increased by the end of the century simply to maintain present levels of nutrition. Desertification of once-productive land poses a threat to the health of the world's people.

Responding to These Environmental Trends

As the population continues to expand onto undeveloped land, care must be taken to plan this expansion to avoid destruction of land features and an undue drain on natural resources. Care must be taken to preserve the habitats of the many species of plants and animals in these regions that give our planet its rich biological diversity.

LESSON 2 *Review*

Reviewing Facts and Vocabulary

1. Use the term *hazardous waste* in a sentence that explains the seriousness of toxic dumping.
2. Explain the difference between deforestation and desertification.

Thinking Critically

3. *Synthesizing.* Find examples in newspapers and magazines of land pollution and its effects on the global environment. Write a summary of your findings.
4. *Comparing and Contrasting.* Use both a current and an older world map or atlas to compare the growing effects of deforestation and desertification.

Applying Health Skills

5. *In Your School.* Conduct an informal questionnaire in your school to find out what students know about the problem of toxic landfills. Use the results as a springboard for a campaign that could be used to raise the consciousness of all members of your community to this serious problem.

HAZARDOUS WASTE PROHIBITED

Being an Involved Citizen

At last count, the earth's population was 6 billion. With so many people in the world, you may well wonder how you can make a difference in the health of the environment. Actually, each one of us can—and *must*—do something about the problems discussed in Lessons 1 and 2. The survival of our planet hangs in the balance, but you can make a difference.

HEALTH TERMS

conservation

recycling

HEALTH CONCEPTS

- Every citizen is responsible for doing his or her share to improve and maintain the fragile health of our planet.
- Conservation of water, energy, and natural resources and recycling are the keys to the future health of the global community.

Conservation

The health of the environment is influenced by many factors, but the actions people take can have a far-reaching effect. **Conservation,** *protection and preservation of the environment,* is more important than ever. Much of the power and responsibility for conservation today rests with you, the health-literate citizen. You can help conserve precious natural resources and reduce waste by being aware of environmental issues and by making others aware of them. You can also protect the environment through the sound decisions you make as a consumer.

Guidelines for Home Conservation

About 70 percent of the energy we use at home is for heating or cooling. An additional 20 percent is used to heat water, and the remaining 10 percent goes toward lighting, cooking, and running small appliances. What can you and the adults in your home do to conserve energy? The following are a few of the actions you can take:

HEATING AND COOLING

- Keep doors and windows shut during the air-conditioning season. Close fireplace vents.
- Keep air-conditioning at a constant temperature.
- During cold weather, turn the thermostat down at bedtime.

WATER

- Wash clothes in warm or cold, not hot, water.
- Fix leaky faucets.
- Never let hot water run unnecessarily.

LIGHTING

- Use fluorescent bulbs when possible.
- Use one higher-watt bulb instead of two lower-watt bulbs in a two-bulb fixture.

COOKING

- Be sure a gas stove has a blue flame in the pilot light.
- When possible, cook on the stove top rather than in the oven.

Building Health Skills

Being a Wise Consumer: Rules of Precycling

MANY COMPANIES ARE NOW doing their part in the recycling effort by taking steps to reduce the amount of waste they create. You can do your part right inside the store by *precycling* as you shop. Here are some tips:

1. **Be selective about packaging.** Determine whether the package a product comes in can be reused or refilled.

2. **Choose products packaged in recyclable materials.** These include paper, glass, aluminum, and cardboard. Avoid products packaged in polystyrene, which contains CFCs.

3. **Avoid disposable items.** These include disposable razors, diapers, cups, and plates.

4. **Buy in bulk.** In addition to saving money, bulk quantities use less packaging than small or single-serving sizes.

How can you limit the amount of waste you create by reducing, reusing, and recycling? Learn about this and other environmental issues, such as air and water polution, at **health.glencoe.com**. Test your knowledge by solving an online crossword puzzle.

Recycling

Recycling is *the treating of waste so that it can be reused, as well as an awareness of such practices.* Recycling pays dividends to the environment in many ways:

- Recycling saves energy. For example, making a can out of recycled aluminum takes only 10 percent of the energy needed to make a brand-new can from raw materials.
- Recycling saves resources by reducing the need for cutting trees, mining, and drilling.
- Recycling can produce six times as many jobs as when landfills and incineration are used. Whatever does not have to be burned or buried, moreover, is money saved.

Guidelines for Recycling

More than 80 percent of household waste can be recycled. The following guidelines apply to individual recyclable materials.

- **Aluminum.** Rinse cans and other aluminum receptacles such as pie pans and frozen food trays. Crush them to save space.
- **Cardboard.** Flatten cardboard boxes and tie them together.
- **Clothing and household items.** Recycle these by donating them to a community organization for refurbishing and resale.
- **Glass.** Check with your recycling center to see which of the three types of glass—clear, green, and brown—it accepts. Rinse bottles and jars well, and remove any caps or lids.
- **Oil.** Take used motor oil to a service station or oil change shop for proper disposal.
- **Paper.** Reuse the backs of envelopes and paper from junk mail. Reuse grocery bags, and replace paper towels with rags.
- **Tires.** Use old tires for play equipment, gardening containers, and bumpers.
- **Computer printer toner cartridges.** Some computer printers now use recyclable toner cartridges. Consult your manual, or contact the manufacturer.

➤ *Check packaging for symbols that show the item is recyclable.*

ACTIVITY *Explain what recycling methods are used in your community.*

Protecting the Environment

Here are some practical suggestions for becoming involved in protecting the environment:

- **Become an informed consumer.** Evaluate advertising, labels, contents, and packaging as it relates to the environment. Give feedback to companies on positive ways they can affect the environment. Write letters also to newspapers, and seek opportunities to express your opinions about the environment.

- **Contact organizations that conserve resources, and educate people on environmental issues.** Ask for information and ideas for conservation. Review how your own habits and lifestyle affect the environment. Better still, join an environmental organization. Most of these organizations can provide you with resources for understanding current issues. Being part of such a group can often provide you with suggestions on ways you can promote environmental health.

- **Take action against local polluters.** The environmental problems in your community directly affect your health and way of life. Targeting local polluters is a very effective way of protecting your health and that of your family and neighbors. Unfortunately, this is not an easy task. Local and national laws may not be adequately enforced. Some companies continue to pollute for years before the government can make them stop. Even then, the fines are often small compared with the cost of modernizing the facilities or cleaning up toxic wastes. Joining with others to let elected officials become aware of the problem is a start.

LESSON 3 *Review*

Reviewing Facts and Vocabulary

1. Name two steps you can take to conserve energy and water in your home.
2. How does recycling contribute to protecting the environment?

Thinking Critically

3. ***Analyzing.*** At present, only 10 percent of recyclable household products are actually recycled. Why do you think this is so? How can you help implement a change in this area?
4. ***Evaluating.*** Explain in what ways you as an individual can most make a difference in environmental matters.

What skills and powers do you possess that could be useful?

Applying Health Skills

5. ***In Your Home.*** Make an inspection of your home, looking for ways in which your family currently conserves energy and water. Discuss areas that could be improved with parents or other adults in your household.

Health Skills Activities

Activity 1 — Your Environmental Health

The news is filled with stories about environmental problems throughout the world. Although addressing these hazards is important, action must start "at home." How can you improve the environmental health of your community?

Directions

1. With a group, browse newspaper articles. Identify three local community health problems related to the environment. For each, describe the problem itself, how it impacts the environment, and possible solutions.
2. Prepare a brief report summarizing your findings. Include actions that can be taken now by students in you school.
3. Compile your findings into an article to be published in a school or community newspaper.

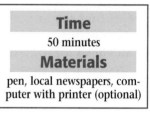

Time

50 minutes

Materials

pen, local newspapers, computer with printer (optional)

Self-Assessment

✓ Suggested at least one solution for each environmental problem.
✓ Report clearly and accurately summarized the problem and possible solutions.

Activity 2 — Save our Local Species

The health of the environment is influenced by many factors. Yet, the actions people take can have a far-reaching impact, especially on the health of other species. Imagine you were hired to develop an ad to save a species.

Directions

1. In a group, research endangered or threatened species. Choose one, and take notes on its habitat, current population size, and factors that threaten or endanger this species. Learn in addition what actions, if any, environmental groups are taking to protect this species.
2. With your group, brainstorm ways of getting others involved in a "Save the Species" campaign for the species you have researched. Possibilities might include slogans, TV commercials, or public service announcements.

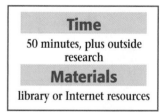

Time

50 minutes, plus outside research

Materials

library or Internet resources

Self-Assessment

✓ Accurately described the problems facing a specific species.
✓ Created a persuasive message urging support for preserving remaining members of this species.

HEALTH NEWS
ARTICLE

Ozone Layer Will Take Time to Heal

For decades we've been cutting our use of aerosol cans and foam cups because the chemicals they use–CFCs–harm the atmosphere. Now researchers believe that the ozone layer may still take half a century or more to heal. A recent study revealed that up to 70 percent of the ozone layer over the North Pole has been lost.

"Even though levels of organic chlorine in the stratosphere are going down, we saw severe ozone depletion in the Arctic this past winter," said National Oceanic and Atmospheric Administration scientist Dale Hurst.

The extreme cold in the Arctic stratosphere intensifies ozone depletion. Atmospheric physicist Paul Newman says the cold slows the decay of CFCs and causes them to destroy ozone faster.

The ozone layer is important to the protection of human life. Ozone reduces ultraviolet radiation, the kind that burns skin. Loss of that protection has predictable results, Newman says. "Skin cancer rates will go up. Sunburns will occur at a faster rate . . . because of enhanced ultraviolet radiation from a lowering of ozone."

"This is a wakeup call that although we have cut emissions of ozone depleting chemicals, these ozone holes may continue for a long time into the future," Hurst warns.

Read This ▼

Ozone 101

Here's a quick refresher on ozone:
- Ozone is colorless gas.
- A layer of ozone surrounds the Earth in a zone called the stratosphere. This ozone layer acts like a pair of sunglasses. It absorbs dangerous ultraviolet radiation from the sun.
- CFCs, or chloro-fluorocarbons, are chemicals that were used in refrigerants, industrial solvents, cleaning fluids, and to make foam.
- When CFCs are released at ground level, they rise into the stratosphere. When they reach the ozone layer, the molecules break down and release chlorine, which destroys ozone.

Source: Environment Canada–The Ozone Layer

Think About It

1. How do CFCs affect the ozone layer?
2. How can the destruction of the ozone layer affect people's health?

Using Health Terms

On a separate sheet of paper, write the term that best matches each definition below.

LESSON 1

1. Able to be broken down by microorganisms in the environment.
2. Tiny particles suspended and carried through air.
3. A slowdown of the rate at which the earth loses heat, causing an increase in the earth's temperature.
4. A mineral occurring in the form of fibers.
5. Compounds of chlorine, fluorine, and carbon.
6. A by-product of nitrogen oxides or sulfur oxides mixed with rain.

LESSON 2

7. The conversion of grasslands, rain-fed cropland, or irrigated cropland to desert-like conditions.
8. Any substances that are explosive, corrosive, flammable, or toxic to human or other life forms.
9. Destruction of forests.

LESSON 3

10. The treating of waste so that it can be reused, as well as having an awareness of such practices.
11. Concern about the preservation of the environment.

Recalling the Facts

Using complete sentences, answer the following questions.

LESSON 1

1. What aspects of modern life have led to environmental problems such as pollution?
2. What are the advantages of carbon dioxide in the atmosphere? What are the disadvantages?
3. What is acid rain?
4. What is the major cause of damage to the ozone layer?
5. Why are CFCs dangerous?
6. List three ways in which water can become polluted, and identify the effects.

LESSON 2

7. What are the pros and cons of using land-fills to store solid waste?
8. What are the risks associated with the use of nuclear power?

9. How does ever-expanding development pose a threat to forests?
10. How does deforestation affect rainfall?

LESSON 3

11. Give four suggestions that can be used in support of the statement: *Each home owner has it in his or her power to help conserve precious energy.*
12. What does recycling involve?
13. Identify three actions a responsible citizen can take to help save the environment from future abuse.

Review

Thinking Critically

LESSON 1

1. ***Comparing and Contrasting.*** Identify two similarities and two differences between harmful gases and particulates.
2. ***Synthesizing.*** Explain why the greenhouse effect poses a serious threat to the future of the planet.
3. ***Analyzing.*** What simple actions can the individual consumer take to reduce the pollution of the world's waterways?

LESSON 2

4. ***Synthesizing.*** Working alone or with several classmates, invent one or more environmentally sound ways for society to dispose of trash or garbage. Be creative. Present your plan to the class, along with illustrative pictures or diagrams of your process.

LESSON 3

5. ***Evaluating.*** Of the environmental problems addressed in this chapter, to which do you feel you could make the strongest commitment? Support your answer with valid reasons. Then take the next step and make the commitment.

Making the Connection

1. ***Science.*** Fill a shallow pan with water until it is half full. Pour in one cup of cooking oil or salad oil. Devise several ways to remove the oil from the water. You might try a lettuce leaf or a suction tube. Which of your cleanup devices worked best? Which could be best applied on a large scale?

2. ***Social Studies.*** The *Exxon Valdez* spill was the worst oil spill on record. It is not, sadly, the only such environmental catastrophe. Learn about another such catastrophe. Determine when the event happened, what happened, and what the long-term consequences have been. Share your findings in a brief report.

BEYOND THE CLASSROOM

PARENTAL INVOLVEMENT Observe and keep track of your trash at home for a week. Then talk to your parents or other adults at home about a family trash reduction program. Identify items thrown away that could be recycled, such as glass jars or plastic bottles. Develop a plan whereby each family member takes a responsibility for one kind of material to recycle.

COMMUNITY INVOLVEMENT Find out about the water treatment facility used by your community to treat water before it is consumed. Where is this facility located, how large an area does it serve, and what process is water exposed to before it is ready for human consumption? Report your findings to the class.

SCHOOL-TO-CAREER

Interpersonal. Rachel Carson was a marine biologist by profession. Find out about the work done by people in this field. What training—including education—and interpersonal skills are necessary for a career in this area? What are some of the struggles faced by people in this line of work? Write a report of your findings for a classroom resource folder.

CHAPTER 34

Your Safety and Well-Being

HEALTH Online

PRACTICING HEALTHFUL BEHAVIORS

Make a difference and promote safe riding behaviors at your school or in your neighborhood. Follow the steps in the Interactive Project, "Safety on Wheels Fair," at **health.glencoe.com**.

Personal Health Inventory

Self-Inventory Write the numbers 1–10 on a sheet of paper. Read each statement below and respond by writing *yes, no,* or *sometimes* for each item. Write a *yes* only for items that you practice regularly. Save your responses.

1	I do not use an electrical appliance if my body, clothing, or the floor is wet.
2	I do not rebottle or repackage products that might cause harm to someone else.
3	I stay within my abilities and limits when taking part in sports and recreational activities.
4	I don't risk my health or the health of others to show off.
5	I read and follow labels when using chemicals.
6	When I drive a vehicle or a motorcycle, I follow traffic guidelines.
7	I follow posted speed limits when driving or cycling.
8	I wear seat belts.
9	I do not open the door of my home to anyone I do not know or trust.
10	When going out with someone I do not know well, I make sure we go with other friends of mine.

Follow-up After completing the chapter, retake this self-inventory. Pick two items that you need to work on and set a goal to improve your health behaviors.

> **Simple things make a difference.**
>
> —Dr. Tedd Mitchell
> Director, Wellness Program, Cooper Clinic

Quick Write Divide a sheet of paper into three columns and list the steps you can take *at home, in school,* and *in your community* to reduce the risk of accidents and other preventable injuries.

Safety at Home

Home should be the one place where you can feel safe and secure. Yet every year, thousands of people are injured as a result of home accidents. Accidents involving fire, falls, and electric shock cause more disabling injuries than any other kind. This lesson will look at the nature of accidents in the home and explore ways of preventing them.

HEALTH TERMS

accident chain

situation

smoke detector

fire extinguisher

electrocution

HEALTH CONCEPTS

- Although accidents do happen, exercising safety sense can help prevent accidents or at least diminish the severity of their effects.
- Safety measures in the home include the use of working smoke detectors and periodic inspection of electrical outlets and power cords.

The Accident Chain

Although accidents seem to be random, haphazard events, safety experts have observed an **accident chain**, *a recurring pattern that is present in all mishaps.* They have found that nearly all accidents include four steps that are connected, much like the links of a chain. In order for the accident to occur, all four of the following steps must be present:

- **The Situation.** The **situation** is *the circumstance or event leading up to an accident.* A situation can be something seemingly innocent, such as heading to your room to listen to CDs with a friend.
- **The Risk Factor.** The risk factor may be either an isolated unsafe act or an unsafe habit. An example is routinely leaving your

books on the stairway as you go up to your room after school. Rushing is another habit that is involved in many accidents.

- **The Accident.** The accident is the result or consequence of one or more risk factors. For example, as your friend hurries down the stairs after listening to CDs, she trips over the books you have left on the stairway and falls.

- **The Aftermath.** The aftermath may take the form of personal injury, destruction of property, or both. For example, in the aftermath of your friend's fall, she might have broken her arm.

As you will see in the sections and lessons that follow, a single preventive behavior is often sufficient to break the accident chain.

Fires

What needs to be present for a fire to take place? Three elements (fuel, heat, and air) must be present. Fuel for a fire can be carelessly stored rags, wood, coal, oil, gasoline, or paper. A heat source could be a match, an electrical wire, or a cigarette. The oxygen in the air feeds and fans the flames. Recognition of the three links in the "fire chain" is the basis of fire prevention.

Fire Prevention Devices

Because household fires kill thousands of people each year, it is essential that each home be equipped with two life-saving devices: a smoke detector and a fire extinguisher. A **smoke detector** is *an alarm that is triggered by the presence of smoke.* Safety experts recommend one smoke detector on each floor or level of a home. They also advise testing the detector periodically and replacing the battery. Smoke detectors are now universally installed in new homes.

A **fire extinguisher** is *a portable device that puts out small fires by ejecting fire-extinguishing chemicals.* If you are confident that you can control a fire quickly with an extinguisher, use it promptly and properly. Stand away from the flames; aim it at the source of the fire, not at the flames; and move the spray from side to side. If you have any doubt at all, forget the extinguisher, get out of the house, and call the fire department.

When selecting a fire extinguisher for the home, be certain that you and your family understand the manufacturer's specifications and directions. Check the dial on the equipment from time to time to be certain that it still has sufficient pressure to be useful in an emergency.

Fire Safety Action

Most fatal home fires occur during the night, when it is easy to become disoriented by smoke or flame. The best protection against injury or death from home fires is to establish escape plans and conduct practice drills periodically.

keeping Fit

Think Fast!

If you are caught near or in an actual fire, acting quickly and remaining calm could save your life and the lives of others. Remember the following:

➤ Most deaths caused by fire result from smoke inhalation rather than burns. The chemical by-products of combustion combine quickly with oxygen, preventing smoke-inhalation victims from getting oxygen from the air. Because smoke rises, stay low to the floor to escape.

➤ Cover your mouth and nose with a wet towel or pillowcase to filter the smoke when evacuating a room.

➤ If you cannot escape your room, stuff towels and clothing in door cracks and vents.

➤ If a fire starts in a frying pan, put a lid on the fire. Never put water on a grease fire, because it will make the grease and the fire spread.

➤ If a fire starts in the oven, turn off the oven, and smother the fire with baking soda.

➤ Do not use water to put out an electrical fire. Use dry materials such as sand, salt, flour, or baking soda.

➤ If your clothes catch on fire, remember to *stop, drop,* and *roll.* Roll on the ground or roll up in a rug or blanket to smother the flames. If you remain upright or run, the flames will spread.

You and your family should draw a floor plan, including doors, hallways, and windows, of each story of your home. Use arrows to point out two ways of escape, if possible, from each room. Alternate escape routes are necessary in case one route is blocked. For example, if an upstairs door is blocked by fire, a ladder or a readily available rope coil is essential for escape through windows. Use a predetermined signal to alert everyone to the fire. Smoke detectors, which should be in every household, will do this job.

After escaping, meet outside at a safe prearranged place. Do not go back into the house. Call the fire department from a neighbor's house. If a person is trapped inside a burning building, rescue is safer and usually faster if left to the fire department.

Use a safe stepping-stool to reach high places.

Falls

Even though young children and the elderly are the most susceptible to injury from falls, this type of accident can happen to anyone.

Preventing Falls

Although falls are not usually serious, in some instances they can be deadly. You can take steps to help break the accident chain associated with many falls.

Stairways should be well lighted, in good repair, equipped with sturdy handrails and nonskid stair strips, and free of clutter. A loose rug is always a danger. Make sure that all bare wood and tile floors are not slippery. All bathtubs and showers should be equipped with safety rails and nonskid mats.

Outdoor steps and sidewalks should be maintained in good repair and kept free of ice, leaves, toys, and other obstacles.

If there are small children in the home, install adjustable safety latches so that windows can open only a few inches. (Be sure they are removable in case of an emergency.)

Electric Shock

Shocks from electrical appliances can kill. Each year, more than 1,000 Americans are killed by accidental **electrocution**, *death resulting from passage through the body of a high-voltage current.*

Preventing Electric Shock

You should take precautions when using home electrical appliances and power tools. Whenever anything seems to be wrong with an appliance or power tool, unplug it immediately. Inspect cords occasionally for signs of cracked insulation and have frayed cords replaced. Cords should not be placed under a carpet or rug because they can be damaged when walked on.

Disconnect appliances by pulling on the plug, not on the cord. Never use an electrical appliance or power tool if your body, clothing, or the floor is wet. Keep outlet protectors in sockets if small children are in the home.

Poisoning

Everyday products, not just those marked with a skull and crossbones, can be poisonous. Most of these products are typically found in the kitchen, bathroom, utility area, basement, and garage. Poisoning, which is especially prevalent among young children, can result from either swallowing a toxic substance or breathing in a lethal gas. Still another type of poisoning, **food poisoning**, is covered in Chapter 6.

Preventive Behaviors

In families with children, household products and medicines should be kept in locked cabinets or out of the reach of children. Never place any **medicine** in an unlabeled vial or a container other than the one it was originally packaged in. Periodically check the medicine cabinet, read labels carefully, and discard any medicine that is past its expiration date.

LESSON 1 *Review*

Reviewing Facts and Vocabulary

1. Explain the purpose of a smoke detector and a fire extinguisher.
2. Give some examples of hazards that cause falls in the home.

Thinking Critically

3. **Evaluating.** For a school report that is due in a month, Todd is keeping back issues of newsmagazines. He has piled a dozen copies on a stair landing leading down to the family basement. Identify at least two accidents that could result from this situation.
4. **Analyzing.** Analyze the saying: *Safety begins at home.* What assumptions does this saying make?

5. **Synthesizing.** Marta has a three-year-old brother. What special steps do Marta and her family need to take to minimize her brother's risk of injury due to a fall if the family lives in an apartment?

Applying Health Skills

6. **In Your Home and School.** Design a fire escape plan for your classroom and your home. For your home, include two escape routes from each room.

Safety Outside the Home

Although many accidents occur at home, the potential for danger lurks outside the home as well. Accidents occur during leisure-time activities, in the workplace, and even in acts of nature. As with accidents in the home, a single preventive behavior can often break the accident chain.

HEALTH TERMS

Occupational Safety and Health Administration (OSHA)

hurricane

tornado

blizzard

HEALTH CONCEPTS

- Many accidents, especially among teens, occur when people show off, get overly confident, or accept a dare.
- Safety on the job is the responsibility of each and every employee.
- Careful planning and preparation can help you survive a natural disaster.

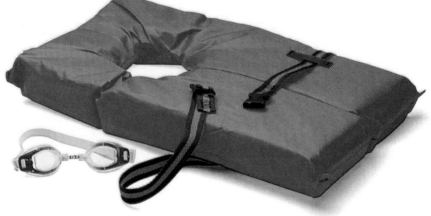

Recreational Safety

Do you enjoy swimming? Maybe you participate in a sport. Recreational activities such as these can be fun, but all too often such activities are "accidents waiting to happen." By exercising common sense and caution, you can break the accident chain.

Accidents In or On Water

Drowning is the second leading cause of injury-related death for children in the United States today. Each year 4,300 people drown, and another 3,000 are hospitalized for near-drownings. The majority of drownings and near-drownings occur in residential swimming pools. Children under the age of four are especially at risk and account for over 60 percent of all pool drownings.

Among teens, accidents involving water occur most often when a person is showing off, gets overly confident, uses alcohol near or on the water, or accepts a dare.

Water Safety

When the behaviors described above happen in or around water, the price can be high—even deadly. Whether you are swimming, diving, or boating, following these simple rules will reduce your risk of accidents:

SWIMMING

■ Know your swimming abilities. Never swim so far out that you are not sure you can make it safely back to your starting point. Learn to swim well.

■ Swim only in supervised areas, where a lifeguard is present. If possible, swim with a companion who knows lifesaving techniques.

■ If you get a **muscle cramp**, do not panic. Relax, float, and press and squeeze the muscle until it relaxes.

■ If you are pulled offshore by rapid currents or undertows, swim toward shore at a 45-degree angle until you are freed by the current.

■ Never swim or dive when using any form of medication or when under the influence of alcohol or another drug.

keeping Fit

Pool Rules

The high incidence of pool-related drownings can be greatly reduced by following a few simple, common-sense rules.

➤ Never leave a small child alone near the water.

➤ Remove toys that are in and around the pool when they are not being used. Toys can attract young children to a pool.

➤ With above-ground pools, steps and ladders leading from the ground to the pool should be secured and locked.

➤ A first-aid kit, a phone, and emergency phone numbers should be in a convenient nearby location.

➤ High fences or walls should protect outsiders from getting in your pool.

➤ For a young child, a bathtub can be as dangerous as a pool.

h⊙t link

muscle cramp For more information on muscle cramps and ways to treat this problem, see Chapter 4, page 84.

◄ *Drowning is a constant danger for all swimmers, no matter how well they swim. That is why it is important to always swim with a lifeguard present.*

ACTIVITY *What can you do to improve your swimming skills?*

DIVING

- Always check the water depth before diving.
- Never dive into unfamiliar water or into shallow breaking waves. Make sure the area is clear of swimmers and floating objects.
- Always dive straight ahead and not off the side of the diving board.
- Do not jump into shallow water. This could cause a spinal injury by jolting the body.

BOATING

- Learn how to handle a boat or canoe correctly. Some states require a boating class or have age requirements.
- Wear approved flotation devices on boats and other watercraft. Rubber tubes and floats are no substitute in the event of a mishap.
- Follow basic highway and driving safety rules when it comes to alcohol and drugs: Don't drink or use drugs and drive a boat.

▼ *Camping can be fun when safety precautions are followed.*

ACTIVITY *Name other precautions that campers should follow in addition to campfire safety.*

Accidents on the Trail

Outdoor pastimes, such as hiking, camping, hunting, and climbing are wonderful forms of **physical activity**. Yet, they can turn disastrous when rules of safety are not followed. When taking part in any nature activity or sport, keep the following safety tips uppermost in mind:

- Stay in specified campsites, and hunt only in approved areas.
- Never camp, hike, or hunt alone. Always make sure someone knows where you are going and when you will return.
- Be knowledgeable about poisonous plants, insects, and snakes in the area.
- Carry plenty of fresh water on the trail.
- Never cook inside a tent, and smother all campfires with dirt and water.
- Never include alcohol or drugs in any outdoor activity.

h⊙tlink

physical activity For more information on physical activity and its benefits to total health, see Chapter 4, page 72.

Safety on the Job

Do you have an after-school or weekend job? Even if you do not, some day you will be part of the workforce. Thus, it is important for you to know that precautions in the workplace are a vital part of safety.

Since the early 1990s accidental deaths on the job have been reduced by three quarters, largely due to the efforts of the **Occupational Safety and Health Administration (OSHA),** a *federal agency responsible for promoting safe and healthful conditions in the workplace.* A

Making Responsible Decisions

Selling Safety Short

Herb and Ramon, two friends and classmates, are working in the same factory over the summer. During their two-week training period, the boys' supervisor emphasized the importance of wearing safety goggles at all times while in the factory. Recently, Ramon started noticing that Herb wears his goggles only when the supervisor is nearby. When confronted by Ramon, Herb made it clear that he finds the goggles uncomfortable and hot. Ramon is concerned for his friend and remembers being told during training about employees who were injured on the job. He wants to tell the supervisor but is afraid it might cost his friend his job.

What Would You Do?

Apply the six steps of the decision-making process to Ramon's problem.

1. **State the situation.**
2. **List the options.**
3. **Weigh the possible outcomes.**
4. **Consider your values.**
5. **Make a decision and act.**
6. **Evaluate the decision.**

division of the U.S. Department of Labor, OSHA develops and enforces health regulations and job safety. It also is involved in keeping employers and employees aware of industrial hazards. OSHA deals with fire prevention, protective clothing, and acceptable levels of exposure to asbestos and lead. OSHA workers inspect work sites to ensure compliance with their standards.

Responsibility for maintaining a safe work environment also rests with the employer and the employee. Employers can do their part by making sure that workers are adequately trained and are made aware of potential hazards and safety rules. Employees can help ensure a healthful and accident-free environment by:

- arriving at work well rested and alert.
- learning the proper use of machinery and other equipment.
- following established safety measures, including the wearing of protective gear.

Natural Disasters

The sky turns suddenly dark, an ominous funnel appears at the horizon. You are sitting at home when suddenly the floor begins to vibrate beneath your feet, and objects come crashing to the floor. These and similar situations, all acts of nature, affect not only the individual but entire communities. Yet, as with other situations, careful planning and preparation can help you survive should a natural disaster hit your area.

HEALTH
Online

A natural disaster can occur just about anywhere and at any time. Learn how to prepare for and stay safe during natural disasters from the American Red Cross Disaster Services at **health.glencoe.com**.

Hurricanes and Tornadoes

A **hurricane** is *a powerful rainstorm, characterized by driving winds.* Hurricanes occur near coastal areas of the United States, mainly on the eastern and southern seaboards. In general, preparation for a hurricane includes securing your property and then either going to a shelter or evacuating the area as the National Weather Service instructs. The farther inland you go, the safer you will be. Hurricanes have been known to build up enough momentum to carry their destructive winds inland for hundreds of miles.

A **tornado** is *a powerful, twisting windstorm.* Although tornadoes were once largely confined to the central United States, in recent times they have begun to strike sporadically in all areas of the country. Knowing what to do in case of a hurricane or a tornado could save your life.

A storm cellar or basement is the safest place to go for protection from a tornado. If neither option is available, a hallway or bathtub away from windows will suffice. If you are caught outside, get into a ditch and lie face down. Cover yourself with a mattress, blanket, rug, or bulky winter clothing, if possible, to protect yourself from flying objects.

Floods

Flooding is often the result of severe rains of the type that accompany hurricanes. Some streams and rivers may also overflow as a result of melting mountain snow. If you live in an area that is prone to flooding, an emergency plan is your best first course of action. It is also important to learn under what conditions to abandon your home, as well as when it is safer to stay put until help arrives. Some people refuse to leave, and they drown in their homes.

If you are in a car that stalls because of rising waters, abandon the car and seek higher ground immediately. When driving, be on the lookout as well for signs warning that bridges and roads may be "out" because of flood conditions.

Earthquakes

Heavy ground tremors from earthquakes occur often in some parts of the United States. California averages almost 5,000 weak but detectable quakes per year. Knowing what to do during and after an earthquake is important to your safety.

Most casualties during an earthquake are not a direct result of the ground movement but result from falling objects or collapsing structures. If you are inside a building and feel a tremor, follow these safety procedures:

1. Stay in the building.
2. Select a safe spot away from falling objects within a few steps of where you are standing, and go to it. If there is a heavy desk or table with enough space for you to fit underneath, crawl under it

and then hold on to it to keep it from moving away from you.

3. If you live in an area prone to tremors, safeguard your home by bolting bookcases and other tall or heavy furniture to the wall. If you are outdoors when an earthquake hits, stay away from buildings, trees, and power lines.

Blizzards

A **blizzard** is *a snowstorm with winds of 35 miles per hour (56 km per hour) or greater.* Visibility is less than 500 feet (152 m), so it is easy for a person to get lost. The safest place to be during a blizzard is indoors. If you are caught outside, try to keep your mouth and nose covered, and keep moving so that you do not freeze. Try to follow a road or a fence to the closest safe place. If you live in snow country, carry jumper cables, a blanket, and shovel in your car during the winter.

If you must go outside in a blizzard, wear protective clothing. All of the following will help protect you from freezing temperatures and **frostbite:** thermal undergarments; outer garments that repel wind and moisture; head, face, and ear coverings; extra socks; warm boots; and wool-lined mittens. Many thin layers of clothing provide the best protection from the cold.

Blizzards and other natural disasters can strike without warning.

ACTIVITY *Identify measures established in your community to prepare for disasters.*

h◦t link

frostbite For more information on frostbite, see Chapter 4, page 87.

LESSON 2

Review

Reviewing Facts and Vocabulary

1. List five rules of safety on or near water.
2. Describe the purpose of OSHA.

Thinking Critically

3. **Synthesizing.** Develop a plan that would help reduce the number of recreational accidents in your community.
4. **Analyzing.** Compare safe and unsafe behavior when camping or hiking.
5. **Comparing and Contrasting.** Tell in what ways hurricanes, tornadoes, and earthquakes are similar. In what ways are they not alike?

Applying Health Skills

6. **In Your Home.** Research the kinds of natural disasters common to your area of the United States. Speak with someone at your local chapter of the American Red Cross, Salvation Army, or National Guard about what action should be taken in disasters of this type. Summarize your findings, and share them with the class.

Safety on Wheels

It is a frightening fact that automobile accidents are the leading cause of death for people between the ages of 15 and 20 in the United States. The fatality rate for teenage drivers is about four times higher than the rate for drivers 25 to 65 years old. What is perhaps even more sobering is that many of these fatal accidents are preventable.

HEALTH TERMS

vehicular safety

road rage

HEALTH CONCEPTS

- Vehicular safety is obeying the rules of the road, as well as exercising common sense and good judgment.
- Most automobile accidents among teens do not involve a second vehicle.
- Every driver accepts some responsibility to protect his or her personal life as well as the lives of others.

Automobile Safety

When teenagers are entrusted with the family car, they are taking on a big responsibility to themselves, their own families, their passengers, and the passengers of other vehicles. That responsibility is to behave in a manner that reduces the risk of death or injury. Behaving responsibly means exercising **vehicular safety**—*obeying the rules of the road, as well as exercising common sense and good judgment.* Obeying the rules means driving within the speed limit, yielding the right-of-way when called for, and observing local traffic regulations. Exercising common sense and good judgment includes:

- **Paying attention to road conditions.** This means reducing your speed when the road is icy or rain-slicked, when a lane narrows, or when there is construction or congestion.

- **Paying attention to other drivers.** A popular TV commercial that aired several years ago, sponsored by the National Safety Council, advised drivers to "watch out for the other guy." This advice is still sound. When it is dark or inclement weather reduces visibility, turn on your headlights. This makes it possible for other drivers to see *you*. In general, drive as though the other driver is going to act irresponsibly. That way you will always be ready for some unforeseen action.

- **Paying attention to your physical state.** If you are tired, don't drive. Pull over at the nearest rest stop and call home. *Under no circumstances should you drive when you have been using alcohol, other drugs, or prescription or over-the-counter medications.* The National Highway Traffic Safety Administration (NHTSA) reports that almost 38 percent of young drivers killed in crashes in 1999 were **intoxicated**.

- **Paying attention to your emotional state.** If you are angry or feeling other strong emotions, don't drive. Your mental state can affect your judgment and reaction time as much as your physical state. Taking an approved driver's education course can help you develop better driving skills and habits. Such a course can help you learn to anticipate problems before they occur.

Road Rage

Sometimes people who are otherwise emotionally stable become enraged when they get behind the wheel. *When intense anger and driving mix,* the results—known as **road rage**—can be deadly. Road rage has been linked to a number of incidents, such as disputes over a parking space, obscene gestures, loud music, overuse of the horn, and slow driving. A driver consumed with road rage may run red lights, tailgate, or pass on a shoulder. Some individuals have even been known to use guns or other weapons.

If you see someone who is truly a danger on the road, keep your distance. Get the vehicle's license plate number, and report it promptly to the police.

ROAD RAGE: SOME STRATEGIES

You can protect yourself when you are behind the wheel by taking these measures:

- avoid blocking the right-hand turn lane.
- assume other drivers' mistakes are not personal.
- be polite and courteous, even if the other driver is not.
- pull over and allow traffic to pass if moving slowly.
- avoid unnecessary use of high-beam headlights.
- avoid all conflict if possible. If another driver challenges you, take a deep breath and get out of the way.

Did You Know?

➤ The National Highway Traffic Safety Administration maintains that 15,900 highway deaths could be prevented if everyone wore seat belts.

➤ Your chances of being killed in a motorcycle accident or motor scooter accident are 17 times greater than if you are in a car.

➤ Persons on in-line skates can reach speeds as high as 30 miles per hour and often have difficulty stopping.

hot link

intoxicated For more on what it means to be intoxicated and the dangers of driving under the influence of alcohol, see Chapter 25, page 550.

Other Preventive Behaviors

For every 100 young people killed in a motor vehicle accident in the United States last year, 80 would still be alive if they had been wearing a seat belt. Yet, according to the CDC's *Youth Risk Behavior Survey,* about 19 percent of students nationwide rarely, or never, use seat belts when riding in a car or truck driven by someone else. Drivers and passengers who fail to use seat belts are more likely to become flying missiles during a crash. This is true whether they are in the front or back seat.

When you use a seat belt, you are practicing accident and injury prevention. If your friends do not buckle up, ask them to do so. Most states have laws requiring the use of seat belts.

up date
▶ *Looking at the Issues*

Should More Restrictions Be Put on Teen Drivers?

Although driver training helps save lives, some safety experts feel that where teens are concerned, driver's ed and safety courses are "too little, too late." Many states have now implemented measures to restrict teen drivers. These include raising the minimum driving age, revoking licenses for criminal offenses, limiting the kinds of roads on which teens may drive, and keeping teens off the roads after dark. Not everyone agrees with these policies.

ANALYZING DIFFERENT VIEWPOINTS

▶ **Viewpoint One**

Many teens believe that just because some teens drive unsafely, other law-abiding and safe-driving teens should not have to pay the price. They state that many teens are good citizens who care about their own and others' safety and are respectful of others' rights on the road.

▶ **Viewpoint Two**

Advocates of stricter driving restrictions state that some teens, unaccustomed to cars and driving, make dangerous mistakes on the road. Other teens, they say, are guilty of daredevil tactics, showing off for friends, and driving under the influence of alcohol and other drugs. They also point to statistics that reveal that 16-year-old drivers are less responsible and more likely to have accidents than 17-year-olds.

EXPLORING YOUR VIEWS

1. Do you believe that teen drivers should have restrictions placed on them? Why or why not?

2. How does the topic of driving restrictions relate to the issue of rights vs. responsibility?

Being an Alert Consumer: Helmet Hints

ACCORDING TO THE NHTSA, an estimated half of all cyclists between the ages of 15 and 20 who die in crashes each year were not wearing helmets. When buying a helmet, remember to consider:

1. **Visibility.** A helmet should be bright-colored so that motorists can see you clearly. Helmets that are black or some neutral color may be stylish, but they can also be deadly if they cause you to blend in with your surroundings.

2. **Dependability.** A properly fitting helmet should cover the top of your forehead. It should also have straps that prevent it from shifting or, worse still, falling off in the event you hit a bump.

3. **Reliability.** Buy only a helmet that is certified by the Snell Memorial Foundation or approved by the American National Standards Institute.

Use your head when buying a helmet. This is your best safeguard against losing it.

Safety on Two Wheels

Although the phrase *safety on wheels* may prompt you to think only of cars and trucks, remember that motorcycles, mopeds, and even bicycles are also vehicles. Like cars, they are subject to vehicular safety as well as traffic laws.

Motorcycle and Moped Safety

Motorcyclists and moped drivers are 17 times more likely to be killed in an accident than people traveling in a car. Part of the reason is that motorized two-wheeled vehicles slide more easily and weigh less than those with four wheels. Such vehicles are also more difficult for other motorists to see.

Besides following safety rules on the road, cyclists can increase their protection by:

- wearing safety helmets and proper clothing, including eye protection.
- being extra cautious in wet weather when tire traction on wet surfaces is poor.
- avoiding "wheelies" and other forms of showing off.
- carrying an additional rider *only* when your vehicle has an attached second seat, foot rests, and a spare helmet.
- avoiding touching or grabbing on to another moving vehicle.

keeping
Fit

Glove Compartment Checklist

When you are driving alone, your car's glove compartment can be a lifesaver–provided it contains the following items:

➤ a flashlight with working batteries.

➤ a notepad and pen or pencil.

➤ change for a telephone call.

➤ a tire pressure gauge.

➤ number of a 24-hour towing service.

➤ an insurance card for the car you are traveling in.

➤ a pump-spray product that can be used to fix a flat tire instantly.

- being on the lookout for potential sudden hazards, such as a car door opening or pedestrians darting out from between parked cars.
- taking a motorcycle safety course, required in some states.

Bicycle Safety

Bicycles are a main form of transportation in many nations around the world, and their popularity in the United States has grown dramatically in recent years. Because bicycles use "human power" rather than motor power, they also represent a pleasant way to stay fit.

At the same time, like motorcycles and mopeds, bicycles are legitimate vehicles and need to be taken seriously. An estimated 53,000 bicycle injuries occur each year, some 750 of them fatal. The most common and potentially most serious mishap is a **head injury**, which can be as minor as a scalp wound or as serious as a traumatic brain injury. Four out of five collisions between bicycles and cars are caused by cyclists who disregard traffic rules. The most frequent mistake that cyclists make is riding on the wrong side of the road, against—rather than with—the flow of traffic.

Follow these guidelines for safe cycling:

- Ride on the right, keeping close to the side of the road. When riding with others, ride in a straight, single-file line.
- Always yield the right-of-way. You will not win against a car or truck.
- Watch for parked cars pulling into traffic and for car doors that swing open suddenly in your path.
- Obey the same rules as drivers, such as signaling before you turn and stopping for red lights and stop signs.

h⬡t l⬤nk

head injury For more information on head injuries and ways to reduce their risk, see Chapter 16, page 373.

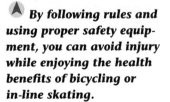

▲ *By following rules and using proper safety equipment, you can avoid injury while enjoying the health benefits of bicycling or in-line skating.*

- Except when signaling, keep both hands on the handlebars at all times.
- Wear a properly fitting hard-shell helmet.
- Make sure your bike has a bright headlight and a red rear light and reflector for night riding.
- Wear reflective, or at least light-colored, clothing when riding at dawn, dusk, after dark, or in the rain.

Skating Safety

Skateboards, roller skates, and in-line skates can be a lot of fun. They can also lead to disaster when precautions are not followed. When roller skating, skateboarding, or using in-line skates, heed the following:

- Wear protective equipment—wrist guards, elbow and knee pads, a hard-shell helmet, and light gloves.
- Watch for and slow down around pedestrians.
- Keep your speed under control.
- Do not hold anything in your hand, such as a portable radio. In the event of a fall, your natural reflex will be to save the item you are holding, rather than to protect your body.
- If you do begin to fall, try to curl up into a ball and roll, staying loose. Tensing up will increase your chances of injury.

LESSON 3 *Review*

Reviewing Facts and Vocabulary

1. What is vehicular safety?
2. List three safety tips for operators of each of the following: cars, motorcycles, and bicycles.

Thinking Critically

3. *Synthesizing.* Write a one-page editorial emphasizing the importance of wearing a helmet when riding a two-wheel vehicle or while skating.
4. *Evaluating.* Since the federal speed limit of 65 was abolished, many states have increased their speed limits to 70 or 75, and in a few states there is no daytime speed limit whatsoever. Do you feel this is a mistake? Support your views.

5. *Analyzing.* What does it mean to say that it is "better to be alive than right" when it comes to vehicular safety?

Applying Health Skills

6. *In Your Home.* Collect several newspaper articles about accidents in and around your community. Try to identify each of the links of the accident chain and ways the chain might have been broken.

LESSON 4

Personal Safety

Up until now, the focus of this chapter has been safety procedures that can minimize the risk of accidents and injury. Yet, in life there are "non-accident" situations that are every bit as serious and require the same preparedness and alert action. This lesson will explore such situations.

HEALTH TERMS

date rape

acquaintance rape

HEALTH CONCEPTS

- When safety sense is used, the likelihood of physical attack can be reduced.
- Rape and sexual assault are crimes of violence, not passion.

h⊙t link

violence For more information on violence in its many forms and ways to prevent it, see Chapter 14, page 324.

Physical Attack

Anyone can be a victim of physical **violence**. In fact, it is estimated that one out of three Americans will become the victim of a sexual assault or attempted attack sometime in his or her lifetime. Although this usually happens to females, males can also be victims. Teens who are involved with—or have friends who are involved with—gangs, guns, alcohol, or drugs are especially at risk.

In many instances, physical attack occurs in conjunction with some other crime, such as robbery. In other cases, the attack can be purely random and happen for no apparent reason. Such crimes, moreover, can take place anywhere, although there are well-defined circumstances under which they are more likely to occur. These include deserted streets, dark parking lots, and other isolated situations, particularly during nighttime hours.

Preventive Behaviors

Some suggestions for preventing and surviving physical violence are addressed in Chapter 14. Other measures include the following:

- Give up jewelry, shoes, a bike, or other personal property, if that is what the attacker is after. You are better off losing a possession, even one that at the time seems priceless, rather than risking personal injury.
- Avoid parts of town or places with a high incidence of known crime.
- Avoid walking alone at night, in wooded areas, or in dark alleys. If you must walk at night, walk under lights and by the curb. Avoid doorways.
- At night, have your car keys ready when you are going to your car. Before entering, check the back seat to make sure no one is inside your car. Lock all the doors.
- Park in well-lighted areas.
- Don't put your wallet or purse in an easy-to-grab place.
- Take down license plate numbers and descriptions of suspicious cars in your neighborhood and report them to the police.
- Stay alert to what is going on around you.
- Walk briskly; act assertively, as though you know where you are going and what you are doing.
- Be cautious with anyone who gives you undue attention.
- Avoid placing yourself in isolated, risky situations.
- Don't hitchhike or give rides to hitchhikers.
- Ask anyone giving you a ride to wait until you have safely entered where you're going.
- Get on and off buses in well-lit areas.

▲ *How are these teens demonstrating safe behavior while walking at night?*

SOME INNER TOOLS OF SELF-DEFENSE

When people talk about self-defense, they often mean learning physical strategies for stopping attacks. They imagine quick kicks and tricky moves. However, mental or emotional strategies are also important. You may already have the following valuable self-defense tools within you.

- **Self-esteem.** This includes the confidence you have in yourself. People with high self-esteem are not likely to be bullied or chosen as easy targets, particularly by people who know them.
- **Assertiveness.** Assertiveness is bold and confident behavior. **Assertive** people speak with definite conviction, leaving no doubt as to their feelings or intentions. Many attackers want easy victims they can overpower quickly. Phrases such as "Leave me alone" or "I'm not going with you" may throw an attacker off guard.

h⚬t link

assertive For more information on an assertive posture and how to use assertiveness in high-pressure situations, see Chapter 13, page 308.

hotlink

rape For more information on rape and how to avoid becoming a victim, see Chapter 14, page 331.

▼ *Taking a class in self-defense can improve your chances of withstanding an attack.*

ACTIVITY *Name four mental and emotional self-defense tools.*

■ **Body language.** Your body language can project your thoughts in a forceful way. Making direct eye contact, using a strong voice, keeping your body erect and chin held high, and using a deliberate stride can send the message that you are in charge of your safety.

■ **A self-protective attitude.** Realize that you are worthy and have a right to be treated with respect and to be safe. Don't be afraid of insulting someone by walking away or by being overly cautious.

Sexual Assault and Rape

As noted in Chapter 14, some physical attacks have a sexual component. These crimes, sexual assault and **rape**, are crimes of violence, not passion. The attacker is motivated not by sexual desire but by the prospect of forcing another person to do something he or she doesn't want to do.

Often, victims of rape know their attacker. *When rape occurs between two people who are dating,* it is called **date rape. Acquaintance rape** is *rape by someone who is known casually by the victim or someone thought to be a friend.* Though these crimes are technically different, for the victim the consequences are equally devastating. These include a feeling of having been violated, which can leave deep emotional scars.

Preventive Behaviors

Sexual assault and rape can happen anywhere. They can even happen in the confines of a house—your own or someone else's. Among the measures you can take to prevent becoming a victim are the following:

■ Have sexual limits and communicate them clearly.
■ Do not drink or use drugs or date anyone who does.
■ Do not go out alone or ride in a car with a person you do not know well.
■ Do not put others' feelings ahead of your own safety.
■ Take classes in karate or other forms of self-defense.
■ Never open your door to anyone you do not know or trust.
■ Use locks on doors and windows.
■ Do not let strangers use your phone.
■ Do not get into an elevator alone with a stranger.
■ Do not hitchhike or pick up hitchhikers.
■ Do not park your car, walk, or jog in remote areas.
■ If you are being followed, hurry to a place where there are other people, such as to a store.
■ If your car is rammed from behind or breaks down, stay in your car with the doors locked and flasher lights on.

Escaping and Surviving an Attack

If you become the target of a sexual attack, try to run for help. If you cannot run, decide on another course of action. Scream or yell "Fire!" If possible, physically disable or stun the person in some way. Watch for a moment when the attacker may be caught off guard so you can escape. Use your wits. Try different approaches. Don't assume you can't get away. You have a greater chance of escaping than you might think. If all else fails, you may have to submit in order to survive.

Help for Rape Victims

If you or someone you know is raped, get help from your family or a friend after an attack and get it quickly. *Call law enforcement agents immediately.* Get medical help right away. You should undergo medical tests for pregnancy, **STDs**, and **HIV** infection.

Call a rape crisis center and get counseling or join a support group. You will need help to recover from the emotional shock of being raped. Be patient. It takes time to recover from the trauma of an attack. Remember that any person who becomes a victim of rape is the *victim,* not the cause, and has no reason to be ashamed.

h◦t link

STDs For more information on STDs and their treatment, see Chapter 29, page 642.

HIV For more information on HIV, the virus that causes AIDS, see Chapter 30, page 656.

LESSON 4 *Review*

Reviewing Facts and Vocabulary

1. What are three ways of reducing your chances of becoming a victim of physical attack?
2. Explain the similarities and differences between date rape and acquaintance rape.

Thinking Critically

3. *Synthesizing.* Most incidences of rape are not reported. Why do you think this is so?
4. *Analyzing.* What steps can teens in particular take to prevent becoming victims of attack, sexual or otherwise?
5. *Synthesizing.* Summarize the major considerations when it comes to the decision of resisting or not resisting in the case of an assault.

6. *Evaluating. People make a "big deal" out of sexual harassment. It really becomes an issue only when someone wants to "get back" at an individual.* Is this an accurate statement? Explain.

Applying Health Skills

7. ***In Your Home.*** Read about crime statistics in your community. Create a public service announcement offering specific ways of reducing the incidence of physical attack (e.g., by cleaning up certain neighborhoods). If possible, broadcast the announcement over a local radio station.

Health Skills Activities

Activity 1 — In Case of Fire

Does your family have a fire escape plan in place in case of an emergency? If they do not, here is your chance to help.

Directions

1. On a computer or working freehand, create a "blueprint" of your family home. Show stairways, and note windows and doors by drawing short breaks, or spaces, in walls.
2. Draw red arrows to indicate a main escape route and a secondary route (in case the main one is blocked) from every room.
3. Include a meeting spot outside the home where all family members are to gather.
4. Share your escape route with all members of your family at a family meeting. Rehearse the main and secondary routes.

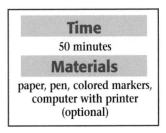

Time
50 minutes
Materials
paper, pen, colored markers, computer with printer (optional)

Self-Assessment

✓ House "blueprint" was neat and easy to read with each room clearly labeled.
✓ Both escape routes were clearly marked and easy to use in an emergency situation.

Activity 2 — Personal Safety Video

Anyone can become a victim of physical violence. However, there are some preventive measures you can take to increase your personal safety. You and classmates will show these in an instructional video.

Directions

1. Using the information in your text, create a list of topics for a "Personal Safety Instructional Video." Among the topics to be explored are how to prevent and survive physical violence, tools of self-defense, reducing the risk of sexual assault, and escaping and surviving a sexual attack.
2. Group members are to convert their findings into a script detailing the kinds of measures a person can take to increase his or her chances of safety.
3. Record your video to be shared with other classes.

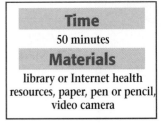

Time
50 minutes
Materials
library or Internet health resources, paper, pen or pencil, video camera

Self-Assessment

✓ Included all the information requested.
✓ Video was clear, engaging, and targeted to a teen audience.

Cell Phone Safety Survey

An estimated 3 percent of American drivers are talking on handheld cell phones at any given time, according to the first-of-its-kind survey conducted by the federal government.

The National Highway Traffic Safety Administration (NHTSA) found that about a half-million drivers are holding a phone to their ears at any given time.

The survey found that rates of use can double during times outside rush hour. The survey covered drivers of all types of passenger vehicles, including cars, vans, sport-utility vehicles, and pickups.

While the report looked at cell phone use across the country, it did not try to assess how cell phones contribute to car crashes. However, other NHTSA data suggests cell phones contribute to approximately 20 to 30 percent of all crashes.

Data collected in the survey found:
- Drivers of vans and SUVs used their cell phones the most.
- Use by drivers was highest during times outside rush hour.
- Women use their cell phones more then men. In the case of SUV drivers it was almost twice as high.
- Senior citizens use cell phones less than any other age group.
- Cell phones are used more during the week than on weekends.

The study is based on data collected nationwide by researchers who observed more than 12,000 vehicles between 8 a.m. and 6 p.m. during October and November.

Read This

No Hands? Still Risky

Some drivers have shifted to using "hands free" cell phones. They hope that these speaker phones will allow them to drive and talk safely.

Unfortunately, a new study suggests that driving with a hands-free cell phone is just as dangerous as a hand-held phone. The National Safety Council found that having any type of phone conversation slows down a driver's responses. Slower responses are directly linked to poor driving and traffic collisions.

Source: CNN.com

Think About It

1. How is driving while talking on a cell phone dangerous?

2. What is being done to curb this danger?

Using Health Terms

On a separate sheet of paper, write the term that best matches each definition below.

LESSON 1

1. A recurring pattern that is present in all mishaps.
2. A portable device that puts out small fires by ejecting fire-extinguishing chemicals.
3. Death resulting from passage through the body of a high-voltage current.
4. The circumstance or event leading up to an accident.
5. An alarm that is triggered by the presence of smoke.

LESSON 2

6. A powerful, twisting windstorm.
7. A federal agency responsible for promoting safe and healthful conditions in the workplace.

8. A powerful rainstorm, characterized by driving winds.
9. A snowstorm with winds of 35 miles per hour (56 km per hour) or greater.

LESSON 3

10. When intense anger and driving mix.
11. Obeying the rules of the road, as well as exercising common sense and good judgment.

LESSON 4

12. Rape by someone who is known casually by the victim or someone thought to be a friend.
13. When rape occurs between two people who are dating.

Recalling the Facts

Using complete sentences, answer the following questions.

LESSON 1

1. What is a good way to prevent smoke inhalation during a fire?
2. What can be done to reduce the number of falls that occur on stairways?
3. How should poisonous products in the home be stored to minimize their dangers?

LESSON 2

4. Why should everyone learn to swim?
5. What is a major cause of spinal injuries that can result in paralysis?
6. How can employers minimize the risk of work-related accidents?
7. How can employees minimize the risk of work-related accidents?

LESSON 3

8. What is the leading cause of death among people between 15 and 20?
9. How can bike riders minimize the risk of injury in case of an accident?
10. What five pieces of protective equipment should people wear when roller skating or skateboarding?
11. What should you do if you fall while using in-line skates?

LESSON 4

12. Name four inner self-defense tools you can use to help protect yourself from an attack.
13. Give examples of body language that can help protect someone from harm.
14. What measures can you take to help prevent rape?

Thinking Critically

LESSON 1

1. *Analyzing.* What parts of the accident chain are the easiest to break?
2. *Synthesizing.* Name three flammable liquids that might be used in or around a home. Tell what preventive behaviors should be taken in using each.
3. *Synthesizing.* What would you include in a home fire escape plan? Why?

LESSON 2

4. *Evaluating.* How would you measure the worth of wearing safety goggles on the job?

5. *Synthesizing.* Explain the importance of planning for a natural disaster.

LESSON 3

6. *Evaluating.* Some states have laws requiring a person to use a seat belt while driving or riding in a car and to wear a helmet while operating a motorcycle. Explain your opinion of such laws.

LESSON 4

7. *Evaluating.* List, in order, the five most important things you think a person should do after a rape. Why did you rate each one as you did?

Making the Connection

1. *Math.* Conduct a survey in your school and in your community to find out the following: how many homes have smoke detectors, how many people periodically test the battery to make sure it is in proper working order, and how many people have disengaged the battery. Compute the percentages and share your findings with the class.

2. *Social Studies.* Do research to find out how so-called push-out doors—the variety with bar handles found in gyms, schools, theaters, and public buildings—first came to be used. If possible, learn why these doors were originally called "panic doors." Share your findings in a brief report.

BEYOND THE CLASSROOM

PARENTAL INVOLVEMENT Speak with parents or other adults in your home about safety precautions that are necessary at their jobs. Ask them what they are required to do regarding safety in the workplace.

COMMUNITY INVOLVEMENT Find the telephone numbers for the fire department, the police department, and the poison control center in your community. Post these and other emergency numbers in your home by the phone. Interview a person from each of these agencies to find out what action they take when they receive a call.

SCHOOL-TO-CAREER

Technology. Learn how technology is used in the field of accident prevention and quick response time to accidents. Investigate the use of computers and other high technology to enable rescuers to arrive on the scene more quickly than ever in response to 911 calls. Write a report on your findings.

CHAPTER 35

Providing First Aid and Handling Emergencies

GOAL SETTING

Are you inspired to give assistance when you know someone needs help? Find out what's involved in training as an Emergency Medical Technician in the Career Corner at **health.glencoe.com**.

Personal Health Inventory

Self-Inventory Write the numbers 1–10 on a sheet of paper. Read each statement below and respond by writing *yes*, *no*, or *sometimes* for each item. Write a *yes* only for items that you practice regularly. Save your responses.

1	I make a point of knowing the names of all my family's health care professionals.
2	I keep a list of emergency phone numbers near a telephone in my home.
3	I can help someone who has swallowed poison.
4	I take small bites of food when eating and chew each bite slowly before swallowing.
5	I know what action to take to help victims of choking.
6	I am trained in rescue breathing for adults and children.
7	I know how to administer CPR.
8	I know what steps to take to stop heavy bleeding.
9	I am able to tell the difference between minor and serious burns and can treat each kind.
10	I know how to help with common emergencies such as nosebleed, fainting, heat cramps, or frostbite.

Follow-up After completing the chapter, retake this self-inventory. Pick two items that you need to work on and set a goal to improve your health behaviors.

> ❝ *The best place to find a helping hand is at the end of your own arm.* ❞
>
> —SWEDISH PROVERB

Quick Write Think of a time when you were hurt and someone came to your aid or when you helped someone else. Write about the experience in a paragraph. Include the words *caring, responsibility,* and *safety* in your paragraph.

Administering First Aid

Imagine you happened upon the scene of a traffic accident in which people had been hurt. Suppose you were on a bus and someone fainted. Would you know what to do in either of these emergency situations? In this chapter, you will learn about responses to accidents and emergencies that could save a life.

HEALTH TERMS

first aid

poison

pressure point

shock

HEALTH CONCEPTS

- Actions taken in the first minutes of an emergency can make the difference between life and death.
- The most important considerations in treating open wounds are stopping the bleeding and seeking help.

First Aid

First aid is *the immediate, temporary care given to a person who has become sick or who has been injured.* First aid is administered in the seconds and minutes following an accident or a person's becoming sick. Administering first aid until a proper medical authority arrives on the scene can mean the difference between life and death.

Priorities in an Emergency

The first five minutes of an emergency situation are the most critical. During this crucial time, it is important to remain calm and to keep these six priorities in mind:

1. **Check the immediate surroundings for possible dangers.** Move the victim only if his or her life is threatened. Some life-threatening conditions include water deep enough for drowning, a car that might catch on fire, or a room filled with smoke or poisonous fumes.

2. **Check to see if the victim is conscious.** If not, call for an ambulance at once.

3. **Check breathing.** Be sure the victim has an open airway. If he or she does not, attempt to clear the airway. Then administer rescue breathing if necessary. More on this lifesaving technique is presented in Lesson 3.

4. **Control severe bleeding.** If blood is bright red and spurting, an artery has been damaged. You can control the bleeding by applying direct pressure to the wound. Use gloves or other protective barrier to prevent the spread of infectious diseases.

5. **Check the victim for poisoning.** A poison is *any substance—solid, liquid, or gas—that causes injury, illness, or death when introduced into the body.* Treatment for poisoning is detailed in the next lesson.

6. **Send for medical help.** Emergency Medical Services (EMS) can be summoned in most areas by dialing either 911 or 0. Learn the numbers for EMS in your area.

Secondary Emergency Measures

Once you have taken steps to ensure the victim's safety and have administered life support procedures, you should attend to the following secondary measures:

- Learn as much as you can about what happened, and devise a plan of action.
- Look after the victim's continued safety and comfort. Keep the victim still and in the position most suited to his or her injury or condition.
- Make sure the victim maintains normal body temperature. Provide blankets or a coat for warmth, or provide shade for cooling protection from the hot sun.
- Loosen tight or binding clothing. Take care not to jar the victim's neck or spine.

As you work, keep reassuring the victim. Part of your job is to keep him or her calm. Above all else, know your own limits. Do not try to do more than you have been trained to do.

keeping Fit

Read My Wrist!

Another important procedure when treating an accident victim is to look for a piece of emergency medical identification on or near the victim. He or she may have a bracelet, necklace, or card carried in a wallet or purse advising of a medical condition that demands special attention.

People with diabetes or heart conditions and those subject to seizures or severe allergic reactions are among those who wear or carry emergency medical identification. The tag or card gives vital information to those who might be called upon to give the wearer first aid.

Dialing 911 will summon emergency help in most areas.

ACTIVITY *Make a list of situations for which it would be appropriate to call 911. Also, make a list of those situations that require first aid but do not require that you call 911.*

Proper Use
of Emergency Services

Have you ever needed to call for an ambulance or paramedic? If you have, you know how important time and availability can be. One way to show your **concern for others** is to make sure that you use emergency services properly and only when truly necessary. For example, you can ensure that emergency services are there for people who need them by going to the emergency room *only* for serious ailments.

Character Check Brainstorm a *Do and Don't List* for the proper use of emergency services. Ask students to give examples of the proper use of each kind of service.

Did You Know?

➤ Removing adhesive bandages from minor cuts can be made painless by rubbing an alcohol-moistened cotton ball across the bandage.

➤ Most accidents take place between 2 A.M. and 7 A.M. and again during the period between 2 P.M. and 5 P.M.

➤ The manufacturing industry is the most dangerous in terms of worker injuries.

Types of Emergencies

There are many different kinds of emergencies. Some, such as nosebleeds and splinters, are relatively minor. Others—including situations in which an individual is rendered unconscious, as was the case with Jamal in the chapter-opening story—can be life-threatening. Among the most serious emergencies are open wounds and severe burns.

Open Wounds

Open wounds are caused by a variety of accidents, including falls and the mishandling of sharp tools and machinery. The correct response to an open wound depends on the type of wound:

■ **Abrasion.** Also known as a scrape, an abrasion damages the outer layers of skin. Abrasions are accompanied by little or no bleeding but may easily become infected. Abrasions are caused by scraping or rubbing.

■ **Laceration.** A laceration, or cut, is generally caused by a sharp object such as a knife or broken glass, though lacerations also can be the result of a hard blow from a blunt object. Lacerations can have jagged or smooth edges and are usually accompanied by bleeding. Deep cuts can result in heavy bleeding, as well as damage to nerves, large blood vessels, and other soft tissues.

■ **Puncture.** A puncture is a wound caused by a pin, splinter, or other pointed object piercing the skin. Although external bleeding is usually limited, puncture wounds carry the potential for internal bleeding and damage to internal organs as well as an increased possibility of infection. The risk of infection becomes even greater when the object remains in the skin.

■ **Avulsion.** This is a wound that results when tissue is separated partly or completely from a person's body. Avulsions often occur in auto accidents and from animal bites. Because severed body parts can sometimes be reattached surgically, they should be sent along with the victim to the hospital, packed in ice or ice water if possible to preserve the tissue.

First Aid for Open Wounds

As with any emergency, treating an open wound requires thinking quickly and remaining calm. It also requires a knowledge of four steps. These are as follows.

1. **Stop the bleeding.** Apply direct pressure to the top of the wound or to a **pressure point**, *one of a number of points along the main artery supplying blood to an affected limb.* This prevents blood loss without interfering with circulation. When applying direct pressure, use a thick, clean cloth and press firmly with the heel of your hand, adding fresh layers as the blood soaks through. To

protect yourself from **infectious diseases**, wear disposable latex gloves, and wash your hands as soon as possible after giving care.

2. **Protect the wound.** Normally, a clean cloth over an open wound will help protect it from infection. If a cloth is not available, a coat, undershirt, or any other clean covering will do.

3. **Treat for shock.** Shock is *the failure of the cardiovascular system to keep adequate blood circulating to the vital organs of the body.* Shock can result from severe bleeding, heart attack, **electrocution**, poisoning, burns, or sudden changes in temperature. Symptoms of shock include confusion, accelerated or slowed pulse rate, trembling, weakness in the arms and legs, pale or clammy skin, pale or bluish lips and fingernails, and enlarged pupils. When treating for shock, it is important to keep the victim lying down, maintain his or her normal body temperature, and get medical help as quickly as possible. Unless a head injury is suspected—in which case the person should not be moved—a shock victim should be kept on his or her back with the feet elevated on a book bag or large purse about 8 to 12 inches (20 to 30 cm) above the head. This helps return blood to the heart. Shock victims should never be given food or drink.

4. **Get help.** See to it that the wounded victim gets immediate medical attention. Send someone for help, or if you are alone, shout for help. Leave the victim only after you have performed first aid and feel that you have lessened the risk of further injury or death. If you know the victim's blood type, you will want to communicate this information to the emergency medical technician. You should also know your own blood type, in case you become the victim of an emergency.

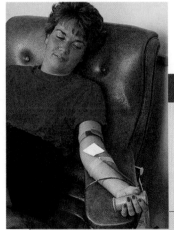

h⚫tl⚫nk

infectious diseases For more information on infectious diseases and how to prevent their spread, see Chapter 28, page 632.

electrocution For more on electrocution and how to prevent it, see Chapter 34, page 746.

◀ *Giving blood helps save lives.*

ACTIVITY *Find out what organizations in your community conduct blood drives.*

Blood Types

Human blood is classified into four types: **TYPE A, TYPE B, TYPE AB,** and **TYPE O.** For transfusions to work, the blood types must match. Hospitals and blood banks take extreme care in checking blood types before giving transfusions. Knowing your blood type can save your life.

A person who has **TYPE O BLOOD** is referred to as a *universal donor* because that person can give blood to a person with any blood type.

A person with **TYPE AB BLOOD** is referred to as a *universal recipient* because he or she can receive any type of blood.

Another important consideration regarding blood transfusions is **RH FACTOR,** a protein present in the blood of some 85 percent of the U.S. population. Individuals with Rh-negative blood–blood that does not have the factor–should not be given Rh-positive blood.

Severe Burns

Burns can be a minor inconvenience, as when your finger touches a hot stove. When a burn destroys vital tissue, however, it can be a life-and-death emergency. There are three types of burns.

1. **First-degree.** These are superficial burns, like most sunburns, and involve the top layer of skin. Healing takes five to six days.
2. **Second-degree.** Second-degree burns involve the top several layers of skin. The skin will have blisters and appear blotchy. Healing takes three to four weeks.
3. **Third-degree.** The most serious burns, third-degree burns destroy all layers of skin as well as nerves, muscles, fat, and bones. The burn looks black or brown.

▲ *Sunburn is typically a first-degree burn.*

ACTIVITY *How can sunburn be avoided? How should more serious burns be treated?*

FIRST AID FOR SEVERE BURNS

A severe burn—one in which more than one part of the body is affected or where the skin is blistered and charred—requires immediate medical attention. While waiting for help to arrive, ease the burn with plenty of cool water and place a clean, dry dressing over the burned area to prevent infection. If possible, raise the burned area above the level of the heart. Treat for shock. *Do not attempt to remove clothing that is stuck to the burn or to treat burns where the skin has been burned away.*

LESSON 1 *Review*

Reviewing Facts and Vocabulary
1. Use the term *first aid* in a paragraph that also specifies the six tasks that should be completed first in an emergency.
2. Name the four types of open wounds.

Thinking Critically
3. *Analyzing.* While cycling fast, your friend takes a bad spill. You rush to help and find that her skin is clammy and blood is spurting from her head. Describe the first aid you would administer.
4. *Evaluating.* If it is a stranger in need of first aid, and you ask the person if he or she wants your help, and the answer is no, should you walk away?

Should you be held accountable if you cause some harm to an injured person while trying to administer first aid?

Applying Health Skills
5. *In Your School.* Prepare a talk on first aid for younger students in a school in your community. Think about specific points to emphasize that relate to potential local accident sites.

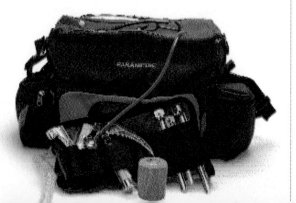

Poisonings

W hat do medicines, snakebites, auto exhaust, household cleaners, and many plants have in common? All are potentially poisonous to the human body. Do you remember from the previous lesson what a poison is? A poison is any substance that causes injury, illness, or death when introduced into the body.

HEALTH TERMS

poison control center

emetic

venom

HEALTH CONCEPTS

- Poisoning can occur through swallowing or inhaling a toxic substance, through snakebite, or through contact with a poisonous plant or chemical.
- Victims of poisoning require immediate treatment.
- Poisoning is a life-threatening situation.

Poisons

The American Red Cross estimates that between 1 and 2 million poisonings occur in the United States every year. About half of these involve medicines or household products that are swallowed or inhaled. Poisoning can also result from insect or animal bites and even from touching certain substances, such as poison ivy and certain chemicals. Most poisonings involve children under the age of six.

Swallowing Poison

Today, most household cleaners, medications, and other potentially dangerous products come in containers with safety tops that are hard for children to remove. Yet, in spite of these precautions, many poisonings still occur.

Even though the signs of oral poisoning are not as obvious as those in many other emergency situations, telltale symptoms do exist. These symptoms include sharp abdominal cramps, extreme drowsiness followed by a loss of consciousness, vomiting, chemical odor on the breath or chemical burns on the lips, and the presence of an open container of a potentially poisonous substance.

First Aid for Swallowing Poison

When you suspect someone has swallowed a poison, look for and save the container of the suspected poison. Then do the following:

- Call the nearest **poison control center,** *a 24-hour hot line that provides emergency medical advice on treating poisoning victims.* Such centers are part of a nationwide network that has been set up in and around large cities. A toll-free number for the poison control center in your locality may be listed in your local telephone directory. This number should be posted in a highly visible place in your home.
- Be prepared to give information about the victim and the poison to the person on the phone. This information should include the age and weight of the victim, the name of the suspected poison,

Building Health Skills

Goal Setting: Planning a Safe Home Environment

ALTHOUGH KNOWING WHAT TO DO in the event of a poisoning is important, a prior step that is every bit as important is *prevention.* The following are steps that can be taken to help safeguard any home against poisoning accidents.

1. **Make sure all potentially poisonous products have child-resistant caps.** Even in homes where there are no small children, the presence of such caps can alert family members to a medicine's or product's potential for poisoning.

2. **Keep household products and medicines out of children's reach.** Install childproof locks on cabinets and closets that contain anything that could poison a child.

3. **Carefully read the directions when using poisonous products and medicines.** Reseal and safely store these products after use. In the case of medicines, be mindful of the expiration date on the label, and flush away all medicines that are past this date.

4. **Be prepared.** Look in the phone book and write the phone number of the nearest poison control center on a card. Place it next to the phone on the family's emergency number list.

the amount of poison swallowed, and the time it was swallowed, if known. The person at the control center will then offer assistance with the situation and tell you where to go for further help. Depending on the poison, you may be instructed to give the victim a substance that dilutes the poison, such as large quantities of water or milk, or you may be told to administer an **emetic** (ee-MEH-tik). This is *an agent that induces vomiting,* such as a tablespoon of salt dissolved in warm water. *An emetic should never be administered to a person who is unconscious.*

- Treat the victim for shock. Use the same procedure you read about in the section on treating wounds in Lesson 1. It may also be necessary to help the victim maintain respiration and circulation through rescue breathing or CPR. You will learn about these techniques in the next lesson.

Knowing which snakes are poisonous can help you steer clear of danger.

ACTIVITY *Find out what kinds of snakes are found in your community. Share this information with classmates.*

Snakebite

People who think of snakebites as hazards of life found only in rural areas are only partly right. Suburban environments and city parks can also be home to poisonous snakes.

Of the hundreds of varieties of snakes, only four poisonous types are found in the United States: the rattlesnake, the copperhead, the water moccasin (also called the *cottonmouth*), and the coral snake. More than half of all poisonous snakebites occur in Texas, North Carolina, Florida, Georgia, Louisiana, and Arkansas.

Only about 1 percent of the people bitten by poisonous snakes die. A large number of deformities and amputations do result from poisonous snakebites, so they should be treated immediately.

First Aid for Snakebite

If you are unsure whether a snakebite came from a poisonous snake, treat the bite as though it had. You can administer first aid by following these steps:

➤ **Get the victim to a hospital.** This is the most important task. Keep the victim as quiet as possible, preferably in a reclining position. The more the victim moves, the greater the risk that the venom will be circulated throughout the body. **Venom** is *a poisonous substance secreted by a snake or other animal.*

➤ **Keep the bitten area at or below the level of the heart.** If the bitten area is on a limb, keep the affected part immobile.

➤ **Call, or have someone call, EMS.** Take careful note of any instructions you are given.

➤ **Delay the absorption of venom.** Because snakes are cold-blooded animals, their venom does the most damage in a cold environment. For this reason, avoid putting anything cold on the bite or giving the victim alcohol or sedatives. Aspirin, which can adversely affect blood coagulation, should also be avoided.

➤ **Maintain breathing and prevent aggravation of the wound.** If you are the victim of a snakebite and are alone, walk slowly and rest periodically. This will help to minimize blood circulation.

Poison oak

Poison sumac

Poison ivy

▲ **Common poisonous plants.**
ACTIVITY *Describe the reaction caused by contact with these plants.*

Contact Poisoning

Poisons that come into contact with the skin fall into two categories: those found on plants and those found in some chemicals.

First Aid for Poisonous Plants

The most common poisonous plants have the word *poison* in their names. These are poison ivy, poison oak, and poison sumac. A first defense against poisoning by any of these plants is to learn what they look like. Some people have no reaction to poisonous plants. Others develop a severe skin rash at the point of contact, followed later by blistering, swelling, burning, itching, and possibly a fever.

First aid for plant poisoning begins by removing any clothing that may be contaminated. Pour large quantities of water over the affected areas and wash thoroughly with soap and water. Calamine lotion can be used to relieve itching. If pain is severe, seek medical attention.

First Aid for Poisonous Chemicals

Pesticides, solvents, household cleaning agents, and highly abrasive cleaners are among the chemicals that can cause poisoning. To protect against such poisoning, make sure safety caps on these products are securely in place when the products are not being used. In addition, the products should be stored out of the reach of small children.

Poisoning through direct contact with a chemical is usually characterized by a burning of the skin, resembling a sunburn. Treatment should begin as soon after the contact as possible.

1. Remove any clothing that has come into contact with the chemical.
2. Remove as much of the chemical from the surface of the skin as you can by flooding the area with water for 15 minutes.
3. Contact the nearest poison control center.

LESSON 2 *Review*

Reviewing Facts and Vocabulary

1. Use the terms *poison control center* and *emetic* in a paragraph that defines the terms and explains their relationship.
2. Identify three steps to take in treating the two types of contact poisoning.

Thinking Critically

3. *Comparing and Contrasting.* In what ways are first aid for swallowing a poison and touching a poison similar? How are they different?

4. *Synthesizing.* Which of the first-aid techniques covered in the lesson would be especially important for a camper or a hiker to know? Explain your choices.

Applying Health Skills

5. *In Your School.* Have a horticulturist, a person who works with plants, come to your class and discuss poisonous plants in your area, how they can be recognized, and what to do in case of exposure.

First Aid for Choking, Rescue Breathing, and CPR

Each year more than 2,800 Americans choke to death, and many of the victims are children under four years of age. Choking is, in fact, the sixth leading cause of death in the overall population. What is even more sobering is that many who died could have been rescued. This lesson will explore first aid for choking, rescue breathing, and CPR.

HEALTH TERMS

abdominal thrusts

respiratory failure

rescue breathing

carotid pulse

cardiovascular failure

cardiopulmonary resuscitation (CPR)

xiphoid process

HEALTH CONCEPTS

- The main objectives of rescue breathing are maintaining an open airway and supplying a victim with oxygen.
- CPR is a lifesaving measure in which a heart that has stopped is forced to pump blood to the body by means of applied pressure.
- The method for applying CPR differs between adults and children.

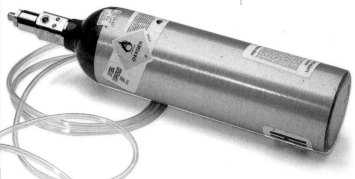

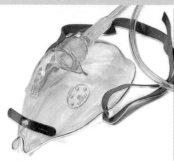

h⚬tlink

trachea For more information on the trachea and habits that can help prevent choking, see Chapter 17, page 402.

First Aid for Choking

In the majority of cases, choking occurs when a piece of food becomes lodged in the **trachea**. No matter what the cause, the first step in first aid for choking is recognizing the symptoms of choking and attempting to dislodge the offending particle or object. The "universal" choking signal is both hands placed at the throat.

Choking in Children and Adults

If you suspect a child or adult is choking, ask the person, "Are you choking?" If the victim is unable to breathe, cough, or speak, begin first aid immediately by administering abdominal thrusts. Also known as the *Heimlich maneuver,* **abdominal thrusts** are *the application of sudden pressure on the victim's diaphragm so as to expel the substance blocking the airway.*

When administering abdominal thrusts to a conscious victim:

STEP 1   STEP 2

1. Wrap your arms around the victim's waist, thumb side of your wrist against the victim's abdomen. Make sure the victim's feet are spread apart so that you have a good base of support. Place your hand halfway between the lower tip of the victim's breastbone, or sternum, and the navel.
2. Grasp your fist with the other hand, and press into the abdomen with quick upward thrusts until the blockage is dislodged.

If no other person is present, a choking victim can perform abdominal thrusts on himself or herself by leaning over the back of a chair or over the edge of a table.

Choking in Infants

For children age one and under, abdominal thrusts are not recommended, since this technique may result in damage to the abdomen and internal organs. Families with very small children are urged to take a course in first aid for choking from the local Emergency Medical Services (EMS) or local chapter of the American Red Cross or the American Heart Association. Briefly, the technique is as follows and should be performed only on conscious choking infants:

1. Place the infant on a downward angle over your arm.
2. Using the heel of your other hand, give four quick blows to the baby's back between the shoulder blades.
3. Turn the infant over, supporting its head, neck, and back between the shoulders. Press two fingers into the middle of the baby's sternum. This action is known as a *chest thrust.* Repeat four times.
4. Alternate administering back blows and chest thrusts until the object is dislodged.

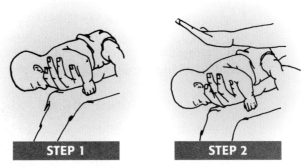

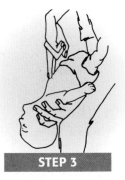

STEP 1   STEP 2   STEP 3

Respiratory Failure

When choking blockage is severe, **respiratory failure**—a *state in which air is unable to reach the lungs*—occurs. This condition can also result from the lungs filling with water, as in drowning, or from gas poisoning, an overdose of **narcotics**, or electrocution. Signs of respiratory failure include an absence of breathing movements, dilated pupils, and a bluish color to the lips, tongue, or fingernails. Blood and oxygen circulation must be restored to the brain within four minutes to prevent irreversible brain damage. In such an emergency, the best course of action is *artificial respiration,* or **rescue breathing**. This technique may be administered mouth to mouth or mouth to nose. The American Red Cross recommends using a special protective face shield to avoid direct contact with body fluids.

h⊙t link

narcotics For more information on narcotics and the dangers of using these and other drugs, see Chapter 26, page 583.

Rescue Breathing for Adults

Check to see whether the victim is conscious. Tap the person's shoulder and ask, "Are you all right?" If there is no response, direct someone else at the scene to call EMS for help. To administer rescue breathing for adults, follow these steps:

1. Tilt the victim's head backward by placing one hand under the bony part of the victim's chin and lifting while placing the other hand on the victim's forehead and pressing downward. This action moves the jaw and tongue forward, opening the airway.

   Determine whether the victim is breathing. Look, listen, and feel. Look to see whether the chest is rising and falling. Listen for air being expelled from the lungs. Feel whether air is being expelled by placing your cheek close to the victim's mouth, or hold a mirror in front of the victim's mouth.

2. If the victim is not breathing, pinch the victim's nostrils together with your index finger and thumb. Take a deep breath and, with your mouth sealed over the victim's, exhale. Give the person two full breaths (1 to 1½ seconds each).

3. Keeping the victim's head tilted, look, listen, and feel again. Determine whether the victim's heart is beating by feeling for the **carotid** (ku-RAH-tid) **pulse.** This is *the heartbeat found on each side of the neck.* To locate the carotid pulse, place your index and middle finger on the Adam's apple and slide them into the groove at the side of the neck.

4. If there is a pulse but still no breathing, continue to administer breaths at the rate of one every five seconds.

RESCUE BREATHING FOR ADULTS

STEP 1

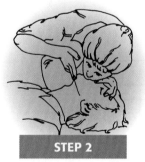

STEP 2

STEP 3

STEP 4

HEALTH Online

Visit **health.glencoe.com** to review the steps for giving CPR to adults, children, and infants. Knowing how to perform CPR in an emergency can mean the difference between life and death.

Periodically, check the victim's chest to see whether it is rising and falling. If it is moving, you know that air is getting into the lungs. Continue artificial respiration until the victim has started breathing again or medical help arrives and takes over.

Rescue Breathing for Infants and Children

Rescue breathing for infants and children parallels rescue breathing for adults, with these exceptions:

1. When positioning the child's head to clear the airway, do not tilt the head as far back as you would for an adult.
2. For infants, cover and form an airtight seal by placing your mouth over *both* the infant's mouth and nose rather than only the mouth.
3. Administer not-quite-full breaths, and breathe into the infant's mouth and nose at a rate of one breath every three seconds. For a child, give one breath about every four seconds.

CPR

Among the most serious life-threatening situations a person can face is *failure of the heart to pump blood*. This condition, **cardiovascular failure**, can be brought on by respiratory failure, a drug overdose, blockage in a **blood vessel**, electric shock, or poisoning. In such situations, **cardiopulmonary resuscitation (CPR)**—*a lifesaving technique in which a heart that has stopped is forced to pump blood to the body by means of applied pressure*—is the victim's only hope. CPR requires no special tools or equipment to perform. Yet, learning this technique is like giving the gift of life.

Unlike abdominal thrusts, before a person can administer CPR, he or she must receive certification by taking an approved course with a local chapter of the American Red Cross.

CPR for Adults

CPR consists of three basic steps. A convenient way of remembering these steps and the order in which they occur is to think of them as the ABC's of CPR: **A**irway, **B**reathing, **C**irculation.

AIRWAY

When you witness a person collapsing or come upon a person who has collapsed, your first task is to determine whether the victim is conscious. Tap the person's shoulder and ask, "Are you all right?" If the victim does not respond, dial 911 or contact your local EMS before beginning CPR. If someone is nearby, direct that person to make the call.

If the victim is not lying flat on his or her back, you need to carefully roll the person into this position. Do not turn the upper body first, then the lower body. Once the victim is lying flat, open his or her airway as described in Step 2 of rescue breathing on page 781.

BREATHING

Check for breathing, as in Step 3 of rescue breathing. Check to see if the chest is rising and falling. Listen and feel for signs that air is being expelled from the lungs. If the victim shows no signs of breathing, you must get air into his or her lungs at once by administering Step 4 of rescue breathing.

CIRCULATION

The third and most critical step in CPR is to move blood through the body to supply oxygen to the cells. The heart is located beneath the sternum. Compressions on the sternum force blood out of the heart and into the blood vessels. *Remember that you must be properly trained before administering this procedure to anyone.*

First, check the victim's carotid pulse for 5 to 10 seconds. This is a very important step because chest compressions can harm the victim if his or her heart is beating. If you find no pulse, begin artificial circulation. *Never practice this technique on someone whose heart is beating.*

Finding the correct position to give effective compressions is essential. The pressure must be directly on the sternum to avoid injury to the ribs and above the xiphoid (ZY-foyd) process so that internal organs will not be damaged. The **xiphoid process** is *the lower part of the sternum that projects downward to the point where the sternum meets the lower ribs.*

After locating the correct position for hand placement, you should position your body so that your shoulders are directly above your hands and your elbows are locked. Push straight down. Each compression should push the sternum down 1½ to 2 inches (3.8 to 5.1 cm). When the pressure is released, blood flows into the heart. Apply compressions in short, rhythmic thrusts about one per second. Every 15 seconds or so, you should apply mouth-to-mouth respiration, alternating two full breaths for every 15 chest compressions. Even if no signs of revival are apparent, continue the procedure until help arrives.

keeping Fit

Do's and Don'ts of CPR

When you happen upon an accident or other emergency situation, it is important to know when to jump in and help and when to wait for trained help to arrive. Here are some guidelines on administering CPR and rescue breathing.

➤ *Don't* take action unless **you know what you are doing.** This is especially true of administering CPR if you have not taken a course and become certified in the procedure. Taking the wrong action could cost a life. Call 911, and wait for help to arrive.

➤ *Do* call out for help when you lack the necessary first-aid skills. Someone at the accident scene or a passerby may have such skills.

➤ *Do* protect yourself against risk of infection with hepatitis or HIV. The American Red Cross encourages the public to use some sort of barrier between themselves and someone's blood and other body fluids when performing emergency lifesaving techniques.

CPR FOR ADULTS

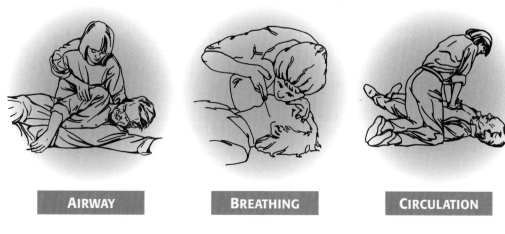

AIRWAY   BREATHING   CIRCULATION

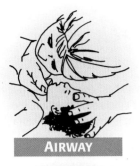

AIRWAY

BREATHING

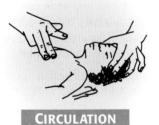

CIRCULATION

CPR for Children

Because of differences in size, some adjustments need to be made when administering CPR to infants and children up to age eight. The first two steps are the same as those for rescue breathing.

AIRWAY

Tip the child's head back only a little. Tilting the head back too far will close the airway.

BREATHING

Cover the child's mouth and nose with your mouth rather than pinching the nose shut. For infants, give small puffs of air.

CIRCULATION

In infants, check the pulse at the inner arm just above the elbow. For a child, check the carotid pulse. If no pulse is detected, administer chest compressions as follows.

For infants, draw an imaginary line between the nipples. Place two or three fingers on the sternum, one finger width below the imaginary line, and compress ½ to 1 inch (1.3 cm to 2.5 cm) at a rate of 100 compressions per minute.

For children, place the middle and index fingers of one hand on the xiphoid process, and with the heel of the other hand, compress the sternum about 1 to 1½ inches (2.5 cm to 3.8 cm) at a rate of 80 to 100 compressions per minute. For both infants and children, administer a breath after every five chest compressions.

Remember, never try this on a well person. *Do not attempt CPR at all without training!*

LESSON 3 *Review*

Reviewing Facts and Vocabulary

1. Give another name for each of the terms *abdominal thrust* and *artificial respiration,* and use each in an original sentence.
2. What is CPR, and who can administer it?

Thinking Critically

3. *Comparing and Contrasting.* Compare first aid for choking in infants with first aid for choking in children and adults.

4. *Synthesizing.* In an emergency, if plastic gloves or rescue breathing masks are not available, what could you do to avoid contact with body fluids?

Applying Health Skills

5. *In Your Home.* Discuss with your family the importance of learning CPR. Report on their reactions to your discussion.

More Common Emergencies

I n addition to such life-threatening emergencies as severe bleeding and poisoning, life has its share of minor mishaps. For example, you and your friend are going out the door when your friend slips and sprains an ankle. As with major emergencies, knowing proper first aid in these and other common emergencies can help prevent further injury or complication.

HEALTH TERMS

rabies

gangrene

HEALTH CONCEPTS

■ Every type of injury, minor or severe, has its own specific and general first-aid procedures.

■ Animals are frequently carriers of diseases that are harmful to humans.

■ Weather conditions are always a consideration when participating in any outdoor recreational activity.

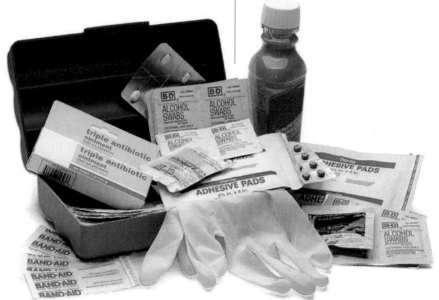

Fractures

When a body part, such as a leg or an arm, is under stress and you hear a popping sound, it is usually a good indication that a bone has been fractured. Always treat such an injury as if the bone were broken.

In applying first aid to fractures, your main objective is to keep the bone end from moving. Never attempt to set the bone.

Keep the body part in the position it is in, and immobilize it by securing a splint to the body part with clean lengths of cloth. You can fashion a splint from everyday materials, such as rolled newspapers and heavy cardboard. Seek medical care immediately.

hotlink

sprain For more information about sprains and strategies for reducing their risk when exercising, see Chapter 4, page 85.

R.I.C.E. procedure For more information on the *R.I.C.E.* procedure, which is effective for treating sprains and other minor injuries, see Chapter 4, page 85.

➤ **Sprains are among the less serious mishaps that require medical attention.**

ACTIVITY *Speak with a member of your family or a neighbor who suffered a sprain. Find out what type of medical care was administered and how long the recovery period took. Share your findings with classmates.*

Sprains

A sprain is a condition caused by a stretching or tearing of the soft tissue bands, or ligaments, that hold bones together at a joint. Wrists, knees, and ankles are among the areas most frequently sprained. To treat a sprain, use the ***R.I.C.E. procedure*** outlined in Chapter 4.

Fainting

Fainting is a temporary loss of consciousness brought on by a reduced supply of blood to the brain. People who faint usually recover within a few minutes. First aid for fainting includes the following steps:

1. Do not prop the person up. Leave the individual lying down on her or his back. If possible, elevate the legs 8 to 12 inches.
2. Loosen any tight or binding clothing.
3. Maintain an open airway, as explained in Lesson 3.
4. Sponge the person's face with water. Do not splash water over the face, because this may cause the person to choke.
5. If the person fails to revive promptly, seek medical help.

Animal Bites

Dogs and other animals can transmit diseases to humans by biting them. Any animal bite, and especially one in which the animal's teeth have pierced the skin, should be washed with soap and warm water, then covered with a clean dressing or bandage. It is also important to get the person to a hospital or doctor's office at once. Some animals carry **rabies**—*a viral disease of the nervous system that eventually causes madness and death.* In addition to dogs, common carriers of the disease include cats, squirrels, skunks, foxes, bats, raccoons, and rats.

If you find the animal that inflicted the wound, do not try to capture it yourself. Contact the proper authorities to capture the animal and call the local health center to learn where the animal has been taken for examination. If the animal is not captured, the bitten individual will need to undergo a series of daily injections with a rabies vaccine. If this vaccine is not administered to a person who is indeed infected with the rabies virus, the person will die.

Bee Stings

In most cases, bee stings are minor emergencies and are easily treated. For people who are allergic to bee

Acting in an Emergency

Sally and several friends were driving along the interstate. It was raining, and the road was slick. As Sally was approaching her exit, she saw a recreational vehicle spin out of control ahead of her and veer off the road. Upon reaching the accident scene, Sally and her friends discovered two people in the RV. Neither of them was responsive. Neither Sally nor her friends knew what steps to take at this point, though all agreed something needed to be done—and fast.

What Would You Do?

Apply the six steps of the decision-making process to the problem facing Sally and her friends.

1. **State the situation.**
2. **List the options.**
3. **Weigh the possible outcomes.**
4. **Consider your values.**
5. **Make a decision and act.**
6. **Evaluate the decision.**

---

stings, however, stings can be serious and sometimes even fatal. To treat bee stings, use a piece of cardboard, a credit card, or other flat, sharp-edged object to scrape the stinger away from the skin until you pull out the venom sac. Wash the area thoroughly with soap and water.

Once the stinger is out, watch for allergic reactions. An allergic person will usually carry a kit with adrenaline to open the airways.

Objects in the Eye

If a foreign object comes into contact with the surface of your eye, resist the impulse to rub the eye or you may scratch the cornea. Instead, gently flush the eye with water, starting at the edge nearest the nose and working outward. If this measure fails to dislodge the object, cover both eyes and seek medical attention.

Minor Burns

When burns are severe, they are potentially life-threatening. When burns are minor, do the following:

1. Stop the burning by removing the victim from the source of the burn.
2. Cool the burn by soaking the burned area in cool water or using wet towels.
3. Cover the burn with dry, sterile dressings. This action helps prevent infection and reduces pain.

Chemical burns should be flushed with large quantities of cool running water. Remove any clothing that has the chemical on it.

What should you do if one of your friends needs first aid? Learn about first aid for emergencies such as broken bones, burns, cuts, and insect stings at **health.glencoe.com**.

Nosebleeds

Nosebleeds can happen when the nose is struck or when the mucous membranes in the nose become dried out. Occasional minor nosebleeds are not a cause for alarm. People whose noses bleed often, however, should see their health care professional.

To treat a nosebleed, do the following:

1. Keep the person quiet. Walking, talking, and blowing the nose may cause an increase in bleeding.
2. Place the person in a sitting position and have him or her lean forward. You do not want to tilt the head back, because doing so may cause the person to choke as the blood runs down the throat.
3. Use a protective barrier and apply direct pressure by pressing on the bleeding nostril.
4. Apply a cold towel to the person's nose and face.
5. Place a piece of cotton or gauze between the upper lip and teeth to stop the bleeding.

If these measures fail to stop the bleeding, the person should seek medical help immediately.

▼ *Frostbite occurs only when exposure to extreme temperatures is prolonged.*

ACTIVITY *Identify four measures people can take during cold weather to guard against frostbite.*

Weather-Related Emergencies

Extremes of heat and cold can bring on conditions that require immediate care. You should be familiar with these problems.

Frostbite

In extremely cold conditions, the body tries to conserve heat for its more vital internal organs. As a result, less blood is sent to the extremities. If the temperature in body cells gets low enough, frostbite may occur. Frostbite is a condition in which ice crystals form in the spaces between the cells. This ice expands and kills tissue and, in the process, causes the skin to lose color and become numb.

Frostbitten skin is yellowish or gray in color and feels clammy or doughy. Treat frostbite by doing the following:

1. Never rub the affected area. Rewarm the frozen body part by soaking it in lukewarm water (about 100° to 105° F [37.8° to 40.6° C]).
2. Bandage the injured part, placing sheets of gauze between the warmed fingers and toes.
3. Seek professional medical attention as soon as possible.

Cold Weather Advisory

When you plan to spend prolonged periods outdoors during cold weather, it is vital to dress properly. Wearing several layers of clothing will help retain body heat. Footgear and headgear are also important.

Be mindful, too, of the windchill. Any windchill of -25° F (-31° C) or colder presents a danger, with -72° F (-57.8° C) presenting a critical danger.

If a frostbitten body part goes untreated, gangrene may set in. **Gangrene** is *the death of tissue in a part of the body.* Gangrene often requires amputation of the affected part.

Heat Cramps

When a person is exposed to high temperatures over a prolonged period of time, the body loses essential water and salt. The resulting condition is known as **heat cramps**. Heat cramps are characterized by muscle cramps, heavy sweating, headache, and dizziness.

Here are some procedures to follow when heat cramps strike:

1. Move the victim, or help the victim move, out of the heat.
2. Using your hands, apply firm pressure to the cramped muscle. Gently massage the muscle to relieve the spasm.
3. Give the victim sips of plain water or a commercial sports drink, which will replace the lost salt and water. The victim should consume about 4 ounces (118 ml) every 15 minutes. Be careful that the victim does not take in too much of the liquid at once.

Heatstroke

In some cases, prolonged exposure to extremely high heat causes a life-threatening condition known as *heatstroke.* Unlike heat cramps, which are accompanied by profuse sweating, a warning sign of heatstroke is *lack* of perspiration. Other signs include vomiting, confusion, and an irregular pulse. The victim may lose consciousness.

Prompt action is essential. Get the person to a shaded area immediately and, if possible, immerse the victim in cold water or place ice packs around the neck, in the groin, and under the arms. Monitor the person's symptoms while waiting for emergency help to arrive.

h⬤t link

heat cramps For more information on heat cramps and precautions against them, see Chapter 4, page 87.

LESSON 4 *Review*

Reviewing Facts and Vocabulary

1. What should you *not* do in treating a fracture? In treating frostbite?
2. Describe first aid for minor burns.

Thinking Critically

3. *Evaluating.* Of the first-aid measures mentioned in the chapter, which are most important for someone living in your locality? Explain your answer.
4. *Synthesizing.* While out hiking, Simon is bitten by a raccoon. Tell what health risk Simon faces, what type of treatment he can expect, and what information he needs to provide to authorities.

Applying Health Skills

5. *In Your School.* Interview at least ten students and teachers in your school about common emergencies the person has faced in the past six months. Learn about the steps the person took and the way in which the problem was resolved. Share your findings with the class in a report on the general level of safety knowledge in your school.

Activity 1 — Prepared for Emergencies

Since the outbreak of deadly HIV in the early 1980s, emergency medical teams have worn plastic gloves and rescue breathing masks when attending to accident victims. Do you have the proper equipment for an emergency situation?

Directions

1. Work in pairs to locate supply facilities in your community where one could obtain the protective gear mentioned at the left.
2. Determine the average cost for each item.
3. Research different types of breathing masks that may be available.
4. Present your findings to the class in an oral presentation, using illustrations or visual aids.
5. After your presentation, ask classmates to list items that should be included in a well-stocked first-aid kit.

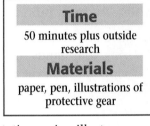

Time
50 minutes plus outside research

Materials
paper, pen, illustrations of protective gear

Self-Assessment

✓ Collected information on at least three different protective devices.
✓ Explained how each protective item should be properly used.

Activity 2 — First Aid Handbook

Administering first aid in an emergency situation can mean the difference between life and death. Would you know what to do in an emergency situation? You and members of your community will after your class publishes a "First Aid Handbook."

Directions

1. In groups, review or research these topics: "First Steps to Take," "Wounds," "Treating Shock," "Burns," "Bites and Stings," "Poisons," and "CPR."
2. Discuss the most effective way of communicating each topic (i.e., through lists, illustrations, or both).
3. Appoint one or more class members to input the handbook on the classroom computer.
4. Include an appendix with emergency telephone numbers for your area.
5. Share copies of your handbook with family and community members.

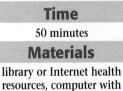

Time
50 minutes

Materials
library or Internet health resources, computer with design software and color printer

Self-Assessment

✓ Covered various areas of first aid.
✓ Included accurate emergency telephone numbers.
✓ Completed book is clear, well-organized, and attractively designed.

HEALTH NEWS

VIDEO

Coping with Emergencies Every Day

When a medical crisis hits, the experts are ready. Emergency workers arrive at the scene. Trauma surgeons and operating room staff wait at the hospital, ready to tend wounds. Later, others nurses and doctors take over to help patients heal. But who takes care of these caregivers? Working in urgent medical situations takes a heavy emotional toll.

All trauma workers need to find their own ways of coping with the daily stress of handling emergencies. Off-the-job relaxation is key. Talking about job stress with a counselor is another essential tool.

Play the Video

Think About It

❯ What are the particular stressors linked with providing emergency medical care? Describe the programs that often are available to help workers handle these stressors.

❯ Suppose that you are interviewing someone who wants to be an emergency medical worker. What strengths would you look for?

❯ Make a list of the kinds of workers who might be involved in one emergency medical situation. Consider each person's unique perspective on the event.

Using Health Terms

On a separate sheet of paper, write the term that best matches each definition below.

LESSON 1

1. One of a number of points along the main artery supplying blood to an affected limb.
2. The immediate, temporary care given to a person who has become sick or injured.
3. The failure of the cardiovascular system to keep adequate blood circulating to the vital organs of the body.

LESSON 2

4. An agent that induces vomiting.
5. A poisonous substance secreted by a snake or other animal.
6. A 24-hour hot line that provides emergency medical advice on treating poisoning victims.

LESSON 3

7. Failure of the heart to pump blood.
8. A state in which air is unable to reach the lungs.
9. The lower part of the sternum that projects downward to the point where the sternum meets the lower ribs.
10. A lifesaving technique in which a heart that has stopped is forced to pump blood to the body by means of applied pressure.
11. The heartbeat found on each side of the neck.

LESSON 4

12. The death of tissue in a part of the body.
13. A viral disease of the nervous system that eventually causes madness and death.

Recalling the Facts

Using complete sentences, answer the following questions.

LESSON 1

1. In your own words, describe the four secondary measures one should attend to in an emergency situation.
2. Explain the four steps in treating an open wound.
3. What are the symptoms of shock?

LESSON 2

4. What is the proper first aid for poisoning by swallowing?
5. What information should you give when you call a poison control center?
6. What is a characteristic of chemical poisoning by touch?

LESSON 3

7. What is the best thing to do if one is alone and choking?
8. Outline the steps in giving artificial respiration.
9. What are the two main objectives in rescue breathing?
10. What is the purpose of CPR?

LESSON 4

11. If one suspects someone has suffered a fracture, should the victim be told to move the injured part to see if it works? Why or why not?
12. What is the first-aid procedure for fainting?
13. What factors can play a role in frostbite? Which of these factors is within a person's control?

Thinking Critically

LESSON 1

1. ***Analyzing.*** Methods of first aid sometimes change as new information becomes available. What implications does this hold for people who have studied first aid?

LESSON 2

2. ***Analyzing.*** How would treatment for poison ivy and treatment for a battery-acid burn on the skin differ?

LESSON 3

3. ***Analyzing.*** Why is it important to know any universal distress signal?
4. ***Synthesizing.*** Analyze this statement: *Two people are better than one when it comes to administering CPR.*

LESSON 4

5. ***Evaluating.*** In some areas, emergency medical technicians decide whether to transport victims to a hospital for further treatment. In other areas, anyone in an emergency is transported to a hospital. Which procedure do you feel is better?

Making the Connection

1. ***Science.*** Using information from Chapter 17 and the current chapter, draw a diagram of the respiratory system that shows how abdominal thrusts force the diaphragm upward, dislodging a foreign object.
2. ***Language Arts.*** Research the universality of body language by interviewing individuals in your community who speak languages in addition to English. Make a poster showing eight foreign words and drawings of their body language equivalents. Present your poster to the class. Consider how interpreting body language in emergency situations would be important in the case of language differences.

BEYOND THE CLASSROOM

PARENTAL INVOLVEMENT Share with your parents or other adults in your home information you learned in this chapter. Then, together, make your home more first-aid ready. Find and post the phone numbers for the nearest poison control center and other emergency numbers. Assemble or update a first-aid kit.

COMMUNITY INVOLVEMENT In this chapter, you have learned first aid for many different kinds of wounds and situations. Make a separate poster for each kind of first aid discussed. Post each one in a location in the school where it is most appropriate. For example, a poster on how to treat chemical burns may be best suited for the chemistry lab.

SCHOOL-TO-CAREER
Exploring Careers. Interview an emergency medical technician in your community. Learn about the training and interpersonal skills needed for this job. Share your findings with the class in a brief report. If a video camera is available, you may want to record your interview so classmates can learn first-hand about this important profession.

Glossary

A

Abdominal thrusts The application of sudden pressure on the victim's diaphragm so as to expel the substance blocking the airway. (Ch. 35, 780)

Absorption The passage of digested food from the digestive tract into the circulatory system. (Ch. 18, 412)

Abstinence The conscious decision to avoid harmful behaviors, including sexual activity before marriage and the use of tobacco, alcohol, and other drugs. (Ch. 1, 21; Ch. 21, 484)

Abuse The intentional physical, emotional, sexual, and/or verbal maltreatment or injury of one person by another. (Ch. 14, 330)

Accident chain A recurring pattern that is present in all mishaps. (Ch. 34, 744)

Acid rain A by-product of nitrogen oxides or sulfur oxides mixed with rain. (Ch. 33, 727)

Acne A clogging of the pores of the skin. (Ch. 7, 165)

Acquaintance rape Rape by someone who is known casually by the victim or someone thought to be a friend. (Ch. 14, 330)

Acquired immune deficiency syndrome (AIDS) HIV infection combined with severe immune deficiency. (Ch. 30, 658)

Action plan A multi-step strategy for identifying and achieving goals. (Ch. 2, 38)

Active immunity Immunity your body develops to protect you from disease. (Ch. 28, 633)

Active listening Really paying attention to what someone is saying and feeling. (Ch. 11, 265)

Addiction A physiological or psychological dependence on a substance or activity. (Ch. 24, 529)

Additive interaction When medicines work together in a positive way. (Ch. 23, 516)

Adolescence The stage between childhood and adulthood. (Ch. 21, 478)

Adrenal glands Two glands located on the top of the kidneys. (Ch. 16, 379)

Adrenaline The "emergency hormone" secreted by the adrenal glands to prepare the body to respond to a stressor. (Ch. 9, 216)

Advocate Someone who speaks out for another person or a cause. (Ch. 32, 716)

Aerobic exercise Vigorous activity in which oxygen is continuously taken in for a period of at least 20 minutes. (Ch. 3, 57)

Aesthetic Artistic. (Ch. 8, 193)

Affective disorder A psychological illness or condition that relates to emotions and involves mood swings or mood extremes that interfere with everyday living. (Ch. 10, 241)

Affirmation Positive input that helps others feel appreciated and supported. (Ch. 12, 281)

Aggravated assault Unlawful attack with an intent to hurt or kill. (Ch. 14, 325)

Aggressive Overly forceful, pushy, hostile, or otherwise attacking in approach. (Ch. 13, 307)

Agility The ability to control the body's movements and to change the body's position quickly. (Ch. 4, 74)

AIDS-opportunistic illnesses (AIDS-OIs) Infections and other diseases caused by organisms that do not usually produce illness in healthy people with unimpaired immune systems. (Ch. 30, 666)

Al-Anon A worldwide self-help organization for people who are close to alcoholics. (Ch. 27, 612)

Alarm The first stage in the stress response when the body and mind go on high alert. (Ch. 9, 216)

Alateen A support program for people ages 12 to 20 whose parents, other family members, or friends have drinking problems. (Ch. 27, 613)

Alcohol poisoning A dangerous toxic condition that occurs when a person drinks a large amount of alcohol in a short period of time. (Ch. 25, 563)

Alcoholism A physical and psychological dependence on the drug ethanol. (Ch. 25, 563)

Americans with Disabilities Act A law prohibiting discrimination against people with physical or mental disabilities in the workplace, transportation, public accommodations, and telecommunications. (Ch. 31, 697)

Amino acids Chemical substances that make up body proteins. (Ch. 5, 103)

Amniocentesis A procedure in which a syringe is inserted through the pregnant female's abdominal wall into the amniotic fluid surrounding the developing fetus. (Ch. 20, 466)

Anabolic steroids Chemicals similar to the male hormone testosterone. (Ch. 4, 80)

Anaerobic exercise Intense bursts of activity in which the muscles work so hard that they produce energy without using oxygen. (Ch. 3, 58)

Analgesics Pain relievers. (Ch. 23, 515)

Angina pectoris Pain and tightness in the chest caused by the lack of oxygen to the heart. (Ch. 31, 679)

Anorexia nervosa A disorder in which the irrational fear of becoming obese results in severe weight loss from self-induced starvation. (Ch. 6, 142)

Antagonistic interaction When the effect of a medicine is canceled or reduced when taken with another medicine. (Ch. 23, 517)

Antibodies Proteins that destroy or neutralize invading pathogens. (Ch. 28, 626)

Anxiety disorder An illness or condition in which real or imagined fears prevent a person from enjoying life. (Ch. 10, 239)

Apgar test Diagnostic test that determines an infant's physical condition at birth. (Ch. 20, 460)

Appendicitis Inflammation of the appendix. (Ch. 18, 421)

Appendicular skeleton The 126 bones of the shoulders, arms, hands, hips, legs, and feet. (Ch. 15, 346)

Appetite A desire, rather than a need, to eat. (Ch. 5, 97)

Arteries The blood vessels that carry blood away from the heart. (Ch. 17, 392)

Arteriosclerosis Hardening of the arteries. (Ch. 31, 679)

Arthritis At least 100 different conditions that cause aching, pain, and swelling in joints and connective tissue throughout the body. (Ch. 31, 692)

Asbestos A mineral occurring in the form of fibers. (Ch. 33, 728)

Assailant A person who commits a violent act against another. (Ch. 14, 324)

Assertive Standing up for your own rights, in firm but positive ways. (Ch. 13, 307)

Asthma An inflammatory condition in which the small airways in the lungs become narrowed, causing difficulty in breathing. (Ch. 17, 404)

Athlete's foot A fungal infection of the skin between the toes. (Ch. 15, 343)

Autonomy The confidence that one can control one's own body, impulses, and environment. (Ch. 20, 469)

Axial skeleton The 80 bones of the skull, spine, ribs, and sternum, or breastbone. (Ch. 15, 346)

B

Balance The ability to remain upright while either standing still or moving. (Ch. 4, 74)

Basal metabolism The minimum amount of energy required to maintain the life processes in a body. (Ch. 3, 54)

Benign Noncancerous. (Ch. 31, 683)

Bile A yellowish green, bitter fluid important in the breakdown of fats. (Ch. 18, 416)

Binge drinking Periodic excessive drinking. (Ch. 25, 562)

Biodegradable Able to be broken down by microorganisms in the environment. (Ch. 33, 729)

Biopsy A laboratory analysis of a section of tissue taken from a site where abnormal cell growth is suspected. (Ch. 31, 687)

Bipolar disorder A psychological illness characterized by extreme mood swings between depression and extreme happiness, or mania. (Ch. 10, 241)

Bladder A hollow, muscular organ that acts as a reservoir for urine. (Ch. 18, 426)

Blizzard A snowstorm with winds of 35 miles per hour (56 km per hour) or greater. (Ch. 34, 753)

Blood alcohol concentration (BAC) The amount of alcohol in a person's blood expressed as a percentage. (Ch. 25, 557)

Body composition The ratio of body fat to lean body tissue, including muscle, bone, water, and connective tissue such as ligament, cartilage, and tendons. (Ch. 3, 47)

Body language Nonverbal communication through gestures, facial expressions, and behaviors. (Ch. 11, 266)

Body mass index (BMI) The ratio of weight to height. (Ch. 6, 135)

Brain stem A 3-inch-long (7.6-cm-long) stalk of nerve cells and fibers that connects the spinal cord to the rest of the brain. (Ch. 16, 369)

Bronchi The airways that connect the trachea to the lungs. (Ch. 17, 402)

Bulimia nervosa A disorder in which cycles of overeating are followed by some form of purging or clearing of the digestive tract. (Ch. 6, 142)

C

Calories Units of heat. (Ch. 3, 54)

Cancer Uncontrolled abnormal cell growth. (Ch. 31, 683)

Capillaries The vessels that carry blood between arterioles and small vessels called venules. (Ch. 17, 392)

Carbohydrate loading Storing extra glycogen in the muscle. (Ch. 6, 148)

Carbohydrates The starches and sugars found in foods. (Ch. 5, 101)

Carbon monoxide A colorless, odorless, poisonous gas in cigarette smoke that passes through the lungs into the blood. (Ch. 24, 530)

Carcinogens Cancer-causing substances. (Ch. 24, 530; Ch. 31, 684)

Cardiac muscle A special type of striated tissue that forms the walls of the heart. (Ch. 15, 354)

Cardiopulmonary resuscitation (CPR) A lifesaving technique in which a heart that has stopped is forced to pump blood to the body by means of applied pressure. (Ch. 35, 782)

Cardiorespiratory endurance The ability of the heart, lungs, and blood vessels to send fuel and oxygen to the body's tissues during long periods of vigorous activity. (Ch. 3, 48)

Cardiovascular diseases (CVDs) Medical disorders that affect the heart and blood vessels. (Ch. 31, 676)

Cardiovascular failure Failure of the heart to pump blood. (Ch. 35, 782)

Carjacking Hijacking or stealing a car by force. (Ch. 14, 328)

Carotid pulse   The heartbeat found on each side of the neck. (Ch. 35, 781)

Cartilage   Strong, flexible connective tissue. (Ch. 15, 346)

Cerebellum   The second largest part of the brain. (Ch. 16, 368)

Cerebral palsy   A group of nonprogressive neurological disorders that are the result of damage to the brain before birth, during birth, in the newborn period, or in early childhood. (Ch. 16, 376)

Cerebrum   The largest, most complex part of the brain. (Ch. 16, 367)

Cervix   Neck of the uterus. (Ch. 19, 444)

Chemotherapy   The use of anti-cancer medications in the treatment of cancer. (Ch. 31, 688)

Child abuse   Physical harm, including sexual abuse, or emotional harm to a child. (Ch. 12, 287)

Chlamydia   An infection caused by a bacteria that affects the vagina in females and the urethra in males. (Ch. 29, 646)

Chlorofluorocarbons (CFCs)   Compounds of chlorine, fluorine, and carbon. (Ch. 33, 728)

Cholesterol   A fatlike substance produced in the liver of all animals and, therefore, found only in foods of animal origin. (Ch. 5, 106)

Chorionic villi sampling   A test in which a small piece of membrane is removed from the chorion, a layer of tissue that develops into the placenta. (Ch. 20, 467)

Choroid   The middle layer of the eyeball wall. (Ch. 7, 172)

Chromosomes   Tiny structures within the nuclei of cells that carry information about hereditary traits. (Ch. 20, 461)

Chyme   A creamy, fluid mixture of food and gastric juices. (Ch. 18, 415)

Circumcision   Surgical removal of the foreskin of the penis. (Ch. 19, 438)

Cirrhosis   A condition in which liver tissue is destroyed and then replaced with useless scar tissue. (Ch. 25, 559)

Clinical psychologist   A psychologist who diagnoses and treats emotional and behavioral disorders but cannot prescribe medications. (Ch. 10, 250)

Clique   A small, narrow circle of friends, usually with similar backgrounds or tastes, that excludes people they view as outsiders. (Ch. 13, 300)

Closure   A coming to an end of the most intense parts of the grieving process. (Ch. 9, 231)

Cluster suicides   A rash of suicides occurring within a short space of time and involving several people in the same school or community. (Ch. 10, 246)

Codependents   People who become overly concerned with another's addiction problem and feel driven to fix or control it. (Ch. 27, 608)

Cognition   The ability to reason and think out abstract solutions. (Ch. 21, 479)

Commitment   A promise or a pledge. (Ch. 22, 498)

Communication   A process through which you send messages to and receive messages from others. (Ch. 11, 263)

Compromise   The result of each person's giving up something in order to reach a solution that satisfies everyone. (Ch. 11, 261)

Confidentiality   Respecting the privacy of both parties and keeping details secret. (Ch. 14, 323)

Confirmatory test   A highly accurate test used to confirm the results of a reactive ELISA (EIA). (Ch. 30, 664)

Conflict   Any disagreement, struggle, or fight. (Ch. 14, 316)

Conflict resolution   The process of ending a conflict by cooperating and problem solving. (Ch. 14, 320)

Congenital   Occurring at birth. (Ch. 17, 397)

Congestive heart failure   A slow, gradual weakening of the heart muscle from overwork. (Ch. 31, 680)

Conservation   Concern about the preservation of the environment. (Ch. 33, 734)

Constructive criticism   Nonhostile comments that point out problems and have the potential to help a person change. (Ch. 11, 268)

Contaminant   A substance that spoils or infects. (Ch. 6, 151)

Cool-down   Engaging in activity to gradually decrease activity. (Ch. 3, 64)

Cooperation   Working together for the good of all. (Ch. 11, 261)

Coordination   The ability to use two or more body parts together well, or to use the senses along with the body parts. (Ch. 4, 74)

Cornea   The main lens of the eye that performs most of the focusing. (Ch. 7, 172)

Crisis   An extreme change in a person's life. (Ch. 12, 287)

Crisis center   A facility equipped to handle emergencies and make referrals for persons who need help. (Ch. 12, 288)

Cross-contamination   The spreading of bacteria from one food to another. (Ch. 6, 153)

Cross-training   Combining various exercise routines to help work different body systems. (Ch. 3, 62)

Culture   The collective beliefs, customs, and behaviors of a group. (Ch. 1, 14)

Custody   A legal decision about who has the right to make decisions that affect the children and who has the physical responsibility of caring for them. (Ch. 12, 286)

Cystitis   A bacterial infection of the bladder that occurs most frequently in females. (Ch. 18, 428)

D

Dandruff   A condition in which the outer layer of dead skin cells is shed from the scalp. (Ch. 7, 166)

Date rape   When rape occurs between two people who are dating. (Ch. 34, 762)

Defense mechanisms   Strategies used to deal with strong or stressful emotions and situations. (Ch. 8, 204)

Deforestation   Destruction of forests. (Ch. 33, 732)

Delayed grief response   A putting off of the most intense stages of grief. (Ch. 9, 231)

Delirium tremens (DTs)   The dramatic physical and psychological effects of alcohol withdrawal. (Ch. 25, 565)

Depressants   Drugs that tend to slow down the central nervous system. (Ch. 26, 582)

Depression   Feelings of helplessness, hopelessness, and sadness. (Ch. 10, 243)

Dermis   The inner, thicker layer of skin. (Ch. 15, 341)

Desertification   The conversion of grasslands, rain-fed cropland, or irrigated cropland to desertlike conditions. (Ch. 33, 733)

Designated drivers   People in social settings who choose not to drink so that they can safely drive themselves and others. (Ch. 25, 559)

Designer drugs   Synthetic substances meant to imitate the effects of narcotics and hallucinogens. (Ch. 26, 590)

Detachment   The process of pulling back or separating from involvement with someone else's addiction and refusing to let that addiction rule one's life any longer. (Ch. 27, 612)

Detoxification   The removal of all drugs from the body. (Ch. 27, 605)

Developmental task   Something that needs to occur during a particular stage for a person to continue his or her growth toward becoming a healthy, mature adult. (Ch. 20, 468)

Diabetes   A chronic disease that affects the way body cells convert food into energy. (Ch. 31, 689)

Diaphragm   A muscle that separates the chest and abdominal cavities. (Ch. 17, 401)

Digestion   The mechanical and chemical breakdown of foods for use by the body's cells. (Ch. 18, 412)

Disability   Any physical or mental impairment that limits normal activities. (Ch. 31, 694)

Distress   Negative stress. (Ch. 9, 215)

Domestic violence   Any acts of violence involving family members. (Ch. 12, 286)

Drug watches   Organized community efforts by neighborhood residents to patrol, monitor, report, and otherwise help try to stop drug deals and drug use. (Ch. 26, 595)

Drug-Free School Zones   Areas within 1,000 feet of schools and designated by signs, within which people caught selling drugs receive especially tough penalties. (Ch. 26, 593)

E

Electrocution   Death resulting from passage through the body of a high-voltage current. (Ch. 34, 746)

Electrolytes   Nutrients that become electrically charged when in solution. (Ch. 6, 146)

Elimination   The expulsion of undigested food or body wastes. (Ch. 18, 412)

ELISA (EIA)   A test that screens for the presence of HIV antibodies in the blood. (Ch. 30, 664)

Embryo   Cluster of developing cells following implantation. (Ch. 20, 455)

Emetic   An agent that induces vomiting. (Ch. 35, 777)

Emotional abuse   A pattern of behavior that attacks a child's emotional development and sense of self-worth. (Ch. 12, 287)

Emotional intimacy   The ability to experience a caring, loving relationship with another person with whom you can share your innermost feelings. (Ch. 22, 497)

Emotional maturity   The state at which the mental and emotional capabilities of an individual are fully developed. (Ch. 22, 495)

Emotions   Signals that tell your mind and body how to react. (Ch. 8, 197)

Empathy   The ability to imagine and understand how someone else feels. (Ch. 8, 199; Ch. 11, 262)

Empty-nest syndrome   Feelings of despair or loneliness that accompany children leaving home and entering adulthood. (Ch. 22, 504)

Enabling   Trying to protect the person having trouble with alcohol or drugs from facing the consequences of his or her drug-related problems. (Ch. 27, 609)

Endocrine glands   Ductless, or tubeless, structures that secrete hormones. (Ch. 16, 377)

Enriched food   A food in which nutrients lost in processing have been added back. (Ch. 5, 123)

Environment   The sum total of your surroundings—your family, where you grew up, where you live now, and all of your experiences. (Ch. 1, 11)

Epidemic   An outbreak of an infectious disease that affects a large population. (Ch. 29, 642)

Epidemiology   The scientific study of epidemics. (Ch. 32, 719)

Epidermis   The outer, thinner layer of skin. (Ch. 15, 341)

Epilepsy   A disorder of the nervous system that is characterized by recurrent seizures—sudden episodes of uncontrolled electrical activity in the brain. (Ch. 16, 376)

Escalate   Grow into a situation that is unhealthful and even unsafe. (Ch. 14, 318)

Ethanol   The type of alcohol found in alcoholic beverages. (Ch. 25, 550)

Euphoria   A temporary feeling of intense well-being or elation that may be followed by a complete "crash" or letdown. (Ch. 26, 581)

Eustress   Positive stress. (Ch. 9, 215)

Exploitation   Being used for someone else's benefit. (Ch. 12, 287)

Extensors   Muscles that open out a joint. (Ch. 15, 354)

External auditory canal   A passageway in the ear about 1 inch (2.5 cm) long. (Ch. 7, 176)

F

Fallopian tubes   A pair of tubes with fingerlike projections that draw the ovum in. (Ch. 19, 443)

Family counseling   Therapy to restore healthy relationships in a family. (Ch. 12, 290)

Famine   A widespread shortage of food. (Ch. 32, 719)

Fatigue   The third stage of the stress response, resulting in a tired feeling that lowers one's level of activity. (Ch. 9, 218)

Fatty liver   A condition in which fats build up in the liver and cannot be broken down. (Ch. 25, 559)

Feedback   Messages from others that indicate who they think you are or what they think you are like. (Ch. 8, 189)

Fermentation   The chemical action of yeast on sugars. (Ch. 25, 550)

Fertilization   The union of a reproductive cell from a male and one from a female. (Ch. 19, 438)

Fetal alcohol syndrome (FAS)   A condition in which a fetus has been adversely affected mentally and physically by its mother's heavy alcohol use during pregnancy. (Ch. 25, 561)

Fetus   The name by which the embryo is known from the end of the eighth week until birth. (Ch. 20, 455)

Fibrillation   The rapid, ineffective beating of the heart in one of two chambers called ventricles. (Ch. 31, 680)

Fire extinguisher   A portable device that puts out small fires by ejecting fire-extinguishing chemicals. (Ch. 34. 745)

First aid   The immediate, temporary care given to a person who has become sick or who has been injured. (Ch. 35, 770)

Flexibility   The ability to move a body part through a full range of motion. (Ch. 3, 47)

Flexors   Muscles that close a joint. (Ch. 15, 354)

Follicles   Tiny pits in the skin. (Ch. 7, 165)

Food additives   Substances added to food intentionally to produce a desired effect. (Ch. 5, 123)

Food allergy   A condition in which the body's immune system overreacts to substances in some foods. (Ch. 6, 154)

Foodborne illness   Food poisoning. (Ch. 6, 151)

Food intolerance   A negative reaction to a food or an ingredient in food that is not related to the body's immune system or to food poisoning. (Ch. 6, 155)

Fortification   The addition of nutrients that are not naturally present. (Ch. 5, 123)

Foster care   Under the guidance and supervision of a family headed up by parents or a parent who is not related to the child by birth. (Ch. 12, 289)

Friendship   A significant relationship between two people based on caring, consideration, and trust. (Ch. 11, 259)

Frostbite   A condition that results when body tissue becomes frozen. (Ch. 4, 87)

G

Gametes   Reproductive cells produced by the gonads. (Ch. 21, 479)

Gangrene   The death of tissue in a part of the body. (Ch. 35, 789)

Gastric juices   Secretions from the stomach lining that contain pepsin and hydrochloric acid. (Ch. 18, 414)

Gateway drugs   Drugs that often lead to other serious and dangerous drug use. (Ch. 26, 575)

Generativity   A shift of attention away from oneself in the present to concerns for future generations. (Ch. 22, 502)

Generic   A less-expensive version of a medicine that may be substituted for a brand-name medication. (Ch. 32, 712)

Genes   Segments of DNA molecules. (Ch. 20, 461)

Genital herpes   Blisterlike sores in the genital area. (Ch. 29, 648)

Genital warts   Reddish warts with cauliflowerlike tops that appear on the genitals. (Ch. 29, 648)

Glucose   A simple sugar and the body's chief fuel. (Ch. 5, 102)

Glycogen   A starchlike substance. (Ch. 5, 102)

Goal   Something you aim for that takes planning and work. (Ch. 2, 36)

Gonads   The ovaries and testes. (Ch. 16, 378)

Gonorrhea   An STD caused by bacteria that affect the genital mucous membrane, primarily in the lining of the urethra of the male and in the cervix and vagina of the female. (Ch. 29, 647)

Greenhouse effect   A slowdown of the rate at which the earth loses heat, causing an increase in the earth's temperature. (Ch. 33, 727)

Grief reaction   An individual's total response to a major loss. (Ch. 9, 229)

H

Halfway houses   Continuing-care facilities that offer people housing, counseling, and support meetings as they are recovering from a severe addiction. (Ch. 27, 607)

Hallucinogens Drugs that alter moods, thoughts, and sense perceptions, including vision, hearing, smell, and touch. (Ch. 26, 584)

Hardy personality A personality type that seems able to stay healthy despite major or even traumatic stressors. (Ch. 9, 220)

Hashish The dark brown resin collected from the tops of the cannabis plant. (Ch. 26, 587)

Hazardous wastes Any substances that are explosive, corrosive, flammable, or toxic to human or other life forms. (Ch. 33, 730)

Health The combination of your physical, mental/emotional, and social well-being. (Ch. 1, 4)

Health-care facility Any place staffed by health-care professionals and equipped for the delivery of health services. (Ch. 32, 706)

Health-care providers Professionals trained in the health fields. (Ch. 32, 704)

Health consumer A person who uses health products or services. (Ch. 32, 709)

Health insurance A plan to cover part or most costs of expenses and care associated with medical treatment. (Ch. 32, 707)

Health literacy An individual's capacity to obtain, interpret, and understand basic health information and services and use such information to promote his or her health and wellness. (Ch. 1, 10)

Health maintenance organization (HMO) A group of physicians of different specialties who work together to provide medical services to members. (Ch. 32, 708)

Health skills Specific tools and strategies that lead to better and more informed health choices. (Ch. 2, 28)

Heat cramps Muscle spasms that are the result of loss of large amounts of salt and water through perspiration. (Ch. 4, 87)

Heat exhaustion An overheating of the body resulting in cold, clammy skin and symptoms of shock. (Ch. 4, 87)

Hemodialysis A technique in which an artificial kidney machine removes waste products from the blood. (Ch. 18, 429)

Hemoglobin The oxygen-carrying part of blood. (Ch. 17, 390)

Heredity All the traits and properties that are passed along biologically from parent to child. (Ch. 1, 11)

Hernia Protrusion of an organ or tissue through a weak area in the muscle. (Ch. 15, 357)

Hiatal hernia A condition in which part of the stomach pushes through an opening in the diaphragm. (Ch. 18, 419)

Hierarchy of needs A ranked list of those needs essential to human growth and development pre-sented in ascending order from most basic to most fulfilling or satisfying. (Ch. 8, 191)

HIV-reactive Infected with HIV. (Ch. 30, 663)

Homicide The willful killing of one human being by another. (Ch. 14, 324)

Hormones Chemical substances produced by duct-less glands that regulate the activities of different body cells. (Ch. 16, 377)

Hostility The intentional use of unfriendly or nasty behavior. (Ch. 8, 200)

Human immunodeficiency virus (HIV) A virus that attacks the body's immune system. (Ch. 30, 658)

Hunger A natural drive that protects us from starvation. (Ch. 5, 97)

Hurricane A powerful rainstorm, characterized by driving winds. (Ch. 34, 752)

Hydration The addition of body fluids. (Ch. 4, 80)

Hypertension High blood pressure. (Ch. 31, 677)

Hypochondria Preoccupation with the body and fear of diseases that are not present. (Ch. 10, 240)

Hypothermia A condition in which body temperature becomes dangerously low. (Ch. 4, 87)

I

"I" message A statement in which a person tells how he or she feels using the pronoun "I." (Ch. 11, 264)

Illegal drugs Street drugs. (Ch. 26, 575)

Illicit drug use The use or sale of any substances that are illegal or otherwise not permitted. (Ch. 26, 575)

Immunity The body's natural defenses against infection. (Ch. 28, 624)

Immunization A program whereby communities or other large populations are systematically made immune to a disease. (Ch. 28, 630)

Impaired glucose tolerance (IGT) A condition in which blood sugar levels are higher than normal but not high enough to be classified as diabetes. (Ch. 31, 691)

Incontinence The inability of the body to control the bladder and the elimination of waste. (Ch. 18, 428)

Indigestion A burning discomfort in the upper abdomen. (Ch. 18, 418)

Infatuation Exaggerated feelings of passion for another person. (Ch. 13, 301)

Infectious disease A disease caused by organisms that enter and multiply within the human body. (Ch. 28, 620)

Infertility The inability of a woman to become pregnant. (Ch. 19, 445)

Ingestion The taking of food into the body. (Ch. 18, 413)

Inhalants Substances with breathable fumes that are sniffed and inhaled to give a hallucinogenic or mind-altering high. (Ch. 26, 589)

Inpatient treatment Medical and psychological care during which a person stays at a medical or rehabilitation facility. (Ch. 27, 606)

Insulin A hormone that is produced in the pancreas and that helps the body convert glucose to energy. (Ch. 31, 690)

Integrity A feeling of wholeness and contentment. (Ch. 22, 505)

Integumentary system The body system that includes your skin, hair, nails, sebaceous glands, and sweat glands. (Ch. 15, 340)

Internal conflicts Struggles within yourself. (Ch. 14, 317)

Interpersonal conflicts Disagreements between groups of any size, from two people to entire nations. (Ch. 14, 316)

Intervention Interruption of the addiction continuum before the addict or alcoholic hits bottom. (Ch. 27, 604)

Intoxication Physical and mental impairment resulting from the use of alcohol. (Ch. 25, 550)

Intravenous (IV) drugs Drugs that are injected into the veins. (Ch. 30, 659)

Isokinetic exercise Activity that involves resistance through an entire range of motion. (Ch. 3, 58)

Isometric exercise Activity that uses muscle tension to improve muscular strength with little or no movement of the body part. (Ch. 3, 58)

Isotonic exercise Activity that combines muscle contraction with repeated movement. (Ch. 3, 58)

L

Labyrinth Inner ear. (Ch. 7, 177)

Lacrimal gland The gland responsible for producing tears. (Ch. 7, 171)

Larynx Voice box. (Ch. 17, 402)

Latency A stage when the virus is present but not active. (Ch. 30, 664)

Leukoplakia Thickened, white, leathery-appearing spots on the inside of a smokeless tobacco user's mouth that can develop into cancer of the mouth. (Ch. 24, 535)

Lifestyle activities Forms of physical activity that are a normal part of your daily routine or recreation that promote good health throughout a lifetime. (Ch. 4, 73)

Lifestyle factors Personal behaviors and habits related to the way a person lives that help determine his or her level of health. (Ch. 1, 8)

Ligaments Tough bands of fibrous, elastic tissue that bind the bone ends at the joint. (Ch. 15, 348)

Linoleic acid An essential fatty acid not made in the body but that is essential for growth and healthy skin. (Ch. 5, 105)

Lipid A fatty substance that does not dissolve in water. (Ch. 5, 105)

Look-alike drugs Drugs made so as to physically resemble specific illegal drugs. (Ch. 26, 590)

Lymph A clear yellow fluid that fills the spaces around body cells. (Ch. 17, 393)

Lymphocytes White blood cells that protect the body against pathogens. (Ch. 17, 394)

M

Mainstream smoke The smoke that a smoker blows off. (Ch. 24, 536)

Malignant Cancerous. (Ch. 31, 683)

Manipulation A sneaky or dishonest way to control or influence others. (Ch. 13, 305)

Marijuana Cannabis that is smoked, eaten, or drunk for intoxicating effects. (Ch. 26, 587)

Marital adjustment How well people adjust and adapt to marriage and to each other. (Ch. 22, 499)

Mastication The process of chewing. (Ch. 18, 413)

Mediation A process in which specifically trained people help others to resolve their conflicts peacefully. (Ch. 14, 323)

Mediator A person who helps others resolve issues to the satisfaction of both parties. (Ch. 12, 290)

Medicaid An assistance program of medical aid for people of all ages who are unable financially to afford medical care. (Ch. 32, 708)

Medical history Complete and comprehensive information about immunizations and any health problems to date. (Ch. 32, 711)

Medicare A health insurance program that is available to people 65 years of age or older and to people who receive Social Security disability benefits. (Ch. 32, 708)

Medicine misuse Using a medicine in a way other than the one intended. (Ch. 23, 520)

Medicines Substances that, when taken internally or applied to the body, help prevent or cure a disease or other medical problem. (Ch. 23, 512)

Megadoses Very large amounts of nutrient supplements. (Ch. 6, 150)

Melanin The pigment that gives skin, hair, and the iris of the eyes their coloring. (Ch. 15, 341)

Melanoma Often deadly type of skin cancer. (Ch. 31, 685)

Menopause The stopping of ovulation and menstruation. (Ch. 22, 503)

Menstrual cycle The time from the beginning of one menstrual period to the onset of the next. (Ch. 19, 444)

Mental disorder An illness of the mind that can affect the thoughts, feelings, and behaviors of a person, preventing him or her from leading a happy, healthful, and productive life. (Ch. 10, 238)

Mental health Generally having a positive outlook, being comfortable with yourself and others, and being able to meet life's challenges and demands. (Ch. 8, 186)

Mental retardation   Below-average intellectual ability present from birth or early childhood and associated with difficulties in learning and social adaptation. (Ch. 31, 696)

Metabolism   The process by which your body gets energy from food. (Ch. 3, 54)

Metastasis   Spread of cancer from the point where it originated to other parts of the body. (Ch. 31, 683)

Minerals   Inorganic substances that the body cannot manufacture but that act as catalysts, regulating many vital body processes. (Ch. 5, 109)

Miscarriage   A spontaneous abortion. (Ch. 20, 460)

Modeling   Copying the behaviors of those you are exposed to. (Ch. 8, 196)

Mucous membranes   The soft, skinlike lining of many parts of the body. (Ch. 28, 624)

Muscle cramp   A spasm or sudden tightening of a muscle. (Ch. 4, 84)

Muscle tone   The natural tension in the fibers of a muscle. (Ch. 15, 355)

Muscular endurance   The ability of the muscles to do difficult physical tasks over a period of time without causing fatigue. (Ch. 3, 48)

Muscular strength   The amount of force a muscle can exert. (Ch. 3, 47)

N

Narcotics   Drugs derived from the opium plant which have a sedative effect. (Ch. 26, 583)

Neglect   A failure to provide a child's physical or emotional needs. (Ch. 12, 287)

Negotiation   A process in which compromise is used to reach agreement. (Ch. 14, 322)

Nephrons   The functional units of the kidneys. (Ch. 18, 425)

Neurologist   A physician who specializes in organic disorders of the brain and nervous system. (Ch. 10, 250)

Neurons   Nerve cells. (Ch. 16, 365)

Neutrophils   The chief phagocyte involved in the process of phagocytosis. (Ch. 28, 625)

Nicotine   The addictive drug in cigarettes. (Ch. 24, 529)

Nicotine substitutes   Manufactured forms of nicotine that deliver small amounts of the drug into the user's system while he or she is trying to give up the tobacco habit. (Ch. 24, 539)

Nicotine withdrawal   The process that occurs when nicotine, an addictive drug, is no longer used. (Ch. 24, 539)

Nongonococcal urethritis   An infection caused by several different kinds of bacterialike organisms that infect the urethra in males and the cervix in females. (Ch. 29, 646)

Noninfectious diseases   Diseases that are not transmitted by means of a pathogen. (Ch. 31, 676)

Nutrient supplements   Pills, powders, liquids, and other synthetic forms of nutrients. (Ch. 6, 149)

Nutrient-dense   Foods high in nutrients relative to their caloric content. (Ch. 6, 138)

Nutrients   Substances in food that your body needs to function properly, such as in growing, in repairing itself, and in having a supply of energy. (Ch. 5, 96)

Nutrition   The process by which the body takes in and uses food. (Ch. 5, 100)

O

Obesity   Excess body fat, or adipose tissue. (Ch. 5, 99; Ch. 6, 133)

Occupational Safety and Health Administration (OSHA)   A federal agency responsible for promoting safe and healthful conditions in the workplace. (Ch. 34, 750)

Ossicles   Three tiny, linked, movable bones behind the eardrum. (Ch. 7, 176)

Ossification   The process by which bone is formed, renewed, and repaired. (Ch. 15, 346)

Osteoarthritis   A disease in the weight-bearing joints of the knees and hips, causing aches and soreness especially when moving. (Ch. 31, 693)

Otosclerosis   A hereditary disorder in which an overgrowth of bone causes the ossicles to lose their ability to move. (Ch. 7, 179)

Outpatient surgical facility   A place where surgery is performed on patients who are released the same day. (Ch. 32, 707)

Outpatient treatment   On-site medical and psychological care for a person trying to become alcohol-free and drug-free. (Ch. 27, 607)

Ova   Female reproductive cells. (Ch. 19, 442)

Ovaries   The female sex glands that house the ova and produce female sex hormones. (Ch. 19, 443)

Overdose   A strong or even fatal reaction to taking a large amount of a drug. (Ch. 26, 576)

Overexertion   Overworking the body. (Ch. 4, 86)

Overload   Working the body harder than it is normally worked. (Ch. 3, 62)

Over-the-counter (OTC) medicines   Medicines you can buy without a doctor's prescription. (Ch. 23, 519)

Overweight   Weighing more than 10 percent over the standard weight for height. (Ch. 6, 133)

Ovulation   The process of releasing one mature ovum each month. (Ch. 19, 443)

P

Pancreas   A gland that serves two systems—the digestive and the endocrine. (Ch. 16, 380)

Paranoia Irrational suspiciousness or distrust of others. (Ch. 26, 581)

Parasites Organisms that live in or on another organism and derive nourishment from it. (Ch. 28, 620)

Parathyroid glands Structures that produce parathyroid hormone, which regulates the body's calcium and phosphorus balance. (Ch. 16, 379)

Particulates Tiny particles suspended and carried through air. (Ch. 33, 728)

Passive Giving up, giving in, or backing down without standing up for your own rights and needs. (Ch. 13, 306)

Passive immunity The temporary immunity that an infant acquires from its mother. (Ch. 28, 633)

Passive smoke Cigarette, cigar, or pipe smoke inhaled by nonsmokers as well as smoke that remains in a closed environment after the smoker is through smoking. (Ch. 24, 536)

Pasteurized Treated by a process of heating to destroy or slow the growth of pathogens. (Ch. 6, 152)

Peer mediators Students trained to help other students in conflict find fair ways to settle their differences. (Ch. 14, 323)

Peer pressure The control and influence people your age may have over you. (Ch. 1, 14; Ch. 13, 304)

Peers People the same age who share a similar range of interests. (Ch. 1, 14)

Penis A tube-shaped organ attached to the trunk of the body just above the testes. (Ch. 19, 437)

Peptic ulcer A sore in the lining of the digestive tract. (Ch. 18, 422)

Periodontal disease An inflammation of the periodontal structures. (Ch. 7, 168)

Periodontium The area immediately around the teeth. (Ch. 7, 167)

Perishable Liable to spoil. (Ch. 6, 153)

Peristalsis A series of involuntary muscular contractions. (Ch. 18, 414)

Personal identity The factors you believe make you unique, or unlike anyone else. (Ch. 21, 482)

Personality A complex set of characteristics that makes you unique and sets you apart from everyone else. (Ch. 8, 194)

Personality disorders A variety of psychological illnesses and conditions that affect a person's ability to get along with others. (Ch. 10, 241)

Phagocytosis The process by which phagocytes engulf and destroy pathogens. (Ch. 28, 625)

Pharynx Throat. (Ch. 17, 402)

Phobias Irrational fears. (Ch. 8, 200)

Physical activity Any form of movement, whether purposeful, as in exercise and sports or recreation, or incidental, as when carrying out domestic chores. (Ch. 4, 72)

Physical fitness The ability to carry out daily tasks easily and have enough reserve energy to respond to unexpected demands. (Ch. 3, 46)

Physical maturity The state at which the physical body and all its organs are fully developed. (Ch. 22, 495)

Pituitary gland Structure that regulates and controls the activities of all other endocrine glands. (Ch. 16, 378)

Placenta A blood-rich tissue developed from an outer layer of cells from the embryo and tissue from the mother (Ch. 20, 455)

Planned pregnancy Making a decision to get pregnant before the baby is conceived. (Ch. 22, 500)

Plaque A sticky, colorless film that acts on sugar to form acids that destroy tooth enamel and irritate gums. (Ch. 7, 168)

Plasma The fluid in which the other parts of blood are suspended. (Ch. 17, 390)

Platelets The cells that prevent the body's loss of blood. (Ch. 17, 391)

Platonic friendship A relationship with a member of the opposite gender in which there is affection, but no sexual activity. (Ch. 13, 299)

Pleurisy An inflammation of the membrane lining the lungs and chest cavity. (Ch. 17, 405)

Pneumonia Inflammation of the lungs. (Ch. 28, 628)

Poison Any substance—solid, liquid, or gas—that causes injury, illness, or death when introduced into the body. (Ch. 35, 771)

Poison control center A 24-hour hot line that provides emergency medical advice on treating poisoning victims. (Ch. 35, 776)

Power The ability to use force with great speed. (Ch. 4, 74)

Preferred provider organization (PPO) A type of health insurance in which medical providers agree to charge less to members. (Ch. 32, 708)

Prejudice Negative feeling toward someone or something that is based not on experience but, rather, on stereotypes. (Ch. 13, 300)

Prescription medicines Medicines that cannot be used safely without the written approval of a licensed physician. (Ch. 23, 519)

Pressure point One of a number of points along the main artery supplying blood to an affected limb. (Ch. 35, 772)

Prevention Practicing healthy habits to keep a person well and free from disease and other ailments. (Ch. 1, 9)

Primary care physician A medical professional who provides the first line of health care. (Ch. 32, 704)

Priorities Those goals, tasks, or activities that you judge as more important to do than others. (Ch. 9, 227; Ch. 21, 484)

Profound deafness   A hearing loss so severe that a person affected cannot benefit from mechanical amplification such as a hearing aid. (Ch. 31, 695)

Progression   A gradual increase in overload necessary for achieving higher levels of fitness. (Ch. 3, 63)

Proteins   Nutrients that help build and maintain body tissues. (Ch. 5, 103)

Psychiatric social worker   One who has concentrated on psychiatric casework, doing fieldwork in a mental hospital, mental health clinic, or family service agency that provides guidance and treatment for clients with emotional problems. (Ch. 10, 251)

Psychiatrist   A medical doctor who specializes in diagnosing and treating mental disorders and can prescribe medications. (Ch. 10, 249)

Psychoactive drugs   Chemicals that affect the central nervous system and interfere with the normal functioning of the brain. (Ch. 26, 580)

Psychologists   Professionals with doctoral degrees who diagnose and treat emotional and behavioral disorders. (Ch. 8, 194)

Psychosomatic response   A physical disorder that results from stress rather than from an injury or illness. (Ch. 9, 222)

Puberty   The period of time when males and females become physically able to reproduce. (Ch. 21, 478)

Public health   A community-wide effort to monitor and promote the welfare of the population. (Ch. 32, 717)

Pulp   The living tissue inside the tooth. (Ch. 7, 167)

Q

Quackery   A type of medical fraud. (Ch. 32, 713)

R

Rabies   A viral disease of the nervous system that eventually causes madness and death. (Ch. 35, 786)

Random violence   Violence committed for no particular reason. (Ch. 14, 325)

Rape   Sexual intercourse by force. (Ch. 14, 331)

Reaction time   The rate of movement once a person realizes the need to move. (Ch. 4, 74)

Rechanneling   Transferring or redirecting your energies. (Ch. 9, 226)

Recommended Dietary Allowances (RDA)   The amounts of nutrients that will prevent deficiencies and excesses in most healthy people. (Ch. 5, 112)

Recovery   Learning to live an alcohol-free or drug-free life. (Ch. 27, 605)

Recycling   The treating of waste so that it can be reused, as well as having an awareness of such practices. (Ch. 33, 736)

Reflex   A spontaneous response of the body to a stimulus. (Ch. 16, 371)

Refusal skills   Techniques that can help you refuse when you are urged to take part in unsafe or unhealthful behaviors. (Ch. 2, 29; Ch. 13, 308)

Rehydration   Restoring lost body fluids. (Ch. 6, 146)

Relapses   Slips from recovery, or periodic returns to drinking and drug use. (Ch. 27, 605)

Relationship   A bond or connection between people. (Ch. 11, 258)

Relaxation response   A state of deep rest that can be reached if one or more relaxation techniques are practiced regularly. (Ch. 9, 226)

Repetitive motion injury   Damage to tissues caused by prolonged, repeated movements. (Ch. 15, 352)

Rescue breathing   Artificial respiration. (Ch. 35, 781)

Resilience   The ability to adapt effectively and recover from disappointment, difficulty, or crisis. (Ch. 8, 207)

Resistance   The second stage in the stress response, when the body tries to repair its damage from the stressful event and return to its normal state. (Ch. 9, 216)

Respiration   The exchange of gases between your body and your environment. (Ch. 17, 400)

Respiratory failure   A state in which air is unable to reach the lungs. (Ch. 35, 781)

Resting heart rate   The number of times your heart beats in one minute when you are not active. (Ch. 3, 65)

Retina   The light-sensitive membrane on which images are cast by the cornea and lens. (Ch. 7, 172)

Rheumatoid arthritis   A destructive and disabling inflammation of the joints. (Ch. 31, 692)

Risk factors   Actions or behaviors that represent a potential health threat. (Ch. 1, 17)

Road rage   When intense anger and driving mix. (Ch. 34, 755)

Role   A part that you play in a relationship. (Ch. 11, 260)

Rubella   German measles. (Ch. 29, 630)

S

Schizophrenia   A serious mental illness disorder meaning "split mind." (Ch. 10, 242)

Sclera   The tough white outer coat of the eye. (Ch. 7, 172)

Sebaceous glands   Structures within the skin that produce an oily secretion called sebum. (Ch. 7, 165)

Sedentary lifestyle   A way of life that requires little movement or exercise. (Ch. 3, 54)

Self-actualization   The striving to become the best that you can be. (Ch. 8, 193)

Self-control   A person's ability to use sense to override emotions. (Ch. 21, 485)

Self-directed Making correct decisions about behavior when adults are not there to enforce rules. (Ch. 22, 501)

Self-esteem The confidence and worth that you feel about yourself. (Ch. 2, 30)

Semen A thick fluid containing sperm and other secretions from the male reproductive organs. (Ch. 19, 438)

Sex characteristics Those traits related to one's gender. (Ch. 21, 478)

Sexual assault Any intentional sexual attack against another person. (Ch. 14, 331)

Sexually transmitted diseases (STDs) Infectious diseases spread from person to person through sexual contact. (Ch. 21, 486; Ch. 29, 642)

Shock The failure of the cardiovascular system to keep adequate blood circulating to the vital organs of the body. (Ch. 35, 773)

Sibling Brother or sister. (Ch. 12, 279)

Side effects Reactions to medicine other than the one intended. (Ch. 23, 516; Ch. 34, 744)

Sidestream smoke The smoke that comes from burning tobacco. (Ch. 24, 536)

Situation The circumstance or event leading up to an accident. (Ch. 34, 744)

Skeletal muscles The striped, or striated, muscles attached to bones that cause body movements. (Ch. 15, 354)

Smoke detector An alarm that is triggered by the presence of smoke. (Ch. 34, 745)

Smokeless tobacco Tobacco that is sniffed through the nose or chewed. (Ch. 24, 531)

Smooth muscles The type of muscle concerned with the movements of internal organs. (Ch. 15, 354)

Somatoform disorder An illness or condition in which a person complains of disease symptoms, but no physical cause can be found. (Ch. 10, 240)

Specialist A physician who has received additional training in a particular area. (Ch. 32, 703)

Specificity Principle that states that particular exercises and activities improve particular areas of health-related fitness. (Ch. 3, 63)

Speed The ability to move a distance or complete a body movement in a short period of time. (Ch. 4, 74)

Sperm Male reproductive cells. (Ch. 19, 436)

Sprain An injury to tissues surrounding a joint. (Ch. 4, 85)

Spousal abuse Domestic abuse directed at a spouse. (Ch. 12, 287)

Stereotype An exaggerated and oversimplified belief about an entire group of people. (Ch. 13, 300)

Sterility A condition in which a person is unable to reproduce. (Ch. 19, 440)

Stillbirth The birth of a dead fetus. (Ch. 20, 460)

Stimulant A drug that increases the action of the central nervous system, the heart, and other organs. (Ch. 24, 530; Ch. 26, 581)

Strain A condition in which muscles have been overworked. (Ch. 4, 85)

Strep throat A bacterial infection of the throat. (Ch. 28, 628)

Stress The body's and mind's demands and reactions to everyday demands or threats. (Ch. 9, 214)

Stress tolerance The amount of stress that you can handle before you reach a state of too much stress. (Ch. 9, 219)

Stressor Any stimulus that produces a stress response. (Ch. 9, 215)

Stroke An interruption of the flow of blood to any part of the brain. (Ch. 31, 680)

Substance abuse Any unnecessary or improper use of chemical substances for nonmedical purposes. (Ch. 26, 575)

Suicide The taking of one's own life. (Ch. 10, 243)

Support group An informal or a formal gathering of people who meet and share experiences, feelings, and trust. (Ch. 9, 227)

Sweat glands Structures within the skin that secrete perspiration through ducts to pores on the skin's surface. (Ch. 7, 163)

Synergistic effect The interaction of two or more medicines that results in a greater effect than when the medicines are taken independently. (Ch. 23, 516)

Synthetic drugs Chemical substances produced artificially in a laboratory. (Ch. 26, 575)

Syphilis An STD that attacks many parts of the body and is caused by a small bacterium called a spirochete. (Ch. 29, 649)

T

Tar A thick, sticky, dark fluid produced when tobacco burns. (Ch. 24, 530)

Tartar A hard, crustlike substance. (Ch. 7, 169)

Tendinitis The inflammation of a tendon. (Ch. 15, 357)

Tendons Fibrous cords that join muscle to bone or to other muscles. (Ch. 15, 348)

Testes Two small glands that produce sperm. (Ch. 19, 437)

Testosterone Male sex hormone. (Ch. 19, 436)

Therapeutic communities Residential treatment centers. (Ch. 26, 593)

Thyroid gland Structure that produces hormones that regulate metabolism—the use of nutrients by the body's cells—body heat production, and bone growth. (Ch. 16, 379)

Time management skills Specific strategies for planning and using time in effective, healthful ways. (Ch. 9, 227)

Tinnitus A condition in which a ringing, buzzing, whistling, hissing, or other noise is heard in the ear in the absence of external sound. (Ch. 7, 179)

Tolerance Accepting others' differences and allowing them to be who they are without expressing disapproval. (Ch. 14, 321)

Tolerance A condition in which the body becomes used to the effect of a medicine. (Ch. 23, 517)

Tornado A powerful, twisting windstorm. (Ch. 34, 752)

Trachea Windpipe. (Ch. 17, 402)

Training program A program of formalized physical preparation for participation in a sport. (Ch. 4, 79)

Transitions Critical changes that occur at all stages of life. (Ch. 22, 502)

Transmission Spread. (Ch. 28, 623)

Trichomoniasis A vaginal infection that can lead to urethra and bladder infections. (Ch. 29, 647)

Tuberculosis (TB) A highly contagious bacterial infection that most often affects the lungs. (Ch. 28, 628)

Tumors Masses of tissue. (Ch. 31, 683)

Type A personality A competitive, high-achieving personality type most likely to develop heart disease. (Ch. 9, 220)

Type B personality A "laid back," noncompetitive personality type less likely to suffer from heart disease. (Ch. 9, 220)

U

Ultrasound A test in which sound waves are used to project light images on a screen. (Ch. 20, 467)

Umbilical cord A tube through which nutrients and oxygen pass from the mother's blood into the embryo's blood. (Ch. 20, 455)

Undernutrition Not consuming enough essential nutrients or calories for normal body functions. (Ch. 6, 134)

Underweight Being 10 percent or more below normal weight. (Ch. 6, 134)

Unit pricing A strategy for recognizing the relative cost of a product based on the cost of a standard unit, such as an ounce or a gram. (Ch. 5, 125)

Ureters Tubes that connect the kidneys with the bladder. (Ch. 18, 425)

Urethra The tube that leads from the bladder to the outside of the body. (Ch. 18, 426)

Urethritis An inflammation of the urethra. (Ch. 18, 428)

Urine Liquid waste material. (Ch. 18, 424)

Uterus A small, muscular, pear-shaped organ, about the size of a fist. (Ch. 19, 443)

V

Vaccine A preparation containing weakened or dead pathogens that provides immunity by causing the body to produce antibodies to the pathogen. (Ch. 23, 513; Ch. 28, 629)

Vagina A muscular, elastic passageway that extends from the uterus to the outside of the body. (Ch. 19, 442)

Vaginitis A common inflammation of the female genitals. (Ch. 29, 648)

Values Beliefs and standards of conduct that you find important. (Ch. 1, 20)

Vegans Vegetarians who eat only foods of plant origin. (Ch. 6, 148)

Vehicular safety Obeying the rules of the road, as well as exercising common sense and good judgment. (Ch. 34, 754)

Veins The vessels that return deoxygenated blood toward the heart from the body's organs and tissues. (Ch. 17, 393)

Venom A poisonous substance secreted by a snake or other animal. (Ch. 35, 777)

Violence The use of physical force to injure or abuse another person or persons. (Ch. 14, 324)

Virus The smallest known type of infectious agent. (Ch. 28, 621)

Vitamins Compounds that help regulate many vital body processes, including the digestion, absorption, metabolism, and use of other nutrients. (Ch. 5, 107)

W

Warm-up Engaging in activity that prepares the muscles for the work that is to come. (Ch. 3, 63)

Weight cycling The cycle of losing, regaining, losing, and regaining weight. (Ch. 6, 140)

Wellness An overall state of well-being, or total health. (Ch. 1, 7)

Withdrawal The process that occurs when a person stops using a medicine or other substance to which he or she has a physiological dependence. (Ch. 23, 517)

X

Xiphoid process The lower part of the sternum that projects downward to the point where the sternum meets the lower ribs. (Ch. 35, 783)

Z

Zygote The cell that results from the union of sperm and ovum. (Ch. 19, 443)

Glossary/Glosario

A

Abdominal thrusts/compresiones abdominales La aplicación de presión brusca sobre el diafragma de la víctima para expulsar la sustancia que está bloqueando la tráquea.

Absorption/absorción Paso del alimento digerido desde el sistema digestivo al sistema circulatorio.

Abstinence/abstinencia Decisión consciente de evitar conductas nocivas, incluyendo las relaciones sexuales prematrimoniales y el consumo de tabaco, alcohol y otras drogas.

Abuse/maltrato El maltrato o daño físico, emocional, sexual y/o verbal que una persona causa intencionalmente a otra.

Accident chain/concatenación de eventos previos a un accidente Patrón recurrente de acontecimientos que se presenta en todos los percances.

Acid rain/lluvia ácida Derivados del óxido de nitrógeno o sulfuro mezclados con la lluvia.

Acne/acné Oclusión de los poros de la piel.

Acquaintance/conocido Persona que te resulta superficialmente familiar.

Acquaintance rape/violación por un conocido Violación por alguien a quien la víctima conoce superficialmente, o por alguien a quien considera un amigo.

Acquired immune deficiency syndrome (AIDS)/síndrome de inmunodeficiencia adquirida (sida) Infección por VIH combinada con inmunodeficiencia severa.

Action plan/plan de acción Estrategia de etapas múltiples para identificar y lograr objetivos.

Active immunity/inmunidad activa Inmunidad que desarrolla el cuerpo para protegerse de las enfermedades.

Active listening/escucha activa Prestar verdadera atención a lo que alguien dice y siente.

Addiction/adicción Dependencia fisiológica o psicológica respecto de una sustancia o actividad.

Additive interaction/interacción aditiva Situación en la que dos medicamentos obran juntos de manera positiva.

Adolescence/adolescencia Etapa entre la niñez y la edad adulta.

Adrenal glands/glándulas suprarrenales Dos glándulas ubicadas sobre los riñones.

Adrenaline/adrenalina La "hormona de la emergencia" secretada por las glándulas suprarrenales que prepara al cuerpo para responder a una situación de estrés.

Advocate/defensor Alguien que habla en nombre de otra persona o de una causa.

Aerobic exercise/ejercicio aeróbico Actividad vigorosa en la que se inhala y exhala oxígeno de forma continua por un período de por lo menos 20 minutos.

Aesthetic/estético Artístico.

Affective disorder/trastorno afectivo Trastorno o enfermedad psicológica relacionada con las emociones que se presenta con cambios de humor o variaciones extremas del estado anímico que interfieren con la vida cotidiana.

Affirmation/reafirmación Proveer apoyo que ayude a otros a sentirse apreciados y respaldados.

Aggravated assault/agresión grave Ataque ilegal cometido con la intención de herir o matar.

Aggressive/agresivo Excesivamente brusco, insistente, hostil, o que se conduce con agresividad.

Agility/agilidad La destreza para controlar el movimiento del cuerpo y para cambiar la posición del cuerpo con rapidez.

AIDS-opportunistic illnesses (AIDS-OIs)/enfermedades oportunistas del sida Infecciones y otras enfermedades que no suelen afectar a personas sanas inmunocompetentes.

Al-Anon/Al-Anon Organización mundial de autoayuda para familiares y amigos de alcohólicos.

Alarm/alarma La primera etapa en la respuesta al estrés, cuando el cuerpo y la mente entran en alerta.

Alateen/Alateen Programa de apoyo para personas entre 12 y 20 años de edad cuyos padres, parientes o amigos tienen problemas de alcoholismo.

Alcohol poisoning/intoxicación alcohólica Grave trastorno tóxico que ocurre cuando alguien consume gran cantidad de alcohol en poco tiempo.

Alcoholism/alcoholismo Dependencia física y psicológica de la droga etanol.

Americans with Disabilities Act/Ley sobre Discapacitados de Estados Unidos Ley que prohíbe la discriminación de personas discapacitadas física o mentalmente en el lugar de trabajo, los medios de transporte, instalaciones públicas y telecomunicaciones.

Amino acids/aminoácidos Sustancias químicas que componen las proteínas del cuerpo.

Amniocentesis/amniocentesis Procedimiento en el que se introduce una jeringa a través de la pared abdominal de la mujer embarazada para extraer algo del líquido amniótico que rodea al feto en desarrollo.

Anabolic steroids/esteroides anabólicos Sustancias químicas similares a la hormona masculina testosterona.

Anaerobic exercise/ejercicio anaeróbico Arranques de actividad intensa en los que los músculos se esfuerzan tanto que producen energía sin utilizar oxígeno.

Analgesics/analgésicos Medicinas para aliviar el dolor.

Angina pectoris/angina de pecho Dolor y presión en el pecho causada por la falta de oxígeno en el corazón.

Anorexia nervosa/anorexia nerviosa Trastorno en el que el miedo irracional a la obesidad resulta en la pérdida severa de peso debido al ayuno autoimpuesto.

Antagonistic interaction/interacción antagónica Cuando el efecto de una medicina se cancela o reduce al combinarla con otra medicina.

Antibodies/anticuerpos Proteínas que destruyen o neutralizan los patógenos invasores.

Anxiety disorder/trastornos de ansiedad Enfermedad o trastorno en el que los miedos reales o imaginarios impiden a alguien disfrutar la vida.

Apgar test/prueba de Apgar Examen diagnóstico de rutina que determina la condición física de un recién nacido.

Appendicitis/apendicitis Inflamación del apéndice.

Appendicular skeleton/esqueleto apendicular Los 126 huesos de los hombros, los brazos, las manos, las caderas, las piernas y los pies.

Appetite/apetito El deseo, más que la necesidad, de comer.

Arteries/arterias Los vasos sanguíneos que transportan la sangre desde el corazón.

Arteriosclerosis/arterioesclerosis Endurecimiento de las arterias.

Arthritis/artritis Al menos 100 trastornos diferentes que causan molestia, dolor e hinchazón en las articulaciones y el tejido conjuntivo de todo el cuerpo.

Asbestos/asbesto Mineral fibroso

Assailant/atacante Aquel que comete un acto violento en contra de otra persona.

Assertive/firme Defender los derechos propios de manera enérgica pero positiva.

Asthma/asma Trastorno inflamatorio en el que se angostan los pequeños conductos de los pulmones, llamados bronquiolos, causando dificultad para respirar.

Athlete's foot/pie de atleta Infección por hongos de la piel entre los dedos de los pies.

Autonomy/autonomía La seguridad de poder controlar el propio cuerpo, impulsos y medio ambiente.

Axial skeleton/esqueleto axial Los 80 huesos del cráneo, la columna vertebral, las costillas y el esternón.

B

Balance/equilibrio La capacidad de mantenerse erguido, ya sea parado o en movimiento.

Basal metabolism/metabolismo basal La cantidad mínima de energía requerida para mantener los procesos vitales del cuerpo.

Benign/benigno Que no es canceroso.

Bile/bilis Fluido verde amarillento y amargo que desempeña un papel importante en la descomposición de las grasas.

Binge drinking/borrachera Tomar alcohol en exceso periódicamente.

Biodegradable/biodegradable Que puede ser descompuesto por los microorganismos del medio ambiente.

Biopsy/biopsia Análisis en un laboratorio de una porción de tejido tomada de una zona donde se sospecha la presencia de crecimiento anormal de células.

Bipolar disorder/trastorno maníaco-depresivo Enfermedad psicológica caracterizada por cambios extremos en el estado de ánimo entre depresión y euforia o manía.

Bladder/vejiga Órgano muscular hueco que funciona como reservorio de orina.

Blizzard/ventisca Tormenta de nieve con vientos de 35 millas (56 km) por hora o más.

Blood alcohol concentration (BAC)/concentración de alcohol en la sangre La cantidad de alcohol en la sangre de un individuo expresada en forma de porcentaje.

Body composition/composición corporal La relación entre la grasa corporal y los tejidos magros, incluyendo músculos, huesos, agua y tejidos conjuntivos como ligamentos, cartílago y tendones.

Body language/lenguaje corporal Comunicación no verbal a través de gestos, expresiones faciales y comportamientos.

Body mass index (BMI)/índice de masa corporal (IMC) La relación entre peso y estatura.

Brain stem/médula oblonga o bulbo raquídeo Tallo de fibras y células nerviosas de 3 pulgadas (7.6 cm) de largo que conecta la espina dorsal con el resto del cerebro.

Bronqui/bronquios Conductos que conectan la tráquea con los pulmones.

Bulimia nervosa/bulimia Trastorno en el que ciclos de comer en exceso se suceden de alguna forma de purga o limpieza del trayecto digestivo.

C

Calories/calorías Unidades de calor.

Cancer/cáncer Crecimiento anormal y descontrolado de las células.

Capillaries/capilares Vasos que transportan la sangre entre las arteriolas y otros vasos pequeños llamados vénulas.

Carbohydrate loading/almacenamiento de carbohidratos Almacenar glicógeno extra en los músculos.

Carbohydrates/carbohidratos Almidones y azúcares presentes en el alimento.

Carbon monoxide/monóxido de carbono Gas venenoso inodoro e incoloro, presente en el humo de cigarrillo, que pasa a la sangre a través de los pulmones.

Carcinogens/carcinógenos Sustancias que causan cáncer.

Cardiac muscle/músculo cardíaco Un tipo especial de tejido estriado que forma las paredes del corazón.

Cardipulmonary resuscitacion (CPR)/resucitación cardiopulmonar (RCP) Una técnica para salvar vidas en la que se fuerza al corazón a bombear sangre al cuerpo por medio de la aplicación de presión.

Cardiorespiratory endurance/resistencia cardiovascular La capacidad del corazón, los pulmones y los vasos sanguíneos para enviar energía y oxígeno a los tejidos del organismo durante largos períodos de actividad vigorosa.

Cardiovascular diseases (CVDs)/enfermedades cardiovasculares Trastornos de salud que afectan el corazón y los vasos sanguíneos.

Cardiovascular failure/insuficiencia cardíaca Situación en la que el corazón no bombea sangre.

Carjacking/secuestro de un auto Robar o secuestrar un auto por la fuerza.

Carotid pulse/pulso carotídeo El latido cardíaco que se siente a ambos lados del cuello.

Cartilage/cartílago Tejido conjuntivo fuerte y flexible.

Cerebellum/cerebelo La segunda parte del cerebro en tamaño.

Cerebral palsy/parálisis cerebral Un grupo de trastornos neurológicos no progresivos que resultan de daños al cerebro antes de nacer, durante el parto, en el período neonatal o en la primera infancia.

Cerebrum/cerebro La parte más grande y más compleja del encéfalo.

Cervix/cérvix El cuello del útero.

Chemotherapy/quimioterapia El uso de medicamentos en el tratamiento del cáncer.

Child abuse/maltrato infantil Daño físico, incluyendo abuso sexual, o daño emocional que se hace a un niño o niña.

Chlamydia/clamidia Infección causada por una bacteria que afecta la vagina en las mujeres y la uretra en los hombres.

Chlorofluorocarbons (CFCs)/clorofluorocarbonos Compuestos del cloro, el flúor y el carbón.

Cholesterol/colesterol Sustancia semejante a la grasa que se produce en el hígado de todos los animales y, como consecuencia, presente únicamente en alimentos de origen animal.

Chorionic villi sampling/biopsia de vellosidades coriónicas Examen en el que se extrae una pequeña muestra de membrana del corion, una capa de tejido que se desarrolla en la placenta.

Choroid/coroides La capa media de la pared del globo ocular.

Chromosomes/cromosomas Estructuras diminutas dentro del núcleo de las células que contienen información sobre los rasgos hereditarios.

Chyme/quimo Mezcla cremosa y líquida de alimento y jugos gástricos.

Circumcision/circuncisión Procedimiento quirúrgico por el que se extirpa el prepucio del pene.

Cirrhosis/cirrosis Trastorno en el que se destruye el tejido del hígado y es reemplazado por tejido fibroso.

Clinical psychologist/psicólogo clínico Psicólogo o psicóloga que diagnostica y trata los trastornos emocionales y de comportamiento, pero no puede recetar medicamentos.

Clique/camarilla Grupo de amigos pequeño y restringido, cuyos miembros suelen venir de medios similares o compartir gustos, y que excluye a otros que considera ajenos a su círculo.

Closure/cierre La conclusión de una de las partes más intensas del proceso de duelo.

Cluster of suicides/suicidios múltiples Proliferación de suicidios que ocurren dentro de un período corto de tiempo e involucran a varias personas de la misma escuela o comunidad.

Codependents/codependientes Personas que se preocupan demasiado con el problema de adicción de otro y sienten el impulso de arreglarlo o controlarlo.

Cognition/entendimiento La capacidad de razonar y deducir soluciones abstractas.

Commitment/compromiso Una promesa o voto.

Communication/comunicación Proceso por el cual uno envía mensajes y recibe mensajes de otros.

Compromise/acuerdo Arreglo en el que cada persona cede algo para lograr una solución que satisfaga a todos.

Confidentiality/confidencialidad Respetar la privacidad de ambas partes y mantener en secreto los detalles.

Confirmatory test/análisis de confirmación Prueba altamente eficaz utilizada para confirmar los resultados de un ELISA (EIA) positivo.

Conflict/conflicto Cualquier desacuerdo, lucha o pelea.

Conflict resolution/resolución de conflictos Proceso dar solución a un conflicto por medio de la cooperación y la búsqueda de soluciones en común.

Congenital/congénito Que está presente al nacer.

Congestive heart failure/insuficiencia cardíaca congestiva Debilitamiento lento y progresivo del corazón debido a la sobrecarga.

Conservation/conservación   Preocupación por preservar el medio ambiente.

Constructive criticism/crítica constructiva   Comentarios hechos sin hostilidad que señalan problemas y potencialmente pueden ayudar a alguien a cambiar.

Contaminant/contaminante   Sustancia que echa a perder o infecta.

Cool-down/enfriamiento   Actividad que se inicia para reducir gradualmente la actividad.

Cooperation/cooperación   Trabajar en conjunto para beneficio de todos.

Coordination/coordinación   La capacidad para usar juntas y bien dos o más partes del cuerpo, o de usar los sentidos junto con las partes del cuerpo.

Cornea/córnea   Lente principal del ojo que realiza la mayor parte de la tarea de enfocar.

Crisis/crisis   Un cambio extremo en la vida de una persona.

Crisis center/centro de emergencias   Establecimiento equipado para manejar emergencias y para orientar a personas que necesitan ayuda.

Cross-contamination/contaminación cruzada   La propagación de bacterias de uno a otro alimento.

Cross-training/entrenamiento combinado   Combinar varias rutinas de ejercicio para ejercitar distintos sistemas del cuerpo.

Culture/cultura   Las creencias, costumbres y comportamientos colectivos de un grupo.

Custody/custodia   Una decisión legal sobre quién tiene la responsabilidad de tomar decisiones que afectan a los niños y quién tiene la responsabilidad física de cuidarlos.

Cystitis/cistitis   Infección bacteriana de la vejiga que ocurre con mayor frecuencia en las mujeres.

D

Dandruff/caspa   Trastorno en que se cae la capa más superficial de células de piel muertas del cuero cabelludo.

Date rape/violación durante una cita   La violación que ocurre entre dos personas que están saliendo juntas.

Defense mechanisms/mecanismos de defensa   Estrategias que se usan para hacer frente a sentimientos y situaciones muy fuertes o estresantes.

Deforestation/deforestación   La destrucción de los bosques.

Delayed grief response/Reacción tardía del duelo   La postergación de las etapas más intensas del duelo.

Delirium tremens (DTs)/delirium tremens   Los dramáticos efectos físicos y psicológicos del síndrome de abstinencia del alcohol.

Depressants/depresores   Drogas que tienden a desacelerar el sistema nervioso central.

Depression/depresión   Sentimientos de desamparo, desesperanza y tristeza.

Dermis/dermis   La capa interna y gruesa de la piel.

Desertification/desertificación   La transformación de praderas y campos de lluvia o regadío en zonas de condiciones desérticas.

Designated drivers/conductores designados   Personas en un contexto social que deciden no tomar para así poder conducir un auto y evitar riesgos para ellos y para otros.

Designer drugs/drogas ilegales de preparado especial   Sustancias sintéticas cuyo fin es imitar los efectos de los narcóticos y alucinógenos.

Detachment/desapego   El proceso de desligarse o dejar de estar involucrado en la adicción de otro, rehusando a que esa adicción controle nuestra vida.

Detoxification/desintoxicación   El proceso de limpiar el cuerpo de drogas.

Developmental task/tarea del desarrollo   Algo que debe ocurrir en una etapa en particular para que la persona continúe su crecimiento para convertirse en un adulto sano y maduro.

Diabetes/diabetes   Enfermedad crónica que afecta el modo en que las células del cuerpo convierten el alimento en energía.

Diaphragm/diafragma   Músculo que separa la cavidad torácica de la cavidad abdominal.

Digestion/digestión   La descomposición física y química del alimento para su uso por las células del cuerpo.

Disability/incapacidad   Cualquier impedimento físico o mental que limita la actividad normal, incluyendo, ver, oír, caminar o hablar.

Distress/aflicción   Tensión negativa.

Domestic violence/violencia doméstica   Cualquier acto de violencia que involucre a miembros de una misma familia.

Drug watches/agrupaciones vecinales antidrogas   Esfuerzos comunitarios organizados en los que residentes de un vecindario tratan de impedir la compraventa y el consumo de drogas patrullando, vigilando, denunciando y de otras formas.

Drug-Free School Zones/zonas libres de drogas alrededor de las escuelas   Áreas dentro de los 1,000 pies de distancia de una escuela señalizadas con letreros, dentro de las cuales aquel que sea hallado vendiendo drogas recibe penas particularmente severas.

E

Electrocution/electrocución   Muerte que resulta de una descarga eléctrica de alto voltaje que pasa por el cuerpo.

Electrolytes/electrólitos   Nutrientes que se cargan de electricidad al ser sumergidos en una solución.

Elimination/eliminación   La expulsión de alimento sin digerir o desechos corporales.

ELISA (EIA)/ELISA Prueba que detecta la presencia de anticuerpos del VIH en la sangre.

Embryo/embrión Racimo de células en desarrollo que se forma después de la implantación.

Emetic/emético Un agente que induce el vómito.

Emotional abuse/maltrato emocional Patrón de comportamiento que atenta contra el desarrollo emocional y la autovaloración de un niño o niña.

Emotional initmacy/intimidad emocional La capacidad de vivir una relación cariñosa y afectuosa con otra persona con quien puedes compartir tus sentimientos más intimos.

Emotional maturity/madurez emocional Estado en el que las capacidades mentales y emocionales de un individuo se han desarrollado plenamente.

Emotions/emociones Sentimientos.

Empathy/empatía La capacidad para imaginar y comprender cómo se siente otra persona.

Empty-nest syndrome/síndrome del nido vacío Sentimientos de desesperación y soledad que suceden cuando los hijos se van de la casa y entran en la edad adulta.

Enabling/posibilitar Tratar de proteger a una persona que tiene problemas con el alcohol o las drogas para que no tenga que enfrentar las consecuencias de su problema de adicción.

Endocrine glands/glándulas endócrinas Estructuras de secreción interna que producen hormonas.

Enriched food/alimentos enriquecidos Alimento al cual se le agregan los nutrientes que ha perdido durante el procesamiento.

Environment/medio ambiente La suma total de lo que te rodeaótu familia, el lugar adonde te has criado, el lugar donde vives ahora y la totalidad de tus experiencias.

Epidemic/epidemia Brote de una enfermedad infecciosa que afecta a una población numerosa.

Epidemiology/epidemiología El estudio científico de las epidemias.

Epidermis/epidermis La capa delgada exterior de la piel.

Epilepsy/epilepsia Trastorno del sistema nervioso que se caracteriza por ataques recurrentesóepisodios repentinos de actividad eléctrica descontrolada en el cerebro.

Escalate/escalar Avanzar a una situación que no es sana e incluso puede ser peligrosa para todas las partes involucradas.

Ethanol/etanol El tipo de alcohol que se encuentra en las bebidas alcohólicas.

Euphoria/euforia Sentimiento temporario de bienestar intenso o felicidad que puede verse sucedido por un "bajón" o derrumbe anímico completo.

Eustress/estrés positivo Tensión benéfica.

Exploited/explotado Utilizado para beneficio de otro.

Extensors/extensores Músculos que abren una articulación.

External auditory canal/canal auditivo externo Un conducto de más o menos 1 pulgada (2.5 cm) de largo.

F

Fallopian tubes/trompas de Falopio Un par de trompas con extensiones similares a dedos que atraen al óvulo.

Family counseling/terapia familiar Terapia para restaurar las relaciones sanas en una familia.

Famine/hambruna Escasez generalizada de alimento.

Fatigue/fatiga Tercera etapa de la respuesta al estrés que se manifiesta en un sentimiento de cansancio que reduce el nivel de actividad.

Fatty liver/hígado graso Trastorno en el que se acumula en el hígado grasa que no puede ser descompuesta.

Feedback/retroalimentación Mensajes de otros que nos indican lo que piensan sobre quiénes somos y cómo somos.

Fermentation/fermentación La acción química de la levadura sobre los azúcares.

Fertilization/fertilización La unión de una célula reproductiva masculina con una femenina.

Fetal alcohol syndrome/síndrome de alcoholismo fetal Trastorno en el que un feto se ha visto afectado en forma negativa mental y físicamente por la ingestión de mucho alcohol por parte de su madre durante el embarazo.

Fetus/feto Nombre que se le da al embrión desde la octava semana hasta el nacimiento.

Fibrillation/fibrilación El latido rápido e ineficaz del corazón en una de dos cámaras llamadas ventrículos.

Fire extinguisher/extintor de incendios Aparato portátil que apaga pequeños incendios al lanzar sustancias químicas que extinguen el fuego.

First aid/primeros auxilios La atención médica inmediata y temporaria que se presta a alguien que se ha enfermado o lesionado.

Flexibility/flexibilidad La capacidad de mover una parte del cuerpo a través de todo un espectro de movimiento.

Fexors/flexores Músculos que cierran una articulación.

Follicles/folículos Pequeños sacos o bolsas de la piel.

Food additives/aditivos Sustancias que se añaden a los alimentos con el propósito de obtener un efecto deseado.

Food allergy/alergia alimenticia Trastorno en el que el sistema inmune del cuerpo reacciona exageradamente a ciertos alimentos.

Foodborne illness/intoxicación alimenticia
Enfermedad causada por los alimentos.

Fortification/fortificación El proceso de añadir nutrientes que no están presentes por naturaleza.

Foster care/acogimiento familiar Bajo la guía y supervisión de una familia encabezada por padres o una padre o madre que no tiene relación sanguinea con el niño.

Friendship/amistad Una relación significativa entre dos personas basada en el cariño, la consideración y la confianza.

Frostbite/congelación Condición que ocurre cuando se congela el tejido del cuerpo.

G

Gametes/gametos Células reproductivas que producen las gónadas.

Gangrene/gangrena La muerte de tejido en alguna parte del cuerpo.

Gastric juices/jugos gástricos Secreciones de la capa interior del estómago que contienen pepsina, y ácido hidroclorídrico.

Gateway drugs/drogas precursoras Drogas que a menudo conducen al consumo serio y peligroso de drogas.

Generativity/capacidad de generar Volver la atención más allá de uno mismo en el presente y empezar a ocuparse de las generaciones futuras.

Generic/genérico Versión más barata de un medicamento que puede reemplazar a un medicamento de marca.

Genes/genes Pequeños segmentos de las moléculas de ADN (ácido desoxirribonucleico).

Genital herpes/herpes genital Llagas similares a ampollas en la zona genital.

Genital warts/verrugas genitales Verrugas rosadas o rojizas con una textura similar a la coliflor que aparecen en la zona genital.

Glucose/glucosa Azúcar simple que representa la principal fuente de energía del cuerpo.

Glycogen/glucógeno Sustancia similar al almidón.

Goal/meta Objetivo que quieres lograr y para el cual hay que planificar y trabajar.

Gonads/gónadas Los ovarios y los testículos.

Gonorrhea/gonorrea Enfermedad de transmisión sexual causada por bacterias que afectan la membrana mucosa genital, principalmente en el revestimiento de la uretra en los hombres y en el cuello del útero y la vagina en las mujeres.

Greenhouse effect/efecto invernadero
Desaceleración del ritmo al que la tierra despide calor, lo cual causa un aumento en la temperatura de la tierra.

Grief reaction/reacción al duelo La totalidad de la respuesta de un individuo a una pérdida significativa.

H

Halfway houses/establecimientos de transición
Entidades de tratamiento continuado que ofrecen alojamiento, asesoramiento y reuniones de apoyo a quienes se están recuperando de una adicción severa.

Hallucinogens/alucinógenos Drogas que alteran el estado de ánimo, los pensamientos y las percepciones sensitivas, incluyendo la vista, el oído, el olfato y el tacto.

Hardy personality/personalidad robusta Un tipo de personalidad que parece poder mantener un buen estado de salud pese a sufrir estrés grave o incluso traumático.

Hashish/hachís Resina color café oscuro que se obtiene de la punta del cáñamo.

Hazardous wastes/residuos peligrosos Cualquier sustancia que sea explosiva, corrosiva, inflamable o tóxica para la vida humana u otras formas de vida.

Health/salud La combinación del bienestar físico, mental-emocional y social.

Health care facility/establecimiento de atención médica Cualquier lugar atendido por profesionales de la salud y equipado para prestar servicios de salud.

Health-care providers/prestadores de servicios de salud Profesionales entrenados en el campo de los servicios de salud.

Health consumer/consumidor de servicios de salud Persona que utiliza productos o servicios de salud.

Health insurance/seguro médico Plan para cubrir una parte o la totalidad de los gastos asociados al tratamiento médico.

Health literacy/educación sobre salud La capacidad de un individuo para obtener, interpretar y comprender información básica relacionada con la salud, y de utilizar tal información y servicios con el fin de promover su salud y bienestar.

Health maintenance organization HMO)/organización para el mantenimiento de la salud Un grupo de médicos de distintas especialidades que trabajan juntos para prestar servicios médicos a los socios de la organización.

Health skills/recursos de salud Instrumentos y estrategias específicos que conducen a decisiones mejores y más informadas en lo que concierne a la salud.

Heat cramps/calambres Espasmos musculares que resultan de la pérdida de grandes cantidades de sal y agua a través de la transpiración.

Heat exhaustion/golpe de calor Calentamiento excesivo del cuerpo que se manifiesta por piel fría y húmeda y síntomas de choque.

Hemodialysis/hemodiálisis Técnica por la cual se limpia la sangre de desechos con un riñón artificial.

Hemoglobin/hemoglobina La parte de la sangre que lleva oxígeno.

Heredity/herencia   Todos los rasgos y propiedades que se transmiten biológicamente de padres a hijos.

Hernia/hernia   Protuberancia de un órgano o tejido a través de un área débil del músculo.

Hiatal hernia/hernia hiatal   Trastorno en el que parte del estómago sobresale a través de una abertura en el diafragma.

Hierarchy of needs/jerarquía de necesidades   Lista categorizada de las necesidades esenciales para el crecimiento y desarrollo humano, presentadas en orden ascendente desde las más básicas hasta las que producen mayor satisfacción y sentimiento de realización.

HIV reactive/VIH positivo   Infectado con el VIH.

Homicide/homicidio   El asesinato intencional de un ser humano por otro.

Hormones/hormonas   Sustancias químicas producidas por glándulas de secreción internas que regulan la actividad de distintas células del organismo.

Hostility/hostilidad   El uso intencional de comportamiento poco amable o antipático.

Human immunodeficiency virus (HIV)/virus de inmunodeficiencia humana (VIH)   Virus que ataca el sistema inmune del cuerpo.

Hunger/hambre   Impulso natural que nos protege de la inanición.

Hurricane/huracán   Tormenta fuerte con lluvia y vendavales.

Hydration/hidratación   El proceso de agregar fluidos al cuerpo.

Hypertension/hipertensión   Presión arterial alta.

Hypochondria/hipocondria   Preocupación por el cuerpo y miedo a supuestas enfermedades que son inexistentes.

Hypothermia/hipotermia   Condición en que la temperatura del cuerpo baja a niveles peligrosos.

I

"I" message/mensaje "yo"   Declaración en la que alguien expresa sus sentimientos usando el pronombre "yo".

Illegal drugs/drogas ilegales   Drogas que se compran ilícitamente en la calle.

Illicit drug use/consumo ilegal de drogas   El consumo o venta de cualquier sustancia ilegal o prohibida.

Immunity/inmunidad   Las defensas naturales del cuerpo contra la infección.

Immunization/vacunación   Programa por el cual se inmuniza contra una enfermedad a una comunidad u otra población numerosa.

Impaired glucose tolerance (IGT)/Alteración en la tolerancia a la glucosa   Trastorno en el que los niveles de azúcar en la sangre son más altos que lo normal, pero no tan altos como para ser clasificados como diabetes.

Incontinence/incontinencia   La incapacidad del cuerpo para controlar la vejiga y la eliminación de desechos.

Indigestion/indigestión   Malestar y ardor en la boca del estómago.

Infatuation/amor desmedido   Sentimientos de pasión exagerada por otra persona.

Infectious disease/enfermedad infecciosa   Enfermedad causada por organismos que entran en el cuerpo humano y se multiplican.

Infertility/infertilidad   La incapacidad de una mujer para quedar embarazada.

Ingestion/ingestión   La introducción de alimento en el cuerpo.

Inhalants/inhalantes   Sustancias con vapores que se huelen y se aspiran para inducir un estado de alucinación.

Inpatient treatment/tratamiento de pacientes internados   Atención médica o psicológica durante la cual una persona permanece en un establecimiento médico o de rehabilitación.

Insulin/insulina   Hormona que se produce en el páncreas y que ayuda al cuerpo a transformar glucosa en energía.

Integrity/entereza   Sentimiento de integridad y satisfacción.

Integumentary system/sistema integumentario   El sistema corporal que incluye la piel, el cabello, las uñas, las glándulas sebáceas y las glándulas sudoríparas.

Internal conflicts/conflictos internos   Luchas dentro de uno mismo.

Interpersonal conflicts/conflictos interpersonales   Desacuerdos entre grupos de cualquier tamaño, ya sean dos personas o dos países.

Intervention/intervención   La interrupción del ciclo continuo de adicción antes de que el adicto o el alcohólico toque fondo.

Intoxication/ebriedad   Disminución de la capacidad física y mental como resultado del consumo de alcohol.

Intravenous (IV) drugs/drogas intravenosas   Drogas que se inyectan en las venas.

Isokinetic exercise/ejercicio isoquinético   Actividad que implica resistencia a lo largo de un espectro completo de movimiento.

Isometric exercise/ejercicio isométrico   Actividad que usa la tensión muscular para mejorar la fuerza muscular con poco o ningún movimiento de la parte del cuerpo.

Isotonic exercise/ejercicio isotónico   Actividad que combina la contracción muscular con movimientos repetitivos.

L

Labyrinth/laberinto   Oído interno.

Lacrimal gland/lagrimal   La glándula encargada de producir lágrimas.

Larynx/laringe   Órgano encargado de la voz.

Latency/latencia   Etapa en la que el virus está presente pero inactivo.

Leukoplakia/leucoplasia   Manchas gruesas, blanquecinas y apergaminadas presentes en de la boca de quienes mascan tabaco y que pueden evolucionar hacia el cáncer de boca.

Lifestyle activities/actividades del estilo de vida   Formas de actividad física, incorporadas a la rutina diaria normal o al esparcimiento, que promueven la buena salud a lo largo de la vida.

Lifestyle factors/factores del estilo de vida   Hábitos y comportamientos personales relacionados con el modo de vida que afectan el nivel de salud.

Ligaments/ligamentos   Cordones resistentes de tejido fibroso y algo elástico que unen los extremos de los huesos a la altura de la articulación.

Linoleic acid/ácido linoleico   Ácido graso esencial que es fundamental para el crecimiento y la salud de la piel, pero que no se produce en el cuerpo.

Lipid/lípido   Sustancia grasosa que no se disuelve en agua.

Look-alike drugs/drogas de imitación   Drogas que se fabrican de manera tal que se parezcan a drogas ilegales específicas.

Lymph/linfa   Fluido amarillo transparente que rellena los espacios alrededor de las células del cuerpo.

Lymphocytes/linfocitos   Un tipo de glóbulo blanco que protege al organismo contra los patógenos.

M

Mainstream smoke/humo directo   El humo que exhala el fumador.

Malignant/maligno   Canceroso.

Manipulation/manipulación   Forma solapada o deshonesta de controlar o influir en los demás.

Marijuana/marihuana   La planta del cáñamo (cannabis) que se fuma, se come o se toma por sus efectos intoxicantes.

Marital adjustment/adaptación al matrimonio   La forma en que las personas se ajustan o se adaptan entre sí y al matriomio.

Mastication/masticación   El proceso de mascar.

Mediator/mediador   Persona que ayuda a otros a resolver cuestiones para satisfacción de ambas partes.

Meditation/mediación   Proceso en el que personas específicamente entrenadas ayudan a otras a resolver sus conflictos de manera pacífica.

Medicaid/Medicaid   Programa de ayuda para asistencia médica destinado a personas de todas las edades que no tienen los recursos para financiar su atención médica.

Medical history/historial clínico   Información completa y amplia sobre vacunaciones y enfermedades pasadas de un paciente.

Medicare/Medicare   Programa de seguro de salud accesible a personas de 65 años de edad o más y a aquellos que reciben beneficios por incapacidad a través del seguro social.

Medicine misuse/mal uso de medicamentos   Utilizar un medicamento para un fin distinto al que tiene.

Medicines/medicamentos   Sustancias que, al ser ingeridas o introducidas en el cuerpo, ayudan a prevenir o curar enfermedades u otros problemas médicos.

Megadoses/megadosis   Grandes cantidades de suplementos nutricionales.

Melanin/melanina   El pigmento que da su coloración a la piel, el cabello y el iris de los ojos.

Melanoma/melanoma   Un tipo frecuentemente mortal de cáncer de la piel.

Menopause/menopausia   El detenimiento permanente de la ovulación y la menstruación.

Menstrual cycle/ciclo menstrual   El tiempo que transcurre entre el comienzo de un periodo menstrual y el inicio del siguiente.

Mental disorder/trastorno mental   Enfermedad de la mente que puede afectar los pensamientos, sentimientos y comportamientos de una persona, impidiéndole llevar una vida feliz, sana y productiva.

Mental health/salud mental   Tener una actitud general positiva, sentirse cómodo con uno mismo y los demás, y ser capaz de enfrentar los desafíos y las demandas de la vida.

Mental retardation/retardo mental   Capacidad intelectual inferior al promedio presente desde el nacimiento o la primera infancia y asociada a dificultades en el aprendizaje y la adaptación social.

Metabolism/metabolismo   El proceso por el cual el cuerpo obtiene energía del alimento.

Metastasis/metástasis   La propagación del cáncer desde el lugar donde se originó a otras partes del cuerpo.

Minerals/minerales   Sustancias inorgánicas que el cuerpo no puede producir pero que actúan como catalizadores, regulando muchos procesos vitales del cuerpo.

Miscarriage/aborto espontáneo   Pérdida espontánea de un embarazo.

Modeling/imitar   Copiar los comportamientos de aquellos a quienes uno está expuesto.

Mucous membranes/membranas mucosas   Revestimiento suave semejante a la piel de muchas partes del cuerpo.

Muscle cramp/calambre muscular   Espasmo o contractura súbita de un músculo.

Muscle tone/tono muscular La tensión natural de las fibras musculares.

Muscular endurance/resistencia muscular La capacidad de los músculos para realizar tareas físicas difíciles durante un período de tiempo sin fatigarse.

Muscular strength/fuerza muscular La cantidad de fuerza que puede ejercer un músculo.

N

Narcotics/narcóticos Drogas derivadas de la planta del opio que tienen un efecto sedante.

Neglect/descuido No proveer para las necesidades físicas y emocionales de una niño o niña.

Negotiation/negociación Proceso en el que se hacen concesiones recíprocas para llegar a un acuerdo.

Nephrons/nefrones Las unidades funcionales de los riñones.

Neurologist/neurólogo Médico especializado en los trastornos orgánicos del cerebro y el sistema nervioso.

Neurons/neuronas Células nerviosas.

Neutrophils/neutrófilos Los fagocitos principales involucrados en el proceso de fagocitosis.

Nicotine/nicotina La droga adictiva presente en los cigarrillos.

Nicotine substitutes/sustitutos de la nicotina Formas manufacturadas de nicotina que envían pequeñas cantidades de la droga al organismo de quien las usa mientras él o ella está intentando dejar el hábito del tabaco.

Nicotine withdrawal/síndrome de abstinencia de la nicotina El proceso que ocurre cuando se deja de consumir nicotina, una droga adictiva.

Nongonococcal urethritis/uretritis no gonocóxica Infección causada por varios tipos diferentes de organismos similares a las bacterias que infectan la uretra en los hombres y el cuello del útero en las mujeres.

Noninfectious diseases/enfermedades no infecciosas Enfermedades que no son transmitidas por medio de un patógeno.

Nutrient supplements/suplementos nutricionales Píldoras, polvos, líquidos y otros nutrientes sintéticos.

Nutrient-dense/de alto valor nutritivo Alimentos ricos en nutrientes en relación a su contenido calórico.

nutrients/nutrientes Sustancias presentes en el alimento que el cuerpo necesita para ejercer adecuadamente funciones como crecer, reconstituirse y disponer de una provisión de energía.

Nutrition/nutrición Proceso por el cual el cuerpo incorpora y utiliza los alimentos.

O

Obesity/obesidad Exceso de grasa o tejido adiposo en el cuerpo.

Occupational Safety and Health Administration (OSHA)/Departamento de Seguridad y Sanidad Laboral Agencia federal responsable de promover condiciones seguras y sanitarias en el lugar de trabajo.

Ossicles/huesillos del oído Tres huesillos móviles unidos entre sí.

Ossification/osificación El proceso por el que se forman, renuevan y reparan los huesos.

Osteoarthritis/osteoartritis Enfermedad que afecta principalmente las articulaciones que soportan peso de las rodillas y caderas, causando molestias y dolores, especialmente al moverse.

Otosclerosis/otoesclerosis Trastorno hereditario en el que un sobrehueso impide el movimiento de los huesillos del oído.

Outpatient surgical facility/establecimiento de cirugía para pacientes ambulatorios Lugar adonde se opera a pacientes que son dados de alta el mismo día.

Outpatient treatment/tratamiento de pacientes ambulatorios Atención médica y psicológica en una institución para alguien que quiere dejar el alcohol y las drogas.

Ova/óvulos Células reproductivas femeninas.

Ovaries/ovarios Glándulas sexuales femeninas que contienen los óvulos y producen hormonas sexuales femeninas.

Overdose/sobredosis Reacción grave o hasta mortal a la ingestión de una gran cantidad de droga.

Overexertion/esfuerzo excesivo Ejercitar el cuerpo en exceso.

Overload/sobrecarga Ejercitar el cuerpo en forma más exigente que lo normal.

Over-the-counter (OTC) medicines/medicamentos sin receta Remedios que se pueden comprar sin receta médica.

Ovulation/ovulación El proceso de liberar un óvulo maduro cada mes.

P

Pancreas/páncreas Glándula que cumple funciones en dos sistemasóel digestivo y el endócrino.

Paranoia/paranoia Suspicacia irracional o recelo hacia los demás.

Parasites/parásitos Organismos que viven en o dentro de otro organismo y obtienen su alimento de él.

Parathyroid glands/glándulas paratirodes Estructuras que producen la hormona paratiroides, que regula el equilibrio de calcio y fósforo del organismo.

Particulates/partículas Pequeños fragmentos suspendidos de materia que son transportados por el aire.

Passive/pasivo El que renuncia, cede o retrocede sin hacer valer sus derechos y necesidades.

Passive immunity/inmunidad pasiva La inmunidad temporaria que un recién nacido obtiene de su madre.

Passive smoke/humo indirecto Humo de cigarrillo, cigarro o pipa que inhalan los no fumadores, y también el humo que permanece en un ambiente cerrado una vez que el fumador ha terminado de fumar.

Pasteurized/pasteurizado Sometido a un proceso de calentamiento para destruir o retrasar el crecimiento de patógenos.

Peer mediators/mediadores paritarios Estudiantes entrenados para ayudar a otros estudiantes a encontrar formas justas de arreglar sus diferencias.

Peer pressure/presión del grupo de pares El control y la influencia que pueden ejercer sobre ti las personas de tu misma edad.

Peers/grupo de pares Personas de la misma edad que comparten intereses similares.

Penis/pene Órgano en forma de tubo que se une al cuerpo justo encima de los testículos.

Peptic ulcer/úlcera péptica Llaga en el revestimiento interno del trayecto digestivo.

Periodontal disease/enfermedad periodontal Inflamación de las estructuras periodontales.

Periodontium/periodonto La área que rodea los dientes.

Perishable/perecedero Que puede echarse a perder.

Peristalsis/peristalsis Una serie de contracciones musculares involuntarias.

Personal identity/identidad personal Los factores que nos hacen únicos y diferentes a todos los demás.

Personality/personalidad Conjunto complejo de características que nos hace únicos y diferentes a todo los demás.

Personality disorders/trastornos de la personalidad Una variedad de enfermedades psicológicas que afectan la capacidad de una persona para relacionarse con los demás.

Phagocytosis/fagocitosis El proceso por el cual los fagocitos rodean y destruyen los patógenos.

Pharynx/faringe Garganta.

Phobias/fobias Miedos irracionales.

Physical activity/actividad física Cualquier forma de movimiento, ya sea intencional, como en el caso de los deportes y el entretenimiento, o incidental, como en el caso de realizar las tareas hogareñas.

Physical fitness/buen estado físico La capacidad de realizar fácilmente las tareas diarias y tener suficiente energía de reserva para responder a demandas inesperadas.

Physical maturity/madurez física Estado en el cual el cuerpo y todos sus órganos han alcanzado un nivel completo de desarrollo.

Pituitary gland/glándula pituitaria Estructura que regula y controla la actividad de todas las otras glándulas endócrinas.

Placenta/placenta Capa exterior de células del embrión con tejido materno rico en sangre.

Planned pregnancy/embarazo planeado Tomar la decisión de quedar encinta antes de concebir.

Plaque/placa dental Película pegajosa e incolora que actúa sobre el azúcar formando ácidos que destruyen el esmalte dental e irritan las encías.

Plasma/plasma El líquido en el que están suspendidos los demás componentes de la sangre.

Platelets/plaquetas Células que previenen la pérdida de sangre.

Platonic friendship/amistad platónica Una relación con un miembro del sexo opuesto en la que hay afecto pero no hay actividad sexual.

Pleurisy/pleuresía Inflamación de la membrana interna que reviste los pulmones y la cavidad torácica.

Pneumonia/neumonía Grave inflamación de los pulmones.

Poison/veneno Una sustancia, ya sea sólida, líquida o gaseosa, que causa daño, enfermedad o la muerte al ser introducida en el cuerpo.

Poison control center/centro de control de intoxicaciones Línea telefónica que funciona las 24 horas y provee asesoramiento sobre cómo tratar a las víctimas de envenenamiento.

Power/potencia La capacidad de ejercer fuerza con mucha rapidez.

Preferred provider organization (PPO)/plan de salud Un tipo de seguro de salud en el que los prestadores de servicios médicos acuerdan cobrar menos a los socios del plan.

Prejudice/prejuicio Sentimiento negativo hacia alguien o hacia algo que no está basado en la experiencia sino más bien en estereotipos.

Prescription medicines/medicamentos con receta Remedios que no pueden ser usados en forma segura sin la aprobación por escrito de un médico acreditado.

Pressure point/punto de presión Uno de varios puntos a lo largo de la arteria mayor que provee de sangre a una extremidad afectada.

Prevention/prevención Practicar hábitos sanos para mantenerse bien y libre de enfermedades y otros malestares.

Primary care physician/médico de cabecera Un profesional de la medicina que provee la atención de salud primaria.

Priorities/prioridades Aquellas metas, tareas o actividades que uno juzga más importantes que otras.

Priorities/prioridades Aquellas cosas que están en primer lugar en cuanto a su importancia.

Profound deafness/sordera profunda Pérdida del oído tan severa que la persona afectada no puede beneficiarse del uso de amplificación mecánica como la de un audífono.

Progression/progresión Aumento gradual del esfuerzo necesario para lograr un nivel de estado físico más alto.

Proteins/proteínas Nutrientes que ayudan a producir y mantener los tejidos del cuerpo.

Psychiatric social worker/trabajador social para casos psiquiátricos Alguien especializado en casos psiquiátricos que trabaja en un hospital psiquiátrico, clínica de salud mental o agencia de servicios familiares y provee asesoramiento y tratamiento a personas con problemas emocionales.

Psychiatrist/psiquiatra Médico especializado en el diagnóstico y tratamiento de trastornos mentales que puede recetar medicamentos.

Psychoactive drugs/drogas psicoactivas Sustancias químicas que afectan el sistema nervioso central e interfieren con el funcionamiento normal del cerebro.

Psychologists/psicólogos Profesional con título doctoral especializado en el diagnóstico y tratamiento de trastornos emocionales.

Psychosomatic response/respuesta psicosomática Trastorno físico que resulta del estrés más bien que de una lesión o enfermedad.

Puberty/pubertad La etapa en la que hombres y mujeres adquieren la capacidad física de reproducirse.

Public health/salud pública Esfuerzo comunitario para controlar y promover el bienestar de la población.

Pulp/pulpa El tejido vivo situado dentro de los dientes.

Q

Quackery/curanderismo Un tipo de fraude médico.

R

Rabies/rabia Enfermedad viral del sistema nervioso que eventualmente conduce a la locura y la muerte.

Random violence/violencia al azar Violencia cometida sin ninguna razón en particular.

Rape/violación Relación sexual forzada.

Reaction time/tiempo de reacción La velocidad del movimiento tan pronto una persona se da cuenta de que debe moverse.

Rechanneling/reorientación Transferir o recanalizar tus energías.

Recommended Dietary Allowances (RDA)/Raciones Dietéticas Recomendadas (RDR) Las cantidades de nutrientes que previenen deficiencias y excesos en la mayoría de las personas saludables.

Recovery/recuperación Aprender a vivir sin alcohol ni drogas.

Recycling/reciclaje El tratamiento de la basura de forma que pueda volver a usarse, y la conciencia de que tales prácticas existen.

Reflex/reflejo Respuesta espontánea del cuerpo a un estímulo.

Refusal skills/técnicas para rehusarse Habilidades que te ayudan a rehusarte cuando te instan a participar en comportamientos poco seguros o poco sanos.

Rehydration/rehidratación Restaurar los líquidos que el cuerpo ha perdido.

Relapses/recaídas Deslices en la recuperación, o retornos periódicos a la bebida y el consumo de drogas.

Relationship/relación Vínculo o conexión entre las personas.

Relaxation response/respuesta a la relajación Estado de reposo profundo que puede alcanzarse al practicar regularmente una o más técnicas de relajación.

Repetitive motion injury/lesión por uso repetido Daño a los tejidos causado por la reiteración prolongada de movimientos.

Rescue breathing/asistencia respiratoria de emergencia Respiración artificial.

Resilience/flexibilidad La capacidad de adaptarse de forma efectiva y recuperarse de una desilusión, una dificultad o una crisis.

Resistance/resistencia La segunda etapa de la respuesta al estrés, cuando el cuerpo busca reparar el daño sufrido a raíz del hecho estresante y volver a su estado normal.

Respiration/respiración El intercambio de gases entre el cuerpo y el medio ambiente.

Respiratory failure/insuficiencia respiratoria Estado en el que el aire no puede llegar a los pulmones.

Resting heart rate/frecuencia cardíaca basal La cantidad de veces que late el corazón en un minuto cuando está en reposo.

Retina/retina Membrana sensible a la luz en la que la córnea y el cristalino proyectan las imágenes.

Rheumatoid arthritis/artritis reumatoidea Inflamación destructiva e incapacitante de las articulaciones.

Risk factors/factores de riesgo Actos o comportamientos que representan un riesgo potencial para la salud.

Road rage/furia del conductor Cuando se combinan la ira intensa y el acto de conducir un vehículo.

Role/papel La función o papel que juegas en una relación.

Rubella/rubéola Erupción semejante a la del sarampión.

S

Schizophrenia/esquizofrenia Serio trastorno mental que significa "mente dividida".

Sclera/esclerótica La capa externa blanca y resistente del ojo.

Sebaceous glands/glándulas sebáceas Estructuras de la piel que producen una secreción aceitosa llamada sebo.

Sedentary lifestyle/estilo de vida sedentario Estilo de vida que requiere poco movimiento o ejercicio.

Self-actualization/autorrealización El esfuerzo por llegar a ser lo mejor posible.

Self-control/autocontrol La capacidad para usar la sensatez en lugar de las emociones.

Self-directed/por voluntad propia Tomar decisiones correctas en cuanto al comportamiento cuando no hay adultos que hagan cumplir las reglas.

Self-esteem/autoestima La confianza y valoración que uno siente respecto de sí mismo.

Semen/semen Líquido espeso que contiene espermatozoides y otras secreciones del órgano reproductivo masculino.

Sex characteristics/características sexuales Los rasgos relacionados con el sexo.

Sexual assault/agresión sexual Cualquier ataque sexual intencional contra otra persona.

Sexually transmitted diseases (STDs)/enfermedades de transmisión sexual (ETS) Enfermedades infecciosas que se contagian a través del contacto sexual.

Shock/choque La imposibilidad del sistema cardiovascular de mantener un flujo adecuado de sangre circulando por los órganos vitales del cuerpo.

Sibling/hermano Hermano o hermana.

Side effects/efectos secundarios Reacciones no buscadas a los medicamentos.

Sidestream smoke/corriente de humo El humo que sale del tabaco que se está quemando.

Situation/situación La circunstancia o evento previo a un accidente.

Skeletal muscles/músculos del esqueleto Los músculos estriados pegados a los huesos que causan los movimientos del cuerpo.

Smoke detector/detector de humo Alarma que suena ante la presencia de humo.

Smokeless tobacco/tabaco sin humo Tabaco que se aspira por la nariz o se masca.

Smooth muscles/músculos lisos El tipo de músculo que se encarga de mover los órganos internos.

Somatoform disorder/trastorno somatoforme Enfermedad o trastorno en el que una persona se queja de síntomas para los cuales no se puede hallar una causa física.

Specialist/especialista Médico que ha recibido formación adicional en un área particular de la medicina.

Specificity/especificidad Principio que establece que determinados ejercicios y actividades mejoran ciertas áreas del estado físico relacionadas con la salud.

Speed/velocidad La capacidad de trasladarse una distancia o completar un movimiento del cuerpo en un periodo corto de tiempo.

Sperm/espermatozoides Células reproductivas masculinas.

Spousal abuse/maltrato conyugal Maltrato doméstico dirigido a un cónyuge.

Sprain/torcedura Lesión de los tejidos que rodean a una articulación.

Stereotype/estereotipo Opinión exagerada o demasiado simplificada acerca de todo un grupo de personas, frecuentemente basada en la raza, la religión o la orientación sexual.

Sterility/esterilidad Trastorno en el que una persona es incapaz de reproducirse.

Stillbirth/parto de un feto muerto Nacimiento de un bebé muerto.

Stimulant/estimulante Droga que aumenta la actividad del sistema nervioso central, el corazón y otros órganos.

Strain/distensión Condición en la que los músculos han trabajado en exceso.

Strep throat/inflamación de la garganta Infección bacteriana de la garganta.

Stress/estrés Las demandas y reacciones del cuerpo y la mente ante las exigencias diarias.

Stress tolerance/tolerancia al estrés La cantidad de estrés que puedes sobrellevar antes de llegar al punto en que el estrés es demasiado.

Stressor/factor estresante Cualquier estímulo que produce una respuesta de estrés.

Stroke/accidente cerebrovascular Interrupción del flujo de sangre a cualquier parte del cerebro.

Substance abuse/abuso de sustancias Uso innecesario o impropio de sustancias químicas sin un propósito médico.

Suicide/suicidio Quitarse la propia vida.

Support group/grupo de apoyo Reunión formal o informal de personas que se encuentran y comparten experiencias, sentimientos y confianza mutua.

Sweat glands/glándulas sudoríparas Estructuras dentro de la piel que secretan tranpiración a través de conductos hacia los poros en la superficie de la piel.

Synergistic effect/effecto sinérgico La interacción de dos o más medicamentos que resulta en un efecto mayor que cuando se toman las medicinas independientemente una de la otra.

Synthetic drugs/drogas sintéticas Sustancias químicas producidas artificialmente en un laboratorio.

Syphilis/sífilis Una ETS que ataca muchas partes del cuerpo y es causada por una pequeña bacteria llamada espiroqueta.

T

Tar/alquitrán Líquido espeso, pegajoso y oscuro que se produce al quemar tabaco.

Tartar/sarro dental Sustancia dura como una costra.

Tendinitis/tendinitis Inflamación de un tendón.

Tendons/tendones Cuerdas fibrosas que unen el músculo con el hueso o con otros músculos.

Testes/testículos Dos glándulas pequeñas que producen espermatozoides.

Testosterone/testosterona Hormona sexual masculina.

Therapeutic communities/comunidades terapéuticas Centros de tratamiento donde residen los pacientes.

Thyroid gland/glándula tiroides Estructura que produce hormonas que regulan el metabolismoóel uso de nutrientes por las célulasóla producción de calor corporal y el crecimiento de los huesos.

Time management skills/técnicas de administración del tiempo Estrategias específicas para planificar y utilizar el tiempo de forma efectiva y sana.

Tinnitus/tiniteo Trastorno en el que se oyen retintineos, zumbidos, silbidos, siseos y otros sonidos en la ausencia de sonido externo.

Tolerance/tolerancia Aceptar las diferencias de otros y permitirles ser como son sin expresar desaprobación.

Tolerance/tolerancia Situación en la que el cuerpo se acostumbra al efecto de un medicamento.

Tornado/tornado Tormenta de viento fuerte y giratorio.

Trachea/tráquea Conducto para el aire.

Training/entrenamiento Programa formal de preparación física para participar en un deporte.

Transitions/transiciones Cambios críticos que ocurren en todas las etapas de la vida.

Transmission/transmisión Propagación.

Trichomoniasis/tricomoniasis Infección vaginal que puede llevar a infecciones de la uretra y la vegija.

Tuberculosis (TB)/tuberculosis (TB) Infección bacteriana altamente contagiosa que casi siempre afecta los pulmones.

Tumors/tumores Masas de tejido.

Type A personality/personalidad del Tipo A Tipo de personalidad competitiva y orientada a los logros que es la más propensa a desarrollar enfermedades cardíacas.

Type B personality/personalidad del Tipo B Tipo de personalidad apacible y no competitiva que es menos propensa a sufrir enfermedades cardíacas.

U

Ultrasound/ecografía o estudio de ultrasonido Examen en el que se utilizan ondas de sonido para proyectar imágenes de luz en una pantalla.

Umbilical cord/cordón umbilical Tubo por el que pasan nutrientes y oxígeno desde la sangre de la madre hacia la sangre del embrión.

Undernutrition/malnutrición No consumir suficientes nutrientes esenciales o calorías para el funcionamiento normal del organismo.

Underweight/bajo peso Estar por debajo del peso normal un 10 por ciento o más.

Unit pricing/precio por unidad Estrategia para establecer el costo relativo de un producto basándose en el costo por unidad estándar, como una onza o gramo.

Ureters/uréteres Tubos que conectan los riñones con la vejiga.

Urethra/uretra El tubo que va desde la vejiga hacia el exterior del cuerpo.

Urethritis/uretritis Inflamación de la uretra.

Urine/orina Material de desecho líquido.

Uterus/útero Órgano muscular pequeño en forma de pera, aproximadamente del tamaño de un puño.

V

Vaccine/vacuna Preparación que contiene patógenos debilitados o muertos y provee inmunidad al estimular al cuerpo a producir anticuerpos para ese patógeno.

Vagina/vagina Conducto muscular y elástico que se extiende desde el útero hasta el exterior del cuerpo.

Vaginitis/vaginitis Inflamación común de los genitales femeninos.

Values/valores Creencias y normas de comportamiento que crees importantes.

Vegans/vegetalistas Vegetarianos que sólo consumen alimentos de origen vegetal.

Vehicular safety/seguridad vehicular Obedecer las reglas del tránsito, así como utilizar el sentido común y el buen criterio.

Veins/venas Los vasos que regresan al corazón la sangre desoxigenada desde los órganos y tejidos del cuerpo.

Venom/ponzoña Sustancia venenosa secretada por una serpiente u otro animal.

Violence/violencia El uso de fuerza física para dañar o maltratar a otra persona o personas.

Virus/virus El agente infeccioso más pequeño que se conoce.

Vitamins/vitaminas Compuestos que ayudan a regular varios procesos vitales, incluyendo la digestión, la absorción, el metabolismo y el uso de otros nutrientes.

W

Warm-up/precalentamiento Actividad que prepara los músculos para el trabajo por venir.

Weight cycling/oscilación de peso El ciclo de perder peso, ganarlo, volver a adelgazar y recuperar peso.

Wellness/bienestar Estado general de contento, o de salud total.

Withdrawal/síndrome de abstinencia El proceso que ocurre cuando una persona deja de consumir un medicamento u otra sustancia de la cual es fisiológicamente dependiente.

X

Xiphoid process/apéndice xifoides Extremo inferior del esternón que se proyecta hacia abajo hasta el punto donde el esternón se toca con las costillas.

Z

Zygote/cigota Célula que resulta de la unión de un óvulo y un espermatozoide.

Index

A

AA. *See* Alcoholics Anonymous
Abdominal thrusts, 779–80
Abrasion, 772
Absorption, 412
Abstinence, 21
  addiction recovery and, 605
  alcohol, 567, 605
  choice, 484–85
  drinking, 554
  drugs, 592–93, 669
  sex, 645, 662, 669
  smoking, 543
Abuse, 330–33. *See also* Substance abuse
  alcohol, 562–63
  child, 287, 331, 565
  emotional, 287
  Making Responsible Decisions, 332
  sexual, 331. *See also* Date rape; Sexual assault
  spousal, 286, 331
Acceptance, 229, 262
Accident chain, 744–45
Acetaminophen, 515
Acetylsalicylic acid, 515
Acid rain, 727
Acne, 165, 343, 479
Acquaintance rape, 762
Acquired immune deficiency syndrome (AIDS), 486, 644, 658
  diagnosis, 664
  education about, 669
  research and treatment, 667–68
Action plan, 38
Active immunity, 632–33
Active listening, 265
Activity triangle, 61
Addiction, 577, 602–4. *See also* Enabling; Intervention; Recovery
  tobacco, 529
  treatment options, 605–7
Additive interaction, medicines, 516
Additives
  food, 123
  generally recognized as safe (GRAS), 123
Adipose tissue. *See* Fat
Adolescence, 478
  changes during, 479–80
  emotions and, 201. *See also* Dating relationships
  stress and, 217, 221
Adoption, 280
Adrenal glands, 379
Adrenaline, 216
Adulthood, 495. *See also* Late adulthood; Middle adulthood
Advertising
  alcohol, 552–54
  media and, 552–53
  nutrition, 98
  self-image and, 189
  tobacco, 536
Aerobic exercise, 57–59, 61
  circulatory system and, 396
Aesthetic needs, 193

Affective disorder, 240
Affirmation, 281
Age, 677
Agency for Health Care Policy and Research, 718
Agency for Toxic Substances and Disease Registry, 718
Aggravated assault, 325
Aggressive approach, to peer pressure, 307
Agility, 74
Aging, nutrition and, 150
AIDS. *See* Acquired immune deficiency syndrome (AIDS)
AIDS-opportunistic illnesses (AIDS-OIs), 666–67
AIDS-Related Cognitive Motor Dysfunction, 667
Air pollution, 726–28
Al-Anon, 612
Alarm, 216
Alateen, 565, 613
Alcohol. *See also* Addiction; Codependency; Drinking
  abstinence, 566–67
  accidents, 749
  driving and, 554, 557–59
  family and, 553, 565
  fetal alcohol syndrome (FAS), 458, 461
  Making Responsible Decisions, 458
  physical effects, 550, 555–57, 559–60
  poisoning, 563
  pregnancy and, 458
  teens and, 551–54
  treatment centers, 606–7
  violence and, 328
Alcoholics Anonymous (AA), 289, 565, 593, 606
Alcoholism, 563–66. *See also* Addiction; Codependency
Aldosterone, 379
Allergies, 154–55. *See also* Bee sting
Allergist, 705
Allied medical professionals, 706
Alveoli, 401
Alzheimer's disease, 375, 505
Amblyopia, 174
American Association of Retired Persons (AARP), 505
American College of Obstetricians and Gynecologists (ACOG), 447
American Medical Association (AMA), 25, 330, 715
American Public Health Association, 25
Americans with Disabilities Act, 382, 697
Amino acids, 103
Amniocentesis, 466
Amniotic sac, 455
Amphetamines, 581
Amygdala, 198
Amylase, 416
Anabolic steroids
  Making Responsible Decisions, 587
  risks from, 80–81, 587

Anaerobic exercise, 58
Analgesics, 515
Anemia, 398
Anger, 200, 204–5, 229
  Making Responsible Decisions, 205
Angina pectoris, 679
Angioplasty, 682
Anorexia nervosa, 142
Antacids, 420–21
Antagonistic interaction, medicines, 517
Anthrax, 514
Antiarrhythmics, 515
Antibiotics, 175, 513–15, 517, 628
Antibodies, 104, 390, 513, 626
Antidiuretic hormone (ADH), 378
Antitoxins, 513
Anus, 415
Anxiety disorders, 239
Apgar test, 460
Appendicitis, 421
Appendicular skeleton, 346
Appetite, 97
  vs. hunger, 99
Arrhythmia, 556
Arteries, 392
  diseases, 679
Arteriosclerosis, 679
Arthritis, 351, 505, 692–93
Asbestos, 728
Ascorbic acid, 108
Aspartame, 123
Aspirin, 515, 631
Assailant, 324
Assertive approach, 761
  communication, 308
  to peer pressure, 307–8
Asthma, 62, 222, 404–5
Astigmatism, 174
Athlete's foot, 343
Atrium, 389
Attitudes, 8–9
Auditory canal, external, 176
Auricle, 176
Autonomic nervous system (ANS), 370
Autonomy, 469
Avulsion, 772
Axial skeleton, 346
Axon, 365
AZT. *See* Zidovudine

B

Bacteria, 620–21
Balance, 74–75
Barbiturates, 582, 583
Bargaining, 229
B cells, 394, 626, 659
Beef, 122
Bee sting, 786–87
Behavior
  cardiovascular disease and, 677
  environment and, 15–16
  habits and, 18–19
  modeling, 196
Benign tumor, 683
Beta blockers, 515
Bile, 416

Credits

DESIGN AND PRODUCTION
Design Office/San Francisco

PHOTOGRAPHS

© Aaron Haupt; 526
© Aaron Haupt/Stock Boston/PNI; 154T
© Aaron Haupt/Stock Boston; 275
© Aaron Haupt/Photo Researchers; 455T
© John Henley/The Stock Market; 212, 479
© Michal Heron/The Stock Market; 429
© Ken Highfill/Photo Researchers; 777R
© Kevin Horan/Tony Stone Images; 579
Susan Hunt; 463
© Robert Huntzinger/The Stock Market; 661, 213T, 496, 540, 758L
© Richard Hutchings/Photo Researchers; 213T, 496, 540, 758L
© IFA/Leo deWys Inc. NY; 215
© Image Club Graphics; 71B, 213B
© Institut Pasteur/CNRI/PHOTOTAKE; 15
© Jacobsen/Index Stock Imagery; 141L
© Jasmine/PNI; 12R, 208
© Johns Hopkins Children's Center, courtesy of the Carson Scholars Fund; 369
© William Johnson/Stock Boston; 71M, 78
© Jump Run Productions/The Image Bank; 640
© Henryk Kaiser/Leo de Wys Inc.; 619B, 660TL
© Dr. Michael Klein/Peter Arnold; 693B
© Bruce Kliewe/The Picture Cube; 743T
© David Klutho/Allsport USA; 219, 223
© L. Kolvoord/The Image Works; 217M
© J. Koontz/The Picture Cube; 338
© Bob Krist/Corbis; Interior of CNN Room
© Mehau Kulyk, Science Source/Photo Researchers; 364 background, 667, 682
© Dr. Dennis Kunkel/PHOTOTAKE; 620M, 621B
© Susan Lapides; 469T, 609R, 731
© Calvin Larsen/Photo Researchers; 527B
© Ken Lax/Photo Researchers; 493B
© Andrew M. Levine/Photo Researchers; 587L
© Rob Lewine/The Stock Market; 226TR
© David Lissy/Leo de Wys Inc. N.Y.; 586
© Andy Lyons/Allsport USA; 372, 376, 503
© Rafael Macia/Photo Researchers; 593
© Stephen Marks/The Image Bank; 634T
© Doug Martin; 386, 768
© Doug Martin, courtesy of Dr. Clayton N. Hicks; 160
© Court Mast/FPG International LLC; 238
© Tom McCarthy/Leo de Wys Inc.; 675
© Tom & DeeAnn McCarthy/The Stock Market; 758R
© Patti McConville/The Image Bank; 753
© Tom McHugh/Photo Researchers; 727B
© Will & Deni McIntyre/Photo Researchers; 500, 656, 706
© Mednet/PHOTOTAKE; 635
© Peter Menzel/Stock Boston; 718
© Lawrence Migdale/Photo Researchers; 277M, 751
© Bill Miles/The Stock Market; 648
© Roy Morsch/The Stock Market; 220R, 277BR
© Prof. P. Motta, Science Source/Photo Researchers; 339T, 436, 442, 693T
© Mugshots/The Stock Market; 482
© Bob Mullinex; 70, 510
© Larry Mulvehill/Photo Researchers; 773
© Dr. Gopal Murti, Science Source/Photo Researchers; 454
© Joseph Nettis/Photo Researchers; 332B
© Joseph Nettis/Stock Boston/PNI; 306
© NIBSC, Science Source/Photo Researchers; 659
© Richard T. Nowitz/Photo Researchers; 565, 769B
© Michael Paras/International Stock; 600

© Alfred Pasieka, Science Source/Photo Researchers; xM, 387, 650T
© Jose Pelaez/The Stock Market; 226TL, 435M
© Brent Petersen/The Stock Market; 198B
© Petit Format/Nestle/Photo Researchers; 457
© Mark D. Phillips/Photo Researchers; 411T
© David Phillips/Photo Researchers; 464L
© Phyllis Picardi/International Stock; 131T
© Picture Perfect; 403, 591–592
© Noah Poritz/Photo Researchers; 629
© James Prince/Photo Researchers; 495T
© Patrick Ramesy/International Stock; 94
© Alon Reininger/Leo de Wys Inc. N.Y.; 657T
© Claude Revy, Jean/PHOTOTAKE; 684
© D. Richardson/Custom Medical Stock Photo; 462
© Tim Rollins; 13
© Marc Romanelli/The Image Bank; 445, 625, 685B (girl)
© Martin M. Rotker/Photo Researchers; 560B
© Rouchon/Explorer/Photo Researchers; 143
© R. Rowan/Photo Researchers; 389
© Nancy Santullo/The Stock Market; 787
© Chuck Savage/The Stock Market; 61 row 1
© Karelle Scharff; 326, 594
© B. Seitz/Photo Researchers; 622B
© Blair Seitz/Photo Researchers; 703B
© Frank Siteman/Stock Boston; 477B
© SIU/Photo Researchers; 560T
© Ariel Skelley/The Stock Market; 277T
© A. Sofianopoulos/Ace Photo Agency/PHOTOTAKE; 511T
© St. Bartholomew's Hospital, Science Source/Photo Researchers; 680
© Stock Image/Zephyr Images; 71T
© SuperStock; 279, 297
© Karl H. Switak; 777B
© Tektoff-Merieux, CNRI, Science Photo Library/Custom Medical Stock Photo; 619T
© Telegraph Colour Library/FPG International; 131B, 131M, 226BL, 229, 413L, 574, 583, 587R, 599, 601T, 623B, 676–677
© Sheila Terry, Science Source/Photo Researchers; 530L, 774T
© Terry Wild Studio; 8, 45T 57T, 142, 217T, 275T, 308, 368T, 419, 446, 513
© Jay Thomas/International Stock; 368B
© Arthur Tilley/FPG International; 453T
© Geoff Tompkinson, Science Source/Photo Researchers; 511B, 618
© USDA, Science Source/Photo Researchers; 660TR
© Vanessa Vick/Photo Researchers; 277BL, 669
© E. H. Wallop/The Stock Market; 61 row 2R
© Westerman/International Stock; 226ML
© Keith Wood/Tony Stone Images; 184
© Yellow Dog Productions/The Image Bank; 439
© Robert Zappalorti/Photo Researchers; 777M

ILLUSTRATIONS

Matt Meadows; 341
Judith Tulenko Morley; 346, 347, 348
Network Graphics; 172
Betsy Paley; 392
Felipe Passalacqua; 349
Rolin Graphics Inc.; 413R, 426
Charles S. Scogins; 355, 356T, 366
Gretchen Shields; 780, 781, 782, 783, 784